Building Python Programs

Stuart Reges
University of Washington

Marty Stepp
Stanford University

Allison Obourn
University of Arizona

330 Hudson Street, NY, NY 10013

Senior Vice President Courseware Portfolio Management: Marcia Horton
Vice President, Portfolio Management: Engineering, Computer Science & Global Editions: Julian Partridge
Executive Portfolio Manager: Matt Goldstein
Portfolio Management Assistant: Meghan Jacoby
Field Marketing Manager: Demetrius Hall
Product Marketing Manager: Yvonne Vannatta
Marketing Assistant: Jon Bryant
Managing Producer: Scott Disanno
Content Producer: Amanda Brands
Project Manager: Rose Kernan, RPK Editorial Services

Manufacturing Buyer, Higher Ed, Lake Side Communications, Inc. (LSC): Maura Zaldivar-Garcia
Cover Design: Pearson CSC
R&P Manager: Ben Ferrini
Inventory Manager: Bruce Boundy
Cover Art: Matt Walford/Cultura/Getty Images
Full Service Vendor: Pearson CSC
Full-Service Project Management: Pearson CSC/Rose Kernan
Composition: Pearson CSC
Printer/Binder: LSC Communications, Inc

Library of Congress Cataloging-in-Publication Data
Names: Reges, Stuart, author. | Stepp, Martin, author. | Obourn, Allison, author.
Title: Building Python programs / Stuart Reges, University of Washington, Marty Stepp, Stanford University, Allison Obourn, University of Arizona.
Description: First edition. | New York, NY : Pearson, [2019] | Includes index.
Identifiers: LCCN 2018028848| ISBN 9780135205983 | ISBN 0135205980
Subjects: LCSH: Python (Computer program language)
Classification: LCC QA76.73.P98 R445 2019 | DDC 005.13/3—dc23
LC record available at https://lccn.loc.gov/2018028848
1 18

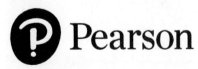

ISBN 10:   0-13-520598-0
ISBN 13: 978-0-13-520598-3

Preface

The Python programming language has become enormously popular in recent years. Many people are impressed with how quickly you can learn Python's simple and intuitive syntax and that has led many users to create popular libraries. Python was designed by Guido van Rossum who has been affectionaly dubbed "Benevolent Dictator For Life (BDFL)" by the Python community. He has said that he chose the name Python because he was "in a slightly irreverent mood" and that he is "a big fan of Monty Python's Flying Circus" (a British comedy show). Who wouldn't want to learn a programming language named after a group of comedians?

Our new *Building Python Programs* text is designed for use in a first course in computer science. We have class-tested it with hundreds of undergraduates at the University of Arizona, most of whom were not computer science majors. This textbook is based on our previous text, *Building Java Programs*, now in its fourth edition. The Java text has proven effective in our class testing with thousands of students including our own at the University of Washington since 2007.

Introductory computer science courses have a long history at many universities of being "killer" courses with high failure rates. But as Douglas Adams says in *The Hitchhiker's Guide to the Galaxy*, "Don't panic." Students can master this material if they can learn it gradually.

Python has many attributes that make it an appealing language for a first computer science course. It has a simple and concise yet powerful syntax that makes it pleasant to learn and great for writing many common programs. A student can write their first Python program with only a single line of code, as opposed to several lines in most other languages such as Java or C++. Python includes a built-in interpreter and read-evaluate-print loop (REPL) for quickly running and testing code, encouraging students to test and explore the language. Python also offers a rich set of libraries that students can use for graphics, animation, math, scientific computing, games, and much more. This text has been built from the start for Python 3, the most modern version of the language as of this writing, and it embraces the modern features and idioms of that version of the language.

Our teaching materials are based on a "back to basics" approach that focuses on procedural programming and program decomposition. This is also called the "objects later" approach, as opposed to the "objects early" approach taught in some schools. We know from years of experience that a broad range of scientists, engineers, and others can learn how to program in a procedural manner. Once we have built a solid foundation of procedural techniques, we turn to object-oriented programming. By the end of the text, students will have learned about both styles of programming.

iii

The following are the key features of our approach and materials:

- **Focus on problem solving.** Many textbooks focus on language details when they introduce new constructs. We focus instead on problem solving. What new problems can be solved with each construct? What pitfalls are novices likely to encounter along the way? What are the most common ways to use a new construct?

- **Emphasis on algorithmic thinking.** Our procedural approach allows us to emphasize algorithmic problem solving: breaking a large problem into smaller problems, using pseudocode to refine an algorithm, and grappling with the challenge of expressing a large program algorithmically.

- **Thorough discussion of topics.** The authors have found that many introductory texts rapidly cover new syntax and concepts and then quickly race on to the next topic. We feel that the students who crack open their textbook are exactly the sort that want more thorough and careful explanation and discussion of tricky topics. In this text we favor longer explanations, with more verbiage, figures, and code examples than in many other texts.

- **Layered approach.** Programming involves many concepts that are difficult to learn all at once. Teaching a novice to code is like trying to build a house of cards; each new card has to be placed carefully. If the process is rushed and you try to place too many cards at once, the entire structure collapses. We teach new concepts gradually, layer by layer, allowing students to expand their understanding at a manageable pace.

- **Emphasis on good coding style.** We show code that uses proper and consistent programming style and design. All complete programs shown in the text are thoroughly commented and properly decomposed. Throughout the text we discuss common idioms, good and bad style choices, and how to choose elegant and appropriate ways to decompose and solve each new category of problem.

- **Carefully chosen language subset.** Rather than a "kitchen sink" approach that tries to show the student every language construct and feature, we instead go out of our way to explain and use a core subset of the Python language that we feel is most well suited to solving introductory level problems.

- **Case studies.** We end most chapters with a significant case study that shows students how to develop a complex program in stages and how to test it as it is being developed. This structure allows us to demonstrate each new programming construct in a rich context that cannot be achieved with short code examples.

Layers and Dependencies

Many introductory computer science texts are language-oriented, but the early chapters of our approach are layered. For example, Python has many control structures (including loops and `if`/`else` statements), and many texts include all of these control structures in a single chapter. While that might make sense to someone who already knows how to program, it can be overwhelming for a novice who is learning how to program. We find that it is much more effective to spread these control structures into different chapters so that students learn one structure at a time rather than trying to learn them all at once.

The following table shows how the layered approach works in the first seven chapters:

Layers in Chapters 1–7

Chapter	Control Flow	Data	Techniques	Input/Output
1	functions	string literals	decomposition	`print`
2	definite loops (`for` loops)	expressions/ variables, integers, real numbers	local variables, global constants, pseudocode	
3	parameters, return	using objects	decomposition with param/return	console input, graphics
4	conditionals (`if`/`else`)	strings	pre/postconditions, raising exceptions	
5	indefinite loops (`while` loops)	Boolean logic	assertions, robust programs	
6		file objects	line-based processing, line-based processing	file I/O
7		lists	traversals	files as lists

Chapters 1–5 are designed to be worked through in order, with greater flexibility of study then beginning in Chapter 6. Chapter 6 (File I/O) may be skipped, although the case study in Chapter 7 (Lists) involves reading from a file, a topic that is covered in Chapter 6.

The following figure represents a dependency chart for the book. A strong dependency is drawn as a solid arrow; we recommend not covering chapters outside of their strong dependency order. A weak dependency is drawn as a dashed arrow. Weak dependencies are ones where the later chapter briefly mentions a topic from the earlier chapter, but the chapter can still be read and explored without having covered the earlier chapter if necessary.

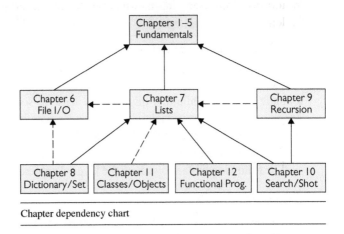

Chapter dependency chart

Here are more detailed explanations of the weak dependencies between chapters:

- A few examples from Chapter 7 on lists, and from Chapter 8 on dictionaries and sets, read data from files. File input/output is covered in Chapter 6. But overall file-reading is not required in order to discuss lists or other collections, so Chapter 6 can be skipped if desired.
- A few examples from Chapter 11 on classes and objects mention the concept of reference semantics, which is introduced in Chapter 7 on lists. But the concept of references is re-explained in Chapter 11, so classes can be covered early before lists if desired.
- Some of the recursive functions in Chapter 9 process lists, and one recursive function recursively reverses the lines of a file. So Chapter 9 weakly depends on Chapter 7. But almost every recursive function written in Chapter 9 can be written and understood using only the Chapter 1–5 core material.

As you can see from the diagram, Chapter 7 on Lists is perhaps the most important chapter after the first five, and its material is used by many other chapters. A common chapter order swap would be to cover Chapters 1–5, then do Chapter 7 on Lists, then go back to Chapter 6 on Files with the extra knowledge of lists to help you.

Supplements

Answers to all self-check problems appear on our web site and are accessible to anyone: http://www.buildingpythonprograms.com/

In addition, our web site also has the following additional resources available for students:

- Online-only supplemental content
- Source code and data files for all case studies and other complete program examples.
- The `DrawingPanel` class used in Chapter 3.
- Links to web-based programming practice tools.

Instructors can access the following resources from our web site:

- PowerPoint slides suitable for lectures.
- Solutions to exercises and programming projects, along with homework specification documents for many projects.
- Sample Exams and solution keys.

To access instructor resources, contact us at authors@buildingpythonprograms.com. For other questions related to resources, contact the authors and/or your Pearson representative.

MyLab Programming

MyLab Programming helps students fully grasp the logic, semantics, and syntax of programming. Through practice exercises and immediate, personalized feedback, MyLab Programming improves the programming competence of beginning students, who often struggle with the basic concepts and paradigms of popular high-level programming languages. A self-study and homework tool, the MyLab Programming course consists of hundreds of small practice exercises organized around the structure of this textbook. For students, the system automatically detects errors in the logic and syntax of their code submissions and offers targeted hints that enable students to figure out what went wrong—and why. For instructors, a comprehensive gradebook tracks correct and incorrect answers and stores the code inputted by students for review.

MyLab Programming is offered to users of this book in partnership with Turing's Craft, the makers of the CodeLab interactive programming exercise system. For a full demonstration, to see feedback from instructors and students, or to get started using MyLab Programming in your course, visit: http://www.pearson.com/mylab/programming.

Acknowledgments

We would also like to thank the staff at Pearson who helped produce the book. Rose Kernan managed the project and was our primary point of contact during book production. Rose did a phenomenal job; she was diligent, responsive, and helpful at every step of the process. Amanda Brands was our content producer, and she also provided excellent support along the way. Thank you to Martha McMaster for proofreading the text, and thanks to Shelly Gerger-Knechtl for copy editing and indexing. We thank Yvonne Vannatta, our marketing manager, and Meghan Jacoby, our editorial assistant. We also want to thank the team of artists and compositors from Pearson's partner institutions who helped produce the chapters of this text.

We would like to thank our lead editor at Pearson, Matt Goldstein. Over a decade ago Matt believed in our work and partnered with us to create the original *Building Java Programs* on which this text is based. Matt has been a stalwart supporter and is always a pleasure to work with.

Last but not least, the authors would like to thank the CSC 110 students at the University of Arizona who class-tested our chapters in rough draft form. Students provided helpful suggestions for improving the content and also submitted corrections for typos and errors in drafts of chapters.

Stuart Reges, *University of Washington*
Marty Stepp, *Stanford University*
Allison Obourn, *University of Arizona*

MyLab Programming

Through the power of practice and immediate personalized feedback, MyLab Programming™ helps students master programming fundamentals and build computational thinking skills.

PROGRAMMING PRACTICE

With MyLab Programming, your students will gain first-hand programming experience in an interactive online environment.

IMMEDIATE, PERSONALIZED FEEDBACK

MyLab Programming automatically detects errors in the logic and syntax of their code submission and offers trageted hints that enables students to figure out what went wrong and why.

GRADUATED COMPLEXITY

MyLab Programming breaks down programming concepts into short, understandable sequences of exercises. Within each sequence the level and sophistication of the exercises increase gradually but steadily.

DYNAMIC ROSTER

Students' submissions are stored in a roster that indicates whether the submission is correct, how many attempts were made, and the actual code submissions from each attempt.

PEARSON eTEXT

The Pearson eText gives students access to their textbook anytime, anywhere

STEP-BY-STEP VIDEONOTE TUTORIALS

These step-by-step video tutorials enhance the programming concepts presented in select Pearson textbooks.

For more information and titles available with MyLab Programming, please visit www.pearson.com/mylab/programming

Brief Contents

Contents

## Chapter 1

Introduction to Python Programming

Introduction

This chapter begins with a review of some basic terminology about computers and computer programming. Many of these concepts will come up in later chapters, so it will be useful to review them before we start delving into the details of how to program in Python.

We will begin our exploration of Python by looking at simple programs that produce text output to a console window. This discussion will allow us to explore many elements that are common to all Python programs, while working with programs that are fairly simple in structure.

After we have reviewed the basic elements of Python programs, we will explore the technique of procedural decomposition by learning how to break up a Python program into several functions. Using this technique, we can break up complex tasks into smaller subtasks that are easier to manage and we can avoid redundancy in our program solutions.

1.1 Basic Computing Concepts

Computers are pervasive in our daily lives, and, thanks to the Internet, they give us access to nearly limitless information. Some of this information is essential news, like the headlines at cnn.com. Computers let us share photos with our families and map directions to the nearest pizza place for dinner.

Lots of real-world problems are being solved by computers, some of which don't much resemble the one on your desk or lap. Computers allow us to sequence the human genome and search for DNA patterns within it. Computers in recently manufactured cars monitor each vehicle's status and motion. Digital devices such as Apple's iPhone actually have computers inside their small casings. Even the Roomba vacuum-cleaning robot houses a computer with complex instructions about how to dodge furniture while cleaning your floors.

But what makes a computer a computer? Is a calculator a computer? Is a human being with a paper and pencil a computer? The next several sections attempt to address this question while introducing some basic terminology that will help prepare you to study programming.

Why Programming?

At most universities, the first course in computer science is a programming course. Many computer scientists are bothered by this because it leaves people with the impression that computer science is programming. While it is true that many trained computer scientists spend time programming, there is a lot more to the discipline. So why do we study programming first?

A Stanford computer scientist named Don Knuth answers this question by saying that the common thread for most computer scientists is that we all in some way work with *algorithms*.

> **Algorithm**
>
> A step-by-step description of how to accomplish a task.

Knuth is an expert in algorithms, so he is naturally biased toward thinking of them as the center of computer science. Still, he claims that what is most important is not the algorithms themselves, but rather the thought process that computer scientists employ to develop them. According to Knuth:

> It has often been said that a person does not really understand something until after teaching it to someone else. Actually a person does not really understand something until after teaching it to a computer, i.e., expressing it as an algorithm.[1]

---

[1] Knuth, Don. *Selected Papers on Computer Science*. Stanford. CA: Center for the Study of Language and Information, 1996.

Knuth is describing a thought process that is common to most of computer science, which he refers to as algorithmic thinking. We study programming not because it is the most important aspect of computer science, but because it is the best way to explain the approach that computer scientists take to solving problems.

The concept of algorithms is helpful in understanding what a computer is and what computer science is all about. The Merriam-Webster dictionary defines the word "computer" as "one that computes." Using that definition, all sorts of devices qualify as computers, from calculators to GPS navigation systems to children's toys. Prior to the invention of electronic computers, it was common to refer to humans as computers. The nineteenth-century mathematician Charles Peirce, for example, was originally hired to work for the U.S. government as an "Assistant Computer" because his job involved performing mathematical computations.

In a broad sense, then, the word "computer" can be applied to many devices. But when computer scientists refer to a computer, they are usually thinking of a universal computation device that can be programmed to execute any algorithm. Computer science, then, is the study of computational devices and the study of computation itself, including algorithms.

Algorithms are expressed as computer programs, and that is what this book is all about. But before we look at how to program, it will be useful to review some basic concepts about computers.

Hardware and Software

A computer is a machine that manipulates data and executes lists of instructions known as *programs*.

> **Program**
> A list of instructions to be carried out by a computer.

One key feature that differentiates a computer from a simpler machine like a calculator is its versatility. The same computer can perform many different tasks (playing games, computing income taxes, connecting to other computers around the world), depending on what program it is running at a given moment. A computer can run not only the programs that exist on it currently, but also new programs that haven't even been written yet.

The physical components that make up a computer are collectively called *hardware*. One of the most important pieces of hardware is the central processing unit, or CPU. The CPU is the "brain" of the computer: It is what executes the instructions. Also important is the computer's *memory* (often called random access memory, or RAM, because the computer can access any part of that memory at any time). The computer uses its memory to store programs that are being executed, along with their data. RAM is limited in size and does not retain its contents when the computer is turned off. Therefore, computers generally also use a *hard disk* as a larger permanent storage area.

Computer programs are collectively called *software*. The primary piece of software running on a computer is its operating system. An *operating system* provides an environment in which many programs may be run at the same time; it also provides a bridge among those programs, the hardware, and the user (the person using the computer). The programs that run inside the operating system are often called *applications* or *apps*.

When the user selects a program for the operating system to run (e.g., by double-clicking the program's icon on the desktop), several things happen: The instructions for that program are loaded into the computer's memory from the hard disk, the operating system allocates memory for that program to use, and the instructions to run the program are fed from memory to the CPU and executed sequentially.

The Digital Realm

In the previous section, we saw that a computer is a general-purpose device that can be programmed. You will often hear people refer to modern computers as *digital* computers because of the way they operate.

> **Digital**
>
> Based on numbers that increase in discrete increments, such as the integers 0, 1, 2, 3, etc.

Because computers are digital, everything that is stored on a computer is stored as a sequence of integers. This includes every program and every piece of data. An MP3 file, for example, is simply a long sequence of integers that stores audio information. Today we're used to digital music, digital pictures, and digital movies, but in the 1940s, when the first computers were built, the idea of storing complex data in integer form was fairly unusual.

Not only are computers digital, storing all information as integers, but they are also *binary*, which means they store integers as *binary numbers*.

> **Binary Number**
>
> A number composed of just 0s and 1s, also known as a base-2 number.

Humans generally work with *decimal* or base-10 numbers, which match our physiology (10 fingers and 10 toes). However, when we were designing the first computers, we wanted systems that would be easy to create and very reliable. It turned out to be simpler to build these systems on top of binary phenomena (e.g., a circuit being open or closed) rather than having 10 different states that would have to be distinguished from one another (e.g., 10 different voltage levels).

From a mathematical point of view, you can store things just as easily using binary numbers as you can using base-10 numbers. But since it is easier to construct a physical device that uses binary numbers, that's what computers use.

This does mean, however, that people who aren't used to computers find their conventions unfamiliar. As a result, it is worth spending a little time reviewing how binary numbers work. To count with binary numbers, as with base-10 numbers, you start with 0 and count up, but you run out of digits much faster. So, counting in binary, you say:

```
0
1
```

And already you've run out of digits. This is like reaching 9 when you count in base-10. After you run out of digits, you carry over to the next digit. So, the next two binary numbers are:

```
10
11
```

And again, you've run out of digits. This is like reaching 99 in base-10. Again, you carry over to the next digit to form the three-digit number 100. In binary, whenever you see a series of ones, such as 111111, you know you're just one away from the digits all flipping to 0s with a 1 added in front, the same way that, in base-10, when you see a number like 999999, you know that you are one away from all those digits turning to 0s with a 1 added in front. Table 1.1 shows how to count up to the base-10 number 8 using binary.

We can make several useful observations about binary numbers. Notice in the table that the binary numbers 1, 10, 100, and 1000 are all perfect powers of 2 (2^0, 2^1, 2^2, 2^3). In the same way that in base-10 we talk about a ones digit, tens digit, hundreds digit, and so on, we can think in binary of a ones digit, twos digit, fours digit, eights digit, sixteens digit, and so on.

Computer scientists quickly found themselves needing to refer to the sizes of different binary quantities, so they invented the term *bit* to refer to a single binary digit and the term *byte* to refer to 8 bits. (The less commonly used term "*nibble*" refers to 4 bits, or half a byte.) To talk about large amounts of memory, they invented the terms kilobytes (KB), megabytes (MB), gigabytes (GB), and so on. Many people think that these correspond to the metric system, where "kilo" means 1000, but that is only

Table 1.1 Decimal vs. Binary

Decimal	Binary
0	0
1	1
2	10
3	11
4	100
5	101
6	110
7	111
8	1000

approximately true. We use the fact that 2^{10} is approximately equal to 1000 (it actually equals 1024). Table 1.2 shows some common units of memory storage.

Table 1.2   Units of Memory Storage

Measurement	Power of 2	Actual Value	Example
kilobyte (KB)	2^{10}	1,024	500-word paper (3 KB)
megabyte (MB)	2^{20}	1,048,576	typical book (1 MB) or song (5 MB)
gigabyte (GB)	2^{30}	1,073,741,824	typical movie (4.7 GB)
terabyte (TB)	2^{40}	1,099,511,627,776	20 million books in the Library of Congress (20 TB)
petabyte (PB)	2^{50}	1,125,899,906,842,624	10 billion photos on Facebook (1.5 PB)

The Process of Programming

The word *code* describes program fragments ("these four lines of code") or the act of programming ("Let's code this into Python."). Once a program has been written, you can *execute* it.

> **Program Execution**
>
> The act of carrying out the instructions contained in a program.

The process of execution is often called *running*. This term can also be used as a verb ("When my program runs it does something strange") or as a noun ("The last run of my program produced these results").

A computer program is stored internally as a series of binary numbers known as the *machine language* of the computer. In the early days, programmers entered numbers like these directly into the computer. Obviously, this is a tedious and confusing way to program a computer, and we have invented all sorts of mechanisms to simplify this process.

Modern programmers write in what are known as high-level programming languages, such as Python. Such programs cannot be run directly on a computer: They first have to be translated into a form that can be executed. Translating a program from a language such as Python into executable binary instructions can be done two ways: all at once (called *compiling*) or incrementally (called *interpreting* the program). Python is an *interpreted language*, which means that after you type and save your program, you directly execute it without any other steps. Each command written in your program is executed in sequence by a special program called an *interpreter*. When you download and install Python on your computer, the Python interpreter is installed for you so that you can run Python programs.

> **Interpreter**
>
> A program that dynamically reads, translates, and executes instructions from a computer program.

Many other languages such as Java and C are *compiled languages*. Compiled languages require you to use a special program known as a *compiler* to explicitly translate the entire program before it runs. A compiler often translates a program directly into machine language and creates a program file that can be executed directly on the computer, known as an *executable*. Interpreted languages like Python do not usually produce a separate executable program file.

> **Compiler**
>
> A program that translates an entire computer program written in one language into an equivalent program in another language (often, but not always, translating from a high-level language into machine language).

You can write Python code in two ways. The first way is called *interactive mode*, also called the *Python shell*, where you type individual Python commands and immediately watch them execute and see their results. Interactive mode is useful for trying out commands quickly to experiment and learn more about them. But the commands you type in interactive mode are not saved anywhere and will be gone when you exit your Python editor or shut off your computer. The second way is *normal mode*, where you type a program that can consist of many Python commands, save it to a file, and then execute the program to run all of the commands in sequence. Normal mode is the way to write complete programs that will persist on your computer so they can be executed many times.

Why Python?

Python was created as a hobby project by a Dutch programmer named Guido van Rossum. The first public versions of Python were released in 1989. As of this writing the current major version of the language is **Python 3**, which is the version taught in this text. The language is named after the classic comedy TV show *Monty Python's Flying Circus*, of which van Rossum was a big fan. Python currently ranks fifth on the TIOBE index of programming language popularity.

The language's official web site, python.org, says, "Python is a programming language that lets you work quickly and integrate systems more effectively" and that it is "easy to learn and use." Python has a plain and simple structure that allows you to write basic programs more quickly and with less conceptual overhead than many other popular languages.

Python also includes a large amount of prewritten software that programmers can utilize to enhance their programs. Such off-the-shelf software components are often called *libraries*. For example, if you wish to write a program that connects to a site on the Internet, Python contains a library to simplify the connection for you. Python contains libraries to draw graphical user interfaces (GUIs), retrieve data from databases, create games, and perform complex scientific and mathematical computations, among many other things. The richness of Python libraries has been an important factor in the rise of Python as a popular language.

> **Library**
>
> A collection of preexisting code that provides solutions to common programming problems.

Another reason to use Python is that it has a vibrant programmer community. Extensive online documentation and tutorials are available to help programmers learn new skills. The Python official web site contains detailed descriptions of the language's features, and many other web sites have written documentation and tutorials for the language.

Python is platform independent; unlike programs written in some other languages, the same Python program can be executed on many different operating systems, such as Windows, Mac OS X, and Linux.

Python is used extensively for both research and business applications, which means that a large number of programming jobs exist in the marketplace today for skilled Python programmers. Many companies and organizations such as Google, Facebook, Yahoo, IBM, Quora, and NASA use Python as part of their code base. A sample Google search for the phrase "Python jobs" returned around 2,000,000 results at the time of this writing.

The Python Programming Environment

You must become familiar with your computer setup before you start programming. Each computer provides a different environment for program development, but there are some common elements that deserve comment. No matter what environment you use, you will follow the same basic three steps:

1. Type a Python program into your editor.
2. Save the program as a file that ends with .*py*.
3. Run the program using the Python interpreter.

Try typing the following one-line program into your Python editor:

```
print("Hello, world!")
```

Don't worry about the details of this program right now. We will explore those in the next section.

Once you have created your program file, move to step 2 and save it. The basic unit of storage on most computers is a *file*. Every file has a name. A file name ends with an *extension*, which is the part of a file's name that follows the period. A file's extension indicates the type of data contained in the file. For example, files with the extension .*txt* are text files, and files with the extension .*mp3* are MP3 audio files.

By convention, the Python program files that we will write in this text will use the extension .*py*. Python programs can use other extensions, but .*py* is expected and is most commonly used.

Most Python programmers use what are known as Integrated Development Environments, or *IDEs*, which provide an all-in-one environment for creating, editing, compiling, and executing program files. As of this writing, some of the more popular choices for introductory computer science classes are IDLE, Eclipse, IntelliJ IDEA, PyDev, Sublime Text, and Komodo. Your instructor will tell you what environment you should use.

Once you have successfully saved your program to a file, you are ready to move to step 3, running the program. The command to run the program will be different in each development environment, but the process is the same (typically you click a "Run" button with a Play icon or an icon of a running person on it). If you mistyped the program, an error might be displayed when you run it; if so, go back to the editor, carefully check the code to make sure you typed it exactly as shown, fix any mistakes, save it, and try to run the program again. Some IDEs (such as PyDev or Eclipse) automatically check your code for errors and underline potential errors as you type. (We'll discuss errors in more detail later in this chapter.)

The diagram in Figure 1.1 summarizes the steps you would follow in creating a program called *hello.py*.

When your program is executed, it will typically interact with the user in some way. The *hello.py* program involves an onscreen window known as a *console*.

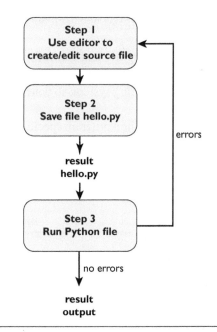

Figure 1.1   Creation and execution of a Python program

> **Console Window**
>
> A special text-only window in which Python programs interact with the user.

A console window is a classic interaction mechanism wherein the computer displays text on the screen and sometimes waits for the user to type responses. This is known as *console interaction* or *terminal interaction*. The text the computer prints to the console window is known as the *output* of the program. Any information typed by the user while the program is running is known as the *console input*.

To keep things simple, most of the sample programs in this text involve console interaction. Keeping the interaction simple will allow you to focus your attention and effort on other aspects of programming. Once you have mastered the basics of programming, you will be ready to learn how to write programs that use more modern graphical user interfaces.

1.2 And Now: Python

It's time to look at a complete Python program. It is a tradition in computer science that when you describe a new programming language, you should start with a program that produces a single line of output with the words, "Hello, world!" The "hello world" tradition isn't practical in every language, but writing a "hello world" program is relatively simple in Python, so we will continue the tradition.

Here is our "hello world" program, which we have saved into a file named *hello.py*:

```
print("Hello, world!")
```

If you save this program and run it in your editor, a console window should appear displaying the following output, as shown in Figure 1.2. A console window looks different on each operating system, so your window may not exactly match the appearance in our figure.

Each line of a Python program specifies an action the computer should perform when it executes. We refer to these as the *statements* of the program. Just as you put together an essay by writing a sequence of complete sentences, you put together a program by writing a sequence of statements. There are lots of different kinds of statements that you can write in Python, but for now, we'll focus on `print` statements.

Console

    Hello, world!

Figure 1.2   Console window displaying program output

> **Statement**
>
> An executable unit of code that represents a single complete command.

The sample "hello world" program has just a single statement that is known as a `print` statement: Each statement occupies a single line in your program file. The end of the line is implicitly also the end of the statement on that line. More generally, a `print` statement is written in the following format:

```
print("message to display")
```
Syntax template: print statement

An overall program can consist of many `print` statements in sequence, such as:

```
print("message 1")
print("message 2")
print("message 3")
...
print("message N")
```
Syntax template: Sequence of print statements

This type of description is known as a *syntax template* because it describes the basic form of a Python construct. Python has rules that determine its legal *syntax* or grammar. Each time we introduce a new element of Python, we'll begin by looking at its syntax template. By convention, we use an italic font appearance in a syntax template to indicate items that need to be filled in (in this case, the message to be printed). When we write ". . ." in a list of elements, we're indicating that any number of those elements may be included.

In the basic "hello world" program there is just a single command to produce a line of output, but the following variation (saved as *hello2.py*) has four statements to be executed:

```
1  print("Hello, world!")
2  print()
3  print("This program produces four")
4  print("lines of output.")
```

The numbers shown to the left of the code are not part of the program's code; they are just line numbers included to make it easier to refer to each line when we talk about programs in this text. The statements are executed in the order in which they appear, starting with line 1, from first to last. So the *hello2* program produces the following output:

```
Hello, world!
This program produces
four lines of output.
```

(In general, when we show the output of a program in this text, we will not show the entire console window with its title and border and so on. We will show only the text of the output.)

Now that you've seen an overview of the structure, let's examine some of the details of Python programs.

Common Programming Error

Typing Program in Interactive Mode Instead of Saving to a File

One of Python's greatest strengths is its interactive mode, which lets you type individual Python statements and see their results immediately. But the statements typed into the interactive command prompt are only for testing and are not permanently saved or stored as a program. This can be confusing to new programmers who are intending to type and save a program to a file such as *hello.py* but instead accidentally type their Python commands into the interactive prompt.

Every editor handles this issue differently, and we cannot discuss every Python editor here; but let's look at one specific example to get the general idea. The following screenshots come from IDLE, a simple Python editor that comes included with Python when you install it.

Figure 1.3 shows a screenshot of the IDLE editor. When you first run IDLE, it displays a Python Shell window containing the interactive mode prompt, indicated by the characters >>>. Notice that in the screenshot, the programmer has typed a command, and its resulting output has appeared immediately on the screen. This is because in interactive mode, the interpreter immediately runs each command you type as soon as you press Enter to complete the command.

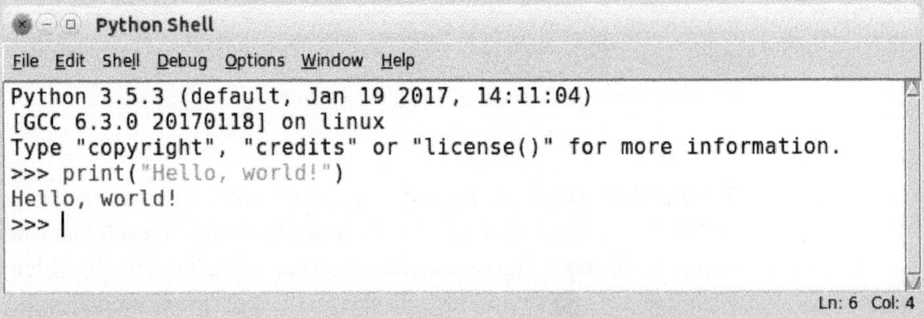

```
⊗ ⊖ ▢   Python Shell

File  Edit  Shell  Debug  Options  Window  Help

Python 3.5.3 (default, Jan 19 2017, 14:11:04)
[GCC 6.3.0 20170118] on linux
Type "copyright", "credits" or "license()" for more information.
>>> print("Hello, world!")
Hello, world!
>>> |

                                                            Ln: 6  Col: 4
```

Figure 1.3   IDLE editor in interactive mode

Continued on next page

Continued from previous page

To switch from interactive mode to normal mode in IDLE, you must click
File → New File. This pops up a second window for you to edit and save your
program as a file, as shown in Figure 1.4.

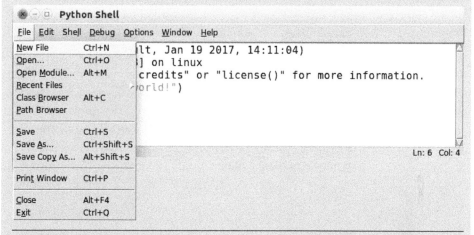

Figure 1.4   IDLE editor creating a new file

Notice that when you are in normal mode editing a file, the Python statements
you type do not display their results immediately. This allows you to write a larger
program containing several commands, then save and run that program, seeing the
results of all of the commands at once, as shown in Figure 1.5.

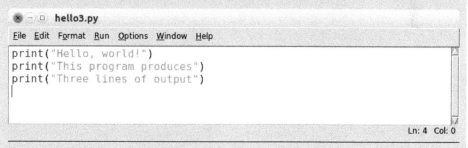

Figure 1.5   IDLE editor in normal mode

Once you have finished typing all of the commands into the program, you can run
it. In many editors, there is a "Play" or "Run" button near the top of the window.
In IDLE, you must click Run → Run Module from the top text menu bar. When
you run the program, the results of all of its statements appear in the output console
window as shown in Figure 1.6.

Continued on next page

Continued from previous page

Figure 1.6   IDLE editor running program and displaying its output

Every editor is different, and this was just one example. But no matter what software you use to type your Python programs, make sure to learn how to distinguish between typing individual commands into an interactive mode and editing a program file.

Did You Know?

Hello, World!

The "Hello, world" tradition was started by Brian Kernighan and Dennis Ritchie. Ritchie invented a programming language known as C in the 1970s and, together with Kernighan, coauthored the first book describing C, published in 1978. The first complete program in their book was a "Hello, world" program. Kernighan and Ritchie, as well as their book *The C Programming Language*, have been affectionately referred to as "K & R" ever since.

Many major programming languages have borrowed the basic C syntax as a way to leverage the popularity of C and to encourage programmers to switch to it. Languages such as C++, C#, and Java borrow a great deal of their core syntax from C. Python is also heavily influenced by C and its related family of languages, so we continue the "Hello, world" tradition in this text.

Printing Output

As you have seen, a Python program contains a series of statements for the computer to carry out. They are executed sequentially, starting with the first statement, then the second, then the third, and so on until the final statement has been executed. One of the simplest and most common statements is print, which is used to produce a line of output that is sent to the console window.

The simplest form of the `print` statement has nothing inside its parentheses and produces a blank line of output. You need to include the parentheses even if you don't have anything to put inside them.

```
print()
```

More often, however, you use `print` to output a line of text:

```
print("This line is a print statement.")
```

The above statement commands the computer to produce the following line of output:

```
This line is a print statement.
```

Each `print` statement produces a different line of output. For example, consider the following three statements:

```
print("This is the first line of output.")
print()
print("This is the third, below a blank line.")
```

Executing these statements produces the following three lines of output (the second line is blank):

```
This is the first line of output.

This is the third, below a blank line.
```

String Literals (Strings)

When you are writing Python programs (such as the preceding "hello world" program), you'll often want to include some literal text to send to the console window as output. Programmers have traditionally referred to such text as a *string* because it is composed of a sequence of characters that we string together. The Python language specification uses the term *string literals*.

In Python you specify a string literal by surrounding the literal text in quotation marks, as in:

```
"This is a string of text surrounded by quotation marks."
```

Python allows you to use either double quotation marks (") or single quotation apostrophe (') marks. The following is also a valid string literal:

```
'This string of text is surrounded by single-quote marks.'
```

Neither kind of quotation mark is inherently better or worse than the other. A string wrapped in one kind of quote marks can contain the other kind of quote marks inside it as part of the output. For example, the following are both valid string literals:

```
"This is a string even with 'these' quotes inside."
'This is also a string even with "these quotes" in it.'
```

A string literal must contain a quote at its start and end, and they must be the same type of quote. The following are not valid string literals:

```
"Wrong type of ending quote in this string.'
'Wrong type of ending quote in this string, too."
'I forgot my ending quote entirely.
And I forgot my beginning quote!"
```

String literals must not span more than one line of a program. The following is not a valid string literal:

```
"This is really bad stuff
right here."
```

If you do want to print a large multi-line message, you can enclose a string in three consecutive apostrophes, `'''`, at its start and end. For example, the following single `print` statement produces three lines of output:

```
print('''An old silent pond
A frog jumps into the pond
Splash! Silence again''')
```

However, the authors find the multi-line string style to be awkward to write and read, so we will not use it further in this text. We prefer to make each line of output its own `print` statement that uses a standard single-line string:

```
print("An old silent pond")
print("A frog jumps into the pond")
print("Splash! Silence again")
```

Escape Sequences

Any system that involves quoting text will lead you to certain difficult situations. For example, string literals are contained inside quotation marks, so how can you include a single quotation mark and a double quotation mark inside the same string literal?

   The solution is to embed what are known as *escape sequences* in the string literals. Escape sequences are two-character sequences that are used to represent special characters. They all begin with the backslash character (\). Table 1.3 lists some of the more common escape sequences.

Table 1.3   Common Escape Sequences

Sequence	Represents
\t	tab character
\n	new line character
\"	quotation mark (in a double-quoted string)
\'	apostrophe (in a single-quoted string)
\\	backslash character

Keep in mind that each of these two-character sequences actually stands for just a single character. For example, consider the following statement:

```
print("What \"characters\" does \\ this \\\\\\ print?")
```

If you executed this statement, you would get the following output:

```
What "characters" does \ this \\\ print?
```

The string literal has several escape sequences, each of which is two characters long and produces a single character of output.

While most string literals do not span multiple lines, you can use the \n escape sequence to embed a line break in a string. This leads to the odd situation where a single print statement can produce more than one line of output. For example, consider this statement:

```
print("This\nproduces 3 lines\nof output.")
```

If you execute it, you will get the following output:

```
This
produces 3 lines
of output.
```

The print itself produces one line of output, but the string literal contains two new-line characters that cause it to be broken up into a total of three lines of output. To produce the same output without newline characters, you would have to issue three separate print statements.

This is another programming habit that tends to vary according to taste. Some people (including the authors) find it hard to read string literals that contain \n escape sequences, but other people prefer to write fewer lines of code. Once again, you should make up your own mind about when to use the newline escape sequence.

Printing a Complex Figure

The `print` statement can be used to draw text figures as output. Consider the following more complicated program example (notice that it uses two empty `print` statements to produce blank lines):

```
 1  # This program draws several text figures, including
 2  # a diamond, an X, and a rocket ship.
 3
 4  print("   /\\")
 5  print("  /  \\")
 6  print(" /    \\")
 7  print(" \\    /")
 8  print("  \\  /")
 9  print("   \\/")
10  print()
11  print(" \\    /")
12  print("  \\  /")
13  print("   \\/")
14  print("   /\\")
15  print("  /  \\")
16  print(" /    \\")
17  print()
18  print("   /\\")
19  print("  /  \\")
20  print(" /    \\")
21  print("+------+")
22  print("|      |")
23  print("|      |")
24  print("+------+")
25  print("|United|")
26  print("|States|")
27  print("+------+")
28  print("|      |")
29  print("|      |")
30  print("+------+")
31  print("   /\\")
32  print("  /  \\")
33  print(" /    \\")
```

The following is the output the program generates. Notice that the program includes double backslash characters (\\), but the output has single backslash characters. This is an example of an escape sequence, as described previously.

```
   /\
  /  \
 /    \
 \    /
  \  /
   \/

  \    /
   \  /
    \/
    /\
   /  \
  /    \

   /\
  /  \
 /    \
+------+
|      |
|      |
+------+
|United|
|States|
+------+
|      |
|      |
+------+
  /\
 /  \
/    \
```

Comments, Whitespace, and Readability

Blank characters that appear in a program such as spaces, tabs, and line breaks are called *whitespace*. Python uses whitespace as part of its syntax; for example, pressing Enter to go to a new line marks the end of the current statement. Python also gives a special meaning to whitespace indentation at the start of lines, which we will discuss in the next section.

But otherwise, the language allows you to put in as many or as few spaces and blank lines as you like throughout the program. However, you should bear in mind that the layout of a program can enhance (or detract from) its readability. The following program is legal but hard to read:

```
print (
"Look at this beautiful program!"
    )

print(
"Isn't it great?"   )

print("I do believe it is")
print ( "The best program in the world." )
```

Here are some simple rules to follow that will make your programs more readable:

- Put each statement on a single line by itself.
- Use a consistent spacing style around `print` statements, parentheses, and other syntax.
- Use blank lines to separate groups of statements or related parts of the program.
- (As discussed in the next section) Indent functions by a consistent number of spaces or a tab. (A common choice is four spaces per level of indentation.)

Using these rules to rewrite the ugly program yields the following code:

```
1  print("Look at this beautiful program!")
2  print("Isn't it great?")
3
4  print("I do believe it is")
5  print("The best program in the world.")
```

The preceding rules and examples may lead you to believe that the goal is to produce shorter programs. But sometimes a program is too compact and becomes harder to read. For example, the following version of the ugly program requires only two lines, but we prefer the prior version that had better vertical separation of its statements and output.

```
1  print("Look at this beautiful program!\nIsn't it great?")
2  print("I do believe it is\nThe best program in the world.")
```

Well-written Python programs can be quite readable, but often you will want to include some explanations that are not part of the program itself. You can annotate programs by putting notes called *comments* in them.

> **Comment**
>
> Text that programmers include in a program to explain their code. The interpreter ignores comments.

There are two comment forms in Python. In the first and most common form, you write a hash character (#) to indicate that the rest of the current line (everything to the right of the hash sign) is a comment. The general form of a comment is the following:

```
# text of the comment
```
Syntax template: single-line comment

A common usage is to put a brief comment line before the start of a group of statements to describe the purpose of those statements:

```
# give an introduction to the user
print("Welcome to the game of blackjack.")
print()
print("Let me explain the rules.")
...
```

You can also put a comment at the end of a line after a statement, which is often used to make a note to the programmer about that particular statement:

```
print("You win!")    # Good job!
```

You can put almost any text you like inside the comment. If you want to write a multi-line message, you can write multiple lines that each begin with a hash sign. A common pattern is to write a *comment header* at the top of a program indicating the author, the course/instructor, and an overall description of the program:

```
# Thaddeus Martin
# Assignment #1
# Instructor: Professor Walingford
# Grader: Bianca Montgomery
#
# Program Description: This program displays a complex figure
# that draws patterns of repeating text characters.
```

Python also provides a second comment form that allows longer multi-line comments. You can use three apostrophe (') marks or three quotation (") marks in a row to begin a multi-line comment; the comment extends until you write another three apostrophes or quotation marks in a row to end it. For example, the following is a comment header equivalent to the one previously shown:

```
'''
Thaddeus Martin
Assignment #1
Instructor: Professor Walingford
Grader: Bianca Montgomery

Program Description: This program displays a complex figure
that draws patterns of repeating text characters.
'''
```

Technically the multi-line comment is actually a multi-line string. But if you don't print that string to the console using a `print` statement, it won't produce any output on the console and is therefore equivalent to a comment.

Some people prefer to use the multi-line comment form for long comments that span multiple lines, but it is safer to use the single-line form because you don't have to remember to close the comment. It also makes the comment stand out more. The authors tend to prefer the single-line comment style and will use it in most of the examples in this text. But this is a case where there is no true "correct" or "best" answer. If your instructor or manager does not tell you to use a particular comment style, you should decide for yourself which style you prefer and use it consistently.

Don't confuse comments with the text of `print` statements. The text of your comments will not be displayed as output when the program executes. The comments are there only to help readers examine and understand the program.

Commenting becomes more useful in larger and more complicated programs, as well as in programs that will be viewed or modified by more than one programmer. Clear comments are extremely helpful to explain to another person, or to yourself at a later time, what your program is doing and why it is doing it.

1.3 Program Errors

In 1949, Maurice Wilkes, an early pioneer of computing, expressed a sentiment that still rings true today:

> As soon as we started programming, we found out to our surprise that it wasn't as easy to get programs right as we had thought. Debugging had to be discovered. I can remember the exact instant when I realized that a large part of my life from then on was going to be spent in finding mistakes in my own programs.

You also will have to face this reality as you learn to program. You're going to make mistakes, just like every other programmer in history, and you're going to need strategies for eliminating those mistakes. Fortunately, the computer itself can help you with some of the work.

There are three kinds of errors that you'll encounter as you write programs:

- *Syntax errors* occur when you misuse Python. They are the programming equivalent of bad grammar and are caught by the Python interpreter.
- *Logic errors* occur when you write code that doesn't perform the task it is intended to perform.
- *Runtime errors* are logic errors that are so severe that Python stops your program from executing.

Syntax Errors

Human beings tend to be fairly forgiving about minor mistakes in speech. For example, we might find it to be odd phrasing, but we generally understand Master Yoda when he says, "Unfortunate that you rushed to face him . . . that incomplete was your training. Not ready for the burden were you."

The Python interpreter will be less forgiving. The interpreter reports syntax errors as it attempts to translate your program from Python into executable instructions if your program breaks any of Python's grammar rules. For example, if you forget a closing " quotation mark on a string or a closing) parenthesis in your program, you can send the interpreter into a tailspin of confusion. The interpreter may report several error messages, depending on what it thinks is wrong with your program.

A program will stop running when it reaches a statement that contains a syntax error. If you try to run your program and the interpreter reports errors, you must fix the errors and re-run the program. A program that contains syntax errors is considered to be incorrect, even if it executes some useful behavior before the error occurs, so you should get into the habit of fixing any errors you see in your programs.

Some development environments, such as PyDev or Eclipse, help you along the way by underlining syntax errors as you write your program. This makes it easy to spot errors and fix them even before you run the program to test it.

If your program reports an error but you can't figure out its cause, try looking at the error's line number and comparing the contents of that line with similar lines in other programs. You can also ask someone else, such as an instructor or lab assistant, to examine your program.

Common Programming Error

Misspelled Words

Python (like most programming languages) is very picky about spelling. You need to spell each word correctly, including proper capitalization. Suppose, for example, that you were to replace the `print` statement in the "hello world" program with the following:

```
# a print statement with a spelling error
prunt("Hello, world!")
```

Continued on next page

Continued from previous page

When you try to run this program, it will generate an error message similar to the following:

```
Traceback (most recent call last):
  File "<hello.py>", line 1, in <module>
NameError: name 'prunt' is not defined
```

It's a bit hard to read this error output if you are a new programmer. The interpreter is showing a "traceback," which is a listing of what state of execution the program was in when the error occurred. The next line of this output indicates that the error occurs in the file *hello.py* on line 1. The third line indicates that kind of error is a `NameError`, which means that Python did not understand a name that was written in the code. That same line gives more detail and says that the name it doesn't understand is `prunt`. That's because there is no such function or command; the function is called `print`.

The error message you see will take different forms depending on what you have misspelled, but it should always contain a line number and a description of what went wrong. Syntax errors are not always very clear, but if you pay attention to the line number of the error and learn to understand the error messages, you'll have a pretty good sense of where the error occurred and a start toward fixing it.

Common Programming Error

Not Closing a String Literal or Comment

Every string literal has to have an opening quote and a closing quote, but it's easy to forget the closing quotation mark, as shown in the following code:

```
# a print statement with a missing closing quote mark
print("Hello, world!)
```

This produces the following error message:

```
  File "<hello.py>", line 1
    print("Hello, world!)
                        ^
SyntaxError: EOL while scanning string literal
```

The error is harder to understand in this case. "EOL while scanning string literal"? "EOL" in this case stands for "end-of-line," indicating that the Python interpreter is upset because it sees the end of the line/statement without seeing a closing " mark for your string. If you forget to close a ' ' ' multi-line string, you'll see a similar

Continued on next page

Continued from previous page

error message, but it will complain about "EOF," which stands for "end-of-file." Learning to program can seem overwhelming because of jargon and acronyms like this, but it will get better the more you learn and practice. And you can always Google for definitions of terms you haven't seen before.

A similar problem occurs when you forget to write a closing parenthesis at the end of a `print` statement. Here is a program with two `print` statements, each of which has an error:

```
print("Hello, world!"
print("How are you?)"
```

The first `print` statement is missing its closing parenthesis. The second has its closing quotation mark and closing parenthesis out of order. The program produces the following error message when you try to run it:

```
File "bug3.py", line 2
    print("How are you?)"
        ^
SyntaxError: invalid syntax
```

This error message is particularly unhelpful. For starters, it lists the error as simply, "invalid syntax," which gives us no detail about what is wrong. Second, the interpreter lists line 2 as the cause of the problem, not line 1, where the parenthesis was actually forgotten. This is because the interpreter keeps looking forward for a closing parenthesis and isn't upset until it finds something that isn't a parenthesis, which it does when it reaches the word `print` on line 2. Unfortunately, as this case demonstrates, error messages don't always direct you to the correct line to be fixed.

Luckily, many Python editors color the parts of a program to help you identify them visually. If you forget to close a string literal or comment, usually the rest of your program will turn the wrong color, which can help you spot the mistake.

Logic Errors (Bugs)

Logic errors are also called *bugs*. Computer programmers use words like "bugridden" and "buggy" to describe poorly written programs, and the process of finding and eliminating bugs from programs is called debugging.

The word "bug" is an old engineering term that predates computers; early computing bugs sometimes occurred in hardware as well as software. Admiral Grace Hopper, an early pioneer of computing, is largely credited with popularizing the use of the term in the context of computer programming. She often told the true story of a group of programmers at Harvard University in the mid-1940s who couldn't figure out what was wrong with their programs until they opened up the computer and found an actual moth trapped inside.

The form that a bug takes may vary. Sometimes your program will simply behave improperly. For example, it might produce the wrong output. Other times it will ask the computer to perform some task that is clearly a mistake, in which case your program will have a runtime error that stops it from executing. In this chapter, since your knowledge of Python is limited, generally the only type of logic error you will see is a mistake in program output from an incorrect `print` statement or function call.

1.4 Procedural Decomposition

Brian Kernighan, coauthor of The C Programming Language, has said, "Controlling complexity is the essence of computer programming." People have only a modest capacity for detail. We can't solve complex problems all at once. Instead, we structure our problem solving by dividing the problem into manageable pieces and conquering each piece individually. We often use the term *decomposition* to describe this principle as applied to programming.

> **Decomposition**
>
> A separation into discernible parts, each of which is simpler than the whole.

With procedural programming languages like Python, decomposition involves dividing a complex task into a set of subtasks. This is a very verb- or action-oriented approach, involving dividing up the overall action into a series of smaller actions. This technique is called *procedural decomposition*. There are other kinds of decomposition, such as object-oriented decomposition, which we will explore later.

As a computer scientist, you should be familiar with many types of problem solving. This book devotes many chapters to mastering various aspects of the procedural approach. After you have thoroughly practiced procedural programming, we will turn to other kinds of decomposition.

As an example of procedural decomposition, consider the problem of baking a cake. You can divide this problem into the following subproblems:

- Make the batter.
- Bake the cake.
- Make the frosting.
- Frost the cake.

Each of these four tasks has details associated with it. To make the batter, for example, you follow these steps:

- Mix the dry ingredients.
- Cream the butter and sugar.
- Beat in the eggs.
- Stir in the dry ingredients.

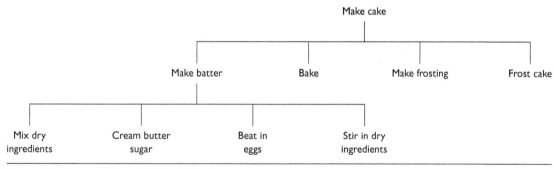

Figure 1.7   Decomposition of "Make cake" task

Thus, you divide the overall task into subtasks, which you further divide into even smaller subtasks. Eventually, you reach descriptions that are so simple they require no further explanation.

A partial diagram of this decomposition is shown in Figure 1.7. "Make cake" is the highest-level operation. It is defined in terms of four lower-level operations called "Make batter," "Bake," "Make frosting," and "Frost cake." The "Make batter" operation is defined in terms of even lower-level operations, and the same could be done for the other three operations. This diagram is called a structure diagram and is intended to show how a problem is broken down into subproblems. In this diagram, you can also tell in what order operations are performed by reading from left to right. That is not true of most structure diagrams. To determine the actual order in which subprograms are performed, you usually have to refer to the program itself.

One final problem-solving term has to do with the process of programming. Professional programmers develop programs in stages. Instead of trying to produce a complete working program all at once, they choose some piece of the problem to implement first. Then they add another piece, and another, and another. The overall program is built up slowly, piece by piece. This process is known as *iterative enhancement* or *stepwise refinement*.

Iterative Enhancement

The process of producing a program in stages, adding new functionality at each stage. A key feature of each iterative step is that you can test it to make sure that piece works before moving on.

Functions

In this section we will look at a construct that will allow you to iteratively enhance your Python programs to improve their structure and reduce their redundancy: functions. Other Python texts often do not discuss functions as early as we do here; instead, they show other techniques for decomposing problems. But even though functions require a bit of work to create, they are powerful and useful tools for improving basic Python programs.

Consider the following program, which draws two text boxes on the console:

```
1   # This program draws two text boxes. (version 1)
2   print("+------+")
3   print("|        |")
4   print("|        |")
5   print("+------+")
6   print()
7   print("+------+")
8   print("|        |")
9   print("|        |")
10  print("+------+")
```

The program works correctly, but the four lines used to draw the box appear twice. This redundancy is undesirable for several reasons. For example, you might wish to change the appearance of the boxes, in which case you'll have to make all of the edits twice. Also, you might wish to draw additional boxes, which would require you to type additional copies of (or copy and paste) the redundant lines.

A preferable program would include a Python command that specifies how to draw the box and then executes that command twice. Python doesn't have a "draw a box" command, but you can create one. Such a named command is called a *function*.

> **Function**
>
> A block of Python statements that is given a name and can be executed as a group.

Functions are units of procedural decomposition. We typically break a program into several functions, each of which solves some piece of the overall problem. A simple function is like a verb: It commands the computer to perform some action. Inside a Python program, you can define as many functions as you like.

Working with functions involves two major steps:

1. *Defining* the function, which means writing down the function's name and the set of statements it will contain.

2. *Calling* the function, which means indicating that you want to execute the statements contained in the function.

Let's look at each of these two steps in order. The definition of a function has the following general syntax:

```
def name():
    statement
    statement
    ...
    statement
```

Syntax template: Defining a function

For example, the following is the definition of a function named `draw_box` that draws a box of text:

```
def draw_box():
    print("+------+")
    print("|      |")
    print("|      |")
    print("+------+")
```

The first line is known as the function header. The word "`def`" here is short for "define," since we are defining a new function for Python to execute. You'll need to write `def`, followed by the name you want to give the function, followed by a set of parentheses and a colon. (The parentheses are needed because of a Python feature called parameters that we will learn in Chapter 3.)

The colon character in this context in Python indicates the beginning of a sequence of statements. As in the overall program, the statements of the function are executed in order from first to last. After the header in our sample function, a series of `print` statements makes up the body of our `draw_box` function.

Each statement that belongs to the function must be indented. You typically press the Tab character on your keyboard to increase your code's indentation level, which adds a given number of spaces (often 4) to the start of the line. The increased indentation is used in Python to group together related statements, such as the statements in a function. All of the statements must be indented exactly the same amount; if they are not, the program contains a syntax error. Most Python code editing programs will help you to keep your indentation consistent by auto-indenting each line to the right level after the first one.

Defining a function is like adding a new command to the Python language, giving a named alias to execute a sequence of commands. By defining the function `draw_box`, you are essentially saying to the Python interpreter, "Whenever I tell you to "draw_box," I really mean that you should execute all four of the `print` statements in the `draw_box` function."

But the command won't actually be executed unless our program explicitly says that it wants to do so. The act of executing a function is called a *function call*. The concept of defining and calling functions is a bit like recipes for cooking. Defining a function is like writing down a recipe for how to bake a cake. Calling a function is like following the recipe to actually bake the cake. If you define a function but don't call it, you don't get any cake.

> **Function Call**
>
> A command to execute a function, which causes all of the statements inside that function to be executed.

The syntax for calling a function is to write its name followed by two parentheses. You don't include the colon or the rest of the function, only its name and the parentheses.

```
function_name()
```
Syntax template: Calling a function

For example, to call the `draw_box` function and execute the statements inside it, include this line in your program below the `draw_box` definition, not indented:

```
draw_box()
```

Remember that our original program is supposed to draw two boxes. We can achieve this by executing the `draw_box` command twice in a row. The following program produces the same output as the original program but uses the `draw_box` function to do so:

```
 1   # This program draws two text boxes using a function. (v2)
 2   def draw_box():
 3       print("+------+")
 4       print("|      |")
 5       print("|      |")
 6       print("+------+")
 7
 8   draw_box()
 9   print()
10   draw_box()
```

The three unindented lines of code underneath the `draw_box` function consist of two calls on `draw_box` (which causes the function be executed twice) with a blank line between them. In programs with functions, the portion of the program that is unindented contains code that specifies which functions to execute, in what order, what number of times. We sometimes call this the *main program*.

> **Main Program**
>
> The unindented part of a Python program that specifies which statements and functions the overall program should execute.

This program is better than its predecessor, but once you start using functions, it is generally considered poor style to have any code that is outside of a function. For this reason, throughout this text we will also follow the convention of creating a function named `main` in which we will write the overall program code to execute. Some languages require a main function. Python does not, but we will follow this convention in all programs in this text.

Main Function

A function containing the main program code, specifying which statements and functions the overall program should execute.

The following program contains a `main` function. You'll notice that the last line of the program is simply `main()`, which tells Python to execute the `main` function. You can think of the program as having three parts: a definition of a `draw_box` function, a definition of a `main` function, and a call to execute the `main` function. The programs we write going forward will follow this format.

```
1   # This program draws two text boxes using a function. (v3)
2   # It also contains a main function to represent the program.
3   def draw_box():
4       print("+------+")
5       print("|      |")
6       print("|      |")
7       print("+------+")
8
9   def main():
10      draw_box()
11      print()
12      draw_box()
13
14  main()
```

Flow of Control

The most confusing thing about functions is that programs with functions do not seem to execute sequentially from top to bottom. Rather, each time the program encounters a function call, the execution of the program "jumps" to that function, executes each statement in that function in order, and then "jumps" back to the point where the call began and resumes executing. The order in which the statements of a program are executed is called the program's *flow of control*.

Flow of Control

The order in which the statements of a program are executed.

Let's look at the control flow of the program shown previously. Its `main` function contains the following statements:

```
draw_box()
print()
draw_box()
```

In a sense, the execution of this program is sequential: Each statement listed in the `main` function is executed in turn, from first to last. But this code includes two different calls on the `draw_box` function. This program will do three different things: execute `draw_box`, execute a `print`, then execute `draw_box` again, in that order.

Figure 1.8 indicates the flow of control produced by this program.

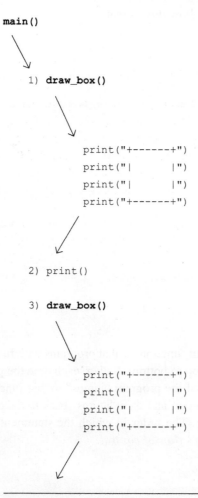

Figure 1.8 Control flow of function calls

Following the diagram, you can see that nine `print` statements are executed. First the program transfers control to the `draw_box` function and executes its four statements. Then it returns to the `main` function and executes the middle `print` statement. Then it transfers control a second time to `draw_box` and once again executes its four statements. Making these function calls is almost like copying and pasting the code of the function into the `main` function. As a result, this program has the exact same behavior as the nine-line main program code of the original program, whose code was:

```
# This program draws two text boxes. (version 1)
print("+------+")
print("|      |")
print("|      |")
print("+------+")
print()
print("+------+")
print("|      |")
print("|      |")
print("+------+")
```

The first version we wrote was simpler in terms of its flow of control, but the version with the function avoids the redundancy of having the same sequence `print` statements appear multiple times. It also gives a better sense of the structure of the solution. In the version with the function it is clear that there is a subtask of drawing a box that is being performed twice. Also consider what would happen if you wanted to add a third box to the output. You would have to add five more `print` statements again, whereas in the programs that use the `draw_box` function you can simply add one more `print` and a third call to the function.

A program can contain multiple functions, and Python allows you to define and call functions in any order you like. It is a common convention to put the `main` function last at the end of the program, and we will follow that convention in this text. The following program contains two functions aside from `main` and calls each of them multiple times:

```
1   # This program draws faces and text boxes using functions.
2   def draw_wide_box():
3       print("+------------+")
4       print("|            |")
5       print("+------------+")
6
7   def draw_face():
8       print("   _____   ")
9       print("  /      \\")
10      print("  |o    o|")
11      print("  |  .   |")
12      print("  | \_/  |")
13      print("   \_____/")
```

Continued on next page

Continued from previous page

```
14
15  def main():
16      draw_face()
17      draw_wide_box()
18      draw_wide_box()
19      draw_face()
20      draw_wide_box()
21
22  main()
```

The program produces the following output. Notice that the order of the figures that appear matches the order of the calls in the `main` function. The `main` function will always be the starting point for execution of our programs, and from that starting point you can determine the order in which other functions are called.

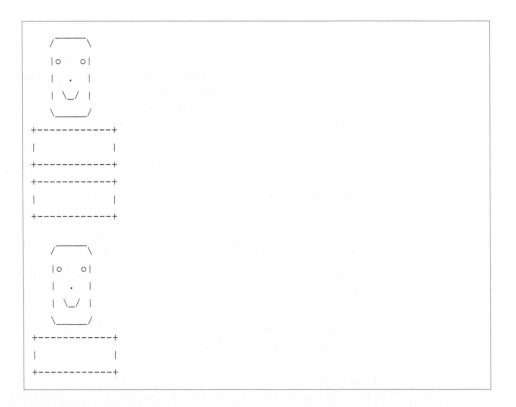

Identifiers and Keywords

Now that we are writing programs with functions and giving names to those functions, let's examine Python's rules about naming. The words used to name parts of a Python program are called *identifiers*.

> **Identifier**
>
> A name given to an entity in a program, such as a function.

Identifiers must start with a letter, which can be followed by any number of letters or digits. The following are all legal identifiers:

```
first            hiThere        numStudents        TwoBy4
```

The Python language specification allows identifiers to include the underscore character (_), which means that the following are legal identifiers as well:

```
two_plus_two      _count        _2__donuts         MAX_COUNT
```

The following are illegal identifiers:

```
two+two          hi there       hi-There       2by4          $money
```

Python has conventions for capitalization that are followed fairly consistently by programmers. Function names should be lowercase. When you are putting several words together to form a function name, place an underscore before each word after the first, such as `batten_down_the_hatches`. In a later chapter we'll discuss constants, which have yet another capitalization scheme, with all letters in uppercase. Following a strict naming scheme might seem like a tedious constraint, but using consistent capitalization in your code allows the reader to quickly identify the various code elements.

Python is case sensitive, so the identifiers `hello`, `Hello`, `HELLO`, and `hElLo` are all considered different. Keep this in mind as you read error messages from the interpreter. People are good at understanding what you write, even if you misspell words or make little mistakes like changing the capitalization of a word. However, mistakes like these cause the Python interpreter to become hopelessly confused.

Don't hesitate to use long identifiers. The more descriptive your names are, the easier it will be for people (including you) to read your programs. Descriptive identifiers are worth the time they take to type. A function name such as `search_for_account_late_fees` is a lot to type, but it is easier to understand than something terse like `find_late`.

Python has a set of predefined identifiers called *keywords* that are reserved for particular uses. As you read this book, you will learn many of these keywords and their uses. Table 1.4 shows the complete list of reserved keywords. You must use keywords only for their intended purposes; you should not use a keyword as the name of a function in your program, for example. For example, if you name a function `def` or `in`, this will cause a problem, because those are reserved keywords.

Table 1.4   List of Python Keywords (reference: Python.org)

and	as	assert	break	class
continue	def	del	elif	else
except	False	finally	for	from
global	if	import	in	is
lambda	None	nonlocal	not	or
pass	raise	return	True	try
while	with	yield		

Functions That Call Other Functions

The `main` function is not the only place where you can call a function. In fact, any function may call any other function. As a result, the flow of control can get quite complicated. Consider, for example, the following rather strange program. We use nonsense words like "foo," "bar," and "mumble" on purpose because the program is not intended to make sense.

```
1   # This program demonstrates functions that call other functions.
2   def foo():
3       print("foo")
4
5   def quux():
6       print("quux")
7
8   def bar():
9       print("bar 1")
10      quux()
11      print("bar 2")
12
13  def main():
14      foo()
15      bar()
16      print("mumble")
17
18  main()
```

You can't tell easily what output this program produces, so let's explore in detail what the program is doing. Remember that execution will always begin with the contents of the `main` function. In this program, `main` calls the `foo` function and the `bar` function and then executes a `print` statement, as shown in Figure 1.9.

This helps to make our picture of the flow of control more complete, but notice that `bar` calls the `quux` function, so we have to expand that as well, as shown in Figure 1.10.

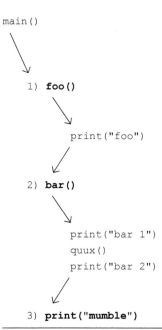

```
main()

    1) foo()

            print("foo")

    2) bar()

            print("bar 1")
            quux()
            print("bar 2")

    3) print("mumble")
```

Figure 1.9   Control flow of foobar function calls, v1

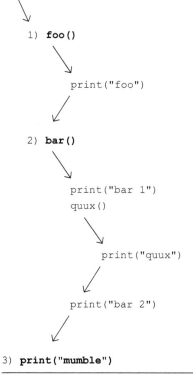

```
main()

    1) foo()

            print("foo")

    2) bar()

            print("bar 1")
            quux()

                print("quux")

            print("bar 2")

3) print("mumble")
```

Figure 1.10   Control flow of foobar function calls, v2

Finally, we have finished our picture of the flow of control of this program. It should make sense, then, that the program produces the following output:

```
foo
bar 1
quux
bar 2
mumble
```

We will see a much more useful example of functions calling functions when we go through the case study at the end of the chapter.

An Example Runtime Error

Runtime errors occur when a bug causes your program to be unable to continue executing. What could cause such a thing to happen? One example is if you asked the computer to calculate an invalid value, such as 1 divided by 0. Another example would be if your program tries to read data from a file that does not exist.

We haven't discussed how to compute values or read files yet, but there is a way you can "accidentally" cause a runtime error. The way to do this is to write a function that calls itself. If you do this, your program will not stop running, because the function will keep calling itself indefinitely, until the computer runs out of memory. When this happens, the program prints a large number of lines of output, and then eventually stops executing with an error message called a RecursionError. Here's an example:

```
1   # This program contains a runtime error.
2   def oops():
3       print("Make it stop!")
4       oops()
5
6   def main():
7       oops()
8
9   main()
```

This ill-fated program produces the following output (with large groups of identical lines represented by "..."):

```
Make it stop!
Make it stop!
Make it stop!
...
Make it stop!

Traceback (most recent call last):
  File "infinite.py", line 6, in <module>
    oops()
  File "infinite.py", line 4, in oops
    oops()
  File "infinite.py", line 4, in oops
    oops()
  File "infinite.py", line 3, in oops
    print("Make it stop!")
RecursionError: maximum recursion depth exceeded while calling a Python
object
```

Notice the distinction between a runtime error and a syntax error. A syntax error is when the programmer does not correctly follow the grammar rules of the Python language. A runtime error is when the program is legal but does not behave in a way that allows it to complete executing successfully. Our infinite program follows legal Python syntax, but it does not behave properly because of the programmer's mistake. This illustrates one of the simultaneous joys and frustrations of programming, which is that the computer will do exactly what you tell it to do, even if what you tell it to do is wrong.

Runtime errors are, unfortunately, something you'll have to live with as you learn to program. You will have to carefully ensure that your programs not only have proper syntax so that they can run successfully, but also do not contain any bugs that will cause a runtime error. The most common way to catch and fix runtime errors is to run the program several times to test its behavior.

1.5 Case Study: Drawing Figures

Earlier in the chapter, you saw a program that produced the following output:

```
     /\
    /  \
   /    \
   \    /
    \  /
     \/

    \    /
     \  /
      \/
      /\
     /  \
    /    \

     /\
    /  \
   /    \
  +------+
  |      |
  |      |
  +------+
  |United|
  |States|
  +------+
  |      |
  |      |
  +------+
    /\
   /  \
  /    \
```

It did so with a long sequence of `print` statements without any functions. In this section you'll improve the program by using functions for procedural decomposition to capture structure and eliminate redundancy. The redundancy might be more obvious, but let's start by improving the way the program captures the structure of the overall task.

Structured Version

If you look closely at the output, you'll see that it has a structure that would be desirable to capture in the program structure. The output is divided into three subfigures: the diamond, the X, and the rocket.

You can better indicate the structure of the program by dividing it into functions. Since there are three subfigures, you can create three functions, one for each subfigure. You should also create a `main` function that calls the other three. The following program produces the same output as the previous version:

```
 1   # This program draws several text figures, including
 2   # a diamond, an X, and a rocket ship.
 3   # (Version 2 with functions for structure.)
 4
 5   def draw_diamond():
 6       print("   /\\")
 7       print("  /  \\")
 8       print(" /    \\")
 9       print(" \\    /")
10       print("  \\  /")
11       print("   \\/")
12       print()
13
14   def draw_x():
15       print(" \\    /")
16       print("  \\  /")
17       print("   \\/")
18       print("   /\\")
19       print("  /  \\")
20       print(" /    \\")
21       print()
22
23   def draw_rocket():
24       print("   /\\")
25       print("  /  \\")
26       print(" /    \\")
27       print("+------+")
28       print("|      |")
29       print("|      |")
30       print("+------+")
```

Continued on next page

Continued from previous page

```
31        print("|United|")
32        print("|States|")
33        print("+------+")
34        print("|      |")
35        print("|      |")
36        print("+------+")
37        print("   /\\")
38        print("  /  \\")
39        print(" /    \\")
40
41  def main():
42        draw_diamond()
43        draw_x()
44        draw_rocket()
45
46  main()
```

The program has four functions defined within it. Each of the first three functions represents one of the three figures to be drawn: a diamond, an X, and a rocket ship. The `main` function appears last and calls the three other functions in order.

   This second version of the program is better than the first, but it can still be improved, which we will explore in the next section.

Final Version without Redundancy

Adding functions to our figure drawing program improves its structure, but the program still contains redundancy. Each of the three subfigures in our program has individual elements, and some of those elements appear in more than one of the three subfigures. For example, the program prints the following redundant group of lines several times:

The redundant sections are the top and bottom halves of the diamond shape and the box used in the rocket. A better version of our program adds an additional function for each redundant section of output. Here is the improved program:

```
1  # This program draws several text figures, including
2  # a diamond, an X, and a rocket ship.
3  # (Version 3 with functions for structure and redundancy.)
4
5  def draw_cone():
```

Continued on next page

Continued from previous page

```
 6        print("    /\\")
 7        print("   /  \\")
 8        print("  /    \\")
 9
10   def draw_v():
11        print(" \\    /")
12        print("  \\  /")
13        print("   \\/")
14
15   def draw_box():
16        print("+------+")
17        print("|      |")
18        print("|      |")
19        print("+------+")
20
21   def draw_diamond():
22        draw_cone()
23        draw_v()
24        print()
25
26   def draw_x():
27        draw_v()
28        draw_cone()
29        print()
30
31   def draw_rocket():
32        draw_cone()
33        draw_box()
34        print("|United|")
35        print("|States|")
36        draw_box()
37        draw_cone()
38
39   def main():
40        draw_diamond()
41        draw_x()
42        draw_rocket()
43
44   main()
```

This program has seven functions defined within it. The main function calls three of these functions. These three functions in turn call three other functions.

Analysis of Flow of Execution

The structure diagram in Figure 1.11 shows which functions `main` calls and which functions each of them calls. As you can see, this program has three levels of structure and two levels of decomposition. The overall task is split into three subtasks, each of which has two subtasks.

A program with functions has a more complex flow of control than one without them, but the rules are still fairly simple. Remember that when a function is called, the computer executes the statements in the body of that function. Then the computer proceeds to the next statement after the function call. Also remember that the program starts with the `main` function, executing its statements from first to last.

So, to execute the program, the computer first executes its `main` function. That, in turn, first executes the body of the function `draw_diamond`. `draw_diamond` executes the functions `draw_cone` and `draw_v` (in that order). When `draw_diamond` finishes executing, control shifts to the next statement in the body of the `main` function: the call to the `draw_x` function. A complete breakdown of the flow of control from function to function is shown in Figure 1.12.

Recall that the order in which you define functions does not have to parallel the order in which they are executed. The order of execution is determined by the `main` function and by the bodies of functions called from it. A function definition is like a dictionary entry: it defines a word, but it does not specify how the word will be used. The body of this program's `main` function says to first execute `draw_diamond`, then `draw_x`, then `draw_rocket`. This is the order of execution, regardless of the order in which the functions are defined. Consistency is important, though, so that you can easily find a function later in a large program.

It is important to note that the three versions of this program produce exactly the same output to the console. While the first version may be the easiest program for a novice to read, the second and particularly the third have many advantages over it. For one, a well-structured solution is easier to comprehend, and the functions themselves become a means of explaining the program. Also, programs with functions are more flexible and can more easily be

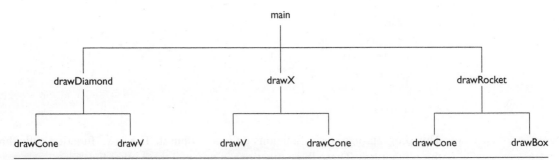

Figure 1.11   Decomposition of third version of figure-drawing program

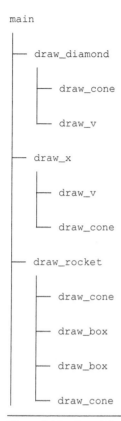

```
main

  ├── draw_diamond
  │      ├── draw_cone
  │      └── draw_v
  ├── draw_x
  │      ├── draw_v
  │      └── draw_cone
  ├── draw_rocket
         ├── draw_cone
         ├── draw_box
         ├── draw_box
         └── draw_cone
```

Figure 1.12 Control flow of third version of figure-drawing program

adapted to similar but different tasks. You can take the six functions defined and write a new program to produce a larger and more complex output. Building functions to create new commands increases your flexibility without adding unnecessary complication. For example, you could replace the `main` function code with a version that calls the other functions in the following new order. What output would it produce?

```python
def main():
    draw_cone()
    draw_cone()
    draw_rocket()
    draw_x()
    draw_rocket()
    draw_diamond()
    draw_box()
    draw_diamond()
    draw_x()
    draw_rocket()
```

Chapter Summary

- Computers execute sets of instructions called programs. Computers store information internally as sequences of 0s and 1s (binary numbers).
- Programming and computer science deal with algorithms, which are step-by-step descriptions for solving problems.
- Python is a modern programming language with a simple syntax that has a large set of libraries you can use to build complex programs.
- A program is translated from text into computer instructions by another program called an interpreter. Python's interpreter reads and executes each statement of your program to run it. Python programmers typically complete their work using an editor called an Integrated Development Environment (IDE). The commands may vary from environment to environment, but the same three-step process is always involved:

  1. Type in a Python program into your editor.
  2. Save the program to a file ending with `.py`.
  3. Run the program using the interpreter.

- Python uses a command called `print` to display text on the console screen.
- Written words in a program can take different meanings. Keywords are special reserved words that are part of the language. Identifiers are words defined by the programmer to name entities in the program. Words can also be put into strings, which are pieces of text that can be printed to the console.
- Python programs that use proper spacing and layout are more readable to programmers. Readability is also improved by writing notes called comments inside the program.
- The Python language has a syntax, or a legal set of commands that can be used. A Python program that does not follow the proper syntax will not run. A program that does follow proper syntax but that is written incorrectly may still contain errors that occur when the program runs. A third kind of error is a logic or intent error, which occurs when the program runs but does not do what the programmer intended.
- Commands in programs are called statements. A program can group statements into larger commands called functions. Functions help the programmer group code into reusable pieces.
- Iterative enhancement is the process of building a program piece by piece, testing the program at each step before advancing to the next.
- Complex programming tasks should be broken down into the major tasks the computer must perform. This process is called procedural decomposition. Correct use of functions aids procedural decomposition.

Self-Check Problems

Section 1.1: Basic Computing Concepts

1. Why do computers use binary numbers?

2. Convert each of the following decimal numbers into its equivalent binary number:

   a. 6
   b. 44
   c. 72
   d. 131

3. What is the decimal equivalent of each of the following binary numbers?

   a. 100
   b. 1011
   c. 101010
   d. 1001110

4. In your own words, describe an algorithm for baking cookies. Assume that you have a large number of hungry friends, so you'll want to produce several batches of cookies!

Section 1.2: And Now: Python

5. Which of the following can be used in a Python program as identifiers?

  a. `printed`
  b. `first-name`
  c. `annual_salary`
  d. `"hello"`
  e. `abc`
  f. `42isTheAnswer`
  g. `sum_of_data`
  h. `>average`
  i. `b4`

6. Which of the following is the correct syntax to output a message?

  a. `print(Hello, world!)`
  b. `print("Hello, world!')`
  c. `print("Hello, world!")`
  d. `print "Hello, world!"`
  e. `print"(Hello, world!)"`

7. What is the output produced from the following statements?

```
print("\"Quotes\"")
print("Slashes \\//")
print("How '\"confounding' \"\\\" it is!")
```

8. What is the output produced from the following statements?

```
print("name\tage\theight")
print("Archie\t17\t5'9\"")
print("Betty\t17\t5'6\"")
print("Jughead\t16\t6'")
```

9. What is the output produced from the following statements?

```
print("Shaq is 7'1")
print("The string \"\" is an empty message.")
print("\\'\"\"")
```

10. What is the output produced from the following statements? (Notice that the strings in this problem have single quotes.)

```
print('\ta\tb\tc"')
print('\\\\')
print('"')
print('\'\'\'')
print('C:\nin\the downward spiral')
```

11. What is the output produced from the following statements?

```
print("Dear \"DoubleSlash\" magazine,")
print()
print("\tYour publication confuses me. Is it")
print("a \\\\ slash or a //// slash?")
print("\nSincerely,")
print("Susan \"Suzy\" Smith")
```

12. What series of `print` statements would produce the following output?

```
"Several slashes are sometimes seen,"
said Sally. "I've said so." See?
\ / \\ // \\\ ///
```

13. What series of `print` statements would produce the following output?

```
This is a test of your
knowledge of "quotes" used
in 'string literals.'

You're bound to "get it right"
if you read the section on
''quotes.''
```

14. Write a `print` statement that produces the following output:

```
/ \ // \\ /// \\\
```

Section 1.3: Program Errors

15. Name the three errors in the following program:

```
my_program:
    print("This is a test of the"
    print(emergency broadcast system.)
```

16. Name the three errors in the following program:

```
def main:
print("Speak friend")
print("and enter)
```

Section 1.4: Procedural Decomposition

17. Which of the following function headers uses the correct syntax?

```
a. def example():
b. def example() {
c. def example()
d. example def():
e. def example[]:
```

18. What is the output of the following program? (You may wish to draw a structure diagram first.)

```
def main():
    message1()
    message2()
    print("Done with main.")

def message1():
    print("This is message1.")

def message2():
    print("This is message2.")
    message1()
    print("Done with message2.")

main()
```

19. What is the output of the following program? (You may wish to draw a structure diagram first.)

```
def first():
    print("Inside first function")

def second():
    print("Inside second function")
    first()

def third():
    print("Inside third function")
    first()
    second()

def main():
    first()
    third()
    second()
    third()

main()
```

20. What would have been the output of the preceding program if the third function had contained the following statements?

```
def third():
    first()
    second()
    print("Inside third function")
```

21. What would have been the output of the last full program if the `main` function had contained the following statements? (Use the original version of third, not the modified version from the most recent exercise.)

```
def main():
    second()
    first()
    second()
    third()
```

22. The following program contains at least eight syntax errors. What are they?

```
def main():
        print(Hello, world!)
    essage()


def message
    print('This program surely cannot '
    print("have any "errors" in it");
```

Exercises

1. Write a complete Python program that prints the following output:

```
//////////////////////
|| Victory is mine! ||
\\\\\\\\\\\\\\\\\\\\\\
```

2. Write a complete Python program that prints the following output:

```
  \/
 \\//
\\\///
///\\\
 //\\
  /\
```

3. Write a complete Python program that prints the following output:

```
A well-formed Python program has a main
function with : at the end of the line.

A print statement has ( and ) and usually
a string that starts and ends with a
" or ' character.
(But we type \" or \' instead!)
```

4. Write a complete Python program that prints the following output:

```
What is the difference between
a ' and a \'? Or between a " and a \"?
' and " can be used to define strings
\' and \" are used to print quotes
```

5. Write a complete Python program that prints the following output. Use at least one function besides main to help you.

```
There's one thing every coder must understand:
showing output with the print command.

There's one thing every coder must understand:
showing output with the print command.
```

6. Write a complete Python program that prints the following output. Use at least one function besides main to help you.

```
/////////////////////
|| Victory is mine! ||
\\\\\\\\\\\\\\\\\\\\\
|| Victory is mine! ||
\\\\\\\\\\\\\\\\\\\\\
|| Victory is mine! ||
\\\\\\\\\\\\\\\\\\\\\
|| Victory is mine! ||
\\\\\\\\\\\\\\\\\\\\\
|| Victory is mine! ||
\\\\\\\\\\\\\\\\\\\\\
```

7. Write a program that displays the following output:

```
     /‾‾‾‾‾‾\
    /        \
 _"_'_"_'_"_
    \        /
     _____/
```

8. Modify the program from the previous exercise so that it displays the following output. Use functions as appropriate.

9. Write a Python program that generates the following output. Use functions to show structure and eliminate redundancy in your solution. Note that there are two rocket ships next to each other. What redundancy can you eliminate using functions? What redundancy cannot be eliminated?

```
    /\          /\
   /  \        /  \
  /    \      /    \
 +------+ +------+
 |      | |      |
 |      | |      |
 +------+ +------+
 |United| |United|
 |States| |States|
 +------+ +------+
 |      | |      |
 |      | |      |
 +------+ +------+
    /\          /\
   /  \        /  \
  /    \      /    \
```

10. Write a program that produces this output. Use at least two functions to show structure and eliminate redundancy in your solution.

```
Go, team, go!
You can do it.

Go, team, go!
You can do it.
You're the best,
In the West.
Go, team, go!
You can do it.

Go, team, go!
You can do it.
You're the best,
in the West.
Go, team, go!
You can do it.

Go, team, go!
You can do it.
```

11. Write a Python program that generates the following output. Use functions to show structure and eliminate redundancy in your solution.

```
*****
*****
 *  *
  *
 *  *

*****
*****
 *  *
  *
 *  *
*****
*****

  *
  *
  *
*****
```

Continued on next page

Continued from previous page

```
*****
 *   *
   *
 *   *
```

12. Write a Python program that generates the following output. Use functions to show structure and eliminate redundancy in your solution.

```
      /‾‾‾‾‾\
     /       \
     \       /
      \_____/


      /‾‾‾‾‾\
     /       \
     \       /
      \_____/
   +--------+


      /‾‾‾‾‾\
     /       \
     |  STOP  |
     \       /
      \_____/
   +--------+
```

Programming Projects

1. Write a program to spell out MISSISSIPPI using block letters like the following (one per line):

```
M       M    IIIII     SSSSS      PPPPP
MM     MM      I      S     S     P     P
M M M M        I      S           P     P
M   M   M      I       SSSSS      PPPPP
M       M      I            S     P
M       M      I      S     S     P
M       M    IIIII     SSSSS      P
```

2. Sometimes we write similar letters to different people. For example, you might write to your parents to tell them about your classes and your friends and to ask for money; you might write to a friend about your love life, your classes, and your hobbies; and you might write to your brother about your hobbies and your friends and to ask for money. Write a program that prints similar letters such as these to three people of your choice. Each letter should have at least one paragraph in common with each of the other letters. Your main program should have three function calls, one for each of the people to whom you are writing. Try to isolate repeated tasks into functions.

3. Write a program that produces as output the words of "The Twelve Days of Christmas." (Functions simplify this task.) Here are the first two verses and the last verse of the song:

```
On the first day of Christmas, my true love sent to me
a partridge in a pear tree.

On the second day of Christmas, my true love sent to me
two turtle doves, and
a partridge in a pear tree.


...


On the twelfth day of Christmas, my true love sent to me
Twelve drummers drumming,
eleven pipers piping,
ten lords a-leaping,
nine ladies dancing,
eight maids a-milking,
seven swans a-swimming,
six geese a-laying,
five golden rings,
four calling birds,
three French hens,
two turtle doves, and
a partridge in a pear tree.
```

4. Write a program that produces as output the words of "The House That Jack Built." Use methods for each verse and for repeated text. Here are lyrics to use:

```
This is the house that Jack built.

This is the malt
That lay in the house that Jack built.

This is the rat,
That ate the malt
That lay in the house that Jack built.

This is the cat,
That killed the rat,
That ate the malt
That lay in the house that Jack built.

This is the dog,
That worried the cat,
That killed the rat,
That ate the malt
That lay in the house that Jack built.

This is the cow with the crumpled horn,
That tossed the dog,
That worried the cat,
That killed the rat,
That ate the malt
That lay in the house that Jack built.

This is the maiden all forlorn
That milked the cow with the crumpled horn,
That tossed the dog,
That worried the cat,
That killed the rat,
That ate the malt
That lay in the house that Jack built.
```

## Chapter 2

Data and Definite Loops

Introduction

Now that you know something about the basic structure of Python programs, you are ready to learn how to solve more complex problems. For the time being we will still concentrate on programs that produce output, but we will begin to explore some of the aspects of programming that require problem-solving skills.

The first half of this chapter fills in two important areas. First, it examines expressions, which are used to perform simple computations in Python, particularly those involving numeric data. Second, it discusses program elements called variables that can change in value as the program executes.

The second half of the chapter introduces your first control structure: the for loop. You use this structure to repeat actions in a program. This is useful whenever you find a pattern in a task such as the creation of a complex figure, because you can use a for loop to repeat the action to create that particular pattern. The challenge is finding each pattern and figuring out what repeated actions will reproduce it.

The for loop is a flexible control structure that can be used for many tasks. In this chapter we use it for definite loops, where you know exactly how many times you want to perform a particular task. In Chapter 5 we will discuss how to write indefinite loops, where you don't know in advance how many times to perform a task.

2.1 Basic Data Concepts

Programs manipulate information, and information comes in many forms. For example, a program to keep track of library book rentals might store each book's title, author, ISBN number, date it was checked out, name of the person to whom it was checked out, and more. Each of these pieces of data is a different kind of data: the title and author are words of text, the ISBN is an integer, the checkout time is a calendar date, and so forth. The idea of different pieces of data coming in different forms and having different allowed sets of values is related to the notion of data types, which we will explore in this section.

Types

Python programs can manipulate data, such as performing numerical computations similar to a calculator (1 + 1 equals 2) or searching through a body of text for a given keyword (display all dictionary words that begin with the letter "k"). Every piece of data that you manipulate in a Python program will be of a certain *type*, where a type describes a set of related values along with a set of operations you can perform on those values. One example of a type is integers, which includes values like 0, 1, 2, −4, 65536, and so on; and operations such as addition, subtraction, and multiplication. As you write code you will often find yourself thinking about what types of data you intend to use.

> **Data Type**
>
> A name for a category of data values that are all related, such as type `int` in Python that represents integer values.

Some programming languages have a syntax that insists on the programmer explicitly referring to types of data throughout the code. Python has a shorter and simpler syntax where the type of each piece of data you mention in your program is generally automatically inferred from the data value itself. For example, if you write a Python program that asks to compute the result of 1 + 1, the Python interpreter infers that you are performing a calculation on integers.

Python includes a wide variety of built-in types. We will not explore all of them in this chapter or even in this text as a whole, since some of them are not needed for basic programs. Table 2.1 lists some of Python's built-in data types.

Let's begin our exploration of data and types by looking at calculations with numbers. We will focus on two numeric data types in Python: `int`, which represents integers

Table 2.1   Commonly Used Data Types in Python

Type	Description	Examples
int	integers (whole numbers)	42, 3, 18, 20493, 0
float	real numbers	7.35, 14.9, 19.83423, 6.022e23
str	sequences of text characters (strings)	"hello", 'X', "abc 1 2 3!", ""
bool	logical values	True, False

(whole numbers) such as 42; and `float`, which represents real numbers with a decimal point such as 3.14. The type names `int` and `float` are Python keywords, and we will explore the usage of those keywords later in this chapter.

It may seem odd to use one type for integers and another type for real numbers. Isn't every integer a real number? The answer is yes, but these are fundamentally different types of numbers. The difference is so great that we make this distinction even in English. We don't ask, "How much sisters do you have?" or "How many do you weigh?" We realize that sisters come in discrete integer quantities (0 sisters, 1 sister, 2 sisters, 3 sisters, and so on), and we use the word "many" for integer quantities ("How many sisters do you have?"). Similarly, we realize that weight can vary by tiny amounts (175 pounds versus 175.5 pounds versus 175.25 pounds, and so on), and we use the word "much" for these real-number quantities ("How much do you weigh?").

In programming, this distinction is even more important, because integers and real numbers are represented in different ways in the computer's memory: Integers are stored exactly, while real numbers are stored as approximations with a limited number of digits of accuracy. You will see that storing values as approximations can lead to round-off errors when you use real number values.

The name `float` for real values is not very intuitive. It's an accident of history in much the same way that we still talk about "dialing" a number on our telephones even though modern telephones don't have dials. Real numbers in computing are often referred to as *floating-point numbers* because of the way that a computer's central processing unit (CPU) represents and handles them. In 1972 the C programming language introduced a data type called `float` for storing real numbers; the name caught on and was used by later languages as well. A more intuitive name might be `real`, which is what they're called in some languages, but the old C name of `float` is familiar and used by Python and many other languages. So programmers will continue to use the word `float` for real numbers, and people will still talk about "dialing" people on the phone even if they've never touched a telephone dial.

Expressions

When you write programs, you will often need to include values and calculations. The technical term for these elements is *expressions*.

> **Expression**
>
> A simple value or a set of operations that produces a value.

The simplest expression is a specific value, like 42 or 28.9. We call these "literal values," or *literals* for short. More complex expressions involve combining simple values. Suppose, for example, that you want to know how many bottles of water you have. If you have two 6-packs, four 4-packs, and two individual bottles, you can compute the total number of bottles with the following expression:

```
(2 * 6) + (4 * 4) + 2
```

Notice that we use an asterisk to represent multiplication and that we use parentheses to group parts of the expression. The computer determines the value of an expression by *evaluating* it.

> **Evaluation**
>
> The process of obtaining the value of an expression.

The value obtained when an expression is evaluated is called the *result*. Complex expressions are formed using *operators*.

> **Operator**
>
> A special symbol (like + or *) that is used to indicate an operation to be performed on one or more values.

The values used in the expression are called *operands*. For example, consider the following simple expressions:

```
3 + 29
4 * 5
```

The operators here are the + and *, and the operands are simple numbers.

```
     3              +            29
     |              |             |
  operand       operator      operand
     |              |             |
     4              *             5
```

When you form complex expressions, these simpler expressions can in turn become operands for other operators. For example, consider the following expression:

```
(3 + 29) - (4 * 5)
```

This expression has two levels of arithmetic operators:

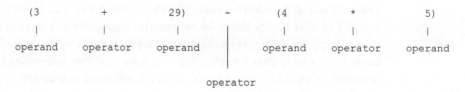

```
    (3          +          29)        -        (4          *          5)
     |          |           |         |         |          |           |
  operand   operator    operand       |      operand   operator    operand
                                      |
                                  operator
```

The addition operator has simple operands of 3 and 29 and the multiplication operator has simple operands of 4 and 5, but the subtraction operator has operands that are each parenthesized expressions with operators of their own. Thus, complex expressions can be built from smaller expressions. At the lowest level, you have simple numbers. These are used as operands to make more complex expressions, which in turn can be used as operands in even more complex expressions.

There are many things you can do with expressions. One of the simplest things you can do is to type expressions into the Python Shell, which causes the interpreter to evaluate them and display their results. This is a great way to learn more about expressions and operators:

```
>>> 1 + 1
2
>>> (3 + 29) - (4 * 5)
12
```

If you are writing a program to be saved in a file, you can print the result of an expression using a `print` statement. For example, the following three `print` statements produce the following three lines of output:

```
print(75)
print(2 + 2)
print((3 + 29) - (4 * 5))
```

```
75
4
12
```

Notice that for the second `print`, the computer evaluates the expression (adding 2 and 2) and prints the result (in this case, 4). For the third `print`, the computer evaluates all of the arithmetic operators and prints the result. You will see many different operators as you progress through this book, all of which can be used to form expressions. Expressions can be arbitrarily complex, with as many operators as you like. For that reason, when we tell you, "An expression can be used here," we mean that you can use arbitrary expressions that include complex expressions as well as simple values.

The spacing in expressions is optional; you can write 3+4 or 3 + 4 and achieve the same result. We prefer to put spaces between an operator and its operands, and that is the style we'll follow in this textbook. The designers of Python have written a Python official style guide "PEP" that also recommends a single space on each side of an operator.

Literals

The simplest expressions refer to values directly using what are known as *literals*. An integer literal (considered to be of type `int`) is a sequence of digits with or without a leading + or – sign:

```
3    482    -29434    0    92348    +9812
```

A real number literal (considered to be of type `float`) is any number that includes a decimal point:

```
298.4    0.284    207.    .2843    42.0    -17.452    -.98
```

Notice that `207.` and `42.0` are considered to be type `float` even though they coincide with integers, because of the decimal point. Literals of type `float` can also be expressed in scientific notation (a number followed by e followed by an integer):

```
2.3e4    1e-5    3.84e92    2.458e12
```

The first of these numbers represents 2.3 times 10 to the 4th power, which equals 23,000. Even though this value happens to coincide with an integer, it is considered to be of type `float` because it is expressed in scientific notation. The second number represents 1 times 10 to the negative 5th power, which is equal to 0.00001. The third number represents 3.84 times 10 to the 92nd power. The fourth number represents 2.458 times 10 to the 12th power.

We have seen that textual information can be represented as strings that contain a sequence of characters. Strings in quotation marks are considered literal values of type `str`. In later chapters we will explore strings in more detail, including how to examine and manipulate the characters of a string. As we saw previously, a string literal consists of zero or more characters enclosed in single or double quotation marks:

```
'abc'    "hello"    "I'm happy!"    'Michael "Air" Jordan'    "X"    ""
```

Finally, the type `bool` stores logical information. We won't be exploring the use of type `bool` until we reach Chapter 4 and see how to introduce logical tests into our programs, but for completeness, we include the `bool` literal values here. Logic deals with just two possibilities: `True` and `False`. These two Python keywords are the two literal values of type `bool`:

```
True    False
```

Arithmetic Operators

The basic arithmetic operators are shown in Table 2.2. The addition and subtraction operators will, of course, look familiar to you, as should the asterisk as a multiplication operator and the forward slash as a division operator.

Table 2.2 Arithmetic Operators in Python

Operator	Meaning	Example	Result
+	addition	2 + 2	4
-	subtraction	53 - 18	35
*	multiplication	3 * 8	24
/	division	9 / 2	4.5
//	integer division	9 // 2	4
%	remainder or mod	19 % 5	4
**	exponentiation	3 ** 4	81

The `**` syntax for exponentiation may seem unusual, but the behavior matches what you would expect. An expression such as 3 `**` 5 means 3^5, or 3 raised to the 5th power, which is 3 `*` 3 `*` 3 `*` 3 `*` 3, which evaluates to 243.

Division is the most complex of the basic arithmetic operations, so it deserves further discussion. Dividing with the / operator produces a real number result represented as a `float` value. The result will be of type `float` even if both operands are integers. The following interaction in the Python Shell shows some examples of this:

```
>>> 11.0 / 4.0
2.75
>>> 1 / 2
0.5
>>> 12 / 2
6.0
>>> 119 / 5
23.8
```

But as we'll see throughout this textbook, there are often situations where we want to perform integer division and produce an integer (`int`) quotient. As you learned from doing long division in school, the results of integer division can be expressed as two integers, a quotient and a remainder:

```
119 divided by 5 = 23 (quotient) with 4 (remainder)
```

You can compute the integer quotient and remainder from division using the // and % operators, respectively. Here are some examples in the Python Shell that show these arithmetic operators:

```
>>> 119 // 5
23
>>> 119 % 5
4
```

These two division operators should be familiar if you recall how long-division calculations are performed. Consider the result you'd get when dividing 1079 by 34 longhand on paper:

```
        31
34 ) 1079
     102

       59
       34

       25
```

Here, dividing 1079 by 34 yields 31 with a remainder of 25. Using arithmetic operators, the problem would be described like this:

```
1079 // 34 evaluates to 31
1079 %  34 evaluates to 25
```

It takes a while to get used to integer division in Python. When you are using the integer division operator (//), the key thing to keep in mind is that it truncates (discards) anything after the decimal point. So, if you imagine computing an answer on a calculator, just think of ignoring anything after the decimal point, as shown in the following examples in the Python Shell. Notice that the number is never rounded up; even if its fractional component is above 0.5, the integer division result is always rounded down by discarding the portion after the decimal point.

```
>>> 19 // 5     # 19 / 5 is  3.8 on a calculator
3
>>> 207 // 10   # 207 / 10 is 20.7 on a calculator
20
>>> 7 // 8      # 7 / 8 is 0.875 on a calculator
0
```

The operator % computes the remainder left over from integer division. It is usually referred to as the "modulus" or "mod" operator. The mod operator lets you know how much was left unaccounted for by the truncating // division operator. For example, given the previous examples, you'd compute the mod results as shown in Table 2.3.

In each case, you figure out how much of the number is accounted for by the truncating division operator. The mod operator gives you any excess (the remainder). When you put this into a formula, you can think of the mod operator as behaving as follows:

```
x % y = x - (x // y) * y
```

Table 2.3   Examples of % Mod Operator

Mod problem	First divide	What does division account for?	How much is left over?	Answer
19 % 5	19 // 5 is 3	3 * 5 is 15	19 - 15 is 4	4
207 % 10	207 // 10 is 20	20 * 10 is 200	207 - 200 is 7	7
7 % 8	7 // 8 is 0	0 * 8 is 0	7 - 0 is 7	7

It is possible to get a result of 0 for the mod operator. This happens when one number divides evenly into another. For example, each of the following expressions evaluates to 0 because the second number goes evenly into the first number:

```
>>> 28 % 7
0
>>> 95 % 5
0
>>> 44 % 2
0
```

A few special cases are worth noting because they are not always immediately obvious to novice programmers:

- **Numerator smaller than denominator:** In this case division produces 0 and mod produces the original number.
- **Numerator of 0:** In this case both division and mod produce 0.
- **Denominator of 0:** In this case, both division and mod are undefined and produce a runtime error. For example, a program that attempts to evaluate any of 7 / 0, 7 // 0, or 7 % 0 will produce an error.

The following interactions in the Python Shell demonstrate these special cases:

```
>>> 7 // 10      # numerator smaller than denominator
0
>>> 7 % 10
7
>>> 0 // 10      # numerator of 0
0
>>> 0 % 10
0
>>> 7 // 0       # denominator of 0
Traceback (most recent call last):
  File "<stdin>", line 1, in <module>
ZeroDivisionError: integer division or modulo by zero
```

The mod operator has many useful applications in computer programs. Here are just a few:

- Testing whether a number is even or odd (`number % 2` is `0` for evens, and `number % 2` is `1` for odds).
- Finding individual digits of a number (e.g., `number % 10` is the final digit).
- Finding the last four digits of a social security number (`number % 10000`).

The remainder operator can be used with `floats` as well as with integers, and it works similarly: You consider how much is left over when you take away as many "whole" values as you can. For example, the expression `10.1 % 2.4` evaluates to `0.5` because you can take away four `2.4` values from `10.1`, leaving you with `0.5` left over. But the use of `%` is much more common with integers than `float` values.

The integer division operator `//` can also be used with `floats`. It performs an exact division but then truncates the fractional component, replacing it with `.0`. For example, the expression `7.0 // 2.0` evaluates to `3.0`.

Precedence

Python expressions are like complex noun phrases in English in that they are subject to ambiguity. For example, consider the phrase, "the man on the hill by the river with the telescope." Is the river by the hill or by the man? Is the man holding the telescope, or is the telescope on the hill, or is the telescope in the river? We don't know how to group the various parts together.

You can get the same kind of ambiguity if parentheses aren't used to group the parts of a Python expression. For example, the expression `2 + 3 * 4` has two operators. Which operation is performed first? You could interpret this as `(2 + 3) * 4`, which would evaluate to `5 * 4` or `20`. Or it could be `2 + (3 * 4)`, which would be `2 + 12` or `14`.

To deal with this kind of ambiguity, Python has a set of rules called *precedence* that determine the order in which various parts of an expression will be grouped together and evaluated.

> **Precedence**
> The binding power of an operator, which determines how to group and evaluate parts of an expression.

The computer applies rules of precedence when the grouping of operators in an expression is ambiguous. An operator with high precedence is evaluated first, followed by operators of lower precedence. Within a given level of precedence the operators are evaluated in one direction, usually left to right.

Table 2.4 Python Operator Precedence

Description	Operators
exponentiation	`**`
unary operators	`+, -`
multiplicative operators	`*, /, //, %`
additive operators	`+, -`

For the expressions we have seen, parentheses receive the highest level of precedence. After that, the exponentiation operator `**` has the highest precedence. The multiplicative operators `*, /, //, %` are next, followed by the additive operators `+` and `-`.

Table 2.4 lists these levels of precedence in descending order. (Placing a `+` or `-` sign in front of a number is considered a "unary" operator that modifies only a single operand, and those unary operators are listed in the table for completeness.) The order of precedence is the same as in the "PEMDAS" acronym many students are taught in school, short for "Parentheses, Exponents, Multiplication / Division, Addition / Subtraction."

Thus, the expression `2 + 3 * 4` is evaluated to `14` as follows:

```
2   +   3   *   4
            \___/
2   +       12
_____/
      14
```

Within the same level of precedence, arithmetic operators are evaluated from left to right. This often doesn't make a difference in the final result, but occasionally it does. Consider, for example, the expression `40 - 25 - 9`, which evaluates to `6` as follows:

```
40   -   25   -   9
_____/
     15    -   9
     _____/
          6
```

The expression would produce a different result if the second subtraction were evaluated first.

You can always override precedence with parentheses. For example, if you really want the second subtraction to be evaluated first, you can force that to happen by introducing parentheses and writing `40 - (25 - 9)`. The expression would then evaluate as follows:

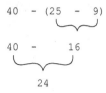

```
40  -  (25  -  9)
           ⌣

40  -      16
  ⌣

      24
```

Another concept in arithmetic is *unary* plus and minus, which take a single operand, as opposed to the binary operators we have seen thus far (e.g., `*`, `/`, and even binary + and –), all of which take two operands. For example, we can find the negation of `8` by asking for `-8`. These unary operators have a higher level of precedence than the multiplicative operators. Consequently, we can form expressions like `12 * -8`, which evaluates to `-96`.

We will see many other types of operators in the next few chapters. As we introduce more operators, we'll update the precedence listing in Table 2.4 to include them as well.

Before we leave this topic, let's look at a complex expression and see how it is evaluated step by step. Consider the following expression:

```
13 * 2 + 239 // 10 % 5 - 2 * 2
```

It has a total of six operators: two multiplications, one integer division, one mod, one subtraction, and one addition. The multiplication, division, and mod operations will be performed first, because they have higher precedence, and they will be performed from left to right because they are all at the same level of precedence. Now we evaluate the additive operators from left to right. The final result of the long expression is `25`.

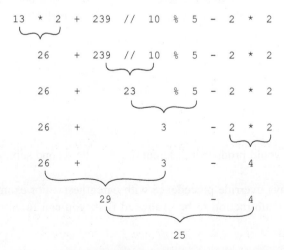

```
13  *  2  +  239  //  10  %  5  -  2  *  2
  ⌣

   26  +  239  //  10  %  5  -  2  *  2
              ⌣

   26  +       23      %  5  -  2  *  2
                        ⌣

   26  +               3      -  2  *  2
                                 ⌣

   26  +               3      -     4
     ⌣

         29                   -     4
           ⌣

                   25
```

Mixing and Converting Types

You'll often find yourself mixing values of different types and wanting to convert from one type to another. Python has simple rules to avoid confusion and provides a mechanism for requesting that a value be converted from one type to another.

Two types that are frequently mixed are `int`s and `float`s. You might, for example, ask Python to compute `2 * 3.6`. This expression includes the `int` literal 2 and the `float` literal `3.6`. In this case, Python converts the `int` into a `float` and performs the computation entirely with `float` values. This is always the rule when Python encounters an `int` where it was expecting a `float`. These rules hold true even if there is an equivalent `int` that could have been used to represent the result. For example, `2 * 3.0` evaluates to the `float` value of `6.0` and not the `int` value of `6`.

The preceding is called an *implicit conversion* between types. But sometimes you want to perform an *explicit conversion* between types, such as turning a `float` into an `int`. You can ask Python for this conversion by writing the desired type name followed by the value or expression to convert in parentheses. The general syntax template for converting one type to another is:

type(expression)
Syntax template: Type conversion

For example, the expression `int(4.75)` will convert the `float` value of `4.75` into the `int` value 4. When you convert a `float` value to an `int`, it does not round to the nearest integer; it simply truncates anything after the decimal point. There is also a `float` conversion that turns an integer value into a real number.

```
>>> int(4.75)       # convert to int
4
>>> int(17.3)
17
>>> int(3.14159)
3
>>> float(42)       # convert to float
42.0
```

Perhaps it's unclear why you would want to explicitly convert `4.75` into `4`. Why not just write `4` in the code in the first place? The more likely case where you'd use a type conversion is when you're computing the result of a more complex expression.

If you want to convert the result of an expression, you have to be careful to use the parentheses properly. For example, suppose that you have some books that are each

0.15 feet wide and you want to know how many of them will fit in a bookshelf that is 2.5 feet wide. You could do a straight division of `2.5 / 0.15`, but that evaluates to a `float` result that is between 16 and 17. Americans use the phrase "16 and change" as a way to express the idea that a value is larger than 16 but not as big as 17. Even if you use the integer division `//` operator and write `2.5 // 0.15`, the result is a `float` result of `16.0`. In this case, we don't care about the "change"; we only want to compute the 16 part. You might form the following expression:

```
>>> int(2.5) / 0.15
13.333333333333334
```

Unfortunately, this expression evaluates to the wrong answer because the type conversion is applied to whatever is in the parentheses (here, the value `2.5`). This converts `2.5` into the integer 2, divides by 0.15, and evaluates to 13 and change, which isn't an integer and isn't the right answer. Instead, you want to form this expression:

```
>>> int(2.5 / 0.15)
16
```

This expression first performs the division to get 16 and change, and then converts that value to an `int` by truncating it. It thus evaluates to the `int` value 16, which is the answer you're looking for.

Some languages call a conversion between types a type *cast*, as in, "casting a value in a different light."

2.2 Variables

As you write larger programs with data and expressions, you will find that you end up with calculations that you want to use multiple times in your program. For example, you might write the following code to calculate the cost of some purchased items before and after taxes:

```
# cost of items before/after 10% tax
print("Subtotal:")
print(30 + 22 + 17 + 46)
```

Continued on next page

Continued from previous page

```
print("Taxes:")
print((30 + 22 + 17 + 46) * 0.1)
print("Total:")
print((30 + 22 + 17 + 46) * 1.10)
```

```
Subtotal:
115
Taxes:
11.5
Total:
125.5
```

Notice that the subtotal amount of (30 + 22 + 17 + 46) is used three times in the code, which is redundant. We'd like to eliminate the redundancy by calculating the subtotal amount a single time and then referring to the resulting value throughout the code. Python has a feature called variables that is made for just this kind of situation. A *variable* is a location in the computer's memory that is given a name and a value. The program can store a value and retrieve it for use later.

> **Variable**
>
> A memory location with a name that stores a value.

Think of the computer's memory as being like a giant spreadsheet that has many cells where data can be stored. When you create a variable in Python, you are asking it to set aside one of those cells for this new variable. When you define the variable, you store an initial value in the cell. And as with a spreadsheet, you will have the option to change the value in that cell later.

When you create a variable, you have to decide on a name to use to refer to this memory location. The normal rules of Python identifiers apply (the name must start with a letter or underscore, which can be followed by any combination of letters, underscores, and digits). The standard convention in Python is for variable names to consist of lowercase letters, as in `number` or `digits`. If you want a multi-word variable name, place an underscore in front of any subsequent words, as in `number_of_students` or `average_age`.

To use a variable in a Python program, they must state its name and the value you want to store in it. The line of code that creates a variable and gives a value to it is called a *variable definition*.

> **Variable Definition**
>
> A request to set aside memory for a new variable with a given name and value.

A variable definition uses the following syntax:

```
name = expression
```

When the Python interpreter reaches a variable definition, it first calculates the result of the expression on the right side of the = sign. Then it stores that value into the computer's memory and associates it with the `name` on the left side of the = sign.

Once you have defined a variable, you can use that variable in your code. If you write the variable's name in an expression, it is equivalent to writing the value stored in that variable. For example, the following code has the same output as the previous code but uses a variable named `subtotal` to store the cost of the items rather than rewriting and recalculating that expression three times:

```
# cost of items before/after 10% tax (using a variable)
subtotal = 30 + 22 + 17 + 46
print("Subtotal:")
print(subtotal)
print("Taxes:")
print(subtotal * 0.1)
print("Total:")
print(subtotal * 1.10)
```

You can also try out variables in the Python Shell. If you define a variable and then type its name afterward, the shell will report its value to you:

```
>>> x = 1 + 1
>>> x
2
>>> y = x + 3
>>> y
5
>>> x * 3 + y
11
```

It is an error to refer to a variable that has not been defined. If there is no variable named x, the following code will result in an error:

```
# bug: try to print a variable
# that has not been defined
print("The value of x is:")
print(x)
```

```
The value of x is:
Traceback (most recent call last):
  File "undefined.py", line 7, in <module>
    main()
  File "undefined.py", line 5, in main
    print(x)
NameError: name 'x' is not defined
```

One very common variable definition statement that points out the difference between algebraic relationships and program statements is:

```
x = x + 1
```

Remember not to think of this as "x equals x + 1." There are no numbers that satisfy that mathematical equation. We read this as, "x's value should be updated to become the value of x plus one." This may seem a rather odd statement, but you should be able to decipher it given the rules outlined earlier. Suppose that the current value of x is 19. To execute the statement, you first evaluate the expression to obtain the result 20. The computer stores this value in the variable named on the left, x. Thus, this statement adds one to the value of the variable. We refer to this as *incrementing* the value of x. It is a fundamental programming operation because it is the programming equivalent of counting (1, 2, 3, 4, and so on). The following statement is a variation that counts down, which we call *decrementing* a variable:

```
x = x - 1      # decrement a variable (decrease its value)
```

We will discuss incrementing and decrementing in more detail later in the following section.

You can also define several variables in a single statement. The syntax is to write their names separated by commas, followed by an equals sign, followed by their values in the same order separated by commas:

```
name, name, ..., name = expression, expression, ..., expression
```
Syntax template: Defining multiple variables in a single statement

The following example defines three variables named height, weight, and age. It sets height to store 70, sets weight to store 195, and sets age to store 40.

```
# define several variables and set their values
height, weight, age = 70, 195, 40
```

The authors find the preceding syntax hard to read and prefer to define only a single variable on each line.

A Program with Variables

To explore more uses of variables, let's examine a larger program that computes a value called the *basal metabolic rate* (BMR), which is the number of calories a person burns in 24 hours if their body is completely at rest. Of course, a person does not remain completely at rest for 24 straight hours, and an active person burns more calories in a day than their BMR. But BMR can still be an interesting estimation of a lower bound for the minimum number of calories a person would need to eat in a day to sustain their vital organs.

Given an individual's height, weight, age, and sex, we can compute that person's BMR using the following formulas:

- men: BMR $= 10 \times$ (weight in kg) $+ 6.25 \times$ (height in cm)
$- 5 \times$ (age in years) $+ 5$
- women: BMR $= 10 \times$ (weight in kg) $+ 6.25 \times$ (height in cm)
$- 5 \times$ (age in years) $- 161$

Or if you use American units of measurement, as we'll do in the rest of this section, the formulas are the following:

- men: BMR $= 4.54545 \times$ (weight in lb) $+ 15.875 \times$ (height in inches)
$- 5 \times$ (age in years) $+ 5$
- women: BMR $= 4.54545 \times$ (weight in lb) $+ 15.875 \times$ (height in inches)
$- 5 \times$ (age in years) $- 161$

The height, weight, and age are important parts of the BMR formula. A program to calculate BMR, then, would naturally have three variables for these three pieces of information. There are several details that we need to discuss about variables, but it can be helpful to look at a complete program first to see the overall picture. The following program computes and prints the BMR for a 40-year-old male and female who are 5 feet 10 inches tall and weigh 195 pounds:

```
 1   # This program calculates a person's Basal Metabolic Rate (BMR),
 2   # which is the number of calories burned when at rest for 24 hours.
 3
 4   def main():
 5       # define variables
 6       height = 70
 7       weight = 195
 8       age = 40
 9
10       # compute BMR for male and female
11       bmr_m = 4.54545 * weight + 15.875 * height - 5 * age + 5
12       bmr_f = 4.54545 * weight + 15.875 * height - 5 * age - 161
13
```

Continued on next page

Continued from previous page

```
14      # print results
15      print("Your Basal Metabolic Rate (BMR) is the number")
16      print("of calories that your body burns when you are")
17      print("at rest for 24 hours.")
18      print()
19      print("Current BMR (male):")
20      print(bmr_m)
21      print("Current BMR (female):")
22      print(bmr_f)
23
24  main()
```

Notice that the program includes blank lines to separate the sections and comments to indicate what the different parts of the program do. It produces the following output:

```
Your Basal Metabolic Rate (BMR) is the number
of calories that your body burns when you are
at rest for 24 hours.

Current BMR (male):
1802.61275
Current BMR (female):
1636.61275
```

Let's now examine the details of this program to understand how its variables work. For example, in the following code, the first line defines a variable named `height` and sets its value to `70`. The second line defines a variable named `weight` and sets its value to `195`. The third line defines a variable named `age` and sets its value to `40`.

```
height = 70
weight = 195
age = 40
```

Once a variable is defined, Python sets aside a memory location to store its value. Our variable definition stores the value `70` in the memory location for the variable `height`, indicating that this person is 70 inches tall (5 feet 10 inches).

We sometimes draw pictures of variables as boxes to indicate the memory used for them, with the variable's value inside the box. After the Python interpreter executes the three statements above, the memory looks like this:

height | 70 | weight | 195 | age | 40 |

You can think of a variable as being a named alias for a given value. By setting `height` to be `70`, you can now refer to `height` later in your program and the program will substitute the value `70` in its place.

Variable definitions can appear anywhere a statement can occur. Every variable stores a value of a particular type. Our variable named `height` stores the value `70`, which is of type `int`. We don't have to explicitly write the type of the variable in the code; the Python interpreter figures it out based on the context of the code. Some other programming languages require the programmer to explicitly specify what type of data the variable will hold, but Python does not.

The value stored in a variable does not have to be a simple literal value. You can write a more complex expression; that expression will be evaluated, and its result will be stored into the variable. For example, the following variable definition defines the variable `height` to store the value `77`:

```
height = 44 + 3 * 11
```

When the statement executes, the computer first evaluates the expression on the right side of the = sign; then, it stores the result in the memory location for the given variable. The next two lines of our program contain two more definitions for variables named `bmr_m` and `bmr_f`. These definitions each use a formula (an expression to be evaluated):

```
bmr_m = 4.54545 * weight + 15.875 * height - 5 * age + 5
bmr_f = 4.54545 * weight + 15.875 * height - 5 * age - 161
```

The Python interpreter calculates the value of each expression and stores the result into each variable. When the expression refers to a variable such as `weight`, `height`, or `age`, the interpreter substitutes the value of that variable as defined previously. All of the same operator behavior and precedence still apply when using variables in an expression. The following diagram breaks down the evaluation of the value for the `bmr_m` variable:

```
                    195              70           40
                     |                |            |
bmr_m = 4.54545 * weight + 15.875 * height - 5 * age + 5
                  ᴗᴗᴗ

          886.36275    + 15.875 * height - 5 * age + 5
                               ᴗᴗᴗ

          886.36275    +     1111.25     - 5 * age + 5
                                              ᴗᴗᴗ

          886.36275    +     1111.25     -  200   + 5
                    ᴗᴗᴗᴗᴗᴗ

                 1997.61275                -  200   + 5
                      ᴗᴗᴗᴗᴗᴗ

                       1797.61275                  + 5
                            ᴗᴗᴗᴗᴗᴗ

bmr_m =                                      1802.61275
```

So, after the computer has executed the `bmr_m` variable definition, the memory looks like this:

height `70`   weight `195`   age `40`   bmr_m `1802.61275`

The `bmr_f` variable is calculated in a similar way. The last lines of the program report the BMR result using `print` statements:

```
print("Current BMR (male):")
print(bmr_m)
print("Current BMR (female):")
print(bmr_f)
```

Notice that we can include a variable in a `print` statement the same way that we include literal values and other expressions to be printed.

As its name implies, a variable can take on different values at different times. The first time a variable is defined is called an *initialization*, while a change to the value of a variable is called an *assignment*.

Initialization

Defining a variable for the first time in your program.

Assignment

Storing a new value into an already existing variable, replacing the previous value.

For example, consider the following variation of the BMR program, which computes a new BMR for a male user, assuming the person lost 15 pounds (going from 195 pounds to 180 pounds).

```
1  # This program calculates a male user's Basal Metabolic Rate
2  # (BMR) both before and after losing 15 pounds.
3
4  def main():
5      # define variables
6      height = 70
7      weight = 195
8      age = 40
9
```

Continued on next page

Continued from previous page

```
10       # compute and print BMR for male user before weight loss
11       bmr_m = 4.54545 * weight + 15.875 * height - 5 * age + 5
12       print("Previous BMR (male):")
13       print(bmr_m)
14
15       # compute and print BMR for male user after weight loss
16       weight = 180
17       bmr_m = 4.54545 * weight + 15.875 * height - 5 * age + 5
18       print("Current BMR (male):")
19       print(bmr_m)
20
21   main()
```

The program begins the same way, setting the variables to the following values and reporting this initial value for the male BMR:

height	70	weight	195	age	40	bmr_m	1802.61275

But the new program then includes the following definition:

```
weight = 180
```

This changes the value of the `weight` variable:

height	70	weight	**180**	age	40	bmr_m	1802.61275

You might think that this would also change the value of the `bmr_m` variable. After all, earlier in the program we said that the following should be true:

```
bmr_m = 4.54545 * weight + 15.875 * height - 5 * age + 5
```

This is a place where the spreadsheet analogy is not as accurate. A spreadsheet can store formulas in its cells and when you update one cell it can cause the values in other cells to be updated. The same is not true in Python.

You might also be misled by the use of an equals sign for assignment. Don't confuse this statement with a statement of equality. The assignment statement does not represent an algebraic relationship. In algebra, you might say:

```
x = y + 2
```

In mathematics you state definitively that x is equal to y plus two, a fact that is true now and forever. If x changes, y will change accordingly, and vice versa. Python's variable definition statement is very different.

The definition statement is a command to perform an action at a particular point in time. It does not represent a lasting relationship between variables. That's why we usually say "stores" or "becomes" rather than saying "equals" when we read variable definition statements.

Getting back to the program, resetting the variable called `weight` does not reset the variable called `bmr_m`. To recompute `bmr_m` based on the new value for `weight`, we must include the second assignment statement:

```
weight = 180
bmr_m = 4.54545 * weight + 15.875 * height - 5 * age + 5
```

Otherwise, the variable `bmr_m` would store the same value as before. That would be an incorrect outcome to report to someone who's just lost 15 pounds. By including both of these statements, we reset both the `weight` and `bmr_m` variables so that memory looks like this:

height	70		weight	180		age	40		bmr_m	**1734.431**

The output of the new version of the program is:

```
Previous BMR (male):
1802.61275
Current BMR (male):
1734.431
```

Increment/Decrement Operators

In addition to standard assignment with =, Python has several special operators that are useful for a particular family of operations that are common in programming. As we mentioned earlier, you will often find yourself increasing the value of a variable by a particular amount, an operation called *incrementing*. You will also often find yourself decreasing the value of a variable by a particular amount, an operation called *decrementing*. To accomplish this, you write statements like the following:

```
x = x + 1
y = y - 1
z = z + 2
```

Likewise, you'll frequently find yourself wanting to double or triple the value of a variable or to reduce its value by a factor of 2, in which case you might write code like the following:

```
x = x * 2
y = y * 3
z = z // 2
```

Python has a shorthand for these situations. You glue together the operator character (+, -, *, etc.) with the equals sign to get a special *assignment operator* (+=, -=, *=, etc.). This variation allows you to rewrite assignment statements like the previous ones as follows:

```
x += 1
y -= 1
z += 2

x *= 2
y *= 3
z //= 2
```

This convention is yet another detail to learn about Python, but it can make the code easier to read. Think of a statement like x += 2 as saying, "add 2 to x." That's more concise than saying x = x + 2.

Some other languages have special operators ++ and -- for the operation of incrementing or decrementing a variable by 1. (The C++ language got its name because it is one "increment" above its predecessor language, C.) Python does not include ++ or -- operators because the language designers felt the existing += and -= operators were more clear.

Printing Multiple Values

You saw in Chapter 1 that you can output string literals using print. You can also output numeric expressions and variables' values using print. The statement in the following code causes the interpreter first to evaluate the expression, which yields the value 14, and then to write that value to the console window.

```
print(12 + 3 - 1)
```

You have also seen that you can also include the value of a variable in a print statement. The following code prints the number of years until a person of a given age can retire from their job at age 65:

```
age = 40
years_until_retirement = 65 - age
```

Continued on next page

Continued from previous page

```
print("You will retire in this many years:")
print(years_until_retirement)
```

```
You will retire in this many years:
25
```

You'll often want to output more than one value on a line, such as a variable or expression's value with text before it. In our preceding example it might be better to print the retirement information on a single line, such as:

```
You will retire in 25 years.
```

To do so, Python allows you to supply multiple values in a `print` statement, separated by commas. All of the values or expressions you provide will be printed, with a blank space between them. The general syntax is the following:

```
print(expression, expression, ..., expression)
```
Syntax template: Printing multiple values

For example, to print the desired single line of retirement output, we can write:

```
age = 40
years_until_retirement = 65 - age
print("You will retire in", years_until_retirement, "years.")
```

```
You will retire in 25 years.
```

You need to pay close attention to the quotation marks and commas in a line like this to keep track of which parts are "inside" a string literal and which are outside. This line of output begins with the text "You will retire in", then a space, then the value of the variable `years_until_retirement`, then another space, and finally the text "years." By contrast, the following line is incorrect and does not insert the variable's value because it is inside the quotation marks of the string:

```
print("You will retire in, years_until_retirement, years.")
```

Providing multiple values in a `print` statement is related to the concept of function *parameters*, which we will discuss in detail in the next chapter. You will often use the multiple-value `print` syntax in conjunction with variables. For example, consider the following program that computes the number of hours, minutes, and seconds in a standard year: Notice that the three `print` commands at the end each have a string literal followed by a comma and a variable name.

```
 1  def main():
 2      hours = 365 * 24
 3      minutes = hours * 60
 4      seconds = minutes * 60
 5
 6      print("Hours   in a year =", hours)
 7      print("Minutes in a year =", minutes)
 8      print("Seconds in a year =", seconds)
 9
10  main()
```

```
Hours   in a year = 8760
Minutes in a year = 525600
Seconds in a year = 31536000
```

You can print arbitrarily complex expressions. For example, if you had variables named x, y, and z, you might want to display their values in coordinate format with parentheses and commas as shown in the following code. Notice the careful placement of quotation marks and commas. If x, y, and z had the values 8, 19, and 23, respectively, this statement would produce the following output:

```
print("(", x, ",", y, ",", z, ")")
```

```
( 8 , 19 , 23 )
```

By default the multiple values in a `print` statement are separated by single spaces. If you want to change the separator between values, you can do so using a special syntax. Just before the closing) parenthesis in the `print` statement, you write `sep=` followed by the string to print between the multiple values. The general syntax is the following:

```
print(expression, expression, ..., expression, sep="text")
```
Syntax template: Printing with a custom separator between values

For example, to print a date in year / month / day format, you could write the following code:

```
year = 2021
month = 1
day = 20
print("Today is", year, month, day, sep="/")
```

```
Today is 2021/1/20
```

We won't use the sep= syntax much in this text, but it is useful in the cases where you need precise control over your output format.

Another syntax for printing multiple values is to use the str function, which converts any value into a string, and then concatenate these strings together using + operators. The following code is equivalent to the previous example but using str:

```
year = 2021
month = 1
day = 20
print("Today is " + str(year) + "/" + str(month) + "/" + str(day))
```

```
Today is 2021/1/20
```

The authors prefer to avoid the use of str in most cases and will tend to favor the comma-separated style whenever reasonably possible. But you may see code examples online and in other texts that use str heavily, partly because the str style is more similar to the way multiple values are printed in other languages such as Java and C++.

2.3 The for Loop

Programming often involves specifying redundant tasks. The for loop helps to avoid such redundancy by repeatedly executing a sequence of statements over a particular range of values.

Suppose you want to write a program that repeats a printed message several times, like a chant being repeated by sports fans at your university. If your school's team is the Wildcats, you could write a program like this:

```
1   # This program prints a repeating chant.
2   def main():
3       print("Go, Cats, Go!")
4       print("Go, Cats, Go!")
```

Continued on next page

Continued from previous page

```
5      print("Go, Cats, Go!")
6      print("Go, Cats, Go!")
7      print("BEAR DOWN!")
8
9  main()
```

The program produces the following output:

```
Go, Cats, Go!
Go, Cats, Go!
Go, Cats, Go!
Go, Cats, Go!
BEAR DOWN!
```

This code approach is tedious because the program has four `print` statements that are exactly the same. You could put the `print` statement into a function and call that function four times instead, but now the function calls themselves are redundant. The more repeated copies of the chant, the worse this redundancy would get.

Python's `for` loop is made for exactly this kind of situation. A `for` loop is a statement that instructs the interpreter to execute a line or lines a given number of times. The `for` loop has the following general syntax:

```
for name in range(max):
    statements
```
Syntax template: for loop

For example, to print the same output as the previous program with a `for` loop, you could write the following code:

```
1  # This program prints a repeating chant using a for loop.
2  def main():
3      for i in range(4):
4          print("Go, Cats, Go!")
5      print("BEAR DOWN!")
6
7  main()
```

An oversimplified mental model of the `for` loop is, whatever number you write in the parentheses after `range` is the number of times the statement in the loop will repeat. If you changed the preceding program to say `range(10)`, the message would print 10 times. Notice that the last line printing "BEAR DOWN!" is not indented; it is not part of the `for` loop and will print only a single time.

You can try out `for` loops in the Python Shell. If you type the loop's header and press Enter, the shell will show a second line with a "..." in front of it, and you can type the loop's indented body on that line. After typing a blank line, the shell will run the loop and display its output:

```
>>> for i in range(3):
...     print("Hello, Python Shell")
...
Hello, Python Shell
Hello, Python Shell
Hello, Python Shell
```

The `for` loop is the first example of a *control structure* that we will study. A control structure is a language element that controls other statements.

Control Structure

A syntactic structure that controls other statements.

The initial line that contains the word `for` is called the *header* or *heading* of the loop, and the indented statement or statements being repeated are called the *body* of the loop. A `for` loop can repeat one statement or multiple statements. For example, the following program has a `for` loop containing two statements:

```
1   # This program prints part of a song.
2   # It demonstrates a for loop with two lines in its body.
3
4   def main():
5       print("My Coding Song:")
6       for i in range(3):
7           print("'C' is for 'Coding'")
8           print("That's good enough for me!")
9       print("Oh!")
10      print("Coding, Coding, Coding starts with 'C'!")
11  main()
```

The `print` statement that comes before the `for` loop, and the two `print` statements after the `for` loop, will not be repeated. These statements are not indented and are not included as part of the loop's body. The program produces the follow-ing output:

```
My Coding Song:
'C' is for 'Coding'
That's good enough for me!
'C' is for 'Coding'
That's good enough for me!
'C' is for 'Coding'
That's good enough for me!
Oh!
Coding, Coding, Coding starts with 'C'!
```

Notice the order of the lines in the output. The two indented lines inside the `for` loop are repeated three times. The repeated lines appear in pairs; it prints the first line, then the second line, then the first, then the second, and so on.

Be careful to use consistent indentation to indicate controlled statements. All con-secutive indented lines after the loop header are considered to be part of the body of that loop.

A program can contain multiple `for` loops. The following new version of our song program produces similar output to the original, but with two repetitions of the final line of the song:

```
 1  # This program prints part of a song.
 2  # It demonstrates a for loop with two lines in its body.
 3
 4  def main():
 5      print("My Coding Song:")
 6      for i in range(3):
 7          print("'C' is for 'Coding'")
 8          print("That's good enough for me!")
 9      print("Oh!")
10      for i in range(2):
11          print("Coding, Coding, Coding starts with 'C'!")
12
13  main()
```

Common Programming Error

Forgetting to Indent

You should use indentation to indicate the body of a for loop. If you intend to have a loop that contains two statements, it's easy to forget the additional lines of the body after the first one. Suppose, for example, that you want to print 20 alternating copies of the strings "Hi!" and "Ho!". You might mistakenly write the following incorrect code:

```
for i in range(20):
    print("Hi!")
print("Ho!")
```

The indentation indicates to the interpreter which statements are part of the loop body. Since we did not indent the second print statement, it is not included in the loop body and is therefore not repeated. The code would produce 20 lines of output that all say "Hi!" followed by one line of output that says "Ho!" To include both print statements in the loop body and therefore repeat both of them, you need to indent both lines:

```
for i in range(20):
    print("Hi!")
    print("Ho!")
```

Using a Loop Variable

A for loop can help you write code to process a range of numbers. We'll take advantage of that in this next program. Suppose you want to write out the squared values of the integers 0 through 5. You could write a redundant program like this:

```
1  def main():
2      print(0, "squared =", 0 * 0)
3      print(1, "squared =", 1 * 1)
4      print(2, "squared =", 2 * 2)
5      print(3, "squared =", 3 * 3)
6      print(4, "squared =", 4 * 4)
7      print(5, "squared =", 5 * 5)
8
9  main()
```

```
0 squared = 0
1 squared = 1
2 squared = 4
3 squared = 9
4 squared = 16
5 squared = 25
```

But this approach is tedious because the program has six statements that are very similar. They are all of the form:

```
print(number, "squared =", number * number)
```

In this case, `number` is either 0, 1, 2, 3, 4, or 5. What we are really trying to say here is, "execute this `print` statement for each of the values 0 through 5." The `for` loop can help us do exactly that.

What a `for` loop actually does is to execute a piece of code once for each element in a range of integers. The expression `range(max)` includes the range of integers that begins with 0 and ends just before `max`. For example, the expression `range(4)` includes 0, 1, 2, and 3, but not 4 itself. Note that `range(max)` is a range that contains exactly `max` integers in it.

The `for` loop also contains a `name` that we have called `i` in our examples. The `i` here is an example of a *loop variable* (also called a *control variable*), which is a special variable that exists inside a loop that you can use in the loop's code.

> **Loop Variable**
>
> The variable defined in the heading of a `for` loop, which can be used in the loop's code and changes on each repetition of the loop.

When we say the following, the loop executes the statement once for each integer in the range, temporarily storing that integer as a variable named `i`:

```
for i in range(max):
    statement
```

- Define a variable named `i` storing the value 0, then run the statement.
- Now assign `i` to be 1, then run the statement again.
- Now assign `i` to be 2, then run the statement again.
- ...
- Now assign `i` to be `max` - 2, then run the statement again.
- Now assign `i` to be `max` - 1, then run the statement again.

The key insight about a loop variable is that you can use it in the statement inside the loop. For example, consider the following code:

```
for i in range(5):
    print(i)
```

```
0
1
2
3
4
```

The `for` loop is running the code once for each number in the range 0 through 4, referring to that number as `i` each time. Figure 2.1 shows essentially what the `for` loop expands to become when it executes.

Each execution of the controlled statement of a loop is called an *iteration* of the loop, as in, "The loop finished executing after four iterations." Iteration also refers to looping in general, as in, "I solved the problem using iteration."

With all of this in mind, here is a version of our squared numbers program that uses a `for` loop to eliminate the redundant statements:

```
1  def main():
2      for i in range(6):
3          print(i, "squared =", i * i)
4
5  main()
```

All of our examples have used a loop variable named `i`. But the loop variable's name can be any legal identifier. By convention, we often use names like `i`, `j`, and `k` for loop variables because those names are short and meaningless. But if the numbers you are printing represent something important, you can give the loop variable a more

```
for i in range(5):        i = 0
    print(i)              print(i)
                          i = 1
                          print(i)
                          i = 2
                          print(i)
                          i = 3
                          print(i)
                          i = 4
                          print(i)
```

Figure 2.1 Expansion of for loop using loop variable i

descriptive name, such as a or z_coordinate or student_id. Here is an example of a for loop with a loop variable named num:

```
# loop with 'num' as variable name instead of 'i'
for num in range(10):
    print(num)
```

Details about Ranges

The for loops we have written interacted with ranges of numbers produced from a command called range. The range command is actually a function that your code calls that creates a range of numbers for your program to process. The form we have seen so far was to supply a maximum integer in parentheses, which would produce a range from 0 (inclusive) through that maximum (exclusive). But there are situations where you don't want to start at 0, and/or when you don't want to process every integer in the range. In such cases you can supply additional information to the range function to customize the range of numbers produced. Table 2.5 shows the various forms of the range function.

For example, if you want to print the integers 1–10 inclusive, you could write the following code. Note that the max is exclusive, so we write 11 if we want 10 to be the last number included in the range.

```
# print the integers 1-10
for i in range(1, 11):
    print(i)
```

There is also a form of range where you supply a minimum value, a maximum value, and a step value to indicate how much the loop variable should increase on each iteration. For example, if the step is 2, the loop will process the numbers min, min+2, min+4, ... The following code prints a sequence of numbers in a song:

```
# range with a step of 2
for i in range(2, 9, 2):
    print(i)
print("Who do we appreciate?")
```

Continued on next page

Table 2.5 **Ways to Create Ranges**

Range Form	Description	Example	Numbers in Range
range(max)	range from 0 (inclusive) to max (exclusive)	range(5)	0, 1, 2, 3, 4
range(min, max)	range from min (inclusive) to max (exclusive)	range(3, 7)	3, 4, 5, 6
range(min, max, step)	range from min (inclusive) to max (exclusive), increasing by step each time	range(4, 22, 3)	4, 7, 10, 13, 16, 19

Continued from previous page

```
2
4
6
8
Who do we appreciate?
```

The `for` loop is running the code once for each number in the range 2 (inclusive) through 9 (exclusive, meaning that the range stops at 8), stepping upward by 2 each time. The code refers to each number as `i`. In a previous section we showed an expansion of a basic `for` loop; Figure 2.2 shows a similar expansion of this loop.

Sometimes we want to process a range of numbers in reverse order, counting down rather than up. You can achieve this by providing a negative number as the step to your range. You can accomplish this by using a decrement rather than an increment, so we sometimes refer to this as a *decrementing loop*. For example, the following code counts down from 5 to 1. Notice that the second value is written as 0 rather than 1, to make sure that 1 is included in the range.

```
# range with a negative step (count down)
for i in range(5, 0, -1):
    print(i)
print("Kaboom!")
```

```
5
4
3
2
1
Kaboom!
```

```
for i in range(2, 9, 2):        ⎱   i = 2
    print(i)                         print(i)
                                     i += 2
                                     print(i)
                                     i += 2
                                     print(i)
                                     i += 2
                                     print(i)
                                     i += 2
                                     print(i)
```

Figure 2.2   Expansion of for loop with a step

The values used in the range do not have to be integer literals. You can write any arbitrary integer expression:

```
# range using variables and expressions
a = 17
b = 2
c = 3
for i in range(c, a + 1, b * 2):
    print(i)
```

```
3
7
11
15
```

This loop will use a min of 3, a max of 18, and a step of 4, producing the integers 3, 7, 11, 15.

It is also possible to provide a combination of integers that iterates only once, or no times at all. The following range contains only a single integer, the number 42, so the loop prints only a single line of output:

```
# range containing a single value
for i in range(42, 43):
    print(i)
```

```
42
```

The following range does not contain any integers at all, so no output is produced. This loop performs no iterations at all. It will not cause an error; it just won't execute the print statement in the loop body.

```
# empty range (prints no output)
for i in range(7, 7):
    print(i)
```

The integers we write inside the parentheses when creating a range are called *parameters*. Parameters are values that are provided to a function that modify or customize its behavior. In this case, the numbers we write in the parentheses customize the range of numbers that the function creates. We will explore parameters in much more detail in the next chapter.

Common Programming Error

Off-By-One Bug (OBOB) in Range Boundary

The fact that Python's `range` function has an inclusive min value and an exclusive max value is hard to remember for new programmers. This can lead to frequent bugs where your code loops over a range of numbers that is off by 1 from the correct range. We find that students are especially likely to make this mistake when using the form of `range` where you supply both a minimum and maximum value. For example, if you want to print the integers from 1 through 4 inclusive, you might write the code below:

```
# print integers from 1-4 inclusive (incorrect!)
for i in range(1, 4):
    print(i)
```

```
1
2
3
```

When writing these kinds of loops, remember that if you want to include a value max in your output, your loop must specify its maximum value as `max + 1`.

```
# print integers from 1-4 inclusive (correct)
for i in range(1, 5):
    print(i)
```

Common Programming Error

Float as Range Boundary

Many students who are new to `for` loops accidentally try to loop over a non-integer range. The `range` function raises an error if you write a real number as the range boundary:

```
>>> range(3.14159)
Traceback (most recent call last):
  File "<stdin>", line 1, in <module>
TypeError: 'float' object cannot be interpreted as an integer
```

The more subtle and common case is when the student computes the loop boundary using expressions on variables. It is easy to forget that the `/` operator on integers

Continued on next page

Continued from previous page

produces a float result, not int. The following code crashes because the variable
class_size is a float with the value 5.4, which is not a valid range boundary:

```
 1  # This buggy program contains a for loop that uses
 2  # a float value as its loop range boundary.
 3  def main():
 4      courses = 5
 5      students = 27
 6      class_size = students / courses
 7
 8      for i in range(class_size):
 9          print(i)
10
11  main()
```

```
Traceback (most recent call last):
  File "float_loop.py", line 11, in <module>
    main()
  File "float_loop.py", line 8, in main
    for i in range(class_size):
TypeError: 'float' object cannot be interpreted as an integer
```

The program will work properly if you convert the class size to an int explicitly,
and/or if you use the // operator when dividing integers.

String Multiplication and Printing Partial Lines

We have talked about the * operator for performing multiplication on integers and real
numbers. Interestingly, Python also allows you to use * on a string, which replicates
the string a given number of times:

```
"text" * int
```
Syntax template: String multiplication

This operation is called *string multiplication*. For example, the expression "hello" * 3
replicates the string "hello" three times, evaluating to a result of "hellohellohello".
The following interaction in the Python Shell shows more examples:

```
>>> "Go Cats " * 4
"Go Cats Go Cats Go Cats Go Cats "
>>> "x" * 10
```

```
"xxxxxxxxxx"
>>> "Python" * 1
"Python"
>>> "times zero!" * 0
""
```

You can print a multiplied string to see repeated text patterns in the program's output. For example:

```
print("hello" * 3)
```

```
hellohellohello
```

If you want to repeat part of a line of output, you can use the syntax shown in this chapter where multiple comma-separated values are provided in a `print` statement. For example, in the following song code, the word "la" needs to be repeated, but the initial word "Fa" does not. So we supply them separately with commas in the `print` statement on that line of output:

```
print("Deck the halls with boughs of holly")
print("Fa", "la " * 8)
```

```
Deck the halls with boughs of holly
Fa la la la la la la la la
```

You can use the combination of `for` loops and string multiplication to produce interesting patterns of characters. For example, the following code prints five lines of output, each of which contains ten # characters. Notice that we name our loop variable `line` here because each iteration of the loop produces a line of a figure:

```
for line in range(5):
    print("#" * 10)
```

```
##########
##########
##########
##########
##########
```

You can use the loop variable to alter the number of characters printed. In the previous code, the `for` loop always does exactly the same thing: It prints exactly 10 characters on a line of output. But if we change the code to make use of the loop's control variable `i`, the output is very different. The following code prints 1 character on line 1, 2 characters on line 2, and so on, producing a triangular figure as output.

```
for line in range(1, 6):
    print("#" * line)
```

```
#
##
###
####
#####
```

Suppose we want to print a more complex pattern, such as the following figure of output:

```
#++#
##++++##
###++++++###
####++++++++####
#####++++++++++#####
```

This pattern is hard to print in a single statement because each line contains a complex pattern. To help us break down the task, we will use a new variation of the `print` statement that prints a partial line of output. This new form prints the text you provide, but it does not drop the output down to the next line. The consequence is that you can place several `print` statements in sequence and all of their output will appear on the same line on the console.

The general syntax for printing a partial line of output is to place a comma followed by `end=""` inside the parentheses of your `print` statement:

```
print(expression, end="")
```
Syntax template: Printing partial line of output

The `end=""` syntax looks a bit odd; here's what it is really doing. The `print` statement has a notion of an `end` marker that it will print after whatever text you write in parentheses. By default the end marker is `"\n"`, which is a line break character. This means that after printing the text you provide, a `"\n"` is printed, causing the console to move to the next line. By writing `end=""` we are changing the `end` marker into an empty string, because we don't want any line break or other characters to print after the text or value we're printing. This causes the console to remain on the same line after printing. You can actually set the `end` marker to be any arbitrary string, but that is not a common style and we won't use it in this text.

If we use our previous code as a starting point, it contains a loop with a `range(1, 6)` and a loop variable named `i` to print exactly `i` copies of the `"#"` character on each line. For this new figure we want that same number of `"#"` characters, followed by twice that many `"+"` signs, followed by the original number of `"#"` characters a second time. To print all three of those character sequences on the same line, we will use three `print` statements inside the `for` loop as follows:

```
# printing a complex pattern using string multiplication
# and partial lines of output
for line in range(1, 6):
    print("#" * line, end="")
    print("+" * (2 * line), end="")
    print("#" * line)
```

```
#++#
##++++##
###++++++###
####++++++++####
#####++++++++++#####
```

Notice that the last `print` statement does not include `end=""` because we do want to end the line of output after the final sequence of # characters has printed. If we accidentally did include `end=""` on the final `print` statement, the output would be the following jumbled mess with no line breaks:

```
#++##+++####++++######+++++++#########+++++++++############+++++++++++#####
```

Earlier in this chapter we saw that we can write multiple values to print, separated by commas. We also saw the `sep="text"` notation for controlling what characters should appear between each of those values. An alternative style for printing the previous figure would be to write all three sequences of characters (the initial # signs; the + signs; and the final # signs) of each line in a single `print` statement. We want these sequences of characters to appear with no separation between them, indicated by `sep=""`. In this form, you no longer need the `end=""`, because the single `print` statement contains the entire contents of the line of output to print.

```
# printing multiple sequences of repeated characters
# in a single print statement
for line in range(1, 6):
    print("#" * line, "+" * (2 * line), "#" * line, sep="")
```

Though this latter form is shorter and requires fewer lines of code, the authors find it difficult to read and consider it poor style. We will favor using individual `print` statements for each repeated sequence of characters, and we recommend that you do the same in your programs.

Nested for Loops

Suppose you want to print a multiplication table such as the following:

1	2	3	4	5	6	7	8	9
2	4	6	8	10	12	14	16	18
3	6	9	12	15	18	21	24	27
4	8	12	16	20	24	28	32	36
5	10	15	20	25	30	35	40	45

You can print such a table using standard `for` loops, but the code is lengthy and redundant:

```
 1  # This redundant program prints a multiplication table using loops.
 2  def main():
 3      for x in range(1, 10):
 4          print(1 * x, end="\t")
 5      print()
 6
 7      for x in range(1, 10):
 8          print(2 * x, end="\t")
 9      print()
10
11      for x in range(1, 10):
12          print(3 * x, end="\t")
13      print()
14
15      for x in range(1, 10):
16          print(4 * x, end="\t")
17      print()
18
19      for x in range(1, 10):
20          print(5 * x, end="\t")
21      print()
22
23  main()
```

Earlier in this chapter we discussed string multiplication, but that feature can't help us print this particular output. String multiplication helps us when we are repeating the exact same character, but in this case the numbers are changing.

Notice the pattern in the redundant lines. There is a trio of lines containing a `for` loop header, the loop body, and a `print` statement to end the line of output. This trio of lines repeats five times in the program, with the only difference being the integer to multiply by x each time. This integer, which we could call y, takes on the values 1, 2, 3, 4, and 5 in our code.

Luckily we can remove the redundancy by embedding the trio of repeated lines inside a second loop. Such a loop is called a *nested loop*. The `for` loop controls a statement, and the `for` loop is itself a statement, which means that one `for` loop can control another `for` loop.

The following program prints the same multiplication table using nested `for` loops. We take advantage of the end marker in our `print` statement, setting it to `"\t"` to separate each number by a tab character so that they line up nicely on the console.

```
1   # This program prints a multiplication table using nested loops.
2   def main():
3       for y in range(1, 6):
4           for x in range(1, 10):
5               print(y * x, end="\t")
6           print()
7
8   main()
```

The behavior of this code is consistent with how standard `for` loops behave. The outer loop executes once for each value in the specified numeric range. The outer loop's range is specified as `range(1, 6)` and the outer loop variable's name is y, which means that the inner code should execute with y = 1, then with y = 2, and so on, up to y = 5. Figure 2.3 shows an expansion of what the nested loops are doing along with the console output produced by each pass of the outer loop.

The outer loop is the more long-lived of the two, the one that takes longer for each of its iterations to finish. The outer loop defines y to be 1 and then executes the entire inner loop. Then the outer loop assigns y to be 2 and then executes the entire inner loop again, and so on.

Nested loops and string multiplication both involve repetition, but nested loops are more versatile and powerful. Many programming languages don't support string multiplication, but you can achieve a similar effect using a nested loop. For example, we previously saw the following program for printing a triangular figure:

```
# print triangular figure w/ string multiplication
for i in range(1, 6):
    print("#" * i)
```

```
for y in range(1, 6):
    for x in range(1, 10):
        print(y * x, end="\t")
    print()
```

Code (expanded)   Output

```
y = 1
for x in range(1, 10):
    print(y * x, end="\t")   ⟶   1   2   3   4   5   6   7   8   9
print()


y = 2
for x in range(1, 10):
    print(y * x, end="\t")   ⟶   2   4   6   8   10  12  14  16  18
print()


y = 3
for x in range(1, 10):
    print(y * x, end="\t")   ⟶   3   6   9   12  15  18  21  24  27
print()


y = 4
for x in range(1, 10):
    print(y * x, end="\t")   ⟶   4   8   12  16  20  24  28  32  36
print()


y = 5
for x in range(1, 10):
    print(y * x, end="\t")   ⟶   5   10  15  20  25  30  35  40  45
print()
```

Figure 2.3 Nested loop expansion

The purpose of the string multiplication was to print a given character a given number of times. If Python did not support string multiplication, you could still print the same figure using a nested loop as follows, where each iteration of the inner loop prints a single character:

```
# print triangular figure w/out string multiplication
for i in range(1, 6):
    for j in range(i):
        print("#")
```

```
#
##
###
####
#####
```

Of course, the string multiplication version of the code is cleaner and simpler, so we will favor that approach over a nested loop when it is viable to do so.

2.4 Managing Complexity

You've learned about several new programming constructs in this chapter, and it's time to put the pieces together to solve some complex tasks. As Brian Kernighan, one of the coauthors of *The C Programming Language*, once said, "Controlling complexity is the essence of computer programming." In this section we will examine several techniques that computer scientists use to solve complex problems without being overwhelmed by complexity.

Scope

As programs get longer, it is increasingly likely that different parts of the program will interfere with each other. Python helps us to manage this potential problem by enforcing rules of *scope*.

> **Scope**
> The part of a program in which a particular definition is valid.

You've seen that when it comes to defining functions, you can put them in any order whatsoever. The scope of a function is the entire program file in which it appears. Variables work differently. The simple rule is that the scope of a variable definition extends from the point where it is defined to the end of the function that encloses it.

This scope rule has several implications. Consider first what it means for different functions. Each function has its own set of statements to be executed when the function is called. Any variables defined inside a function's indented set of statements won't be available outside that function. We refer to such variables as *local variables*.

> **Local Variable**
> A variable defined inside a function that is accessible only in that function.

Let's look at a simple example involving two functions. In this example, the `main` function defines local variables x and y and gives them initial values. Then it calls the function `compute_sum`, which tries to use the values of x and y to compute a sum. However, because the variables x and y are local to the `main` function and are not visible inside of the `compute_sum` function, this doesn't work, so the interpreter displays a runtime error called a `NameError`.

```
 1   # This program produces an error because
 2   # a variable is used out of scope.
 3
 4   def compute_sum():
 5       sum = x + y              # error!
 6       print("sum =", sum)
 7
 8   def main():
 9       x = 3
10       y = 7
11       compute_sum()
12
13   main()
```

```
Traceback (most recent call last):
  File "scope1.py", line 13, in <module>
    main()
  File "scope1.py", line 11, in main
    compute_sum()
  File "scope1.py", line 5, in compute_sum
    sum = x + y
NameError: name 'x' is not defined
```

A loop variable defined in the header of a `for` loop can be accessed after the loop. Its value after the loop will be equal to the value the loop variable held on the last iteration of the loop. For example, in the following code, the loop variable `i` has the value 3 as it exits the loop:

```
# access a loop variable after the loop
for i in range(4):
    print("inside loop:", i)
print("after loop:", i)
```

```
inside loop: 0
inside loop: 1
inside loop: 2
inside loop: 3
after loop: 3
```

In general you will want to define variables inside of functions. It is possible, though, to define variables outside of functions. Such variables, called *global variables*, are visible to the entire program. At first glance, this sounds like an incredibly useful feature. You might wonder, why not just define every variable as global?

> **Global Variable**
>
> A variable defined outside of your functions that is accessible to the entire program. Global variables are generally considered to be poor style and are discouraged from use.

Using global variables certainly sounds simpler and more powerful. But remember that if you write large programs, you will inevitably spend a lot of time trying to find and fix bugs. A very common category of software bugs involves accidentally setting a variable to the wrong value. How do you find and fix such a bug? You need to examine all of the parts of the program that might have corrupted the variable's value. If the variable is local, to find the bug you only need to examine the function in which the variable was defined. But if the variable is global, literally any part of your program could have caused the bug. Localizing variables provides more security to your code because it minimizes the amount of your program that could modify a given variable's value.

As a nonprogramming analogy, consider the use of refrigerators in student dormitories. A dormitory building might have a large shared communal refrigerator that anybody can use. The last time we were in a dorm we noticed that most of the rooms also had individual refrigerators in them. This seems redundant, since everyone could use the shared refrigerator to store all of their food, but the reason for the duplication is obvious. Having your own private refrigerator protects your important food items from being accessed or modified (eaten) by a roommate. If you put a sandwich into the dorm's shared refrigerator and it goes missing, the culprit could be anyone, and it will be difficult to figure out who took it.

Python programs use variables to store values just as students use refrigerators to store ice cream, drinks, and other valuables. If you want to guarantee the security of something, you put it where nobody else can access it. You will use local variables in your programs in much the same way. If each individual function has its own local variables to use, you don't have to consider possible interference from other parts of the program.

(Don't worry about the loss of the power of global variables. In the next chapter we will learn about a technique called parameters that will allow us to selectively share data values from one function to another.)

Pseudocode

As you write more complex algorithms, you will find that you can't just write the entire algorithm correctly all at once. If the desired behavior or output is very complex, you will need to reason about the proper code before starting to write it. As Brian Kernighan, one of the coauthors of *The C Programming Language*, once said,

"Controlling complexity is the essence of computer programming." Experienced programmers use several techniques to break down and solve complex problems without being overwhelmed by their complexity. In this section we will explore one such technique called *pseudocode*, which is when you write out a rough description of the program in plain text rather than in actual Python code.

> **Pseudocode**
>
> English-like descriptions of algorithms. Programming with pseudocode involves successively refining an informal description until it is easily translated into Python.

For example, you can describe the problem of drawing a box as the following:

```
Print a box with 50 lines and 30 columns of asterisks.
```

While this statement describes the figure, it does not give specific instructions about how to draw it (that is, what algorithm to use). Do you draw the figure line by line or column by column? In Python, figures like these must be generated line by line, because once a `print` statement has been performed on a line of output, that line cannot be changed. There is no command for going back to a previous line in the output. Therefore, you must output the first line in its entirety, then the second line in its entirety, and so on. As a result, your decompositions for figures such as these will be line-oriented at the top level. Thus, a pseudocode that is closer to Python would be:

```
for each of 50 lines:
    Print a line of 30 asterisks.
```

Using pseudocode, you can gradually convert an English description into something that is easily translated into a Python program. The simple examples we've looked at so far are hardly worth the application of pseudocode, so we will now examine the problem of generating a more complex figure:

```
*********
 *******
  *****
   ***
    *
```

This figure must also be generated line by line:

```
for each of 5 lines:
    Print one line of the triangle.
```

Unfortunately, each line is different. Therefore, you must come up with a general rule that fits all the lines. The first line of this figure has a series of asterisks on it with no leading spaces. Each of the subsequent lines has a series of spaces followed by a series of asterisks. Using your imagination a bit, you can say that the first line has 0 spaces on it followed by a series of asterisks. This allows you to write a general rule for making this figure:

```
for each of 5 lines:
    Print some spaces (possibly 0) on the output line.
    Print some asterisks on the output line.
    End the output line.
```

In order to proceed, you must determine a rule for the number of spaces and a rule for the number of asterisks. Assuming that the lines are numbered 1 through 5, looking at the figure, you can fill in Table 2.6 with the number of each kind of character on each line.

Table 2.6 **Analysis of Triangle Output Figure**

Line	Spaces	Asterisks	Output
1	0	9	* * * * * * * * *
2	1	7	* * * * * * *
3	2	5	* * * * *
4	3	3	* * *
5	4	1	*

You want to find a relationship between line number and the other two columns. This is simple algebra, because these columns are related in a linear way. The second column is easy to get from the line number. It equals (line $-$ 1). The third column is a little tougher. Because it goes down by 2 every time and the first column goes up by 1 every time, you need a multiplier of -2. Then you need an appropriate constant. The number 11 seems to do the trick, so you can make the third column equal (11 $-$ 2 * line). You can improve your pseudocode, then, as follows:

```
for each line from 1 through 5:
    Print (line - 1) spaces on the output line.
    Print (11 - 2 * line) asterisks on the output line.
    End the output line.
```

This pseudocode is simple to turn into a program:

```
1  # This program draws a downward
2  # triangular figure using loops.
3  def main():
4      for line in range(1, 6):
5          print(" " * (line - 1), end="")
```

Continued on next page

Continued from previous page

```
6              print("*" * (11 - 2 * line))
7
8  main()
```

```
* * * * * * * *
 * * * * * * *
  * * * * *
   * * *
    *
```

Sometimes we manage complexity by taking advantage of work that we have already done. For example, how would you produce a similar triangle figure that points upward?

```
    *
   * * *
  * * * * *
 * * * * * * *
* * * * * * * *
```

You could follow the same process you did before and find new expressions that produce the appropriate number of spaces and asterisks. However, there is an easier way. This figure is the same as the previous one, except the lines appear in reverse order. This is a good place to use a decrementing loop to run the `for` loop backward. Instead of starting at 1 and going up through 5, you can start at 5 and go down through 1 using a step of -1. The simple way to produce the upward-pointing triangle, then, is with the following code:

```
1  # This program draws an upward
2  # triangular figure using loops.
3  def main():
4      for line in range(5, 0, -1):
5          print(" " * (line - 1), end="")
6          print("*" * (11 - 2 * line))
7
8  main()
```

```
    *
   * * *
  * * * * *
 * * * * * * *
* * * * * * * *
```

Suppose you wanted to draw both of these figures in a single program. It would be tempting to try to come up with a single `for` loop that draws both figures, but there is no simple way to make a single range that contains both an increasing and decreasing sequence of numbers. Instead, you could turn each figure into a function and call both of them from `main` with a blank line between them:

```
 1   # This program draws two triangular
 2   # figures using loops.
 3
 4   # Draws a 5-line downward-facing triangle of stars.
 5   def downward_triangle():
 6       for line in range(1, 6):
 7           print(" " * (line - 1), end="")
 8           print("*" * (11 - 2 * line))
 9
10   # Draws a 5-line upward-facing triangle of stars.
11   def upward_triangle():
12       for line in range(5, 0, -1):
13           print(" " * (line - 1), end="")
14           print("*" * (11 - 2 * line))
15
16   def main():
17       downward_triangle()
18       print()
19       upward_triangle()
20
21   main()
```

```
*********
 *******
  *****
   ***
    *

    *
   ***
  *****
 *******
*********
```

Once you get practice at writing pseudocode, you'll find that it is often simple to translate well-written pseudocode into correct Python code. This is partly because of Python's clean and simple syntax. Some programmers even jokingly call Python "executable pseudocode" since its syntax is so similar to the way a person might write down an algorithm in pseudocode format.

Constants

The triangle-drawing programs in the previous section draw a figure where each region has five lines. How would you modify the code to produce similar triangle figures but with only three lines in each part? Your first thought might be to simply change the occurrences of 5 in the code to 3. However, making that change to the most recent version of the program would produce the following incorrect output:

```
*********
  *******
   *****



   *****
  *******
*********
```

If you work through the geometry of the figure, you will discover that the problem is with the use of the number 11 in the expressions that calculate the number of asterisks to print. The number 11 actually comes from this formula:

```
2 * (number of lines) + 1
```

So when the number of lines is 5, the appropriate value is 11, but when the number of lines is three, the appropriate value is 7. Programmers call numbers like these *magic numbers*. They are magic in the sense that they seem to make the program work, but their definition is not always obvious. Glancing at the `draw_triangle` program, one is apt to ask, "Why 5? Why 11? Why 3? Why 7? Why me?"

   To make programs more readable and more adaptable, you should try to avoid magic numbers whenever possible. You do so by storing the magic numbers as variables. You could use a local variable to store these values, but there are two problems with that approach. The first problem is that any variable you define in one function, such as `downward_triangle`, won't be visible in the other function due to scope. The second problem is that programmers expect that variables might have values that change over time, but we don't want this value to be modified after it is defined.

   In cases like these, we define special variables called *constants* that are expected not to be modified after they are defined. We most often define *global constants*, which have a large scope so that they can be accessed throughout the entire program.

> **Constant**
>
> A variable that is defined once and never to be changed afterward. A global constant can be accessed anywhere in the program (i.e., its scope is the entire program file).

You can choose a descriptive name for a constant that explains what it represents. You can then use that name instead of referring to the specific value to make your programs more readable and adaptable. For example, in the *draw_triangle* program, you might want to introduce a constant called LINES that represents the number of lines. (We follow the common convention of using all uppercase letters for constant names.) You can use that constant in place of the magic number 5 and as part of an expression to calculate a value. This approach allows you to replace the magic number 11 with the formula from which it is derived (2 * LINES + 1).

Python does not have any special syntax for defining constants; they are just like any other variable. What differs is where you define the constant; rather than defining it indented inside a function, it is defined near the top of your program, unindented, before any of your functions. For example:

```
LINES = 5
```

You can define a constant anywhere you can define a variable, but because constants are often used by several different functions, we generally define them outside functions. We can avoid using a magic number in the *draw_triangle* program by instead referring to our constant for the number of lines. We can replace the 5 in the outer loop with this constant and replace the 11 in the second inner loop with the expression 2 * LINES + 1. The result is the following program:

```
1   # This program draws two triangular
2   # figures using loops.
3   LINES = 3
4
5   # Draws a downward-facing triangle of stars.
6   def downward_triangle():
7       for line in range(1, LINES + 1):
8           print(" " * (line - 1), end="")
9           print("*" * (2 * LINES + 1 - 2 * line))
10
11  # Draws an upward-facing triangle of stars.
12  def upward_triangle():
13      for line in range(LINES, 0, -1):
14          print(" " * (line - 1), end="")
15          print("*" * (2 * LINES + 1 - 2 * line))
16
17  def main():
18      downward_triangle()
19      print()
20      upward_triangle()
21
22  main()
```

```
*****
 ***
  *

  *
 ***
*****
```

This new program is more adaptable and can produce figures of different sizes with only a single change. If the LINES constant is changed to 7, the program's output becomes the following:

```
*************
 ***********
  *********
   *******
    *****
     ***
      *

      *
     ***
    *****
   *******
  *********
 ***********
*************
```

Some programming languages allow the programmer to specify that a given variable is a constant, which then produces an error if the code tries to modify the constant's value after it has been defined. Unfortunately Python does not include this feature. By defining our constant in a global scope, Python does provide us with a bit of protection against code that tries to change the constant's value. For example, if you try to modify the value of a constant from inside a function, the interpreter raises an error:

```
# Bad code; tries to modify a global constant.
def upward_triangle():
    LINES += 3    # error!
    for line in range(LINES, 0, -1):
        ...
```

```
+--------+
Traceback (most recent call last):
  File "hourglass2_error.py", line 43, in <module>
    main()
  File "hourglass2_error.py", line 39, in main
    draw_top()
  File "hourglass2_error.py", line 14, in draw_top
    LINES += 3
UnboundLocalError: local variable 'LINES'
                   referenced before assignment
```

But unfortunately the protection is imperfect; if we instead wrote `LINES = 7`, the code would run successfully and would draw the `upward_triangle` with a `LINES` value of 7 rather than 4. Therefore Python constants are technically just global variables and are held constant only through convention and through the good behavior of the programmer writing the code. Modifying the value of a global constant variable is considered very poor style and strongly discouraged. The expectation followed by Python programmers is that if a variable is named in UPPERCASE, it is to be treated as a constant, and its value is not to be modified after it is defined. The language cannot force us to obey this convention, but we are expected to take care to do so when writing our code.

2.5 Case Study: Hourglass Figure

Now we'll consider an example that is even more complex. This program will draw an "hourglass" figure made out of patterns of repeating characters. The desired output is the following:

```
+----------+
|\12345678/|
| \123456/ |
|  \1234/  |
|   \12/   |
|    \/    |
|    /\    |
|   /21\   |
|  /4321\  |
| /654321\ |
|/87654321\|
+----------+
```

To solve it, we will follow three basic steps:

1. Decompose the task into subtasks, each of which will become a function.
2. For each subtask, make a table for the figure and compute formulas for each column of the table in terms of the line number.
3. Convert the tables into actual `for` loops and code for each function.

Problem Decomposition and Pseudocode

To generate this figure, you have to first break it down into subfigures. In doing so, you should look for lines that are similar in one way or another. The first and last lines are exactly the same. The five "top half" lines after the first line all fit one pattern, and the five "bottom half" lines after that fit another. Figure 2.4 shows the patterns of characters.

```
+----------+   line

|\12345678/|
| \123456/ |   top half
|  \1234/  |
|   \12/   |
|    \/    |

|    /\    |
|   /21\   |
|  /4321\  |   bottom half
| /654321\ |
|/87654321\|

+----------+   line
```

Figure 2.4   Hourglass figure character patterns

Thus, you can break down the overall problem into the following pseudocode:

```
Draw a solid line.
Draw the top half of the hourglass.
Draw the bottom half of the hourglass.
Draw a solid line.
```

You should solve each subproblem independently. Eventually you'll want to incorporate a constant to make the program more flexible, but let's first solve the problem without worrying about the use of a constant.

The "Draw a solid line" task can be further specified as:

```
Draw a solid line:
    Print a plus on the output line.
    Print 10 dashes on the output line.
    Print a plus on the output line.
    End the line of output.
```

This set of instructions translates easily into a function:

```
# Prints a solid line of dashes.
def draw_line():
```

Continued on next page

Continued from previous page

```
print("+", end="")
print("-" * 10, end="")
print("+")
```

The top half of the hourglass is more complex. Here is a typical line:

```
|  \1234/  |
```

There are four individual characters, separated by spaces and numbers.

```
 |               \           1234        /              |
bar      spaces      backslash      numbers     slash      spaces      bar
```

Thus, a first approximation in pseudocode might look like this:

```
for each of 5 lines:
    Print a bar.
    Print some spaces.
    Print a backslash.
    Print some numbers.
    Print a slash.
    Print some spaces.
    Print a bar.
    End the line of output.
```

Again, you can make a table to figure out the required expressions. Writing the individual characters will be easy enough to translate into Python, but you need to be more specific about the spaces and numbers. Each line in this group contains two sets of spaces and one set of numbers. Table 2.7 shows how many to use. We do not list the |, \, and / characters in the table because they always appear exactly once on each line.

The two sets of spaces go from 0 to 4 when the line number goes from 1 to 5; this can be expressed as (line - 1). The range of numbers on each line is more complicated.

Table 2.7 Analysis of Hourglass Figure

Line	Spaces	Numbers	Spaces	Output
1	0	1--8	0	`|\12345678/|`
2	1	1--6	1	`| \123456/ |`
3	2	1--4	2	`|  \1234/  |`
4	3	1--2	3	`|   \12/   |`
5	4	none	4	`|    \/    |`

As the line number goes up 1 to 2 to 3 and so on, the max value appearing in the output goes down by 2 each time from 8 to 6 and so on. One way of figuring out the pattern would be to think of this as an algebraic equation between the line number and the max number value. You could also think about what the max number value would be if there were a line number 0; by the pattern we've seen, the max would be 10. Therefore, the general formula for the range's max is $(10 - 2 * line)$. But we have to write our loop using a Python range, and ranges exclude the max value you write, so we need to shift our formula by $+1$ to account for this. That means we actually want a `range(1, 11 - 2 * line)`.

```
for each line from 1 through 5:
    Print a bar.
    Print (line - 1) spaces.
    Print a backslash.
    Print the range of integers from 1 to (11 - 2 * line).
    Print a slash.
    Print (line - 1) spaces.
    Print a bar.
    End the line of output.
```

Initial Structured Version

The pseudocode for the top half of the hourglass is easily translated into a function called `draw_top`. A similar solution exists for the bottom half of the hourglass, which we will call `draw_bottom`. The `main` function calls the functions to draw the top and bottom halves with lines around them.

Our code uses the `end=""` modifier for many of its `print` statements so that we can print each chunk of a line's complex sequence of characters using a separate `print` statement.

We can produce most of the repeated sequences of characters using string multiplication with the `*` operator. The one exception is the sequences of integers in the middle of each line, which require us to use a nested `for` loop.

Put together, the program looks like this:

```
1   # This program draws an hourglass figure
2   # of characters and numbers using nested loops.
3
4   # Prints a solid line of dashes.
5   def draw_line():
6       print("+", end="")
7       print("-" * 10, end="")
8       print("+")
```

Continued on next page

Continued from previous page

```
9
10  # Produces the top half of the hourglass figure.
11  def draw_top():
12      for line in range(1, 6):
13          print("|", end="")
14          print(" " * (line - 1), end="")
15          print("\\", end="")
16          for i in range(1, 11 - 2 * line):
17              print(i, end="")
18          print("/", end="")
19          print(" " * (line - 1), end="")
20          print("|")
21
22  # Produces the bottom half of the hourglass figure.
23  def draw_bottom():
24      for line in range(1, 6):
25          print("|", end="")
26          print(" " * (5 - line), end="")
27          print("/", end="")
28          for i in range(2 * line - 2, 0, -1):
29              print(i, end="")
30          print("\\", end="")
31          print(" " * (5 - line), end="")
32          print("|")
33
34  def main():
35      draw_line()
36      draw_top()
37      draw_bottom()
38      draw_line()
39
40  main()
```

Adding a Constant

The hourglass program produces the desired output, but it is not very flexible. What if we wanted to produce a similar figure of a different size? The original problem involved an hourglass figure that had five lines in the top half and five lines in the bottom half. What if we wanted the following output, with three lines in the top half and three lines in the bottom half?

```
+------+
|\1234/|
| \12/ |
|  \/  |
|  /\  |
| /21\ |
|/4321\|
+------+
```

Obviously the program would be more useful if we could make it flexible enough to produce either output. We do so by eliminating the magic numbers with the introduction of a constant. You might think that we need to introduce two constants, one for the height and one for the width, but because of the regularity of this figure, the height is determined by the width and vice versa. Consequently, we only need to introduce a single constant. Let's use the height of the hourglass halves:

```
SUB_HEIGHT = 5
```

We've called the constant SUB_HEIGHT rather than HEIGHT because it refers to the height of each of the two halves, rather than the figure as a whole. Notice how we use the underscore character to separate the different words in the name of the constant.

So, how do we modify the original program to incorporate this constant? We look through the program for any magic numbers and insert the constant or an expression involving the constant where appropriate. For example, both the draw_top and draw_bottom functions have a for loop that executes 5 times to produce 5 lines of output. We change this to 3 to produce 3 lines of output, and more generally, we change it to SUB_HEIGHT to produce SUB_HEIGHT lines of output.

In other parts of the program we have to update our formulas for the number of dashes, spaces, and dots. Sometimes we can use educated guesses to figure out how to adjust such a formula to use the constant. If you can't guess a proper formula, you can use the table technique to find the appropriate formula. Using this new output with a subheight of 3, you can update the various formulas in the program. We also show what the formulas would be for a subheight of 4. Table 2.8 shows the various formulas.

Table 2.8 **Analysis of Different Height Figures**

Sub Height	Dashes in line	Spaces in top	Numbers in top	Spaces in bottom	Numbers in bottom
3	6	line-1	range(1, 7-2*line)	3-line	range(2*line-2, 0, -1)
4	8	line-1	range(1, 9-2*line)	4-line	range(2*line-2, 0, -1)
5	10	line-1	range(1, 11-2*line)	5-line	range(2*line-2, 0, -1)

We then go through each formula (each column in the table) and figure out how to replace it with a new formula involving the constant:

- The number of dashes increases by 2 when the subheight increases by 1, so the general expression is twice the subfigure height, or 2 * SUB_HEIGHT.

- The number of spaces in draw_top does not change when the subheight changes, so the expression does not need to be altered.

- The range of numbers in draw_top involves the number 7 for a subheight of 3, the number 9 for a subheight of 4, and the number 11 for a subheight of 5. The general expression for this is 2 * SUB_HEIGHT + 1, and substituting this into the original range formula leads to an overall range of range(1, 2 * SUB_HEIGHT + 1 - 2 * line).

- The number of spaces in draw_bottom involves the value 3 for a subheight of 3, the value 4 for a subheight of 4, and the value 5 for a subheight of 5. This is clearly just the subfigure height, and substituting it into the expression yields SUB_HEIGHT - line.

- The range of numbers in draw_bottom does not change when subheight changes, so the expression does not need to be altered.

Here is the new version of the program with a constant for the subheight. It uses a SUB_HEIGHT value of 3, but we could change this to other values to produce figures of other sizes.

```
1   # This program draws an hourglass figure
2   # of characters and numbers using nested loops.
3   # This version uses a global constant for the figure size.
4   SUB_HEIGHT = 4
5
6   # Prints a solid line of dashes.
7   def draw_line():
8       print("+", end="")
9       print("-" * (2 * SUB_HEIGHT), end="")
10      print("+")
11
12  # Produces the top half of the hourglass figure.
13  def draw_top():
14      for line in range(1, SUB_HEIGHT + 1):
15          print("|", end="")
16          print(" " * (line - 1), end="")
17          print("\\", end="")
18          for i in range(1, 2 * SUB_HEIGHT + 1 - 2 * line):
19              print(i, end="")
20          print("/", end="")
```

Continued on next page

Continued from previous page

```
21              print(" " * (line - 1), end="")
22              print("|")
23
24   # Produces the bottom half of the hourglass figure.
25   def draw_bottom():
26       for line in range(1, SUB_HEIGHT + 1):
27              print("|", end="")
28              print(" " * (SUB_HEIGHT - line), end="")
29              print("/", end="")
30              for i in range(2 * line - 2, 0, -1):
31                  print(i, end="")
32              print("\\", end="")
33              print(" " * (SUB_HEIGHT - line), end="")
34              print("|")
35
36   def main():
37       draw_line()
38       draw_top()
39       draw_bottom()
40       draw_line()
41
42   main()
```

Notice that the SUB_HEIGHT constant is defined at the top of the program, giving it program-wide scope, rather than locally in the individual functions. While localizing variables is a good idea, the same is not true for constants. We localize variables to avoid potential interference, but that argument doesn't hold for constants, since they are guaranteed not to change. Another argument for using local variables is that it makes functions more independent. That argument has some merit when applied to constants, but not enough. It is true that constants introduce dependencies between functions, but often that is what you want. For example, the three functions in the program should not be independent of each other when it comes to the size of the figure. Each subfigure has to use the same size constant. Imagine the potential disaster if each function had its own SUB_HEIGHT, each with a different value; none of the pieces would fit together.

Chapter Summary

- Python groups data into types. Some of Python's built-in types are int for integers, float for real numbers, str for sequences of text characters, and bool for logical values.
- Values and computations are called expressions. The simplest expressions are individual values, also called literals. Some example literals are: 42, 3.14, "Q", and

False. Expressions may contain operators, as in (3 + 29) - 4 * 5. The division operation is split into exact division (/), integer division (//), and remainder (%) operators. You can test expressions and operators in the Python Shell.
- Rules of precedence determine the order in which multiple operators are evaluated in complex expressions.

Multiplication and division are performed before addition and subtraction. Parentheses can be used to force a particular order of evaluation.

- Variables are memory locations in which values can be stored. A variable is defined with a name and an initial value. The variable's value can be used later in the program or modified.

- Data can be printed on the console using the `print` function, just like text strings. Multiple comma-separated values can be printed to produce a more complex line of output, or you can use the `str` function to convert values into strings for printing.

- A loop is used to execute a group of statements several times. The `for` loop is one kind of loop that can be used to apply the same statements over a range of numbers or to repeat statements a specified number of times. A loop can contain another loop, called a nested loop.

- A variable exists from the line where it is defined to the end of the function that encloses it. This range, also called the scope of the variable, constitutes the part of the program where the variable can legally be used. A program can also contain constants, which are variables defined in a global scope that are not supposed to be modified after they are defined.

- An algorithm can be easier to write if you first write an English description of it. Such a description is also called pseudocode.

Self-Check Problems

Section 2.1: Basic Data Concepts

1. Trace the evaluation of the following expressions, and give their resulting values:

a. `2 + 3 * 4 - 6`

b. `14 // 7 * 2 + 30 // 5 + 1`

c. `(12 + 3) // 4 * 2`

d. `(238 % 10 + 3) % 7`

e. `(18 - 7) * (43 % 10)`

f. `2 + 19 % 5 - (11 * (5 // 2))`

g. `813 % 100 // 3 + 2.4`

h. `26 % 10 % 4 * 3`

i. `22 + 4 ** 1 * 2`

j. `23 % 8 % 3`

k. `12 - 2 ** 2 - 3 ** 2`

l. `6/2 + 7//3`

m. `6 * 7 % 4`

n. `3 * 4 + 2 * 3`

o. `177 % 100 % 10 // 2`

p. `89 % (5 + 5) % 5`

q. `392 // 10 % 10 // 2`

r. `8 * 2 - 7 // 4`

s. `37 % 20 % 3 * 4`

t. `17 % 10 // 4`

2. Trace the evaluation of the following expressions, and give their resulting values:

a. `4.0 / 2 * 9 / 2`

b. `2.5 * 2 + 8 / 5.0 + 10 // 3`

c. `12 // 7 * 4.4 * 2 // 4`

d. 4 * 3 // 8 + 2.5 * 2

e. (5 * 7.0 / 2 - 2.5) / 5 * 2

f. 41 % 7 * 3 // 5 + 5 // 2 * 2.5

g. 10.0 / 2 / 4

h. 8 // 5 + 13 // 2 / 3.0

i. (2.5 + 3.5) / 2

j. 9 // 4 * 2.0 - 5 // 4

k. 9 / 2.0 + 7 // 3 - 3.0 / 2

l. 813 % 100 // 3 + 2.4

m. 27 // 2 / 2.0 * (4.3 + 1.7) - 8 // 3

n. 53 // 5 / (0.6 + 1.4) / 2 ** 1 + 13 // 2

o. 2.5 * 2 + 8 / 5.0 + 10 // 3

p. 2 * 3 // 4 * 2 / 4.0 + 4.5 - 1

q. 89 % 10 // 4 * 2.0 / 5 + (1.5 + 1.0 / 2) * 2

r. 1 ** 5 + 7 ** 2 / 2.0

Section 2.2: Variables

3. Which of the following choices is the correct syntax for defining a real number variable named grade and initializing its value to 4.0?

   a. int grade = 4.0

   b. grade = float 4.0

   c. float grade = 4.0

   d. grade = 4

   e. grade = 4.0

4. Suppose you have an variable called number that stores an integer. What Python expression produces the last digit of the number (the 1s place)?

5. The following program contains 4 mistakes! What are they?

```
def main():
    x = 2
    print("x is" x)
    x = 15.2    # set x to 15.2
    print("x is now , x")
    y = 0               # set y to 1 more than x
    y = int x + 1
    print("x and y are " , x , and , y)
main()
```

6. Suppose you have a variable called number that stores an integer. What Python expression produces the second-to-last digit of the number (the 10s place)? What expression produces the third-to-last digit of the number (the 100s place)?

7. What are the values of a, b, and c after the following statements?

```
a = 5
b = 10
c = b

a = a + 1
b = b - 1
c = c + a
```

8. What are the values of `first` and `second` at the end of the following code? How would you describe the net effect of the code statements in this exercise? Consider the following code:

```
first = 8
second = 19
first = first + second
second = first - second
first = first - second
```

9. Rewrite the code from the previous exercise to be shorter, by defining the variables together and by using the special assignment operators (e.g., `+=` , `-=`, `*=`, and `/=`) as appropriate.

10. What are the values of `i`, `j`, and `k` after the following statements?

```
i = 2
j = 3
k = 4
x = i + j + k

i = x - i - j
j = x - j - k
k = x - i - k
```

11. What is the output from the following code?

```
max = 0
min = 10
max = 17 -   4 // 10
max = max + 6
min = max -   min
print(max * 2)
print(max + min)
print(max)
print(min)
```

12. The following program redundantly repeats the same expressions many times. Modify the program to remove all redundant expressions using variables.

```
def main():
    # Calculate pay at work based on hours worked each day
    print("My total hours worked:")
    print(4 + 5 + 8 + 4)

    print("My hourly salary:")
    print("8.75")

    print("My total pay:")
    print((4 + 5 + 8 + 4) * 8.75)

    print("My taxes owed:")   # 20% tax
    print((4 + 5 + 8 + 4) * 8.75 * 0.20)


main()
```

Section 2.3: The `for` Loop

13. Complete the following code, replacing the "FINISH ME" parts with your own code:

```
def main():
    for i in range("FINISH ME"):
        print("FINISH ME")
main()
```

to produce the following output:

```
2 times 1 = 2
2 times 2 = 4
2 times 3 = 6
2 times 4 = 8
```

14. Assume that you have a variable called `count` that will take on the values 1, 2, 3, 4, and so on. You are going to formulate expressions in terms of `count` that will yield different sequences. For example, to get the sequence 2, 4, 6, 8, 10, 12, ... , you would use the expression (2 * `count`). Fill in the following table, indicating an expression that will generate each sequence.

Sequence	Expression
2, 4, 6, 8, 10, 12, . . .	
4, 19, 34, 49, 64, 79, . . .	
30, 20, 10, 0, 210, 220, . . .	
−7, −3, 1, 5, 9, 13, . . .	
97, 94, 91, 88, 85, 82, . . .	

15. Complete the code for the following `for` loop:

```
for i in range(1, 7):
    # your code here
```

```
-4
14
32
50
68
86
```

The loop should print the following numbers, one per line:

16. What is the output of the following `odd_stuff` function?

```
def odd_stuff():
    number = 4
    for count in range(1, number + 1):
        print(number)
        number = number // 2
```

17. What is the output of the following loop?

```
total = 10
for number in range(1, total // 2):
    total = total -  number
    print(total, number)
```

18. What is the output of the following loop?

```
print("+---+")
for i in range(1, 4):
    print("\\    /")
    print("/    \\")
print("+---+")
```

19. What is the output of the following loop?

```
print("T-minus ", end="")
for i in range(5, 0, -1):
    print(i, end=", ")
print("Blastoff!")
```

20. What is the output of the following sequence of loops?

```
for i in range(1, 6):
    for j in range(1, 11):
        print(i * j, end=" ")
    print()
```

21. What is the output of the following sequence of loops?

```
for i in range(1, 3):
    for j in range(1, 4):
        for k in range(1, 5):
            print("*", end="")
        print("!", end="")
    print()
```

Section 2.4: Managing Complexity

22. Suppose that you have a variable called `line` that will take on the values 1, 2, 3, 4, and so on, and a constant named `SIZE` that takes one of two values. You are going to formulate expressions in terms of `line` and `SIZE` that will yield different sequences of numbers of characters. Fill in the table below, indicating an expression that will generate each sequence.

`line` Value	Constant `SIZE` Value	Number of Characters	Expression
a. 1, 2, 3, 4, 5, 6, ...	1	4, 6, 8, 10, 12, 14, ...	
1, 2, 3, 4, 5, 6, ...	2	6, 8, 10, 12, 14, 16, ...	
b. 1, 2, 3, 4, 5, 6, ...	3	13, 17, 21, 25, 29, 33, ...	
1, 2, 3, 4, 5, 6, ...	5	19, 23, 27, 31, 35, 39, ...	
c. 1, 2, 3, 4, 5, 6, ...	4	10, 9, 8, 7, 6, 5, ...	
1, 2, 3, 4, 5, 6, ...	9	20, 19, 18, 17, 16, 15, ...	

23. Write a table that determines the expressions for the number of each type of character on each of the 6 lines in the following output.

```
!!!!!!!!!!!!!!!!!!!!!!!!
\\!!!!!!!!!!!!!!!!!!!!//
\\\\!!!!!!!!!!!!!!!!////
\\\\\\!!!!!!!!!!!!//////
\\\\\\\\!!!!!!!!////////
\\\\\\\\\\!!!!!!//////////
```

24. Suppose that a program has been written that produces the output shown in the previous problem. Now the author wants the program to be scalable using a constant called SIZE. The previous output used a constant height of 6, since there were 6 lines. The following is the output for a constant height of 4. Create a new table that shows the expressions for the character counts at this new size of 4, and compare these tables to figure out the expressions for any size using the SIZE constant.

```
!!!!!!!!!!!!!!!!
\\!!!!!!!!!!!!//
\\\\!!!!!!!!////
\\\\\\!!!!!!//////
```

Exercises

1. Write a for loop that produces the following output:

```
1 4 9 16 25 36 49 64 81 100
```

For added challenge, try to modify your code so that it does not need to use the * multiplication operator. (It can be done! Hint: Look at the differences between adjacent numbers.)

2. The Fibonacci numbers are a sequence of integers in which the first two elements are 1, and each following element is the sum of the two preceding elements. The mathematical definition of each kth Fibonacci number is the following:

$$F(k) = \begin{cases} F(k-1) + F(k-2), & k > 2 \\ 1, & k <= 2 \end{cases}$$

The first 12 Fibonacci numbers are

```
1 1 2 3 5 8 13 21 34 55 89 144
```

Write a for loop that computes and prints the first 12 Fibonacci numbers.

3. Write `for` loops to produce the following output:

```
*****
*****
*****
*****
```

4. Write `for` loops to produce the following output:

```
*
**
***
****
*****
```

5. Write `for` loops to produce the following output:

```
1
22
333
4444
55555
666666
7777777
```

6. It's common to print a rotating, increasing list of single-digit numbers at the start of a program's output as a visual guide to number the columns of the output to follow. With this in mind, write nested `for` loops to produce the following output, with each line 60 characters wide:

```
    |         |         |         |         |         |
123456789012345678901234567890123456789012345678901234567890
```

7. Modify your code from the previous exercise so that it could easily be modified to display a different range of numbers (instead of 1234567890) and a different number of repetitions of those numbers (instead of 60 total characters), with the vertical bars still matching up correctly. Use constants instead of "magic numbers." Here are some example outputs that could be generated by changing your constants:

```
    |    |    |    |    |    |    |    |    |    |
123401234012340123401234012340123401234012340123401234012340
    |       |       |       |       |       |       |
123456701234567012345670123456701234567012345670123456701234567012345670
```

8. Write a function called `print_design` that produces the following output. Use `for` loops to capture the structure of the figure.

```
-----1-----
----333----
---55555---
--7777777--
-999999999-
```

9. Write a Python program that produces the following output. Use `for` loops and string multiplication to capture the structure of the figure.

```
!!!!!!!!!!!!!!!!!!!!!!!
\\!!!!!!!!!!!!!!!!!!!//
\\\\!!!!!!!!!!!!!!!////
\\\\\\!!!!!!!!!!!//////
\\\\\\\\!!!!!!!////////
\\\\\\\\\\!!!//////////
```

10. Modify your program from the previous exercise to use a constant for the figure's height. (You may want to make loop tables first.) The previous output used a constant height of 6. The following are the outputs for constant heights of 4 and 8:

```
Height 4              Height 8
!!!!!!!!!!!!!!!       !!!!!!!!!!!!!!!!!!!!!!!!!!!!!!!
\\!!!!!!!!!!!//        \\!!!!!!!!!!!!!!!!!!!!!!!!!!!//
\\\\!!!!!!!////        \\\\!!!!!!!!!!!!!!!!!!!!!!!////
\\\\\\!!!//////        \\\\\\!!!!!!!!!!!!!!!!!!!//////
                       \\\\\\\\!!!!!!!!!!!!!!!////////
                       \\\\\\\\\\!!!!!!!!!!!//////////
                       \\\\\\\\\\\\!!!!!!!////////////
                       \\\\\\\\\\\\\\!!!//////////////
```

11. Write a Python program that produces the following output. Use `for` loops and string multiplication to capture the structure of the figure. Once you get it to work, add a constant so that the size of the figure can be changed simply by changing the constant's value.

```
+===+===+
|   |   |
|   |   |
|   |   |
+===+===+
|   |   |
|   |   |
|   |   |
+===+===+
```

12. Write a Python program that produces the following output. Use `for` loops to capture the structure of the figure.

```
//////////////////\\\\\\\\\\\\\\\\\\
////////////********\\\\\\\\\\\\\\
////////****************\\\\\\\\
////********************\\\\
********************************
```

13. Modify the program from the previous exercise to use a constant for the figure's height. (You may want to make loop tables first.) The previous output used a constant height of 5. The following are the outputs for constant heights of 3 and 6:

```
Height 3                Height 6
////////\\\\\\\\        //////////////////////\\\\\\\\\\\\\\\\\\\\\\
////********\\\\        ///////////////********\\\\\\\\\\\\\\\\\\
****************        ////////////****************\\\\\\\\\\\\\\
                        ////////****************************\\\\\\\\
                        ////********************************\\\\
                        ****************************************
```

Programming Projects

1. Write a program that produces the following output using nested `for` loops and string multiplication:

```
****** ////////////  ******
*****  ///////////\\   *****
****   //////////\\\    ****
***    ///////\\\\\\      ***
**     ////\\\\\\\\\       **
*      //\\\\\\\\\\\        *
       \\\\\\\\\\\\
```

2. Write a program that produces the following output using nested `for` loops:

```
+---------+
|    *    |
|   /*\   |
|  //*\\  |
| ///*\\\ |
| \\\*/// |
|  \\*//  |
|   \*/   |
|    *    |
+---------+
| \\\*/// |
|  \\*//  |
|   \*/   |
|    *    |
|    *    |
|   /*\   |
|  //*\\  |
| ///*\\\ |
+---------+
```

3. Write a program that produces the following hourglass figure as its output using nested `for` loops and string multiplication:

```
|"""""""""|
 \:::::::/
  \::::::/
   \::::/
    \::/
    ||
    /::\
   /::::\
  /::::::\
 /:::::::\
|_____|
```

4. Write a program that produces the following rocket ship figure as its output using nested `for` loops and string multi-plication. Use a constant to make it possible to change the size of the rocket (the following output uses a size of 3).

```
      /**\
     //**\\
    ///**\\\
   ////**\\\\
  /////**\\\\\
 +=*=*=*=*=*=*+
 |../\..../\..|
 |./\/\../\/\.|
 |/\/\/\/\/\/\|
 |\/\/\/\/\/\/|
 |.\/\/..\/\/.|
 |..\/....\/..|
 +=*=*=*=*=*=*+
 |\/\/\/\/\/\/|
 |.\/\/..\/\/.|
 |..\/....\/..|
 |../\..../\..|
 |./\/\../\/\.|
 |/\/\/\/\/\/\|
 +=*=*=*=*=*=*+
      /**\
     //**\\
    ///**\\\
   ////**\\\\
  /////**\\\\\
```

5. Write a program that produces the following figure (which vaguely resembles the Seattle Space Needle) as its output using nested `for` loops and string multiplication. Use a constant to make it possible to change the size of the figure (the following output uses a size of 4).

```
                | |
                | |
                | |
                | |
              __/| |\__
           __/:::| |:::\__
        __/::::::| |::::::\__
     __/:::::::::| |:::::::::\__
     |"""""""""""""""""""""""""|
     \_/\/\/\/\/\/\/\/\/\/\/\_/
       \_/\/\/\/\/\/\/\/\/\_/
         \_/\/\/\/\/\/\_/
           \_/\/\/\/\_/
                | |
                | |
                | |
                | |
             |%%| |%%|
             |%%| |%%|
             |%%| |%%|
             |%%| |%%|
             |%%| |%%|
             |%%| |%%|
             |%%| |%%|
             |%%| |%%|
             |%%| |%%|
             |%%| |%%|
             |%%| |%%|
             |%%| |%%|
             |%%| |%%|
             |%%| |%%|
             |%%| |%%|
             |%%| |%%|
              __/| |\__
           __/:::| |:::\__
        __/::::::| |::::::\__
     __/:::::::::| |:::::::::\__
     |"""""""""""""""""""""""""|
```

6. Write a program that produces the following figure (which vaguely resembles a textbook) as its output using nested `for` loops and string multiplication. Use a class constant to make it possible to change the size of the figure (the following output uses a size of 10).

```
                    +------------------------------+
          /                                  ___/
         /                              ___/___//
        /                          ___/___/___///
       /                       ___/___/___/___////
      /                    ___/___/___/___/___/////
     /                 ___/___/___/___/___/___//////
    /              ___/___/___/___/___/___/___///////
   /           ___/___/___/___/___/___/___/___////////
  /        ___/___/___/___/___/___/___/___/___/////////
 /     ___/___/___/___/___/___/___/___/___/__//////////
/___/___/___/___/___/___/___/___/___/__///////////
 +------------------------------+//////////
 |    Building Python Programs    |//////////
 |    Building Python Programs    |////////
 |    Building Python Programs    |//////
 |    Building Python Programs    |////
 |    Building Python Programs    |//
 +------------------------------+
```

7. Write a program that produces the following figure (which vaguely resembles a saguaro cactus) as its output using nested `for` loops and string multiplication. Use a class constant to make it possible to change the size of the figure (the following output uses a size of 3).

```
 XXX      XXXXXX
X---X   X/-----X
X---X   X//----X
X---X   X///---X
X---X   X////--X
X---X   X/////-X
 XXXXXXX~~~~~~X      XXX
            X-----\X   X---X
            X----\\X   X---X
            X---\\\X   X---X
            X--\\\\X   X---X
            X-\\\\\X   X---X
            X~~~~~~Xxxxxxx
            X~~~~~~X
            X~~~~~~X
            X~~~~~~X
            X~~~~~~X
            X~~~~~~X
            X~~~~~~X
```

Parameters and Graphics

Introduction

Chapter 2 introduced techniques for managing complexity, including the use of constants, which make programs more flexible. This chapter explores a more powerful technique for obtaining such flexibility. Here, you will learn how to use parameters to create functions that solve not just single tasks, but whole families of tasks. Creating such functions requires you to generalize, or look beyond a specific task to find the more general category of task that it exemplifies. The ability to generalize is one of the most important qualities of a good software engineer, and the generalization technique you will study in this chapter is one of the most powerful techniques programmers use.

After exploring parameters, we'll discuss some other issues associated with functions, such as the ability of a function to "return" a value. Returning values will allow us to learn about some useful Python libraries for mathematical calculations and random number generation.

This chapter will also explore how to create interactive programs that obtain values from the user. This feature will allow you to write programs that prompt the user for input as well as producing output.

The chapter will conclude with an introduction to drawing graphics using an instructor-provided library called `DrawingPanel`.

3.1 Parameters

Humans are very good at learning new tasks. When we learn, we often develop a single generalized solution for a family of related tasks. For example, someone might ask you to take 10 steps forward or 20 steps forward. These are different tasks, but they both involve taking a certain number of steps forward. We think of this action as a single task of taking steps forward, and we understand that the number of steps will vary from one task to another. In programming terms, we refer to the number of steps as a *parameter* that allows us to generalize the task.

Parameter (Parameterize)

Any of a set of characteristics that distinguish different members of a family of tasks. To parameterize a task is to identify a set of its parameters.

We will explore how parameters can improve a Python program by looking at a specific example. Suppose you want to write a program that draws box-shaped figures. Each box is a square with the same number of characters wide as it is tall, with asterisks around its border and dots in its interior. The following function draws a box of size 6 × 6:

```python
# Prints a 6x6 box filled with dots.
def draw_box():
    print("*" * 6)
    for line in range(4):
        print("*", "." * 4, "*", sep="")
    print("*" * 6)
```

```
******
*....*
*....*
*....*
*....*
******
```

Now suppose we want to draw three boxes of various sizes. The following program does this using three functions named `draw_box1`, `draw_box2`, and `draw_box3`:

```
 1   # This program draws square box figures.
 2   # This initial version is redundant.
 3
 4   # Prints a 6x6 box filled with dots.
 5   def draw_box1():
 6       print("*" * 6)
 7       for line in range(4):
 8           print("*", "." * 4, "*", sep="")
 9       print("*" * 6)
10
11   # Prints a 9x9 box filled with dots.
12   def draw_box2():
13       print("*" * 9)
14       for line in range(7):
15           print("*", "." * 7, "*", sep="")
16       print("*" * 9)
17
18   # Prints a 4x4 box filled with dots.
19   def draw_box3():
20       print("*" * 4)
21       for line in range(2):
22           print("*", "." * 2, "*", sep="")
23       print("*" * 4)
24
25   def main():
26       print("This program draws three boxes.")
27       draw_box1()
28       print()
29       draw_box2()
30       print()
31       draw_box3()
32
33   main()
```

```
This program draws three boxes.
******
*....*
*....*
*....*
*....*
******
```

Continued on next page

Continued from previous page

```
********

*......*

*......*

*......*

*......*

*......*

*......*

*......*

********

****

*..*

*..*

****
```

As you can see, the code for the three box-drawing functions is almost exactly the same, so this is a suboptimal solution. Notice the relationship between the various integers in the box-drawing code. The number of characters to draw on each line is related to the size of the box. Suppose we want to rewrite the box-drawing code in a way that is generalized to work for a square box of any size. To figure out loop expressions for repeating character patterns, you can use reasoning similar to the reasoning we used in the the tables and equations in Chapter 2.

The 6 × 6 box begins with a line of print("*" * 6), and the 9 × 9 box begins with print("*" * 9), so in general the code prints a number of stars equal to the box size. The middle of the 6 × 6 box has a loop that repeats 4 times drawing a star, 4 dots, and a star. The middle of the 9 × 9 box has a loop that repeats 7 times drawing a star, 7 dots, and a star. The general formula is that the middle should have a loop that repeats 2 less than the size of the box. Based on all of this, we could write a draw_box function that defines a size variable and then draws the various characters:

```
# Prints a 6×6 box filled with dots.
def draw_box():
    size = 6
    print("*" * size)
    for line in range(size - 2):
        print("*", "." * (size - 2), "*", sep="")
    print("*" * size)
```

The problem with this new code is that we would need to run draw_box with three different values for size: 6, 9, and 4. One approach might be to set the size variable to a particular value before the draw_box function is called:

```
# attempt to use a variable to control the
# number of spaces (this does not work)
def main():
    size = 6
    draw_box()
    ...
```

Unfortunately, this approach won't work. With the code structured in this way, scope limitations prevent `main` from being able to change the value of the `size` variable. Any variable being defined by `main` would be a local variable in `main` that could not be seen inside `draw_box`. A global constant might seem like a better choice, but remember that we want to run `draw_box` with different sizes at different points in the program. Constants by nature have values that do not change, so they won't work in this case.

We want the `draw_box` code to depend on the value of a `size` variable. But we also want the value of that variable to be supplied by the part of the code that is calling `draw_box`, which is `main` in our case. This is exactly the functionality that is provided by a parameter.

A parameter is a variable that is defined in the header of a function. Parameters are different from other variables in that their values are set by code outside of the function at the moment the function is called. The general syntax for defining a function with a parameter is:

```
def name(parameter_name):
    ...
```

Syntax template: Function definition with parameter

The parameter appears in the function header, after the name and inside the parentheses that you have, up to this point, been leaving empty. Notice that you write the parameter's name but not its value. This is on purpose; the parameter doesn't have a single fixed value, but rather the value is provided by `main` when the function is called. The following is the definition of `draw_box` with a parameter for the box size:

```
# Prints a box filled with dots using a size parameter.
def draw_box(size):
    print("*" * size)
    for line in range(size - 2):
        print("*", "." * (size - 2), "*", sep="")
    print("*" * size)
```

The idea is that instead of writing a function that performs just one version of a task, you write a more flexible version that solves a family of related tasks that all differ by one or more parameters. In the case of the `draw_box` function, the parameter is the size of the box.

Now that the `draw_box` function uses a parameter, you must modify the syntax for calling the function. You can no longer call the parameterized function by using just its name:

```
draw_box()
```

Instead, `main` must supply a value that will be used for the `size` parameter while the function is running. The syntax for calling a function is to write the value you want to give the parameter inside the parentheses of the function call:

name(expression)

Syntax template: Function call with parameter

For example, to draw a box of size 6, you would write:

```
draw_box(6)
```

When a call like this is made, the value `6` is used to define the `size` parameter. You can think of this as information flowing from the call into the function, as shown in Figure 3.1.

The parameter `size` is a local variable, but it gets its initial value from the call. The call of `draw_box(6)` is the same as saying, "Run the `draw_box` function with `size` set to the value 6."

The flexibility of the `size` parameter means that we can call it with different `size` values to draw boxes of different sizes, such as `draw_box(14)` to draw a 14 × 14 box.

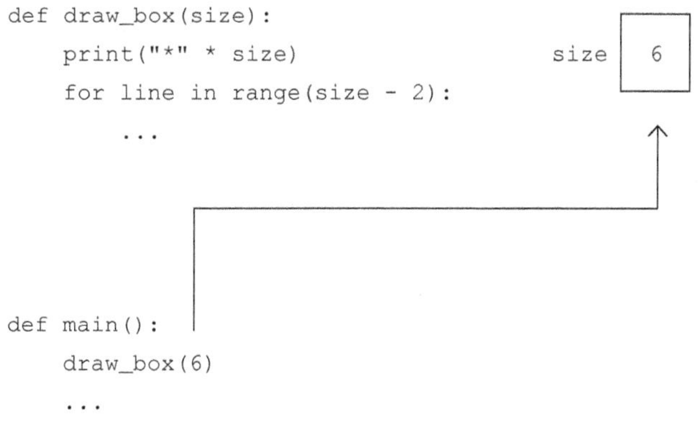

Figure 3.1 Information flow of function call with parameter

The following is a complete version of the box-drawing program that uses parameters to draw three square boxes:

```
1   # This program draws square box figures.
2   # This second version uses a parameter.
3
4   # Prints a box of the given height filled with dots.
5   def draw_box(height):
6       print("*" * (height * 2))
7       for line in range(height - 2):
8           print("*", "." * (height * 2 - 2), "*", sep="")
9       print("*" * (height * 2))
10
11  def main():
12      print("This program draws three boxes.")
13      draw_box(5)
14      print()
15      draw_box(7)
16      print()
17      draw_box(3)
18
19  main()
```

Python also allows you to optionally write the parameter's name and an = sign as you are calling the function. This is called a *named parameter* or a *keyword argument*. The general syntax for a function call with a named parameter is the following:

```
name(parameter_name = expression)
```
Syntax template: Function call with named parameter

Writing the parameter's name does not change the behavior of the function call, but some programmers understand this syntax better because the intent of the value 6 becomes more explicit. For example, the call to draw a box of size 6 could also be written as:

```
# call draw_box using named parameter
draw_box(size = 6)
```

In this text we will generally not use the named parameter syntax. It is more verbose and longer to write, and most other programming languages do not support that syntax.

(You have actually seen named parameters before in Chapter 2, when we discussed variations of the print statement that used end= and sep=; those are examples of named parameters to the print function.)

The value you pass for a parameter does not have to be a simple literal value. You can use an integer expression such as:

```
draw_box(3 * 5 - 6)
```

In this case, Python first evaluates the expression to get the value 9 and then calls `draw_box(9)`.

The variable definition inside the parentheses of the function header is called a *formal parameter*, while the value provided in `main` in a given function call is called an *actual parameter*. Computer scientists sometimes use the word "parameter" loosely to mean both formal and actual parameters.

Formal Parameter

A variable that appears inside parentheses in the header of a function that is used to generalize the function's behavior.

Actual Parameter

A specific value or expression that appears inside parentheses in a function call.

The term "formal parameter" does not describe its purpose. A better name might be "generalized parameter." In the `draw_box` function, `size` is the generalized parameter that appears in the function header. It is a placeholder for some unspecified value. The values appearing in the function calls are the actual parameters, because each call indicates a specific task to perform. In other words, each call provides an actual value to fill the placeholder.

The word *argument* is often used as a synonym for "parameter," as in "These are the arguments I'm passing to this function." Some people prefer to reserve the word "argument" for actual parameters and the word "parameter" for formal parameters.

The Mechanics of Parameters

When Python executes a call on a function, it defines the function's parameters. For each parameter, it first evaluates the expression passed as the actual parameter and then uses the result to define the local variable whose name is given by the formal parameter. Suppose the `main` function of our previous box-drawing program had been the following:

```
def main():
    box_size_1 = 5
    box_size_2 = 3

    draw_box(box_size_1)
    print()
    draw_box(box_size_2)
    print()
    draw_box(box_size_1 * box_size_2 - 9)
```

In the first two lines of the main function, the interpreter finds instructions to allocate and define two variables:

box_size_1 [5]   box_size_2 [3]

The next lines of code call the draw_box function and pass box_size_1 as the parameter value.

```
draw_box(box_size_1)
```

When Python executes the call on draw_box, it must set up its parameter. To set up the parameter, Python first evaluates the expression being passed as the actual parameter. The expression is simply the variable box_size_1, which has the value 5. Therefore, Python sends the value 5 to the draw_box function and uses that value to define the draw_box function's local parameter variable called size.

The following diagram indicates how the computer's memory would look as the draw_box function is called the first time. Because there are two functions involved (main and draw_box), the diagram indicates which variables are local to main (box_size_1 and box_size_2) and which are local to draw_box (the parameter size):

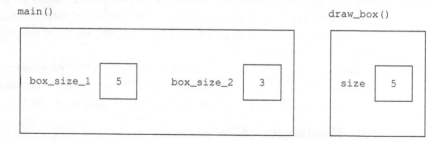

The net effect of this process is that the draw_box function has a local copy of the value stored in the variable box_size_1 from the main function.

The main function then calls draw_box again, this time with the variable box_size_2 as its actual parameter. The computer evaluates this expression, obtaining the result 3. This value is used to define size inside the draw_box function:

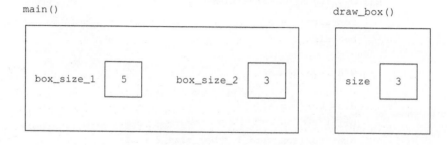

Because `size` has a different value this time (3 instead of 5), the function produces a box with a different size. Finally, the last call from the `main` function is:

```
draw_box(box_size_1 * box_size_2 - 9)
```

This time the actual parameter is an expression, not just a variable or literal value. Thus, before the call is made, the computer evaluates the expression to determine its value:

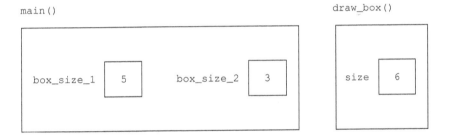

The interpreter uses this result to define the `size` parameter:

```
main()                                                    draw_box()
```

```
box_size_1   5        box_size_2   3            size   6
```

We should mention that `print` is also a function, and that when you call it and write values in parentheses, you are passing parameters to the `print` function. When you write a message in quotes to `print`, you are actually passing a string parameter (a value of type `str`). We will learn more about strings in the next chapter.

Limitations of Parameters

We've seen that a parameter can be used to provide input to a function. But while you can use a parameter to send a value into a function, you can't use a parameter to get a value out of a function.

When a parameter is set up, a local variable is created and is defined to the value being passed as the actual parameter. The net effect is that the local variable is a copy of the value coming from the outside. Since it is a local variable, it can't influence any variables outside the function. Consider the following sample program:

```
 1   # This buggy program shows the limitations of parameters.
 2
 3   # Prints a number before and after doubling its value.
 4   def double_number(num):
 5       print("in double_number, initial value =", num)
 6       num *= 2
 7       print("in double_number, final value =", num)
 8
 9   def main():
10       x = 17
11       double_number(x)
12       print("in main, x =", x)
13       print()
14
15       num = 42
16       double_number(num)
17       print("in main, num =", num)
18
19   main()
```

This program begins by defining an integer variable called x with the value 17:

main()

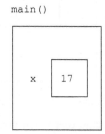

It then calls the function double_number, passing x as a parameter. The value of x is used to define the parameter num as a local variable of the function:

main()   double_number()

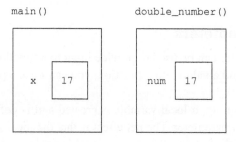

The program then executes the statements inside of `double_number`. First, `double_number` prints the initial value of `num`, which is `17`. Then it doubles the value of `num`:

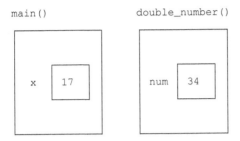

Notice that this has no effect on the `x` variable in `main`. The parameter called `num` is a copy of x, so even though they started out the same, changing the value of number does not affect x. Next, `double_number` reports the new value of `num`, which is `34`. At this point, `double_number` finishes executing and we return to `main`:

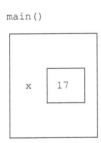

The next statement in the `main` function prints the value of `x`, which is still `17`. Then it defines a variable called `num` with the value `42`:

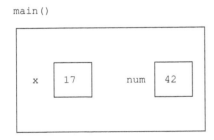

The following statement calls `double_number` again, this time passing it the value of `num`. This is an odd situation because the parameter has the same name as the variable in `main`, but Python doesn't care. It always creates a new local variable for the `double_number` function:

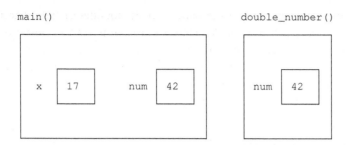

So, at this point there are two different variables called num, one in each function. Now it's time to execute the statements of double_number again. It first reports the value of num, which is 42, then doubles it:

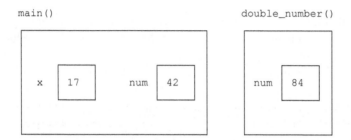

Again, notice that doubling number inside double_number has no effect on the original variable number in main. These are separate variables, even though they have the same name. This is allowed because they exist in separate scopes. The function then reports the new value of num, which is 84, and returns to main:

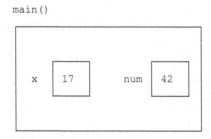

The program then reports the value of num and terminates. So, the overall output of the program is as follows:

```
in double_number, initial value = 17
in double_number, final value = 34
in main, x = 17

in double_number, initial value = 42
in double_number, final value = 84
in main, num = 42
```

The local manipulations of the parameter do not change these variables outside the function. The fact that variables are copied is an important aspect of parameters. On the positive side, we know that the variables are protected from change because the parameters are copies of the originals. On the negative side, it means that although parameters will allow us to send values into a function, they will not allow us to get values back out of a function.

Multiple Parameters

A function can accept more than one parameter. The syntax is to write all of the parameters' names inside the parentheses of the function header, separated by commas:

```
def name(parameter_name, parameter_name, ..., parameter_name):
    ...
```
Syntax template: Function definition with multiple parameters

Whether you knew it or not, you have passed multiple parameters to a function before. When you printed multiple values in a `print` statement separated by commas, you were actually passing multiple parameters to `print`.

As an example of writing a function that accepts multiple parameters, let's consider a variation of our `draw_box` function from earlier in this chapter. The function draws square boxes of a given size. What if we want to be able to draw rectangular boxes that have a different width and height? We can generalize the box-drawing task even further by defining the function with two parameters to represent its size in each dimension. (When we talk about functions with parameters, we often say that the function "accepts" or "takes" these parameters from the caller.)

Here is the original version of `draw_box`, followed by a new version that accepts two parameters:

```
# Prints a square box filled with dots.
def draw_box(size):
    print("*" * size)
    for line in range(size - 2):
        print("*", "." * (size - 2), "*", sep="")
    print("*" * size)


# Prints a rectangular box filled with dots.
def draw_box(width, height):
    print("*" * width)
    for line in range(height - 2):
        print("*", "." * (width - 2), "*", sep="")
    print("*" * width)
```

To call a function that accepts multiple parameters, write the function's name followed by the values for each parameter in parentheses separated by commas. You must supply the same number values as are defined in the function's header, in the same order. The general syntax is the following:

```
name(expression, expression, ..., expression)
```

For example, to call our new rectangular `draw_box` function to create a 10 × 5 box, you would write:

```
def main():
    draw_box(10, 5)
```

```
**********
*........*
*........*
*........*
**********
```

The preceding code executes `draw_box` with the parameter `width` set to `10` and the parameter `height` set to `5`. Python lines up the parameters in sequential order, with the first actual parameter going into the first formal parameter and the second actual parameter going into the second formal parameter, as shown in Figure 3.2.

You can include as many parameters as you want when you define a function. Each function call must provide exactly that number of parameters, in the same order. In the

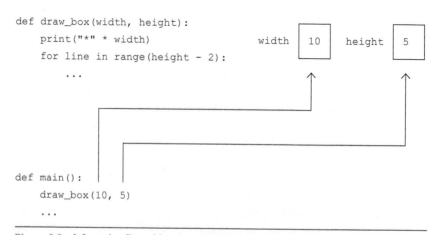

Figure 3.2   Information flow of function call with multiple parameters

case of `draw_box`, if the call does not have exactly two parameters, the program will generate an error:

```
# this bad code passes the
# wrong number of parameters
def main():
    draw_box(10)
    draw_box(5, 8, 19)
```

```
Traceback (most recent call last):
  File "boxes3.py", line 15, in <module>
    main()
  File "boxes3.py", line 12, in main
    draw_box(10)
TypeError: draw_box() missing 1 required
          positional argument: 'height'
```

It is interesting that the interpreter calls this a `TypeError`. Python thinks of functions as having a "type" that is related to the parameters they require. When you call a function and pass the wrong number of parameters, you are treating it as the wrong type of function. The type of a function based on its number of parameters is also called its *signature*.

Function Signature

The name of a function, along with its number of parameters.

We've seen that functions can call other functions. This is equally true of functions that take parameters. For example, suppose you want to draw a "hut" figure that is similar to the rectangular boxes we have drawn previously, but with a triangular "roof" on top of it. You can write a `draw_hut` function that calls `draw_box` to draw the base of the hut figure, passing appropriate parameters to it:

```
# Prints a "hut" figure with a triangular roof
# and rectangular base of the given size.
def draw_hut(size):
    for line in range(1, size):
        print(" " * (size - line), end="")
        print("*" * (line * 2 - 1))
    draw_box(size * 2 - 1, size)
```

```
        *
       ***
      *****
     *******
    *********
   ***********
  *.........*
  *.........*
  *.........*
  *.........*
  ***********
```

Notice that `draw_hut` accepts a parameter called `size` and this parameter is used to form expressions that are passed as values to the two parameters of `draw_box`. In `main`, the call of `draw_hut(6)` would produce the figure shown as output.

When you're calling functions that accept many parameters, the line of code can become very long. Python allows you to wrap long lines (ones that exceed roughly 80 characters in length) by inserting a backslash followed by line break and increased indentation:

```
# wrap a long line onto a second and third line
my_function_call(a + 7, b * c - 19, \
    d + e + f + g, \
    h, i, j, k)
```

Parameters versus Constants

In Chapter 2, you saw that constants are a useful mechanism to increase the flexibility of your programs. By using such constants, you can make it easy to modify a program to behave differently. Parameters provide much of the same flexibility, and more. Consider the `draw_box` function. Suppose you wrote it using a constant:

```
BOX_SIZE = 10
```

This approach would give you the flexibility to produce a box of a certain size, but it has one major limitation: The constant can change only when modified by the programmer between runs of the program; you must open your Python program file, change the constant's value, save the file, and run the program again. It is not possible to change the constant's value in the middle of a single execution of the program.

Parameters are more flexible. Because you specify the value to be used each time you call the function, you can use several different values in a single program execution. As you have seen, you can call the function many different times within a single program execution and have it behave differently every time. However, using parameters involves more work for the programmer than using constants. It makes your function headers and function calls more tedious, not to mention making the execution (and, thus, the debugging) more complex.

Therefore, you will probably find occasion to use each technique. The basic rule is to use a constant when you only want to change the value from execution to execution. If you want to use different values within a single execution, use a parameter.

Optional Parameters

Python allows you to write a single function that accepts optional parameters. An *optional parameter* is one for which the caller can pass an explicit value or can omit the parameter to receive a default value instead. Optional parameters can make a function more flexible by allowing it to be called in multiple ways. The syntax for an optional parameter is to define it in the function's header with a name and a value, separated by an = sign.

```
def name(parameter_name = value):
    ...
```

Syntax template: Function definition with optional parameter

For example, in the last section we wrote a draw_hut function that accepts a size parameter. The following code makes the size parameter optional and sets its default value to 6:

```
# Draws a hut of the given size, with a
# default size of 6 if none is provided.
def draw_hut(size = 6):
    ...
```

This allows the caller to execute draw_hut in two different ways. If the caller supplies a parameter value in parentheses, that value will be used as the figure's size; if not, the default value of 6 will be used:

```
def main():
    draw_hut(11)     # pass a size of 11
    draw_hut()       # default size of 6
```

A function can have multiple optional parameters. For example, we could modify our previous draw_box function to use a default width and height of 10 and 5, respectively:

```
# Draws a box of the given size.
# If no width and/or height are provided, uses a default of 10 x 5.
def draw_box(width = 10, height = 5):
    ...
```

Since both parameters are optional, the caller can now call draw_box in three different ways. If two parameters are passed, they are used as the width and height. If only one parameter is passed, it is used as the box's width, and the default height is used. If no parameters are passed, the default values are used for both the width and height.

```
def main():
    draw_box(7, 3)      #  7 x 3 (pass both width and height)
    print()
    draw_box(8)         #  8 x 5 (pass width of 8; default height)
    print()
    draw_box()          # 10 x 5 (default width and height)
```

You can even write a function that uses a combination of required and optional parameters. The following is a version of draw_box with a required width parameter and an optional height parameter. This version can be called with one or two parameters in the parentheses; if no parameters are written, the interpreter will generate a TypeError.

```
# Draws a box of the given size.
# Width must be passed, height is optional (default 5).
def draw_box(width, height = 5):
    ...
```

The default value given to a parameter must be a constant value such as 10 or 5. It might be useful to write a version of draw_box where the width parameter is mandatory, and if the height parameter is omitted, the height will take the same value as the width, making a square box. You might try to achieve this by writing a draw_box heading where the height parameter's default value is set to width, but Python does not allow this because width is not a constant value. The code generates a NameError when it runs.

```
# Draws a box of the given size.
# If no height is provided, makes a square box.
# (This does not work.)
def draw_box(width, height = width):
    ...
```

We don't have a good way of working around this limitation yet, but we will see one later in this chapter.

Python's optional parameter syntax is a useful feature. Many programming languages don't support optional parameters and instead require you to write a separate entire function for each combination of parameters you want to allow. Each of the separate versions of the function uses the same name but with different parameters listed in its header. That is called *overloading* the function. Python does not allow you to write two functions with the same name in the same program's scope, but the optional parameter syntax removes the need to do so in the first place.

3.2 Returning Values

The last few functions we've looked at have been action-oriented functions that perform some specific task. You can think of them as being like commands that you could give someone, as in "Draw a box" or "Draw a triangle." Parameters allow these commands to be more flexible, as in "Draw a box of size 10 by 5."

You will also want to be able to write functions that compute values. These functions are more like questions, as in, "What is the square root of 6.5?" or, "What do you get when you raise 2.3 to the 4th power?"

Python has a built-in function named `round` that accepts a number as a parameter and rounds that number to the nearest integer. For example, `round(3.2)` is 3 and `round(4.8)` is 5. It might seem that this function would print its result to the console as output. But you may want to use the rounded integer as part of a larger expression or computation.

A better solution is for the rounding function to allow the program to use the rounded result as an expression or value. If the rounded result is part of an expression, you can store it in a variable, or print it to the console. Such a command is a new type of function that is said to *return* a value.

> **Return**
>
> To send a value out as the result of a function that can be used in an expression in your program.

You could use the `round` function to store the rounded integer nearest to `3.647` by writing code like the following Python Shell interaction:

```
>>> x = 3.647
>>> y = round(x)
>>> y
4
```

The `round` function has a parameter (the number whose rounded integer form you want to find), and it also returns a value (the rounded number). The actual parameter `3.647` goes "into" the function, and the rounded integer comes "out." In the preceding code, the returned result is stored in a variable called `y`. A function can return any type of data: an `int`, a `float`, or any other type.

If you want to round to a given decimal place rather than to the nearest integer, you can pass an optional second parameter to `round` indicating the maximum number of digits to leave after the decimal. For example, a call of `round(value, 2)` rounds the value to 2 decimal places, which is to the nearest hundredth.

Instead of storing the result into a variable as we did in our previous code, you can also directly print the returned result of a call to `round` as shown in the following code. Notice that the call to `round` on x does not modify the value of x afterward:

```
x = 3.647
print("nearest integer is", round(x))
print("nearest tenth is", round(x, 1))
print("nearest hundredth is", round(x, 2))
print("x is", x)
```

```
nearest integer is 4
nearest tenth is 3.6
nearest hundredth is 3.65
x is 3.647
```

A key insight into functions that return values is that the function call itself becomes an expression that can be used in your code anywhere an expression is expected. This includes the fact that you can use a function call as part of a larger expression or calculation. For example, the following diagram shows the evaluation of an expression containing a call to round:

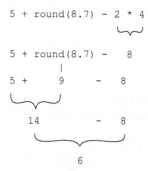

Python includes several other useful built-in functions that return values. Table 3.1 lists some of them. You can read a complete list of these functions at:

https://docs.python.org/3/library/functions.html

Table 3.1   Built-In Global Functions

Function	Description	Example	Result
abs	absolute value	abs(-308)	308
max	largest of two or more values	max(11, 8)	11
min	smallest of two or more values	min(7, 2, 4, 3)	2
pow	exponentiation (like **)	pow(3, 4)	81
round	number rounded to a given	round(3.647)	4
	decimal place	round(3.647, 1)	3.7

The math Module

Python includes many useful functions that represent mathematical operations. These functions are part of a library known as `math`. In this section we will explore the math library and how to introduce libraries into your programs in general.

In Chapter 1 we mentioned that a great deal of predefined code, collectively known as the Python libraries, has been written for Python. Each individual library available is called a *module*. One of the most useful modules is named `math`. It includes predefined mathematical constants and a large number of common mathematical functions. The `math` module is available on any machine on which Python is installed.

> **Module**
> An individual unit of Python library functionality with a name.

To use a library in your program, you must place a new kind of statement at the top of your program called an *import statement*. An import statement instructs the Python interpreter to load a given library and utilize its functionality in your program. We haven't needed an import statement until now because some of Python's features and functions like `print` and `round` are globally available to every program.

> **Import Statement**
> A request to access a specific Python library in your code.

The syntax for an import statement is to write the keyword `import` followed by the library's name:

```
import module
```
Syntax template: import statement

For example, in order to use `math` functions in your program, you must place the following statement at the top of your code:

```
import math
```

The `math` module has a function called `sqrt` that computes the square root of a number. Whenever you want to call a function from a module, the syntax is different from calling a function you defined yourself. You must write the module's name followed by a dot and then the function's name:

```
module.function_name(parameters)
```
Syntax template: Calling a function from a library

In the case of computing a square root, a call of `math.sqrt(value)` will compute and return the square root of the given value. Here are some example calls in the Python Shell. Notice that you must type `import math` into the shell before the math functions will be recognized:

```
>>> import math
>>> math.sqrt(4.0)
2.0
>>> math.sqrt(22)
4.69041575982343
```

The following is a complete program that uses the module. Notice that the code also uses the `round` function from the last section to show the roots with two digits after the decimal. Also note that this code uses the \ backslash syntax to split a long line into two lines:

```
1   # This program uses the math module to compute
2   # the square roots of the integers 1-20.
3
4   import math
5
6   def main():
7       for i in range(1, 11):
8           root = math.sqrt(i)
9           print("square root of", i, \
10              "is", round(root, 2))
11
12  main()
```

```
square root of 1 is 1.0
square root of 2 is 1.41
square root of 3 is 1.73
square root of 4 is 2.0
square root of 5 is 2.24
square root of 6 is 2.45
square root of 7 is 2.65
square root of 8 is 2.83
square root of 9 is 3.0
square root of 10 is 3.16
```

Notice that we passed a value of type `int` to `math.sqrt`, but the function expects a value of type `float`. Remember that if Python is expecting a `float` and gets an `int`, it converts the `int` into a corresponding `float`.

Table 3.2 lists some of the most useful functions from the `math` module. The table is a partial list of math functions, but you can see a complete list of functions defined in the `math` module by checking out the Python Standard Library documentation for your version of Python:

https://docs.python.org/3/library/math.html

Table 3.2   Useful Functions in the math Module

Function	Description	Example	Result
ceil	ceiling (round upward)	math.ceil(2.13)	3.0
cos	cosine (radians)	math.cos(math.pi)	-1.0
degrees	radians to degrees	math.degrees(math.pi)	180.0
exp	exponent base e	math.exp(1)	2.7182818284590455
factorial	product of [1 .. n]	math.factorial(5)	120
floor	floor (rounds downward)	math.floor(2.93)	2.0
gcd	greatest common divisor	math.gcd(24, 36)	12
log	logarithm	math.log(math.e)	1.0
	(default is base e);	math.log(8, 2)	3.0
	pass base as optional		
	second parameter		
log10	logarithm base 10	math.log10(1000)	3.0
pow	power (exponentiation)	math.pow(3, 4)	81.0
radians	degrees to radians	math.radians(270.0)	4.71238898038469
sin	sine (radians)	math.sin(3 * math.pi / 2)	-1.0
sqrt	square root	math.sqrt(2)	1.4142135623730951

The library documentation describes how to use the standard libraries that are available to Python programmers. It can be a bit overwhelming, because the Python libraries are vast. Wander around a bit if you are so inclined, but don't be dismayed that there are so many functions and libraries to choose from in Python. Even an experienced programmer does not memorize them all. The right tactic is to learn a useful subset and keep a reference to documentation to remember important library function names and parameters.

The math module also defines some constants for frequently used mathematical values, such as *pi* (π) and *e*. You can refer to these values as math.pi and math.e, respectively. Table 3.3 lists several of the most useful constants.

There is another syntax for importing libraries. You can say:

```
from module import *
```

For example, in the case of the math library, you would write:

```
# import math library into global namespace
# (this is bad style)
from math import *
```

Table 3.3   Math Constants

Constant	Description	Value
e	base used in natural logarithms	2.718281828459045
inf	a special `float` value representing infinity	∞
nan	"not a number"; represents results of invalid math operations	nan
pi	π ratio of circumference of a circle to its diameter	3.141592653589793
tau	τ twice as large as `pi`	6.283185307179586

This second import style is interesting because it makes the `math` functions global to our program. That means that you can call them by writing just their names without the `math.` prefix, such as `sqrt(2.5)` instead of `math.sqrt(2.5)`. Though this might seem more convenient and easier to write, the authors of this textbook consider it poor style. The problem is that these math function names would now collide with the names that you give to your own functions. For example, using the earlier import style you could still write a function in your own program named `abs` or `pow` or `sqrt`, but with this second style, your names would conflict with math function names and would make it harder to call the math functions. So we will not use this second style of import with math functions in our programs. (Collisions between names like this are sometimes referred to as *namespace pollution*.)

The `random` Module

Python's standard libraries include a module named `random` that contains many useful functions related to generating random numbers and values. Random numbers can be fun because they lead to programs with unpredictable or varying behavior. Technically the numbers generated by the library are called *pseudo-random numbers* because they are actually based on mathematical functions and the system clock. But the numbers are unpredictable and varied enough to be considered random for our purposes.

To use the `random` library module in your code, you will need an import statement like you used with the `math` library:

```
import random
```

Table 3.4 lists several useful functions of the `random` library module. The table is a partial list of random functions, but you can see a complete list of functions defined in the `random` module by checking out the Python Standard Library documentation for your version of Python:

https://docs.python.org/3/library/random.html

The random function we'll use the most is `randint`, which accepts two parameters representing a range of integers and returns a randomly chosen integer from within that range. For example, a call of `random.randint(1, 10)` returns a random integer

Table 3.4   Functions of random Module

Function Name	Description	Example

`choice,`
`choices,`
`shuffle`
	choosing random elements from lists and sequences	(seen later)

`randrange`	integer in range(start, stop, step)	`random.randrange(1, 100, 3)`
`randint`	integer in [min, max]	`random.randint(1, 10)`
`random`	real number in [0.0, 1.0)	`random.random()`
`seed`	sets value that influences sequence of numbers generated	`random.seed(42)`
`uniform`	real number in [min, max]	`random.uniform(2.5, 10.75)`

from 1 through 10 inclusive. It is a bit confusing that `randint` includes the end number of 10 in its range of values, while the `range` function does not include the stop value in its range. Unfortunately this is an instance where the designers of Python chose inconsistent models, and you'll just need to be aware of it and be careful to avoid bugs.

Here are some example calls to `random.randint` in the Python Shell. Notice that each call produces a new random value:

```
>>> import random
>>> random.randint(1, 5)
5
>>> random.randint(1, 5)
2
>>> random.randint(1, 5)
1
>>> random.randint(1, 5)
2
```

The following simple program generates and prints four random numbers from 1 to 10 inclusive. An output from the program is also shown, but remember that the program would choose new random numbers if it were run again.

```
1  # This program prints random numbers.
2
3  import random
4
5  def main():
6      r1 = random.randint(1, 10)
7      r2 = random.randint(1, 10)
8      r3 = random.randint(1, 10)
```

Continued on next page

Continued from previous page

```
9        r4 = random.randint(1, 10)
10       print("Four random numbers:", r1, r2, r3, r4)
11
12  main()
```

```
Four random numbers: 6 3 10 6
```

Notice that in this particular run, the number 6 happened to occur twice; this is expected behavior. The random generator tries to distribute the numbers evenly, but it doesn't have any logic to limit how often a particular value comes up. You might even get the same number many times in a row, though the odds of that are low.

Even if you don't directly print the random number you generate, you can use a random number to affect your program's output. The following program contains a loop that generates random numbers and uses them to draw lines of characters. An output from the program is also shown, but remember that the program would choose new random numbers if it were run again.

```
1   # This program prints lines of characters
2   # of randomly chosen lengths between 1-20.
3
4   import random
5
6   def main():
7       for i in range(10):
8           r = random.randint(1, 20)
9           print("#" * r)
10
11  main()
```

```
######
############
##################
#############
####
###
######
#########
##################
######
```

Another common use of random numbers is to choose between a fixed set of available choices. For example, suppose you want to write a program that draws a character whose position moves left or right randomly as each line is printed. This is sometimes called a *random walk*. You can produce this random movement by randomly choosing either −1 or +1 and adding it to the character's current position. But if you ask for `random.randint(-1, 1)` that will include the value 0, which you don't want to include. Instead, the call of `random.randrange(-1, 2, 2)` will produce a range from −1 to 2 by a step of 2, which ends up including the numbers −1 and 1 only.

The program is more fun if you insert a delay between each printed line to produce a simple animation effect. To do this we will very briefly look at one more Python standard library named `time` that contains some functions related to timing. To use the `time` library you must import it:

```
import time
```

Once you've imported the `time` library, you can pause your program by calling its `sleep` function and passing a given number of seconds to pause. If you pass a `float` value less than 1, you can sleep for a fraction of a second; for example, passing `0.1` sleeps for 100 milliseconds.

```
time.sleep(seconds)
```

Putting all of this together, here is our program that prints the random walk, along with output from one random run of the program. You cannot see the pausing and delays in a printed text, of course, so we show the program's completed output. Try downloading this program, increasing the number of steps, and running it for yourself to see the character animate left and right as it moves down the screen.

```
1   # This program prints a "random walk" of a
2   # character that randomly moves left or right.
3
4   import random
5   import time
6
7   def main():
8       # initial position and number of steps to move
9       STEPS = 20
10      position = 10
11
12      for i in range(STEPS):
13          # pause for 200ms
14          time.sleep(0.2)
15
16          # randomly adjust position by -1 or +1
17          rnd = random.randrange(-1, 2, 2)
18          position += rnd
19
20          # print character at its current position
```

Continued on next page

Continued from previous page

```
21              print(" " * position, "*")
22
23  main()
```

```
                   *
                  *
                 *
                 *
                  *
                   *
                    *
                   *
                    *
                     *
                    *
                     *
                    *
                    *
                   *
                    *
                     *
                    *
                   *
                    *
```

Defining Functions That Return Values

We can write our own functions that return values by using a special statement known as a *return statement*. For example, we often use a function that returns a value to express an equation or calculation.

There is a famous story about the mathematician Carl Friedrich Gauss that illustrates the use of such a function. When Gauss was a boy, his teacher asked the class to add up the integers 1 through 100, thinking that it would take a while for students to complete the task. Gauss immediately found a formula and presented his answer to the teacher. He used a simple trick of adding two copies of the series together, one in forward order and one in backward order. This function allowed him to pair up values from the two copies so that their sum was the same (see Table 3.5).

Every entry in the right-hand column of this table is equal to 101 and there are 100 rows in this table, so the overall sum is 100 * 101 = 10100. Of course, that's the sum of two copies of the sequence, so the actual answer is half that. Using this approach,

Table 3.5   Sum of a Sequence of Integers

First Series	Second Series	Sum
1	100	101
2	99	101
3	98	101
4	97	101
. . .	. . .	. . .
100	1	101

Gauss determined that the sum of the first 100 integers is 5050. When the series goes from 1 to n, the sum is $(n + 1) * n/2$.

We can use the Gauss formula to write a function that computes the sum of the first n integers. A function can return a value to its caller by using a *return statement*. The syntax for a return statement is:

```
return expression
```
Syntax template: Return statement

For example, the following is the definition of a function that returns the sum of the first n integers:

```
# Returns the sum of the integers 1--n.
def sum_of(n):
    return (n + 1) * n // 2
```

The `sum_of` function could be used by the `main` function in much the same way as the functions we've seen in this chapter such as `round` or `math.sqrt`. The following code calls `sum_of` and stores and prints its result:

```
def main():
    answer = sum_of(100)
    print("sum of 1-100 is", answer)
```

```
sum of 1-100 is 5050
```

A diagram of what happens when this code is executed follows. The function is called with the parameter n being defined to `100`. Plugging this value into the formula, we get a value of `5050`, which is sent back to be stored in the variable called `answer`:

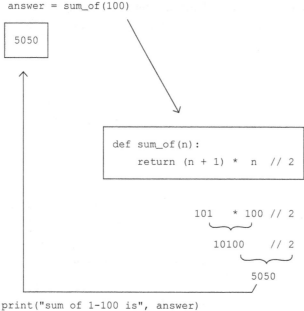

```
answer = sum_of(100)
```

```
def sum_of(n):
    return (n + 1) * n // 2
```

```
print("sum of 1-100 is", answer)
```

When Python encounters a `return` statement, it evaluates the given expression and immediately terminates the function, returning the value it obtained from the expression. As a result, it's not useful to have any other statements after a `return` statement inside a function, because they will not be executed.

There are exceptions to the previous rule, as you'll see later. For example, it is possible for a function to have more than one return statement; this will come up in the next chapter, when we discuss conditional execution using `if` and `if/else` statements.

Let's look at another example function that returns a value. In *The Wizard of Oz*, the Scarecrow after being given a diploma demonstrates his intelligence by saying, "The sum of the square roots of any two sides of an isosceles triangle is equal to the square root of the remaining side. Oh, joy, oh, rapture. I've got a brain!" Probably he was trying to state the Pythagorean theorem, although it's not clear whether the writers were bad at math or whether they were making a comment about the value of a diploma. In an episode of *The Simpsons*, Homer repeats the Scarecrow's mistaken formula after putting on a pair of Henry Kissinger's glasses that he finds in a bathroom at the Springfield nuclear power plant.

The correct Pythagorean theorem refers only to right triangles and says that the length of the hypotenuse of a right triangle is equal to the square root of the sums of the squares of the two remaining sides. If you know the lengths of two sides *a* and *b* of a right triangle and want to find the length of the third side *c*, you compute it as follows:

$$c = \sqrt{a^2 + b^2}$$

Say you want to print out the lengths of the hypotenuses of two right triangles, one with side lengths of 5 and 12, and the other with side lengths of 3 and 4. You could write code such as the following:

```
# compute and print two hypotenuse lengths
c1 = math.sqrt(5 ** 2 + 12 ** 2)
print("hypotenuse 1 =", c1)
c2 = math.sqrt(3 ** 2 + 4 ** 2)
print("hypotenuse 2 =", c2)
```

The preceding code is correct, but it's a bit hard to read, and you'd have to duplicate the same complex math a third time if you wanted to include a third triangle. A better solution would be to create a function that computes and returns the hypotenuse length when given the lengths of the two other sides as parameters. Such a function would look like this:

```
def hypotenuse(a, b):
    c = math.sqrt(a ** 2 + b ** 2)
    return c
```

This function can be used to craft a more concise and readable `main` function, as shown here.

```
 1  # Compute and prints two hypotenuse lengths
 2  # using a function with return values.
 3
 4  import math
 5
 6  # Returns the length of the hypotenuse c of a
 7  # right triangle with given side lengths a and b.
 8  def hypotenuse(a, b):
 9      c = math.sqrt(a ** 2 + b ** 2)
10      return c
11
12  def main():
13      print("hypotenuse 1 =", hypotenuse(5, 12))
14      print("hypotenuse 2 =", hypotenuse(3, 4))
15
16  main()
```

```
hypotenuse 1 = 13.0
hypotenuse 2 = 5.0
```

A few variations of this program are possible. For one, it isn't necessary to store the hypotenuse function's return value into the variable c. If you prefer, you can simply compute and return the value in one line. In this case, the body of the hypotenuse function would become the following:

```
return math.sqrt(a ** 2 + b ** 2)
```

Also, some programmers avoid using the `**` operator for low powers such as 2 and just manually do the multiplication. Using that approach, the body of the hypotenuse function would look like this:

```
return math.sqrt(a * a + b * b)
```

Common Programming Error

Ignoring the Returned Value

When you call a function that returns a value, the expectation is that you'll do something with the value that's returned. You can print it, store it in a variable, or use it as part of a larger expression. It is legal (but unwise) to simply call the function and ignore the value being returned from it:

```
sum_of(1000)    # doesn't do anything
```

The preceding call doesn't print the sum or have any noticeable effect. If you want the value printed, you must include a print statement:

```
answer = sum_of(1000)    # better
print("sum of 1-1000 is", answer)
```

A shorter form of the fixed code would be the following:

```
print("sum of 1-1000 is", sum_of(1000))
```

One place it can be helpful to call a function without using its return value is in the interpreter. If you type a call to a function in the interpreter, it displays the returned value. This can be a useful way to test your functions.

```
>>> sum_of(1000)
5050
```

Common Programming Error

Statement after Return

It's a bug to place other statements immediately after a return statement, because those statements can never be reached or executed. New programmers often accidentally do this when trying to print the value of a variable after returning. Say you've written the `hypotenuse` function but have accidentally written the parameters to `math.pow` in the wrong order, so the function is not producing the right answer. You would try to debug this by printing the value of `c` that is being returned. Here's the faulty code:

```
# trying to find the bug in this buggy version of hypotenuse
def hypotenuse(a, b):
    c = math.sqrt(2 ** a + 2 ** b)
    return c
    print(c)    # this doesn't work
```

The buggy code does not produce an error, but the message will never print. The fix is to move the `print` statement earlier in the function, before the `return` statement:

```
# trying to find the bug in this buggy version of hypotenuse
def hypotenuse(a, b):
    c = math.sqrt(2 ** a + 2 ** b)
    print(c)    # this doesn't work
    return c
```

Returning Multiple Values

Just as a function can accept multiple parameters, it can also return multiple values. This is an unusual feature of Python; most programming languages allow the programmer to return only a single value.

The syntax for returning multiple values is to write a `return` statement where you list all of the values to return, separated by commas:

```
return expression, expression, ..., expression
```
Syntax template: Returning multiple values

For example, suppose you want to write a function named `quadratic` that solves quadratic equations and returns their roots. Recall that a quadratic equation is one of the following form expressed in terms of a variable x, where a, b, and c are integer coefficients:

$$ax^2 + bx + c = 0$$

A quadratic equation can be solved to find its roots, which are the values of x that satisfy the equation. Roots of quadratic equations are found using the quadratic formula:

$$x = \frac{-b \pm \sqrt{b^2 - 4ac}}{2a}$$

When writing a quadratic equation solver function, the parameters should be the coefficients that distinguish one equation from another: a, b, and c:

```
# Computes the roots of the given quadratic equation.
def quadratic(a, b, c):
    ...
```

Depending on the values of a, b, and c, a given quadratic equation might have 0, 1, or 2 real number roots. The number of roots is related to the sign of the discriminant, which is the square root portion of the quadratic formula. To simplify our discussion, we will assume that we are dealing with an equation with 2 real roots. Our function should calculate these roots and return them. Since there are 2 roots, we will have to return multiple values.

```
 1  # This program solves for roots of quadratic equations
 2  # (ones of the form ax^2 + bx + c = 0).
 3  # It is a demonstration of returning multiple values.
 4
 5  import math
 6
 7  # Computes/returns the roots of the quadratic equation
 8  # with the given integer coefficients a, b, and c.
 9  def quadratic(a, b, c):
10      disc = math.sqrt(b * b - 4 * a * c)
11      root1 = (-b + disc) / (2 * a)
12      root2 = (-b - disc) / (2 * a)
13      return root1, root2
14
15  def main():
16      r1, r2 = quadratic(1, -5, 6)
17      print("The roots are", r1, "and", r2)
18
19      r1, r2 = quadratic(2, 6, 4)
20      print("The roots are", r1, "and", r2)
21
22  main()
```

```
The roots are 3.0 and 2.0
The roots are -1.0 and -2.0
```

When your function returns multiple values, the calls to that function should have the same number of variables listed before the = sign. Because the quadratic function returns two values, we wrote the names of two variables in each call to main r1 and r2. If the number of variables listed does not match the number of values that are returned by the function, the interpreter raises an error.

3.3 Interactive Programs

As you've seen, you can easily produce output in the console window by calling the print function. You can also write programs that pause and wait for the user to type a response. Such a program is known as an *interactive program*, and the responses typed by the user are known as *console input*.

> **Console Input (User Input)**
> Responses typed by the user when an interactive program pauses for input.

Using console input allows a program to go beyond simply computing a few specific expressions in a program. A program that uses console input can interact with its user and behave differently depending on the user's responses. Without modifying the code, the program can have different results on each run.

Console input is performed using a built-in function called input. The input function accepts a string parameter indicating a message to show to users to indicate what they should type. This message is called a *prompt*. When the interpreter reaches a call to input, the interpreter shows the prompt message as output, then pauses and waits for the user to type a value and press Enter. Once the user has done so, this value is returned from input and the program continues running. Typically, you will use a variable to keep track of the value returned by these functions. The general syntax for calling the input function to read a string is the following:

```
variable_name = input("message ")
```
Syntax template: Read user input as a string

The input function reads input as a string of text (str), which is a type we will discuss in detail in the next chapter. The simplest way you can use input is to store the user's input as a string value. In our output log, we show the user's typed input in bold **like this**.

```
name = input("What is your name? ")
print("Hello", name)
```

```
What is your name? Evelyn
Hello Evelyn
```

Asking the user to type strings can be very useful, and we will explore strings in more detail in the next chapter. But there are also many situations where you will want to ask the user to type a value of a different type, such as an integer or real number. For example, suppose you are writing a program to manage a college student's personal information. The student's name, age in years, and school grade point average (GPA) values would be a `str`, `int`, and `float`, respectively. If you want to treat the user's input as an integer, real number, or other type, you must explicitly convert the input result into that type using the conversion functions we saw in Chapter 2. The general syntax for reading and converting user input is the following:

```
variable_name = type(input("message "))
```
Syntax template: Read user input of a given type

For example, if you want to ask the user to type his or her age and school GPA, you might write the following code:

```
# read two values as input
age = int(input("How many years old are you? "))
gpa = float(input("What is your GPA? "))
print("Your age is", age, "and GPA is", gpa)
```

```
How many years old are you? 19
What is your GPA? 3.25
Your age is 19 and your GPA is 3.25
```

The conversion between input types can be confusing, especially for new programmers. The lines above that read and convert input are performing two operations: reading the user input as a string, and then passing it to the `int` or `float` conversion function. These two operations could be separated into two statements:

```
>>> age_string = input("How old are you? ")
How old are you? 45
>>> age_string
'45'
>>> age = int(age_string)
>>> age
45
```

At first glance it may be hard to discern the difference between the variables `age_string` and `age` in our previous code. They both seem to store the value 45. But if you look carefully, you will see quotation marks around the value of `age_string`; it is actually `'45'`. This is our indication that its value is actually a string and not an integer.

It is a string whose characters happen to be numeric, but there is a difference between the string `'45'` and the integer `45`.

The main difference between a numeric string and an integer is the set of operations they support. As we saw in Chapter 2, Python allows you to perform mathematical calculations on integer values using operators like +. Python does not allow math calculations on strings, even if those strings consist of numeric characters:

```
>>> 11 + 22
33
>>> 11 + "22"
Traceback (most recent call last):
  File "<stdin>", line 1, in <module>
TypeError: unsupported operand type(s) for +: 'int' and 'str'
```

But if you pass a numeric string to the `int` or `float` conversion functions, they will return an `int` or `float` value that is equivalent to the numeric string, allowing you to use it for calculations:

```
>>> 11 + int("22")
33
```

If you are ever unsure of the type of a variable or expression in your code, you can ask the Python Shell to display it. Python has a built-in function called `type` that accepts an expression as a parameter and returns information about the type of that expression. The expression you provide can be a variable, a literal value, or a complex expression.

```
>>> type(42)
<class 'int'>
>>> type(3.14)
<class 'float'>
>>> type("hello")
<class 'str'>
>>> type(age_string)
<class 'str'>
>>> type(age)
<class 'int'>
```

If a user types something that cannot be converted to the type in question, such as `"xyzzy"` when you ask for an `int`, the code generates a `ValueError` and the program halts.

```
How many years old are you? Timmy

Traceback (most recent call last):
  File "userinput1.py", line 9, in <module>
    main()
  File "userinput1.py", line 5, in main
    age = int(input("How many years old are you? "))
ValueError: invalid literal for int() with base 10: 'Timmy'
```

You will see in a later chapter how to test for type errors using new syntax called a try/except statement. In the meantime, we will assume that the user provides appropriate input.

Sample Interactive Program

Using the input function, we can write a complete interactive program that performs a useful computation for the user. If you ever find yourself buying a house, you'll want to know what your monthly mortgage payment is going to be. The formula for computing monthly mortgage payments involves the loan amount in dollars, the total number of months involved (a value we call n), and the monthly interest rate (a value we call c). The payment formula is given by the following equation:

$$\text{payment} = \text{loan}\,\frac{c(1 + c)^n}{(1 + c)^n - 1}$$

The following is a complete program that asks for information about a loan and prints the monthly payment using this formula:

```
1   # This program prompts for information about a
2   # loan and computes the monthly mortgage payment.
3
4   def main():
5       # obtain values
6       print("Monthly Mortgage Payment Calculator")
7       loan = float(input("Loan amount? "))
8       years = int(input("Number of years? "))
9       rate = float(input("Interest rate? "))
10
11      # compute payment result
12      n = 12 * years
13      c = rate / 12.0 / 100.0
14      payment = loan * c * (1 + c) ** n / ((1 + c) ** n - 1)
15
16      # report result to user
```

Continued on next page

Continued from previous page

```
17        print()
18        print("Monthly payment is: $", round(payment, 2))
19
20  main()
```

```
Monthly Mortgage Payment Calculator
Loan amount? 275000
Number of years? 30
Interest rate? 6.75


Monthly payment is: $ 1783.64
```

The first part of the program prints an explanation of what the program is going to do. This is essential for interactive programs. You don't want a program to pause for user input until you've explained to the user what is going to happen.

Next the program calls the input function three different times to obtain details about the loan. The values are read in as strings but are converted to numeric values by the calls on float and int. The resulting numbers are stored in variables called loan, years, and rate. After prompting for the three values, the program performs the necessary calculations. Notice in the program that we use the ** operator for exponentiation to translate this formula into a Python expression.

The final line of the program prints out the monthly payment. Since the payment is stored in a variable of type float and may contain many digits after the decimal, we use the round function to print it to a maximum of two decimal places. Without rounding, the code might print a number with too many digits such as 1783.6447655625927, which would be rather strange-looking for someone who is used to dollars and cents.

As in past chapters, it is important to break down larger problems into functions to better indicate the structure of the program. The following is a second version of the mortgage calculator that is decomposed using functions. Notice that the first function, read_input, performs the prompting and returns the multiple values that the user typed. The second function, compute_payment, accepts these same values as parameters and calculates and returns the monthly mortgage payment. The main function calls these other two functions and then prints the ending output showing the mortgage payment.

```
1  # This program prompts for information about a
2  # loan and computes the monthly mortgage payment.
3  # This version is decomposed into functions.
4
5  # Obtains and returns needed values from the user.
6  def read_input():
7      print("Monthly Mortgage Payment Calculator")
8      loan = float(input("Loan amount? "))
9      years = int(input("Number of years? "))
```

Continued on next page

Continued from previous page

```
10       rate = float(input("Interest rate? "))
11       print()
12       return loan, years, rate
13
14   # Computes and returns the monthly payment for a
15   # loan with the given values.
16   def compute_payment(loan, years, rate):
17       # compute payment result
18       n = 12 * years
19       c = rate / 12.0 / 100.0
20       payment = loan * c * (1 + c) ** n / ((1 + c) ** n - 1)
21       return payment
22
23   def main():
24       # compute payment and report result to user
25       loan, years, rate = read_input()
26       payment = compute_payment(loan, years, rate)
27       print("Monthly payment is: $", round(payment, 2))
28
29   main()
```

3.4 Graphics

One of the most compelling reasons to learn about parameters is that they allow us to draw graphics in Python. Graphics are used for games, computer animations, and modern graphical user interfaces (GUIs), and they are used to render complex images. In this section we will use an instructor-provided library based on Python's built-in graphical framework to draw patterned two-dimensional figures of shapes and text onto the screen.

In most 2D graphics systems, all onscreen coordinates are specified as integers. Each (x, y) position corresponds to a different pixel on the computer screen. The word *pixel* is shorthand for "picture element" and represents a single dot on the computer screen.

> **Pixel**
>
> A single small dot on a computer screen.

The coordinate system assigns the upper-left corner of a panel the position (0, 0). As you move to the right of this position, the x value increases. As you move down from this position, the y value increases. For example, suppose that you create a `DrawingPanel` with a width of 200 pixels and a height of 100 pixels. The upper-left corner will have the coordinates (0, 0), and the lower-right corner will have the coordinates (199, 99), as shown in Figure 3.3.

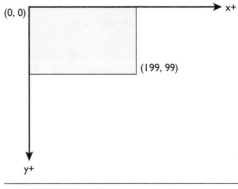

Figure 3.3 x/y coordinate space

This is likely to be confusing at first, because you're probably used to coordinate systems where *y* values decrease as you move down. However, you'll soon get the hang of it.

Introduction to `DrawingPanel`

There are many different graphical libraries you can use to draw graphics in Python. The Python standard library includes a graphical system called *Tkinter*, and we will use that in this section. To keep things simple, we introduce a custom library called `DrawingPanel` that we have written to simplify some of the details of Python graphics. A *drawing panel* is an onscreen window that keeps track of an overall image onto which you can draw various lines and shapes.

You will need to download the file `DrawingPanel.py` from our web site and place it in the same folder as your program. You will also need to import the library using the following statement:

```
from DrawingPanel import *
```

Notice that this is the second import style shown earlier in this chapter. We didn't use this second import style with math functions, because the `math` library would otherwise clutter our global namespace with lots of global math functions. But we use the second import style here with `DrawingPanel` because the library does not contain any functions that would interfere with the namespace of the programs we will write. Using the first import style would not work properly with the code shown in the rest of this section.

(If you see an error such as `ImportError: No module named 'DrawingPanel'`, double-check that you have saved the `.py` file into the same directory as your program with exactly the right file name and spelling.)

You can create a graphical window on your screen by defining a `DrawingPanel` variable. You must specify the width and height of the drawing area. The following general syntax creates a drawing panel window:

```
name = DrawingPanel(width, height)
```
Syntax template: Creating a DrawingPanel

When the line executes, a window appears immediately on the screen. For example, to create a drawing panel named `panel` of size 400 × 300, you would write:

```
# create a DrawingPanel of size 400 x 300
panel = DrawingPanel(400, 300)
```

The preceding line is a variable definition; you are creating a new window on the screen and storing it as a variable named `panel`. We can use that variable `panel` to draw shapes and lines on the panel's graphical canvas.

Each `DrawingPanel` has functions that can be called to perform drawing tasks, but these functions are contained within the `DrawingPanel`. A function that exists inside of an object is called a *method*. As a result, we have to use the same dot notation that we used for calling functions inside of a library. So in the same way that we refer to `math.sqrt` to refer to the `sqrt` function that is part of the `math` library, we will give commands such as `panel.draw_line` to call the line drawing method inside the `DrawingPanel`. The general syntax for calling methods on a drawing panel is the following:

```
panel.method_name(parameters)
```

For example, to draw a line from (20, 40) to (50, 75), you write:

```
panel.draw_line(20, 40, 50, 75)
```

The `DrawingPanel` also has properties, which are like variables within the panel that you can set to impact its behavior. The general syntax for setting properties on a drawing panel is the following:

```
panel.property_name = value
```

For example, to set a panel's background color to green, you write:

```
panel.background = "green"
```

The reason for all of this special syntax is because the `DrawingPanel` is a new kind of Python entity called an object. We will be discussing objects in detail later in this text. But for now, all you'll need to know is that you need to write "`panel.`" in front of your drawing function calls and property accesses.

A `DrawingPanel` has many useful public methods and properties, listed in Tables 3.6 and 3.7. We will explore many of these in the upcoming sections. You can view a complete list of the available methods and properties by looking at the authors' provided `DrawingPanel` library documentation on the following web page:

http://www.buildingpythonprograms.com/drawingpanel/

Table 3.6   Useful DrawingPanel Methods (Functions)

Method	Description
`panel = DrawingPanel(width, height)`	creates and returns a new window of the given size
`panel.clear()`	erases all drawn shapes and resets canvas to initial state
`panel.close()`	hides and closes the window
`panel.draw_arc(x, y, w, h,` `             angle, extent)`	outlined arc (partial oval) over the given angle range
`panel.draw_image("filename", x, y)`	image from a file with top-left corner at (x, y)
`panel.draw_line(x1, y1, x2, y2)`	line from (x1, y1) to (x2, y2)
`panel.draw_oval(x, y, w, h)`	outlined oval with bounding box's top-left corner (x, y) of given size
`panel.draw_polyline(x1, y1, x2, y2, ...)`	outlined multiple line segments between given endpoints
`panel.draw_polygon(x1, y1, x2, y2, ...)`	outlined many-sided polygon with given endpoints
`panel.draw_rect(x, y, w, h)`	outlined rectangle with top-left corner at (x, y) of given width/height
`panel.draw_string("text", x, y)`	text with top-left corner at (x, y)
`panel.fill_arc(x, y, w, h,` `             angle, extent)`	filled arc (partial oval) over the given angle range
`panel.fill_oval(x, y, w, h)`	filled oval with bounding box's top-left corner at (x, y) of given width/height
`panel.fill_polygon(x1, y1, x2, y2, ...)`	filled many-sided polygon with given endpoints
`panel.fill_rect(x, y, w, h)`	filled rectangle with top-left corner at (x, y) of given width/height
`panel.get_pixel_color(x, y)`	returns color of pixel at position (x, y) as a hexadecimal string
`panel.get_pixel_color_rgb(x, y)`	returns color of the pixel at position (x, y) as three integer values
`panel.sleep(ms)`	pauses program for given number of milliseconds

Table 3.7   Useful DrawingPanel Properties

Property	Description
`panel.background`	background color of panel's drawing canvas
`panel.color`	outline color used for future shapes
`panel.fill_color`	fill color used for future shapes
`panel.font`	font used for future text
`panel.height`	height of panel's canvas in pixels
`panel.location`	drawing panel window (x, y) location on screen

Continued on next page

Continued from previous page

Property	Description
panel.size	width and height of panel's canvas in pixels
panel.stroke	thickness of shape outlines in pixels
panel.title	window title text as a string
panel.width	height of panel's canvas in pixels
panel.x	drawing panel window x location on screen
panel.y	drawing panel window y location on screen

Drawing Lines and Shapes

One of the simplest drawing commands is `draw_line`, which accepts four integer parameters. For example, the following call draws a line from the point ($x1$, $y1$) to the point ($x2$, $y2$).

```
panel.draw_line(x1, y1, x2, y2)
```

Here is a sample program that demonstrates drawing two lines along with its graphical output. Although the program's behavior appears graphically rather than on the console as in previous chapters, we'll still refer to this as the "output" of the program.

```
1   # Draws two lines onto a DrawingPanel.
2
3   from DrawingPanel import *
4
5   def main():
6       # create the drawing panel
7       panel = DrawingPanel(300, 200)
8
9       # draw two lines on the panel
10      panel.draw_line(25, 75, 175, 25)
11      panel.draw_line(10, 170, 150, 80)
12
13  main()
```

The first statement in `main` creates a `DrawingPanel` with a width of 300 and a height of 200. Once it has been created, the window will pop up on the screen. The second statement draws a line from (25, 75) to (175, 25). The first point is in the lower-left part of the window (25 over from the left, 75 down from the top). The second point is in the upper-right corner (175 over from the left, 25 down from the top). The third statement draws a line from (10, 170) to (150, 80).

Let's look at a more complicated example. This program draws three different lines to form a triangle. The lines are drawn between three different points. In the lower-left corner we have the point (25, 75). In the middle at the top we have the point (100, 25). And in the lower-right corner we have the point (175, 75). The various calls on `draw_line` simply draw the lines that connect these three points.

```
1   # Draws three lines to make a triangle.
2
3   from DrawingPanel import *
4
5   def main():
6       panel = DrawingPanel(200, 100)
7       panel.draw_line(25, 75, 100, 25)
8       panel.draw_line(100, 25, 175, 75)
9       panel.draw_line(25, 75, 175, 75)
10
11  main()
```

The `DrawingPanel` also has methods for drawing several kinds of shapes. For example, you can draw rectangles and squares with the `draw_rect` method:

panel.draw_rect(*x, y, width, height*)

This draws a rectangle with its upper-left corner at (*x, y*) and the given height and width. Another figure you'll often want to draw is a circle, or, more generally, an oval. But how do you specify where it appears and how big it is? What you actually specify is what is known as the "bounding rectangle" of the circle or oval. Python will draw the largest oval possible that fits inside that rectangle. So, the following call draws the largest oval that fits within the rectangle with upper-left coordinates (*x, y*) and the given height and width.

panel.draw_oval(*x, y, width, height*)

Notice that the first two values passed to `draw_rect` and `draw_oval` are coordinates, while the next two values are a width and a height. For example, here is a short program that draws two rectangles and two ovals:

```
1   # Draws several shapes.
2
```

Continued on next page

Continued from previous page

```
3   from DrawingPanel import *

4

5   def main():
6       panel = DrawingPanel(200, 100)
7       panel.draw_rect(25, 50, 20, 20)
8       panel.draw_rect(150, 10, 40, 20)
9       panel.draw_oval(50, 25, 20, 20)
10      panel.draw_oval(150, 50, 40, 20)

11

12  main()
```

The first rectangle has its upper-left corner at the coordinates (25, 50). Its width and height are each 20, so this is a square. The coordinates of its lower-right corner would be (45, 70), or 20 more than the (x, y) coordinates of the upper-left corner. The program also draws a rectangle with its upper-left corner at (150, 10) that has a width of 40 and a height of 20 (wider than it is tall). The bounding rectangle of the first oval has upper-left coordinates (50, 25) and a width and height of 20. In other words, it's a circle. The bounding rectangle of the second oval has upper-left coordinates (150, 50), a width of 40, and a height of 20 (it's an oval that is wider than it is tall).

Sometimes you don't just want to draw the outline of a shape; you want to paint the entire area with a particular color. There are variations of the draw_rect and draw_oval functions known as fill_rect and fill_oval that do exactly that, drawing a rectangle or oval and filling it in with the current color of paint (the default is black). Let's change two of the calls in the previous program to be "fill" operations instead of "draw" operations:

```
1   # Draws several filled shapes.

2

3   from DrawingPanel import *

4

5   def main():
6       panel = DrawingPanel(200, 100)
7       panel.fill_rect(25, 50, 20, 20)
8       panel.draw_rect(150, 10, 40, 20)
9       panel.draw_oval(50, 25, 20, 20)
10      panel.fill_oval(150, 50, 40, 20)

11

12  main()
```

Colors

All of the shapes and lines drawn by the preceding programs were black, and all of the panels had a white background. These are the default colors, but you can change the background color of the panel, and you can change the color being used by the panel to draw each shape.

A color can be specified in several ways to a `DrawingPanel`:

- As a color name string such as `"red"` or `"light sky blue"`.
- As a color constant such as `Color.RED` or `Color.LIGHT_SKY_BLUE`.
- As a color hexadecimal string representing the red, green, and blue components of the color from 0 to 255 in base-16, such as `"#ff00b6"`.
- As a trio of integers in parentheses, representing the red, green, and blue components of the color from 0 to 255 such as `(255, 0, 182)`.

There are a number of predefined colors that you can refer to directly as strings in quotes. A useful subset of commonly used color names is shown in Table 3.8. A complete list of available color names can be found at: http://wiki.tcl.tk/16166

The `DrawingPanel` has a `background` property that can be used to change the background color that covers the entire panel:

```
panel.background = color
```

For example, to set your panel's background color to yellow, you could write:

```
panel.background = "yellow"
```

You can also set the color used to draw shapes and lines. There are two ways to do this. If you want to specify the color of an individual shape, pass it as an extra parameter to

Table 3.8 Common Color Names

azure	beige	blue	brown	cyan
dark blue	dark green	gold	gray	green
hot pink	lavender	light blue	light gray	light green
magenta	maroon	orange	pink	purple
red	royal blue	salmon	sienna	slate gray
tan	turquoise	violet	white	yellow

the drawing function to draw that shape. For example, the following call draws a filled red rectangle:

```
# draw a filled red rectangle
panel.fill_rect(25, 50, 20, 20, "red")
```

The second way to specify shape colors is to use the color property of the panel to set a default color to be used for all subsequent shapes. This saves you the trouble of passing the same color over and over if you intend to draw many shapes of the same color. For example, the following call draws two filled blue ovals:

```
# draw two filled blue ovals
panel.color = "blue"
panel.fill_oval(25, 50, 20, 20)
panel.fill_oval(80, 73, 100, 50)
```

Modifying the panel's color is like dipping your paintbrush in a different color of paint. From that point on, all drawing and filling will be done in the specified color. The following is another version of our previous program that uses a yellow background color and uses a color for each shape. (The figures shown in this text may not match the colors you would see on your screen.)

```
 1  # Draws several colored shapes.
 2
 3  from DrawingPanel import *
 4
 5  def main():
 6      panel = DrawingPanel(200, 100)
 7      panel.background = "yellow"
 8      panel.fill_rect(25, 50, 20, 20, "red")
 9      panel.fill_rect(150, 10, 40, 20, "blue")
10      panel.color = "green"
11      panel.fill_oval(50, 25, 20, 20)
12      panel.fill_oval(150, 50, 40, 20)
13
14  main()
```

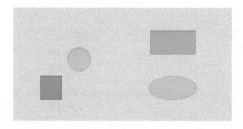

It's also possible to create custom colors of your own, rather than using the constant color names provided. Computer monitors use red, green, and blue (RGB) as their primary colors, so you can specify a color as a trio of integers from 0 to 255, with the integers representing the redness, greenness, and blueness of the color.

(*red*, *green*, *blue*)

The red/green/blue components should be integer values between 0 and 255 inclusive. The higher the value, the more of that color is mixed in. All 0 values produce black, and all 255 values produce white. Values of (0, 255, 0) produce a pure green, while values of (128, 0, 128) make a dark purple color (because red and blue are mixed). Search for "RGB table" in your favorite search engine to find tables of many common colors.

Earlier in this chapter we learned how to generate random numbers with the random library. You can use random numbers to generate a random color by asking for three random numbers between 0 and 255 inclusive. The following program generates random RGB values from 0 to 255 and uses them to draw several rectangles at randomly chosen *x/y* positions on the screen:

```
 1   # Draws many rectangles at random x/y positions
 2   # filled in with randomly chosen colors.
 3
 4   import random
 5   from DrawingPanel import *
 6
 7   # constants
 8   WIDTH = 300
 9   HEIGHT = 200
10   SIZE = 30
11   NUM_RECTS = 20
12
13   def main():
14       panel = DrawingPanel(WIDTH, HEIGHT)
15       for i in range(NUM_RECTS):
16           # choose random rectangle location
17           x = random.randint(0, WIDTH - SIZE)
18           y = random.randint(0, HEIGHT - SIZE)
19
20           # create a random RGB color for the rectangle
21           red = random.randint(0, 255)
22           green = random.randint(0, 255)
23           blue = random.randint(0, 255)
24
25           panel.fill_rect(x, y, SIZE, SIZE, (red, green, blue))
26
27   main()
```

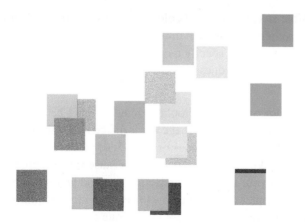

There is one more way to specify a color. You can write a string that consists of a "#" hash sign followed by six characters that we call *hexadecimal* or *hex* characters. These are digit values from 0 through 9 or letters from a through f.

```
"#ff0088" ==> RGB color
   ^ ^ ^
   r g b
```

The idea is that the characters represent numbers in base-16, such that 0 is the smallest number and f is the largest (15). Each pair of characters represents one of the three color components from left to right: red, green, and blue. For example, the color "#ff0088" has a lot of red, no green, and a medium amount of blue, making it a purplish red color. DrawingPanel supports this hex format partly because that format is used commonly in web programming and because it is more compact than writing out a trio of base-10 integers as described previously. We won't go into hexadecimal notation here or use it much in our examples, but you can search the web to learn more about it if you like.

The following program demonstrates the use of colors in several formats:

```
1   # Draws colored shapes using various color syntax.
2
3   from DrawingPanel import *
4
5   def main():
6       panel = DrawingPanel(230, 120)
7       panel.background = "#ffff88"   # light yellow
8       panel.color = "red"
9       panel.fill_rect(25, 50, 20, 20)
10      panel.fill_rect(150, 10, 40, 20)
11
12      # use a custom color
```

```
13      panel.color = (255, 128, 0)      # orange
14      panel.fill_oval(50, 25, 20, 20)
15      panel.fill_oval(100, 50, 40, 20)
16
17      # pass custom color as a parameter (sky bluish)
18      panel.fill_oval(150, 80, 30, 30, (64, 128, 196))
19
20  main()
```

Drawing with Loops

In each of the preceding examples we used simple integer values for the drawing and filling commands, but it is possible to use expressions. For example, suppose that we stick with our panel size of 200 × 100 pixels and we want to produce a diagonal series of four rectangles that extend from the upper-left corner to the lower-right corner, each with a yellow oval inside. In other words, we want to produce the output shown in the following figure.

The overall width of 200 and overall height of 100 are divided evenly into four rectangles, which means that they must all be 50 pixels wide and 25 pixels high. So, width and height values for the four rectangles are the same, but the positions of their upper-left corners are different. The first rectangle's upper-left corner is at (0, 0), the second is at (50, 25), the third is at (100, 50), and the fourth is at (150, 75). We need to write code to generate these different coordinates.

This is a great place to use a `for` loop. Using the techniques introduced in Chapter 2, we can make a table and develop a formula for the coordinates. Here is a program that makes a good first stab at generating the desired output:

```
1   # Draws boxed ovals using a for loop.
2   # (This version does not work properly.)
3
4   from DrawingPanel import *
5
6   def main():
7       panel = DrawingPanel(200, 100)
8       panel.background = "cyan"
9       for i in range(4):
10          panel.fill_oval(i * 50, i * 25, 50, 25, "yellow")
11          panel.fill_rect(i * 50, i * 25, 50, 25, "red")
12
13  main()
```

The coordinates and sizes are right, but where are the ovals? The ovals are being drawn correctly, but they aren't visible on the screen because the rectangles are being drawn on top of them. The drawing panel draws each shape in order, and if two shapes occupy the same pixels, the one drawn later is the one that appears to be "on top." The fix is to swap the order of the drawing statements in the loop:

```
1   # Draws boxed ovals using a for loop.
2
3   from DrawingPanel import *
4
5   def main():
6       panel = DrawingPanel(200, 100)
7       panel.background = "cyan"
8       for i in range(4):
9           panel.fill_rect(i * 50, i * 25, 50, 25, "red")
10          panel.fill_oval(i * 50, i * 25, 50, 25, "yellow")
11
12  main()
```

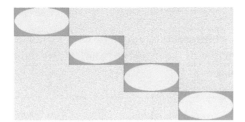

The following program demonstrates the use of custom colors. It uses a constant for the number of rectangles to draw and produces a blend of colors from black to white:

```
1   # Draws a smooth color gradient from black to white.
2
3   from DrawingPanel import *
4
5   RECTS = 32    # constant for number of rectangles
6
7   def main():
8       panel = DrawingPanel(256, 256)
9       panel.background = (255, 128, 0)    # orange
10
11      # from black to white, top left to bottom right
12      for i in range(RECTS):
13          c = i * 256 // RECTS
14          panel.fill_rect(c, c, 20, 20, (c, c, c))
15
16  main()
```

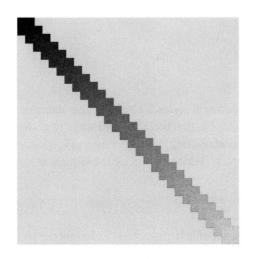

Text and Fonts

Another drawing command worth mentioning can be used to include text in your drawings. The `draw_string` function of the `DrawingPanel` draws the given string with its lower-left corner at coordinates (x, y):

```
panel.draw_string("message", x, y)
```

This is a slightly different convention than we used for `draw_rect`. With `draw_rect`, we specified the coordinates of the upper-left corner. Here we specify the coordinates of the lower-left corner. By default, text is drawn approximately 10 pixels high. Here is a sample program that uses a loop to draw a particular string 10 different times, each time indenting it 5 pixels to the right and moving it down 10 pixels from the top. Notice that we are using the \ backslash notation on line 9 to allow it to be continued on line 10 so that the line doesn't become too long.

```
 1  # Draws a message several times.
 2
 3  from DrawingPanel import *
 4
 5  def main():
 6      panel = DrawingPanel(240, 120)
 7      panel.background = "yellow"
 8      for i in range(10):
 9          panel.draw_string("There is no place like home", \
10              i * 5, i * 10)
11
12  main()
```

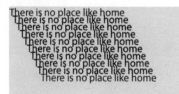

Fonts are used to describe different styles for writing characters on the screen. Setting fonts is similar to setting colors in that there are two ways to do it. One way is to pass a font as an additional parameter string when calling `draw_string`. The other way is to set the panel's `font` property, which affects all subsequent text.

> **Font**
>
> An overall design for a set of text characters, including the style, size, weight, and appearance of each character.

Table 3.9   Font Descriptors

Font Name	Description	Example
Courier	monospaced characters for showing code	This is Courier text.
Helvetica	a font without curves (serifs) at letter edges, such as Helvetica or Arial	This is Helvetica text.
Times	a font with curved edges, such as Times New Roman	This is Times text.

Table 3.10   Font Styles

normal	bold	roman
italic	underline	overstrike

This function changes the text size and style in which strings are drawn. A font is represented as a string with three space-separated parts: the font's name, its size as an integer, and its style such as bold or italic:

```
"name size style"
```

What fonts are available differs by operating system and by computer. You can learn what fonts are available on your system by going to your Control Panel or System Settings. There are some font names called generic *font descriptors* that are available on all systems. Table 3.9 lists the three most common font descriptors. Table 3.10 lists the various font styles that are supported. Some font styles can be combined by separating them with spaces, such as "bold italic underline".

As in the case of colors, setting the font affects only strings that are drawn after the font is set. The following program sets several fonts and uses them to draw strings:

```
1  # Draws several messages using different fonts.
2
3  from DrawingPanel import *
4
5  def main():
6      panel = DrawingPanel(250, 120)
7      panel.background = "pink"
8
9      panel.font = "Courier 36"
10     panel.draw_string("Too big", 20, 5)
11
12     panel.font = "Helvetica 10 italic"
13     panel.draw_string("Too small", 30, 60)
14
15     panel.font = "Times 18 bold italic"
16     panel.draw_string("Just right", 40, 90)
```

Continued on next page

Continued from previous page

```
17
18  main()
```

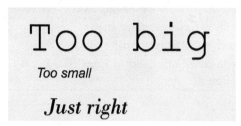

Images

The `DrawingPanel` is also capable of displaying images loaded from files in formats such as PNG and GIF. (Unfortunately Python's built-in libraries do not support JPG images.) To display an image, first you must find an image file, such as one on the Internet or on your computer, and save it into the same directory as your program. Then you can draw it onto the screen using the panel's `draw_image` function:

```
panel.draw_image("filename", x, y)
```

The *x* and *y* coordinates passed when drawing the image represent its top/left corner pixel position. For example, the following program displays two images: one that looks like a drawing of a rainbow, and one that looks like a smiley face (drawn twice):

```
1   # Displays a rainbow from an image file.
2
3   from DrawingPanel import *
4
5   def main():
6       panel = DrawingPanel(300, 200)
7       panel.draw_image("rainbow.png", 5, 5)
8       panel.draw_image("smiley.png", 10, 10)
9       panel.draw_image("smiley.png", 160, 10)
10      panel.draw_string("Rainbow!", 10, 170)
11
12  main()
```

Rainbow!

Procedural Decomposition with Graphics

If you write complex drawing programs, you will want to break them down into several functions to structure the code and to remove redundancy. When you do this, you'll have to pass your `DrawingPanel` as a parameter to each function that you introduce.

Let's explore this by writing a slightly more complicated program to draw the largest diamond figure that will fit into a box of a particular size. The largest diamond that can fit into a box of size 50 × 50 is shown in Figure 3.4.

The code to draw such a diamond would be the following:

```
# draw a 50x50 diamond at (0, 0)
panel.draw_rect(0, 0, 50, 50)
panel.draw_line(0, 25, 25, 0)
panel.draw_line(25, 0, 50, 25)
panel.draw_line(50, 25, 25, 50)
panel.draw_line(25, 50, 0, 25)
```

Now imagine that we wish to draw three such 50 × 50 diamonds at different locations. We want to turn this diamond-drawing code into a `draw_diamond` function that can be called three different times. By putting the code in a function, we will avoid redundancy by writing it once. But this requires figuring out how to generalize the code so that it can draw all three diamonds. Figure 3.5 shows a different 50 × 50 diamond with its top-left corner at the location (78, 22).

We can write code just as we did before for this new figure by filling in appropriate values to pass to the calls on the `draw_rect` and `draw_line` functions. In the following code we compare the original diamond at (0, 0) with the code we would write for the new diamond at (78, 22).

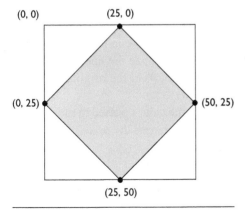

Figure 3.4   Diamond figure

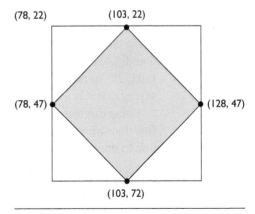

Figure 3.5   Diamond figure offset to (78, 22)

```
# draw a 50x50 diamond at (0, 0)
panel.draw_rect(0, 0, 50, 50)
panel.draw_line(0, 25, 25, 0)
panel.draw_line(25, 0, 50, 25)
panel.draw_line(50, 25, 25, 50)
panel.draw_line(25, 50, 0, 25)

# draw a 50x50 diamond at (78, 22)
panel.draw_rect(78, 22, 50, 50)
panel.draw_line(78, 47, 103, 22)
panel.draw_line(103, 22, 128, 47)
panel.draw_line(128, 47, 103, 72)
panel.draw_line(103, 72, 78, 47)
```

Our task is to generalize this to write a single function that can be used to draw each of the diamonds. When you find yourself trying to eliminate redundancy in this way, you should ask yourself what is different between the two code fragments. In the call on `draw_rect` the first two values passed to the function are different because the rectangle is to be drawn at a different location (at (0, 0) for the first and at (78, 22) for the second). To capture this difference, we should plan on including the x and y coordinates as parameters to our function. This (x, y) location is called an *offset*.

Given that we also need to pass the drawing panel as a parameter, we know that our function header will look like this:

```
def draw_diamond(panel, x, y):
    ...
```

This allows us to write a single version of the call on `draw_rect` that works for both:

```
panel.draw_rect(x, y, 50, 50)
```

Notice that the third and fourth values passed to `draw_rect` are the same because both are intended to draw a figure of size 50 × 50. There are many other numbers that differ in the calls to `draw_line`, but it turns out that these can be computed from the (x, y) coordinates and the size of 50. For example, we'll generalize the line from (78, 47) to (103, 22) in the new diamond and from (0, 25) to (25, 0) in the original diamond by saying that it is a line from $(x, y + 25)$ to $(x + 25, y)$.

Using this technique to compute expressions for the values passed to the `draw_line` function, we end up with the following program, which uses the `draw_diamond` function to draw three diamonds without redundancy:

```
1  # Draws several diamond figures of size 50×50.
2
3  from DrawingPanel import *
4
5  # Draws a diamond in a 50×50 box.
```

Continued on next page

Continued from previous page

```
 6  def draw_diamond(panel, x, y):
 7      panel.draw_rect(x, y, 50, 50)
 8      panel.draw_line(x, y + 25, x + 25, y)
 9      panel.draw_line(x + 25, y, x + 50, y + 25)
10      panel.draw_line(x + 50, y + 25, x + 25, y + 50)
11      panel.draw_line(x + 25, y + 50, x, y + 25)
12
13  def main():
14      panel = DrawingPanel(250, 150)
15      draw_diamond(panel, 0, 0)
16      draw_diamond(panel, 78, 22)
17      draw_diamond(panel, 19, 81)
18
19  main()
```

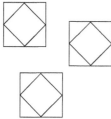

It's possible to draw patterned figures in loops and to have one drawing function call another. For example, if we want to draw five diamonds, starting at (12, 15) and spaced 60 pixels apart, we just need a `for` loop that repeats five times and shifts the *x* coordinate by 60 each time. Here's an example loop:

```
for i in range(5):
    draw_diamond(panel, 12 + 60 * i, 15)
```

3.5 Case Study: Projectile Trajectory

It's time to pull together the threads of this chapter with a more complex example that will involve parameters, functions that return values, mathematical computations, and console input. We will also add graphical output to our final version of the program.

Physics students are often asked to calculate the trajectory that a projectile will follow, given its initial velocity and its initial angle relative to the horizontal. For example, the projectile might be a football that someone has kicked. We want to compute the path it follows given Earth's gravity. To keep the computation reasonable, we will ignore air resistance.

There are several questions relating to this problem that we might want to answer:

- When does the projectile reach its highest point?
- How high does it reach?
- How long does it take to come back to the ground?
- How far does it land from where it was launched?

There are several ways to answer these questions. One simple approach is to provide a table that displays the trajectory step by step, indicating the *x* position, *y* position, and elapsed time.

To make such a table, we need to obtain three values from the user: the initial velocity, the angle relative to the horizontal, and the number of steps to include in the table we will produce. We could ask for the velocity in either meters/second or feet/second, but given that this is a physics problem, we'll stick to the metric system and ask for meters/second.

We also have to think about how to specify the angle. Unfortunately, most of the Python functions that operate on angles require angles in radians rather than degrees. We could request the angle in radians, but that would be highly inconvenient for the user, who would be required to make the conversion. Instead, we can allow the user to enter the angle in degrees and then convert it to radians using the built-in function `math.radians`.

So, the interactive part of the program will look like this:

```
velocity = float(input("velocity (meters/second)? "))
angle = math.radians(float(input("angle (degrees)? ")))
steps = int(input("number of steps to display? "))
```

Notice that for the velocity and angle we convert the input to `float`, because we want to let the user specify any number (including one with a decimal point), but for the number of steps we convert to `int`, because the number of lines in our table needs to be an integer.

Look more closely at this line of code:

```
angle = math.radians(float(input("angle (degrees)? ")))
```

Some beginners would write this as two separate steps:

```
angle_degrees = float(input("angle (degrees)? ")))
angle = math.radians(angle_degrees)
```

Both approaches work and are reasonable, but keep in mind that you don't need to divide this operation into two separate steps. You can write it in the more compact form as a single line of code.

Once we have obtained these values from the user, we are ready to begin the computations for the trajectory table. The x/y-position of the projectile at each time increment is determined by its velocity in each dimension and by the acceleration on the projectile due to gravity. Figure 3.6 shows the projectile's initial velocity v_0 and angle just as it is thrown and final velocity v_t just as it hits the ground.

We need to compute the x component of the velocity versus the y component of the velocity. As you may remember from physics, these can be computed using the trigonometric cosine and sine functions as follows:

```
# compute the x and y components of velocity
x_velocity = velocity * math.cos(angle)
y_velocity = velocity * math.sin(angle)
```

Because we are ignoring the possibility of air resistance, the x velocity will not change. The y velocity, however, is subject to the pull of gravity. Physics tells us that on the surface of the Earth, acceleration due to gravity is approximately 9.81 meters/second^2. This is an appropriate value to define as a constant:

```
ACCELERATION = -9.81    # acceleration due to gravity
```

Notice that we define gravity acceleration as a negative number because it decreases the y velocity of a projectile (pulling it down as opposed to pushing it away).

Our goal is to display x, y, and elapsed time as the projectile goes up and comes back down again. The y velocity decreases steadily until it becomes 0. From physics, we know that the graph of the projectile will be symmetrical. The projectile will go upward until its y velocity reaches 0, and then it will follow a similar path back down that takes an equal amount of time. Thus, the total time involved in seconds can be computed as follows:

```
total_time = -2.0 * y_velocity / ACCELERATION
```

Now, how do we compute the values of x, y, and elapsed time to include in our table? It is relatively simple to compute two of these. We want steady time increments for each

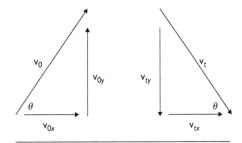

Figure 3.6 Initial and final velocity of projectile

entry in the table, so we can compute the time increment by dividing the total time by the number of steps we want to include in our table:

```
time_increment = total_time / steps
```

As noted earlier, the x velocity does not change, so for each of these time increments, we move the same distance in the x direction:

```
x_increment = x_velocity * time_increment
```

The tricky value to compute here is the y position. Because of acceleration due to gravity, the y velocity changes over time. But from physics, we have the following general formula for computing the displacement of a projectile given the velocity v, time t, and acceleration a:

$$displacement = vt + \tfrac{1}{2} at^2$$

In our case, the velocity we want is the y velocity and the acceleration is from the Earth's gravity constant. Here, then, is a pseudocode description of how to create the table:

```
Set all of x, y, and t to 0.
for given number of steps:
    Report step #, x, y, t.
    Add time_increment to t.
    Add x_increment to x.
    Reset y to y_velocity * t + 0.5 * ACCELERATION * t * t.
```

We are fairly close to having real Python code here, but we have to think about how to report the values of x, y, and t in a table. They will all be of type `float`, which means they are likely to produce a large number of digits after the decimal point. But we aren't interested in seeing all those digits, because they aren't particularly relevant and because our computations aren't that accurate. So we'll use the `round` function to display the numbers rounded to the nearest hundredth.

It would be nice if the values in the table were aligned. To get numbers that line up perfectly, we would have to use formatted output, which we will discuss in a later chapter. For now, we can at least get the numbers to line up in columns by separating them with tab characters (`\t`). We'll pass `sep="\t"` to instruct the `print` statement to use this separator between printed values.

If we're going to have a table with columns, it also makes sense to have a header for the table. And we probably want to include a line in the table showing the initial condition, where x, y, and t are all equal to 0. So we can expand our pseudocode into the following Python code:

```
x = 0.0
y = 0.0
t = 0.0
```

Continued on next page

Continued from previous page

```
print("step", "x", "y", "time", sep="\t")
for i in range(steps + 1):
    print(i, round(x, 2), round(y, 2), round(t, 2), sep="\t")
    t += time_increment
    x += x_increment
    y = y_velocity * t + 0.5 * ACCELERATION * t * t
```

Notice that the boundary on our for loop is steps + 1. This is because we want steps number of steps, along with the trivial 0th step where all values are 0.

Unstructured Solution

We can put all of these pieces together to form a complete program. Let's first look at an unstructured version that includes most of the code in main. This version also includes some new print statements at the beginning that give a brief introduction to the user:

```
1   # This program computes the trajectory of a projectile.
2   import math
3
4   # constant for Earth acceleration in meters/second^2
5   ACCELERATION = -9.81
6
7   def main():
8       # explain program
9       print("This program computes the")
10      print("trajectory of a projectile given")
11      print("its initial velocity and its")
12      print("angle relative to the")
13      print("horizontal.")
14      print()
15
16      # read input from user
17      velocity = float(input("velocity (meters/second)? "))
18      angle = math.radians(float(input("angle (degrees)? ")))
19      steps = int(input("number of steps to display? "))
20      print()
21
22      x_velocity = velocity * math.cos(angle)
23      y_velocity = velocity * math.sin(angle)
24      total_time = -2.0 * y_velocity / ACCELERATION
25      time_increment = total_time / steps
26      x_increment = x_velocity * time_increment
27
28      x = 0.0
```

Continued on next page

Continued from previous page

```
29       y = 0.0
30       t = 0.0
31       print("step", "x", "y", "time", sep="\t")
32       for i in range(steps + 2):
33           print(i, round(x, 2), round(y, 2), round(t, 2), sep="\t")
34           t += time_increment
35           x += x_increment
36           y = y_velocity * t + 0.5 * ACCELERATION * t * t
37
38  main()
```

```
This program computes the
trajectory of a projectile given
its initial velocity and its
angle relative to the
horizontal.

velocity (meters/second)? 30
angle (degrees)? 50
number of steps to display? 10

step    x        y        time
0       0.0      0.0      0.0
1       9.03     9.69     0.47
2       18.07    17.23    0.94
3       27.1     22.61    1.41
4       36.14    25.84    1.87
5       45.17    26.92    2.34
6       54.21    25.84    2.81
7       63.24    22.61    3.28
8       72.28    17.23    3.75
9       81.31    9.69     4.22
10      90.35    0.0      4.69
```

From the log of execution, you can see that the projectile reaches a maximum height of 26.92 meters after 2.34 seconds (the fifth step) and that it lands 90.35 meters from where it began after 4.69 seconds (the tenth step).

This version of the program works, but we don't generally want to include so much code in the main function. The next section explores how to break up the program into smaller pieces.

Structured Solution

There are three major blocks of code in the main function of the Projectile program: a series of print statements that introduce the program to the user, a series of statements that prompt the user for the three values used to produce the table, and then the code that produces the table itself.

So, in pseudocode, the overall structure looks like this:

```
Give introduction.
Prompt for velocity, angle and number of steps.
Produce table.
```

These three steps should be turned into functions.

Another improvement we can make is to turn the physics displacement formula into its own function. It is always a good idea to turn equations into functions. Introducing those functions, we get the following structured version of the program:

```
 1   # This program computes the trajectory of a projectile.
 2   # This version is decomposed into functions.
 3   import math
 4
 5   # constant for Earth acceleration in meters/second^2
 6   ACCELERATION = -9.81
 7
 8   # Explains program to user with print statements.
 9   def intro():
10       print("This program computes the")
11       print("trajectory of a projectile given")
12       print("its initial velocity and its")
13       print("angle relative to the")
14       print("horizontal.")
15       print()
16
17   # Reads input from user for velocity, angle, and steps.
18   # Returns those three values.
19   def read_input():
20       velocity = float(input("velocity (meters/second)? "))
21       angle = math.radians(float(input("angle (degrees)? ")))
22       steps = int(input("number of steps to display? "))
23       print()
24       return velocity, angle, steps
25
26   # Prints the table of x/y position of projectile over time.
27   def print_table(velocity, angle, steps):
28       x_velocity = velocity * math.cos(angle)
29       y_velocity = velocity * math.sin(angle)
30       total_time = -2.0 * y_velocity / ACCELERATION
31       time_increment = total_time / steps
```

Continued on next page

Continued from previous page

```
32      x_increment = x_velocity * time_increment
33
34      x = 0.0
35      y = 0.0
36      t = 0.0
37      print("step", "x", "y", "time", sep="\t")
38      for i in range(steps + 2):
39          print(i, round(x, 2), round(y, 2), round(t, 2), sep="\t")
40          t += time_increment
41          x += x_increment
42          y = y_velocity * t + 0.5 * ACCELERATION * t * t
43
44  def main():
45      intro()
46      velocity, angle, steps = read_input()
47      print_table(velocity, angle, steps)
48
49  main()
```

This version executes the same way as the earlier version.

Take note of the way we have decomposed this program. Each function does a single clear task and then returns any important calculations to main. Since the functions are meant to run in sequence, you might wonder why we don't have each function call the next one, as shown in the following code:

```
def intro():
    print(...)
    read_input()
def read_input():
    ...
    print_table(velocity, angle, steps)

def print_table(velocity, angle, steps):
    ...

def main():
    intro()
```

Having each function call the next function in this way is a poor decomposition of the problem. This is often called *chaining* functions together. Chaining is bad for several reasons. One problem is that chaining unnecessarily couples the functions together; it is no longer possible to call any one function without it also executing every function that comes after it. A second problem is that in a chained program, `main` is often a trivial function containing only a single statement: the call to the first function (in this case, `intro`). Figure 3.7 shows this structure of calls and the data flow of parameters between functions.

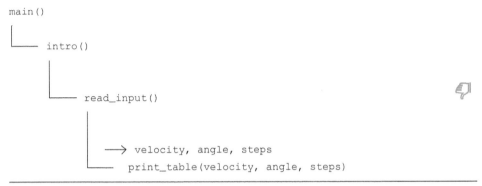

```
main()
    |___ intro()

            |___ read_input()

                    |___  ──→ velocity, angle, steps
                          |___ print_table(velocity, angle, steps)
```

Figure 3.7   Poorly decomposed function structure with chaining

Our original decomposition was better. The `main` function was in control of the overall program, managing the calls to the other various functions. The `main` function also managed the flow of data between functions. Figure 3.8 shows the better structure.

We will talk about chaining and decomposing a program into functions more in the next chapter.

```
main()
    |____ intro()

    |____ read_input()
    |  ←── velocity, angle, steps

    |  ──→ velocity, angle, steps
    |____ print_table(velocity, angle, steps)
```

Figure 3.8   Well-decomposed function structure

Graphical Version

Since our program is about the motion of a projectile through the air, it is only natural to add graphical output to it. We'll incorporate the `DrawingPanel` seen in this chapter. You can leave the existing `print` output in the code; it is fine to have a program that produces both kinds of output.

The first needed step is to import the `DrawingPanel` library:

```
from DrawingPanel import *
```

Now in the `print_table` function we'll write a statement to create a new drawing window. We'll choose a size of 300 × 120 pixels since that size fits the testing data snugly.

```
panel = DrawingPanel(300, 120)
```

We can draw the projectile as a simple black oval using the panel's `fill_oval` function, perhaps representing a ball or rock being thrown. The program already generates *x/y* coordinates, which we can pass directly to `fill_oval`. Let's start with an oval size of 10 × 10 pixels. Inside the `for` loop that performs each step, we will write a statement to draw the projectile as a filled oval:

```
panel.fill_oval(x, y, 10, 10)
```

But this doesn't quite look right; the projectile's path is upside down. This is because our notion of the *y* axis is flipped relative to how drawing panels and computers view the *y* axis. To make a flight path that looks right, you need to flip the *y* coordinates to the other vertical end of the panel. The proper formula is to take our drawing panel's height and subtract the program's existing *y* coordinate. Let's also subtract an additional 10 pixels so that a *y* of 0 puts the top of the projectile oval at the visible bottom of the window. The following rough diagram shows the desired pixel position of the projectile:

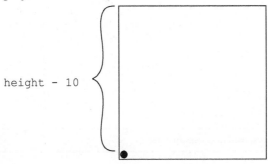

```
draw_y = panel.height - 10 - y
panel.fill_oval(x, draw_y, 10, 10)
```

With the preceding change, the program will produce the correct output. We'll also add a constant for the projectile size of 10:

```
# projectile size on screen
PROJECTILE_SIZE = 10
```

A last fun touch to this program is to incorporate the DrawingPanel's sleep function to produce a bit of animation. We already have a notion of time in our program, so let's tell the panel to sleep by the given amount of time stored as time_increment. The time_increment is stored in seconds, while the panel's sleep function accepts its parameter in milliseconds, so we'll multiply it by 1000 before passing it to the sleep function:

```
panel.sleep(time_increment * 1000)
```

The following is the finished program incorporating all of these changes, along with its text and graphical output:

```
1   # This program computes the trajectory of a projectile.
2   # This version draws graphical output with a DrawingPanel.
3   import math
4   from DrawingPanel import *
5
6   # constant for Earth acceleration in meters/second^2
7   ACCELERATION = -9.81
8
9   # projectile size on screen
10  PROJECTILE_SIZE = 10
11
12  # Explains program to user with print statements.
13  def intro():
14      print("This program computes the")
15      print("trajectory of a projectile given")
16      print("its initial velocity and its")
17      print("angle relative to the")
18      print("horizontal.")
19      print()
20
21  # Reads input from user for velocity, angle, and steps.
22  # Returns those three values.
23  def read_input():
```

Continued on next page

Continued from previous page

```
24        velocity = float(input("velocity (meters/second)? "))
25        angle = math.radians(float(input("angle (degrees)? ")))
26        steps = int(input("number of steps to display? "))
27        print()
28        return velocity, angle, steps
29
30   # Prints the table of x/y position of projectile over time.
31   def print_table(velocity, angle, steps):
32        x_velocity = velocity * math.cos(angle)
33        y_velocity = velocity * math.sin(angle)
34        total_time = -2.0 * y_velocity / ACCELERATION
35        time_increment = total_time / steps
36        x_increment = x_velocity * time_increment
37
38        # create a graphical window
39        panel = DrawingPanel(300, 120)
40
41        x = 0.0
42        y = 0.0
43        t = 0.0
44        print("step", "x", "y", "time", sep="\t")
45        for i in range(steps + 1):
46            print(i, round(x, 2), round(y, 2), round(t, 2), sep="\t")
47            draw_y = panel.height - PROJECTILE_SIZE - y   # flip y axis
48            panel.fill_oval(x, draw_y, PROJECTILE_SIZE, PROJECTILE_SIZE)
49            panel.sleep(time_increment * 1000)
50
51            t += time_increment
52            x += x_increment
53            y = y_velocity * t + 0.5 * ACCELERATION * t * t
54
55   def main():
56        intro()
57        velocity, angle, steps = read_input()
58        print_table(velocity, angle, steps)
59
60   main()
```

Continued on next page

Continued from previous page

```
This program computes the
trajectory of a projectile given
its initial velocity and its
angle relative to the
horizontal.

velocity (meters/second)? 30
angle (degrees)? 50
number of steps to display? 10

step    x        y       time
0       0.0      0.0     0.0
1       9.03     9.69    0.47
2       18.07    17.23   0.94
3       27.1     22.61   1.41
4       36.14    25.84   1.87
5       45.17    26.92   2.34
6       54.21    25.84   2.81
7       63.24    22.61   3.28
8       72.28    17.23   3.75
9       81.31    9.69    4.22
10      90.35    0.0     4.69
```

Chapter Summary

- Functions may be written to accept parameters, which are sets of characteristics that distinguish different members of a family of tasks. Parameters allow data values to flow into a function, which can change the way the function executes. A function defined with a set of parameters can perform an entire family of similar tasks instead of exactly one task.
- Functions can be written to return values to the calling code. This feature allows a function to perform a complex computation and then provide its result back to the calling code.
- Python has a library called math that contains several useful functions that you can use in your programs,

such as powers, square roots, and logarithms. There is also a library called random that generates random numbers.
- Some programs are interactive and respond to input from the user. These programs should print a message to the user, also called a prompt, asking for the input.
- DrawingPanel is a custom library provided by the authors to easily show a graphical window on the screen. A DrawingPanel can be used to draw lines, text, and shapes on the screen in different colors using methods like draw_line and fill_rect. Shapes can be "drawn" (drawing only the outline) or "filled" (coloring the entire shape).

Self-Check Problems

Section 3.1: Parameters

1. What output is produced by the following program?

```
def sentence(num1, num2):
    print(num1, num2)


def main():
    x = 15
    sentence(x, 42)
    y = x - 5
    sentence(y, x + y)


main()
```

2. What output is produced by the following program?

```
def print_odds(n):
    for i in range(1, n + 1):
        odd = 2 * i -  1
        print(odd, end=" ")
    print()


def main():
    print_odds(3)
    print_odds(17 // 2)
    x = 25
    print_odds(37 -  x + 1)


main()
```

3. What is the output of the following program?

```
def half_the_fun(number):
    number = number // 2
    for count in range(1, number + 1):
        print(count, end=" ")
    print()


def main():
    number = 8
    half_the_fun(11)
    half_the_fun(2 - 3 + 2 * 8)
    half_the_fun(number)
```

Continued on next page

Continued from previous page

```
        print("number =", number)

   main()
```

4. What output is produced by the following program?

```
   def sentence(she, who, whom):
       print(who, "and", whom, "like", she)


   def main():
       whom = "her"
       who = "him"
       it = "who"
       he = "it"
       she = "whom"

       sentence(he, she, it)
       sentence(she, he, who)
       sentence(who, she, who)
       sentence(it, "stu", "boo")
       sentence(it, whom, who)


   main()
```

5. What output is produced by the following program?

```
   def touch(elbow, ear):
       print("touch your", elbow, "to your", ear)


   def main():
       head = "shoulders"
       knees = "toes"
       elbow = "head"
       eye = "eyes and ears"
       ear = "eye"

       touch(ear, elbow)
       touch(elbow, ear)
       touch(head, "elbow")
       touch(eye, eye)
       touch(knees, "Toes")
       touch(head, "knees " + knees)


   main()
```

6. What output is produced by the following program?

```
def carbonated(coke, soda, pop):
    print("say", soda, "not", pop, "or", coke)


def main():
    soda = "coke"
    pop = "pepsi"
    coke = "pop"
    pepsi = "soda"
    say = pop

    carbonated(coke, soda, pop)
    carbonated(pop, pepsi, pepsi)
    carbonated("pop", pop, "koolaid")
    carbonated(say, "say", pop)


main()
```

7. Write a function called `print_strings` that accepts a string and a number of repetitions as parameters and prints that string the given number of times with a space after each time. For example, the call

```
print_strings("abc", 5)
```

will print the following output:

```
abc abc abc abc abc
```

Section 3.2: Returning Values

8. What is wrong with the following program?

```
# converts Fahrenheit temperatures to Celsius
def ftoc(tempf, tempc):
    tempc = (tempf - 32) * 5 // 9


def main():
    tempf = 98.6
    tempc = 0.0
    ftoc(tempf, tempc)
    print("Body temp in C is:", tempc)


main()
```

9. Evaluate the following expressions:

   a. `math.abs(-1.6)`

   b. `math.abs(2 + -4)`

   c. `math.pow(6, 2)`

   d. `math.pow(5 // 2, 6)`

   e. `math.ceil(9.1)`

   f. `math.ceil(115.8)`

   g. `math.max(7, 4)`

   h. `math.min(8, 3 + 2)`

   i. `math.min(-2, -5)`

   j. `math.sqrt(64)`

   k. `math.sqrt(76 + 45)`

   l. `100 + math.log10(100)`

   m. `13 + math.abs(-7) - math.pow(2, 3) + 5`

   n. `math.sqrt(16) * math.max(math.abs(-5), math.abs(-3))`

   o. `7 - 2 + math.log10(1000) + math.log(math.pow(math.e, 5))`

   p. `math.max(18 - 5, math.ceil(4.6 * 3))`

10. What output is produced by the following program?

```python
def mystery(z, x, y):
    z -= 1
    x = 2 * y + z
    y = x - 1
    print(y, z)
    return x


def main():
    x = 1
    y = 2
    z = 3
    z = mystery(x, z, y)
    print(x, y, z)
    x = mystery(z, z, x)
    print(x, y, z)
    y = mystery(y, y, z)
    print(x, y, z)


main()
```

11. Write the result of each expression. Note that a variable's value changes only if you reassign it using the = operator.

```
grade = 2.7
count = 25
math.round(grade)                       # grade = _____
grade = math.round(grade)               # grade = _____
min = math.min(grade, math.floor(2.9))  # min   = _____
x = math.pow(2, 4)                       # x     = _____
x = math.sqrt(64)                        # x     = _____
math.sqrt(count)                        # count = _____
count = math.sqrt(count)                # count = _____
a = math.abs(math.min(-1, -3))          # a     = _____
```

12. Write a function called `count_quarters` that takes an integer representing a number of cents as a parameter and returns the number of quarter coins represented by that many cents. Don't count any whole dollars, because those would be dispensed as dollar bills. For example, `count_quarters(64)` would return 2, because 64 cents is equivalent to 2 quarters with 14 cents left over. A call of `count_quarters(1278)` would return 3, because after the 12 dollars are taken out, 3 quarters remain in the 78 cents that are left.

Section 3.3: Interactive Programs

13. Write a program that asks a user how old he or she is and then outputs the number of years until the user can retire. Assume that the user will retire at age 65. A sample run of the program follows.

```
How old are you? 23
You have 42 years until retirement.
```

14. Write Python code to read a number from the user, then print that number multiplied by 2. You may assume that the user types a valid number.

15. Write Python code that prompts the user for a phrase and a number of times to repeat it, then prints the phrase the requested number of times. Here is an example dialogue with the user:

```
What is your phrase? His name is Robert Paulson.
How many times should I repeat it? 3
His name is Robert Paulson.
His name is Robert Paulson.
His name is Robert Paulson.
```

Section 3.4: Graphics

16. Which of the following is the correct syntax to draw a rectangle? Assume p is a `DrawingPanel`.

    a. `p.drawRect(10, 20, 50, 30)`

    b. `p.draw_rectangle(10, 20, 50, 30)`

    c. `p.draw.rect(10, 20, 50, 30)`

    d. `DrawingPanel.draw_rect(10, 20, 50, 30)`

    e. `p.draw_rect(10, 20, 50, 30)`

17. There are two mistakes in the following code, which attempts to draw a line from coordinates (50, 86) to (20, 35). What are they?

```
panel = DrawingPanel(200, 200)
draw_line(50, 20, 86, 35)
```

18. The following code attempts to draw a black-filled outer rectangle with a white-filled inner circle inside it:

```
panel = DrawingPanel(200, 100)
panel.set_color("white")
panel.fill_oval(10, 10, 50, 50)
panel.set_color("black")
panel.fill_rect(10, 10, 50, 50)
```

However, the graphical output looks like the following figure instead. What must be changed for it to look as intended?

19. What sort of figure will be drawn by the following program? Can you draw a picture that will approximately match its appearance without running it first?

```
def main():
    panel = DrawingPanel(200, 200)
    for i in range(20):
        panel.draw_oval(i * 10, i * 10, 200 - (i * 10), 200 - (i * 10))

main()
```

1. Write a function called `print_numbers` that accepts a maximum number as a parameter and prints each number from 1 up to that maximum, inclusive, boxed by square brackets. For example, consider the following calls:

```
print_numbers(15)
print_numbers(5)
```

These calls should produce the following output:

```
[ 1 ] [ 2 ] [ 3 ] [ 4 ] [ 5 ] [ 6 ] [ 7 ] [ 8 ] [ 9 ] [ 10 ] [ 11 ] [ 12 ] [ 13 ] [ 14 ] [ 15 ]
[ 1 ] [ 2 ] [ 3 ] [ 4 ] [ 5 ]
```

You may assume that the value passed to `print_numbers` is 1 or greater.

2. Write a function called `print_powers_of_2` that accepts a maximum number as a parameter and prints each power of 2 from 2^0 (1) up to that maximum power, inclusive. For example, consider the following calls:

```
print_powers_of_2(3)
print_powers_of_2(10)
```

These calls should produce the following output:

```
1 2 4 8
1 2 4 8 16 32 64 128 256 512 1024
```

You may assume that the value passed to `print_powers_of_2` is 0 or greater. (The `math` module may help you with this problem. If you use it, you may need to convert its results from `float` to `int` so that you don't see a `.0` after each number in your output. Also try to write this program without using the `math` module.)

3. Write a function called `print_powers_of_n` that accepts a base and an exponent as parameters and prints each power of the base from $base^0$ (1) up to that maximum power, inclusive. For example, consider the following calls:

```
print_powers_of_n(4, 3)
print_powers_of_n(5, 6)
print_powers_of_n(-2, 8)
```

These calls should produce the following output:

```
1 4 16 64
1 5 25 125 625 3125 15625
1 -2 4 -8 16 -32 64 -128 256
```

You may assume that the exponent passed to `print_powers_of_n` has a value of 0 or greater. (The `math` module may help you with this problem. If you use it, you may need to cast its results from `float` to `int` so that you don't see a `.0` after each number in your output. Also try to write this program without using the `math` module.)

4. Write a function called `print_square` that accepts a minimum and maximum integer and prints a square of lines of increasing numbers. The first line should start with the minimum, and each line that follows should start with the next-higher number. The sequence of numbers on a line wraps back to the minimum after it hits the maximum. For example, the call `print_square(3, 7)` should produce the following output:

```
34567
45673
56734
67345
73456
```

If the maximum passed is less than the minimum, the function produces no output.

5. Write a function called `larger_abs_val` that takes two integers as parameters and returns the larger of the two absolute values. A call of `larger_abs_val(11, 2)` would return 11, and a call of `larger_abs_val(4, -5)` would return 5.

6. Write a function called `quadratic` that solves quadratic equations and prints their roots. Recall that a quadratic equation is a polynomial equation in terms of a variable x of the form `ax2 + bx + c = 0`. The formula for solving a quadratic equation is:

$$ax^2 + bx + c = 0$$

Here are some example equations and their roots:

$$-x^2 - 7x + 12: x = -4, x = -3$$
$$-x^2 + 3x + 2: \ x = -2, x = -1$$

Your function should accept the coefficients a, b, and c as parameters and should print the roots of the equation. You may assume that the equation has two real roots, though mathematically this is not always the case.

7. Write a function called `last_digit` that returns the last digit of an integer. For example, `last_digit(3572)` should return 2. It should work for negative numbers as well. For example, `last_digit(-947)` should return 7.

8. Write a function called `area` that accepts as a parameter the radius of a circle and that returns the area of the circle. For example, the call `area(2.0)` should return roughly `12.566370614359172`. Recall that area can be computed as π times the radius squared and that Python has a constant called `math.pi`.

9. Write a function called `pay` that accepts two parameters: a real number for a teaching assistant (TA)'s salary, and an integer for the number of hours the TA worked this week. The function should return how much money to pay the TA. For example, the call `pay(5.50, 6)` should return `33.0`. The TA should receive "overtime" pay of 1.5 times the normal salary for any hours above 8. For example, the call `pay(4.00, 11)` should return (4.00 * 8) + (6.00 * 3) or `50.0`.

10. Write a function called `sphere_volume` that accepts a radius as a parameter and returns the volume of a sphere with those dimensions. For example, the call `sphere_volume(2.0)` should return roughly `33.510321638291124`. The formula for the volume of a sphere with radius r is the following:

$$\text{volume} = \frac{4}{3}\pi r^3$$

11. Write a function called `pad_string` that accepts two parameters: a string and an integer representing a length. The function should pad the parameter string with spaces until its length is the given length. For example, `pad_string("hello", 8)` should return `"hello   "` with three spaces after the word. (This sort of function is useful when trying to print output that lines up horizontally.) If the string's length is already at least as long as the length parameter, your function should return the original string. For example, `pad_string("congratulations", 10)` should return `"congratulations"` unmodified.

12. Write a function called `vertical` that accepts a string as its parameter and prints each letter of the string on separate lines. For example, a call of `vertical("hey now")` should produce the following output:

```
h
e
y

n
o
w
```

13. Write a program that uses the `DrawingPanel` to draw the following figure.

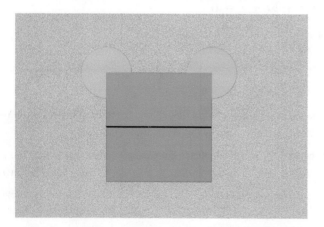

The window is 220 pixels wide and 150 pixels tall. The background is yellow. There are two blue ovals of size 40 by 40 pixels. They are 80 pixels apart, and the left oval's top-left corner is located at position (50, 25). There is a red square whose top two corners exactly intersect the centers of the two ovals. Lastly, there is a black horizontal line through the center of the square.

14. Modify your program from the previous exercise to draw the figure by a function called `draw_figure`. The function should accept three parameters: the `DrawingPanel` on which to draw, and a pair of x/y coordinates specifying the location of the top-left corner of the figure. Use the following heading for your function:

```
def draw_figure(panel, x, y):
```

Set your DrawingPanel's size to 450 by 150 pixels, and use your draw_figure function to place two figures on it, as shown in the following figure. One figure should be at position (50, 25) and the other should be at position (250, 45).

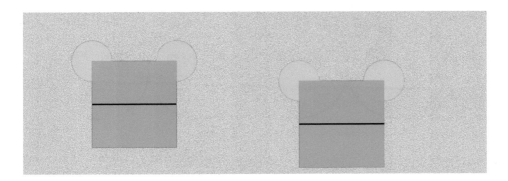

15. Suppose you have the following existing program that uses the DrawingPanel to draw a face. Modify the program to draw the modified output shown in the following figure. Do so by writing a parameterized function that draws a face at different positions. The window size should be changed to 320 × 180 pixels, and the two faces' top-left corners are at (10, 30) and (150, 50).

```
def main():
    panel = DrawingPanel(220, 150)
    panel.draw_oval(10, 30, 100, 100, "black")    # face outline
    panel.fill_oval(30, 60, 20, 20, "blue")        # eyes
    panel.fill_oval(70, 60, 20, 20, "blue")
    panel.draw_line(40, 100, 80, 100, "red")       # mouth

main()
```

16. Modify your previous program to draw the following new output. The window size should be changed to 520 × 180 px, and the faces' top-left corners are at (10, 30), (110, 30), (210, 30), (310, 30), and (410, 30).

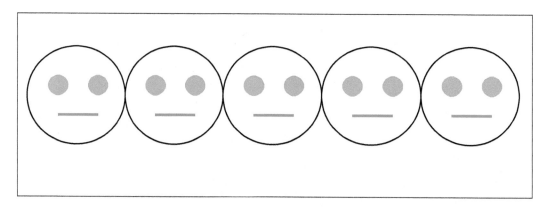

17. Write a program with a function called show_design that uses the DrawingPanel to draw the following figure.

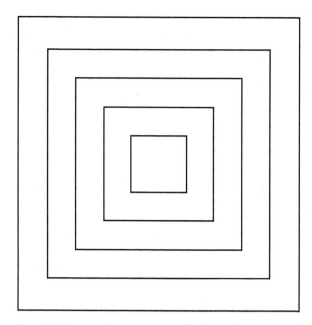

The window is 200 pixels wide and 200 pixels tall. The background is white and the foreground is black. There are 20 pixels between each of the four rectangles, and the rectangles are concentric (their centers are at the same point). Use a loop to draw the repeated rectangles.

18. Modify your `show_design` function from the previous exercise so that it accepts parameters for the window width and height and displays the rectangles at the appropriate sizes. For example, if your `show_design` function was called with values of 300 and 100, the window would look like the following figure.

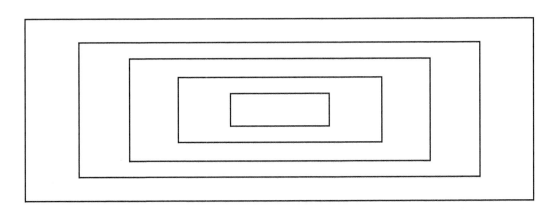

19. Write a program that uses the `DrawingPanel` to draw the following figure. The first stair's top-left corner is at position (5, 5). The first stair is 10 × 10 pixels in size. Each stair is 10 px wider than the one above it. Make a table with the (x, y) coordinates and (width × height) sizes of the first five stairs. Note which values change and which ones stay the same.

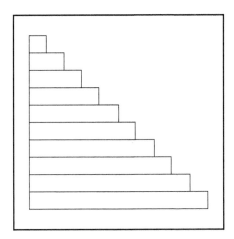

20. Modify your previous program to draw each of the following outputs. Modify only the body of your loop. (You may want to make a new table to find the expressions for x, y, width, and height for each new output.)

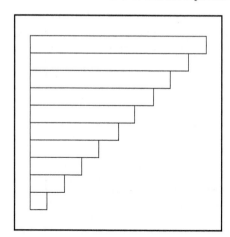

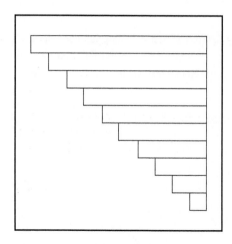

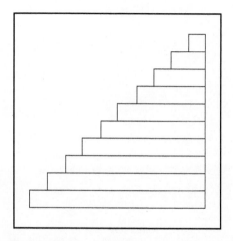

Programming Projects

1. Write a program that produces images of Christmas trees as output. It should have a function with two parameters: one for the number of segments in the tree and one for the height of each segment. For example, the tree shown here on the left has three segments of height 4 and the one on the right has two segments of height 5:

2. A certain bank offers 6.5% interest on savings accounts, compounded annually. Create a table that shows how much money a person will accumulate over a period of 25 years, assuming that the person makes an initial investment of $1000 and deposits $100 each year after the first. Your table should indicate for each year the current balance, the interest, the new deposit, and the new balance.

3. Write a program that shows the total number of presents that the person in the song "The Twelve Days of Christmas" received on each day, as indicated in Table 3.11.

Table 3.11   Twelve Days of Christmas

Day	Presents Received	Total Presents
1	1	1
2	2	3
3	3	6
4	4	10
5	5	15
...	...	...

4. Write a program that prompts for the lengths of the sides of a triangle and reports the three angles.

5. Write a program that produces calendars as output. Your program should have a function that outputs a single month's calendar like the following one, given parameters to specify how many days are in the month and what the date of the first Sunday is on that month. In the month shown, these values are 31 and 6, respectively.

```
    Sun    Mon    Tue    Wed    Thu    Fri    Sat
  +------+------+------+------+------+------+------+
  |      |      |    1 |    2 |    3 |    4 |    5 |
  |    6 |    7 |    8 |    9 |   10 |   11 |   12 |
  |   13 |   14 |   15 |   16 |   17 |   18 |   19 |
  |   20 |   21 |   22 |   23 |   24 |   25 |   26 |
  |   27 |   28 |   29 |   30 |   31 |      |      |
  +------+------+------+------+------+------+------+
```

One tricky part of this program is making the various columns line up properly with proper widths. We will learn better ways of formatting output in the next chapter. For now, you may copy the following helper function into your program and call it to turn a number into a left-padded string of a given exact width. For example, the call of print(padded(7, 5)) prints the number 7 with four leading spaces.

```
# Returns a string of the number n, left-padded
# with spaces until it is at least the given width.
def padded(n, width):
    s = str(n)
    for i in range(len(s), width):
        s = " " + s
    return s
```

## Chapter 4

Conditional Execution

Introduction

In the last few chapters, you've seen how to solve complex programming problems using `for` loops to repeat certain tasks many times. You've also seen how to introduce some flexibility into your programs by using constants and how to read values input by the user with `input`. Now we are going to explore a much more powerful technique for writing code that can adapt to different situations.

In this chapter, we'll look at conditional execution in the form of a control structure known as the `if/else` statement. With `if/else` statements, you can instruct the computer to execute different lines of code depending on whether certain conditions are true. The `if/else` statement, like the `for` loop, is so powerful that you will wonder how you managed to write programs without it.

This chapter will also expand your understanding of common programming situations. It includes an exploration of loop techniques that we haven't yet examined and includes a discussion of text-processing issues. Adding conditional execution to your repertoire will also require us to revisit functions, parameters, and return values so that you can better understand some of the fine points. The chapter concludes with several rules of thumb that help us to design better procedural programs.

4.1 if/else Statements

You will often find yourself writing code that you want to execute some of the time but not all of the time. You can accomplish this by using an if statement. The general form of the if statement is as follows:

```
if test:
    statement
    statement
    ...
    statement
```
Syntax template: if statement

The if statement, like the for loop, is a control structure. Notice that we once again see a Python keyword (if) followed by some other information and a colon with a series of controlled statements indented below.

For example, if you are writing a game-playing program, you might want to print a message each time the user achieves a new high score and store that score. You can accomplish this by putting the required two lines of code inside an if statement:

```
if current_score > max_score:
    print("A new high score!")
    max_score = current_score
```

The idea is that you will sometimes want to execute the two lines of code inside the if statement, but not always. The test in parentheses determines whether or not the statements inside the if statement are executed. In other words, the test describes the conditions under which we want to execute the code.

Figure 4.1 indicates the flow of control for the simple if statement. The computer performs the test, and if it evaluates to True, the computer executes the controlled statements. If the test evaluates to False, the computer skips the controlled statements.

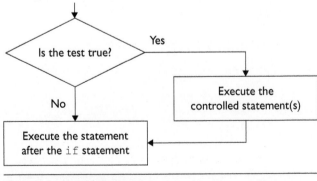

Figure 4.1   Flow of if statement

You'll use the simple `if` statement when you have code that you want to execute sometimes and skip other times. Python also has a variation known as the `if/else` statement that allows you to choose between two alternatives.

The general form of the `if/else` statement is:

```
if test:
    statement
    statement
    ...
    statement
else:
    statement
    statement
    ...
    statement
```

Syntax template: if/else statement

Suppose, for example, that you want to set a variable called `answer` to the square root of a number:

```
answer = math.sqrt(number)
```

You don't want to ask for the square root if the number is negative. To avoid this potential problem, you could use a simple `if` statement:

```
if number >= 0:
    answer = math.sqrt(number)
```

This code will avoid asking for the square root of a negative number, but what value will it assign to `answer` if `number` is negative? In this case, you'll probably want to give a value to `number` either way. In this case it would be better to use an `if/else` statement as it provides two alternatives and executes one or the other. So, in the situation above, you know that `answer` will be assigned a value regardless of whether the condition is true.

Suppose you want `answer` to be -1 when `number` is negative. You can express this pair of alternatives with the following `if/else` statement:

```
if number >= 0:
    answer = math.sqrt(number)
else:
    answer = -1
```

This control structure is unusual in that it has two sets of controlled statements and two different keywords (`if` and `else`). Figure 4.2 indicates the flow of control. The

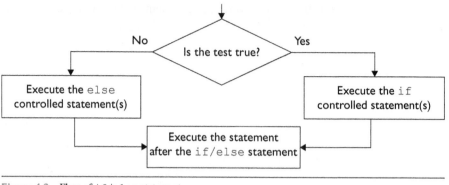

Figure 4.2   Flow of `if/else` statement

computer performs the test and, depending upon whether the code evaluates to `True` or `False`, executes one or the other group of statements.

Relational Operators

An `if/else` statement is controlled by a test. Simple tests compare two expressions to see if they are related in some way. Such tests are themselves expressions of the following form and return either `True` or `False`:

expression   relational operator   expression

Syntax template: relational expressions

To evaluate a test of this form, first evaluate the two expressions and then see whether the given relation holds between the value on the left and the value on the right. If the relation holds, the test evaluates to `True`. If not, the test evaluates to `False`.

`True` and `False` are values of a new type called `bool`. In fact, they are the only two values of type `bool`. The word `bool` is short for Boolean, named for 19th century mathematician George Boole.

The relational operators are listed in Table 4.1. Notice that the equality operator consists of two equals signs (`==`), to distinguish it from the `=` operator that we use to define and assign values to variables.

Table 4.1   Relational Operators

Operator	Meaning	Example	Value
`==`	equal to	`2 + 2 == 4`	`True`
`!=`	not equal to	`3.2 != 4.1`	`True`
`<`	less than	`4 < 3`	`False`
`>`	greater than	`4 > 3`	`True`
`<=`	less than or equal to	`2 <= 0`	`False`
`>=`	greater than or equal to	`2.4 >= 1.6`	`True`

You can try out relational operators in the Python Shell:

```
>>> 2 + 2 == 4
True
>>> 4 < 3
False
```

Because we use the relational operators as a new way of forming expressions, we must reconsider precedence. Table 4.2 is an updated version of our precedence table from Chapter 2 that includes these new operators. You will see that the equality comparisons have a slightly different level of precedence than the other relational operators, but both sets of operators have lower precedence than the arithmetic operators.

Let's look at an operator precedence example that includes relational operators. The following expression is made up of the constants 3, 2, and 9 and contains addition, multiplication, and equality operations:

```
3 + 2 * 2 == 9
```

Which of the operations is performed first? Because the relational operators have a lower level of precedence than the arithmetic operators, the multiplication is performed first, then the addition, then the equality test. In other words, Python will perform all of the "math" operations first before it tests any relationships. This precedence scheme frees you from the need to place parentheses around the left and right sides of a test that uses a relational operator. When you follow Python's precedence rules, the sample expression is evaluated as follows:

```
3 + 2 * 2 == 9

3 +     4    == 9

   7        == 9

        False
```

Table 4.2   Python Operator Precedence

Description	Operators
parentheses	(,)
exponentiation	**
unary operators	+, -
multiplicative operators	*, /, %
additive operators	+, -
relational operators	<, >, <=, >=
equality operators	==, !=
assignment operators	=, +=, -=, *=, /=, %=

You can put arbitrary expressions on either side of the relational operator, as long as the types are compatible. Here is a test with complex expressions on either side:

```
(2 - 3 * 8) // (435 % (7 * 2)) <= 3.8 -  4.5 / (2.2 * 3.8)
```

So far we have only showed examples with one relational operator. However, unlike in some other languages, relational operators can be strung together in Python just as they can in math. For example, the following expressions evaluate just as they would in math:

```
>>> # test whether x is between 1 and 10
>>> x = 5
>>> 1 <= x <= 10
True
>>> 4 < 5 < 90 > 7
True
>>> 4 == 4 != 6 == 7
False
```

We have discussed how the relational operators work between variables and literals of the same type. What happens when you mix types? Python happily mixes integer and float types as they have a clear ordering. It also happily compares between Boolean values and numbers. However, a `TypeError` occurs when you use `<`, `>`, `<=`, or `>=` on a pair of values that includes a string and another type of value such as an `int`.

```
>>> # comparison between int and float
>>> 2 < 2.5
True
>>> # convert string to integer and compare
>>> int("42") > 40
True
>>> # compare == between string and integer
>>> "42" == 42
False
>>> # compare > between string and integer
>>> "42" > 40
Traceback (most recent call last):
  File "<stdin>", line 1, in <module>
TypeError: '>' not supported between instances of 'str' and 'int'
```

The equality operators do work on pairs of values of all different types. Values of different types are considered to be unequal.

Nested `if/else` Statements

Many beginners write code that looks like this:

```
if test1:
    statement1
if test2:
    statement2
if test3:
    statement3
```
Syntax template: non-nested if statements

This sequential structure is appropriate if the tests are independent and you want to execute any combination of the three statements. For example, you might write this code in a program for a questionnaire with three optional parts, any combination of which might be applicable for a given person.

Figure 4.3 shows the flow of the sequential `if` code. Notice that it's possible for the computer to execute none of the controlled statements (if all tests are `False`), just one of them (if only one test happens to be `True`), or more than one of them (if multiple tests are `True`).

Often, however, you only want to execute one of a series of statements. In such cases, it is better to nest the `if` statements, stacking them one inside another:

```
if test1:
    statement1
else:
    if test2:
        statement2
    else:
        if test3:
            statement3
```
Syntax template: nested if statements

When you use this construct, you can be sure that the computer will execute at most one statement: the statement corresponding to the first test that evaluates to `True`. If no tests evaluate to `True`, no statement is executed. If executing at most one statement is your objective, this construct is more appropriate than the sequential `if` statements. It reduces the likelihood of errors and simplifies the testing process.

As you can see, nesting `if` statements like this leads to a lot of indentation. The indentation isn't very helpful, because this construct is really intended to allow the choice of one of a number of alternatives. If an `else` is followed by an `if`, we put them on the same line and combine the words `else` and `if` into a single keyword, `elif`.

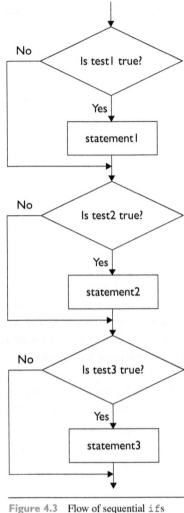

Figure 4.3   Flow of sequential `ifs`

When you follow this convention, the various statements all appear at the same level of indentation.

```
if test1:
    statement1
elif test2:
    statement2
elif test3:
    statement3
```
Syntax template: nested if statements ending in elif

Figure 4.4 shows the flow of the nested `if/else` code. Notice that it is possible to execute one of the controlled statements (the first one that evaluates to `True`) or none (if no tests evaluate to `True`).

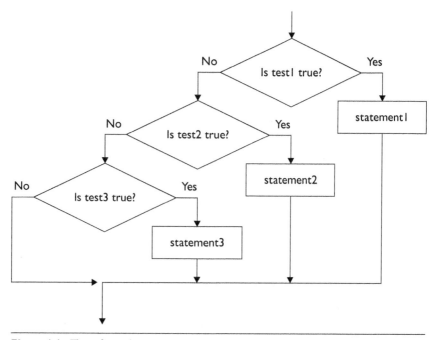

Figure 4.4   Flow of nested ifs ending in test

In a variation of this structure, the final statement is controlled by an else instead of a test:

```
if test1:
    statement1
elif test2:
    statement2
else:
    statement3
```

Syntax template: nested if statements ending in else

In this construct, the computer will always select the final branch when all the tests fail, and thus the construct will always execute exactly one of the three statements. Figure 4.5 shows the flow of this modified nested if/else code.

To explore these variations, consider the task of having the computer state whether a number is positive, negative, or zero. You could structure this task as three simple if statements as follows:

```
# print a message about the sign of an integer (v1)
if number > 0:
    print("Number is positive.")
if number == 0:
    print("Number is zero.")
if number < 0:
    print("Number is negative.")
```

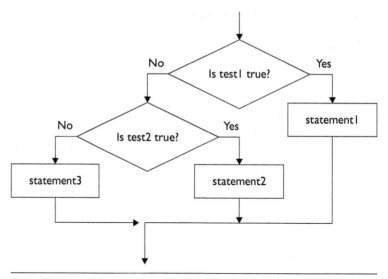

Figure 4.5   Flow of nested `if`s ending in else

To determine how many of the `prints` are potentially executed, you have to stop and think about the tests being performed. But you shouldn't have to put that much effort into understanding this code. The code is clearer if you nest the `if` statements:

```
# print a message about the sign of an integer (v2)
if number > 0:
    print("Number is positive.")
elif number == 0:
    print("Number is zero.")
elif number < 0:
    print("Number is negative.")
```

This solution has a problem, however. You know that you want to execute one and only one `print` statement, but this nested structure does not preclude the possibility of no statement being executed (which would happen if all three tests failed). Of course, with these particular tests that will never happen: If a number is neither positive nor zero, it must be negative. Thus, the final test here is unnecessary and misleading. You must think about the tests to determine whether or not it is possible for all three tests to fail and all three branches to be skipped.

In this case, the best solution is the nested `if/else` approach with a final branch that is always taken if the first two tests fail:

```
# print a message about the sign of an integer (v3)
if number > 0:
    print("Number is positive.")
```

Continued on next page

Continued from previous page

```
elif number == 0:
    print("Number is zero.")
else:
    print("Number is negative.")
```

You can glance at this construct and see immediately that exactly one `print` will be executed. You don't have to look at the tests being performed in order to realize this; it is a property of this kind of nested `if/else` structure. If you want, you can include a comment to make it clear what is going on:

```
# print a message about the sign of an integer (v3)
if number > 0:
    print("Number is positive.")
elif number == 0:
    print("Number is zero.")
else:
    # number must be negative
    print("Number is negative.")
```

One final benefit of this approach is efficiency. When the code includes three simple `if` statements, the computer will always perform all three tests. When the code uses the nested `if/else` approach, the computer carries out tests only until a match is found, which is a better use of resources. For example, in the preceding code we only need to perform one test for positive numbers and at most two tests overall.

When you find yourself writing code to choose among alternatives like these, you have to analyze the particular problem to figure out how many of the branches you potentially want to execute. If it doesn't matter what combination of branches is taken, use sequential `if` statements. If you want one or none of the branches to be taken, use nested `if/else` statements with a test for each statement. If you want exactly one branch to be taken, use nested `if/else` statements with a final branch controlled by an `else` rather than by a test. Table 4.3 summarizes these choices.

Table 4.3   if/else Options

`# sequential ifs:`	`# nested if/else,`	`# nested if/else,`
`# want to execute any`	`# ending in test:`	`# ending in else:`
`# combination of the`	`# want to execute`	`# want to execute`
`# controlled statements`	`# zero or one of the`	`# exactly one of the`
	`# controlled statements`	`# controlled statements`
`if test1:`	`if test1:`	`if test1:`
`    statement1`	`    statement1`	`    statement1`
`if test2:`	`elif test2:`	`elif test2:`
`    statement2`	`    statement2`	`    statement2`
`if test3:`	`elif test3:`	`else:`
`    statement3`	`    statement3`	`    statement3`

| Common Programming Error |

Choosing the Wrong `if/else` Construct

Suppose that your instructor has told you that grades will be determined as follows:

- A for scores $\geq$ 90
- B for scores $\geq$ 80
- C for scores $\geq$ 70
- D for scores $\geq$ 60
- F for scores $<$ 60

You can translate this scale into code as follows:

```
if score >= 90:
    grade = "A"
if score >= 80:
    grade = "B"
if score >= 70:
    grade = "C"
if score >= 60:
    grade = "D"
if score < 60:
    grade = "F"
```

This code will run but you will find that it gives out only two grades: D and F. Anyone who has a score of at least 60 ends up with a D and anyone with a grade below 60 ends up with an F.

The problem here is that you want to execute exactly one of the assignment statements, but when you use sequential `if` statements, it's possible for the program to execute several of them sequentially. For example, if a student has a score of 95, that student's grade is set to "A", then reset to "B", then reset to "C", and finally reset to "D". You can fix this problem by using a nested `if/else` construct:

```
if score >= 90:
    grade = "A"
elif score >= 80:
    grade = "B"
elif score >= 70:
    grade = "C"
elif score >= 60:
    grade = "D"
else:
    # score < 60
    grade = "F"
```

Factoring `if/else` Statements

Suppose you are writing a program that plays a betting game with a user and you want to give different warnings about how much cash the user has left. The nested `if/else` construct that follows distinguishes three different cases: funds less than $500, which is considered low; funds between $500 and $1000, which is considered okay; and funds over $1000, which is considered good. Notice that the user is given different advice in each case:

```
# betting code (unfactored redundant version)
if money < 500:
    print("You have $", money, "left.")
    print("Cash is dangerously low. Bet carefully.")
    bet = int(input("How much do you want to bet?"))
elif money < 1000:
    print("You have $", money, "left.")
    print("Cash is somewhat low. Bet moderately.")
    bet = int(input("How much do you want to bet?"))
else:
    print("You have $", money, "left.")
    print("Cash is in good shape. Bet liberally.")
    bet = int(input("How much do you want to bet?"))
```

This construct is repetitious and can be made more efficient by using a technique called *factoring*. Factoring is when we reorganize our code so that repeated pieces in an `if/else` statement are moved out to reduce the repetition and redundancy.

> **Factoring**
>
> Moving common code out of an `if/else` statement to remove redundancy.

Using this simple technique, you factor out common pieces of code from the different branches of the `if/else` construct. In the preceding program, three different branches can execute, depending on the value of the variable `money`. Start by writing down the series of actions being performed in each branch and comparing them, as in Figure 4.6.

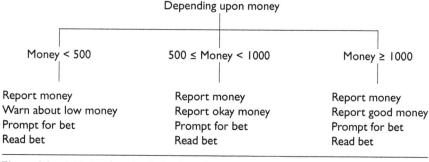

Figure 4.6   `if/else` branches before factoring

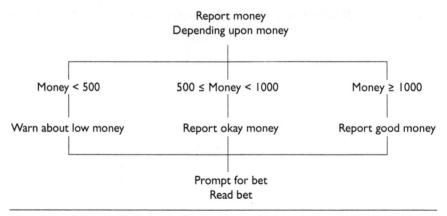

Figure 4.7   `if/else` branches after factoring

You can factor at both the top and the bottom of a construct like this. If you notice that the top statement in each branch is the same, you factor it out of the branching part and put it before the branch. Similarly, if the bottom statement in each branch is the same, you factor it out of the branching part and put it after the loop. You can factor the top statement in each of these branches and the bottom two statements, as in Figure 4.7.

Thus, the preceding code can be reduced to the following more succinct version:

```
# betting code (factored improved version)
print("You have $", money, "left.")
if money < 500:
    print("Cash is dangerously low. Bet carefully.")
elif money < 1000:
    print("Cash is somewhat low. Bet moderately.")
else:
    print("Cash is in good shape. Bet liberally.")
bet = int(input("How much do you want to bet? "))
```

Testing Multiple Conditions

When you are writing a program, you often find yourself wanting to test more than one condition. For example, suppose you want the program to take a particular course of action based on the ages of two users. You might say:

```
# code to test two users' ages
if age1 >= 18:
    if age2 < 18:
        # user 1 is adult, user 2 is child
        do_something()
```

In these lines of code, you had to write two statements: one testing whether the first age was greater than or equal to 18 and one testing whether the second age was less than 18.

Python provides an efficient alternative: You can combine the two tests by using an operator known as the logical and operator. Using the and operator, we can write the preceding code more simply:

```
# code to test two users' ages (with 'and')
if age1 >= 18 and age2 < 18:
    do_something()
```

As its name implies, the and operator forms a test that requires that both parts of the test evaluate to True. There is a similar operator known as logical or that evaluates to True if either of two tests evaluates to True. For example, if you want to test whether a variable num is equal to 1 or 2, you can say:

```
if num == 1 or num == 2:
    process_number(num)
```

We will explore the logical and and logical or operators in more detail in the next chapter.

4.2 Cumulative Algorithms

The more you program, the more you will find that certain patterns emerge. Many common algorithms involve accumulating an answer step by step. In this section, we will explore some of the most common *cumulative algorithms*.

> **Cumulative Algorithm**
>
> An operation in which an overall value is computed incrementally, often using a loop.

For example, you might use a cumulative algorithm over a set of numbers to compute the average value or to find the largest number.

Cumulative Sum

You'll often want to find the sum of a series of numbers. One way to do this is to define a different variable for each value you want to include, but that would not be a practical solution: If you have to add a hundred numbers together, you won't want to define a hundred different variables. Fortunately, there is a simpler way.

The trick is to keep a running tally of the result and process one number at a time. For example, to add to a variable called sum, you would write the following line of code:

```
sum = sum + next
```

Alternatively, you could use the shorthand assignment operator:

```
sum += next
```

The preceding statement takes the existing value of sum, adds the value of a variable called next, and stores the result as the new value of sum. This operation is performed for each number to be summed. Notice that when you execute this statement for the first time, sum does not have a value. To get around this, you initialize sum to a value that will not affect the answer: 0.

Here is a pseudocode description of the cumulative sum algorithm:

```
sum = 0.
for each of the numbers to sum:
    obtain "next".
    sum += next.
```

To implement this algorithm, you must decide how many times to go through the loop and how to obtain a next value. Here is an interactive program that prompts the user for the number of numbers to add together and for the numbers themselves:

```
1   # Finds the sum of a sequence of numbers.
2
3   def main():
4       print("This program adds a sequence of numbers.")
5
6       how_many = int(input("How many numbers do you have? "))
7
8       sum = 0.0
9       for i in range(how_many):
10          next = float(input("Next number?"))
11          sum += next
12
13      print()
14      print("sum =", sum)
15
16  main()
```

The program's execution will look something like this (as usual, user input is boldface):

```
This program adds a sequence of numbers.
How many numbers do you have? 6
Next number? 3.2
Next number? 4.7
Next number? 5.1
```

Continued on next page

Continued from previous page

```
Next number? 9.0
Next number? 2.4
Next number? 3.1
sum = 27.5
```

Let's trace the execution in detail. Before we enter the `for` loop, we initialize the variable `sum` to `0.0`:

sum   `0.0`

On the first execution of the `for` loop, we read in a value of `3.2` from the user and add this value to `sum`:

sum   `3.2`   next   `3.2`

The second time through the loop, we read in a value of `4.7` and add this to the value of `sum`:

sum   `7.9`   next   `4.7`

Notice that the sum now includes both of the numbers entered by the user, because we have added the new value, `4.7`, to the old value, `3.2`. The third time through the loop, we add in the value `5.1`:

sum   `13.0`   next   `5.1`

Notice that the variable `sum` now contains the sum of the first three numbers (`3.2` + `4.7` + `5.1`). Now we read in `9.0` and add it to the sum:

sum   `22.0`   next   `9.0`

Then we add in the fifth value, `2.4`:

sum   `24.4`   next   `2.4`

Finally, we add in the sixth value, `3.1`:

sum   `27.5`   next   `3.1`

We then exit the `for` loop and print the value of `sum`.

There is an interesting scope issue in this particular program. Notice that the variable sum is defined outside the loop, while the variable next is defined inside the loop. We have no choice but to define sum outside the loop because it needs to be initialized and it is used after the loop. But the variable next is used only inside the loop, so it can be defined in that inner scope. It is best to define variables in the innermost scope possible.

The cumulative sum algorithm and variations on it will be useful in many of the programming tasks you solve. How would you do a cumulative product? Here is the pseudocode:

```
product = 1.
for each of the numbers to multiply:
    obtain "next".
    product *= next.
```

Min/Max Loops

Another common programming task is to keep track of the maximum and/or minimum values in a sequence. For example, consider the task of deciding whether it will be viable to build a living area on the Moon inhabited by humans. One obstacle is that the average daily surface temperature on the Moon is a chilly −50 degrees Fahrenheit. But a much more daunting problem is the wide range of values; it ranges from a minimum of −240 degrees to a maximum of 250 degrees.

To compute the maximum of a sequence of values, you can keep track of the largest value you've seen so far and use an if statement to update the maximum if you come across a new value that is larger than the current maximum. This approach can be described in pseudocode as follows:

```
initialize max to 0.
for each of the numbers to examine:
    obtain "next".
    if next > max:
        max = next.
```

Initializing the maximum isn't quite as simple as it sounds. For example, novices often initialize max to 0. But what if the sequence of numbers you are examining is composed entirely of negative numbers? For example, you might be asked to find the maximum of this sequence:

$$-84, -7, -14, -39, -10, -17, -41, -9$$

The maximum value in this sequence is -7, but if you've initialized max to 0, the program will incorrectly report 0 as the maximum.

There are two classic solutions to this problem. First, if you know the range of the numbers you are examining, you can make an appropriate choice for max. In that case, you can set max to the lowest value in the range. That seems counterintuitive because normally we think of the maximum as being large, but the idea is to set max to the smallest possible value it could ever be so that anything larger will cause max to be reset to that value. For example, if you knew that the preceding sequence of numbers were temperatures in degrees Fahrenheit, you would know that they could never be smaller than absolute zero (around −460 degrees Fahrenheit), so you could initialize max to that value.

The second possibility is to initialize max to the first value in the sequence. That won't always be convenient because it means obtaining one of the numbers outside the loop. When you combine these two possibilities, the pseudocode becomes:

```
initialize max either to lowest possible value or to first value.
for each of the numbers to examine:
    obtain "next".
    if next > max:
        max = next.
```

The pseudocode for computing the minimum is a slight variation of this code:

```
initialize min either to highest possible value or to first value.
for each of the numbers to examine:
    obtain "next".
    if next < min:
        min = next.
```

To help you understand this better, let's put the pseudocode into action with a real problem. In mathematics, there is an open problem that involves what is known as a *hailstone sequence*. These sequences of numbers often rise and fall in unpredictable patterns, which is somewhat analogous to the process that forms hailstones.

A hailstone sequence is a sequence of numbers in which each value x is followed by:

- $(3x + 1)$, if x is odd
- $(x/2)$, if x is even

For example, if you start with 7 and construct a sequence of length 10, you get the sequence:

$$7, 22, 11, 34, 17, 52, 26, 13, 40, 20$$

In this sequence, the maximum and minimum values are 52 and 7, respectively. If you extend this computation to a sequence of length 20, you get the sequence:

$$7, 22, 11, 34, 17, 52, 26, 13, 40, 20, 10, 5, 16, 8, 4, 2, 1, 4, 2, 1$$

In this case, the maximum and minimum values are 52 and 1, respectively.

You will notice that once 1, 2, or 4 appears in the sequence, the sequence repeats itself. It is conjectured that all integers eventually reach 1, like hailstones that fall to the ground. This is an unsolved problem in mathematics. Nobody has been able to disprove it, but nobody has proven it, either.

Let's write a function that accepts a starting value and a sequence length as parameters and prints each value in a hailstone sequence of that length, along with the maximum and minimum values obtained along the way. Our function's header will look like this:

```
def print_hailstone_max_min(start, length):
    ...
```

We can use the starting value to initialize `max` and `min`:

```
min = start
max = start
```

We then need a loop that will generate the other values. The user will input a parameter telling us how many times to go through the loop, but we don't want to execute the loop body length times: Remember that the starting value is part of the sequence, so if we want to use a sequence of the given length, we have to make sure that the number of iterations is one less than length. Combining this idea with the max/min pseudocode, we know the loop will look like this:

```
for i in range(length - 1):
    compute next value.
    print the value.
    if value > max:
        max = value.
    elif value < min:
        min = value.

print the max and min.
```

To fill out the pseudocode for "compute next value," we need to translate the hailstone formula into code. The formula is different, depending on whether the current value is odd or even. We can use an `if/else` statement to solve this task. For the test, we can use a "mod 2" test to see what remainder we get when we divide by 2. Even numbers have a remainder of 0 and odd numbers have a remainder of 1. So the test should look like this:

```
if start % 2 == 0:
    do even computation.
else:
    do odd computation.
```

Translating the hailstone mathematical formulas into Python, we get the following code:

```
if value % 2 == 0:
    value = value // 2
else:
    value = 3 * value + 1
```

The only part of our pseudocode that we haven't filled in yet is the part that prints the result. This part comes after the loop and is fairly easy to complete. Here is the complete function:

```
# Computes a hailstone sequence of 'length' steps,
# beginning with the given 'start' value,
# and prints the max and min integer seen in the sequence.
def print_hailstone_max_min(start, length):
    # initialize max/min and current value
    min = start
    max = start
    print(start, end=" ")

    # perform the remaining steps of the sequence
    value = start
    for i in range(length - 1):
        if value % 2 == 0:
            value = value // 2
        else:
            value = 3 * value + 1
        print(value, end=" ")
        if value > max:
            max = value
        elif value < min:
            min = value

    # display max/min values found
    print()
    print("max = ", max)
    print("min = ", min)
```

Cumulative Sum with `if`

Let's now explore how you can use `if/else` statements to create some interesting variations on the cumulative sum algorithm. Suppose you want to read a sequence of numbers and compute the average. This task seems like a straightforward variation of the cumulative sum code. You can compute the average as the sum divided by the number of numbers:

```
average = sum / how_many
print("average =", average)
```

But there is one minor problem with this code. Suppose that when the program asks you how many numbers to process, you enter 0. Then the program will not enter the cumulative sum loop, and your code will try to compute the value of 0 divided by 0. The Python interpreter will then report a ZeroDivisionError and your program will crash. It would be much better for the program to print out some kind of message which indicates that there aren't any numbers to average. You can use an if/else statement for this purpose:

```
if how_many <= 0:
    print("No numbers to average")
else:
    average = sum / how_many
    print("average =", average)
```

Another use of if statements would be to count how many negative numbers the user enters. You will often want to count how many times something occurs in a program.

This goal is easy to accomplish with an if statement and an integer variable called a *counter*. You start by initializing the counter to 0:

```
negatives = 0
```

You can use any name you want for the variable. Here we used negatives because that is what you're counting. The other essential step is to increment the counter inside the loop if it passes the test of interest:

```
if next < 0:
    negatives += 1
```

When you put this all together and modify the comments and introduction, you end up with the following variation of the cumulative sum program:

```
 1  # Finds the average of a sequence of numbers as well as
 2  # reporting how many of the user-specified numbers were negative.
 3
 4  def main():
 5      print("This program examines a sequence")
 6      print("of numbers to find the average")
```

Continued on next page

Continued from previous page

```
 7        print("and count how many are negative.")
 8        print()
 9
10        how_many = int(input("How many numbers do you have? "))
11
12        negatives = 0
13        sum = 0.0
14        for i in range(how_many):
15            next = float(input("Next number?"))
16            sum += next
17            if next < 0:
18                negatives += 1
19
20        print()
21        if how_many <= 0:
22            print("No numbers to average")
23        else:
24            average = sum / how_many
25            print("average =", average);
26
27        print("# of negatives =", negatives)
28
29  main()
```

The program's execution will look something like this:

```
This program examines a sequence
of numbers to find the average
and count how many are negative.

How many numbers do you have? 8
Next number? 2.5
Next number? 9.2
Next number? -19.4
Next number? 208.2
Next number? 42.3
Next number? 92.7
Next number? -17.4
Next number? 8


average = 40.7625
# of negatives = 2
```

Roundoff Errors

As you explore cumulative algorithms, you'll discover a particular problem that you should understand. For example, consider the following execution of the previous program with different user input:

```
This program examines a sequence
of numbers to find the average
and count how many are negative.

How many numbers do you have? 4
Next number? 2.1
Next number? -3.8
Next number? 5.4
Next number? 7.4

average = 2.7750000000000004
# of negatives = 1
```

If you use a calculator, you will find that the four numbers add up to 11.1. If you divide this number by 4, you get 2.775. Yet Python reports the result as 2.7750000000000004. Where do all of those zeros come from, and why does the number end in 4? The answer is that floating-point numbers can lead to *roundoff errors*. A roundoff error is a slightly incorrect floating-point number computed by a program due to imprecision in the way a computer's processor performs calculations on real numbers.

> **Roundoff Error**
>
> A numerical error that occurs because floating-point numbers are stored as approximations rather than as exact values.

Roundoff errors are generally small and can occur in either direction: slightly high or slightly low. In the previous case, we got a roundoff error that was slightly high.

Floating-point numbers are stored in a format similar to scientific notation, with a set of digits and an exponent. Consider how you would store the value one-third in scientific notation using base-10. You would state that the number is 3.33333 (repeating) times 10 to the -1 power. We can't store an infinite number of digits on a computer, though, so we'll have to stop repeating the 3s at some point. Suppose we can store 10 digits. Then the value for one-third would be stored as 3.333333333 times 10 to the -1. If we multiply that number by 3, we don't get back 1. Instead, we get 9.999999999 times 10 to the -1 (which is equal to 0.9999999999).

You might wonder why the numbers we used in the previous example caused a problem when they didn't have any repeating digits. You have to remember that the computer stores numbers in base-2. Numbers like 2.1 and 5.4 might look like simple numbers in base-10, but they have repeating digits when they are stored in base-2.

Roundoff errors can lead to rather surprising outcomes. For example, consider the following short program:

```
# loop that generates roundoff errors
n = 1.0
for i in range(10):
    n += 0.1
    print(n)
```

```
1.1
1.2000000000000002
1.3000000000000003
1.4000000000000004
1.5000000000000004
1.6000000000000005
1.7000000000000006
1.8000000000000007
1.9000000000000008
2.000000000000001
```

This program presents a classic cumulative sum with a loop that adds 0.1 to the variable n each time the loop executes. We start with n equal to `1.0` and the loop iterates 10 times, which we might expect to print the numbers `1.1`, `1.2`, `1.3`, and so on through `2.0`. Instead, it produces the output shown previously that contains roundoff errors.

The problem occurs because 0.1 cannot be stored exactly in base-2 (it produces a repeating set of digits, just as one-third does in base-10). Each time through the loop the error is compounded, which is why the roundoff error gets worse each time.

As another example, consider the task of adding together the values of a penny, a nickel, a dime, and a quarter. If we use numbers without decimals, we will get an exact answer regardless of the order in which we add the numbers:

```
cents1 = 1 + 5 + 10 + 25
cents2 = 25 + 10 + 5 + 1
print("cents =", cents1)
print("cents =", cents2)
```

```
cents = 41
cents = 41
```

Regardless of the order, these numbers always add up to 41 cents. But suppose that instead of thinking of these values as whole cents, we think of them as fractions of a dollar that we store as decimals:

```
dollars1 = 0.01 + 0.05 + 0.10 + 0.25
dollars2 = 0.25 + 0.10 + 0.05 + 0.01
print(dollars1)
print(dollars2)
```

```
0.41000000000000003
0.41
```

Even though we are adding up exactly the same numbers, the fact that we add them in a different order makes a difference in the form of roundoff errors. There are several lessons to draw from this:

- Be aware that when you store floating-point values, you are storing approximations and not exact values. If you need to store an exact value, store it as a whole number.
- Don't be surprised when you see numbers that are slightly off from the expected values.
- Don't expect to be able to compare decimal variables for equality.

To follow up on the third point, consider what the preceding code would lead to if we were to perform the following test:

```
# testing whether two floats are exactly equal
dollars1 = 0.01 + 0.05 + 0.10 + 0.25
dollars2 = 0.25 + 0.10 + 0.05 + 0.01
if dollars1 == dollars2:    # will be false!
    ...
```

The test would evaluate to False because the values are very close, but not close enough for Python to consider them equal. We rarely use a test for exact equality when we work with decimal numbers. Instead, we can use a test like this to see if numbers are close to one another:

```
# testing whether two floats are nearly equal
dollars1 = 0.01 + 0.05 + 0.10 + 0.25
dollars2 = 0.25 + 0.10 + 0.05 + 0.01
if abs(dollars1 -  dollars2) < 0.001:    # will be true
    ...
```

We use the absolute value (`abs`) function to find the magnitude of the difference and then test whether it is less than some small amount (in this case, `0.001`). In fact, this issue is so common that Python has a built-in `math` function called `isclose` to do the same thing as the above code example. It can be used as follows:

```
>>> a = 5.0
>>> b = 4.999999998
>>> math.isclose(a, b)
True
```

Most of the time `float` imprecision doesn't matter but occasionally it can be a problem. Python contains a `Decimal` module for use in these cases. It stores numbers exactly and so doesn't have any precision errors. Since the `Decimal` type is a bit clunky to use, we won't explore it here in detail. But if you are curious, you can read about it on the Python web site:

- https://docs.python.org/3/library/decimal.html

4.3 Functions with Conditional Execution

We introduced a great deal of information about functions in Chapter 3, including how to use parameters to pass values into a function and how to use a `return` statement to have a function return a value. Now that we've introduced conditional execution, we need to revisit these issues so that you can gain a deeper understanding of them.

Preconditions and Postconditions

Every time you write a function you should think about exactly what that function is supposed to accomplish. You can describe how a function works by describing the *preconditions* that must be true before it executes and the *postconditions* that will be true after it has executed.

> **Precondition**
>
> A condition that must be true before a function executes in order to guarantee that the function can perform its task.

> **Postcondition**
>
> A condition that the function guarantees will be true after it finishes executing, as long as the preconditions were true before the function was called.

For example, if you are describing the task of a person on an automobile assembly line, you might use a postcondition like, "The bolts that secure the left front tire are on the car and tight." But postconditions are not the whole story. Employees on an assembly line depend on one another. A line worker can't add bolts and tighten them if the left tire isn't there or if there are no bolts. So, the assembly line worker might have preconditions like, "The left tire is mounted properly on the car, there are at least eight bolts in the supply box, and a working wrench is available." You describe the task fully by saying that the worker can make the postcondition(s) true if the precondition(s) are true before starting.

Like workers on an assembly line, functions need to work together, each solving its own portion of the task in order for them all to solve the overall task. The preconditions and postconditions describe the dependencies between functions.

Raising Exceptions

We have seen several cases in which Python might *raise*, or generate, an exception. For example, if you try to add a string to a number, the code raises a `TypeError`. For now, we just want to explore some of the ways in which exceptions can occur and how you might want to generate them in your own code.

Ideally programs execute without generating any errors, but in practice various problems arise. If you ask the user for an integer, the user may accidentally or perhaps even maliciously type something that is not an integer. Or your code might have a bug in it.

The following program always raises an exception because it tries to compute the value of 1 divided by 0, which is mathematically undefined:

```
1  def main():
2      x = 1 / 0
3      print(x)
4
5  main()
```

```
Traceback (most recent call last):
  File "exception.py", line 5, in <module>
    main()
  File "exception.py", line 2, in main
    x = 1 / 0
ZeroDivisionError: division by zero
```

The problem occurs in line 2, when you ask Python to compute a value that can't exist. What is Python supposed to do? It raises an exception that stops the program from executing and warns you that a zero division error occurred while the program was executing that specific line of code.

You may want to raise exceptions yourself in the code you write. In particular, it is a good idea to raise an exception if a precondition fails. For example, suppose that you want to write a function for computing the factorial of an integer. The factorial of a given integer n, written as "$n!$", is the product of the integers 1 through n inclusive:

$$n! = 1 \times 2 \times 3 \times \ldots \times n$$

You can write a Python function that uses a cumulative product to compute this result:

```
# Computes n!, or the product of the integers 1 through n.
def factorial(n):
    product = 1
    for i in range(2, n + 1):
        product *= i
    return product
```

You can then test the function for various values with a loop:

```
for i in range(0, 11):
    print(str(i) + "! =", factorial(i))
```

The loop produces the following output:

```
0! = 1
1! = 1
2! = 2
3! = 6
4! = 24
5! = 120
6! = 720
7! = 5040
8! = 40320
9! = 362880
10! = 3628800
```

It seems odd that the factorial function should return 1 when it is asked for 0!, but that is actually part of the mathematical definition of a factorial. The code returns 1 because the local variable product in the factorial function is initialized to 1, and the loop is never entered when the parameter n has the value 0. So, this is actually desirable behavior for 0 factorial.

But what if you're asked to compute the factorial of a negative number? Currently the function returns the same value, 1. The mathematical definition of "factorial" says that the function is undefined for negative values of n, so it actually shouldn't even compute an answer when n is negative. Accepting only numbers that are zero or positive is a precondition of the function that can be described in the documentation:

```
# pre : n >= 0
```

Adding comments about this restriction is helpful, but what if someone calls the factorial function with a negative value anyway? You might think that the program should print an error message, but this is not the most common way to deal with such a situation. If a negative value is being passed, it often indicates a bug in the code calling the factorial function, so we want to stop the program immediately to address the problem. The best solution here is to raise an exception, which causes an error to occur that halts the execution of the program. The general syntax for raising an exception is:

```
raise ExceptionType
```

Syntax template: raising an exception

You can also supply an optional string parameter representing a message to include with the exception as you throw it. This message will be printed in the program's console output when it crashes, which helps clarify what caused the program to halt. The general syntax for raising an exception with an error message is:

```
raise ExceptionType("error message")
```

Syntax template: raising an exception and displaying an error message

Python includes several types of exceptions that you can raise in your code. Some of the most common are listed in Table 4.4. For a complete list, see the Python online documentation:

- https://docs.python.org/3/library/exceptions.html

Table 4.4 **Provided Exception Types**

Exception Type	Description
ArithmeticError	invalid numeric operation such as dividing by zero
AttributeError	invalid attempt to access data within an object
ImportError	failure to load a library or module
IndexError	attempt to access an illegal index of a sequence such as a string
IOError	failure to perform input or output (I/O) on a file
KeyError	attempt to look up invalid data in a dictionary
RecursionError	a function that calls itself too many times
RuntimeError	a general error that does not fall into any other category
SyntaxError	invalid syntax in Python code
SystemError	a problem in the operating system or Python interpreter
TypeError	an operation is applied to a value of the wrong type
ValueError	an operation is applied to an inappropriate value

The exception type `ValueError` is meant to cover a case like this where someone has passed an inappropriate value as an argument. Of course, you'll want to do this only when the precondition fails, so you need to include the code inside an `if` statement: You can cause your program to raise a `ValueError` as follows:

```
if n < 0:
    raise ValueError
```

You can also include some text when you construct the exception that will be displayed when the exception is raised:

```
if n < 0:
    raise ValueError("n must be greater or equal to 0")
```

Incorporating the pre/post comments and the exception code into the function definition, you get the following code:

```
# Computes n!, or the product of the integers 1 through n.
# pre : n >= 0
def factorial(n):
    if n < 0:
        raise ValueError("n must be greater or equal to 0")
    product = 1
    for i in range(2, n + 1):
        product *= i
    return product
```

You don't need an `else` after the `if` that raises the exception, because when an exception is raised, it halts the execution of the function. So, if someone calls the `factorial` function with a negative value of *n*, Python will never execute the code that follows the `raise` statement.

You can test this code with the following `main` function:

```
def main():
    print(factorial(-1))


main()
```

When you execute this program, it stops executing and prints the following message:

```
Traceback (most recent call last):
  File "factorial.py", line 13, in <module>
    main()
```

Continued on next page

Continued from previous page

```
  File "factorial.py", line 11, in main
    print(factorial(-1))
  File "factorial.py", line 4, in factorial
    raise ValueError("n must be greater or equal to 0")
ValueError: n must be greater or equal to 0
```

The message indicates that the program `factorial` stopped running because a `ValueError` was raised with a negative *n*. The system then shows you a backward trace of how it got there. The bad value appeared in line 4 of the `factorial` function of the *factorial* program. It got there because of a call in line 11 of the `main` of the *factorial* program. This kind of information is very helpful when you want to find the bugs in your programs.

Raising exceptions is an example of *defensive programming*. We don't intend to have bugs in the programs we write, but we're only human, so we want to build in mechanisms that will give us feedback when we make mistakes. Writing code that will test the values passed to functions and raise a `ValueError` when a value is not appropriate is a great way to provide that feedback.

Revisiting Return Values

In Chapter 3 we looked at some examples of simple calculating functions that return a value, as in this function for finding the sum of the first *n* integers:

```
# Returns the sum of the integers 1 through n.
def sum_of(n):
    return (n + 1) * n // 2
```

Now that you know how to write `if/else` statements, we can look at some more interesting examples involving return values. For example, earlier in this book you saw the `max` function that returns the larger of two values.

Let's write a function similar to the `max` function called `abs_max` that takes two numbers as parameters and returns the one with the larger absolute value. Its header will look like this:

```
# Returns the integer that has the larger absolute
# value between x and y.
def abs_max(x, y):
    ...
```

We want to return either x or y, depending on which absolute value is larger. This is a perfect place to use an `if/else` construct:

```
def abs_max(x, y):
    if abs(x) > abs(y):
        return x
```

Continued on next page

Continued from previous page

```
    else:
        return y
```

This code begins by testing whether x is greater than y. If it is, the computer executes the first branch by returning x. If it is not, the computer executes the else branch by returning y. But what if x and y are equal? The preceding code executes the else branch when the values are equal, but it doesn't actually matter which return statement is executed when x and y are equal.

Remember that when Python executes a return statement, the function stops executing. It's like a command to Python to "get out of this function right now." That means that this function could also be written as follows:

```
def abs_max(x, y):
    if abs(x) > abs(y):
        return x
    return y
```

This version of the code is equivalent in behavior because the statement return x inside the if statement will cause Python to exit the function immediately and Python will not execute the return statement that follows the if. On the other hand, if we don't enter the if statement, we proceed directly to the statement that follows it: return y.

Whether you choose to use the first form or the second in your own programs depends somewhat on personal taste. The if/else construct makes it more clear that the function is choosing between two alternatives, but some people prefer the second alternative because it is shorter.

As another example, let's write a function called dice_game that simulates a dice-rolling game. Our function accepts a parameter indicating the number of times to roll a single six-sided die. We will roll the die up to that many times, printing each rolled value, and accumulating the total of the die values rolled. The function should return the total of all the rolls. If the die rolls a 1, we lose all of our points and the game immediately ends, returning a total of 0.

For example, the call of dice_roll(5) might roll the five die values of 3, 2, 3, 5, 4. If so, the function would return 3 + 2 + 3 + 5 + 4 or 17. On another call, the function might roll the values 4, 5, 1. The instant the 1 is rolled, the function would stop rolling and would return 0. We can describe this function as a cumulative algorithm in pseudocode as follows:

```
def dice_roll(times):
    total = 0.
    repeat 'times' times:
        die = random value from 1 to 6.
        if die is 1: stop.
        otherwise: add die to total.

    if we rolled a 1: return 0.
    otherwise: return total.
```

An important observation about this problem is that if we ever roll a 1, we can stop immediately and not roll the die any more times. To write this code, you have to understand how the `return` statement works in detail. When a `return` statement is executed, Python immediately exits the function. This means that if we have a `return` statement in our loop, the code will break out of the loop and return the value immediately without repeating any more iterations of the loop body.

The code to handle each roll will be the following. In Chapter 3 we saw the `random` module for generating random numbers. Its `randint` function will be useful here to simulate each die roll.

```
die = random.randint(1, 6)
print(die)
if die == 1:
    return 0    # stop immediately
```

Conversely, if we do not roll a 1, we do not want to return immediately. The code should keep going and roll the die more times. So we don't want to include an `else` statement with a `return` inside it. We do, however, want an `else` that adds the die's value to our total if the die roll was not 1. It is often important to recognize when your code should stop early or return early as opposed to when the algorithm should keep going.

The following program contains a complete implementation of the function, along with a `main` function to call it:

```
1   # This program simulates rolling a 6-sided die repeatedly
2   # a given number of times, stopping if a 1 is seen.
3   import random
4
5   # Rolls a 6-sided die the given number of times, returning the
6   # sum of the rolls. If a 1 is seen, stops immediately and returns 0.
7   def dice_roll(times):
8       total = 0
9       for i in range(times):
10          die = random.randint(1, 6)
11          print(die)
12          if die == 1:
13              return 0    # stop immediately
14          else:
15              total += die
16
17      return total    # never rolled a 1
18
19  def main():
20      total = dice_roll(5)
21      print("total is:", total)
22
23  main()
```

Here are outputs from two runs of the program. Notice that if we see a 1, the function stops immediately and returns 0.

```
3
4
3
3
6
total is: 19
5
6
1
total is: 0
```

Reasoning about Paths

The combination of `if/else` and `return` is powerful. It allows you to solve many complex problems in the form of a function that accepts some input and computes a result. But you have to be careful to think about the different paths that exist in the code that you write. At first this process might seem annoying, but when you get the hang of it, you will find that it allows you to simplify your code.

For example, suppose that we want to convert scores on the Scholastic Aptitude Test (SAT) into a rating to be used for college admission. Each of the three components of the SAT ranges from 200 to 800, so the overall total ranges from 600 to 2400. Suppose that a hypothetical college breaks up this range into three subranges with totals below 1200 considered not competitive, scores of at least 1200 but less than 1800 considered competitive, and scores of 1800 to 2400 considered highly competitive.

Let's write a function called `rating` that will take the total SAT score as a parameter and will return a string with the appropriate text.

```
# Returns a string for a rating of an SAT score.
# Not an ideal model to follow.
def rating(total_sat):
    if 600 <= total_sat < 1200:
        return "not competitive"
    elif 1200 <= total_sat < 1800:
        return "competitive"
    elif 1800 <= total_sat <= 2400:
        return "highly competitive"
```

This function has been written in a logical manner with specific tests for each of the three cases, but it isn't ideal.

The function we have written has four paths through it. If the first test succeeds, then the function returns `"not competitive"`. Otherwise, if the second test succeeds, then the function returns `"competitive"`. If both of those tests fail but the third test succeeds, then the function returns `"highly competitive"`. But what if all three tests fail? That case would constitute a fourth path. Since our tests cover all possible cases this fourth path will never be taken. However, it is not good style to include it in your code as it can be confusing to a reader.

Understanding this idea can simplify the code you write. If you think in terms of paths and cases, you can often eliminate unnecessary code. For our function, if we really want to return just one of three different values, then we don't need a third test. We can make the final branch of the nested `if/else` be a simple `else`:

```python
# Returns a string for a rating of an SAT score.
def rating(total_sat):
    if 600 <= total_sat < 1200:
        return "not competitive"
    elif 1200 <= total_sat < 1800:
        return "competitive"
    else:
        # total_sat >= 1800
        return "highly competitive"
```

This version of the function runs and returns the appropriate string for each different case. We were able to eliminate the final test because we know that we want only three paths through the function. Once we have specified two of the paths, then everything else must be part of the third path.

We can carry this idea one step further. We've written a function that runs and computes the right answer, but we can make it even simpler. Consider the first test, for example. Why should we test for the total being greater than or equal to 600? If we expect that it will always be in the range of 600 to 2400, then we can simply test whether the total is less than 1200. Similarly, to test for the highly competitive range, we can simply test whether the score is at least 1800. Of the three ranges, these are the two simplest to test for. So we can simplify this function even further by including tests for the first and third subranges and assume that all other totals are in the middle range:

```python
# Returns a string for a rating of an SAT score.
def rating(total_sat):
    if total_sat < 1200:
        return "not competitive"
    elif total_sat >= 1800:
        return "highly competitive"
    else:
        # 1200 <= total_sat < 1800
        return "competitive"
```

Whenever you write a function like this, you should think about the different cases and figure out which ones are the simplest to test for. This will allow you to avoid writing an explicit test for the most complex case. As in these examples, it is a good idea to include a comment on the final `else` branch to describe that particular case in English.

Before we leave this example, it is worth thinking about what happens when the function is passed an illegal SAT total. If it is passed a total less than 600, then it classifies it as not competitive; and if it is passed a total greater than 2400, it will classify it as highly competitive. Those aren't bad answers for the program to give, but the right thing to do is to document the fact that there is a precondition on the total. In addition, we can add an extra test for this particular case and raise an exception if the precondition is violated. Testing for the illegal values is a case in which the logical `or` is appropriate because illegal values will either be too low or too high (but not both):

```
# Returns a string for a rating of an SAT score.
# pre: 600 <= total_sat <= 2400 (raises ValueError if not)
def rating(total_sat):
    if total_sat < 600 or total_sat > 2400:
        raise ValueError(total_sat)
    elif total_sat < 1200:
        return "not competitive"
    elif total_sat >= 1800:
        return "highly competitive"
    else:
        # 1200 <= total_sat < 1800
        return "competitive"
```

4.4 Strings

Strings are one of the most useful and most commonly used types of objects in Python, so they make a good starting point. Programmers commonly face problems that require them to create, edit, examine, and format text. Collectively, we call these tasks *text processing*. In this section, we'll look in more detail at working with strings.

> **Text Processing**
> Editing and formatting strings of text.

One special property of strings is that there are literal values that represent them (string literals). A string literal is a sequence of characters surrounded by quotation marks or apostrophe marks. We've been using string literals in `print` statements since Chapter 1. What we haven't discussed is that these literal values represent objects of type `str` (instances of the `str` class). We are familiar with code to define an integer variable, that is, a variable of type `int`. The following code defines an integer variable and assigns it the literal value `8`:

```
>>> x = 8
```

In the same way, you can define a string variable, that is, a variable of type `str`. The following code defines a string variable and assigns it a value from the string literal value `"hello"`:

```
>>> s = "hello"
```

You can also write code that involves string expressions with operators. The + operator, when used on two strings, produces the concatenation of those two strings. The * operator, when used on a string and an integer, produces repeated copies of the string. The following code defines two strings that each represent a single word, a third string that represents the concatenation of the two words with a space in between, and a fourth string that is a multiple of another string:

```
>>> # string expressions and operators
>>> s1 = "hello"
>>> s2 = "there"
>>> combined = s1 + " " + s2
>>> combined
'hello there'
>>> repeated = s1 * 3
>>> repeated
'hellohellohello'
```

There are all sorts of operations you might want to perform on a sequence of characters. For example, you might want to know how many characters there are in the string. There is a global function named `len` that returns this information when passed a string as a parameter. The length of a string includes all of its characters, including any spaces and punctuation.

```
>>> # ask for length of a string
>>> s = "hello there"
>>> len(s)
11
```

String Methods

Like the `DrawingPanel` from Chapter 3, strings are objects. This means that they contain data and behavior. The data of a string is its sequence of characters. The behavior of any object is represented by the functions stored inside it that operate on its data. As we discussed in Chapter 3, the functions inside an object are more commonly called methods.

Remember that you call a method of an object by writing your string's variable name, followed by a dot character ., followed by the method name. For example:

```
>>> s = "hello"
>>> s.upper()
'HELLO'
>>> s.count("l")
2
>>> s.endswith("lo")
True
```

Python strings include several useful built-in methods. Table 4.5 lists several of them. You can read a complete list of these methods at:

- https://docs.python.org/3/library/stdtypes.html#string-methods

Table 4.5   Useful String Methods

Method	Description	Example
str.capitalize()	first character capitalized and rest lowercased	"hi".capitalize() returns "Hi"
str.count(text)	number of non-overlapping occurrences of text	"banana".count("an") returns 2
str.endswith(text)	whether the string ends with text	"world".endswith("hi") returns False
str.find(text)	index of first occurrence of text (–1 if not found)	"banana".find("n") returns 2
str.format(args)	perform advanced string formatting operations	"{0} is {1}".format("Bob", 42) returns "Bob is 42"
str.join(list)	the concatenation of the strings with str separating them	"-".join([1, 2, 3]) returns "1-2-3"
len(str)	length of string	len("Hi there!") returns 9
str.lower()	a string with all lowercase letters	"HeLLO".lower() returns "hello"
str.lstrip()	removes leading whitespace	" hello".lstrip() returns "hello"

Continued on next page

Continued from previous page

Method	Description	Example
`str.replace(old, new)`	replaces each old with new	`"seen".replace("e", "o")` returns `"soon"`
`str.rfind(text)`	index of last occurrence of text (−1 if not found)	`"banana".rfind("n")` returns 4
`str.rstrip()`	removes ending whitespace	`" hello ".rstrip()` returns `" hello"`
`str.split(sep)`	list split by sep	`"1:2:3:4".split(":")` returns `["1", "2", "3", "4"]`
`str.splitlines()`	list split by line breaks	`"1\na\nbcd".splitlines()` returns `["1", "a", "bcd"]`
`str.startswith(text)`	whether string begins with text	`"hello".startswith("he")` returns True
`str.strip()`	removes beginning and ending whitespace	`" hello ".strip()` returns `"hello"`
`str.swapcase()`	capitalizes lowercase letters and lowercases uppercase letters	`"HellO".swapcase()` returns `"hELLo"`
`str.title()`	starts each word with uppercase letter and lowercases remaining letters	`"HellO world".title()` returns `"Hello World"`
`str.upper()`	capitalizes all letters	`"hello".upper()` returns `"HELLO"`

Strings in Python are *immutable*, which means that once they are constructed, their values can never be changed.

> **Immutable Object**
>
> An object whose value cannot be changed.

It may seem odd that strings are immutable and yet have functions like `upper` and `lower`. But if you read the descriptions in the table carefully, you'll see that these functions don't actually change a given string; instead they return a new string. Consider the following code:

```
>>> # try (and fail) to convert a string to uppercase
>>> s = "Hello Maria"
>>> s.upper()
'HELLO MARIA'
>>> s
'Hello Maria'
```

You might think that this will turn the string s into its uppercase equivalent, but it doesn't. The second statement in the preceding shell example creates a new string that has the uppercase equivalent of the value of s, but we don't do anything with this new value. In order to turn the string into uppercase, the key is to either store this new string in a different variable or reassign the variable s to point to the new string:

```
>>> # successfully convert a string to uppercase
>>> s = "Hello Maria"
>>> s = s.upper()
>>> s
'HELLO MARIA'
```

Several of the string methods represent logical tests that can be placed into an if/else statement, such as startswith and endswith. For example, you can use startswith to perform a given action only on strings that begin with a certain sequence of characters:

```
>>> # use a string method as a test
>>> name = "Professor Charles Xavier"
>>> if name.startswith("Prof"):
...      print("Welcome, Professor!")
...
Welcome, Professor!
```

The upper and lower functions are particularly helpful when you want to perform string comparisons in which you ignore the case of the letters involved. For example:

```
>>> # compare strings, ignoring case
>>> s1 = "heLlo"
>>> s2 = "HEllO"
>>> s1.lower() == s2.lower()
True
>>> if s1.lower() == s2.lower():
...      print("They are equal!")
...
They are equal!
```

Not all string manipulation is done with the variable name dot syntax shown above. For instance, as was mentioned in the previous section, the len function returns the length of a string. This is a built-in global Python function, not a method inside the string. Therefore it is called by writing len(s) as below:

```
>>> # ask for length of a string
>>> s1 = "hello"
>>> s2 = "how are you?"
>>> len(s1)
5
>>> len(s2)
12
```

Accessing Characters by Index

Python allows you to access individual characters or ranges of characters in a string. Each character is associated with a unique integer called an *index*. You can refer to characters and ranges by their indexes.

> **Index**
>
> An integer used to specify a location in a sequence of values. Python generally uses zero-based indexing (with 0 as the first index value, followed by 1, 2, 3, and so on). It also allows for negative indexes.

Each character of a string object is assigned an index value. These values start with 0 at the beginning of the string and increase. For example, for the variable s1 that refers to the string "hello", the indexes are as shown in Figure 4.8.

It may seem intuitive to consider the letter "h" to be at position 1, but there are advantages to starting with an index of 0. The index can be thought of as an offset; index *i* is the character that is *i* places ahead of the start of the string. It's a convention that was adopted by the designers of the C language and that has been followed by the designers of C++, Java and Python, so it's a convention you'll have to learn to live with.

For another example, for the variable s2 that refers to the string "how are you?", the indexes are as shown in Figure 4.9. Notice that the spaces in this string have positions as well (here, positions 3 and 7). Also notice that the indexes for a given string always range from 0 to one less than the length of the string.

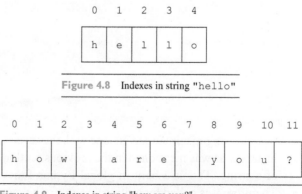

Figure 4.8   Indexes in string "hello"

Figure 4.9   Indexes in string "how are you?"

Using square bracket notation, you can request specific characters of a string. For example:

```
>>> # indexing individual characters of strings
>>> s1 = "hello"
>>> s2 = "how are you?"
>>> s1[1]
'e'
>>> s2[5]
'r'
```

Note that for any string, if you ask for the character at 0, you'll get the first character of the string. If you ask for the character at index `len(str) - 1` you'll get the last character in the string.

Having to use `len(str) - 1` is rather long and clunky. It turns out that there is an easier way to access the last character of a string if we use Python's negative indexes. Every string has a set of negative indexes as well as a set of positive indexes and they can be used interchangeably. Negative indexes always start with the last character of a string as `-1` and decrease as they approach the beginning of the string. Figure 4.10 shows our string `s2` with negative and positive indexes.

Negative indexes make it simpler to do some common string tasks, such as accessing the last character of a string. The last character of a string will always be at index `-1`. The following Python Shell interaction demonstrates negative indexing:

```
>>> # negative indexing on strings
>>> s1 = "hello"
>>> s2 = "how are you?"
>>> s1[-1]
'o'
>>> s1[-5]
'h'
>>> s2[-4]
'y'
>>> s2[-8]
'a'
```

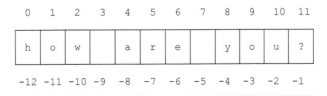

Figure 4.10   Positive and negative string indexes

When you are working with strings, you'll often find it useful to write a `for` loop to handle the different characters of the string. Consider, for example, the following code that prints out the individual characters of `s1` along with their indexes:

```
s1 = "hello"
for i in range(len(s1)):
    print("character", i, "is", s1[i])
```

```
character 0 is h
character 1 is e
character 2 is l
character 3 is l
character 4 is o
```

If you just want to print or examine each letter one at a time, there is a better syntax to traverse a string in Python. Instead of looping over a range of indexes, you can loop directly through the characters of a string. If you do this, your loop variable will represent the current character instead of a number. For example, the below code outputs each letter of a string on its own line:

```
s1 = "hello"
for c in s1:
    print(c)
```

```
h
e
l
l
o
```

Another useful string operation is *slicing*. Slicing allows you to select a substring of a longer string. It uses square bracket notation but the brackets take two integer parameters instead of one, representing a starting and ending index separated by a colon (`:`). The first number is the first character you want and the second is just past the last index that you want. Slicing can be done with positive or negative indexes, as shown in the following interaction:

```
>>> # string slicing
>>> s2 = "how are you?"
>>> s2[0:3]
'how'
>>> s2[8:11]
'you'
>>> s2[-4:-1]
'you'
```

Remember that the second value that you specify is supposed to be one beyond the end of the substring you are forming. So, even though there is a space at position 3 in the original string, it will not be part of what you get from the slicing operation. Instead, you'll get all the characters just before position 3.

Following this rule means that sometimes you could specify a position at which there is no character. For instance, the last character in the string to which s2 refers is at index 11 (the question mark). If you want to get the substring "you?" including the question mark, you could ask for:

```
>>> # slicing at end of string
>>> s2[8:12]
'you?'
```

There is no character at position 12 in s2, but this call asks for characters starting at position 8 that come before position 12, so this actually makes sense.

If you ask for an index outside the length of the string, an empty string will be returned. For example:

```
>>> # slicing out of bounds
>>> s2[16:20]
''
>>> s2[5:100]
're you?'
```

Notice that in the second example above we get all of the string at index 5 and above. Specifying a very large index can allow us to get the string from a specified start point to the end. However, this is a clumsy choice of syntax, and Python has a special syntax designed specifically for this. If you would like to slice from a given index to the end, you can simply leave off the end index. Likewise you can leave off the starting index if you wish to start at the beginning of the string.

```
>>> # slicing with one index omitted
>>> s2[:5]
'how a'
>>> s2[5:]
're you?'
```

You can use strings as parameters to functions. A string parameter is passed using the same syntax as integers and other parameters you have already seen. For example, the following program uses string parameters to eliminate some of the redundancy in a popular children's song:

```
 1  # This program displays the children's song
 2  # "The Wheels on the Bus."
 3
 4  # Displays one verse of the song.
 5  def verse(item, verb, sound):
 6      print("The", item, "on the bus", verb, sound)
 7      print(sound)
 8      print(sound)
 9      print("The", item, "on the bus", verb, sound)
10      print("All through the town")
11      print()
12
13  def main():
14      verse("wheels", "go", "round and round")
15      verse("wipers", "go", "swish swish swish")
16      verse("horn", "goes", "beep beep beep")
17
18  main()
```

```
The wheels on the bus go round and round
round and round
round and round
The wheels on the bus go round and round
All through the town

The wipers on the bus go swish swish swish
swish swish swish
swish swish swish
The wipers on the bus go swish swish swish
All through the town

The horn on the bus goes beep beep beep
beep beep beep
beep beep beep
The horn on the bus goes beep beep beep
All through the town
```

Converting between Letters and Numbers

Individual characters in strings are stored internally as integers. A standard encoding scheme called Unicode determines which integer value represents each character. Since characters are really integers, it is possible to convert between single letter strings and integers. This can sometimes be useful.

The `ord` function accepts a one-character string as a parameter and returns the numeric representation of that character. Conversely, the `chr` function accepts an integer parameter and returns a one-character string that has that integer as its numeric representation. The following shell interaction demonstrates their behavior:

```
>>> # converting characters to/from integer values
>>> ord("a")
97
>>> chr(97)
'a'
```

One example where this conversion is useful is the domain of encryption. *Encryption* involves generating secret codes or *ciphers* that are jumbled versions of messages that are hard to read. Decrypting cipher text reveals the original message. A very simple way to encrypt a string is to add some number to each character's value. We can use the `ord` and `chr` functions to do this:

```
# Shifts each character in s by the given number of letters.
# pre: s consists entirely of lowercase letters from a-z
def encode(s, amount):
    for letter in s:
        num = ord(letter) + amount
        print(chr(num), end="")
    print()
```

Using this simple encoding function, we can pass in a string message and see its encoded form:

```
>>> # encode some messages
>>> encode("hello", 1)
ifmmp
>>> encode("hello", 3)
khoor
```

If you want the original message back, you can pass the negation of the amount of the original shift.

```
>>> # decode a message
>>> encode("khoor", -3)
hello
```

Our encoding function is not very robust because it doesn't behave well with letters near the end of the alphabet. For example, if the message contains a 'z' and you add 3 to that character, you get a character that is outside of the alphabet range. Luckily characters (and their integer representations) can be compared by using relational operators such as < or >=. The following improved version of our encoding function works better for letters at the edges of the alphabet. It now wraps the letters around if needed, which is called a *rotation cipher*.

```
# Prints a rotation cipher of s, shifting each letter in the string
# by the given number of positions in the alphabet.
# pre: s consists entirely of lowercase letters from a-z
# pre: -26 <= amount <= 26
def encode(s, amount):
    for letter in s:
        num = ord(letter) + amount    # shift letter
        if num > ord('z'):                 # wrap around if needed
            num -= 26
        elif num < ord('a'):
            num += 26
        print(chr(num), end="")
    print()
```

Now the function properly handles all letters of the alphabet:

```
>>> # encode/decode with proper wrap-around
>>> encode("zerglings", 1)
afshmjoht
>>> encode("afshmjoht", -1)
zerglings
```

This is not a very strong form of encryption, of course, because anyone who knows our general algorithm can figure out how to decode the message. But it is fun to be able to create jumbled messages, and the weak encoding might be good enough to fool a less savvy observer such as a younger sibling or family member. If you don't know the original message or shifting amount, it can take a while to figure out the original message. For example, if you know that our encoded message is "nzyrclefwletzyd" but don't know the shifting amount, can you figure out the original message and shifting amount that we used? Could you write a program to help you figure it out?

Table 4.6 summarizes the functions shown in this section. You can learn more about the character-to-integer equivalences by searching the Web for Unicode tables.

Table 4.6 Functions to Convert between Characters and Integers

Function	Description
chr(n)	returns a string representing the character with the given numeric value
ord(str)	returns the numeric value equivalent to the given character

Cumulative Text Algorithms

Strings are often used in cumulative algorithms as discussed earlier in this chapter. For example, you might loop over the characters of a string searching for a particular letter. The following function accepts a string (text) and a one-character string (c) and returns the number of times c occurs in text:

```
# Returns the number of occurrences of c in the given string.
def count(text, c):
    found = 0
    for character in text:
        if character == c:
            found += 1
    return found
```

Recall that we have learned about cumulative algorithms in this chapter, such as cumulative sum. The key aspect of a cumulative algorithm is defining a variable before a loop and then incrementally modifying its value in the loop until it has accumulated some useful result. Cumulative algorithms can also be used to build strings, often by growing a result string one character at a time.

You have seen that strings can be concatenated using the + operator. Using this idea, a string can be built using a loop. You start by defining an empty string variable before the loop, and then you concatenate individual characters to that variable in the loop. This is called a *cumulative concatenation*. The following interaction demonstrates repeatedly concatenating the same string to a variable s, achieving an effect similar to the string * multiplication operator:

```
>>> # cumulative concatenation
>>> s = ""
>>> for i in range(4):
...     s += "hello!"
...
>>> s
'hello!hello!hello!hello!'
```

Cumulative concatenation is frequently used with functions, where a result string is accumulated by the function and returned to the caller at the end of the function. For example, the following function accepts a string and returns the same characters in the reverse order. The call of reverse("Tin man") would return "nam niT".

```
# Returns a string that has the same characters as
# the given phrase but in the opposite order.
def reverse(phrase):
    result = ""
    for letter in phrase:
        result = letter + result
return result
```

It is often preferable for a function to return its result rather than directly printing it. This gives more flexibility to the caller in terms of how the result can be used. The following shell interaction tests the reverse function. Notice that the function returns its result, which we can store in a variable, print directly, or manipulate in any way we want.

```
>>> name = "Evelyn"
>>> reverse(name)
'nylevE'
>>> rev = reverse(name)
>>> print("Your name backwards is:", rev)
Your name backwards is nylevE
```

Revisiting the string encoding problem from the previous section, we can modify the encode function to accumulate and return a string rather than directly printing it. This will allow the main function to call encode and print its result in any format it wants. The following is the modified version of the program and its output:

```
1   # This program performs a basic rotation cipher,
2   # shifting each character in a string by a given amount.
3
4   # Returns a rotation cipher of s, shifting each letter in the string
5   # by the given number of positions in the alphabet.
6   # pre: s consists entirely of lowercase letters from a-z
7   # pre: -26 <= amount <= 26
8   def encode(s, amount):
9       result = ""
10      for letter in s:
11          num = ord(letter) + amount    # shift letter
12          if num > ord('z'):            # wrap around if needed
13              num -= 26
```

Continued on next page

Continued from previous page

```
14              elif num < ord('a'):
15                  num += 26
16          result += chr(num)
17      return result
18
19  def main():
20      message = "hello"
21      secret  = encode("hello", 3)
22      print("Your secret message is:", secret)
23
24  main()
```

```
Your secret message is: khoor
```

4.5 Case Study: Basal Metabolic Rate

Basal metabolic rate (BMR) is the number of calories a body burns in 24 hours while at rest. It is a useful biological measure and takes into account height, weight, age and sex. We first introduced BMR and showed the formulas to compute it in Chapter 2. Given an individual's height, weight, age, and sex, we can compute that person's BMR using the following formulas:

- Men: BMR = $4.54545 \times$ (weight in lb) + $15.875 \times$ (height in inches) $- 5 \times$ (age in years) + 5
- Women: BMR = $4.54545 \times$ (weight in lb) + $15.875 \times$ (height in inches) $- 5 \times$ (age in years) $- 161$

In this section, we will write a program that prompts the user for the height, weight, age, and sex of two individuals and reports the overall results for the two people. Here is a sample execution for the program we want to write:

```
This program reads data for two
people and computes their basal
metabolic rate and burn rate.

Enter person 1 information:
height (in inches)? 73.5
weight (in pounds)? 230
age (in years)? 35
sex (male or female)? male
```

Continued on next page

Continued from previous page

```
Enter person 2 information:
height (in inches)? 71
weight (in pounds)? 220.5
age (in years)? 20
sex (male or female)? female


Person 1 basal metabolic rate = 2042.3
high resting burn rate
Person 2 basal metabolic rate = 1868.4
moderate resting burn rate
```

In Chapter 1 we introduced the idea of *iterative enhancement*, in which you develop a complex program in stages. Every professional programmer uses this technique, so it is important to learn to apply it yourself in the programs you write.

In this case, we eventually want our program to explain to the user what it does and compute BMR results for two different people. We also want the program to be well structured. But we don't have to do everything at once. In fact, if we try to do so, we are likely to be overwhelmed by the details. In writing this program, we will go through three different stages:

1. We'll write a program that computes results for just one person, without an introduction. We won't worry about program structure yet.

2. We'll write a complete program that computes results for two people, including an introduction. Again, we won't worry about program structure at this point.

3. We'll put together a well-structured and complete program.

One-Person Unstructured Solution

To compute the BMR for an individual, we will need to know the height, weight, age, and sex of that person. This is a fairly straightforward "prompt and read" task. The only real decision here is with regard to the type we should use for the variables that store height, weight, and age. People often talk about height, weight, and age in whole numbers, but the question to ask is whether or not it makes sense for people to use fractions. Do people ever describe their heights and weights using half-inches and half-pounds? The answer is yes. Do people ever describe their ages in half-years? This is less common, but there's no need to enter a whole number when we can easily also accept partial years. So it makes sense to convert the user input to `float` values:

```
# prompt for one person's information
print("Enter person 1 information:")
height1 = float(input("height (in inches)? "))
weight1 = float(input("weight (in pounds)? "))
age1 = float(input("age (in years)"))
sex1 = input("sex (male or female)? ")
```

Once we have the person's height, weight, age, and sex, we can compute the person's BMR. The following are the formulas for BMR:

- Men: BMR = 4.54545 × (weight in lb) + 15.875 × (height in inches) − 5 × (age in years) + 5
- Women: BMR = 4.54545 × (weight in lb) + 15.875 × (height in inches) − 5 × (age in years) − 161

These formulas can be combined using an if/else fairly easily and translated into Python expressions:

```
# calculate the person's BMR
bmr1 = 4.54545 * weight1 + 15.875 * height1 - 5 * age1
if sex1 == "male":
    bmr1 += 5
else:
    bmr1 -= 161
```

If you look closely at the sample execution, you will see that we want to print blank lines to separate different parts of the user interaction. The introduction ends with a blank line; then there is a blank line after the "prompt and read" portion of the interaction. So, after we add an empty print and put all of these pieces together, our main function looks like this:

```
def main():
    # prompt for one person's information
    print("Enter person 1 information:")
    height1 = float(input("height (in inches)? "))
    weight1 = float(input("weight (in pounds)? ");))
    age1 = float(input("age (in years)? "))
    sex1 = float(input("sex (male or female)? "))
    print()

    # calculate the person's BMR
    bmr1 = 4.54545 * weight1 + 15.875 * height1 - 5 * age1
    if sex1 == "male":
        bmr1 += 5
    else:
        bmr1 -= 161

    ...
```

This program prompts for values and computes the BMR. Now we need to include code to report the results. We could use a print for the BMR:

```
print("Person 1 basal metabolic rate =", bmr1)
```

Table 4.7   **BMR Resting Burn Rate Status**

BMR	Status
below 1200	low
1200 to 2000	moderate
above 2000	high

This would work, but it produces output like the following:

```
Person 1 basal metabolic rate = 2042.2659999999996
```

The long sequence of digits after the decimal point is distracting and implies a level of precision that we simply don't have. It is more appropriate and more appealing to the user to list just a few digits after the decimal point. This is a good place to use the round function. We'll round to a single digit after the decimal point:

```
print("Person 1 basal metabolic rate =", round(bmr1, 1))
```

In the sample execution we also see a report of the relative speed of a person's resting burn rate. Table 4.7 lists the various resting burn rates and their corresponding ranges of BMR values. There are three entries in this table, so we need three different print statements for the three possibilities. We will want to use if or if/else statements to control the four print statements. In this case, we know that we want to print exactly one of the three possibilities. Therefore, it makes most sense to use a nested if/else construct that ends with an else.

The nested if/else construct looks like this:

```
# print person's resting burn rate
if bmr1 < 1200:
    print("low resting burn rate");
elif bmr1 <= 2000:
    print("moderate resting burn rate")
else: # bmr1 > 2000
    print("high resting burn rate")
```

So, putting all this together, we get a complete version of the first program:

```
1  # This program computes a person's basal metabolic rate (BMR).
2  # Initial unstructured version that processes just one person.
3
4  def main():
5      # prompt for one person's information
6      print("Enter person 1 information:")
7      height1 = float(input("height (in inches)? "))
```

Continued on next page

Continued from previous page

```
8          weight1 = float(input("weight (in pounds)? "))
9          age1 = float(input("age (in years)? "))
10         sex1 = input("sex (male or female)? ")
11         print()
12
13         # calculate the person's BMR
14         bmr1 = 4.54545 * weight1 + 15.875 * height1 - 5 * age1
15         if sex1.lower() == "male":
16             bmr1 += 5
17         else:
18             bmr1 -= 161
19         print("Person #1 basal metabolic rate =", round(bmr1, 1))
20
21         # print person's resting burn rate
22         if bmr1 < 1200:
23             print("low resting burn rate");
24         elif bmr1 <= 2000:
25             print("moderate resting burn rate")
26         else: # bmr1 > 2000
27             print("high resting burn rate")
28
29     main()
```

```
Enter person 1 information:
height (in inches)? 73.5
weight (in pounds)? 230
age (in years)? 35
sex (male or female)? male

Person 1 basal metabolic rate = 2042.3
high resting burn rate
```

Two-Person Unstructured Solution

Now that we have a program that computes one person's BMR, let's expand it to handle two different people. Experienced programmers would probably begin by adding structure to the program before trying to make it handle two sets of data, but novice programmers will find it easier to consider the unstructured solution first.

To make this program handle two people, we can copy and paste a lot of the code and make slight modifications. For example, instead of using variables called `height1`, `weight1`, `age1`, `sex1`, and `bmr1`, for the second person we will use variables `height2`, `weight2`, `age2`, `sex2`, and `bmr2`.

We also have to be careful to do each step in the right order. Looking at the sample execution, you'll see that the program prompts for data for both individuals first and then reports results for both. Thus, we can't copy the entire program and simply paste a second copy; we have to rearrange the order of the statements so that all of the prompting happens first and all of the reporting happens later.

We've also decided that when we move to this second stage, we will add code for the introduction. This code should appear at the beginning of the program and should include an empty print to produce a blank line to separate the introduction from the rest of the user interaction.

We now combine these elements into a complete program:

```
1   # This program finds the basal metabolic rate (BMR) for two
2   # individuals.  This version is unstructured and redundant.
3
4   def main():
5       print("This program reads data for two")
6       print("people and computes their body")
7       print("mass index and weight status.")
8       print()
9
10      # prompt for first person's information
11      print("Enter person 1 information:")
12      height1 = float(input("height (in inches)? "))
13      weight1 = float(input("weight (in pounds)? "))
14      age1 = float(input("age (in years)? "))
15      sex1 = input("sex (male or female)? ")
16      print()
17
18      # calculate first person's BMR
19      bmr1 = 4.54545 * weight1 + 15.875 * height1 - 5 * age1
20      if sex1.lower() == "male":
21          bmr1 += 5
22      else:
23          bmr1 -= 161
24
25      # prompt for second person's information
26      print("Enter person 2 information:")
27      height2 = float(input("height (in inches)? "))
28      weight2 = float(input("weight (in pounds)? "))
29      age2 = float(input("age (in years)? "))
30      sex2 = input("sex (male or female)? ")
31      print()
32
```

Continued on next page

Continued from previous page

```
33        # calculate second person's BMR
34        bmr2 = 4.54545 * weight2 + 15.875 * height2 - 5 * age2
35        if sex2.lower() == "male":
36            bmr2 += 5
37        else:
38            bmr2 -= 161
39
40        # report results
41        print("Person 1 basal metabolic rate", round(bmr1, 1))
42        if bmr1 < 1200:
43            print("low resting burn rate");
44        elif bmr1 <= 2000:
45            print("moderate resting burn rate")
46        else: # bmr1 > 2000
47            print("high resting burn rate")
48
49        print("Person 2 basal metabolic rate", round(bmr2, 1))
50        if bmr2 < 1200:
51            print("low resting burn rate");
52        elif bmr2 <= 2000:
53            print("moderate resting burn rate")
54        else: # bmr2 > 2000
55            print("high resting burn rate")
56
57  main()
```

This program works. When we execute it, we get exactly the interaction we wanted. However, the program lacks structure. All of the code appears in `main`, and there is significant redundancy. That shouldn't be a surprise, because we created this version by copying and pasting. Whenever you find yourself using copy and paste, you should wonder whether there isn't a better way to solve the problem. Usually there is.

Two-Person Structured Solution

Let's explore how functions can improve the structure of the program. Looking at the code, you will notice a great deal of redundancy. For example, we have two code segments that look like this:

```
# calculate first person's BMR
bmr1 = 4.54545 * weight1 + 15.875 * height1 - 5 * age1
if sex1.lower() == "male":
    bmr1 += 5
else:
    bmr1 -= 161
```

The only difference between these two code segments is that the first uses variables `height1`, `weight1`, `age1`, `sex1`, and `bmr1`, and the second uses variables `height2`, `weight2`, `age2`, `sex2`, and `bmr2`. When you have a value like this that requires a complex formula to calculate, it is common to write a function that accepts the necessary parameters and returns the calculated value. In this case we'll write a function called `compute_bmr` that does so:

```python
# This function contains the basal metabolic rate formula for
# converting the given height (in inches), weight
# (in pounds), age (in years) and sex (male or female) into a BMR
def compute_bmr(height, weight, age, sex):
    bmr = 4.54545 * weight + 15.875 * height - 5 * age
    if sex.lower() == "male":
        bmr += 5
    else:
        bmr -= 161
    return bmr
```

The code that prompts for each person's information and then initiates the computation of the BMR is also repeated twice. There are two blocks of code that look like the following:

```python
# prompt for first person's information
print("Enter person 1 information:")
height1 = float(input("height (in inches)? "))
weight1 = float(input("weight (in pounds)? "))
age1 = float(input("age (in years)? "))
sex1 = input("sex (male or female)? ")
print()
bmr1 = compute_bmr(height1, weight1, age1, sex1)
```

As with the `compute_bmr` code, the only differences are the person's number and the names of the variables. We can eliminate this redundancy by moving the code into a function that we call twice. So, as a first approximation, we can turn this code into a more generic form as the following function:

```python
# Reads input and calculates BMR for one person.
def read_information(person):
    print("Enter person", person, "information:")
    height = float(input("height (in inches)? "))
    weight = float(input("weight (in pounds)? "))
    age = float(input("age (in years)? "))
    sex = input("sex (male or female)? ")
    print()
    bmr = compute_bmr(height, weight, age, sex)
```

We have to pass the number for the person information prompt from `main` so the function can print the proper output heading. Otherwise we have made all the variables local to this function. From `main` we can call this function twice:

```
read_information(1)
read_information(2)
```

Unfortunately, introducing this change breaks the rest of the code. If we try to run the program, we find that we get error messages in `main` whenever we refer to the variables `bmr1` and `bmr2`. The problem is that the function computes a BMR value that we need later in the program. We can fix this by having the function return the BMR value that it computes:

```
# Reads input and calculates BMR for one person.
# Returns the BMR.
def read_information(person):
    print("Enter person", person, "information:")
    height = float(input("height (in inches)? "))
    weight = float(input("weight (in pounds)? "))
    age = float(input("age (in years)? "))
    sex = input("sex (male or female)? ")
    print()
    bmr = compute_bmr(height, weight, age, sex)
    return bmr
```

We now have to change `main`. We can't just call the function twice the way we would call a function that didn't return anything. Because each call returns a BMR result that the program will need later, for each call we have to store the result coming back from the function in a variable:

```
bmr1 = read_information(1)
bmr2 = read_information(2)
```

Study this change carefully, because this technique can be one of the most challenging for novices to master. When we write the function, we have to make sure that it returns the BMR result. When we write the call, we have to make sure that we store the result in a variable so that we can access it later.

After this modification, the program will run properly. But there is another obvious redundancy in the `main` function: The same nested `if/else` construct appears twice. The only difference between them is that in one case we use the variable `bmr1`, and in the other case we use the variable `bmr2`. The construct is easily generalized with a parameter:

```
# Reports the burn rate for the given BMR value.
def report_status(bmr):
    if bmr < 1200:
        print("low resting burn rate");
    elif bmr <= 2000:
        print("moderate resting burn rate")
    else: # bmr > 2000
        print("high resting burn rate")
```

Using this function, we can replace the code in `main` with two calls:

```
print("Person 1 basal metabolic rate =", round(bmr1, 1))
report_status(bmr1)
print("Person 2 basal metabolic rate =", round(bmr2, 1))
report_status(bmr2)
```

That change takes care of the redundancy in the program, but we can still use functions to improve the program by better indicating structure. It is best to keep the `main` function short if possible, to reflect the overall structure of the program. The problem breaks down into three major phases: introduction, the computation of the BMR, and the reporting of the results. We already have a function for computing the BMR, but we haven't yet introduced functions for the introduction and reporting of results. It is fairly simple to add these functions.

　　Applying all these ideas, we end up with the following version of the program:

```
 1  # This program finds the basal metabolic rate (BMR) for two
 2  # individuals. This variation includes several functions
 3  # other than main.
 4
 5  # Introduces the program to the user.
 6  def give_intro():
 7      print("This program reads data for two")
 8      print("people and computes their basal")
 9      print("metabolic rate and burn rate.")
10      print()
11
12  # Reads input and calculates BMR for one person.
13  # Returns the BMR.
14  def read_information(person):
15      print("Enter person", person, "information:")
16      height = float(input("height (in inches)? "))
17      weight = float(input("weight (in pounds)? "))
18      age = float(input("age (in years)? "))
19      sex = input("sex (male or female)? ")
```

Continued on next page

Continued from previous page

```
20        print()
21        bmr = compute_bmr(height, weight, age, sex)
22        return bmr
23
24  # This function contains the basal metabolic rate formula for
25  # converting the given height (in inches), weight
26  # (in pounds), age (in years) and sex (male or female) into a BMR
27  def compute_bmr(height, weight, age, sex):
28        bmr = 4.54545 * weight + 15.875 * height - 5 * age
29        if sex.lower() == "male":
30            bmr += 5
31        else:
32            bmr -= 161
33        return bmr
34
35  # Reports the overall BMR values and status for two people.
36  def report_results(bmr1, bmr2):
37        print("Person #1 basal metabolic rate =", round(bmr1, 1))
38        report_status(bmr1)
39        print("Person #2 basal metabolic rate =", round(bmr2, 1))
40        report_status(bmr2)
41
42  # Reports the burn rate for the given BMR value.
43  def report_status(bmr):
44        if bmr < 1200:
45            print("low resting burn rate");
46        elif bmr <= 2000:
47            print("moderate resting burn rate")
48        else: # bmr > 2000
49            print("high resting burn rate")
50
51  def main():
52        give_intro()
53        bmr1 = read_information(1)
54        bmr2 = read_information(2)
55        report_results(bmr1, bmr2)
56
57  main()
```

This solution interacts with the user the same way and produces the same results as the unstructured solution, but it has a much nicer structure. The unstructured program is in a sense simpler, but the structured solution is easier to maintain if we want to expand the program or make other modifications. These structural benefits aren't so important in short programs, but they become essential as programs become longer and more complex.

Procedural Design Heuristics

There are often many ways to divide (decompose) a problem into functions, but some sets of functions are better than others. Decomposition is often vague and challenging, especially for larger programs that have complex behavior. But the rewards are worth the effort, because a well-designed program is more understandable and more modular. These features are important when programmers work together or when revisiting a program written earlier to add new behavior or modify existing code. There is no single perfect design, but in this section we will discuss several *heuristics* (guiding principles) for effectively decomposing large programs into functions.

Consider the following alternative poorly structured implementation of a single-person BMR program. We'll use this program as a counterexample, highlighting places where it violates our heuristics and giving reasons that it is worse than the previous complete version of the BMR program.

```
1   # A poorly designed version of the BMR case study program.
2
3   def main():
4       print("This program reads data for one")
5       print("person and computes their basal")
6       print("metabolic rate and burn rate.")
7       print()
8       person()
9
10  # Reads the person's height and weight.
11  def person():
12      print("Enter person 1 information:")
13      height = float(input("height (in inches)? "))
14      weight = float(input("weight (in pounds)? "))
15      get_age_sex(height, weight)
16
17  # Reads the person's age and sex.
18  def get_age_sex(height, weight):
19      age = float(input("age (in years)? "))
20      sex = float(input("sex (male or female)? "))
21      report_status(height, weight, age, sex)
22
23  # Calculates person's BMR and reports their burn rate.
24  def report_status(height, weight, age, sex):
25      bmr = 4.54545 * weight + 15.875 * height - 5 * age
26      if sex.lower() == "male":
27          bmr += 5
```

Continued on next page

Continued from previous page

```
28      else:
29          bmr -= 161
30      print("Person 1 basal metabolic rate", round(bmr, 1))
31      if bmr < 1200:
32          print("low resting burn rate");
33      elif bmr <= 2000:
34          print("moderate resting burn rate")
35      else: # bmr > 2000
36          print("high resting burn rate")
```

The functions of a program are like workers in a company. The author of a program acts like the director of a company, deciding what employee positions to create, how to group employees together into working units, which work to task to which group, and how groups will interact. Figure 4.11 shows a hypothetical company where the director divides the work into three major departments, two of which are overseen by middle managers.

A good structure gives each group clear tasks to complete, avoids giving any particular person or group too much work, and provides a balance between workers and management. These guidelines lead to the first of our procedural design heuristics.

1. **Each function should have a coherent set of responsibilities.** In our analogy to a company, each group of employees must have a clear idea of what work it is to perform. If any of the groups does not have clear responsibilities, it's difficult for the company director to keep track of who is working on what task. When a new job comes in, two departments might both try to claim it, or a job might go unclaimed by any department.

   The analogous concept in programming is that each function should have a clear purpose and set of responsibilities. This characteristic of computer programs is called *cohesion*.

> **Cohesion**
>
> A desirable quality in which the responsibilities of a function or process are closely related to each other.

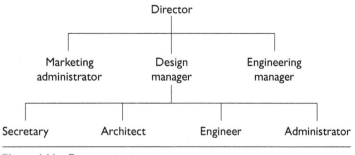

Figure 4.11   Company structure

A good rule of thumb is that you should be able to summarize each of your functions in a single sentence such as "The purpose of this function is to. . ." Writing a sentence like this is a good way to develop a comment for a function's header. It's a bad sign when you have trouble describing the function in a single sentence or when the sentence is long and uses the word "and" several times. Those indications can mean that the function is too large, too small, or does not perform a cohesive set of tasks.

The functions of the `bad_bmr` example have poor cohesion. The `person` function's purpose is vague, and `get_age_sex` is probably too trivial to be its own function. The `report_status` function would be more readable if the computation of the BMR were its own function, since the formula is complex.

A subtler application of this first heuristic is that not every function must produce output. Sometimes a function is more reusable if it simply computes a complex result and returns it rather than printing the result that was computed. This format leaves the caller free to choose whether to print the result or to use it to perform further computations. In the `bad_bmr` program, the `report_status` function both computes and prints the user's BMR. The program would be more flexible if it had a function to simply compute and return the BMR value, such as `compute_bmr` in our last structured version of the code. Such a function might seem trivial because its body is so short, but it has a clear, cohesive purpose: capturing a complex expression that is used several times in the program.

2. **No one function should do too large a share of the overall task.** One subdivision of a company cannot be expected to design and build the entire product line for the year. This system would overwork that subdivision and would leave the other divisions without enough work to do. It would also make it difficult for the subdivisions to communicate effectively, since so much important information and responsibility would be concentrated among so few people.

Similarly, one function should not be expected to comprise the bulk of a program. This principle follows naturally from our first heuristic regarding cohesion, because a function that does too much cannot be cohesive. We sometimes refer to functions like these as "do-everything" functions because they do nearly everything involved in solving the problem. You may have written a do-everything function if one of your functions is much longer than the others, hoards most of the variables and data, or contains the majority of the logic and loops.

In the `bad_bmr` program, the `person` function is an example of a do-everything function. This fact may seem surprising, since the function is not very many lines long. But a single call to `person` leads to several other calls that collectively end up doing all of the work for the program.

3. **Coupling and dependencies between functions should be minimized.** A company is more productive if each of its subdivisions can largely operate independently when completing small work tasks. Subdivisions of the company do need to communicate and depend on each other, but such communication comes

at a cost. Interdepartmental interactions are often minimized and kept to meetings at specific times and places.

When we are programming, we try to avoid functions that have tight *coupling*.

> **Coupling**
>
> An undesirable state in which two functions or processes rigidly depend on each other.

Functions are coupled if one cannot easily be called without the other. One way to determine how tightly coupled two functions are is to look at the set of parameters one passes to the other. A function should accept a parameter only if that piece of data needs to be provided from outside and only if that data is necessary to complete the function's task. In other words, if a piece of data could be computed or gathered inside the function, or if the data isn't used by the function, it should not be defined as a parameter to the function.

An important way to reduce coupling between functions is to use `return` statements to send information back to the caller. A function should return a result value if it computes something that may be useful to later parts of the program. Because it is desirable for functions to be cohesive and self-contained, it is often better for the program to return a result than to call further functions and pass the result as a parameter to them.

None of the functions in the `bad_bmr` program returns a value. Each function passes parameters to the next functions, but none of them returns the value. This is a lost opportunity because several values (such as the user's height, weight, age, sex, or BMR) would be better handled as return values.

4. **The `main` function should be a concise summary of the overall program.**
   The top person in each major group or department of our hypothetical company reports to the group's director. If you look at the groups that are directly connected to the director at the top level of the company diagram, you can see a summary of the overall work: design, engineering, and marketing. This structure helps the director stay aware of what each group is doing. Looking at the top-level structure can also help the employees get a quick overview of the company's goals.

   A program's `main` function is like the director in that it begins the overall task and executes the various subtasks. A `main` function should read as a summary of the overall program's behavior. Programmers can understand each other's code by looking at `main` to get a sense of what the program is doing as a whole.

   A common mistake that prevents `main` from being a good program summary is the inclusion of a do-everything function. When the `main` function calls it, the do-everything function proceeds to do most or all of the real work.

   Another mistake is setting up a program in such a way that it suffers from *chaining*. Chaining is when many functions call each other in a row without properly returning flow of control of the program.

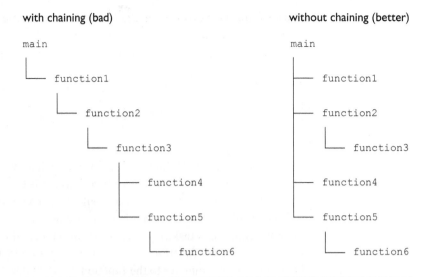

Figure 4.12   Sample code with chaining (left) and without chaining (right)

Chaining

An undesirable design in which a "chain" of several functions call each other without returning the overall flow of control to `main`.

A program suffers from chaining if the end of each function simply calls the next function. Chaining often occurs when a new programmer does not fully understand returns and tries to avoid using them by passing more and more parameters down to the rest of the program. Figure 4.12 shows a hypothetical program with two designs. The flow of calls in a badly chained program might look like the figure.

The `bad_bmr` program suffers heavily from chaining. Each function does a small amount of work and then calls the next function, passing more and more parameters down the chain. The `main` function calls `person`, which calls `get_age_sex`, which calls `report_status`. Never does the flow of execution return to `main` in the middle of the computation. So when you read `main`, you don't get a very clear idea of what computations will be made.

One function should not call another simply as a way of moving on to the next task. A more desirable flow of control is to let `main` manage the overall execution of tasks in the program, as shown in the structured BMR program and on the right side of Figure 4.12. This guideline doesn't mean that it is always bad for one function to call another function; it is okay for one function to call another when the second is a subtask within the overall task of the first, such as in our well-structured BMR program when the `report_results` function calls `report_status`.

5. Data should be "owned" at the lowest level possible. Decisions in a company should be made at the lowest possible level in the organizational hierarchy. For example, a low-level administrator can decide how to perform his or her own work without needing to constantly consult a manager for approval. But the administrator does not have enough information or expertise to design the entire product line; this design task goes to a higher authority such as the manager. The key principle is that each work task should be given to the lowest person in the hierarchy who can correctly handle it.

This principle has two applications in computer programs. The first is that the `main` function should avoid performing low-level tasks as much as possible. For example, in an interactive program `main` should not read the majority of the user input or contain lots of `print` statements.

The second application is that variables should be defined and initialized in the narrowest possible scope. A poor design is for `main` (or another high-level function) to read all of the input, perform heavy computations, and then pass the resulting data as parameters to the various low-level functions. A better design uses low-level functions to read and process the data, and return data to `main` only if they are needed by a later subtask in the program.

It is a sign of poor data ownership when the same parameter must be passed down several function calls, such as the `height` variable in the `bad_bmr` program. If you are passing the same parameter down several levels of calls, perhaps that piece of data should instead be read and initialized by one of the lower-level functions.

Chapter Summary

- An `if` statement lets you write code that will execute only if a certain condition is met. An `if`/`else` statement lets you execute one piece of code if a condition is met, and another if the condition is not met. Conditions are Boolean expressions (type `bool`) and can be written using relational operators such as <, >= , and !=. You can test multiple conditions using the `and` and `or` operators.

- You can nest `if`/`else` statements to test a series of conditions and execute the appropriate block of code on the basis of whichever condition is true.

- Common code that appears in every branch of an `if`/`else` statement should be factored out so that it is not replicated multiple times in the code.

- A string (type `str`) holds a sequence of characters. The characters have indexes, starting with 0 for the first character.

- Cumulative algorithms compute values incrementally. A cumulative sum loop defines a sum variable and incrementally adds to that variable's value inside the loop.

- Since the `float` type does not store all values exactly, small roundoff errors can occur when the computer performs calculations on real numbers. Avoid these errors by providing a small amount of tolerance in your code for values near the values that you expect.

- You can raise exceptions (generate errors) in your own code. This technique can be useful if your code ever reaches an unrecoverable error condition, such as the passing of an invalid parameter value to a function.

Self-Check Problems

Section 4.1: `if/else` **Statements**

1. Translate each of the following English statements into logical tests that could be used in an `if/else` statement. Write the appropriate `if` statement with your logical test. Assume that three integer variables, x, y, and z, have been declared.

   a. z is odd.

   b. z is not greater than y's square root.

   c. y is positive.

   d. Either x or y is even, and the other is odd.

   e. y is a multiple of z.

   f. z is not zero.

   g. y is greater in magnitude than z.

   h. x and z are of opposite signs.

   i. y is a nonnegative one-digit number.

   j. z is nonnegative.

   k. x is even.

   l. x is closer in value to y than z is.

2. Given the following variables:

   ```
   x = 4
   y = -3
   z = 4
   ```

   What are the results of the following relational expressions?

   a. `x == 4`

   b. `x == y`

   c. `x == z`

   d. `y == z`

   e. `x + y > 0`

   f. `x - z != 0`

   g. `y * y <= z`

   h. `y // y == 1`

   i. `x * (y + 2) > y - (y + z) * 2`

3. The following program contains three mistakes! What are they?

   ```
   def main():
       a = 7
       b = 42
       minimum(a, b)
       if smaller = a
           print("a is the smallest!")
   ```

Continued on next page

Continued from previous page

```
def minimum(a, b):
    smaller = 0
    if a < b:
        smaller = a
    else a => b:
        smaller = b
    return smaller
```

4. Consider the following function:

```
def if_else_mystery_1(x, y):
    z = 4
        z = x + 1
    else:
        z = z + 9
    if z <= y:
        y += 1
    print(z, y)
```

What output is produced for each of the following calls?

a. `if_else_mystery_1(3, 20)`
b. `if_else_mystery_1(4, 5)`
c. `if_else_mystery_1(5, 5)`
d. `if_else_mystery_1(6, 10)`

5. Consider the following function:

```
def if_else_mystery_2(a, b):
    if a * 2 < b:
        a = a * 3
    elif a > b:
        b = b + 3
    if b < a:
        b += 1
    else:
        a -= 1
    print(a, b)
```

What output is produced for each of the following calls?

a. `if_else_mystery_2(10, 2)`
b. `if_else_mystery_2(3, 8)`
c. `if_else_mystery_2(4, 4)`
d. `if_else_mystery_2(10, 30)`

6. Write Python code to read an integer from the user; then print `even` if that number is an even number or `odd` otherwise.

7. The following code contains a logic error. Examine the code and describe a case in which the code would print something that is untrue about the number that was entered. Explain why. Then correct the logic error in the code.

```
number = int(input("Type a number: "))
if number % 2 == 0:
    if number % 3 == 0:
        print("Divisible by 6.")
    else:
        print("Odd.")
```

8. Factor out redundant code from the following example by moving it out of the `if/else` statement, preserving the same output.

```
if x < 30:
    a = 2
    x += 1
    print("Python is awesome!", x)
else:
    a = 2
    print("Python is awesome!", x)
```

9. The following code is poorly structured. Rewrite it so that it has a better structure and avoids redundancy. To simplify things, you may assume that the user always types 1 or 2. (How would the code need to be modified to handle any number that the user might type?)

```
sum = 1000
times = int(input("Is your money multiplied 1 or 2 times? "))

if times == 1:
    donation = int(input("And how much are you contributing? "))
    sum = sum + donation
    count1 += 1
    total = total + donation

if times == 2:
    donation = int(input("And how much are you contributing? "))
    sum = sum + 2 * donation
    count2 += 1
    total = total + donation
```

10. Write a piece of code that reads a shorthand text description of a color and prints the longer equivalent. Acceptable color names are B for Blue, G for Green, and R for Red. If the user types something other than B, G, or R, print an error message. Make your program case-insensitive so that the user can type an uppercase or lowercase letter. Here are some example executions:

```
What color do you want? B
You have chosen Blue.

What color do you want? g
You have chosen Green.

What color do you want? Bork
Unknown color: Bork
```

Section 4.2: Cumulative Algorithms

11. What is wrong with the following code, which attempts to add all numbers from 1 to a given maximum? Describe how to fix the code.

```
def sum_to(n):
    for i in range(1, n + 1):
        sum = 0
        sum += i
    return sum
```

12. What is wrong with the following code, which attempts to return the number of factors of a given integer n? Describe how to fix the code.

```
def count_factors(n):
    for i in range(1, n + 1):
        if n % i == 0:    # a factor
            return i
```

13. The following expression should equal 6.8, but in Python it does not. Why not? What can be done to deal with such issues?

```
0.2 + 1.2 + 2.2 + 3.2
```

14. The following code was intended to print a message, but it actually produces no output. Describe how to fix the code to print the expected message.

```
gpa = 3.2
if gpa * 3 == 9.6:
    print("You earned enough credits.")
```

Section 4.3: Functions with Conditional Execution

15. Consider a function `print_triangle_type` that accepts three integer parameters representing the lengths of the sides of a triangle and prints the type of triangle that these sides form. The three types are equilateral, isosceles, and scalene. An equilateral triangle has three sides of the same length, an isosceles triangle has two sides that are the same length, and a scalene triangle has three sides of different lengths. However, certain integer values (or combinations of values) would be illegal and could not represent the sides of an actual triangle. What are these values? How would you describe the precondition(s) of the `print_triangle_type` function?

16. Consider a function `get_grade` that accepts an integer representing a student's grade percentage in a course and returns that student's numerical course grade. The grade can be between 0.0 (failing) and 4.0 (perfect). What are the preconditions of such a function?

17. The following function attempts to return the median (middle) of three integer values, but it contains logic errors. In what cases does the function return an incorrect result? How can the code be fixed?

```
def median_of_3(n1, n2, n3):
    if n1 < n2:
        if n2 < n3:
            return n2
        else:
            return n3
    else:
        if n1 < n3:
            return n1
        else:
            return n3
```

18. Consider the following Python function, which is written incorrectly. Under what cases will the function print the correct answer, and when will it print an incorrect answer? What should be changed to fix the code? Can you think of a way to write the code correctly without any `if`/`else` statements?

```
# This function should return how many of its three
# parameters are odd numbers.
def print_num_odd(n1, n2, n3):
    count = 0
    if n1 % 2 != 0:
        count += 1
    elif n2 % 2 != 0:
        count += 1
    elif n3 % 2 != 0:
        count += 1
    print(count, "of the 3 numbers are odd.")
```

Section 4.4: Strings

19. What output is produced by the following program?

```
def print_range(start_letter, end_letter):
    for i in range(ord(end_letter) - ord(start_letter) + 1):
        letter = chr(ord(start_letter) + i)
        print(letter, end="")
    print()


def main():
    print_range("e", "g")
    print_range("n", "s")
    print_range("z", "a")
    print_range("q", "r")
main()
```

20. Write an if statement that tests to see whether a string begins with an uppercase letter.

21. Consider a string stored in a variable called name that stores a person's first and last name (e.g., "Marla Singer"). Write the expression that would produce the last name followed by the first initial (e.g., "Singer, M.").

22. Write code to examine a string and determine how many of its letters come from the second half of the alphabet (that is, have values of "n" or subsequent letters). Compare case-insensitively, such that values of "N" through "Z" also count. You may assume that every character in the string is a letter.

Exercises

1. Write a function called fraction_sum that accepts an integer parameter n and returns the sum of the first n terms of the sequence:

$$\sum_{i=1}^{n} \frac{1}{i}$$

In other words, the function should generate the following sequence. You may assume that the parameter n is nonnegative.

$$1 + (1/2) + (1/3) + (1/4) + (1/5) + \ldots$$

2. Write a function called repl that accepts a string and a number of repetitions as parameters and returns the string concatenated that many times. For example, the call repl("hello", 3) should return "hellohellohello". If the number of repetitions is zero or less, the function should return an empty string. Do not use the string * operator in your solution; use a cumulative algorithm.

3. Write a function called `days_in_month` that accepts a month (an integer between 1 and 12) as a parameter and returns the number of days in that month in this year. For example, the call `days_in_month(9)` would return 30 because September has 30 days. Assume that the code is not being run during a leap year (that February always has 28 days). The following are the number of days in each month:

#	1	2	3	4	5	6	7	8	9	10	11	12
month	Jan	Feb	Mar	Apr	May	Jun	Jul	Aug	Sep	Oct	Nov	Dec
days	31	28	31	30	31	30	31	31	30	31	30	31

4. Write a function called `print_range` that accepts two integers as parameters and prints the sequence of numbers between the two parameters, enclosed in square brackets. Print an increasing sequence if the first parameter is smaller than the second; otherwise, print a decreasing sequence. If the two numbers are the same, that number should be printed between square brackets. Here are some sample calls to `print_range`:

```
print_range(2, 7)
print_range(19, 11)
print_range(5, 5)
```

The output produced from these calls should be the following sequences of numbers:

```
[2, 3, 4, 5, 6, 7]
[19, 18, 17, 16, 15, 14, 13, 12, 11]
[5]
```

5. Write a function called `xo` that accepts an integer `size` as a parameter and prints a square of `size` by `size` characters, where all characters are `"o"` except that an "x" pattern of `"x"` characters has been drawn from the corners of the square. On the first line, the first and last characters are `"x"`; on the second line, the second and second-from-last characters are `"x"`; and so on. For example, the calls of `xo(5)` and `xo(6)` should produce the following outputs, respectively:

```
xooox
oxoxo
ooxoo
oxoxo
xooox

xooorx
oxooxo
ooxxoo
ooxxoo
oxooxo
xoooox
```

6. Write a function called `smallest_largest` that asks the user to enter numbers, then prints the smallest and largest of all the numbers supplied by the user. You may assume that the user enters a valid number greater than 0 for the number of numbers to read. Here is a sample execution:

```
How many numbers do you want to enter? 4
Number 1: 5
Number 2: 11
Number 3: -2
Number 4: 3
Smallest = -2
Largest = 11
```

7. Write a function called `even_sum_max`. The function should prompt the user for a number of integers, then prompt for an integer that many times. Once the user has entered all the integers, the function should print the sum of all the even numbers the user typed, along with the largest even number typed. You may assume that the user will type at least one nonnegative even integer. Here is an example dialogue:

```
how many integers? 4
next integer? 2
next integer? 9
next integer? 18
next integer? 4
even sum = 24
even max = 18
```

8. Write a function called `longest_name` that accepts an integer n as a parameter and prompts for n names, then prints the longest name (the name that contains the most characters) in the format shown below, which might result from a call of `longest_name(4)`:

```
name #1? Roy
name #2? DANE
name #3? sTeFaNiE
name #4? Mariana
Stefanie's name is longest
```

9. Write a function called `average` that accepts two integers as parameters and returns the average of the two integers.

10. Write a function called `print_palindrome` that prompts the user to enter one or more words and prints whether the entered string is a palindrome (i.e., reads the same forwards as it does backwards, like "abba" or "racecar"). For an added challenge, make the code case-insensitive, so that words like "Abba" and "Madam" will be considered palindromes.

11. Write a function called `swap_pairs` that accepts a string as a parameter and returns that string with each pair of adjacent letters reversed. If the string has an odd number of letters, the last letter is unchanged. For example, the call `swap_pairs("example")` should return `"xemalpe"` and the call `swap_pairs("hello there")` should return `"ehll ohtree"`.

12. Write a function called `word_count` that accepts a string as its parameter and returns the number of words in the string. A word is a sequence of one or more non-space characters (any character other than " "). For example, the call `word_count("hello")` should return 1, the call `word_count("how are you?")` should return 3, the call `word_count("   this    string    has    wide    spaces    ")` should return 5, and the call `wordCount("  ")` should return 0.

Programming Projects

1. Write a program that prompts for a number and displays it in Roman numerals.

2. Write a program that prompts for a date (month, day, year) and reports the day of the week for that date. It might be helpful to know that January 1, 1601 was a Monday.

3. Write a program that compares two college applicants. The program should prompt for each student's GPA, SAT, and ACT exam scores and report which candidate is more qualified on the basis of these scores.

4. Write a program that prompts for two people's birthdays (month and day), along with today's month and day. The program should figure out how many days remain until each user's birthday and which birthday is sooner. Hint: It is much easier to solve this problem if you convert each date into an "absolute day" of year, from 1 through 365.

5. Write a program that computes a student's grade in a course. The course grade has three components: homework assignments, a midterm exam, and a final exam. The program should prompt the user for all information necessary to compute the grade, such as the number of homework assignments, the points earned and points possible for each assignment, the midterm and final exam scores, and whether each exam was curved (and, if so, by how much). Consider writing a variation of this program that reports what final exam score the student needs to get a certain course grade.

6. A useful technique for catching typing errors is to use a check digit. For example, suppose that a school assigns a six-digit number to each student. A seventh digit can be determined from the other digits with the use of the following formula:

$$\text{7th digit} = (1 \times (\text{1st digit}) + 2 \times (\text{2nd digit}) + \ldots + 6 \times (\text{6th digit}))\%10$$

When a user types in a student number, the user types all seven digits. If the number is typed incorrectly, the check digit will fail to match in 90% of the cases. Write an interactive program that prompts for a six-digit student number and reports the check digit for that number, using the preceding formula.

## Chapter 5

Program Logic and Indefinite Loops

Introduction

This chapter begins by examining a new construct called a `while` loop that allows you to loop an indefinite number of times. The `while` loop will allow you to solve a new class of programming problems in which you don't know in advance how many times you want a loop to execute. For example, game-playing programs often involve `while` loops because it is not possible to know beforehand how the user will play the game. We will also explore another class of algorithms known as fencepost algorithms that occur often in loop-programming tasks.

The chapter then discusses Boolean logic using the fourth type that we are going to examine in detail, `bool`. The `bool` type is used to store logical (true/false) information. Once you understand the details of the `bool` type, you will be able to write complex loops involving multiple tests. We'll also briefly examine the important topic of handling user errors.

The chapter concludes with a discussion of assertions. Using assertions, you can reason about the formal properties of programs (what is true at different points in program execution).

5.1 The while Loop

The for loops we have been writing since Chapter 2 are fairly simple loops that execute a predictable number of times. Recall that we call them *definite* loops because we know before the loops begin executing exactly how many times they will execute. Now we want to turn our attention to *indefinite loops*, which execute an unknown number of times. Indefinite loops come up often in interactive programs. For example, you don't know in advance how many times a user might want to play a game, and you won't know before you look at a file exactly how much data it stores.

> Indefinite loop
>
> One that executes an unknown number of times.

The while loop is Python's indefinite loop statement. It has the following syntax:

```
while test:
    statement
    statement
    ...
    statement
```

Syntax template: while loop

Figure 5.1 indicates the flow of control of the while loop. The loop performs its test and, if the test evaluates to True, executes the controlled statements. It repeatedly tests

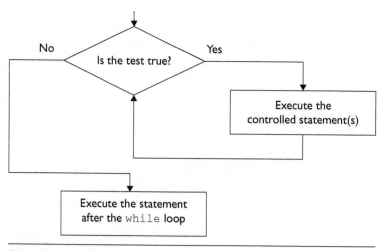

Figure 5.1   Flow of while loop

and executes if the test evaluates to True. Only when the test evaluates to False does the loop terminate.

As Figure 5.1 indicates, the while loop performs its test at the top of the loop, before the body of the loop is executed. A while loop will not execute its controlled statements if its test evaluates to False the first time it is evaluated.

Here is an example of a while loop:

```
# while loop to repeatedly double an integer
number = 1
while number <= 200:
    number *= 2
```

Recall that the *= operator multiplies a variable by a certain amount (in this case, 2). Thus, this loop initializes an integer variable called number to 1 and then doubles it while it is less than or equal to 200. On the surface, this operation is similar to using an if statement:

```
# if statement that doubles an integer a single time
number = 1
if number <= 200:
    number *= 2
```

The difference between the two forms is that the while loop executes multiple times, looping until the test evaluates to False. The if statement executes the doubling statement only once, leaving number equal to 2. The while loop executes the doubling statement repeatedly, with number taking on the values 1, 2, 4, 8, 16, 32, 64, 128, and 256. The loop doesn't stop executing until the test evaluates to False. It executes the assignment statement eight times and terminates when number is set to the value 256 (the first power of 2 that is greater than 200).

Here is a while loop containing two statements:

```
# while loop with two controlled statements;
# prints "Hi there" max times
number = 0
while number < max:
    print("Hi there")
    number += 1
```

This while loop is the same as the following for loop:

```
# equivalent for loop
for number in range(max):
    print("Hi there")
```

A Loop to Find the Smallest Divisor

Suppose you want to find the smallest divisor of an integer, other than 1. Table 5.1 gives examples of what you are looking for. A `while` loop works better than a `for` loop for this situation because you don't know exactly how many times you'll need to repeat before you find the answer.

Here is a pseudocode description of how you might find this value. You start `divisor` at 2 rather than 1 because you are looking for the first divisor greater than 1.

```
Start divisor at 2.
While the current value of divisor does not work:
    Increase divisor.
```

To refine this pseudocode, you must be more explicit about what makes a divisor work. A divisor of a number has no remainder when the number is divided by that divisor. You can rewrite this rule as the following pseudocode:

```
Start divisor at 2.
While the remainder of number/divisor is not 0:
    Increase divisor.
```

To check remainders we can use the mod operator, which gives the remainder for integer division. The following `while` loop performs the task:

```
# find the first divisor other than 1
divisor = 2
while number % divisor != 0:
    divisor += 1
```

One problem you will undoubtedly encounter when you write `while` loops is the infamous *infinite loop*. Consider the following code:

```
# an infinite loop
number = 1
while number > 0:
    number += 1
```

Table 5.1   Examples of Factors

Number	Factors	Smallest Divisor
10	2 * 5	2
15	3 * 5	3
25	5 * 5	5
31	31	31
77	7 * 11	7
105	3 * 5 * 7	3

Because number begins as a positive value and the loop makes it larger, this loop will continue indefinitely. You must be careful when you formulate your `while` loops to avoid situations in which a piece of code will never finish executing. Every time you write a `while` loop, you should consider when and how it will finish executing.

Common Programming Error

Infinite Loop

It is relatively easy to write a `while` loop that never terminates. One reason it's so easy to make this mistake is that a `while` loop doesn't have an update step implicit in its header like a `for` loop does. It's crucial for the programmer to include a correct update step because this step is needed to eventually cause the loop's test to fail.

Consider the following code, which is intended to prompt the user for a number and repeatedly print that number divided in half until 0 is reached. This first attempt doesn't run:

```
while number > 0:
    number = int(input("Type a number: "))
    print(number // 2)
```

The problem with the preceding code is that the variable `number` needs to be in scope during the loop's test, so it cannot be defined inside the loop. An incorrect attempt to fix this error would be to cut and paste the line initializing `number` outside the loop:

```
number = int(input("Type a number: "))    # moved out of loop
while number > 0:
    print(number // 2)
```

This version of the code has an infinite loop; if the loop is entered, it will never be exited. This problem arises because there is no update inside the `while` loop's body to change the value of `number`. If `number` is greater than 0, the loop will keep printing its value and checking the loop test, and the test will evaluate to `True` every time.

The following version of the code solves the infinite loop problem. The loop contains an update step on each pass that divides the integer in half and stores its new value. If the integer hasn't reached 0, the loop repeats:

```
# this code behaves correctly
number = int(input("Type a number: "))    # moved out of loop
while number > 0:
    number = number // 2    # update step: divide in half
    print(number)
```

Continued on next page

> *Continued from previous page*
>
> The key idea is that every `while` loop's body should contain code to update the terms that are tested in the loop test. If the `while` loop test examines a variable's value, the loop body should potentially reassign a meaningful new value to that variable.

Loop Priming

Let's look at a simple program that prints random numbers between 1 and 10 until a particular number comes up. Recall that we explored the `random` library for generating pseudorandom numbers in Chapter 3. We'll use the `random.randint` function for generating numbers in this case.

Our loop should look something like the following pseudocode (where `number` is the value the user has asked us to generate):

```
number = ask user to type a number from 1 - 10.
while result != number:
    result = random number from 1 - 10.
    print result.
```

The preceding pseudocode has the right approach, but if translated directly to Python, the interpreter won't accept it. The code generates an error message that the variable `result` is not defined. This is an example of a loop that needs *priming*.

> **Priming a Loop**
>
> Initializing variables before a loop to "prime the pump" and guarantee that the loop is entered.

The variable `result` needs to be defined before the loop begins, since `result` is part of the loop test. We want to set `result` to something that will cause the loop to be entered, but the exact value we pick isn't important as long as it gets us into the loop. We do want to be careful not to set it to a value the user wants us to generate. We are dealing with values between 1 and 10 in this program, so we could set `result` to a value such as 0 that is clearly outside this range of numbers. We sometimes refer to this as a "dummy" value because we don't actually process it. The following is a correct variable definition and loop heading:

```
# while loop with priming
result = 0
while result != number:
    ...
```

The following is the complete program solution. We include some code to prompt for the desired value and to count the number of repetitions needed until we randomly pick the user's desired number.

```
1   # Prompts the user for a number and then picks random numbers
2   # until the user's number is picked. Outputs the number of times
3   # it picked a number.
4
5   import random
6
7   def main():
8       print("This program picks numbers from 1 to 10")
9       print("until a particular number comes up.")
10      print()
11
12      number = int(input("Pick a number between 1 and 10? "))
13
14      result = 0    # priming; set to 0 to make sure we enter the loop
15      count = 0
16      while result != number:
17          result = random.randint(1, 10)
18          print("next number = ", result)
19          count += 1
20
21      print("Your number came up after", count, "times")
22
23  main()
```

Depending on the sequence of numbers returned by random.randint, the program might end up picking the given number quickly, as in the following sample execution:

```
This program picks numbers from 1 to 10
until a particular number comes up.

Pick a number between 1 and 10? 2
next number = 7
next number = 8
next number = 2
Your number came up after 3 times
```

It's also possible that the program will take a while to pick the number, as in the following sample execution:

```
This program picks numbers from 1 to 10
until a particular number comes up.

Pick a number between 1 and 10? 10
next number = 9
next number = 7
next number = 7
next number = 5
next number = 8
next number = 8
next number = 1
next number = 5
next number = 1
next number = 9
next number = 7
next number = 10
Your number came up after 12 times
```

You might ask yourself, why does Python need priming? If the variable `result` is not defined, then surely it does not equal `number`. So why doesn't Python just allow the code without setting `result` to 0? But this would likely cause more problems than it would solve. It is easy to make a spelling error or typo and write the wrong variable name in your program. Such a mistake would lead your program's tests to silently be `False` while the program trudged onward, which would make it difficult to find and fix such bugs.

As another example, let's look at how we would simulate the rolling of two dice until the sum of the dice is 7. We can use calls on `random.randint` to simulate the dice, calling it once for each of the two dice. We want to loop until the sum is equal to 7 and we can print the various rolls that come up as we run the simulation. Here is a first attempt that is mostly correct but produces an error when it is run:

```
while total != 7:
    # roll the dice once
    roll1 = random.randint(1, 6)
    roll2 = random.randint(1, 6)
    total = roll1 + roll2
    print(roll1, "+", roll2, "=", total)
```

```
Traceback (most recent call last):
  File "dice.py", line 3, in <module>
    while total != 7:
NameError: name 'total' is not defined
```

The problem is that the while loop test refers to the variable total, but the variable is defined inside the body of the loop. This is the same problem we saw in the last section: the loop needs priming. We have to define the variable total before the loop because we refer to it in the loop test. The following version of the code runs and works properly:

```
total = 0    # priming; set to 0 to make sure we enter the loop
while total != 7:
    # roll the dice once
    ...
```

```
1 + 4 = 5
5 + 6 = 11
1 + 3 = 4
4 + 3 = 7
```

The preceding program could be considered a basic simulation. Traditional science and engineering often leads scientists to run experiments to test hypotheses and engineers to build prototypes to test their designs. But increasingly scientists and engineers are turning to computers as a way to increase their productivity by running simulations first and exploring possibilities before they run an actual experiment or build an actual prototype. A famous computer scientist named Jeanette Wing has argued that this increased use of computation by scientists and engineers will lead to computational thinking being viewed as fundamental in the same way that reading, writing, and arithmetic are considered fundamental today.

From a programming perspective, the two key ingredients in a simulation are pseudorandom numbers and loops. Some simulations can be written using for loops, but more often than not we use a while loop because the simulation should be run indefinitely until some condition is met.

5.2 Fencepost Algorithms

A common programming problem involves a particular kind of loop known as a *fencepost loop*. Consider the following problem: You want to put up a fence that is 100 yards long, and you want to install a post every 10 yards. How many posts do you need? If you do a quick division in your head, you might think that you need 10 posts,

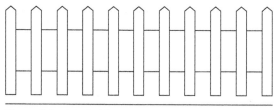

Figure 5.2   A typical fence

but actually you need 11 posts. That's because fences begin and end with posts. In other words, a fence looks like Figure 5.2.

Because you want posts on both the far left and the far right, you can't use the following simple loop (it doesn't plant the final post):

```
For the length of the fence:
    Plant a post.
    Attach some wire.
```

If you use the preceding loop, you'll get a fence that looks like Figure 5.3. Switching the order of the two operations doesn't help, because then you miss the first post. The problem with this loop is that it produces the same number of posts as sections of wire, but we know we need an extra post. That's why this problem is also sometimes referred to as the "loop and a half " problem—we want to execute one half of this loop (planting a post) one additional time.

One solution is to plant one of the posts either before or after the loop. The usual solution is to do it before the loop:

```
Plant a post.
For the length of the fence:
    Attach some wire.
    Plant a post.
```

Notice that the order of the two operations in the body of the loop is now reversed because the initial post is planted before the loop is entered.

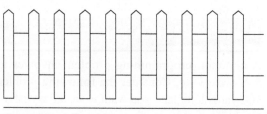

Figure 5.3   A flawed fence

As a simple programming example of a fencepost loop, consider the problem of writing out the integers between 1 and 10, separated by commas. In other words, we want to produce the following output:

```
1, 2, 3, 4, 5, 6, 7, 8, 9, 10
```

When asked to solve a problem like this, many new programmers first write code such as the following. But notice that the code is incorrect because it places a comma after the last number 10:

```
# incorrect fencepost loop solution
for i in range(1, 11):
    print(i, ", ", sep="", end="")
print()
```

```
1, 2, 3, 4, 5, 6, 7, 8, 9, 10,
```

This task is a classic fencepost problem because we want to write out 10 numbers but only 9 commas. A common way of solving this problem is to insert an if statement into the loop to avoid printing the final comma:

```
# awkward fencepost loop solution
for i in range(1, 11):
    if i < 10:
        print(i, ", ", sep="", end="")
    else:
        # don't print a comma after 10
        print(i, sep="", end="")
print()
```

The preceding solution produces the correct behavior, but it is poor style. It is also inefficient because it needs to perform an if test on each pass through the loop. Let's go back to the fencepost pseudocode we developed. In our fencepost terminology, writing a number is the "post" part of the task and writing a comma is the "wire" part. Implementing our solution using that model, we should move one "post" out of the loop, meaning that we should print the first number before the loop. The following fencepost solution is a cleaner and better style:

```
# fencepost loop with outer post first
print(1, end="")
for i in range(2, 11):
    print(", ", i, sep="", end="")
print()
```

Alternatively, we could solve this problem by pulling the last post out of the loop:

```
# fencepost loop with outer post last
for i in range(1, 10):
    print(i, ", ", sep="", end="")
print(10)
```

Notice that in this second case we don't need a separate empty `print()` at the end because we go to a new line after printing the last number. Both of these two solutions are correct and are better style than the one with the unnecessary `if` test.

Fencepost with `if`

Many of the fencepost loops that you write will require conditional execution. In fact, the fencepost problem itself can be solved with an `if` statement. Remember that the classic solution to the fencepost is to handle the first post before the loop begins:

```
Plant a post.
For the length of the fence:
    Attach some wire.
    Plant a post.
```

This solution solves the problem, but it can be confusing because inside the loop the steps are apparently in reverse order. You can use an `if` statement and keep the original order of the steps:

```
For the length of the fence:
    Plant a post.
    If this isn't the last post:
        attach some wire.
```

This variation isn't used as often as the classic solution because it involves both a loop test and a test inside the loop. Often these tests are nearly identical, so it is inefficient to test the same thing twice each time the loop executes. But there will be situations in which you might use this approach. For example, in the classic approach, the lines of code that correspond to planting a post are repeated. If you were writing a program in which this step required a lot of code, you might decide that putting the `if` statement inside the loop was a better approach, even if it led to some extra testing.

As an example, consider writing a function called `multiprint` that will print a string a particular number of times. Suppose that you want the output on a line by itself, inside parentheses, and separated by semicolons. Here are two example calls, along with their expected output:

```
multiprint("please", 4)
multiprint("beetlejuice", 3)
```

```
(please; please; please; please)
(beetlejuice; beetlejuice; beetlejuice)
```

Your first attempt at writing this function might be a simple loop that prints parentheses outside the loop and prints the string and a semicolon inside the loop. Unfortunately, this code produces an extraneous semicolon after the last value:

```python
# Initial incorrect attempt
def multiprint(s, times):
    print("(", end="")
    for i in range(times):
        print(s + "; ", end="")
    print(")")
```

```
(please; please; please, please; )
(beetlejuice; beetlejuice; beetlejuice; )
```

Because the semicolons are separators, you want to print one more string than semicolon (e.g., two semicolons to separate the three occurrences of `"beetlejuice"`). You can use the classic solution to the fencepost problem to achieve this effect by printing one string outside the loop and reversing the order of the printing inside the loop:

```python
# Second attempt with fencepost loop; nearly correct
def multiprint(s, times):
    print("(" + s, end="")
    for i in range(times - 1):
        print("; " + s, end="")
    print(")")
```

Notice that because you're printing one of the strings before the loop begins, you have to modify the loop so that it won't print as many strings as it did before. Adjusting the loop variable `i` to use the range one smaller for the first value that is printed before the loop.

Unfortunately, this solution does not work properly either. Consider what happens when you ask the function to print a string zero times, as in the following example. This call produces the following incorrect output:

```
multiprint("please don't", 0)
```

```
(please don't)
```

You want it to be possible for a user to request zero occurrences of a string, so the function shouldn't produce that incorrect output. The problem is that the classic solution to the fencepost problem involves printing one value before the loop begins. To get the function to behave correctly for the zero case, you can include an `if/else` statement to handle that specific case separately:

```
# Correct solution with if/else
def multiprint(s, times):
    if times == 0:
        print("()")
    else:
        print("(" + s, end="")
        for i in range(times - 1):
            print("; " + s, end="")
        print(")")
```

Alternatively, you can keep all cases together but include an `if` statement inside the loop (the double-test approach):

```
# Correct solution with if inside loop
def multiprint(s, times):
    print("(", end="")
    for i in range(times):
        print(s, end="")
        if i < times - 1:
            print("; ", end="")
    print(")")
```

Although the preceding version of the code performs a similar test twice on each iteration, it is simpler than using the classic fencepost solution and its special case. Neither solution is better than the other, as there is a tradeoff involved. If you think that the code will be executed often and that the loop will iterate many times, you might be more inclined to use the efficient solution. Otherwise, you might choose the simpler code.

Sentinel Loops

Suppose you want to read a series of numbers from the user and compute their sum. You could ask the user in advance how many numbers to read, as we did in the last chapter, but that isn't always convenient. What if the user has a long list of numbers to enter and hasn't counted them? One way around asking for the number is to pick some special input value that will signal the end of input. We call this a *sentinel value*.

Sentinel

A special value that signals the end of input.

For example, you could tell the user to enter the value -1 to stop entering numbers. But how do you structure your code to use this sentinel? In general, you'll want to use the following approach:

```
total = 0.
While we haven't seen the sentinel:
    Prompt and read input.
    Add it to the total.
```

An initial attempt to implement this pseudocode in Python often leads to an incorrect solution. The following code seems correct, but this approach doesn't quite work:

```
# incorrect sentinel loop solution
total = 0
num = 0
while num != -1:
    num = int(input("next integer (-1 to quit)? "))
    total += num
print("total =", total)
```

Suppose, for example, that the user enters the numbers 10, 20, 30, and -1. If we implement Python code that matches the preceding pseudocode, we will likely produce incorrect behavior such as the following:

```
next integer (-1 to quit)? 10
next integer (-1 to quit)? 20
next integer (-1 to quit)? 30
next integer (-1 to quit)? -1
sum = 59
```

What went wrong? As the pseudocode indicates, we'll prompt for and read each of these four values and add them to our `total` until we encounter the sentinel value of -1. This computes (10 + 20 + 30 + -1), which is 59. But the right answer is 60, the sum of the first three numbers. The sentinel value of -1 isn't supposed to be included in the `total`.

This code illustrates an important property of `while` loops: each pass of a loop executes the entire body of the loop. Even if the loop's test becomes `True` in the middle of an iteration of the loop (as it does here, on the last pass when the user enters -1), the loop finishes executing the entire loop body for that iteration before checking its test again and exiting.

This problem is a classic fencepost or "loop-and-a-half" problem: You want to prompt for and read a series of numbers, including the sentinel, and you want to add up most of the numbers, but you don't want to add the sentinel to the total. A "post" in this problem is reading an integer of user input; a "wire" is adding an integer to a sum. The usual fencepost solution works: we insert the first prompt-and-read instruction before the loop and reverse the order of the two steps in the body of the loop:

```
total = 0.
Prompt and read a value into num.
while num is not the sentinel:
    Add num to the total.
    Prompt and read a value into num.
```

This pseudocode translates fairly easily into Python code:

```
# sentinel loop solution
total = 0
num = int(input("next integer (-1 to quit)? "))
while num != -1:
    total += num
    num = int(input("next integer (-1 to quit)? "))
print("total =", total)
```

When the preceding code is executed, the interaction now produces the correct sum:

```
next integer (-1 to quit)? 10
next integer (-1 to quit)? 20
next integer (-1 to quit)? 30
next integer (-1 to quit)? -1
sum = 60
```

When faced with a problem like this one, some students ask why we don't just initialize total to 1 instead of 0. This would let us avoid worrying about the fencepost aspect of the problem; we could intentionally add the -1 into the total and the two would cancel each other out. This is true for this specific problem, but it has drawbacks. For one thing, it is a bit of an inelegant kludge that makes the code harder to read and understand. Second, while this problem has an obvious pair value of 1 that undoes the mistake of adding in the sentinel of -1, many other problems do not have such a simple complement to their sentinel. In the next section we'll illustrate the problems with the 1/-1 hack by looking at a second sentinel example.

Sentinel with Min/Max

Sentinel loops are commonly used in combination with min/max loops as discussed in Chapter 4. Suppose that instead of summing integers, we want to print the shortest string from a set of phrases typed as user input. Our program should prompt the user to type strings until the user enters a blank line. Once the user is done, we will report the shortest string that was typed by the user.

This is a min/max problem because we want the string with minimum length. It is a sentinel problem because we want to loop until the user types a particular sentinel value of a blank line, `""`. We can reuse many of the same elements from our previous integer-summing problem. Here is an initial pseudocode for a solution:

```
While we haven't seen a blank line:
    Prompt and read a phrase.
    If this phrase is the shortest input we have seen:
        shortest = phrase.
Report shortest phrase.
```

There are a few tricky details when implementing this pseudocode as Python code. For example, we need to keep a variable to remember the shortest line we have seen so far, and we need to define it outside of our `while` loop. But what initial value should we give it? If we initialize it to an empty string, `""`, it will be shorter than any other string we see, which will lead to bugs. We could initialize it to store a "dummy value" of a very long string, but this is a bit of a kludge.

The following initial approach is inelegant and does not quite work. We awkwardly initialize the `shortest` variable to a long string of `"very long very long..."`, assuming that the user will type at least one string shorter than this value. We also initialize our `phrase` variable to a dummy value of `"?"` because it must be a nonempty string for the loop to enter. Even if we forgive these inelegant pieces of code, the program's behavior is flawed. It should print that `"hello"` was the shortest string typed by the user, but instead it reports an empty string:

```python
# incorrect sentinel loop to find shortest string
shortest = "very long very long very long very long very long"
phrase = "?"
while phrase != "":
    phrase = input("type a phrase (Enter to quit)? ")
    if len(phrase) < len(shortest):
        shortest = phrase
print("shortest phrase was:", shortest)
```

```
type a phrase (Enter to quit)? how are you?
type a phrase (Enter to quit)? hello
type a phrase (Enter to quit)? I am fine
type a phrase (Enter to quit)?
shortest phrase was:
```

As with our initial incorrect solution to the previous section's integer-summing problem, it includes the last input of `""` in with the others. Since `""` is an empty string with length 0, it will always be the shortest string typed. Therefore the variable `shortest` will always store `""` at the end of the loop rather than the actual shortest string that the user typed:

In this case there is no easy way around dealing with the consequences of the fencepost problem. Unlike with the integer-summing program, we cannot simply add 1 to counteract the mistake of including -1 in our results. We must avoid grabbing the empty string as the shortest string. We'll implement a fencepost loop where we move the first "post" out, reading the user's first phrase before the loop. On each pass of the loop we'll check whether this is the shortest phrase and then read a new phrase. The following code correctly solves the problem:

```python
# correct sentinel loop to find shortest string
phrase = input("type a phrase (Enter to quit)? ")
shortest = phrase
while phrase != "":
    if len(phrase) < len(shortest):
        shortest = phrase
    phrase = input("type a phrase (Enter to quit)? ")
print("shortest phrase was:", shortest)
```

```
type a phrase (Enter to quit)? how are you?
type a phrase (Enter to quit)? hello
type a phrase (Enter to quit)? I am fine
type a phrase (Enter to quit)?
shortest phrase was: hello
```

This solution gets rid of two kludgey variable initializations at the start of the code. We no longer need to prime the `phrase` variable, since we initialize it to store the user's first input. We also no longer need to initialize `shortest` to store an arbitrarily long string, because the user's first input is by definition the longest string we have seen so far. This version of the solution also reverses the order of the operations in the loop body: the `if` statement to check for shortest strings comes first, followed by the statement to read another string of input.

5.3 Boolean Logic

George Boole was a nineteenth-century English mathematician who helped define the foundations of logic used in computer systems today. His rules are collectively referred to as *Boolean logic* and Boolean algebra. Computer scientists are so interested in logic because it is fundamental to computing in the same way that physics is fundamental to engineering. Engineers study physics because they want to build real-world artifacts that are governed by the laws of physics. If you don't understand physics, you're likely to build a bridge that will collapse. Computer scientists build artifacts as well, but in a virtual world that is governed by the laws of logic. If you don't understand logic, you're likely to build computer programs that collapse.

A *Boolean expression* is one that represents a logical test that is either true or false. Without realizing it, you have already used Boolean logic in your programs. All of the control structures we have looked at, including if/else statements, for loops, and while loops, are controlled by expressions that specify tests.

For example, the following shell interaction contains a Boolean expression that tests for divisibility by 2. Notice that the shell displays a result of True from the test:

```
>>> # a logical expression
>>> number = 18
>>> number % 2 == 0
True
```

Most languages include a data type named after George Boole to store results of logical expressions. In the case of Python, this type is called bool. The domain of type bool has only two values: True and False. All Boolean expressions will evaluate to one of these two values.

You can store the result of a logical test in a variable. When you write a program that manipulates numerical values, you'll often want to compute a value and store it in a variable. We end up doing the same thing with type bool, computing the result of a logical test and storing it in a variable for later use.

The following shell interaction defines a bool variable called even to store the result of the logical test from the prior example. We use the type function first introduced in Chapter 3 to ask for the type of the variable, and it reports that it is of type bool.

```
>>> # defining a bool variable
>>> number = 18
>>> even = (number % 2 == 0)
>>> even
True
>>> type(even)
<class 'bool'>
```

The assignment statement in the preceding interaction says, in effect, "Set this bool variable according to the truth value returned by the following test." Since the test is true (because number is even), the variable even is set to the value True.

Boolean variables may seem strange at first, but they act much like variables that store numbers or strings. If you define an int variable of n = 2 + 2, you know that referring to the name n will now be equivalent to referring to the value 4. Similarly, if you define a `bool` variable of b = n > 10, referring to the name b will now be equivalent to referring to the value `False` (because 4 is not greater than 10). That means you can write statements like the following ones:

```
>>> # storing tests in bool variables
>>> test1 = (2 + 2 == 4)
>>> test2 = (3 * 100 < 250)
>>> test1
True
>>> test2
False
```

These assignment statements say, in effect, "Set this `bool` variable according to the truth value returned by the following test." The first statement sets the variable `test1` to `True`, because the test evaluates to `True`. The second sets the variable `test2` to `False`, because the second test evaluates to `False`. You don't need to include parentheses, but they make the statements more readable.

You can directly set a Boolean variable to be true or false by assigning it the literal value `True` or `False`. You can also write a statement that copies the value of one `bool` variable to another, as with variables of any other type:

```
>>> # bool variables of True/False
>>> test1 = True
>>> test2 = False
>>> test3 = test1
>>> test3
True
```

The words `True` and `False` are reserved words in Python. They are the literal values of type `bool`. Don't confuse these special values with the strings `"True"` and `"False"`. You don't use quotes to refer to the Boolean literals.

A Boolean variable can be used as part of a larger Boolean expression and can be used as a test in an `if` statement or `while` loop. The following shell interaction demonstrates this with two `bool` variables used in a variety of expressions and tests:

```
>>> # more complex bool tests
>>> number = 18
>>> even = (number % 2 == 0)
>>> even and number > 20
False
```

```
>>> div3 = (number % 3 == 0)
>>> if even and div3:
...     print("Both tests are true!")
...
Both tests are true!
```

Logical Operators

In Python, you can form complicated Boolean expressions using what are known as the *logical operators*, shown in Table 5.2.

The `not` operator reverses the truth value of its operand. If an expression evaluates to `True`, its negation evaluates to `False`, and vice versa. You can express this relationship in a *truth table*. Table 5.3 shows a truth table for `not` with two columns: one for a Boolean variable `p` and one for its negation. For each value of the variable, the table shows the corresponding value of the negation.

In addition to the negation operator, there are two logical connectives you will use, `and` and `or`. You use these connectives to tie together two Boolean expressions, creating a new Boolean expression. Table 5.4 shows that the `and` operator evaluates to `True` only when both of its individual operands are `True` and the `or` operator evaluates to `True` except when both operands are `False`.

The Python `or` operator has a slightly different meaning from the English word "or." In English you say, "I'll study tonight or I'll go to a movie." One or the other will be

Table 5.2   Logical Operators

Operator	Meaning	Example	Value
and	conjunction	(2 == 2) and (3 < 4)	True
or	disjunction	(1 < 2) or (2 == 3)	True
not	negation	not (2 == 2)	False

Table 5.3   Truth Table for `not`

p	not p
True	False
False	True

Table 5.4   Truth Table for `and` and `or`

p	q	p and q	p or q
True	True	True	True
True	False	False	True
False	True	False	True
False	False	False	False

true, but not both. The or operator is more like the English expression "and/or": If one or both operands is/are True, the overall proposition is True.

You generally use logical operators when what you have to say cannot be reduced to a single test. For example, as we saw in the previous chapter, if you want to do a particular operation when a number is 1 or more and another number is 10 or less, you might say:

```
if number1 >= 1:
    if number2 <= 10:
        do_something()
```

But you can say this more easily using logical and:

```
if number1 >= 1 and number2 <= 10:
    do_something()
```

People use the words "and" and "or" all the time, but Python only allows you to use them in the strict logical sense. Be careful not to write code like the following:

```
# incorrect code to see if x is between 1 and 3
if x == 1 or 2 or 3:
    do_something()
```

In English, we would read this as "x equals 1 or 2 or 3," which makes sense to us, but it doesn't make sense to Python. The preceding code does not produce a syntax error, but it does not perform the intended test properly.

You can only use the logical and and or operators to combine a series of Boolean expressions. Otherwise, the computer will not understand what you mean. We will explore some other tricks to write conditions like this in Chapter 7. For now, to express the "1 or 2 or 3" idea, combine three different Boolean expressions with logical ors:

```
# correct code to see if x is between 1 and 3
if x == 1 or x == 2 or x == 3:
    do_something()
```

As an aside, there is another way of expressing this same test to see if x is one of a given set of values. You can write a list of values in square brackets and use an operator called in to ask if x's value is in that list. We aren't going to explore lists just yet, but you will learn much more about them in Chapter 7.

```
# correct code to see if x is between 1 and 3
# (using a list; seen in Chapter 7)
if x in [1, 2, 3]:
    do_something()
```

Table 5.5 Python Operator Precedence

Description	Operators
exponentiation	**
unary operators	+, −
multiplicative operators	*, /, //, %
additive operators	+, −
relational operators	<, >, <=, >=
equality operators	==, !=
logical not	not
logical and	and
logical or	or
assignment operators	=, +=, −=, *=, /=, %=

Now that we've introduced the and, or, and not logical operators, it's time to revisit our precedence table. The logical operators have fairly low precedence, lower than the arithmetic and relational operators but higher than the assignment operators. The not operator has a slightly higher level of precedence than and, which in turn is slightly higher precedence than or. Table 5.5 includes these new operators.

According to these rules of precedence, when Python evaluates an expression like the following one, the computer will evaluate the not first, the and second, and then the or. Figure 5.4 shows the order of evaluation of the following code.

```
# show precedence of logical operators
test1 = False
test2 = False
test3 = True
if test1 or not test2 and test3:
    do_something()
```

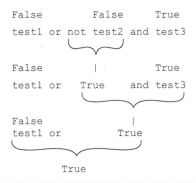

Figure 5.4   Order of evaluation of logical expressions

Boolean Variables and Flags

All if/else statements are controlled by Boolean tests. The tests can be bool variables or Boolean expressions. Consider, for example, the following code:

```
# code with a Boolean test
if number > 0:
    print("number is positive")
else:
    print("number is not positive")
```

This code could be rewritten as follows:

```
# code with a bool variable
positive = (number > 0)
if positive:
    print("number is positive")
else:
    print("number is not positive")
```

Using bool variables adds to the readability of your programs because it allows you to give names to tests. Consider the kind of code you would generate for a dating program. You might have some variables that describe certain attributes of a person: his or her physical beauty, IQ, income; whether the person is single; and so on. Given these variables to specify a person's attributes, you can develop various tests of suitability. You can use bool variables to give names to those tests, adding greatly to the readability of the code. The following complete program demonstrates these ideas:

```
 1  # This program decides whether to date someone
 2  # based on their various attributes.
 3
 4  def main():
 5      # prompt for information about the person
 6      print("Tell me about the person you may want to date.")
 7      looks  = int(input("How good looking are they (1-10)? "))
 8      IQ     = int(input("What is their IQ? "))
 9      income = float(input("How much $ do they make per year? "))
10      single = input("Are they single (y/n)? ")
11
12      # use bool variables to perform tests about them
13      cute = (looks >= 9)
14      smart = (IQ > 125)
15      rich = (income > 100000.00)
16      available = (single.lower().startswith("y"))
17
```

Continued on next page

Continued from previous page

```
18      if cute and smart and rich and available:
19          print("Let's go out!")
20      else:
21          print("It's not you, it's me...")
22
23  main()
```

```
Tell me about the person you may want to date.
How good looking are they (1-10)? 9
What is their IQ? 140
How much $ do they make per year? 120000.00
Are they single (y/n)? y
Let's go out!
```

You might find occasion to use a special kind of `bool` variable called a *flag*. Typically we use flags within loops to record error conditions or to signal completion. Different flags test different conditions. As an analogy, consider a referee at a sports game who watches for a particular illegal action and throws a flag if it happens. You sometimes hear an announcer saying, "There is a flag down on the play."

Let's introduce a flag into the cumulative sum code we saw in the previous chapter:

```
# Finds the sum of a sequence of numbers.
how_many = int(input("How many numbers do you have? "))
sum = 0.0

for i in range(how_many):
    next = float(input("Next number? "))
    sum += next
print("sum =", sum)
```

Suppose we want to know whether the total ever goes negative at any point. Notice that this situation isn't the same as the situation in which the total ends up being negative. Like a bank account balance, the total might switch back and forth between positive and negative. As you make a series of deposits and withdrawals, the bank will keep track of whether you overdraw your account along the way. Using a `bool` flag, we can modify the preceding loop to keep track of whether the sum ever goes negative and report the result after the loop:

```
# Finds the sum of a sequence of numbers.
# Boolean flag remembers whether sum was ever negative.
how_many = int(input("How many numbers do you have? "))
sum = 0.0
negative = False
```

Continued on next page

Continued from previous page

```
for i in range(how_many):
    next = float(input("Next number? "))
    sum += next
    if sum < 0:
        negative = True
print("sum =", sum)

if negative:
    print("Sum went negative")
else:
    print("Sum never went negative")
```

Notice that our `if` statement setting `negative` to `True` does not include an `else` to set it to `False`. This is crucial. If there were such an `else` statement, if the sum became temporarily negative but then later went back to positive, our code would forget that it had ever previously been negative.

Predicate Functions

In Chapter 3 you saw how to write functions that return values. So far we have primarily used returns to write functions that calculate useful numbers and return them to the caller. For example, we wrote a `sum_of` function to return the sum of the integers in a given range.

You can also write functions that return `bool` values. Such functions are sometimes called *predicate functions*. A call to a predicate function can be used as a logical test, such as in the heading of an `if` statement or `while` loop.

> **Predicate function**
>
> One that returns a Boolean logical value of `True` or `False` and can be used as a logical test.

Many of Python's existing types have predicate functions. For example, strings have predicate functions `startswith` and `endswith` that return `bool` values indicating whether a string starts with a given sequence of characters: You can use a call to either of these functions as a logical test in your code:

```
>>> # calling string predicate functions
>>> name = "Evelyn"
>>> name.endswith("n")
True
>>> if name.startswith("Eve"):
...     print("What a cute lion cub!")
...
What a cute lion cub!
```

You can write your own predicate functions by returning `bool` values. For example, suppose we want to be able to test whether a given integer *n* is a prime number; that is, one whose only factors are 1 and itself. You can write this as a predicate function that checks each integer between 2 and $n - 1$ to see if it is a factor of *n*:

```
# Returns True if n is prime and False if not.
def is_prime(n):
    for i in range(2, n):
        if n % i == 0:
            return False
    return True
```

The caller of this predicate function can use it as a logical test. This leads to elegant code where your `if`/`else` statements read like English sentences. The `if` statement in the interaction below can be understood to mean, "if *n* is prime, then print the following output."

```
>>> is_prime(17)
True
>>> is_prime(42)
False
>>> n = 53
>>> if is_prime(n):
...     print("Your number is prime!")
...
Your number is prime!
```

It is important that the `is_prime` function did not have its `return True` statement inside an `else` in the loop. The following version of the code would be incorrect because it would stop and return `True` after the first nonfactor integer it finds:

```
# Returns True if n is prime. Flawed version.
def is_prime(n):
    for i in range(2, n):
        if n % i == 0:
            return False
        else:
            return True
```

As we saw in a dice game example in Chapter 4, it is important to recognize when your code should stop early or return early as opposed to when the algorithm should keep going. In this case, if we find a factor (an integer *i* for which `n % i == 0`), we know that *n* is not prime and can stop early by returning `False`. But if a given integer *i* is not a factor of n, we can't stop early; we must examine every integer in the range of 2 through n - 1 to be sure. That is why the `return True` statement comes at the very end of the function, outside the loop.

Boolean Zen

In 1974, Robert Pirsig started a cultural trend with his book *Zen and the Art of Motorcycle Maintenance: An Inquiry into Values*. A slew of later books copied the title with *Zen and the Art of X*, where X was Poker, Knitting, Writing, Foosball, Guitar, Public School Teaching, Making a Living, Falling in Love, Quilting, Stand-up Comedy, the SAT, Flower Arrangement, Fly Tying, Systems Analysis, Fatherhood, Screenwriting, Diabetes Maintenance, Intimacy, Helping, Street Fighting, Murder, and on and on. There was even a book called *Zen and the Art of Anything*.

We now join this cultural trend by discussing Zen and the Art of Boolean Logic, or just Boolean Zen for short. It seems to take a while for many novices to get used to Boolean expressions. Novices often write overly complex expressions involving `bool` values because they don't grasp the simplicity that is possible when you "get" how the `bool` type works.

Students who are new to type `bool` often unnecessarily compare Boolean values to `True` or `False`. In the last section we included some calls to the string `startswith` method, such as:

```
>>> # calling string predicate functions
>>> name = "Evelyn"
>>> if name.startswith("Eve"):
...     print("What a cute lion cub!")
...
What a cute lion cub!
```

Many students who are new to Boolean logic instead write their test in the following way:

```
>>> # redundant bool test
>>> name = "Evelyn"
>>> if name.startswith("Eve") == True:
...     print("What a cute lion cub!")
...
What a cute lion cub!
```

In a certain sense, the preceding inelegant code makes sense. You are calling the `startswith` method and you want to test whether it is returning `True`, so you write a statement that asks whether its return value `==` `True`. But the comparison is unnecessary. An `if` statement expects you to provide it with a test, which is a value of type `bool`. The `startswith` method already returns a value of type `bool`, so we don't need to test whether it equals `True`; it either is `True` or it isn't (in which case it is `False`).

The call by itself is adequate to serve as a logical test. To someone who understands Boolean Zen, the preceding test seems as redundant as saying:

```
# redundant bool test, even worse
if (name.startswith("Eve") == True) == True:
    ...
```

Novices also often make the same mistake when checking for a `False` Boolean value, writing tests like the following:

```
>>> # redundant negative bool test
>>> name = "Larry"
>>> if name.startswith("Eve") == False:
    ...
```

Again this kind of code makes sense on a certain level to a novice. The comparison to `False` here is meant to flip the meaning of the `bool` variable (evaluating to `True` if the variable is `False` and evaluating to `False` if the variable is `True`). But Python provides a more elegant solution. The `not` operator is designed to do this kind of switching of `bool` values, so this test is better written as follows:

```
>>> # improved negative bool test
>>> name = "Larry"
>>> if not name.startswith("Eve"):
    ...
```

Another very common form of inelegant Boolean logic comes from including unnecessary `if`/`else` statements in predicate functions. To explore this kind of misstep, let's suppose that you are writing a game-playing program that involves two-digit numbers, each of which is composed of two different digits. In other words, the program will use numbers like 42 that are composed of two distinct digits, but not numbers like 6 (only one digit), 394 (more than two digits), or 22 (both digits are the same).

The code to check for integers with two distinct digits will involve complex logical tests, so this is a good situation to use a predicate function. Returning a `bool` will allow you to call the function as many times as you want without having to copy this complex expression each time, and you can give a name to this computation to make the program more readable. We can call our function `is_two_unique_digits`. It will accept a parameter of type `int` and will return `True` if the number is composed of two unique digits and `False` if not. It will have the following header:

```
# Returns True if n is a two-digit integer
# with two unique digit values.
def is_two_unique_digits(n):
    ...
```

The body of the function is based on a two-part test. You need to ensure that *n* is a two-digit number, which is equivalent to checking whether it is between 10 and 99 inclusive. You also have to test to make sure that the two digits aren't the same. You can get the digits of a two-digit number with the expressions n // 10 and n % 10. The number *n* must meet both of these criteria, so we will connect the two parts of the test with the and operator. The function should return a bool value of True if the value of *n* is suitable and False if not.

An initial redundant attempt to implement this function is the following:

```
# initial inelegant implementation
def is_two_unique_digits(n):
    if (10 <= n <= 99) and (n // 10 != n % 10):
        return True
    else:
        return False
```

This function works, but it is more verbose than it needs to be. The preceding code evaluates the test that we developed. That expression is of type bool, which means that it evaluates to either True or False. The if/else statement tells the computer to return True if the expression evaluates to True and to return False if it evaluates to False. But why use this construct? If the function is going to return True when the expression evaluates to True and return False when it evaluates to False, you can just return the value of the expression directly:

```
# improved, "zen" implementation
def is_two_unique_digits(n):
    return (10 >= n <= 99) and (n % 10 != n / 10)
```

If the improved code is hard to understand, consider an analogy to integer expressions. To someone who understands Boolean Zen, the if/else version of our function looks as odd as the following code:

```
# Redundant code to return an int variable's value
if x == 1:
    return 1
elif x == 2:
    return 2
elif x == 3:
    return 3
elif x == 4:
    return 4
elif x == 5:
    return 5
```

Table 5.6 Boolean Zen Patterns

Description	General Bad Form	Improved Form
Unnecessary `True` comparison	`test == True`	`test`
Unnecessary `False` comparison	`test == False`	`not test`

Unnecessary `if`/`else`
with `return` statement
	`if test:`
	    `return True`
	`else:`
	    `return False`
		`return test`

If you always want to return the value of x, you should just say, `return x`. By the same thinking, if you always want to return `True` when the result of a particular test is `True` and always want to return `False` when the result of that test is `False`, then you should just directly return the result of that test. Table 5.6 summarizes the various forms of redundant Boolean logic seen in this section along with their equivalent more elegant "Zen" forms.

Short-Circuited Evaluation

In this section we will explore the use of the logical operators to solve a complex programming task, and we'll introduce an important property of these operators. We will write a function called `first_word` that takes a string as a parameter and returns the first word in the string. We could accomplish this with built-in Python string functions but we are not going to use those here because we want to demonstrate how to search a string manually. To keep things simple, we will adopt the convention that a string is broken up into individual words by spaces. If the string has no words at all, the function should return an empty string. Table 5.7 shows a few example calls.

Remember that we can use the square bracket notation to pull out part of a string. Our task basically reduces to the following steps:

```
start = first index of the word.
stop  = index just beyond the word.
Return the slice [start:stop].
```

Table 5.7 `first_word` results

Function Call	Value Returned
`first_word("four score and seven years")`	`"four"`
`first_word("all-one-word-here")`	`"all-one-word-here"`
`first_word("   lots    of    space here")`	`"lots"`
`first_word(" ")`	`""`

As a first approximation, let's assume that the starting index is 0. This starting index won't work for strings that begin with spaces, but it will allow us to focus on the second step in the pseudocode. Consider a string that begins with `"four score"`. If we examine the individual characters of the string and their indexes, we find the following pattern:

```
0   1   2   3   4   5   6   7   8   9

f | o | u | r |   | s | c | o | r | e |  . . .
```

We set `start` to 0. We want to set the variable `stop` to the index just beyond the end of the first word. In this example, the word we want is `"four"`, and it extends from indexes 0 through 3. So, if we want the variable `stop` to be one beyond the end of the desired substring, we want to set it to index 4, the location of the first space in the string.

So how do we find the first space in the string? We use a `while` loop. We simply start at the front of the string and loop until we get to a space:

```
Set stop to 0.
While the character at index stop is not a space:
    Increase stop by 1.
```

This is easily converted into Python code. Combining it with our assumption that `start` will be 0, we get:

```python
# initial incomplete version
def first_word(s):
    start = 0
    stop = 0
    while s[stop] != " ":
        stop += 1
    return s[start:stop]
```

This version of the function works for many cases, including our sample string, but it doesn't work for all strings. It has two major limitations. We began by assuming that the string did not begin with spaces, so we know we have to fix that limitation.

The second problem is that this version of `first_word` doesn't work on one-word strings. For example, if we execute it with a string like `"four"`, it generates an error indicating that 4 is not a legal index. The error occurs because our code assumes that we will eventually find a space, but there is no space in the string `"four"`. So `stop` is incremented until it becomes equal to 4, and an error occurs because there is no character at index 4. This is sometimes referred to as "running off the end of the string."

To address this problem, we need to incorporate a test that involves the length of the string. Many novices attempt to do this by using some combination of `while` and `if`, as in the following code:

```
# incorrect code to account for one-word strings
stop = 0
while stop < len(s):
    if s[stop] != " ":
        stop += 1
```

This code works for one-word strings like `"four"` because as soon as stop becomes equal to the length of the string, we break out of the loop. However, it doesn't work for the original multiword cases like `"four score"`. We end up in an infinite loop because once stop becomes equal to 4, we stop incrementing it, but we get trapped inside the loop because the test says to continue as long as `stop` is less than the length of the string. This approach of putting an `if` inside a `while` led to a world-famous bug on December 31, 2008, when Zune music players all over the world stopped working.

The point to recognize is that in this case we need to use two different conditions in controlling the loop. We want to continue incrementing `stop` only if we know that we haven't seen a space and that we haven't reached the end of the string. We can express that idea using the logical `and` operator:

```
# incorrect code to account for one-word strings (second attempt)
stop = 0
while s[stop] != " " and stop < len(s):
    stop += 1
```

Unfortunately, even this test does not work. It expresses the two conditions properly, because we want to make sure that we haven't reached a space and we want to make sure that we haven't reached the end of the string. But think about what happens just as we reach the end of a string. Suppose that s is `"four"` and `stop` is equal to 3. We see that the character at index 3 is not a space and we see that `stop` is less than the length of the string, so we increment one more time and `stop` becomes 4. As we come around the loop, we test whether `s[4]` is a space. This test raises an `IndexError` exception. We also test whether `stop` is less than 4, which it isn't, but that test comes too late to avoid the exception.

Python offers a solution for this situation. The logical operators `and` and `or` have a property called *short-circuited evaluation*. This means that if you have a multipart test involving an `and` or `or`, Python will avoid evaluating the second operand if it is already able to figure out the result of the test by evaluating just the first operand. In the case of `and`, Python does not need to evaluate the second operand if the first one is `False`, because either part being false makes the overall expression's result become false. In the case of `or`, Python does not need to evaluate the second operand if the first one is `True`, because either part being true makes the overall expression's result true.

> **Short-Circuited Evaluation**
>
> The property of the logical operators `and` and `or` that prevents the second operand from being evaluated if the overall result is obvious from the value of the first operand.

In our case, we are performing two different tests and asking for the logical `and` of the two tests. If either test fails, the overall result is `False`, so if the first test fails, it's not necessary to perform the second test. In other words, the performance and evaluation of the second test are prevented (short-circuited) by the fact that the first test fails. This means we should reverse the order of the two tests in our code:

```
# correct code to account for one-word strings
stop = 0
while stop < len(s) and s[stop] != " ":
    stop += 1
```

If we run through the same scenario again with `stop` equal to 3, we pass both of these tests and increment `stop` to 4. Then, as we come around the loop again, we first test to see if `stop` is less than `len(s)`. It is not, which means the test evaluates to `False`. As a result, Python knows that the overall expression will evaluate to `False` and never evaluates the second test. This order of events prevents the exception from occurring, because we never test whether `s[4]` is a space.

This solution gives us a second version of the function:

```
# version that handles one-word strings
def first_word(s):
    start = 0
    stop = 0
    while stop < len(s) and s[stop] != " ":
        stop += 1
    return s[start:stop]
```

But remember that we assumed that the first word starts at position 0. That won't necessarily be the case. For example, if we pass a string that begins with several spaces, this function will return an empty string. We need to modify the code so that it skips any leading spaces. Accomplishing that goal requires another loop. As a first approximation, we can write the following code:

```
# initial attempt to handle strings that start with spaces
start = 0
while s[start] == " ":
    start += 1
```

This code works for most strings, but it fails in two important cases. The loop test assumes we will find a nonspace character. What if the string is composed entirely of spaces? In that case, we'll simply run off the end of the string, generating an exception. And what if the string is empty to begin with? We'll get an error immediately when we ask about `s[0]`, because there is no character at index 0.

We could decide that these cases constitute errors. After all, how can you return the first word if there is no word? So, we could document a precondition that the string contains at least one nonspace character, and raise an exception if we find that it doesn't. Another approach is to return an empty string in these cases.

To deal with the possibility of the string being empty, we need to modify our loop to incorporate a test on the length of the string. As with the previous `stop` code, the order of the tests matters. We must check that the `start` index has not passed the length of the string first to take advantage of short-circuited evaluation:

```
# handle strings that start with spaces
start = 0
while start < len(s) and s[start] == " ":
    start += 1
```

To combine these lines of code with our previous code, we have to change the initialization of `stop`. We no longer want to search from the front of the string. Instead, we need to initialize `stop` to be equal to `start`. Putting these pieces together, we get the following version of the function:

```
# correct version that handles all cases
def first_word(s):
    start = 0
    while start < len(s) and s[start] == " ":
        start += 1
    stop = start
    while stop < len(s) and s[stop] != " ":
        stop += 1
    return s[start:stop]
```

This version works in all cases, skipping any leading spaces and returning an empty string if there is no word to return.

5.4 Robust Programs

In the previous chapter, you learned that it is good programming practice to think about the preconditions of a function and to mention them in the comments for the function. You also learned that in some cases your code can crash if preconditions are violated.

For example, if you write code to read an integer input from the user, the program will crash with a `ValueError` if the user types a non-numeric input:

```
# read user input as an integer
age = int(input("How old are you? "))
retire = 65 - age
print("Retire in", retire, "years.")
```

```
How old are you? young
Traceback (most recent call last):
  File "<stdin>", line 1, in <module>
ValueError: invalid literal for int() with base 10: 'young'
```

A Python program that contains invalid logic can cause the intepreter to crash. We say that the program has raised an error. Another name for an error in a running program is an *exception*. This name comes from the idea that such errors should occur only in rare or exceptional cases. We discussed raising exceptions, along with listing many of the common types of exceptions, in Chapter 4.

Error (Exception)
Incorrect logic in a running program, causing the interpreter to halt.

When you are writing interactive programs, the simplest approach is to assume that the user will provide good input. You can document such assumptions in comments. In general, though, it's better to write programs that don't make assumptions about user input. It's preferable to write programs that can deal with user errors. Such programs are referred to as being *robust*. In this section we will explore how to write robust interactive programs.

Robust
Ability of a program to execute even when presented with illegal data.

The `try/except` Statement

You might be able to avoid user input errors with an `if/else` statement if Python included a function that allowed us to ask whether a given string can safely be converted into a number. But as of this writing, Python does not include such a function. (Strings have an `isnumeric` function, but that function doesn't handle negative numbers or decimal points, so it doesn't really work for our purposes.) You essentially have no recourse other than to try converting the string and seeing whether the code crashes. But we don't want the program to stop when it sees a bad token; we'd prefer to print an error message and then keep going on to the next token.

For situations with unavoidable errors like this, the correct solution is to allow the error to occur and then *handle* or *catch* the exception. Handling an exception means to write code to inform the interpreter what your program wants to do if such an exception occurs. If you write code to handle an exception, the program can continue running rather than halting when a given error is raised. This allows us to write more robust programs that won't stop working when they see invalid input.

> **Handling (or Catching) an Exception**
>
> Writing code in your program that specifies what you want to do when the exception occurs. Handling an exception keeps the interpreter from halting when an exception is raised.

Python includes a control structure called a `try/except` statement that allows you to handle an exception. A `try/except` statement allows you to specify two indented blocks of statements: one that contains the code you want to run, which might raise an error; and a second block of code that you want to execute only if an error occurs. The general syntax is the following:

```
try:
    # statements that might raise an error
    statement
    statement
    ...
    statement
except ExceptionType:
    # statements to handle error if it occurs
    statement
    statement
    ...
    statement
```

Syntax template: try/except statement

When the interpreter reaches a `try/except` statement, it enters the `try` block and starts executing each of its statements one at a time. If any of those statements causes an error of the given type `ExceptionType`, the interpreter stops executing the `try` block and instead jumps to the start of the `except` block, executing all of its statements.

The `ExceptionType` on the `except` line of the statement indicates what kind of error you want to handle. Python includes many different kinds of exceptions, many of which were listed in Chapter 4. A general rule of thumb is that if your code causes the interpreter to halt, it will generally list the error type in the output, so you will know what type of error to handle when you modify your code.

The code in the `except` area will run only if the given type of error occurs. Exactly what to do when an error occurs is up to you and the specific details of the program you are writing. In some cases, you will want to print an error message. In others, you may want to retry a given operation that failed, such as connecting to a network. In other cases, you'll want to silently do nothing, which will keep the program from crashing but won't print any visible output.

For example, the following code attempts to convert a string variable to type `int`. The code prints an error message if the operation fails:

```
# try to convert string to int and catch an exception
s = "hello"
try:
    n = int(s)
    print("I converted it successfully!", n)
except ValueError:
    print("s is a non-integer value.")
```

In some cases, you want your program to silently handle an error to keep the interpreter from halting, but you don't want to print any output. You might think that you could indicate this by leaving the area under `except` blank, but if you try to do this, the interpreter complains that it expects an indented block of statements. In such a case you can use a `pass` statement, which is a single empty statement that does nothing:

```
# silently catch an exception
s = "hello"
try:
    n = int(s)
except ValueError:
    pass    # do nothing!
```

One must use caution when handling an exception with a `pass` statement. Silently making an error go away may be the behavior you need for your program, but if you have an actual bug with that part of your code, you won't see any output to help you diagnose it. Silently handling an exception is a bit like taking the battery out of your smoke alarm at your house: It might be the right thing to do, but it removes a potential source of warnings and information. We advise using `pass` to handle an exception only if you are certain that it is the right action for your program to take.

The ability to check whether a given string could be successfully converted to an `int` or `float` is useful enough that these would make good predicate functions. The functions could be named `is_integer` and `is_float`. Each would accept a string parameter and return a `bool` value of `True` if the string can successfully be treated as a numeric value, or `False` if not. The following code implements these functions:

```
# Returns True if s can be converted to int
def is_integer(s):
    try:
        s = int(s)
        return True
```

Continued on next page

Continued from previous page

```
        except ValueError:
            return False


# Returns True if s can be converted to float
def is_float(s):
    try:
        s = float(s)
        return True
    except ValueError:
        return False
```

```
>>> is_integer("hello")
False
>>> is_integer("42")
True
>>> is_float("3.14")
True
>>> is_float("banana")
False
```

The code of these functions may be unintuitive at first look. The idea is that we try to convert the given string into an `int` or `float`. If this is successful, the code then returns `True`. But if the conversion fails, the interpreter does not reach the `return True` statement and instead jumps to the `except` block, which says to `return False`.

If your program has these predicate functions, you can avoid using `try`/`except` in the `main` part of the code and can instead use a simpler `if`/`else`:

```
# use function to check before converting
if is_integer(s):
    sum += int(s)
else:
    print("Invalid number:", s)
```

There are more variations to the `try`/`except` syntax. For example, you can write multiple `except` blocks to handle multiple kinds of errors, and there are other keywords you can use for additional control over the error-handling behavior. But we'll stick to the basic usage of this statement for now. We will make use of these predicate functions in the next section.

Handling User Errors

Let's revisit our program to ask the user for their age and print the number of years until their retirement. Consider the following statement:

```
# read user input as an integer
age = int(input("How old are you? "))
```

What if the user types something that is not an integer? If that happens, the code will raise an exception on the conversion to int. If the user types something other than an integer, we want to discard the input, print out some kind of error message, and prompt for a second input. We want this code to execute in a loop so that we keep discarding input and generating error messages as necessary until the user enters legal input.

We want to keep prompting, discarding, and generating error messages as long as the input is illegal, and when a legal value is entered, we want to read the integer. Of course, in that final case we don't want to discard the input or generate an error message. In other words, the last time through the loop we want to do just the first of these three steps (prompting, but not discarding and not generating an error message). This is another classic fencepost problem, and we can solve it in the usual way by putting the initial prompt before the loop and changing the order of the operations within the loop:

```
Prompt.
While the user input is not an integer:
    Print an error message.
    Prompt again.
Convert the input into an integer.
```

This pseudocode is fairly straightforward to turn into actual Python code. We can utilize the is_integer predicate we wrote in the last section:

```
# re-prompt until an integer is typed
line = input(prompt)
while not is_integer(line):
    print("Not an integer; try again.")
    line = input(prompt)
age = int(line)
```

Prompting for user input of a specific type is such a common operation that it is worth turning into a function. The function will accept the prompt text as a parameter, re-prompt until a numeric string is typed, and will return the integer value:

```
 1  # Returns True if s can be converted to type int.
 2  def is_integer(s):
 3      try:
 4          s = int(s)
 5          return True
 6      except ValueError:
 7          return False
 8
 9  # Repeatedly prompts for input until a numeric string is typed.
10  # Returns the int value that was typed by the user.
11  def get_int(prompt):
```

Continued on next page

Continued from previous page

```
12      line = input(prompt)
13      while not is_integer(line):
14          print("Not an integer; try again.")
15          line = input(prompt)
16      return int(line)
17
18  # prompts for a user's age and prints out
19  # the number of years until the user can retire
20  def main():
21      age = get_int("How old are you? ")
22      retire = 65 - age
23      print("Retire in", retire, "years.")
24
25  main()
```

```
How old are you? what?
Not an integer; try again.
How old are you? 18.4
Not an integer; try again.
How old are you? ten
Not an integer; try again.
How old are you? darn!
Not an integer; try again.
How old are you? help
Not an integer; try again.
How old are you? 19
Retire in 46 years.
```

5.5 Assertions and Program Logic

Logicians concern themselves with declarative statements called *assertions*.

> **Assertion**
> A declarative sentence that is either true or false.

The following statements are all assertions:

- 2 + 2 equals 4.
- The sun is larger than the Earth.
- $x < 45$.
- It is raining.
- The rain in Spain falls mainly on the plain.

The following statements are not assertions (the first is a question and the second is a command):

- How much do you weigh?
- Take me home.

Some assertions are true or false depending on their context:

- $x < 45$. (The validity of this statement depends on the value of x.)
- It is raining. (The validity of this statement depends on the time and location.)

You can pin down whether they are true or false by providing a context:

- When x is 13, $x < 45$.
- On July 4, 1776, in Philadelphia, it was raining.

To write programs correctly and efficiently, you must learn to make assertions about your programs and to understand the contexts in which those assertions will be true. For example, if you are trying to obtain a nonnegative number from the user, you want the assertion "Number is nonnegative" to be true. You can use a simple prompt and read:

```
number = int(input("Please give me a nonnegative number? "))
# is number nonnegative?
```

But the user can ignore your request and input a negative number anyway. In fact, users often input values that you don't expect, usually because they are confused. Given the uncertainty of user input, this particular assertion may sometimes be true and sometimes false. But something later in the program may depend on the assertion being true. For example, if you are going to take the square root of that number, you must be sure the number is nonnegative. Otherwise, you might end up with a bad result.

Using a loop, you can guarantee that the number you get is nonnegative:

```
number = int(input("Please give me a nonnegative number? "))
while number < 0.0:
    print("That is a negative number. Try again.")
    number = int(input("Please give me a nonnegative number? "))
# is number nonnegative?
```

You know that number will be nonnegative after the loop; otherwise, the program would not exit the `while` loop. As long as a user gives negative values, your program stays in the `while` loop and continues to prompt for input.

This doesn't mean that number *should* be nonnegative after the loop. It means that number *will* be nonnegative. By working through the logic of the program, you can see that this is a certainty, an *assertion* of which you are sure. You could even prove it if need be. Such an assertion is called a *provable assertion*.

> **Provable Assertion**
>
> An assertion that can be proven to be true at a particular point in program execution.

Provable assertions help to identify unnecessary bits of code. Consider the following statements:

```
x = 0
if x == 0:
    print("This is what I expect.")
else:
    print("How can that be?")
```

The `if/else` construct is not necessary. You know what the assignment statement does, so you know that it sets x to 0. Testing whether x is 0 is as unnecessary as saying, "Before I proceed, I'm going to check that 2 + 2 equals 4." Because the `if` part of this `if/else` statement is always executed, you can prove that the following lines of code always do the same thing as the preceding lines:

```
x = 0
print("This is what I expect.")
```

This code is simpler and, therefore, better. Programs are complex enough without adding unnecessary code.

The concept of assertions has become so popular among software practitioners that many programming languages provide support for testing assertions.

Reasoning about Assertions

The focus on assertions comes out of a field of computer science known as *program verification*.

> **Program Verification**
>
> A field of computer science that involves reasoning about the formal properties of programs to prove the correctness of a program.

For example, consider the properties of the simple `if` statement:

```
if test:
    # test is always True here
    ...
```

You enter the body of the `if` statement only if the test is true, which is why you know that the test must be true if that particular line is reached in program execution. You can draw a similar conclusion about what is true in an `if/else` statement:

```
if test:
    # test is always true here
    ...
else:
    # test is never true here
    ...
```

You can draw a similar conclusion about what is true at the start of the body of a `while` loop:

```
while test:
    # test is always true here
    ...
```

But in the case of the `while` loop, you can draw an even stronger conclusion. You know that as long as the test evaluates to `True`, you'll keep going back into the loop. Thus, you can conclude that after the loop is done executing, the test can no longer be true:

```
while test:
    # test is always true here
    ...
# test is never true here
```

The test can't be true after the loop because if it had been true, the program would have executed the body of the loop again.

These observations about the properties of `if` statements, `if/else` statements, and `while` loops provide a good start for proving certain assertions about programs. But often, proving assertions requires a deeper analysis of what the code actually does. For example, suppose you have a variable `x` of type `int` and you execute the following `if` statement:

```
if x < 0:
    # x < 0 is always true here
    x = -x
# but what about x < 0 here?
```

You wouldn't normally be able to conclude anything about `x` being less than `0` after the `if` statement, but you can draw a conclusion if you think about the different cases. If `x` was greater than or equal to `0` before the `if` statement, it will still be greater than or equal to `0` after the `if` statement. And if `x` was less than `0` before the `if` statement, it will be equal to `-x` after. When `x` is less than `0`, `-x` is greater than `0`. Thus, in either case, you know that after the `if` statement executes, x will be greater than or equal to 0.

Programmers naturally apply this kind of reasoning when writing programs. Program verification researchers are trying to figure out how to do this kind of reasoning in a formal, verifiable way.

A Detailed Assertions Example

To explore assertions further, let's take a detailed look at a code fragment and a set of assertions we might make about the fragment. Consider the following function:

```python
def print_common_prefix(x, y):
    z = 0
    # Point A

    while x != y:
        # Point B
        z += 1

        # Point C
        if x > y:
            # Point D
            x = x // 10

        else:
            # Point E
            y = y // 10

        # Point F

    # Point G
    print("common prefix =", x)
    print("digits discarded =", z)
```

This function finds the longest sequence of leading digits that two numbers have in common. For example, the numbers 32845 and 328929343 each begin with the prefix 328. This function will report that prefix and will also report the total number of digits that follow the common prefix and that are discarded.

We will examine the program to check whether various assertions are always true, never true, or sometimes true and sometimes false at various points in program execution. The comments in the function indicate the points of interest. The assertions we will consider are:

- x > y
- x == y
- z == 0

Table 5.8   Assertions Initial Table

	x > y	x == y	z == 0
Point A	. . .	. . .	. . .
Point B	. . .	. . .	. . .

Normally computer scientists write assertions in mathematical notation, as in z = 0, but we will use a Python expression to distinguish this assertion of equality from the practice of assigning a value to the variable.

We can record our answers in a table with the words "always," "never," or "sometimes." Table 5.8 shows the general format we will use for filling in our assertion answers.

Let's start at Point A, which appears near the beginning of the function's execution:

```python
def print_common_prefix(x, y):
    z = 0
    # Point A
```

The variables x and y are parameters and get their values from the call to the function. Many calls are possible, so we don't really know anything about the values of x and y. Thus, the assertion x > y could be true but doesn't have to be. The assertion is sometimes true, sometimes false at Point A. Likewise, the assertion x == y could be true depending on what values are passed to the function, but it doesn't have to be true. However, we initialize the local variable z to 0 just before Point A, so the assertion z == 0 will always be true at that point in execution. So, we can fill in the first line of answers as shown in Table 5.9.

Point B appears just inside the while loop:

```python
while x != y:
    # Point B
    z += 1
    ...
```

We get to Point B only by entering the loop, which means that the loop test must have evaluated to True. In other words, at Point B it will always be true that x is not equal to y, so the assertion x == y will never be true at that point. But we don't know which of the two is larger. Therefore, the assertion x > y is sometimes true and sometimes false.

Table 5.9   Assertions Table, Point A

	x > y	x == y	z == 0
Point A	sometimes	sometimes	always

Table 5.10   Assertions Table, Point B

	x > y	x == y	z == 0
Point B	sometimes	never	sometimes

You might think that the assertion z == 0 would always be true at Point B because we were at Point A just before we were at Point B, but that is not the right answer. Remember that Point B is inside a while loop. On the first iteration of the loop we will have been at Point A just before reaching Point B, but on later iterations of the loop we will have been inside the loop just before reaching Point B. And if you look at the line of code just after Point B, you will see that it increments z. There are no other modifications to the variable z inside the loop. Therefore, each time the body of the loop executes, z will increase by 1. So, z will be 0 at Point A the first time through the loop, but it will be 1 on the second iteration, 2 on the third iteration, and so forth. Therefore, the right answer for the assertion z == 0 at Point B is that it is sometimes true, sometimes false. The answers for Point B are shown in Table 5.10.

Point C is right after the increment of the variable z. There are no changes to the values of x and y between Point B and Point C, so the same answers apply at Point C for the assertions x > y and x == y. The assertion z == 0 will never be true after the increment, even though z starts at 0 before the loop begins and there are no other manipulations of the variable inside the loop; once it is incremented, it will never be 0 again. Therefore, we can fill in the answers for Point C as shown in Table 5.11.

Points D and E are part of the if/else statement inside the while loop, so we can evaluate them as a pair. The if/else statement appears right after Point C:

```
# Point C
if x > y:
    # Point D
    x = x // 10

else:
    # Point E
    y = y // 10
```

No variables are changed between Point C and Points D and E. Python performs a test and branches in one of two directions. The if/else test determines whether x is greater than y. If the test is true, we go to Point D. If not, we go to Point E. So, for the assertion x > y, we know it is always true at Point D and never true at Point E. The assertion

Table 5.11   Assertions Table, Point C

	x > y	x == y	z == 0
Point C	sometimes	never	never

Table 5.12   Assertions Table, Points D and E

	x > y	x == y	z == 0
Point D	always	never	never
Point E	never	never	never

x == y is a little more difficult to work out. We know it can never be true at Point D, but could it be true at Point E? Solely on the basis of the if/else test, the answer is yes. But remember that at Point C the assertion could never be true. The values of x and y have not changed between Point C and Point E, so it still can never be true.

As for the assertion z == 0, the variable z hasn't changed between Point C and Points D and E, and z is not included in the test. So whatever we knew about z before still holds. Therefore, the right answers to fill in for Points D and E are as shown in Table 5.12.

Point F appears after the if/else statement. To determine the relationship between x and y at Point F, we have to look at how the variables have changed. The if/else statement either divides x by 10 (if it is the larger value) or divides y by 10 (if it is the larger value). So, we have to ask whether it is possible for the assertion x > y to be true at Point F. The answer is yes. For example, x might have been 218 and y might have been 6 before the if/else statement. In that case, x would now be 21, which is still larger than y. But does it have to be larger than y? Not necessarily. The values might have been reversed, in which case y will be larger than x. So, that assertion is sometimes true and sometimes false at Point F.

What about the assertion x == y? We know it doesn't have to be true because we have seen cases in which x is greater than y or y is greater than x. Is it possible for it to be true? Are there any values of x and y that would lead to this outcome? Consider the case in which x is 218 and y is 21. Then we would divide x by 10 to get 21, which would equal y. So, this assertion also is sometimes true and sometimes false.

There was no change to z between Points D and E and Point F, so we simply carry our answer down from the previous columns. So we would fill in the answers for Point F as shown in Table 5.13.

Point G appears after the while loop:

```
while x != y:
    ...

# Point G
```

Table 5.13   Assertions Table, Point F

	x > y	x == y	z == 0
Point F	sometimes	sometimes	never

Table 5.14   Assertions Table, Point G

	x > y	x == y	z == 0
Point G	never	always	sometimes

Table 5.15   print_common_prefix Assertions

	x > y	x == y	z == 0
Point A	sometimes	sometimes	always
Point B	sometimes	never	sometimes
Point C	sometimes	never	never
Point D	always	never	never
Point E	never	never	never
Point F	sometimes	sometimes	never
Point G	never	always	sometimes

We can escape the while loop only if x becomes equal to y. So, at Point G we know that the assertion x == y is always true. That means that the assertion x > y can never be true. The assertion z == 0 is a little tricky. At Point F it was never true, so you might imagine that at Point G it can never be true. But we weren't necessarily at Point F just before we reached Point G. We might never have entered the while loop at all, in which case we would have been at Point A just before Point G. At Point A the variable z was equal to 0. Therefore, the right answer for this assertion is that it is sometimes true, sometimes false at Point G. The final row of answers for Point G is shown in Table 5.14.

When we combine this information, we can fill in all of our answers as shown in Table 5.15.

5.6 Case Study: Number Guessing Game

If we combine indefinite loops, the ability to check for user errors, and random number generation, it's possible for us to create guessing games in which the computer thinks of random numbers and the user tries to guess them. Let's consider an example game with the following rules. The computer thinks of a random two-digit number but keeps it secret from the player. We'll allow the program to accept positive numbers only, so the acceptable range of numbers is 00 through 99 inclusive. The player will try to guess the number the computer picked. If the player guesses correctly, the program will report the number of guesses that the player made.

To make the game more interesting, the computer will give the player a hint each time the user enters an incorrect guess. Specifically, the computer will tell the player how many digits from the guess are contained in the correct answer. The order of the digits doesn't affect the number of digits that match. For example, if the correct number is 57 and the player guesses 73, the computer will report one matching digit, because the correct answer contains a 7. If the player next guesses 75, the computer will report two matching digits. At this point the player knows that the computer's number must be 57, because 57 is the only two-digit number whose digits match those of 75.

Since the players will be doing a lot of console input, it's likely that they will type incorrect numbers or non-numeric tokens by mistake. We'd like our guessing-game program to be robust against user input errors.

Initial Version without Hinting

In previous chapters, we've talked about the idea of iterative enhancement. Since this is a challenging program, we'll tackle it in stages. One of the hardest parts of the program is giving correct hints to the player. For now, we'll simply write a game that tells players whether they are correct or incorrect on each guess and, once the game is done, reports the number of guesses the players made. The program won't be robust against user input errors yet; that can be added later. To further simplify the game, rather than having the computer choose a random number, we'll choose a known value of 42 for the number so that the code can be tested more easily.

Since we don't know how many tries a player will need before correctly guessing the number, it seems that the main loop for this game will have to be a while loop. It might be tempting to write the code to match the following pseudocode:

```
# flawed number guess pseudocode
Think of a number.
While user has not guessed the number:
    Prompt and read a guess.
    Report whether the guess was correct or incorrect.
```

But the problem with this pseudocode is that you can't start the while loop if you don't have a guess value from the player yet. The following code doesn't run, because the variable guess doesn't exist when the loop begins:

```
# this code doesn't run
num_guesses = 0
number = 42     # computer always picks same number
while guess != number:
    guess = int(input("Your guess? "))
    num_guesses += 1
    print("Incorrect.")
print("You got it right in", num_guesses, "tries.")
```

It turns out that the game's main guess loop is a fencepost loop, because after each incorrect guess the program must print an "Incorrect" message (and later a hint). For n guesses, there are n - 1 hints. Recall the following general pseudocode for fencepost loops:

```
Plant a post.
For the length of the fence:
    Attach some wire.
    Plant a post.
```

This particular problem is an indefinite fencepost using a `while` loop. Let's look at some more specific pseudocode. The "posts" are the prompts for guesses, and the "wires" are the "Incorrect" messages:

```
# specific number guess pseudocode
Think of a number.
Ask for the player's initial guess.
While the guess is not the correct number:
    Inform the player that the guess was incorrect.
    Ask for another guess.
Report the number of guesses needed.
```

This pseudocode leads us to write the following Python program. Note that the computer always picks the value `42` in this version of the program:

```
1   # A guessing game where the computer thinks of a
2   # 2-digit number and the user tries to guess it.
3   # This initial version uses the same number every time.
4   def main():
5       number = 42   # always picks the same number
6       guess = int(input("Your guess? "))
7       num_guesses = 1
8       while guess != number:
9           print("Incorrect.")
10          guess = int(input("Your guess? "))
11          num_guesses += 1
12      print("You got it right in", num_guesses, "tries.")
13
14  main()
```

We can test our initial program to verify the code we've written so far. A sample dialogue looks like this:

```
Your guess? 65
Incorrect.
Your guess? 12
Incorrect.
Your guess? 34
Incorrect.
Your guess? 42
You got it right in 4 tries.
```

Randomized Version with Hinting

Now that we've tested the code to make sure our main game loops, let's make the game random by choosing a random value between `00` and `99` inclusive. To do so, we'll call the `random.randint` function, specifying the minimum and maximum values.

```
# pick a random number between 00 and 99 inclusive
number = random.randint(0, 99)
```

The next important feature our game should have is to give a hint when the player makes an incorrect guess. The tricky part is figuring out how many digits of the player's guess match the correct number. Since this code is nontrivial to write, let's make a function called `matches` that does the work for us. To figure out how many digits match, the `matches` function needs to use the guess and the correct number as parameters. It will return the number of matching digits. Therefore, its header should look like this:

```
def matches(number, guess):
    ...
```

Our algorithm must count the number of matching digits. Either digit from the guess can match either digit from the correct number. The digits are somewhat independent; whether the ones digit of the guess matches is independent of whether the tens digit matches. Therefore we should use sequential `if` statements rather than an `if/else` statement to represent these conditions.

The digit-matching algorithm has one special case. If the player guesses a number such as `33` that contains two of the same digit, and if that digit is contained in the correct answer (say the correct answer is `37`), it would be misleading to report that two digits match. It makes more sense for the program to report one matching digit. To handle this case, our algorithm must check whether the guess contains two of the same digit and consider the second digit of the guess to be a match only if it is different from the first.

Here is the pseudocode for the algorithm:

```
num_matches = 0.
If the first digit of the guess matches
either digit of the correct number:
    We have found one match.

If the second digit of the guess is different from the first digit,
and it matches either digit of the correct number:
    We have found another match.
```

We need to be able to split the correct number and the guess into the two digits that compose each so that we can compare them. Recall from the Boolean Zen section that we can use the integer division and remainder operators to express the digits of any two-digit number n as n `//` 10 for the tens digit and n `%` 10 for the ones digit.

Let's write the statement that compares the tens digit of the guess against the correct answer. Since the tens digit of the guess can match either of the correct number's digits, We'll use an `or` test:

```
num_matches = 0
# check the first digit for a match
if guess // 10 == number // 10 or guess // 10 == number % 10:
    num_matches += 1
```

Writing the statement that compares the ones digit of the guess against the correct answer is slightly trickier, because we have to take into consideration the special case described previously (in which both digits of the guess are the same). We'll account for this by counting the second digit as a match only if it is unique and matches a digit from the correct number:

```
# check the second digit for a match
if guess // 10 != guess % 10 and \
        (guess % 10 == number // 10 or guess % 10 == number % 10):
    num_matches += 1
```

The following version of the program uses the hinting code we've just written. It also adds the randomly chosen number and a brief introduction to the program:

```
 1  # A guessing game where the computer thinks of a
 2  # 2-digit number and the user tries to guess it.
 3  # Two-digit number-guessing game with hinting.
 4
 5  import random
 6
 7  # Reports a hint about how many digits from the given
 8  # guess match digits from the given correct number.
 9  def matches(number, guess):
10      num_matches = 0
11      if guess // 10 == number // 10 or guess // 10 == number % 10:
12          num_matches += 1
13      if guess // 10 != guess % 10 and (guess % 10 == number // 10 or
14              guess % 10 == number % 10):
15          num_matches += 1
16      return num_matches
17
18  def main():
19      print("Try to guess my two-digit number, and I'll tell you")
20      print("how many digits from your guess appear in my number.")
21      print()
```

Continued on next page

Continued from previous page

```
22
23      # pick a random number from 0 to 99 inclusive
24      number = random.randint(0, 99)
25
26      # get first guess
27      guess = int(input("Your guess? "))
28      num_guesses = 1
29
30      # give hints until correct guess is reached
31      while guess != number:
32          num_matches = matches(number, guess)
33          print("Incorrect (hint:", num_matches, "digits match)")
34          guess = int(input("Your guess? "))
35          num_guesses += 1
36
37      print("You got it right in", num_guesses, "tries.")
38
39  main()
```

```
Try to guess my two-digit number, and I'll tell you
how many digits from your guess appear in my number.

Your guess? 13
Incorrect (hint: 0 digits match)
Your guess? 26
Incorrect (hint: 0 digits match)
Your guess? 78
Incorrect (hint: 1 digits match)
Your guess? 79
Incorrect (hint: 1 digits match)
Your guess? 70
Incorrect (hint: 2 digits match)
Your guess? 7
You got it right in 6 tries.
```

Final Robust Version

The last major change We'll make to our program is to make it robust against invalid user input. There are two types of bad input that we may see:

1. Non-numeric tokens.

2. Numbers outside the range of 0–99.

Let's deal with these cases one at a time. Recall the `get_int` function that was discussed earlier in this chapter. It repeatedly prompts the user for input until an integer is typed. Here is its header:

```
def get_int(prompt):
    ...
```

We can make use of `get_int` to get an integer between `0` and `99`. We'll repeatedly call `get_int` until the integer that is returned is within the acceptable range. The postcondition we require before we can stop prompting for guesses is:

```
0 <= guess <= 99
```

To ensure that this postcondition is met, we can use a `while` loop that tests for the opposite condition. The opposite of the previous test would be the following:

```
guess < 0 or guess > 99
```

The reversed test is used in our new `get_guess` function to get a valid guess between `0` and `99`. Now whenever we want to read user input in the `main` program, we'll call `get_guess`. It's useful to separate the input prompting in this way, to make sure that we don't accidentally count invalid inputs as guesses.

The final version of our code is the following:

```
1   # A guessing game where the computer thinks of a
2   # 2-digit number and the user tries to guess it.
3   # Robust two-digit number-guessing game with hinting.
4
5   import random
6
7   # Prints an explanation of how to play the game.
8   def give_intro():
9       print("Try to guess my two-digit number, and I'll tell you")
10      print("how many digits from your guess appear in my number.")
11      print()
12
13  # Returns number of matching digits between the two given numbers.
14  # pre: number and guess are unique two-digit numbers
15  def matches(number, guess):
16      num_matches = 0
17      if guess // 10 == number // 10 or guess // 10 == number % 10:
18          num_matches += 1
19      if guess // 10 != guess % 10 and (guess % 10 == number // 10 or
20              guess % 10 == number % 10):
21          num_matches += 1
22      return num_matches
23
```

Continued on next page

Continued from previous page

```
24   # Prompts until a number in proper range is entered.
25   # post: guess is between 0 and 99
26   def get_guess():
27       guess = get_int("Your guess? ")
28       while guess < 0 or guess > 99:
29           print("Out of range; try again.")
30           guess = get_int("Your guess? ")
31       return guess
32
33   # Returns True if s can be converted to type int.
34   def is_integer(s):
35       try:
36           s = int(s)
37           return True
38       except ValueError:
39           return False
40
41   # Repeatedly prompts for input until a numeric string is typed.
42   # Returns the int value that was typed by the user.
43   def get_int(prompt):
44       line = input(prompt)
45       while not is_integer(line):
46           print("Not an integer; try again.")
47           line = input(prompt)
48       return int(line)
49
50   def main():
51       give_intro()
52
53       # pick a random number from 0 to 99 inclusive
54       number = random.randint(0, 99)
55
56       # get first guess
57       guess = get_guess()
58       num_guesses = 1
59
60       # give hints until correct guess is reached
61       while guess != number:
62           num_matches = matches(number, guess)
63           print("Incorrect (hint:", num_matches, "digits match)")
```

Continued on next page

Continued from previous page

```
64            guess = get_guess()
65            num_guesses += 1
66
67      print("You got it right in", num_guesses, "tries.")
68
69  main()
```

```
Try to guess my two-digit
number, and I'll tell you how
many digits from your guess
appear in my number.

Your guess? 12
Incorrect (hint: 0 digits match)
Your guess? okay
Not an integer; try again.
Your guess? 34
Incorrect (hint: 1 digits match)
Your guess? 35
Incorrect (hint: 1 digits match)
Your guess? 67
Incorrect (hint: 0 digits match)
Your guess? 89
Incorrect (hint: 0 digits match)
Your guess? 3
Incorrect (hint: 2 digits match)
Your guess? 300
Out of range; try again.
Your guess? 30
You got it right in 7 tries.
```

Notice that we're careful to comment our code; by doing so, we document relevant preconditions and postconditions of our functions. The precondition of the matches function is that the two parameters are unique two-digit numbers. The postcondition of our new get_guess function is that it returns a guess between 0 and 99 inclusive. Also, note that the program does not count invalid input (okay and 300 in the previous sample log of execution) as guesses.

Chapter Summary

- Python has a `while` loop in addition to its `for` loop. The `while` loop can be used to write indefinite loops that keep executing until some condition fails.
- Priming a loop means setting the values of variables that will be used in the loop test, so that the test will be sure to succeed the first time and the loop will execute.
- A fencepost loop executes a "loop-and-a-half" by executing part of a loop's body once before the loop begins.
- A sentinel loop is a kind of fencepost loop that repeatedly processes input until it is passed a particular value, but does not process the special value.
- The `bool` type represents logical values of either `True` or `False`. Boolean expressions are used as tests in `if` statements and loops. Boolean expressions can use relational operators such as < or != as well as logical operators such as `and` or `not`.

- Complex Boolean tests with logical operators such as `and` or `or` are evaluated lazily: If the overall result is clear from evaluating the first part of the expression, later parts are not evaluated. This is called short-circuited evaluation.
- `bool` variables (sometimes called "flags") can store Boolean values and can be used as loop tests.
- A robust program checks for errors in user input. Better robustness can be achieved by looping and reprompting the user to enter input when he or she types bad input.
- Assertions are logical statements about a particular point in a program. Assertions are useful for proving properties about how a program will execute. Two useful types of assertions are preconditions and postconditions, which are claims about what will be true before and after a function executes.

Self-Check Problems

Section 5.1: The while Loop

1. For each of the following `while` loops, state how many times the loop will execute its body. Remember that "zero," "infinity," and "unknown" are legal answers. Also, what is the output of the code in each case?

   a.
   ```python
   x = 1
   while x < 100:
       print(x, end=" ")
       x += 10
   ```

   b.
   ```python
   max = 10
   while max < 10:
       print("count down:", max)
       max -= 1
   ```

   c.
   ```python
   x = 250
   while x % 3 != 0:
       print(x)
   ```

   d.
   ```python
   x = 2
   while x < 200:
       print(x, end=" ")
       x *= x
   ```

e.
```
word = "a"
while len(word) < 10:
    word = "b" + word + "b"
print(word)
```

f.
```
x = 100
while x > 0:
    print(x // 10)
    x = x // 2
```

2. Convert each of the following `for` loops into an equivalent `while` loop:

a.
```
for n in range(1, max + 1):
    print(n)
```

b.
```
total = 25
for number in range(1, total // 5 + 1):
    total = total - number
    print(total, number)
```

c.
```
for i in range(1, 3):
    for j in range(1, 4):
        for k in range(1, 5):
            print("*", end="")
        print("!", end="")
    print()
```

3. Consider the following function:

```
def mystery(x):
    y = 1
    z = 0
    while 2 * y <= x:
        y = y * 2
        z += 1
    print(y, z)
```

For each of the following calls, indicate the output that the preceding function produces:

```
mystery(1)
mystery(6)
mystery(19)
mystery(39)
mystery(74)
```

4. Consider the following function:

```
def mystery(x):
    y = 0
    while x % 2 == 0:
        y += 1
```

Continued on next page

Continued from previous page

```
        x = x // 2
    print(x, y)
```

For each of the following calls, indicate the output that the preceding function produces:

```
mystery(19)
mystery(42)
mystery(48)
mystery(40)
mystery(64)
```

5. Write code that generates a random integer between 0 and 10 inclusive.

6. Write code that generates a random odd integer (not divisible by 2) between 50 and 99 inclusive.

Section 5.2: Fencepost Algorithms

7. Consider the flawed function `print_letters` that follows, which accepts a string as its parameter and attempts to print the letters of the string, separated by dashes. For example, the call of `print_letters("Rabbit")` should print R-a-b-b-i-t. The following code is incorrect:

```
def print_letters(text):
    for i in range(0, len(text)):
        print(text[i] + "-", end=" ")
    print() # to end the line of output
```

What is wrong with the code? How can it be corrected to produce the desired behavior?

8. Write a sentinel loop that repeatedly prompts the user to enter a number and, once the number −1 is typed, displays the maximum and minimum numbers that the user entered. Here is a sample dialogue:

```
Type a number (or -1 to stop): 5
Type a number (or -1 to stop): 2
Type a number (or -1 to stop): 17
Type a number (or -1 to stop): 8
Type a number (or -1 to stop): -1
Maximum was 17
Minimum was 2
```

If −1 is the first number typed, no maximum or minimum should be printed. In this case, the dialogue would look like this:

```
Type a number (or -1 to stop): -1
```

Section 5.3: Boolean Logic

9. Consider the following variable definitions:

```
x = 27
y = -1
z = 32
b = False
```

What is the value of each of the following expressions?

a. `not b`
b. `b or True`
c. `(x > y) and (y > z)`
d. `(x == y) or (x <= z)`
e. `not (x % 2 == 0)`
f. `(x % 2 != 0) and b`
g. `b and not b`
h. `b or not b`
i. `(x < y) == b`
j. `not (x / 2 == 13) or b or (z * 3 == 96)`
k. `(z < x) == False`
l. `not ((x > 0) and (y < 0))`

10. Write a function called `is_vowel` that accepts a character as input and returns `True` if that character is a vowel (a, e, i, o, or u). For an extra challenge, make your function case-insensitive.

11. The following code attempts to examine a number and return whether that number is prime (i.e., has no factors other than 1 and itself). A flag named `prime` is used. However, the Boolean logic is not implemented correctly, so the function does not always return the correct answer. In what cases does the function report an incorrect answer? How can the code be changed so that it will always return a correct result?

```
# incorrect code to determine whether an int is prime
def is_prime(n):
    prime = True
    for i in range(2, n):
        if n % i == 0:
            prime = False
        else:
            prime = True
    return prime
```

12. Using Boolean Zen, write an improved version of the following function, which returns whether the given string starts and ends with the same character:

```
def start_end_same(string):
    if string[0] == string[-1]:
        return True
    else:
        return False
```

13. Using Boolean Zen, write an improved version of the following function, which returns whether the given number of cents would require any pennies (as opposed to being an amount that could be made exactly using coins other than pennies):

```
def has_pennies(cents):
    nickels_only = cents % 5 == 0
    if nickels_only == True:
        return False
    else:
        return True
```

14. Consider the following function:

```
def mystery(x, y):
    while x != 0 and y != 0:
        if x < y:
            y -= x
        else:
            x -= y
    return x + y
```

For each of the following calls, indicate the value that is returned:

```
mystery(3, 3)
mystery(5, 3)
mystery(2, 6)
mystery(12, 18)
mystery(30, 75)
```

15. The following code is a slightly modified version of actual code that was in the Microsoft Zune music player in 2008. The code attempts to calculate today's date by determining how many years and days have passed since 1980. Assume the existence of functions for getting the total number of days since 1980 and for determining whether a given year is a leap year:

```
days = get_total_days_since_1980()
year = 1980
```

Continued on next page

Continued from previous page

```
while days > 365:    # subtract out years
    if is_leap_year(year):
        if days > 366:
            days -= 366
            year += 1
    else:
        days -= 365
        year += 1
```

Thousands of Zune music players locked up on January 1, 2009, the first day after the end of a leap year since the Zune was released. (Microsoft quickly released a patch to fix the problem.) What is the problem with the preceding code, and in what cases will it exhibit incorrect behavior? How can it be fixed?

16. Consider the following variable definitions:

```
x = 27
y = -1
z = 32
b = False
```

Write a new expression that is the negation of each of the following expressions. Use De Morgan's laws rather than simply writing a not at the beginning of each entire expression.

a. b
b. (x > y) and (y > z)
c. (x == y) or (x <= z)
d. (x % 2 != 0) and b
e. (x / 2 == 13) or b or (z * 3 == 96)
f. (z < x) and (z > y or x >= y)

Section 5.4: Robust Programs

17. The following code is not robust against invalid user input. Describe how to change the code so that it will not proceed until the user has entered a valid age and grade point average (GPA). Assume that any integer is a legal age and that any real number is a legal GPA.

```
age = int(input("Type your age: "))
gpa = float(input("Type your GPA: "))
```

For an added challenge, modify the code so that it rejects invalid ages (for example, numbers less than 0) and GPAs (say, numbers less than 0.0 or greater than 4.0).

18. Write code that prompts for three integers, averages them, and prints the average. Make your code robust against invalid input.

Section 5.5: Assertions and Program Logic

19. Identify the various assertions in the following code as being always true, never true, or sometimes true and sometimes false at various points in program execution. The comments indicate the points of interest:

```python
def mystery(x):
    y = int(input("Type a number: "))
    count = 0

    # Point A
    while y < x:
        # Point B
        if y == 0:
            count += 1
            # Point C
        y = int(input("Type a number: "))
        # Point D
    # Point E
    return count
```

Categorize each assertion at each point with ALWAYS, NEVER, or SOMETIMES:

	y < x	y == 0	count > 0
Point A			
Point B			
Point C			
Point D			
Point E			

20. Identify the various assertions in the following code as being always true, never true, or sometimes true and sometimes false at various points in program execution. The comments indicate the points of interest:

```python
def mystery(n):
    a = random.randint(1, 3)
    b = 2
    # Point A
    while n > b:
        # Point B
        b = b + a
        if a > 1:
            n -= 1
            # Point C
            a = random.randint(1, b)
```

Continued on next page

Continued from previous page

```
        else:
            a = b + 1
            # Point D
    # Point E
    return n
```

Categorize each assertion at each point with ALWAYS, NEVER, or SOMETIMES:

	n > b	a > 1	b > a
Point A			
Point B			
Point C			
Point D			
Point E			

21. Identify the various assertions in the following code as being always true, never true, or sometimes true and sometimes false at various points in program execution. The comments indicate the points of interest:

```
def mystery():
    prev = 0
    count = 0
    next = int(input("Type a number: "))
    # Point A
    while next != 0:
        # Point B
        if next == prev:
            # Point C
            count += 1
        prev = next
        next = int(input("Type a number: "))
        # Point D
    # Point E
    return count
```

Categorize each assertion at each point with ALWAYS, NEVER, or SOMETIMES:

	next == 0	prev == 0	next == prev
Point A			
Point B			
Point C			
Point D			
Point E			

Exercises

1. Write a function called `show_twos` that shows the factors of 2 in a given integer. For example, consider the following calls:

```
show_twos(7)
show_twos(18)
show_twos(68)
show_twos(120)
```

These calls should produce the following output:

```
7 = 7
18 = 2 * 9
68 = 2 * 2 * 17
120 = 2 * 2 * 2 * 15
```

2. Write a function called `gcd` that accepts two integers as parameters and returns the greatest common divisor (GCD) of the two numbers. The GCD of two integers a and b is the largest integer that is a factor of both a and b. One efficient way to compute the GCD of two numbers is to use Euclid's algorithm, which states the following:

$$GCD(a, b) = GCD(b, a \% b)$$
$$GCD(a, 0) = \text{Absolute value of } a$$

3. Write a function called `to_binary` that accepts an integer as a parameter and returns a string containing that integer's binary representation. For example, the call of `print_binary(44)` should return `"101100"`.

4. Write a function called `random_x` that prints lines that contain a random number of `"x"` characters (between 5 and 20 inclusive) until it prints a line that contains 16 or more characters. For example, the output might look like the following:

```
xxxxxxx
xxxxxxxxxxxxxxx
xxxxxxxxxxxx
xxxxxxxxxxxxxx
xxxxxx
xxxxxxxxxxx
xxxxxxxxxxxxxxxxx
```

5. Write a function called `dice_sum` that prompts for a desired sum, then repeatedly simulates the rolling of 2 six-sided dice until their sum is the desired sum. Here is a sample dialogue with the user:

```
Desired dice sum: 9
4 and 3 = 7
3 and 5 = 8
5 and 6 = 11
5 and 6 = 11
1 and 5 = 6
6 and 3 = 9
```

6. Write a function called `random_walk` that performs steps of a random one-dimensional walk. The random walk should begin at position 0. On each step, you should either increase or decrease the position by 1 (each with equal probability). Your code should continue making steps until a position of 3 or -3 is reached, and then report the maximum position that was reached during the walk. The output should look like the following:

```
position = 1
position = 0
position = -1
position = -2
position = -1
position = -2
position = -3
max position = 1
```

7. Write a function called `print_factors` that accepts an integer as its parameter and uses a fencepost loop to print the factors of that number, separated by the word `"and"`. For example, the factors of the number 24 should print as the following:

```
1 and 2 and 3 and 4 and 6 and 8 and 12 and 24
```

You may assume that the parameter's value is greater than 0, or you may raise an error if it is 0 or negative. Your function should print nothing if the empty string (`""`) is passed.

8. Write a function called `three_heads` that repeatedly flips a coin until the results of the coin toss are three heads in a row. You should use `random.randint` to make it equally likely that a head or a tail will appear. Each time the coin is flipped, display H for heads or T for tails. When three heads in a row are flipped, the function should print a congratulatory message. Here is a possible output of a call to the function:

```
T T H T T T H T H T H H H
Three heads in a row!
```

9. Write a function called `print_average` that uses a sentinel loop to repeatedly prompt the user for numbers. Once the user types any number less than zero, the function should display the average of all nonnegative numbers typed. Here is a sample dialogue with the user:

```
Type a number: 7
Type a number: 4
Type a number: 16
Type a number: -4
Average was 9.0
```

If the first number that the user types is negative, do not print an average:

```
Type a number: -2
```

10. Write a predicate function named called `has_midpoint` that accepts three integers as parameters and returns `True` if one of the integers is the midpoint between the other two integers; that is, if one integer is exactly halfway between them. Your function should return `False` if no such midpoint relationship exists. For example, the call `has_midpoint(7, 4, 10)` should return `True` because 7 is halfway between 4 and 10. By contrast, the call `has_midpoint(9, 15, 8)` should return `False` because no integer is halfway between the other two. The integers could be passed in any order; the midpoint could be the first, second, or third. You must check all cases. If your function is passed three of the same value, return `True`.

11. Write a predicate function named called `month_apart` that accepts four integer parameters, m1, d1, m2, and d2, representing two calendar dates. Each date consists of a month (1-12) and a day (1 through the number of days in that month [28–31]). Assume that all parameter values passed are valid. The function should return `True` if the dates are at least a month apart and `False` otherwise. For example, the call of `month_apart(4, 15, 5, 22)` would return `True` while the call of `month_apart(9, 19, 10, 17)` would return `False`. Assume that all the dates in this problem occur during the same year. Note that the first date could come before or after the second date.

12. Write a function called `digit_sum` that accepts an integer as a parameter and returns the sum of the digits of that number. For example, the call `digit_sum(29107)` returns $2 + 9 + 1 + 0 + 7$ or 19. For negative numbers, return the same value that would result if the number were positive. For example, `digit_sum(-456)` returns $4 + 5 + 6$ or 15. The call `digit_sum(0)` returns 0.

13. Write a function called `first_digit` that returns the first (most significant) digit of an integer. For example, `first_digit(3572)` should return 3. It should work for negative numbers as well; `first_digit(-947)` should return 9.

14. Write a function named called `swap_digit_pairs` that accepts an integer n as a parameter and returns a new integer whose value is similar to n's but with each pair of digits swapped in order. For example, the call of `swap_digit_pairs(482596)` would return 845269. Notice that the 9 and 6 are swapped, as are the 2 and 5, and the 4 and 8. If the number contains an odd number of digits, leave the leftmost digit in its original place. For example, the call of `swap_digit_pairs(1234567)` would return 1325476. You should solve this problem without using a string.

15. Write a function called `is_all_vowels` that returns whether a string consists entirely of vowels (a, e, i, o, or u, case-insensitively). If and only if every character of the string is a vowel, your function should return `True`. For example, the call `is_all_vowels("eIEiO")` returns `True` and `is_all_vowels("oink")` returns `False`. You should return `True` if passed the empty string, since it does not contain any nonvowel characters.

Programming Projects

1. Write an interactive program that reads lines of input from the user and converts each line into "Pig Latin." Pig Latin is English with the initial consonant sound moved to the end of each word, followed by "ay." Words that begin with vowels simply have an "ay" appended. For example, the phrase

   ```
   The deepest shade of mushroom blue
   ```

   would have the following appearance in Pig Latin:

   ```
   e-Thay eepest-day ade-shay of-ay ushroom-may ue-blay
   ```

   Terminate the program when the user types a blank line.

2. Write a program that plays a guessing game with the user. The program should generate a random number between 1 and some maximum (such as 100), then prompt the user repeatedly to guess the number. When the user guesses incorrectly, the game should give the user a hint about whether the correct answer is higher or lower than the guess. Once the user guesses correctly, the program should print a message showing the number of guesses that the user made. Consider extending this program by making it play multiple games until the user chooses to stop and then printing statistics about the player's total and average number of guesses. For an added challenge, consider having the user hint to the computer whether the correct number is higher or lower than the computer's guess. The computer should adjust its range of random guesses on the basis of the hint.

3. Write a program that draws a graphical display of a 2D random walk using a `DrawingPanel`. Start a pixel walker in the middle of the panel. On each step, choose to move 1 pixel up, down, left, or right, and then redraw the pixel. (You can draw a single pixel by drawing a rectangle of size 1 × 1.)

4. Write a program that plays the dice game "Pig." Pig is a two-player game where the players take turns repeatedly rolling a single six-sided die; a player repeatedly rolls the die until one of two events occurs. Either the player chooses to stop rolling, in which case the sum of that player's rolls are added to his/her total points; or if the player rolls a 1 at any time, all points for that turn are lost and the turn ends immediately. The first player to reach a score of at least 100 points wins.

Chapter **6**

File Processing

Introduction

In Chapter 3 we discussed how to use the `input` function to read input from the console. Now we will look at how to read input from files. Many interesting problems can be formulated as file-processing tasks. The idea is fairly straightforward, but it can be complex to read from input files.

Files can be processed in several ways. First we will explore breaking a file apart into lines. Then we will look at examining individual words and tokens of input within each line.

At the end of the chapter we will learn how to write output to files and how to read data from other sources such as the Internet.

6.1 File-Reading Basics

In this section we'll look at the most basic issues related to file processing. What are files and why do we care about them? What are the most basic techniques for reading files in a Python program? Once you've mastered these basics, we'll move on to a more detailed discussion of the different techniques you can use to process files.

Data and Files

People are fascinated by data. When the field of statistics emerged in the nineteenth century, there was an explosion of interest in gathering and interpreting large amounts of data. Mark Twain reported that the British statesman Benjamin Disraeli complained to him, "There are three kinds of lies: lies, damn lies, and statistics."

The advent of the Internet has only added fuel to the fire. Today, every person with an Internet connection has access to a vast array of databases containing information about every facet of our existence. Here are just a few examples:

- If you visit landmark-project.com and click on the link for "Raw Data," you will find data files about earthquakes, air pollution, baseball, labor, crime, financial markets, U.S. history, geography, weather, national parks, a "world values survey," and more.

- At gutenberg.org you'll find thousands of online books, including the complete works of Shakespeare and works by Sir Arthur Conan Doyle, Jane Austen, H. G. Wells, James Joyce, Albert Einstein, Mark Twain, Lewis Carroll, T. S. Eliot, Edgar Allan Poe, and many others.

- Nate Silver's FiveThirtyEight (fivethirtyeight.com) has extensive data on politics, sports, economics, health, and culture.

- A wealth of genomic data is available from sites like ncbi.nlm.nih.gov/guide. Biologists have decided that the vast quantities of data describing the human genome and the genomes of other organisms should be publicly available for everyone to study.

- The U.S. government maintains data.gov, which is described on the web site as "the home of the U.S. Government's open data." Many states and local governments maintain similar sites (e.g., data.seattle.gov, data.wa.gov, and openbooks. az.gov).

- Many popular web sites, such as the Internet Movie Database, make their data available for download as simple data files (see imdb.com/interfaces).

- The U.S. government produces reams of statistical data. The web site usa.gov/ statistics provides a lengthy list of available downloads, including maps and statistics on employment, climate, manufacturing, demographics, health, crime, and more.

Did You Know?

Origin of Data Processing

The field of data processing predates computers by over half a century. It is often said that necessity is the mother of invention, and the emergence of data processing is a good example of this principle. The crisis that spawned the industry came from a requirement in Article 1, Section 2, of the U.S. Constitution, which indicates that each state's population will determine how many representatives that state gets in the House of Representatives. To calculate the correct number, you need to know the population, so the Constitution says, "The actual Enumeration shall be made within three Years after the first Meeting of the Congress of the United States, and within every subsequent Term of ten Years, in such Manner as they shall by Law direct."

The first census was completed relatively quickly in 1790. Since then, every 10 years the U.S. government has had to perform another complete census of the population. This process became more and more difficult as the population of the country grew larger. By 1880 the government discovered that the old-fashioned hand-counting techniques it had been using barely enabled it to complete the census within the 10 years allotted to it. So the government announced a competition for inventors to propose machines that could be used to speed up the process.

Herman Hollerith won the competition with a system involving punched cards. Clerks punched over 62 million cards that were then counted by 100 counting machines. This system allowed the 1890 tabulation to be completed in less than half the time it had taken to hand-count the 1880 results, even though the population had increased by 25 percent.

Hollerith struggled for years to turn his invention into a commercial success. His biggest problem initially was that he had just one customer: the U.S. government. Eventually he found other customers, and the company that he founded merged with competitors and grew into the company we now know as International Business Machines Corporation, or IBM.

We think of IBM as a computer company, but it sold a wide variety of data-processing equipment involving Hollerith cards long before computers became popular. Later, when it entered the computer field, IBM used Hollerith cards for storing programs and data. These cards were still being used when one of this book's authors took his freshman computer programming class in 1978.

When you store data on your own computer, you store it in a *file*.

> **File**
>
> A collection of information that is stored on a computer and assigned a particular name.

As we have just noted, every file has a name. For example, if you were to download the text of *Hamlet* from the Gutenberg site, you might store it on your computer in a file called `hamlet.txt`. A file name often ends with a special suffix that indicates the kind of data it contains or the format in which it has been stored. This suffix is known as a file *extension*. Table 6.1 lists some common file extensions.

Files can be classified into *text files* and *binary files* depending on the format that is used. Text files can be edited using simple text editors. Binary files are stored using an internal format that requires special software to process. Text files are often stored using the `.txt` extension, but other file formats are also text formats, including `.py` and `.html` files. The examples in this chapter will process plain text files.

Files are grouped into *directories*, also called *folders*. Directories are organized in a hierarchy, starting from a root directory at the top. For example, most Windows machines have a disk drive known as `C:`. At the top level of this drive is the root directory, which we can describe as `C:\`. Most Linux and Mac machines do not use disk drive letters like `C:` and instead refer to the root of their file system with a slash, `/`. The root directory of a file system will contain various top-level directories. Each top-level directory can have subdirectories, each of which also has subdirectories, and so on. All files are stored in one of these directories. The description of how to get from the

Table 6.1 Common File Extensions

Extension	Description
.doc	Microsoft Word document
.exe	executable file (Windows)
.html	web page
.java	Java source code file
.jpg	JPEG image file
.mp3	audio file
.pdf	Adobe Portable Document File
.py	Python source code file
.txt	text file
.xls	Microsoft Excel spreadsheet
.zip	ZIP compressed archive

top-level directory to the particular directory that stores a file is known as the *path* of the file.

File Path

A description of a file's location on a computer, starting with a drive and including the path from the root directory to the directory where the file is stored.

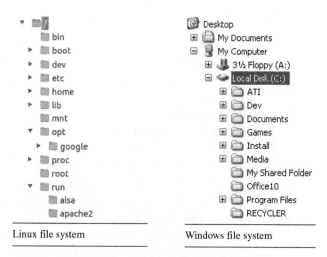

Linux file system   Windows file system

We read the path information from left to right. For example, if the path to a file is */home/kjones12/school/hamlet.txt*, we know that the file system root contains a directory named *home*, which contains a subdirectory named *kjones12*, which contains a subdirectory named *school*, which contains the file *hamlet.txt*.

If you want to read the data from a file in a Python program, you will need to specify the file's name as a string in your code. If your code contains only the file's name, such as "hamlet.txt", the Python interpreter will look in the *current directory* (also called the *working directory*) to find the file. In most environments, the current directory is the one that contains your Python program file. A simple file path like this is called a *relative path*.

You can also specify a relative path containing a directory. For example, the relative path "data/numbers.dat" indicates a file called *numbers.dat* in a subdirectory of the working directory called *data*.

Current Directory (a.k.a. Working Directory)

The directory that Python uses as the default when a program uses a relative file path.

You can also specify a file path as a string containing the entire path to the file, including the directory it is in, such as "/home/kjones12/school/hamlet.txt" (Linux/Mac) or "C:\\Users\\jsmith\\numbers.dat" (Windows). This kind of path is called an *absolute path*. The main difference between an absolute path and a relative path is that an absolute path starts with the file system root, such as / or C:.

We discourage you from using absolute paths in your programs. Absolute paths work well only when you know exactly where your file is going to be stored on your system. If you move the input file into another directory, or if you send your program to a friend who saves it into a different directory, the program will not work properly.

Reading a File in Python

To access a file from inside a Python program, you will use a function called open. The open function accepts a string representing a file path as a parameter and opens that file for reading by your program. It returns an object representing the file, which you can store into a variable. The general syntax is the following:

```
name = open("filename")
```
Syntax template: Opening a file for reading

For example, suppose you have an input file named *poem.txt* located in the same directory as our Python code that contains the following lines of text. You can create such a file with an editor like Notepad++ on a Windows machine or Sublime Text on a Mac.

```
Roses are red,
Violets are blue.
All my base
Are belong to you.
```

The following line of code opens the *poem.txt* file for reading:

```
# read data from poem.txt file
file = open("poem.txt")
```

When this line of code is executed, Python constructs a special *file object* that is linked to the file *poem.txt*. This file object has several methods and features that help you to view and manipulate the data in the file. The simplest way to process a file is to use its read method, which reads the entire contents of the file and returns it as one long string. We don't normally think of a string as containing more than one line of text, but it is possible to embed newline characters ("\n") within the string to indicate the line breaks. This one command will read in all of the lines of text in a file even if the file is thousands of lines long. The following program demonstrates how to use this method:

```
1  # This program prints the entire
2  # text contents of a file.
3
```

Continued on next page

Continued from previous page

```
4   def main():
5       file = open("poem.txt")
6       filetext = file.read()
7       print("Here are the file contents:")
8       print("===========================")
9       print(filetext)
10      print("===========================")
11      print("length:", len(filetext), "characters")
12      file.close()
13
14  main()
```

```
Here are the file contents:
===========================
Roses are red,
Violets are blue.
All my base
Are belong to you.
===========================
length: 63 characters
```

Notice that the last line of main calls a close method on the file object. The close method tells Python that your program is done using the file. The program will still run if you don't call close, though it is considered good practice to always explicitly close any files you are using. Forgetting to close files can also lead to bugs or lost data if you are writing to a file, which we will learn about later in this chapter.

It can be hard to remember to always close files at the end of your code. To help with this, Python has a statement called a with statement that can be used to open a resource, such as a file, and later close it automatically. A with statement contains a heading and then a body of statements indented underneath it. The indented statements can use the opened resource. Once the lines of code in the indented body have finished, Python automatically closes whatever resource was opened in the with statement heading. Its general syntax is the following:

```
with open("filename") as name:
    statement
    statement
    ...
    statement
```

Syntax template: Opening a file using with statement

The syntax of the with heading is a bit odd because the variable's name comes last, after the word as, but it is essentially the same as a normal variable definition. The following is an equivalent version of our previous *print_file* program that uses a `with` statement. Notice that there is no longer a call to `file.close()` because the file will be closed automatically.

```
1   # This program prints the entire contents of a file.
2   # This version uses a 'with' statement, which will
3   # close the file automatically when finished.
4
5   def main():
6       with open("poem.txt") as file:
7           filetext = file.read()
8           print("Here are the file contents:")
9           print("============================")
10          print(filetext)
11          print("============================")
12          print("length:", len(filetext), "characters")
13
14  main()
```

The `with` statement is the recommended way to read and write files in Python, and we will use it for all of the examples in this text.

The `read` method is just one of many that you can call on a Python file object. Table 6.2 lists several of the most useful methods. We will explain some of these in this chapter. You can read about all of the methods in the online Python library documentation:

- https://docs.python.org/3/library/io.html

Table 6.2 Methods of file objects

Method Name	Description
file.close()	indicates that you are done reading/writing the file
file.flush()	writes any buffered data to an open output file
file.read()	reads and returns the entire file as a string
file.readable()	returns True if the file can be read
file.readline()	reads and returns a single line of the file as a string
file.readlines()	reads and returns the entire file as a list of line strings
file.seek(position)	sets the file's current input cursor position
file.tell()	returns the file's current input cursor position
file.writable()	returns True if the file can be written
file.write("text")	sends text to an output file
file.writelines(lines)	sends a list of lines to an output file

You can try out the various methods available with a file object in the Python Shell. For example, the following interaction opens a file and reads two lines from it:

```
>>> # test file-reading methods
>>> file = open("poem.txt")
>>> file.read()
'Roses are red,\nViolets are blue.\nAll my base\nAre belong to you.'
>>> file = open("poem.txt")    # re-open the file
>>> file.readline()
'Roses are red,\n'
>>> file.readline()
'Violets are blue.\n'
>>> file.readline()
'All my base\n'
>>> file.readline()
'Are belong to you.'
>>> file.readline()
''
```

Line-Based File Processing

Printing an entire file is useful, but often you will want to process individual lines of the file one by one. For example, maybe you want to print the lines with extra formatting around them, or perhaps you want to search the file for a given pattern. Examining a file in this way is called *line-based processing*.

> **Line-Based Processing**
>
> The practice of processing input line by line (i.e., reading in entire lines of input at a time).

In Python you can perform line-based processing of an input file in several ways. For example, there is a `readline` method that reads and returns a single line of a file. But the simplest way to read each of the lines in a file is to use a `for` loop. Similar to the way that you can use a string in a `for` loop to iterate over its characters, if you provide a file object after the word `in` in your loop header, the loop will iterate over the lines in the file. The general syntax for this is the following:

```
for line in file:
    statement
    statement
    ...
    statement
```

Syntax template: Reading a file line by line

For example, the following program opens the file *poem.txt* and reads and prints all of its lines to the console, along with a count of the number of lines:

```
1   # This program counts and prints all
2   # of the lines in an input file.
3
4   def main():
5       with open("poem.txt") as file:
6           line_count = 0
7           for line in file:
8               print("next line:", line)
9               line_count += 1
10          print("Line count:", line_count)
11
12  main()
```

```
next line: Roses are red,

next line: Violets are blue.

next line: All my base

next line: Are belong to you.

Line count: 4
```

If you look closely at the output, you'll notice that there are blank lines between each printed line. This is because each line that is read from the file is returned as a string that ends with a newline character (`"\n"`) that signals a line break or end-of-line. Some languages automatically strip these characters off of the end of each line when reading files, but Python does not. If you want to print the file without the blank lines, call the `rstrip` method of the line string to remove any whitespace from the end of the string. You can replace the `print` statement in the loop with the following:

```
print("next line:", line.rstrip())
```

We'll use `rstrip` or `strip` in some of our other examples in this chapter.

Structure of Files and Consuming Input

We think of text as being two-dimensional, like a sheet of paper, but from the computer's point of view, each file is just a one-dimensional sequence of characters. For example, consider the file *poem.txt* that we used in the previous section:

```
Roses are red,
Violets are blue.
All my base
Are belong to you.
```

We think of this as a four-line file with text going across and down. However, the computer views the file differently. When you typed the text in this file, you pressed the Enter key to go to a new line. This key inserts special "newline" characters in the file. You can annotate the file with \n characters to indicate the end of each line:

```
Roses are red,\n
Violets are blue.\n
All my base\n
Are belong to you.\n
```

While it may be easier for us to think of this data as being two-dimensional, the computer doesn't think of a file that way. Really \n is just another character value, and the overall data could be thought of as a one-dimensional sequence of characters:

```
Roses are red,\nViolets are blue.\nAll my base\nAre belong to you.
```

This sequence is how the computer views the file: as a one-dimensional sequence of characters including special characters that happen to represent "new line". On some Windows machines the "new line" marker is a two-character sequence of \r\n, but we'll use just \n here since that is most common. Python's file objects will handle these differences for you, so you can generally ignore them.

When it is processing a file, the file object keeps track of a current position in the file. You can think of this as an *input cursor* or pointer into the file.

> **Input Cursor**
> A pointer to the current position in an input file.

When a file object is first created, the cursor points to the beginning of the file. But as you perform various reading operations, the cursor moves forward. The `print_lines` program from the last section reads the file line-by-line using a `for` loop. Let's take a moment to examine in detail how that works. Again, when the file is first opened, the input cursor will be positioned at the beginning of the file (indicated with an up-arrow pointing at the first character):

```
Roses are red,\nViolets are blue.\nAll my base\nAre belong to you.
↑
input cursor
```

Each iteration of the `for` loop causes the cursor to move forward. For example, after the first iteration of the loop, the cursor will be positioned at the beginning of the second line:

```
Roses are red,\nViolets are blue.\nAll my base\nAre belong to you.
```
↑

input cursor

We refer to this process as *consuming input*. Notice that the entire first line has been consumed, including the newline character at the end of the line. Recall that the string returned includes that newline `"\n"` character.

> **Consuming Input**
> Moving the input cursor forward past some input in a file.

The process of consuming input doesn't actually change the file, it just changes the file object so that it is positioned at a different point in the file. After the second iteration of the loop, the cursor has advanced past another line:

```
Roses are red,\nViolets are blue.\nAll my base\nAre belong to you.
```
↑

input cursor

The program continues reading in this manner until it reaches the end of the file. After it reads the final line, the input cursor is positioned at the end of the file:

```
Roses are red,\nViolets are blue.\nAll my base\nAre belong to you.
```
↑

input cursor

When the input cursor reaches the end of the file, the `for` loop stops.

Python file objects are generally designed for file processing in a forward manner. They provide a great deal of flexibility for looking ahead in an input file, but less support for reading the input backwards or out-of-order.

Reading a file and advancing its input cursor does not modify the file on your computer in any way. The input cursor is entirely a construct of the Python language and its file libraries. If you open a file for reading, you do not need to worry about your program causing damage to that file or erasing its contents.

Trying to Loop Over File Twice

Sometimes you will want to process each line of a file more than once. But if you attempt to do so using two `for` loops over the same file object, you'll find that the second loop does nothing. For example, the following incorrect code attempts to print the lines of the file *poem.txt* twice:

```
with open("poem.txt") as file:
    # print file a first time
    print("First time:")
    for line in file:
        print(line.rstrip())
    print()

    # print file a second time?
    print("Second time:")
    for line in file:
        print(line.rstrip())
```

```
First time:
next line: Roses are red,
next line: Violets are blue.
next line: All my base
next line: Are belong to you.

Second time:
```

Notice that the second time, no output is printed. The reason is that, as discussed in this chapter, a file object maintains an internal position or cursor as it reads input. Whenever you run a `for` loop over a file, the cursor moves forward in the file. After the loop is completed, the cursor is at the end of the file. If you try another `for` loop over that same file object, no lines will come out, because the cursor has already moved past all of the lines.

There are two ways to fix the problem and successfully print the file twice. One is to re-open the file using two separate `with` statements. Each time you re-open the file with a new `with` statement, the cursor is set back to the start of the file, so all of the lines will be printed properly.

```
# print file a first time
with open("poem.txt") as file:
    print("First time:")
    for line in file:
        print(line.rstrip())
    print()

# print file a second time
with open("poem.txt") as file:
    print("Second time:")
    for line in file:
        print(line.rstrip())
```

```
First time:
next line: Roses are red,
next line: Violets are blue.
next line: All my base
next line: Are belong to you.

Second time:
next line: Roses are red,
next line: Violets are blue.
next line: All my base
next line: Are belong to you.
```

Another way to successfully read a file twice is to call the file object's `seek` method. The `seek` method accepts an integer position as a parameter and moves the file object's cursor to that position. Position 0 represents the start of the file, and higher numbers represent positions later in the file. So a call to `seek(0)` will rewind the cursor to the beginning so that the file can be read a second time:

```
with open("poem.txt") as file:
    # print file a first time
    print("First time:")
    for line in file:
        print(line.rstrip())
    print()

    # print file a second time
    file.seek(0)    # rewind cursor to start
    print("Second time:")
    for line in file:
        print(line.rstrip())
```

Continued on next page

Continued from previous page

```
First time:
next line: Roses are red,
next line: Violets are blue.
next line: All my base
next line: Are belong to you.

Second time:
next line: Roses are red,
next line: Violets are blue.
next line: All my base
next line: Are belong to you.
```

Prompting for a File

Sometimes, rather than writing a file's path in the code yourself, you'll ask the user for a file name. This can make the program more flexible.

Prompting for a file name involves reading a string with the `input` function:

```
filename = input("File to open: ")
```

But if the user types the name of a file that does not exist, the program crashes:

```
File to open: oops.txt

Traceback (most recent call last):
  File "prompt_file.py", line 10, in <module>
    main()
  File "prompt_file.py", line 6, in main
    with open(filename) as file:
FileNotFoundError: [Errno 2] No such file or directory: 'oops.txt'
```

You could imagine that the way to avoid this error is to use `if` statements that check for specific file names that we know to exist, such as `"poem.txt"`. But that is inflexible and assumes the existence of particular files; it would fail or need updating if we changed the set of available files on the disk. Notice that the error output indicates that the program has thrown an exception of type `FileNotFoundError`. We could put the file-opening code in a `try/except` block as discussed in Chapter 5 to handle this error.

A better way to avoid such an error is to ask whether the given file exists before trying to open it. To do so, you will need to import a Python library called `os.path` and call its `isfile` function, which returns `True` if a given file exists and `False` if not:

```
import os.path
...
if os.path.isfile(filename):

    ...
```

Since prompting for a file is a generally useful task, we'll make it into a function called `prompt_for_file` that accepts a prompt message as its parameter and uses a `while` loop to repeatedly prompt the user for a file name until they type the name of a file that exists. (The function uses a fencepost loop, as we learned about in the previous chapter.) The function then returns the file name, which is guaranteed to exist, so that `main` can open that file.

Putting it all together, here is a complete program that prompts the user for the file name and then prints the entire contents of that file:

```
 1  # Prompts the user for a file name and
 2  # prints the entire contents of that file.
 3
 4  import os.path
 5
 6  # Prompts the user to type a file name
 7  # using the given prompt message;
 8  # repeatedly re-prompts if file is not found.
 9  # Returns the file name, which must exist.
10  def prompt_for_file(message):
11      filename = input(message)
12      while not os.path.isfile(filename):
13          print("File not found. Try again.")
14          filename = input(message)
15      return filename
16
17  def main():
18      filename = prompt_for_file("File to open? ")
19      with open(filename) as file:
20          filetext = file.read()
21          print(filetext)
22
23  main()
```

```
File to open? oops.txt
File not found. Try again.
File to open? notfound.dat
File not found. Try again.
File to open? poem.txt
Roses are red,
```

Continued on next page

Continued from previous page

```
Violets are blue.
All my base
Are belong to you.
```

The user could also have chosen to type an absolute file path:

```
File to open? /home/ksmith12/data/poem.txt
...
```

The `prompt_for_file` function is fairly standard and could be used without modification in many programs. We refer to reusable code like this as *boilerplate code*.

> **Boilerplate Code**
> Code that tends to be the same from one program to another.

The `os.path` library has several other useful functions. Table 6.3 lists some of the most common ones. You can see complete documentation for `os.path` in the Python library documentation:

- https://docs.python.org/3/library/os.path.html

The following program demonstrates several of the functions of the `os.path` library. For the program to generate the output shown, it would have to exist in a directory */home/ksmith12/data* and there would have to be a file existing in that folder called *poem.txt*.

```
1   # This program prints information about a file.
2   import os.path
3
4   def main():
5       filename = "poem.txt"
6       absfilepath = os.path.abspath(filename)
7       dirname = os.path.dirname(absfilepath)
8       print("abs path :", absfilepath)
9       print("directory:", dirname)
10      print("base name:", os.path.basename(absfilepath))
11      print("file size:", os.path.getsize(filename))
12      print("is file? :", os.path.isfile(filename))
13      print("is dir?  :", os.path.isdir(filename))
14
15  main()
```

```
abs path : /home/ksmith12/data/poem.txt
directory: /home/ksmith12/data
base name: poem.txt
file size: 63
is file? : True
is dir?  : False
```

Table 6.3 Functions of `os.path` library

Function	Description
`os.path.abspath("path")`	returns absolute path string for the given file
`os.path.basename("path")`	returns filename of the given file without directory in front of it
`os.path.dirname("path")`	returns directory the given file is in
`os.path.exists("path")`	returns `True` if the given file or directory exists
`os.path.getmtime("path")`	returns the time the given file was last modified
`os.path.getsize("path")`	returns the size of the given file in bytes
`os.path.isfile("path")`	returns `True` if the given file exists
`os.path.isdir("path")`	returns `True` if the given directory exists

6.2 Token-Based Processing

Reading an input file line-by-line is useful, but so far we have treated each line as an atomic entity. Often the data in each line contains multiple pieces of useful data separated by spaces or other delimiters, such as a collection of names or numbers. In this section we will explore how to access individual words or tokens of input from a file. Examining a file in this way is called *token-based processing*.

> **Token-Based Processing**
>
> Processing input token by token (i.e., one word at a time or one number at a time).

For example, consider the file *shakespeare.txt* containing a selection from Shakespeare's *Hamlet*:

```
To be, or not to be, that is the question:
Whether 'tis nobler in the mind to suffer
The slings and arrows of outrageous fortune,
Or to take Arms against a Sea of troubles,
And by opposing end them.
```

Suppose you want a program to report the number of times that a given word occurs in the file. Rather than looping over the lines of the file, we'd prefer to loop over each individual word.

We have seen that string objects have many useful methods that we can call. Each string has a method called `split` that divides the string into tokens. Strings are split using what are called *delimiters*. You can specify the delimiter yourself with an optional string that you pass as a parameter to `split`. But for our purposes, we want the default behavior of dividing up the string by paying attention to whitespace (sequences of spaces, tabs, line breaks, etc.).

If you first call the `read` method on a file object and then call `split` on the string that is returned, the result is a list of all of the whitespace-separated tokens in the file. The general syntax is the following:

```
for name in file.read().split():
    statement
    statement
    ...
    statement
```

Syntax template: Reading an entire file by tokens

The following code reads and prints every word in the file. This is not our final goal for this example, but it's useful to see the strings that come out for each word. Notice that the punctuation such as commas and periods is still included with each token; if you want it removed, you have to do so yourself.

```
with open("shakespeare.txt") as file:
    for word in file.read().split():
        print(word)
```

```
To
be,
or
not
to
be,
that
is
the
question:
...
```

Now let's revisit the original task of counting word occurrences. The following program prompts the user for a word and counts occurrences of that word. We use a standard cumulative sum to count the occurrences. Notice that we call `lower` on each word to produce a case-insensitive match.

```
1   # This program counts the number of occurrences
2   # of a particular word in a file.
3
4   def main():
5       target = input("Target word? ")
6       count = 0
7       with open("shakespeare.txt") as file:
8           for word in file.read().split():
9               if word.lower() == target.lower():
10                  count += 1
11      print("The word", target, "occurs", count, "times.")
12
13  main()
```

```
Target word? to
The word to occurs 4 times.
```

(This code does not properly handle punctuation at the end of words, such as `"be,"` or `"question."` How would you modify it to get rid of such punctuation marks?)

Numeric Input

Our previous examples handled input tokens that were strings, but many programs process data that consists of numbers. For example, you might want to create a file called *numbers.dat* with the following content:

```
308.2 14.9 7.4
2.8 81

5.0
3.9 4.7 67.0 -15.4
```

Then you might want to write a program that processes this input file and produces some kind of report. For example, suppose you want to add up all of the numbers in the file and report the sum. This is an example of a cumulative sum like you saw in Chapter 4.

The token-based approach of calling `read` and then `split` is a good start. But you cannot directly add each token to a sum because the tokens are strings and not numbers. The following code produces an error:

```
sum = 0.0
with open("numbers.dat") as file:
    for n in line.read().split():
        sum += n
```

```
Traceback (most recent call last):
  File "compute_sum.py", line 13, in <module>
    main()
  File "compute_sum.py", line 10, in main
    sum += n
TypeError: unsupported operand type(s) for +=:
          'float' and 'str'
```

You saw in Chapter 3 that the `input` function always returns the console input as a string, and that if we want to treat the input as a number or other type, you need to pass it to a type conversion function like `int` or `float`. The same applies here, since each token of the split string is also a string. The following program converts each token to a `float` and prints the sum successfully:

```
1   # This program adds numbers from a file
2   # and reports the sum of all the numbers.
3
4   def main():
5       sum = 0.0
6       with open("numbers.dat") as file:
7           for n in file.read().split():
8               sum += float(n)
9       print("Sum is:", round(sum, 1))
10
11  main()
```

```
Sum is: 479.5
```

Handling Invalid Input

In the previous section we wrote a program to read a file of numbers and print their sum. But suppose we want to read a new version of that file called *numbers2.dat* where some tokens are numeric and some are not:

```
308.2 hello 14.9 7.4
2.8 81 how are you?

5.0 :-) oops
badbad 3.9 4.7 67.0 yipes -15.4
```

Suppose we want our program to work with this kind of file; it should sum the numeric tokens in the file but skip over non-numeric tokens. If we try to use the code we wrote previously, it will crash when it reaches a non-numeric token string. The interpreter raises a `ValueError` to indicate that this string cannot be converted into a `float`.

```
Traceback (most recent call last):
  File "compute_sum2.py", line 11, in <module>
    main()
  File "compute_sum2.py", line 8, in main
    sum += float(n)
ValueError: could not convert string to float: 'hello'
```

In Chapter 5 we discussed how to use `try/except` statements to avoid crashing when the user was prompted to enter a number but instead entered a non-numeric input. The approach is similar here when processing a file. We can try to convert each token in the file to a `float`. If we are successful, we will add that number to our sum. If not, we will print an error message indicating that the token of input was invalid.

The following is a version of our *compute_sum* program that uses `try/except` to print an error message when it sees a non-numeric token. This version correctly processes the file without crashing and prints the correct sum:

```
1  # This program adds numbers from a file
2  # and reports the sum of all the numbers.
3  # This version skips non-numeric tokens.
4
5  def main():
6      sum = 0.0
7      with open("numbers2.dat") as file:
```

Continued on next page

Continued from previous page

```
8            for n in file.read().split():
9                # try to convert n to a float, but if it
10               # is not a valid float, print error message
11               try:
12                   sum += float(n)
13               except ValueError:
14                   print("Invalid number:", n)
15       print("Sum is:", round(sum, 1))
16
17   main()
```

```
Invalid number: hello
Invalid number: how
Invalid number: are
Invalid number: you?
Invalid number: :-)
Invalid number: oops
Invalid number: badbad
Invalid number: yipes
Sum is: 479.5
```

Notice that we do not enclose the entire `main` function body in a `try`/`except` statement; we define it narrowly to include only the single operation for which we want to handle errors, which is the string-to-number conversion. It is considered good practice to avoid having `try`/`except` blocks that are unnecessarily long, because otherwise your program may overzealously try to handle errors that you were not actually expecting and cannot actually handle properly.

In Chapter 5 we wrote a predicate function called `is_float` that accepts a string parameter and returns a `bool` value of `True` if the string can successfully be treated as a `float` value, or `False` if not. If we copied that function into this program, we could avoid using `try`/`except` in the `main` part of the code and could instead use the following `if`/`else` statement:

```
# use the Ch. 5 is_float function to check before converting
if is_float(s):
    sum += float(n)
else:
    print("Invalid number:", n)
```

Mixing Lines and Tokens

Some situations require mixing a line-based approach with a token-based approach. For example, consider a file full of actors' names. You have been given a file where each line contains a full name, including a first name, middle name, and last name separated by spaces.

```
Evan Rachel Wood
James Tiberius Kirk
Philip Seymour Hoffman
Sarah Jessica Parker
Tommy Lee Jones
```

Suppose you want to print the actors in `"LastName, FirstName"` format. You'll need to read the individual words on each line that represent the first, middle, and last name.

The `read` and `split` approach from the previous sections doesn't work as well here because there is not a simple way to ask for the tokens in sets of three. But instead you can read the file line-by-line with a `for` loop and then use the `split` method on each line to break the line apart into its three word tokens.

If you know exactly how many words will appear on each line that you are splitting, you can assign them to variables using the following syntax:

```
for line in file:
    name, name, ..., name = line.split()
    ...
```

Syntax template: Splitting each line into tokens by whitespace

The following program splits the preceding *actors.txt* file and then displays each actor by last name:

```
 1  # This program reads names from a file
 2  # in "first middle last" format.
 3
 4  def main():
 5      with open("actors.txt") as file:
 6          for line in file:
 7              first, middle, last = line.split()
 8              print(last, ",", first)
 9
10  main()
```

```
Wood , Evan
Kirk , James
Hoffman , Philip
Anthony , Susan
Jones , Tommy
```

Unlike past file processing programs in this chapter, we don't call `rstrip` on each line here. The `split` method already chews up any whitespace on the line such as line breaks, so `rstrip` is no longer needed.

Handling Varying Numbers of Tokens

Things get more challenging when you don't know exactly how many words or tokens are present on a line. Consider the following file *actors2.txt* of actors' names, where some actors have two names (*FirstName LastName*), but others have three or more:

```
Evan Rachel Wood
Will Smith
Oscar Isaac Hernandez Estrada
Sarah Jessica Parker
Margaret Mary Emily Anne Hyra
Jennifer Lawrence
```

If we modify the preceding *show_actors* program to read from this new file, it crashes after trying to split the second line of input from the file:

```
Wood , Evan

Traceback (most recent call last):
  File "show_actors2.py", line 10, in <module>
    main()
  File "show_actors2.py", line 7, in main
    first, middle, last = line.split()
ValueError: not enough values to unpack (expected 3, got 2)
```

The syntax we showed previously for splitting a string and storing it in multiple variables fails if the line doesn't have exactly the right number of tokens to store in the given number of variables. In our case, the code was splitting the string "Will Smith" into two tokens of "Will" and "Smith" and was therefore unable to store them into three variables.

You might think that a quick fix would be to change the code to split the line into only two variables. But this also fails for similar reasons. If there are too many tokens to store into the given number of variables, the code produces an error:

```
# attempt to print last/first names
for line in file:
    first, last = line.split()
    print(last, first)
```

```
Traceback (most recent call last):
  File "show_actors2.py", line 10, in <module>
    main()
  File "show_actors2.py", line 7, in main
    first, last = line.split()
ValueError: too many values to unpack (expected 2)
```

There is a variation of the splitting syntax that will allow you to gracefully handle varied numbers of tokens. You can declare the minimum number of variables you need and then declare a special additional variable preceded by a * asterisk. This extra variable will be used to store any extra tokens that are not placed into variables. (In this case the * is called the *gather operator* because it gathers the remaining tokens together.) The general syntax is the following:

```
name, name, ..., *name = string.split("delimiter")
```
Syntax template: Splitting a line into arbitrary number of tokens

The following code uses the gather operator as it splits each line. The code does not produce an error, but its output is still incorrect:

```
# second attempt to print last/first names
for line in file:
    first, last, *extra = line.split()
    print(last, first)
```

```
Rachel , Evan
Smith , Will
Isaac , Oscar
Jessica , Sarah
Mary , Margaret
Lawrence , Jennifer
```

The code is assuming that the second word of input is the actor's last name, when in many cases this is the actor's middle name. What we really want in this case is to grab the first and last token into variables and to discard all words between them as "extra" tokens.

Fortunately the * gather operator syntax allows you to do this by placing the gathering variable at different places in the sequence of variables in your splitting statement. If you place the *extra variable at the end of the sequence of variables, as we did in our previous code, any tokens after the first two will be considered extra. If you place the *extra variable at the start of our example, all tokens except the last two will be considered extra. If you place the *extra variable in between first and last, all tokens between the first and last token will be considered extra, which is what we want. Table 6.4 summarizes the behavior of placing *extra at different points in the code.

We want the very first token to be used as the first name and the very last token to be used as the last name, with all others between them considered "extra." Of course, names in real life can be complicated; different cultures and families use different naming conventions, and not every person uses the last word of their name as their family name. We will ignore this for the purposes of this example program. The following code handles all of the names in the file as desired:

```python
1   # This program reads names from a file
2   # in "first middle last" format.
3
4   def main():
5       with open("actors2.txt") as file:
6           for line in file:
7               first, *extra, last = line.split()
8               print(last, ",", first)
9
10  main()
```

```
Wood , Evan
Smith , Will
Estrada , Oscar
Parker , Sarah
Hyra , Margaret
Lawrence , Jennifer
```

Table 6.4   Effect of *extra at different places

# extra at start ***extra**, first, last = ...	Oscar Isaac Hernandez Estrada ⎵___⎵ | | *extra first last
# extra in middle first, ***extra**, last = ...	Oscar Isaac Hernandez Estrada | ⎵___⎵ | first *extra last
# extra at end first, last, ***extra** = ...	Oscar Isaac Hernandez Estrada | | ⎵___⎵ first last *extra

As with any new Python feature, you can try out splitting strings into tokens in the Python Shell. Here are a few lines of interaction when trying to split a string into variables including *extra:

```
>>> "Oscar de la Hoya".split()
['Oscar', 'de', 'la', 'Hoya']
>>> first, last, *extra = "Oscar de la Hoya".split()
>>> first
'Oscar'
>>> last
'de'
>>> extra
['la', 'Hoya']
>>> first, *extra, last = "Oscar de la Hoya".split()
>>> first
'Oscar'
>>> extra
['de', 'la']
>>> last
'Hoya'
```

(The Python Shell output with [ ] around it is an example of a *list*, which we will cover in more detail in the next chapter. A list is an object that can store multiple values; in this case, it is a list of multiple tokens or words from the string. The main takeaway is that the *extra variable stores all of the remaining words left over from the splitting operation.)

This second version of the program is more robust, but there is another variation of this input to consider. What about names that contain only a single word, such as "Madonna" or "Adele"? Such a name is called a mononym. Here is a new version of our input file called *actors3.txt* that contains some mononyms:

```
Evan Rachel Wood
Adele
Will Smith
Oscar Isaac Hernandez Estrada
Cher
Sarah Jessica Parker
Margaret Mary Emily Anne Hyra
Drake
Jennifer Lawrence
```

Our current program would crash if it encountered a line containing a mononym. Even though we are using the helpful *extra syntax, we still defined two variables first and last, meaning that our code demands that each line contain at least two tokens.

In this case, the simplest way to handle lines with mononyms is to put a separate `if/else` test to handle mononyms differently in our code. A mononym has only one token, so it does not need to be split; you can just print it out directly. You can tell whether a line is a multiword name or a mononym by testing to see whether it contains a space character, `" "`. The following program incorporates this change:

```
1   # This program reads names from a file
2   # in "first middle last" format.
3
4   def main():
5       with open("actors3.txt") as file:
6           for line in file:
7               if " " in line:
8                   # multi-word name
9                   first, *extra, last = line.split()
10                  print(last, ",", first)
11              else:
12                  # mononym such as "Adele"
13                  print(line.rstrip())
14
15  main()
```

```
Wood , Evan
Adele
Smith , Will
Estrada , Oscar
Cher
Parker , Sarah
Hyra , Margaret
Drake
Lawrence , Jennifer
```

Complex Input Files

Now that we've looked at strings and numbers as tokens, let's consider a larger example with a mixture of different types of input on each line. The following input file *hours.txt* contains information about how many hours each employee of a company has worked:

```
1234   Erica     7.5 8.5 10.25 8.0 8.5
5678   Erin      10.5 11.5 12.0 11.0 10.75
9012   Simone    8.0 8.0 8.0
3456   Ryan      6.5 8.0 9.25 8.0
7890   Kendall   2.5 3.0
```

Suppose you want to write a program to find out the total number of hours worked by each individual, along with the average number of hours that employee worked per day. The desired output is the following:

```
Erica ID # 1234 : 42.8 hours, 8.6 / day
Erin ID # 5678 : 55.8 hours, 11.2 / day
Simone ID # 9012 : 24.0 hours, 8.0 / day
Ryan ID # 3456 : 31.8 hours, 7.9 / day
Kendall ID # 7890 : 5.5 hours, 2.8 / day
```

In this case, the data is a series of input lines, where each line is a record of data about one employee. Each line begins with the employee's ID number as a four-digit integer. After the name comes the employee's first name as a single word. The rest of the line is a sequence of real numbers representing how many hours the employee worked on each day. Different employees work different numbers of days, so we don't know in advance how many numbers will appear on each line. All of these various tokens are separated by one or more spaces.

So, how do you process each person? Since this problem is larger, it may be helpful to write pseudocode listing the steps to perform.

```
For each employee line in the file:
    Split the line into an ID, name, and sequence of hours.
    For each token in the sequence of hours:
        Add that token to a sum.
        Count the number of tokens.
    Compute average hours per day by dividing sum by count.
    Print results for this employee.
```

As you start writing more complex file-processing programs, you will want to divide the program into functions to break up the code into logical subtasks. In this case, you can open the file in `main` and write a separate function to process a single line from the input file.

The pseudocode maps fairly well to Python code. You can split each line and store the variable number of `"hours"` tokens using the `*` syntax. We'll call it `*hours` rather than `*extra` as we did in other examples because the name is more descriptive:

```
name, id, *hours = line.split()
```

Computing the total hours is a fairly straightforward cumulative sum, as seen in Chapter 4. We'll also count the number of tokens in a variable called `total_days`:

```
total_hours = 0.0
total_days = 0
for hour in hours:
    total_hours += float(hour)
    total_days += 1
```

When you put the parts of the program together, you end up with the following complete program:

```
1   # This program computes hours worked by
2   # employees. Each line of input contains
3   # the name, ID, and hours worked each day.
4
5   # Handles the data line for one employee.
6   # Format: "name ID hours hours ... hours"
7   def process_employee(line):
8       id, name, *hours = line.split()
9       total_hours = 0.0
10      total_days = 0
11      for hour in hours:
12          total_hours += float(hour)
13          total_days += 1
14      hours_per_day = total_hours / total_days
15
16      print(name, "ID #", id, ":", \
17          round(total_hours, 1), "hours,", \
18          round(hours_per_day, 1), "/ day")
19
20  def main():
21      with open("hours.txt") as file:
22          for line in file:
23              process_employee(line)
24
25  main()
```

```
Erica ID # 1234 : 42.8 hours, 8.6 / day
Erin ID # 5678 : 55.8 hours, 11.2 / day
Simone ID # 9012 : 24.0 hours, 8.0 / day
Ryan ID # 3456 : 31.8 hours, 7.9 / day
Kendall ID # 7890 : 5.5 hours, 2.8 / day
```

6.3 Advanced File Processing

In this section we'll explore some advanced topics related to file processing. In particular, we will examine how to process multi-line records of input, we will learn how to write output into a file, and we will learn how to read data from the Web.

Multi-Line Input Records

The examples we have seen so far have all had the property that a single line of input represented a complete piece of data. But in some files, multiple lines are related to each other. The standard `for` loop over a file does not work well for such situations. In this section we'll see techniques for processing a file where groups of lines are examined together.

Consider a file called *dictionary.txt* where each pair of lines is related. The first line in each pair is a dictionary word, and the following line is its definition:

```
abate
to lessen; to subside
abeyance
suspended action
abjure
promise or swear; to give up
...
```

Suppose you want to write a program that allows the user to look up words in this dictionary. The user will be prompted to type a word, and then your code will search for that word in the dictionary file. Once the target word is found, its definition is printed to the console.

To implement this functionality, you should read the data from this file two lines at a time. Python file objects have a `readline` method that reads a single line from the file and returns it, advancing the input cursor past that line. If you call `readline` twice, you read two consecutive lines of the file. The following interaction in the Python Shell demonstrates this functionality:

```
>>> # reading individual lines from dictionary file
>>> file = open("dictionary.txt")
>>> file.readline()
'abate\n'
>>> file.readline()
'to lessen; to subside\n'
>>> file.readline()
'abeyance\n'
>>> file.readline()
'suspended action\n'
```

Notice that the newline "\n" characters that signal a line break are still present in the lines returned, and you may need to strip them from the strings in your code.

The general pattern of reading the file to search for a target word can be expressed with the following pseudocode:

```
Ask the user for their target word.
While we have not reached the end of the file:
    Read a word line.
    Read a definition line.
    If this word is the target word:
        Print its definition.
```

To translate this pseudocode into Python, the trickiest part is the loop test. Unlike with a `for` loop over a file, when you use `while` and `readline` you must explicitly check to see whether there are any more lines left to read in the file. Python indicates that you have reached the end of the file by having `readline` return an empty string, `""`. You can distinguish this case from the case when Python encounters a blank line in the file because in the blank line case `readline` returns `"\n"` instead of `""`.

Reading the file until its end turns out to be a fencepost problem. You need to read at least one pair of lines before you can test for the empty string in your `while` loop header. Then you need to read another pair of lines each time in the loop. The following program demonstrates the correct pattern along with a sample log of execution:

```
 1  # This program looks up words in a dictionary.
 2  # It is an example of multi-line input records.
 3
 4  def main():
 5      target_word = input("Word to look up? ")
 6      with open("dictionary.txt") as file:
 7          word = file.readline()
 8          defn = file.readline()
 9          while word != "":
10              if word.strip() == target_word:
11                  print("Definition:", defn.strip())
12              word = file.readline()    # read next pair
13              defn = file.readline()
14
15  main()
```

```
Word to look up? predilection
Definition: special liking or mental preference
```

Notice that the code calls `strip` on lines before they are compared to the target word or printed. This is because without stripping, you would compare a target word such as `"abate"` with a line such as `"abate\n"`, which is the line we want to find, but the comparison would produce a `False` result.

This program would benefit from procedural decomposition. The task of searching a data set for a given value is often a good candidate to make into a function. The following improved version of the dictionary lookup program has similar behavior, but we have extracted the searching functionality into a function called `find_match` that accepts the file and the target word as parameters, searches the file for the given target word, and then returns its definition. If the word is not found in the dictionary, we return an empty string `""` as the definition to indicate this. The `main` function can test for this result value to tell whether the word is present in the dictionary.

```
1   # This program looks up words in a dictionary.
2   # It is an example of multi-line input records.
3   # This version is decomposed into functions.
4
5   # Searches for the definition of the given word
6   # in the dictionary and returns it.
7   # If not found, returns an empty string.
8   def find_match(file, target_word):
9       word = file.readline()
10      defn = file.readline()
11      while word != "":
12          if word.strip() == target_word:
13              return defn.strip()
14          word = file.readline()    # read next pair
15          defn = file.readline()
16      return ""    # not found
17
18  def main():
19      target_word = input("Word to look up? ")
20      with open("dictionary.txt") as file:
21          defn = find_match(file, target_word)
22          if defn == "":
23              print(target_word, "not found.")
24          else:
25              print("Definition:", defn)
26
27  main()
```

Our example demonstrates how to handle a file where every two lines constitute a complete record of data. But you could generalize the approach to handle a file whose records each contain three, four, or more lines.

File Output

All of the programs we've studied so far have sent their output to the console window by calling `print`. But just as you can read input from a file instead of reading from the console, you can write output to a file instead of writing it to the console.

The first thing you'll need to do in order to write an output file is to open it for writing. The same `open` function that we've used to read files can also be used to write files. This is done by passing an optional second parameter to `open` called a *mode*. Modes are represented as strings. Table 6.5 lists the supported modes for accessing a file.

If no mode is passed to `open`, the default mode is `"r"`, which means reading the file. But if you instead want to write to a file, you can pass `"w"`. The following is the general syntax to open a file for writing:

```
with open("filename", "w") as name):

    ...
```
Syntax template: Opening a file for output

Once you have opened the file for writing, you can send output to it, and the output will be written into that file. There are several ways to accomplish this task. The simplest approach is to use the same `print` statement that you are already familiar with.

By default, the `print` statement sends its output to the console. However, you can instruct a given `print` statement to send its output to other places. You can do this by opening a Python file object and then passing that file object to `print` as an optional named parameter named `file`. The general syntax is the following:

```
print("text", file=file_object)
```
Syntax template: Printing output to a file

For example, to send a line of output to a file called `results.txt`, you can write a `print` statement as follows:

```
with open("results.txt", "w") as outfile:
    print("Hello, world!", file=outfile)
```

If no such file already exists, the program creates it. If such a file does exist, the computer overwrites the current version. Initially, the file will be empty. It will end up containing whatever output you tell it to produce in your `print` statements.

The line of code that opens the file for writing can generate an error if the Python interpreter is unable to create the specified file. There are many reasons that this might

Table 6.5   File open modes

Mode	Description
`"r"`	read the file
`"w"`	write the file, erasing any previous contents
`"a"`	write the file, appending new text at the end after any previous contents
`"x"`	write the file, raising an error if the file already exists
`"b"`	process a binary file

happen: You might not have permission to write to the directory, or the file might be locked because another program is using it.

Let's bring this together into a complete example. In Chapter 1 we looked at a simple "hello world" program that produces several lines of output. Here is a variation that sends its output to a file called *hello.txt*:

```
1   # This program prints output to the console.
2
3   def main():
4       print("Hello, world!")
5       print()
6       print("This program produces four")
7       print("lines of output.")
8
9   main()
```

```
1   # This program writes output to a file.
2
3   def main():
4       with open("hello.txt", "w") as outfile:
5           print("Hello, world!", file=outfile)
6           print("", file=outfile)
7           print("This program produces four", file=outfile)
8           print("lines of output in a file.", file=outfile)
9
10  main()
```

When you run this new version of the program, a curious thing happens. The program doesn't seem to do anything; no output appears on the console at all. You're so used to writing programs that send their output to the console that this might seem confusing at first. We don't see any output in the console window when we run this program because the output was directed to a file instead. After the program finishes executing, you can open up the file called *hello.txt* and you'll find that it contains the following:

```
Hello, world!

This program produces four
lines of output in a file.
```

For all of our examples in this chapter, we have used the `with` statement to open our files. This was so that we did not need to call `close` on the file when we were done using it. The `with` statement is especially important when writing data to a file. If you write data to a file and then forget to close it, the program can terminate without successfully writing the data to the file. This is due to various delays and buffers that the file libraries use to speed up file access. So you should definitely make sure to wrap any file-writing code in a `with` statement, or else make sure to explicitly call `close` on the file when you are done writing text to it.

The `print` statement with a `file` parameter is a syntax that was introduced into the Python language in version 3. Older versions of the language did not have this syntax, but you can still write to an output file in other ways. For example, the file object itself has a `write` method that accepts a string parameter and sends that string as output to the file. The `write` method is not quite the same as `print`; it accepts only a single string parameter, not a list of comma-separated parameters of any type. Also, `write` does not automatically append a line break `\n` after each output, so you need to insert line breaks into your strings manually. The following is an equivalent version of the *hello* program that uses the `write` method:

```
1   # This program writes output to a file.
2   # This version uses the file object's write() method.
3
4   def main():
5       with open("hello.txt", "w") as outfile:
6           outfile.write("Hello, world!\n")
7           outfile.write("\n")
8           outfile.write("This program produces four\n")
9           outfile.write("lines of output in a file.\n")
10
11  main()
```

Reading Data from the Web

The World Wide Web is a rich source of data. Much of the data on the Web is stored in a format called HTML, but the Web also stores plain text files and data in many other formats. In this section we will learn how to read text files from the Web and process them in our Python programs.

A resource on the Web can be accessed using a universal resource locator, or *URL*. Web sites that store data are called servers, and computers that connect to web servers to ask for data are called clients. Asking a server for data is called a *request*, and the data sent back by the server is called a *response*.

Let's look at a specific example of data on the Web. In this chapter we have referred to a file *numbers.dat* containing real numbers. The authors have also placed that file on our web server at the following URL:

- http://www.buildingpythonprograms.com/input/numbers.dat

```
308.2 14.9 7.4
2.8 81

5.0
3.9 4.7 67.0 -15.4
```

Python contains a built-in library called `urllib` that makes it easy for you to download data from a web URL and use it in your program. The specific module we want to use is called `urllib.request`. To access its functionality, include the following `import` statement at the top of your program:

```
import urllib.request
```

The `urllib.request` module has a function `urlopen` that accepts a URL string as a parameter and connects to that URL to request its data. The function returns a response object you can use to access the data at that URL. Python has designed the response object so that you can use it almost exactly the same way that you can manipulate file objects. That means that you can wrap a call to `urlopen` in a `with` statement that will open the URL, allow you to read it, and automatically close the connection when you are finished. The general syntax is the following:

```
with urllib.request.urlopen("url") as name:
      statement
      statement
      ...
      statement
```
Syntax template: Reading data from a URL

Because the returned response object has the same functions and behavior as a local file object, you can treat it much the same way in your code. For example, you can use a `for` loop to iterate over the lines in the file. Or you could call `read` on it to grab the entire contents of the URL as a long string. The following complete program reads the contents of *numbers.dat* from the Web and computes the sum of the numbers in the file. For readability we store the URL as a variable and pass it to the `urlopen` function.

```
 1  # This program adds numbers from a URL
 2  # and reports the sum of all the numbers.
 3
 4  import urllib.request
 5
 6  def main():
 7      URL = "http://buildingpythonprograms.com/input/numbers.dat"
 8      sum = 0.0
 9      with urllib.request.urlopen(URL) as url:
10          for n in url.read().split():
11              sum += float(n)
12      print("Sum is:", round(sum, 1))
13
14  main()
```

```
Sum is: 479.5
```

When you run this program, it is mostly indistinguishable from the version that reads a local file, except that there may be a small delay as the program connects to the Internet and downloads the file. If you are using a computer with a slower Internet connection, the delay may be more noticeable.

If you try to connect to a URL that does not exist or cannot be read, the call to `urlopen` will raise an exception of type `urllib.error.HTTPError`. For example, if you had misspelled the URL of the *numbers.dat* file, the program's output would be the following:

```
Traceback (most recent call last):
  File "compute_sum_url_error.py", line 15, in <module>
    main()
  File "compute_sum_url_error.py", line 8, in main
    with urllib.request.urlopen("http://buildingpythonprograms.com/
input/oops-not-found.dat") as url:
  ...
  File "/usr/lib/python3.5/urllib/request.py", line 590, in
http_error_default
    raise HTTPError(req.full_url, code, msg, hdrs, fp)
urllib.error.HTTPError: HTTP Error 404: Not Found
```

To make your program robust against such potential errors, you can use a `try/except` statement as shown in Chapter 5. The following program demonstrates this error handling with an invalid URL:

```
1   # This program adds numbers from a URL
2   # and reports the sum of all the numbers.
3   # This version handles errors if the URL is invalid.
4
5   import urllib.request
6
7   def main():
8       URL = "http://buildingpythonprograms.com/input/not-found.txt"
9       sum = 0.0
10      try:
11          with urllib.request.urlopen(URL) as url:
12              for n in url.read().split():
13                  sum += float(n)
14      except urllib.error.HTTPError:
15          print("Unable to open URL")
16      print("Sum is:", round(sum, 1))
17
18  main()
```

```
Unable to open URL
Sum is: 0.0
```

You can learn more about `urllib.request` and response objects by reading the Python library documentation:

- https://docs.python.org/3/library/urllib.request.html
- https://docs.python.org/3/library/http.client.html

6.4 Case Study: ZIP Code Lookup

Knowing the distance between two locations turns out to be extremely helpful and valuable. For example, many popular Internet dating sites and apps allow you to search for people on the basis of a target location. On a dating app like OkCupid or Tinder, you can search for potential matches within a particular radius of a given city or ZIP code (5 miles, 10 miles, 15 miles, 25 miles, and so on). Obviously this is an important feature for a dating site because people are most interested in dating other people who live near them.

There are many other applications of this kind of proximity search. In the 1970s and 1980s there was an explosion of interest in what is known as direct mail marketing that has produced what we now call junk mail. Proximity searches are very important in direct mail campaigns. A local store, for example, might decide to mail out a brochure to all residents who live within 5 miles of the store. A political candidate might pay a membership organization like The Sierra Club or the National Rifle Association a fee to get the mailing addresses of all its members who live within a certain distance of a town or a city district.

Massive databases keep track of potential customers and voters. Direct mail marketing organizations often want to find the distance between one of these individuals and some fixed location. The distance calculations are done almost exclusively with ZIP codes. There are over 40,000 five-digit ZIP codes in the United States. Some ZIP codes cover rural areas that are fairly large, but more often a ZIP code determines your location in a city or town to within a fraction of a mile. If you use the more specific ZIP+4 database, you can often pinpoint a location to within a few city blocks.

If you do a web search for "ZIP code database" or "ZIP code software" you will find that there are many people selling the data and the software to interpret the data. There are also some free databases, although the data aren't quite as accurate. The U.S. Census Bureau is the source of much of the free data.

To explore this application, let's write a program that finds all the ZIP codes within a certain proximity of another ZIP code. An app like OkCupid could use the logic of this program to find potential dates within a certain radius. You'd simply start with the ZIP code of interest, find all the other ZIP codes within a particular distance, and then find all the customers who have those ZIP codes. We don't have access to a massive dating database, so we'll be working on just the first part of this task, finding the ZIP codes that are within a specified distance.

As we noted earlier, some free ZIP code databases are available online. Our sample program uses data compiled by software developer Schuyler Erle, whose data are distributed free through a Creative Commons license. The data was obtained from boutell.com/zipcodes.

We have reformatted the data to make it more convenient for us to work with it (a process known as data munging). We will be working with a file called `zipcode.txt` that has a series of entries, with one line per ZIP code. A line entry contains the ZIP code as a five-digit integer, followed by two numbers that represent the latitude and longitude of the ZIP code, followed by the city and state. These tokens on the line are separated by spaces and a colon, " : ". For example, the following is an entry for one of the authors' home ZIP codes:

```
98104 : 47.60252 : -122.32855 : Seattle, WA
```

The overall task is to prompt the user for a target ZIP code and a proximity and to show all ZIP codes within the given proximity of the target. Here is a first attempt at pseudocode for the overall task:

```
Introduce program to user.
Prompt for target ZIP code and proximity.
Display matching ZIP codes from file.
```

This approach doesn't quite work. To display a match, you have to compare the target location to each of the different ZIP codes in the data file. You'll need the latitude and longitude information to make this comparison. But when you prompt the user, you're just asking for a ZIP code and proximity. You could alter the program to prompt for a latitude and longitude, but that wouldn't be a very friendly program for the user. Imagine if OkCupid or Tinder required you to know your latitude and longitude in order for you to search for people who live near you.

Instead, you can use the ZIP code data to find the latitude and longitude of the target ZIP code. As a result, you'll have to search the data twice. The first time through you will be looking for the target ZIP code, so that you can find its coordinates. The second time through you will display all the ZIP codes that are within the distance specified by the user. Here is a new version of the pseudocode:

```
Introduce program to user.
Prompt for target ZIP code and proximity.
Find coordinates for target ZIP code.
Display matching ZIP codes from file.
```

Introducing the program and prompting for the target ZIP code and proximity are fairly straightforward tasks that don't require detailed explanation. The real work of the program involves solving the third and fourth steps in this pseudocode. Each of these steps is sufficiently complex that it deserves to be included in a function.

First consider the problem of finding the coordinates for the target ZIP code. You need to open the file and read from it, and then you need to call the function that will do the search. Let's call this function `find_location`. We'll pass it the Python file object as a parameter so it can search for the ZIP code of interest. It will also need to know what ZIP code you are searching for, so we'll pass that as a second parameter.

But what information should the searching function return? You want the coordinates of the target ZIP code (the latitude and longitude). Once your function finds the line with the right ZIP code, you can return these two values as `floats`. That means that your `main` function will include the following code:

```
lat, lng = find_location(file, zip)
```

The `find_location` function should read the input file line by line, searching for the target ZIP code. Each entry in the file contains four fields separated by " : ". This is slightly different than past examples in this chapter that were separated by spaces. The reason for the colons as delimiters is that city names can have spaces in them, such as `"Carson City, NV"`. To handle this input we will pass " : " as a delimiter when splitting the line strings:

```
# Searches for the given string in the input file.
def find_location(file, target_zip):
    for line in file:
        zip, lat, lng, city = line.rstrip().split(" : ")
        ...
```

As you read various ZIP code entries, you want to test each to see whether it matches the target. If you find a match, you can print it and return the coordinates:

```
# Searches for the given string in the input file.
def find_location(file, target_zip):
    for line in file:
        zip, lat, lng, city = line.rstrip().split(" : ")
        if zip == target_zip:
            print(zip, city)
            return float(lat), float(lng)
    ...
```

Note that we explicitly convert the latitude and longitude to `float` type, but we don't convert the ZIP code to an `int`. This is partly because we want to allow flexibility for ZIP codes that don't follow the typical integer format, such as ones that contain leading zeros or ones that follow the ZIP+4 format with extra characters at the end.

This function is still not complete because you have to consider the case in which the target ZIP code doesn't appear in the file. In that case, you exit the `for` loop without having returned a value. There are many things the program could do at this point, such as printing an error message or generating an error. To keep things simple, let's instead return a set of fake coordinates. If the program returns a latitude and longitude of (0, 0), there won't be any matches unless the user asks for an outrageously high proximity (over 4000 miles).

```
# Searches for the given string in the input file;
# if found, returns coordinates; else returns (0, 0).
def find_location(file, target_zip):
    for line in file:
        zip, lat, lng, city = line.rstrip().split(" : ")
        if zip == target_zip:
            print(zip, city)
            return float(lat), float(lng)

    # at this point we know the ZIP code isn't in the file
    return 0, 0
```

This function completes the first of the two file-processing tasks. In the second task, you have to read the file a second time and search for ZIP codes within the given proximity. But to write this function, you need a way to calculate which matches are within a given distance of the starting ZIP code.

To help with this, you can write a function called `spherical_distance` that computes the distance between two points on Earth, given their latitudes and longitudes. The math is a bit complex, but there is a formula called the spherical law of cosines that can compute the distance between two points on a sphere.

Let φ_1, λ_1, and φ_2, λ_2 be the latitude and longitude of the two points, respectively. $\Delta\lambda$, the longitudinal difference, and $\Delta\varphi$, the angular difference/distance in radians, can be determined from the spherical law of cosines as:

$$\Delta\sigma = \arccos(\sin \varphi_1 \sin \varphi_2 + \cos \varphi_1 \cos \varphi_2 \cos \Delta\lambda)$$

We won't dwell on the math involved here, but a short explanation might be helpful. Imagine forming a triangle by connecting two points with the North Pole. From the two latitudes, you can compute the distance from each point to the North Pole. The difference between the two longitudes tells you the angle formed by these two sides of the triangle. You may recall from geometry class that if you know two sides and the angle between them, then you can compute the third side. We are using a special version of the law of cosines that works for spheres to compute the length of the third side of the triangle (which is the line connecting the two points on our sphere). We have to convert from degrees into radians and we have to include the radius of our sphere (in this case the Earth). The resulting calculation is included in the final version of the program. If you want to read more about spherical distance formulas, you can read an article about the formula on Wikipedia or Wolfram MathWorld.

Now that we can compute spherical distances, let's write a function named `show_matches` to search for ZIP codes within the given proximity. It will accept parameters for the input file, the latitude and longitude of interest, and the number of miles of proximity.

Remember that the `for` loop in `find_location` has already read through the entire file and has therefore moved the file's cursor to the end of the input data. This means that if you want to loop over it again, you need to go back to the beginning of the file. The easiest way to do this is to `seek` the file object to position 0. Thus, your code in `main` will look like the following:

```
with open("zipcode.txt") as file:
    lat, lng = find_location(file, zip)
    file.seek(0)    # rewind file
    show_matches(file, lat, lng, miles)
```

A reasonable pseudocode for the `show_matches` function would be the following:

```
For each line in the file:
    Read line's lat/lng coordinates and other data.
    If this line's lat/lng are within the given proximity:
        Print the match.
```

The code for finding matches involves a similar file-processing loop that reads lines of input and splits them, printing matches as it finds them. To identify matches we will use the `spherical_distance` function we derived earlier.

```
def show_matches(file, lat1, lng1, miles):
    print("ZIP codes within", miles, "miles:")
    for line in file:
        zip, lat2, lng2, city = line.rstrip().split(" : ")
        dist = spherical_distance(lat1, lng1, float(lat2), float(lng2))
        if dist <= miles:
            print(zip, city, round(dist, 2), "miles")
```

Note that you must be careful to convert tokens of input such as latitudes and longitudes into `float`s if you want to perform mathematical calculations on them. We need to convert `lat2` and `lng2` to `float`, but we don't do so for `lat1` and `lng1` because we already converted them earlier in the program.

Bringing together all of these pieces, here is the complete version of the program, along with a sample log of execution:

```
1  # This program uses a file of ZIP code information
2  # to allow a user to find ZIP codes within a
3  # certain distance of another ZIP code.
4
5  import math
6
7  # constant for radius of sphere (Earth), in miles
8  RADIUS = 3956.6
```

Continued on next page

Continued from previous page

```
 9
10  # Introduces the program to the user.
11  def intro():
12      print("Welcome to the ZIP code database.")
13      print("Give me a 5-digit ZIP code and a")
14      print("proximity and I'll tell you where")
15      print("that ZIP code is located along")
16      print("with a list of other ZIP codes")
17      print("within the given proximity.")
18      print()
19
20  # Prompts the user and returns ZIP code and proximity.
21  def read_input():
22      zip = input("ZIP code of interest? ")
23      miles = float(input("Proximity in miles? "))
24      print()
25      return zip, miles
26
27
28  # Searches for the given string in the input file;
29  # if found, returns coordinates; else returns (0, 0).
30  def find_location(file, target_zip):
31      for line in file:
32          zip, lat, lng, city = line.rstrip().split(" : ")
33          if zip == target_zip:
34              print(zip, city)
35              return float(lat), float(lng)
36
37      # at this point we know the ZIP code isn't in the file
38      return 0, 0
39
40  # Shows all matches for given coords within given distance.
41  def show_matches(file, lat1, lng1, miles):
42      print("ZIP codes within", miles, "miles:")
43      for line in file:
44          zip, lat2, lng2, city = line.rstrip().split(" : ")
45          dist = spherical_distance(lat1, lng1, \
46                                    float(lat2), float(lng2))
47          if dist <= miles:
48              print(zip, city, round(dist, 2), "miles")
49
50  # Returns spherical distance in miles given the latitude
51  # and longitude of two points (depends on constant RADIUS).
```

```
52  def spherical_distance(lat1, lng1, lat2, lng2):
53      lat1 = math.radians(lat1)
54      lng1 = math.radians(lng1)
55      lat2 = math.radians(lat2)
56      lng2 = math.radians(lng2)
57      the_cos = math.sin(lat1) * math.sin(lat2) \
58          + math.cos(lat1)  * math.cos(lat2) * math.cos(lng1 - lng2)
59      arc_length = math.acos(the_cos)
60      return arc_length * RADIUS
61
62  def main():
63      intro()
64      zip, miles = read_input()
65      with open("zipcode.txt") as file:
66          lat, lng = find_location(file, zip)
67          file.seek(0)   # rewind file
68          show_matches(file, lat, lng, miles)
69
70  main()
```

```
Welcome to the ZIP code database.
Give me a 5-digit ZIP code and a
proximity and I'll tell you where
that ZIP code is located along
with a list of other ZIP codes
within the given proximity.

ZIP code of interest? 98104
Proximity in miles? 1

98104 Seattle, WA
ZIP codes within 1.0 miles:
98101 Seattle, WA 0.62 miles
98104 Seattle, WA 0.0 miles
98154 Seattle, WA 0.35 miles
98164 Seattle, WA 0.29 miles
98174 Seattle, WA 0.35 miles
```

There is an old saying that you get what you pay for, and these ZIP code data are no exception. There are several web sites that list ZIP codes within a mile of 98104, and they include many ZIP codes not included here. That's because the free ZIP code information is incomplete. Each of those web sites gives you the option of obtaining a better database for a small fee.

Chapter Summary

- Programs can read data from files. A file can be accessed in Python using the open function.
- A file name can be specified as a relative path such as numbers.dat, which refers to a file in the current directory. Alternatively, you can specify an absolute file path such as /home/ksmith12/data/numbers.dat.
- Python file objects treat the text in an input file as a one-dimensional stream of data that is read in order from start to end. As you read the file's data, an internal position called a cursor keeps track of your current place in the file and moves past ("consumes") input lines as they are read and returned to your program.
- In many files, input is structured by lines, and it makes sense to process those files line by line using

a for loop over the file. Some files have complex combinations of tokens on each line, which you can separate and examine by splitting the line string. You may end up using nested loops: an outer loop that iterates over each line of the file and an inner loop that processes the tokens in each line.

- You can write to a file by opening it in "w" mode. The same print function that you used to write output to the console can also send output to a file.
- Other sources of data such as Internet URLs can be accessed similarly to files. Once you have opened the connection to the data source on the Web, you can treat it essentially the same way as a local file on your computer.

Self-Check Problems

Section 6.1: File-Reading Basics

1. What is a file? How can we read data from a file in Python?

2. Write code to open and read the file input.txt, which exists in the same folder as your program.

Section 6.2: Token-Based Processing

3. Given the following line of input, what tokens does a call line.split() return?

```
line = "welcome...to the matrix."
```

a. ["welcome", "to", "the", "matrix"]

b. ["welcome...to the matrix."]

c. ["welcome...to", "the", "matrix."]

d. ["welcome...", "to", "the matrix."]

e. ["welcome", "to the matrix"]

4. Given the following line of input, what tokens does a call line.split() return?

```
lines = "in fourteen-hundred 92\ncolumbus sailed the ocean blue :)"
```

a. ["in", "fourteen-hundred", "92"]

b. ["in", "fourteen-hundred", "92", "columbus", "sailed", "the", "ocean", "blue", ":)"]

c. ["in", "fourteen", "hundred", "92", "columbus", "sailed", "the", "ocean", "blue"]

d. ["in", "fourteen-hundred", "92\ncolumbus", "sailed", "the", "ocean", "blue :)"]

e. ["in fourteen-hundred 92", "columbus sailed the ocean blue :)"]

5. Answer the following questions about a Python program located on a Windows machine in the folder $C:\Users\$ *yana\Documents\programs*:

    a. What are two legal ways you can refer to the file $C:\Users\yana\Documents\programs\numbers.$ *dat*?

    b. How can you refer to the file $C:\Users\yana\Documents\programs\data\homework6\input.$ *dat*?

    c. How many, and in what legal, ways can you refer to the file $C:\Users\yana\Documents\homework\$ *data.txt*?

6. Answer the following questions about a Python program located on a Linux machine in the folder */home/yana/* *Documents/hw6*:

    a. What are two legal ways you can refer to the file */home/yana/Documents/hw6/names.txt*?

    b. How can you refer to the file */home/yana/Documents/hw6/data/numbers.txt*?

    c. How many legal ways can you refer to the file */home/yana/download/saved.html*?

Section 6.3: Advanced File Processing

7. For the next several questions, consider a file called *readme.txt* that has the following contents:

```
6.7          This file has several input lines.

10 20      30   40


test
```

What would be the output from the following code when it is run on the *readme.txt* file?

```
with open("readme.txt") as file:
    count = 0
    for s in file:
        print("input:", s)
        count += 1
    print(count, "total")
```

8. What would be the output from the code in the previous exercise if the `for` loop was modified to have a call to `read` and a call to `split`?

```
for s in file.read().split():
    ...
```

9. Write a program that prints itself to the console as output. For example, if the program is stored in *example.py*, it will open the file *example.py* and print its contents to the console.

10. Write code that prompts the user for a file name and prints the contents of that file to the console as output. Assume that the file exists. You may wish to place this code into a function called `print_entire_file`.

11. Write a program that takes as input a file of lines of text like the following:

```
This is some
text here.
```

The program should produce as output the same text inside a box, as in the following:

```
+--------------+
| This is some |
| text here.   |
+--------------+
```

Your program will have to assume some maximum line length (e.g., 12 in this case).

12. Write code to print the following four lines of text into a file named *message.txt*:

```
Testing,

1, 2, 3.

This is my output file.
```

13. Write code that repeatedly prompts the user for a file name until the user types the name of a file that exists on the system. You may wish to place this code into a function called get_file_name, which will return that file name as a string.

14. In an earlier problem, you wrote a piece of code that prompted the user for a file name and printed that file's contents to the console. Modify your code so that it will repeatedly prompt the user for the file name until the user types the name of a file that exists on the system.

Exercises

1. Write a function called boy_girl that accepts a file name as a parameter. Your function should read input from that file containing a series of names followed by integers. The names alternate between boys' names and girls' names. Your function should compute the absolute difference between the sum of the boys' integers and the sum of the girls' integers. The input could end with either a boy or girl; you may not assume that it contains an even number of names. For example, if the input file contains the following text:

```
Dan 3
Cordelia 7
Tanner 14
Mellany 13
Curtis 4
Amy 12
Nick 6
```

Then the function should produce the following console output, since the boys' sum is 27 and the girls' sum is 32:

```
4 boys, 3 girls
Difference between boys' and girls' sums: 5
```

2. Write a function called `even_numbers` that accepts a file name as a parameter. Your function should read input from the file which contains a series of integers. Report various statistics about the integers to the console. Report the total number of numbers, the sum of the numbers, the count of even numbers and the percent of even numbers. For example, if the input file contains the following text:

```
5 7 2 8
9 10 12
98 7
14
20 22
```

Then the function should produce the following console output:

```
12 numbers, sum = 214
8 evens (66.67%)
```

3. Write a function called `negative_sum` that accepts a file name as a parameter. The input file contains a series of integers, and print a message to the console indicating whether the sum starting from the first number is ever negative. You should also return `True` if a negative sum can be reached and `False` if not. For example, suppose the file contains the following text:

```
38 4 19 -27 -15 -3 4 19 38
```

Your function would consider the sum of just one number (38), the first two numbers (38 + 4), the first three numbers (38 + 4 + 19), and so on to the end. None of these sums is negative, so the function would produce the following output and return `false`:

```
no negative sum
```

If the file instead contains the following numbers:

```
14 7 -10 9 -18 -10 17 42 98
```

The function finds that a negative sum of −8 is reached after adding the first six numbers. It should output the following to the console and return `true`:

```
sum of -8 after 6 steps
```

4. Write a function called `count_coins` that accepts a file name as a parameter. The file's contents is a series of pairs of tokens, where each pair begins with an integer and is followed by the type of coin, which will be `"pennies"` (1 cent each), `"nickels"` (5 cents each), `"dimes"` (10 cents each), or `"quarters"` (25 cents each), case-insensitively. Add up the cash values of all the coins and print the total money. For example, if the input file contains the following text:

```
3 pennies 2 quarters 1 Pennies 23 NiCkeLs 4 DIMES
```

For the input above, your function should produce the following output:

```
Total money: $2.09
```

5. Write a function called `collapse_spaces` that accepts a file name as a parameter. Your function should read that file and output it with all its tokens separated by single spaces, collapsing any sequences of multiple spaces into single spaces. For example, consider the following text:

```
    hello      world!
many      spaces   on    this     line.
```

If this text were a line in the file, the same line should be output as follows:

```
hello world!
many spaces on this line.
```

6. Write a function called `flip_lines` that accepts a file name as a parameter. Your function should read it and write to the console the contents of the file with each pair of lines reversed in order. For example, if the file contains:

```
Twas brillig and the slithy toves
did gyre and gimble in the wabe.
All mimsey were the borogroves,
and the mome raths outgrabe.
```

your function should produce the following output:

```
did gyre and gimble in the wabe.
Twas brillig and the slithy toves
and the mome raths outgrabe.
All mimsey were the borogroves,
```

7. Write a function called `word_wrap` that accepts an input file name as its parameter and outputs each line of the file to the console, word-wrapping all lines that are longer than 60 characters. For example, if a line contains 112 characters, the function should replace it with two lines: one containing the first 60 characters and another containing the final 52 characters. A line containing 217 characters should be wrapped into four lines: three of length 60 and a final line of length 37.

8. Modify the preceding `word_wrap` function so that it outputs the newly wrapped text back into the original file. (Be careful; don't output into a file while you are reading it!) Also, modify it to use a constant for the maximum line length rather than hard-coding 60.

9. Modify the preceding `word_wrap` function so that it only wraps whole words, never chopping a word in half. Assume that a word is any whitespace-separated token and that all words are under 60 characters in length.

10. Write a function called `coin_flip` that accepts an input file name as a parameter. The input file contains coin flips that are heads (H) or tails (T). Consider each line to be a separate set of coin flips and output the number and percentage of heads in that line. If it is more than 50%, print `"You win!"`. Consider the following file:

```
H T H H T
T t    t  T h  H
```

For the input above, your function should produce the following output:

```
3 heads (60.0%)
You win!

2 heads (33.3%)
```

11. Write a function called `most_common_names` that accepts a file name as a parameter. The file contains names on each line separated by spaces. Some names appear multiple times in a row on the same line. For each line, print the most commonly occurring name. If there's a tie, use the first name that had that many occurrences; if all names are unique, print the first name on the line. For example, if the file has this input:

```
Sara Eric    Eric   Kim   Kim Kim Mariana Nancy Nancy  Paul  Paul
Melissa Jamie Jamie Alyssa Alyssa Helene  Helene Jessica Jessica
```

For the input above, your function should produce the following output:

```
Most common: Kim
Most common: Jamie
```

12. Write a function called `plus_scores` that accepts an input file name as a parameter. The input file contains a series of lines that represent student records. Each student record takes up two lines of input. The first line has the student's name and the second line has a series of plus and minus characters. Below is a sample input file:

```
Kane, Erica
--+-+
Chandler, Adam
++-+
Martin, Jake
+++++++
```

For each student you should produce a line of output with the student's name followed by a colon followed by the percent of plus characters. For the input above, your function should produce the following output:

```
Kane, Erica: 40.0% plus
Chandler, Adam: 75.0% plus
Martin, Jake: 100.0% plus
```

13. Write a function called `leet_speak` that accepts two parameters: an input file name, and an output file name. Convert the input file's text to `"leet speak,"` where various letters are replaced by other letters/numbers, and output the new text to the given output file. Replace `"o"` with `"0"`, `"l"` (lowercase `"L"`) with `"1"` (the number one), `"e"` with `"3"`, `"a"` with `"4"`, `"t"` with `"7"`, and an `"s"` at the end of a word with `"Z"`. Preserve the original line breaks from the input. Also wrap each word of input in parentheses. For example, if the input file contains the following text:

```
four score and
seven years ago our
fathers brought forth on this continent
a new nation
```

For the input above, your function should produce the following in the output file:

```
(f0ur) (sc0r3) (4nd)
(s3v3n) (y34rZ) (4g0) (0ur)
(f47h3rZ) (br0ugh7) (f0r7h) (0n) (7hiZ) (c0n7in3n7)
(4) (n3w) (n47i0n)
```

Programming Projects

1. Students are often asked to write term papers containing a certain number of words. Counting words in a long paper is a tedious task, but the computer can help. Write a program that counts the number of words, lines, and total characters (not including whitespace) in a paper, assuming that consecutive words are separated either by spaces or end-of-line characters.

2. Write a program that compares two files and prints information about the differences between them. For example, consider a file *data1.txt* with the following contents:

```
This file has a great deal of
text in it that needs to

be processed.
```

Consider another file *data2.txt* that exists with the following contents:

```
This file has a grate deal of
text in it that needs to

bee proceed.
```

A dialogue with the user running your program might look like the following:

```
Enter a first file name: data1.txt
Enter a second file name: data2.txt
Differences found:
Line 1:
< This file has a great deal of
> This file has a grate deal of

Line 4:
< be processed.
> bee proceed.
```

3. Write a program that reads a file containing data about the changing popularity of various baby names over time and displays the data about a particular name. Each line of the file stores a name followed by integers representing the name's popularity in each decade: 1900, 1910, 1920, and so on. The rankings range from 1 (most popular) to 1000 (least popular), or 0 for a name that was less popular than the 1000th name. The following lines are a sample of the file format:

```
Sally 0 0 0 0 0 0 0 0 0 0 886
Sam 58 69 99 131 168 236 278 380 467 408 466
Samantha 0 0 0 0 0 0 272 107 26 5 7
Samir 0 0 0 0 0 0 0 0 920 0 798
```

Your program should prompt the user for a name and search the file for that name. If the name is found, the program should display data about the name on the screen:

```
This program allows you to search through the
data from the Social Security Administration
to see how popular a particular name has been
since 1900.

Name? Sam
Statistics on name "Sam"
1900: 58
1910: 69
1920: 99
1930: 131
...
```

This program is more fun and challenging if you also draw the name's popularity on a DrawingPanel as a line graph. Plot the decades on the *x*-axis and the popularity on the *y*-axis.

4. Write a program that plays a game where a player is asked to fill in various words of a mostly complete story without being able to see the rest. Then the user is shown his/her story, which is often funny. The input for your program is a set of story files, each of which contains "placeholder" tokens surrounded by < and >, such as:

```
One of the most <adjective> characters in fiction is named
"Tarzan of the <plural-noun>." Tarzan was raised by a/an
<noun> and lives in the <adjective> jungle in the
heart of darkest <place>.
```

The user is prompted to fill in each of the placeholders in the story, and then a resulting output file is created with the placeholders filled in. For example:

```
Input file name? story1.txt
Please enter an adjective: silly
Please enter a plural noun: socks
Please enter a noun: tree
Please enter an adjective: tiny
Please enter a place: Canada
```

The resulting output story would be:

```
One of the most silly characters in fiction is named
"Tarzan of the socks." Tarzan was raised by a/an
tree and lives in the tiny jungle in the
heart of darkest Canada.
```

Chapter 7

Lists

Introduction

So far we have spent some time looking at files but have only examined sequential algorithms: ones that can be performed by examining each data item once, in sequence. An entirely different class of algorithms can be performed when you access the data items multiple times and in an arbitrary order.

This chapter examines a new type called a list that provides this more flexible access. A list allows you to store a sequence of values together in a single variable. The chapter begins with a general discussion of lists and then moves into a discussion of common list manipulations as well as advanced list techniques. The chapter also includes a discussion of special rules known as reference semantics that apply to objects like lists.

Lists have many features, and it can take a while for a novice to learn all of the different ways that a list can be used. But once you master them, you will find that they are one of the most versatile and powerful structures used in Python programming.

7.1 List Basics

Suppose you want to store some different temperature readings. You could keep them in a series of variables, as in the following shell interaction. Figure 7.1 shows the five variables and their values.

```
>>> # defining 5 integer values
>>> temperature1 = 94
>>> temperature2 = 90
>>> temperature3 = 87
>>> temperature4 = 35
>>> temperature5 = 62
```

This isn't a bad solution if you have just a few temperatures, but suppose you need to store a large number of them, such as 3000. Defining 3000 variables to store temperature values would be tedious. The solution with many variables also does not make it easy to process all of the temperatures together, such as calculating the average temperature.

A better solution would be to put all of the temperatures into a single collection. Figure 7.2 depicts the idea of a single variable storing a collection of five integer values.

But if all of the values were stored in a collection with a single name, how would we refer to each individual temperature? The post office serves as a useful analogy. Think of the post office as a collection of numbered "P.O. boxes." The boxes are indexed with numbers, so you can refer to an individual box by using a description like, "Tucson, AZ, USA, P.O. Box 884."

This notion of referring to data by a name and number occurs often in programming. Python has sequenced types of data that contain multiple pieces of state that are accessed by number. One such type is strings; you saw this kind of access by number

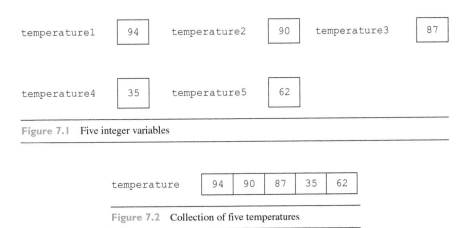

| temperature1 | 94 | temperature2 | 90 | temperature3 | 87 |

| temperature4 | 35 | temperature5 | 62 |

Figure 7.1 Five integer variables

| temperature | 94 | 90 | 87 | 35 | 62 |

Figure 7.2 Collection of five temperatures

when you used indexes to indicate positions within a string. Recall that an expression such as `s[4]` referred to the character at index 4 (the fifth character) within a string `s`.

The *list* is a powerful sequenced type of data where a single variable stores many values, each accessed by an integer index.

> **List**
>
> An ordered collection of values, often accessed using integer indexes.

You can think of a list as a way of storing multiple values in a single variable. The individual values stored in a list are called its *elements*.

> **Element**
>
> An individual value stored in a list.

Each element is accessed using an integer *index*. As with strings, list indexes start with 0, a convention known as *zero-based indexing*. It might seem more natural to start indexes with 1 instead of 0, but most programming languages follow the zero-based convention. As with strings, lists also allow negative indexes, where the last element is given index -1, the second-to-last element is at index -2, and so on.

> **Index**
>
> An integer indicating the position of a particular value in a data structure. Python lists begin at index 0.

In the following sections we will see how to create lists and manipulate the values stored in them.

Creating Lists

A list is defined by writing out a sequence of elements between `[ ]` brackets and separated by commas. When you define a list, you usually store it in a variable. The general syntax for defining a list is the following:

name = [*value, value, ..., value*]

Syntax template: Defining a list with given element values

The following code creates a five-element list called `temperature` that stores the same five integer temperature values seen in the last section:

```
>>> # defining a list of 5 integer values
>>> temperature = [94, 90, 87, 35, 62]
```

```
index        0    1    2    3    4

temperature     94   90   87   35   62

index       -5   -4   -3   -2   -1
```

Figure 7.3   List of temperatures

When you define a list, Python creates a structure that includes those values in that order. Figure 7.3 shows the structure that would result from the previous command. Notice that it has five values because we typed five values when we gave the command. As with the string diagrams in Chapter 4, this diagram indicates both the positive and negative indexes.

Another way to create a list is to use the list function, which accepts any other sequence of values as a parameter and returns a list containing those values:

```
name = list(sequence)
```
Syntax template: Defining a list with multiple copies of a given value

There are many kinds of sequences of values in Python. Two that we have seen previously are ranges and strings. A range is the object produced by the range function that you have used in loops since Chapter 2. If you pass the result of a range call to the list function, it will make a list out of the numbers in that range. The following shell interaction demonstrates:

```
>>> # making a list from a range of integers
>>> mylist = list(range(1, 11))
>>> mylist
[1, 2, 3, 4, 5, 6, 7, 8, 9, 10]
```

Python provides a version of the multiplication operator * that acts on lists. You can "multiply" any list by a constant amount. Although any list can be multiplied, Python programmers most often use this operation to create multiple copies of a single value. The following is the general syntax:

```
name = [value] * length
```
Syntax template: Defining a list with multiple copies of a given value

The value you specify will become the starting value inside each element in the list. The length specifies how many copies of that value will appear in the list. For example,

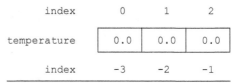

Figure 7.4   List of real numbers of given length

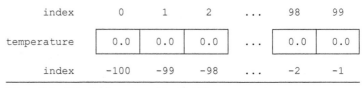

Figure 7.5   List of real numbers of length 100

the following interaction shows the creation of a list of three real numbers, all storing the value `0.0`. Figure 7.4 shows the initial state of this list.

```
>>> # using * operator to create list of a given length
>>> temperature = [0.0] * 3
>>> temperature
[0.0, 0.0, 0.0]
```

Of course, the list isn't very useful if it stores only copies of a single value. In the next section we will see how to access and modify the value of each element. A list also isn't particularly helpful when you have just three values to store, but you can request a much larger list. For example, you could request a list of 100 temperatures by writing the following line of code:

```
>>> temperature = [0.0] * 100
```

This is almost the same line of code you executed before. The only difference is in creating the list, you requested 100 elements instead of 3, which creates a much larger list. Figure 7.5 shows the partial result. Notice that the highest index is 99 rather than 100 because of zero-based indexing.

Yet another way to obtain a list is as a return value from a function. Several library functions return lists. For example, when you read the lines of a file using a file object's `readlines` method, the result returned is a list of strings. And when you break apart a string using its `split` method, the result returned is a list of smaller strings. The following code demonstrates library functions returning lists:

```
>>> # get a list from a string or file
>>> words = "to be or not to be".split()
>>> words
['to', 'be', 'or', 'not', 'to', 'be']
>>> lines = open("poem.txt").readlines()
>>> lines
['Roses are red\n', 'Violets are blue\n',
 'All my base\n', 'Are belong to you']
```

Much of the code in Chapter 6 was really processing lists of strings representing lines and tokens. We chose not to talk about lists in the last chapter so that we could focus on the file-processing concepts, but as you can see, many of the methods we used were actually returning lists to our code.

Accessing List Elements

Once you have created a list, you refer to its individual elements by writing the name of the variable followed by an integer index inside square brackets. The first value goes into index 0, the second value goes into index 1, and so on. The general syntax for accessing a list element by index is the following:

list[index]

Syntax template: Accessing a list element using an index

The following code accesses several list values using an index. Notice that the index can be an arbitrary integer expression, such as 2 + 1 to view index 3.

```
>>> # accessing elements by index
>>> temperature = [94, 90, 87, 35, 62]
>>> temperature[0]
94
>>> temperature[2 + 1]    # access index 3
35
>>> temperature[4]
62
```

You can modify the value at a given index by writing an assignment statement with the list's name and bracketed index followed by an = sign and the value to store. The general syntax is the following:

list[index] = value

Syntax template: Modifying a list element value by index

The following code modifies a list using index. The index and/or value can be an arbitrary integer expression, such as 18 + 23 to produce the value 41 to store in the last index.

```
>>> # modifying elements by index
>>> temperature = [94, 90, 87, 35, 62]
>>> temperature[0] = 72
>>> temperature[1] = 54
>>> temperature[2 + 2] = 18 + 23
>>> temperature
[72, 54, 87, 35, 41]
```

You might find yourself wanting to print various elements of a list. The following code prints the first, middle, and last temperatures in the list we created:

```
# works only for a 5-element list
print("first  =", temperature[0])
print("middle =", temperature[2])
print("last   =", temperature[4])
```

The preceding code is not flexible because it will work only for a list of length 5. A better solution is to use the length of the list to compute an appropriate index. The same len function seen with strings also works with lists, returning the length of the list passed to it. Using half of len as the middle index works properly for a list of any size. And, as with strings, lists allow negative indexes starting from −1 to access the last element of the list. So the following print statements are better because they will work for a list of any size:

```
# works for a list of any length
print("first  =", temperature[0])
print("middle =", temperature[len(temperature) // 2])
print("last   =", temperature[-1])
```

As you learn how to use lists, you will find yourself wondering what types of operations you can perform on a list element that you are accessing. For example, for the list of integers called temperature and an index i, what exactly can you do with temperature[i]? The answer is that you can do anything with temperature[i] that you would normally do with any integer variable. For example, if you have a variable called x that stores an integer, any of the following expressions are valid:

```
>>> # things you can do to an integer
>>> x = 3
>>> x += 1
>>> x *= 2
>>> x -= 1
```

This means that the same expressions are valid for `temperature[i]` if `temperature` is a list containing integers and `i` is some index in that list:

```
>>> # things you can do to an integer element of a list
>>> i = 2
>>> temperature[i] = 3
>>> temperature[i] += 1
>>> temperature[i] *= 2
>>> temperature[i] -= 1
```

From Python's point of view, because `temperature` contains numbers, a list element like `temperature[i]` is a number and can be manipulated as such. Assigning new values to list elements at a given index is especially common if the list was created using the `*` multiplication operator. Once a list of the given length is created, you can store the specific values that are relevant to the problem at specific indexes. Figure 7.6 shows the contents of the list after modifying the elements.

```
>>> # using * operator then modifying element values
>>> temperature = [0.0] * 3
>>> temperature[0] = 74.5
>>> temperature[1] = 68.0
>>> temperature[2] = 70.5
>>> temperature
[74.5, 68.0, 70.5]
```

It is possible to refer to an illegal index of a list, in which case Python raises an exception. For example, in the preceding code with a list of length 3, the legal indexes are

Figure 7.6   List of real numbers after modifying values

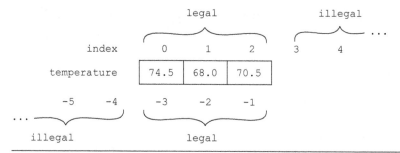

Figure 7.7   Legal/illegal indexes in a list

from 0 to 2 and −1 to −3. Any number less than −3 or greater than 2 is outside the bounds of the list. When you are working with this sample list, if you attempt to refer to temperature[-4] or temperature[3], you are attempting to access a list element that does not exist. If your code makes such an illegal reference, Python will halt your program with an IndexError. Figure 7.7 shows the range of legal indexes for a list of length 3.

```
>>> # index that is out of bounds
>>> temperature = [0.0] * 3
>>> print(temperature[3])
Traceback (most recent call last):
  File "<stdin>", line 1, in <module>
IndexError: list index out of range
>>> print(temperature[-4])
Traceback (most recent call last):
  File "<stdin>", line 1, in <module>
IndexError: list index out of range
```

As we saw with strings in Chapter 3, you can supply more than one integer between [ ] to specify a range of indexes of a list, also called a slice. Slicing a list returns a new list with only a given subset of the indexes. The slice is specified using a start index (the first index to include), a stop index (the first index to exclude), and an optional step (the number of indexes between elements to include in the slice, default of 1 to include all elements in the range), all separated by colon : characters. If you omit the start or stop index, the slice will default to the start or end of the list respectively. The syntax for slicing a list is the following, which is the same as with strings:

list[*start:stop*]
list[*start:stop:step*]
Syntax template: Slicing a list

The following shell interaction demonstrates various slices of a list:

```
>>> # slicing a list
>>> # index  0   1   2   3   4   5   6   7
>>> nums = [10, 20, 30, 40, 50, 60, 70, 80]
>>> nums[2:4]
[30, 40]
>>> nums[:4]
[10, 20, 30, 40]
>>> nums[4:]
[50, 60, 70, 80]
>>> nums[1:7:2]
[20, 40, 60]
>>> nums[::2]
[10, 30, 50, 70]
>>> nums[1::2]
[20, 40, 60, 80]
>>> nums[5:1:-1]
[60, 50, 40, 30]
>>> nums[::-1]
[80, 70, 60, 50, 40, 30, 20, 10]
```

Did You Know?

Buffer Overruns

One of the earliest and still most common sources of computer security problems is a *buffer overrun* (also known as a *buffer overflow*). A buffer overrun is similar to a list IndexError. It occurs when a program writes data beyond the bounds of the buffer that is set aside for that data.

In older programming languages, when you wanted to store data in memory, you had to specify exactly how much memory to allocate for the data. The amount of memory would remain fixed at this amount for the lifetime of the data. For example, suppose that you were coding in an older programming language like C and you wanted to store the string "James T Kirk" in a variable. That string is 12 characters long, counting the spaces, so the program might allocate 12 characters' worth of memory to store it, as shown in Figure 7.8. (Technically strings in C include a special 1-byte "null terminator" at the end, but that is beside the point.)

Continued on next page

Continued from previous page

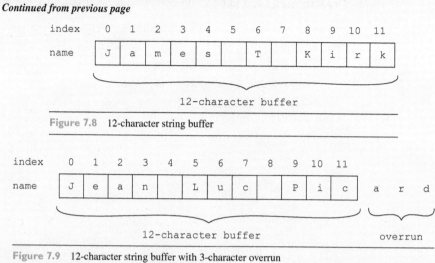

Figure 7.8   12-character string buffer

Figure 7.9   12-character string buffer with 3-character overrun

Suppose that you tell the computer to overwrite this buffer with the string `"Jean Luc Picard"`. There are 15 letters in Picard's name, so if you write all of those characters into the same buffer as before, you "overrun" it by writing three extra characters, as shown in Figure 7.9. You might imagine that the program would simply enlarge the buffer to fit the new contents, but in older languages this was not done automatically.

The last three letters of Picard's name (`"ard"`) would be written to a part of memory that is beyond the end of the buffer. This is a very dangerous situation, because it will overwrite any other data that was already there. An analogy would be a fellow student grabbing three sheets of paper from you and erasing anything you had written on them. You are likely to have had useful information written on those sheets of paper, so the overrun is likely to cause a problem.

When a buffer overrun happens accidentally, the program usually halts with some kind of error condition. However, buffer overruns are particularly dangerous when they are done on purpose by a malicious program. If the attacker can figure out just the right memory location to overwrite, the attacking software can take over your computer and instruct it to do things you haven't asked it to do.

Three of the most famous Internet worms were built on buffer overruns: the 1988 Morris worm, the 2001 Code Red worm, and the 2003 SQLSlammer worm.

You might wonder how such a malicious program could be written if the computer checks the bounds when you access a list. The answer is that older programming languages like C and C++ do not check index bounds by default when you access their data structures. By the time Python was designed in the early 1990s, the danger of buffer overruns was clear and the designers of the language decided to include list-bounds checking so that Python would be more secure.

Traversing a List

Often you will want to do some operation to every element of a list one-by-one. An algorithm that visits each of a list's elements in order is referred to as a *traversal* of the list.

> **List Traversal**
>
> Processing each list element sequentially from the first to the last.

The simplest way to traverse the elements of a list is with a `for` loop. You have seen `for` loops over ranges and strings, and the syntax for lists is no different:

```
for name in list:
    statement
    statement
    ...
    statement
```
Syntax template: for loop over list elements

We will use this traversal pattern often as we explore common list algorithms. The following shell interaction demonstrates a basic `for` loop that prints each element from our temperature list of integers from the previous section.

```
>>> # for loop over list elements
>>> temperature = [94, 90, 87, 35, 62]
>>> for temp in temperature:
...     print(temp)
...
94
90
87
35
62
```

The standard `for` loop is useful for accessing each element, but it has limitations. It does not give you any choice in the order of iteration: it always loops over the elements from first to last. It is also not helpful for modifying elements. Students sometimes think that the following code will increase each element value in a list by 1, but it does not work:

```
>>> # for loop to modify elements (does not work)
>>> temperature = [94, 90, 87, 35, 62]
>>> for temp in temperature:
...     temp += 1
...
>>> temperature
[94, 90, 87, 35, 62]
```

The preceding code does not modify the list because the variable `temp` in the loop stores a copy of each list element. Modifying `temp` does not modify the original list. If you want the flexibility to modify a list or loop over it in a different order, you must instead write a loop over the *indexes* of the list (from 0 through the list's length minus 1) rather than the elements themselves.

We could loop up to the value 5 as the maximum for our range because there are 5 elements in the list. But if we later changed the number of list elements, we would need to carefully update the loop to match. A better solution is to use the `len` function as the endpoint of our range of indexes. The index-based version of the `for` loop has the following general syntax:

```
for name in range(len(list)):
    # do something with list[i]
    statement
    statement
    ...
    statement
```

Syntax template: Indexed for loop over a list

The following shell interaction loops over the list of temperatures to increase each element's value by 1:

```
>>> # for loop to modify elements by index (works)
>>> temperature = [94, 90, 87, 35, 62]
>>> for i in range(len(temperature)):
...     temperature[i] += 1
...
>>> temperature
[95, 91, 88, 36, 63]
```

The indexed `for` loop can be used to set the initial values in a list. This is useful when reading data from another source and storing it into a list. For example, suppose you want to read a series of temperatures from a user. You can read each value using the `input` function and store it at an index in a list:

```
# read values from user input into a list
temperature = [0] * 10
for i in range(len(temperature)):
    temperature[i] = int(input("Type a number: "))
```

A Complete List Program

Let's look at a program in which a list allows you to solve a problem that you couldn't solve before. If you tune in to any local news broadcast at night, you'll hear a report of the high temperature for that day. It is usually reported as an integer, as in, "It got up to 78 today."

Suppose you want to examine a series of daily high temperatures, compute the average high temperature, and count how many days were above that average temperature. You've been using input to solve problems like this, and you can almost solve the problem that way. If you just wanted to know the average, you could use input and write a cumulative sum loop to find it. The following program does a pretty good job. Here is its code along with a sample execution:

```
 1   # Reads a series of high temperatures and reports the average.
 2
 3   def main():
 4       num_days = int(input("How many days' temperatures? "))
 5       total = 0
 6       for i in range(1, num_days + 1):
 7           next = int(input("Day " + str(i) + "'s high temp: "))
 8           total += next
 9
10       average = total / num_days
11       print()
12       print("Average =", average)
13
14   main()
```

```
How many days' temperatures? 5
Day 1's high temp: 78
Day 2's high temp: 81
Day 3's high temp: 75
Day 4's high temp: 79
Day 5's high temp: 71
Average = 76.8
```

But how do you count how many days were above average? You could try to incorporate a comparison to the average temperature in the loop, but that won't work. The problem is that you can't figure out the average until you've gone through all of the data. That means you'll need to make a second pass through the data to figure out how many days were above average. You can't do that with input, because input prompts for new data each time it is called. You'd have to prompt the user to enter the temperature data a second time, which would be silly.

Fortunately, you can solve the problem with a list. As you read numbers in and compute the cumulative sum, you can fill up a list that stores the temperatures. You know the length of the list to use; it should be equal to the number of days' temperatures entered by the user:

```
# define list for storing temperatures
num_days = int(input("How many days' temperatures? "))
temps = [0] * num_days
...
```

Because you're using a list, you'll want to change the input loop to store each day's temperature into the corresponding index in the list. Furthermore, you no longer need the variable next because you'll be storing the values in the list instead. An important change to make to our for loop is to modify its bounds to start from 0 rather than 1. The previous version of the program looped from 1 to num_days inclusive, but since lists begin their indexes at 0, it is better for our code to loop over that range of indexes from 0 to num_days - 1 inclusive. But just because you're using zero-based indexing inside the program doesn't mean that you have to confuse the user by asking for "Day 0's high temp." You can modify the code to prompt for day (i + 1). So the loop code becomes:

```
for i in range(num_days):
    temps[i] = int(input("Day " + str(i + 1) + "'s high temp: "))
    total += temps[i]
```

After this loop executes, you compute the average as you did before. Then you write a new loop that counts how many days were above average using the standard for-each loop. You don't need to use an indexed for loop this time because you just need to use the temperature values; their individual indexes are not important for computing the number of days above average.

```
above = 0
for temp in temps:
    if temp > average:
        above += 1
```

If you put these various code fragments together and include code to report the number of days that had an above-average temperature, you get the following complete program that produces the log of execution shown after the code:

```
 1  # Reads a series of high temperatures and reports the
 2  # average and the number of days above average.
 3
 4  def main():
 5      num_days = int(input("How many days' temperatures? "))
 6      temps = [0] * num_days
 7
 8      # record temperatures and find average
```

Continued on next page

Continued from previous page

```
 9        total = 0
10        for i in range(num_days):
11            temps[i] = int(input("Day " + str(i + 1) + "'s high temp: "))
12            total += temps[i]
13
14        average = total / num_days
15
16        # count days above average
17        above = 0
18        for temp in temps:
19            if temp > average:
20                above += 1
21
22        # report results
23        print()
24        print("Average =", average)
25        print(above, "days above average")
26
27   main()
```

```
How many days' temperatures? 9
Day 1's high temp: 75
Day 2's high temp: 78
Day 3's high temp: 85
Day 4's high temp: 71
Day 5's high temp: 69
Day 6's high temp: 82
Day 7's high temp: 74
Day 8's high temp: 80
Day 9's high temp: 87

Average = 77.88888888888889
5 days above average
```

Common Programming Error

Off-by-One Bug

When you converted the temperature program to one that uses a list, you used the `for` loop that started with 0 to match the range of indexes in the list. But the code prints each day's high temperature starting with 1. Because the output

Continued on next page

Continued from previous page

begins with day 1, it may be tempting to write this same code with a loop that begins at 1:

```
# wrong loop bounds
for i in range(1, num_days + 1):
    temps[i] = int(input("Day " + str(i) + "'s high temp: "))
    sums += temps[i]
```

This loop raises an error when you run the program. On the last iteration of the loop, the code tries to access an index that is one past the end of the list, which raises an `IndexError`. Here's a sample execution:

```
How many days' temperatures? 5
Day 1's high temp: 82
Day 2's high temp: 80
Day 3's high temp: 79
Day 4's high temp: 71
Day 5's high temp: 75
Traceback (most recent call last):
  File "weather.py", line 5, in <module>
    temps[i] = int(input("Day " + str(i) + "'s high temp: "))
IndexError: list assignment index out of range
```

This is a classic off-by-one error. One way to fix it would be to change the loop body statements to refer to `temps[i - 1]` since the loop range now goes from 1 to `num_days`. But the authors generally find it easier to make the list index be the focus of the loop, so that you know the variable `i` refers to a valid index in the list at all times. The better fix is to use a zero-based loop and change the output to shift the number it prints by 1:

```
# correct loop bounds
for i in range(num_days):
    temps[i] = input("Day " + str(i + 1) + "'s high temp: ")
    sums += temps[i]
```

Random Access

Most of the algorithms we have seen so far have involved *sequential access*. A sequential approach means to examine or manipulate each piece of data in order as it arrives, from the first to the last.

> **Sequential Access**
>
> Manipulating values in a sequential manner from first to last.

We have written many sequential algorithms that processed data from user input or from files. These algorithms don't require any lists or data storage in our programs because we only needed to access data from the first element to the last in order. But, as we have seen, there is no way to reexamine old input or easily go back to the beginning. The sample temperature program we just studied uses a list to allow a second pass through the data, but even this is fundamentally a sequential approach because it involves two forward passes through the data.

A list is a powerful data structure that allows a more sophisticated kind of access known as *random access*. Random access is when a structure allows you to look at its contents in any order you like: first to last, or last to first, or jumping around to arbitrary pieces of data.

> **Random Access**
>
> Manipulating values in any order whatsoever to allow quick access to each value.

A list can provide random access because it is allocated as a contiguous block of memory. The computer can quickly compute exactly where a particular value will be stored, because it knows how much space each element takes up in memory and it knows that all the elements are allocated right next to one another in the list.

When you work with lists, you can jump around in the list without worrying about how much time it will take. For example, suppose that you have created a list of temperature readings that has 10,000 elements and you find yourself wanting to print a particular subset of the readings with code like the following:

```
print("#1394 =", temps[1394])
print("#6793 =", temps[6793])
print("#72 =", temps[72])
```

This code will execute quickly even though you are asking for list elements that are far apart from one another. Notice also that you don't have to ask for them in order. You can jump to element `1394`, then jump ahead to element `6793`, and then jump back to element `72`. You can access elements in a list in any order that you like, and you will get fast access.

Later in the chapter we will explore several algorithms that would be difficult to implement without fast random access.

List Methods

Along with all of the syntax you have seen for lists earlier in this chapter, you can also define an empty list by setting it equal to `[]`.

```
data = []
```

This code creates an empty list. It might seem odd to create an empty list; what's the point of making one if it contains no data? The answer is that data can be added to a list after its creation; the length of the list can grow and shrink as data is added to it or removed from it. Lists are objects that provide many methods you can use to add, remove, manipulate, and search the data.

Once you've created a list, you can add a value to the end of the list by calling its `append` method:

```
>>> # adding element to end of list with append
>>> data = []
>>> len(data)
0
>>> data.append("Tool")
>>> data
['Tool']
>>> len(data)
1
>>> data.append("Phish")
>>> data.append("Muse")
>>> data
['Tool', 'Phish', 'Muse']
>>> len(data)
3
```

The `append` method causes the list to increase its length by 1 to accommodate the newly added element. Before any elements are added, the empty list has length 0. As each of the three elements is appended, the length goes to 1, then 2, then 3, as shown by the results of the `len(data)` calls above. This type of code where a list starts out empty and grows over time is sometimes called a *cumulative list* algorithm. Figure 7.10 shows the state of a list before and after an `append` call.

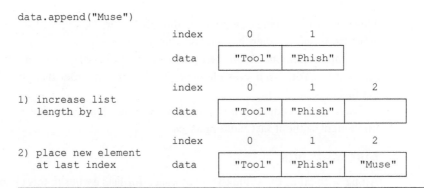

Figure 7.10   List before/after append

The preceding cumulative list code is somewhat similar to code that starts the list at length 3 using the * operator and then fills in each element. The main difference between the two styles is that the * version would create a list of length 3 and then fill in each element. The list's length would not change because it would be created with an initial length of 3. That style is arguably better when you know the length of the list ahead of time. But the style shown in this section is best when you don't know exactly how many elements will be added to the list. Overall the style of making an empty list and adding elements to it over time is the more common pattern.

Lists also have an `insert` method for adding a value at a particular index in the list. It preserves the order of the other list elements, shifting values to the right to make room for the new value. The `insert` method takes two parameters: an index and a value to insert. The new element is inserted just before the value that used to be at that index in the list. Given the preceding list, consider the effect of inserting a value at index 1:

```
>>> # adding element to a list with insert
>>> data
['Tool', 'Phish', 'Muse']
>>> data.insert(1, "U2")
>>> data
['Tool', 'U2', 'Phish', 'Muse']
```

The call on `insert` instructs the computer to insert the new string at index 1. Therefore, the old value at index 1 and everything that follows it gets shifted to the right. Figure 7.11 shows the state of a list before and after an `insert` call.

Python also provides a way to remove a value at a particular index in a list. If you write the `del` keyword (short for "delete") followed by a list name and index in brackets, the value at that index will be removed from the list. Similar to `append`, a `del` operation preserves

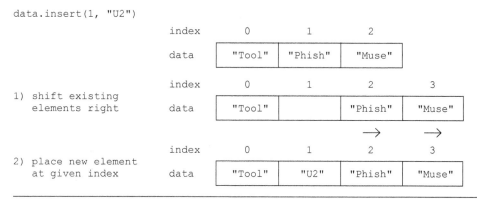

Figure 7.11 List before/after insert

the order of the list by shifting values to the left to fill in any gap. For example, consider what happens to the previous list if we remove the value at position 0 and then at position 1:

```
>>> # removing elements from a list by index
>>> data
['Tool', 'U2', 'Phish', 'Muse']
>>> del data[1]
>>> del data[2]
>>> data
['Tool', 'Phish']
```

This result is a little surprising. We asked the list to remove the value at index 1 and then to remove the value at index 2. You might imagine that this would get rid of the strings "U2" and "Phish", since they were at indexes 1 and 2, respectively, before this code was executed. However, a list is a dynamic structure whose values move around and shift into new indexes in response to your commands. The first `del` statement removes the string "U2" because it's the value currently in index 1. But once that value has been removed, everything else shifts over: the string "Phish" shifts left to index 1, and "Muse" shifts left to index 2. So, when the second `del` is performed for index 2, Python removes "Muse" from the list because it is the value that is in index 2 at that point in time. Figure 7.12 illustrates the result of a deletion from a list.

Lists also have a method called `pop` that is similar to `del` but also returns the removed element. For example, the call of `data.pop(0)` would remove and return "Tool" from the list.

If the list is very large, `insert` and `del` can be expensive in terms of time because the computer has to shift the values around. For example, the following code to replace the value in a list is inefficient. It is not visibly obvious from the output in the shell, but

```
del data[1]
```

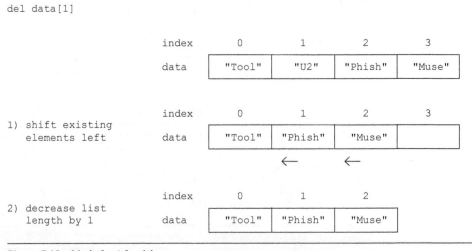

Figure 7.12   List before/after del

the calls to `del` and `insert` in the previous interaction each have to do a lot of work, shifting the list left and then right again. If all you want to do is to replace a value, you should use the square bracket notation shown earlier in this chapter. The subsequent code is equivalent to the previous example and runs more efficiently:

```
>>> # replace value at index 1 in a list (bad style)
>>> data
['Tool', 'U2', 'Phish', 'Muse']
>>> del data[1]
>>> data
['Tool', 'Phish', 'Muse']
>>> data.insert(1, "Drake")
>>> data
['Tool', 'Drake', 'Phish', 'Muse']
```

```
>>> # replace value at index 1 in a list (better style)
>>> data
['Tool', 'U2', 'Phish', 'Muse']
>>> data[1] = "Drake"
>>> data
['Tool', 'Drake', 'Phish', 'Muse']
```

If you don't know the index of the element to remove, you can instead call the list's `remove` method, which accepts a value to remove and searches the list for that value, removing the first occurrence of it. Similar to `del`, the `remove` method shifts any subsequent elements left by 1 and reduces the list's length by 1.

```
>>> # removing elements from a list by value
>>> data
['Tool', 'U2', 'Phish', 'Muse']
>>> data.remove("U2")
>>> data
['Tool', 'Phish', 'Muse']
```

As noted earlier, you can create an empty list. After you have added values to a list, you can remove them one at a time. But what if you want to remove all of the values from the list? In that case, you can call the `clear` method, which removes all elements and sets the list's size to 0.

```
>>> # clear the elements from a list
>>> data
['Tool', 'Drake', 'Phish', 'Muse']
```

Continued on next page

Continued from previous page

```
>>> data.clear()
>>> data
[]
>>> len(data)
0
```

Lists support a + operator that concatenates the elements of two lists into a single new list. There is also an `extend` method that is similar to + except that it modifies a list in place, whereas + produces a new separate list. The following shell interaction demonstrates these operations:

```
>>> # use + operator and extend method
>>> data1 = ["Tool", "Phish", "Muse"]
>>> data2 = ["Drake", "Beyonce"]
>>> data3 = data1 + data2
>>> data3
['Tool', 'Phish', 'Muse', 'Drake', 'Beyonce']
>>> data1
['Tool', 'Phish', 'Muse']
>>> data1.extend(["U2", "KISS"])
>>> data1
['Tool', 'Phish', 'Muse', 'U2', 'KISS']
```

Table 7.1 summarizes the list methods and operations introduced in this section along with other useful operations. A more complete list can be found in the online Python documentation.

There are also a set of global functions that accept a list as a parameter and perform various operations on that list. These functions use the general syntax of `function_name(list)` rather than the list methods' general syntax of `list.method_name()`. The `len` function is an example of such a function. Some others are `min` and `max`, which return the largest and smallest value in a list, respectively. Another is `sum`, which computes a cumulative sum of the elements in the list and returns the total:

```
>>> # demonstrate global list functions
>>> nums = [3, 5, 2, 6, 7, 4]
>>> min(nums)
2
>>> max(nums)
7
>>> sum(nums)
27
```

Table 7.1 **List Operations**

Operation	Description
list[index]	return the element at a given index of a list; IndexError if out of bounds
list[start:stop:step]	return a slice of elements between the given start/stop indexes of a list
list[index] = value	set the element at a given index of a list
del list[index]	removes an item or slice from a given index of list, shifting elements left
del list[index:index]	to cover
list1 + list2	concatenate the elements of two lists to produce a new list
value in list	returns True if the given element occurs in the list
value not in list	returns True if the given element does not occur in the list
list.append(value)	adds an item to the end of the list
list.clear()	removes all items from the list
list.count(value)	returns the number of times the value occurs in the list
list.extend(seq)	extends the list by adding all the elements from the passed in sequence to the end
list.index(value)	returns the first index where the value occurs; raises an error if the value isn't in the list; can optionally also take starting and ending indexes indicating what part of the list to search in
list.insert(index, value)	inserts an item at a given index
list.pop(index)	removes the value at the passed in index and returns it; if no index is passed, will remove and return the last item in list
list.remove(value)	removes first occurrence of specified value from list; raises an error if the value isn't in the list
list.reverse()	reverse the order of list's elements
list.sort()	rearrange list elements into sorted order (or into reverse order,
list.sort(reverse=True)	if reverse=True is passed)

Some of these functions are similar to list methods, except that they create a new list rather than modifying an existing list. For example, lists have a reverse method that reverses the order of the elements in a list. There is also a global reversed function (note the "d" at the end) that accepts a list as a parameter and returns a new list that contains the elements of the original list but in reverse order. The global reversed function does not modify the existing list.

```
>>> # demonstrate reverse method and global reversed function
>>> nums = [3, 5, 2, 6, 7, 4]
>>> nums2 = reversed(nums)
>>> nums2
[4, 7, 6, 2, 5, 3]
```

Continued on next page

Continued from previous page

```
>>> nums
[3, 5, 2, 6, 7, 4]
>>> nums.reverse()
>>> nums
[4, 7, 6, 2, 5, 3]
```

Table 7.2 summarizes the built-in global functions that work with lists. We will discuss some of these functions in Chapter 12 when we discuss functional programming.

The `random` library also has some functions that interact with lists. For example, `random.shuffle` accepts a list parameter, as does `random.choice`. These are not shown in the table, but you may want to look at their online documentation in case you find them useful.

```
>>> # demonstrate random list functions
>>> import random
>>> nums = [3, 5, 2, 6, 7, 4]
>>> random.shuffle(nums)    # randomly rearrange elements
>>> nums
[5, 4, 3, 6, 7, 2]
>>> random.choice(nums)     # return a randomly chosen element
3
>>> random.choice(nums)
7
>>> random.choice(nums)
5
>>> nums
[5, 4, 3, 6, 7, 2]
```

Table 7.2   Global Functions that Operate on Lists

Function	Description
enumerate(list)	returns a sequence of index/value pairs for each element in list
filter(list, predicate)	returns a subset of the elements of the list based on some criteria
len(list)	number of elements in list
map(list, function)	applies a function to each element of the list to make a new list
max(list)	returns the largest value in a list
min(list)	returns the smallest value in a list
reversed(list)	return a new list with the same elements in reverse order
sorted(list)	return a new list with the same elements in sorted order
str(list)	return a string representation of the list
sum(list)	return the sum of the numbers in a list

7.2 List-Traversal Algorithms

So far in this chapter we have presented two standard patterns for manipulating a list. The first is the standard for-each loop, which uses a variable for each element in the list:

```
for name in list:
    statement
    statement
    ...
    statement
```

The second is the indexed `for` loop, which iterates over the integer indexes in the list:

```
for i in range(len(list)):
    # do something with list[i]
    statement
    statement
    ...
    statement
```

In this section we will explore some common list algorithms that can be implemented with these patterns. Of course, not all list operations can be implemented this way; the section ends with an example that requires a modified version of the standard code. We will implement each operation as a function.

Lists as Parameters

When writing larger programs involving lists, you'll want to decompose your solution into functions. Sometimes those functions should accept lists as parameters or return lists as their results. The syntax of passing a list as a parameter is the same as passing any other parameter. When writing a function that accepts a list parameter, you write the list's name in the parentheses of the function's header. When calling a function that accepts a list parameter, you write the list's name, without any [ ] brackets, inside the parentheses of the call. (We won't show a syntax template here because there is no new syntax to show.)

For example, suppose that you want to compute the arithmetic mean (average) value in a list of numbers. This is equal to the sum of the values divided by the number of values. For example, the average of the values 1, 7, 3, and 9 is $(1 + 7 + 3 + 9)/4$, or 5. We can represent this as a function:

```
# Computes the average of the numbers in the given list.
# Example: average([1, 6, 2]) returns 3.0.
def average(numbers):
    sum = 0
    count = 0
```

Continued on next page

Continued from previous page

```
for n in numbers:
    sum += n
    count += 1
return sum / count
```

Notice in the preceding code that there is nothing in particular about the function header that indicates that the parameter `numbers` is a list, since all kinds of parameters use the same syntax. Comment headers on functions are especially important to make clear to the caller what kinds of values should be passed to them.

The syntax for calling the function is to write the list's name in the parentheses of the call. We don't include any `[ ]` brackets here because we are passing the entire list, not any one particular element. For example, the following code calls `average` with the four values mentioned previously, captures the returned result in a variable, and prints the average as output:

```
# calling the average function
numbers = [1, 7, 3, 9]
avg = average(numbers)
print("average of", numbers, "is", avg)
```

```
average of [1, 7, 3, 9] is 5.0
```

Similarly, the syntax for returning a list is the same as returning any other kind of value. Suppose you want a function that computes the squares of integers and stores them in a list. You can write a function called `squares` that builds and returns a list of such integers. This is another example of a cumulative list algorithm as discussed earlier in this chapter. Here is an implementation of the function:

```
# Returns a list of the first N integers squared.
# Example: squares(4) returns [1, 4, 9, 16].
def squares(n):
    result = []
    for i in range(1, n + 1):
        result.append(i * i)
    return result
```

The function is called like any other function. The list that it returns can be stored in a variable and used in the `main` part of the program:

```
# calling the squares function
nums = squares(7)
print("result is", nums)
```

```
result is [1, 4, 9, 16, 25, 36, 49]
```

One interesting detail about lists is that when you pass them as parameters to a function and that function modifies the list, the modification is seen back in `main` (or wherever the function was called). This is related to a concept called reference semantics that we will explore later in this chapter. For now we will focus on the list algorithms and traversals before we dive deeply into parameter passing mechanics.

Searching a List

Once you have built up a list, you might be interested in searching for a specific value in the list. There are several mechanisms for doing so. If you just want to know whether or not something is in the list, you can use the `in` operator, which returns a Boolean value.

```
>>> # testing the 'in' keyword
>>> numbers = [8, 7, 19, 2, 82, 8, 7, 25, 8]
>>> 82 in numbers
True
>>> 7 in numbers
True
>>> 9999 in numbers
False
```

The `in` operator (and its negative variant, `not in`) can be used to filter what elements are added to a list. For example, suppose you have an input file of names that has some duplicates, and you want to get rid of the duplicates. The file might look like this:

```
Maria Derek Erica
Derek Maria Livia Jack
Anita Ed Maria Livia Derek
Jack Erica
```

Notice that some names occur more than once in the file. You can create a list to hold these names and use the `in` operator to ensure that there are no duplicates. We'll implement the code as a function called `unique_words` that accepts the file's name as a parameter, loops over the words of the file, and adds the unique ones to a list that is returned at the end of the code:

```
# Returns a list of the unique words in the given file,
# excluding any duplicate words.
def unique_words(filename):
    with open(filename) as file:
        words = []
        for word in file.read().split():
            if word not in words:
                words.append(word)
        return words
```

When run on the preceding sample input file, this code returns the following list:

```
>>> # testing the unique_words function
>>> unique_words("names.txt")
>>> ['Maria', 'Derek', 'Erica', 'Livia', 'Jack', 'Anita', 'Ed']
```

Notice that only 7 of the original 13 names appear in this list, because the various duplicates have been eliminated. (Python has a different structure called a set that automatically excludes duplicates and would be better suited to this task. We will learn about sets in the next chapter.)

Sometimes it is not enough to know that a value appears in the list. You may want to know exactly where it occurs. Python lists include an index method that accepts a target value as a parameter and returns the index where that value occurs in the list. If the value occurs multiple times in the list, index returns the index of the first occurrence. If the value is not found in the list, index throws a ValueError. There is also a variation of index that takes two additional parameters, a start and stop index, and will search for the value between those two indexes, following the usual convention that the first index is inclusive and the second is exclusive.

```
>>> # index     0  1   2  3   4   5  6   7  8
>>> numbers = [8, 7, 19, 2, 82, 8, 7, 25, 8]
>>> numbers.index(82)
4
>>> numbers.index(7)
1
>>> numbers.index(7, 3, 8)    # search between indexes 3 and 8
6
>>> numbers.index(9999)
Traceback (most recent call last):
  File "<stdin>", line 1, in <module>
ValueError: 9999 is not in list
```

To better understand how index is implemented, let's write a variation called last_index that returns the index of the last occurrence of a given value. Notice in the preceding shell code that the call of numbers.index(7) returned 1 because that was the index of the first occurrence of the value 7. We'd like our function to instead return 6 because that is the index of the last occurrence of the value 7.

The best way to find the last occurrence of a given value is to start at the back of the list and work your way to the front. Because you don't know exactly where you'll find the value, you might try implementing this using a while loop, as in the following pseudocode:

```
i = length of list - 1.
while we haven't found it yet:
    i -= 1
```

However, there is a simpler approach. Because you're writing a function that returns a value, you can return the appropriate index as soon as you find a match. That means you can use an indexed traversal loop to solve this problem. We haven't done as many downward-counting `for` loops as upward-counting, but remember that you can pass three parameters to `range`: a start, a stop, and a step. If we pass a step of -1, the range will count downward. Since the stop parameter of a range is the first index to exclude, we will pass `-1` as the stop index. The loop heading will be the following:

```
# last_index loop heading
for i in range(len(list) - 1, -1, -1):
...
```

You should check the value stored at each index to see if it equals the target value, and if so, you should return the current index `i`. Remember that a `return` statement terminates a function, so you'll break out of the loop as soon as the target value is found. But what if the value isn't found? What if you traverse the entire list and find no matches? In that case, the `for` loop will finish executing without ever returning a value.

There are many things you can do if the value is not found. Some languages choose to return a special value such as `-1` to indicate that the value is not anywhere in the list. But Python allows negative list indexing, so `-1` would be a confusing result to return. Instead, Python's `index` method handles this case by raising a `ValueError`. We can match this behavior by adding an extra `raise` statement after the loop that will be executed only when the target value is not found. Putting all this together, you get the following function:

```
# Returns the index of the last occurrence of the given target
# value in the given list, or raises a ValueError if not found.
def last_index(list, target):
    for i in range(len(list) - 1, -1, -1):
        if list[i] == target:
            return i
    raise ValueError(str(target) + " is not in list")
```

The following example calls test our new function. Notice that we call it with syntax like `last_index(numbers, 7)` rather than `numbers.last_index(7)` because we are writing a function rather than a method. The `list.method_name()` syntax is used only for methods that are built-in parts of Python lists, not functions that we write ourselves in our own programs.

```
>>> # index     0  1   2  3   4  5  6   7   8
>>> numbers = [8, 7, 19, 2, 82, 8, 7, 25, 8]
>>> last_index(numbers, 7)
6
>>> last_index(numbers, 8)
8
```

Continued on next page

Continued from previous page

```
>>> last_index(numbers, 9999)
Traceback (most recent call last):
  File "<stdin>", line 1, in <module>
  File "<stdin>", line 5, in last_index
ValueError: 9999 is not in list
```

As a final searching exercise, you might want to count how many times a particular value appears in a list. Python lists actually already include a count method that accepts a value as a parameter and returns the number of occurrences of that value. For example, the call of numbers.count(8) returns the number of occurrences of the value 8 in the list called numbers:

```
>>> # index    0  1   2  3   4   5  6   7   8
>>> numbers = [8, 7, 19, 2, 82, 8, 7, 25, 8]
>>> numbers.count(8)
3
```

Let's explore how to implement searching algorithms by writing a variation of count called count_between that accepts a list, a minimum value, and a maximum value, and that returns the number of values in the list that are between the min and max values inclusive. Counting occurrences is a relatively simple search task: you just need to loop over each element in the list and check whether it matches the criteria you are looking for. You can accomplish this task with a for loop that keeps a count of the number of occurrences of values that are in the range for which you're searching:

```
# Returns the number of elements in the given list whose values
# are between the given min and max, inclusive.
def count_between(list, min, max):
    occurrences = 0
    for n in list:
        if min <= n <= max:
            occurrences += 1
    return occurrences
```

The following example call counts how many values are between 1 and 10 in the list:

```
>>> numbers = [8, 7, 19, 2, 82, 8, 7, 25, 8]
>>> count_between(numbers, 1, 10)
6
```

As we noted at the beginning of this section, many of our examples involve a list of integers, but they could all be applied to a list of any other type that supports the same operations like <= and ==. For example, we could use last_index and count_between on a list of strings:

```
>>> # index      0    1    2    3    4    5
>>> letters = ["e", "v", "e", "l", "y", "n"]
>>> last_index(letters, "e")
2
>>> count_between(letters, "f", "w")
3
```

Replacing and Removing Values

Often you'll want to make changes to certain elements of a list. For example, suppose you want to write a function to replace the first occurrence of one value in a list with another value. You can use square bracket notation to replace the value, but you have to know where it appears in the list. You can find out the location of a value in the list by calling the index method as described previously.

The index method takes a particular value and returns the index of the first occurrence of the value in the list. If it doesn't find the value, it raises a ValueError. So, you could write a replace function as follows:

```
# Replaces the first occurrence of the given target value
# with the given replacement value in the given list.
def replace(list, target, replacement):
    if target in list:
        index = list.index(target)
        list[index] = replacement
```

This function doesn't return anything, even though it changes the contents of a list. Instead it modifies the list that was passed to it. As we'll explore in more detail later, functions that operate on lists are able to make changes to the lists that are passed to them.

The following code tests the replace function. Notice that the first occurrence of "be" is changed to "beep":

```
>>> words = ["to", "be", "or", "not", "to", "be"]
>>> replace(words, "be", "beep")
>>> words
['to', 'beep', 'or', 'not', 'to', 'be']
```

You might also want to write a replace_all function that replaces all the occurrences of a target value with some new value, rather than just one occurrence. For this function, in and index are not ideal, because we want to find all indexes rather than just one. A better strategy would be to traverse the list looking for the target value and replacing each occurrence of it with the new value. Since we are modifying the list, we must use an indexed `for` loop:

```
# Replaces all occurrences of the given target value with the
# given replacement value in the given list.
def replace_all(list, target, replacement):
    for i in range(len(list)):
        if list[i] == target:
            list[i] = replacement
```

The following example calls test our `replace_all` function:

```
>>> # testing the replace_all function
>>> words = ["to", "be", "or", "not", "to", "be"]
>>> replace_all(words, "be", "beep")
>>> words
['to', 'beep', 'or', 'not', 'to', 'beep']

>>> # index      0   1   2   3    4   5   6    7   8
>>> numbers = [8, 7, 19, 2, 82, 8, 7, 25, 8]
>>> replace_all(numbers, 8, -1)
>>> numbers
[-1, 7, 19, 2, 82, -1, 7, 25, -1]
```

Reversing a List

As another example of common operations, let's consider the task of reversing the order of the elements stored in a list. Python lists have a `reverse` method that reverses the order of the list's elements. The following shell interaction demonstrates this method:

```
>>> # demonstrate reverse method
>>> numbers = [3, 8, 7, -2, 14, 78]
>>> numbers.reverse()
>>> numbers
[78, 14, -2, 7, 8, 3]
```

There is also a global function called `reversed` that accepts a list or other collection as a parameter and returns a new sequence in the reverse order. There are a few differences between `reversed` and `reverse`. One is that `reversed` is a global function, meaning that it is called with the syntax `reversed(list)` rather than `list.reverse()`. The other is that the `reverse` method modifies a given list in-place, while the global `reversed` function instead returns a new sequence that is the reverse of the original without modifying the original list. Oddly, `reversed` does not return a list, but it returns an object that can be examined using a `for` loop or converted into a list with the `list` function. The following shell interaction demonstrates this function:

```
>>> # demonstrate reversed function
>>> numbers = [3, 8, 7, -2, 14, 78]
>>> rev = list(reversed(numbers))
>>> rev
[78, 14, -2, 7, 8, 3]
>>> numbers
[3, 8, 7, -2, 14, 78]
```

The algorithm for reversing a list is interesting and worth examining. How would we reverse a list if there were no `reverse` method or `reversed` function?

One approach would be to create a new list and to store the values from the first list into the second list in reverse order. Although that approach would be reasonable, you should be able to solve the problem in-place without creating a second list. Doing so would involve performing a series of exchanges or swaps.

If we were reversing the list of numbers from the previous shell interaction, the value 3 at the front of the list and the value 78 at the end of the list need to be swapped. After swapping that pair, you can swap the next pair, the values at indexes 1 and 4. Lastly we would need to swap the pair at indexes 2 and 3. Figure 7.13 depicts the swaps that combine to reverse the list.

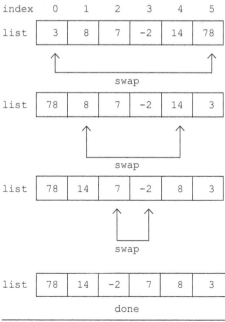

Figure 7.13 Reversing a list by swapping elements

Since our reversal depends on swaps, let's consider the general problem of swapping two values. Suppose you have two integer variables x and y that have the values 3 and 78. How would you swap these values? A naive approach is to simply assign the values to one another, as shown in the following shell interaction:

```
>>> # incorrect code to swap two integers
>>> x = 3
>>> y = 78

>>> x = y
>>> y = x
```

Unfortunately, this doesn't work. When the first assignment statement is executed, you copy the value of y into x. You want x to eventually become equal to 78, but if you attempt to solve the problem this way, you lose the old value of x as soon as you assign the value of y to it. The second assignment statement then copies the new value of x, 78, back into y, which leaves you with two variables equal to 78. Figure 7.14 depicts this process.

The standard solution is to introduce a temporary variable that you can use to store the old value of x while you're giving x its new value. You can then copy the old value of x from the temporary variable into y to complete the swap:

```
>>> # correct code to swap two integers
>>> x = 3
>>> y = 78

>>> temp = x
>>> x = y
>>> y = temp
```

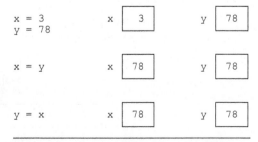

Figure 7.14   Incorrect code to swap two integers

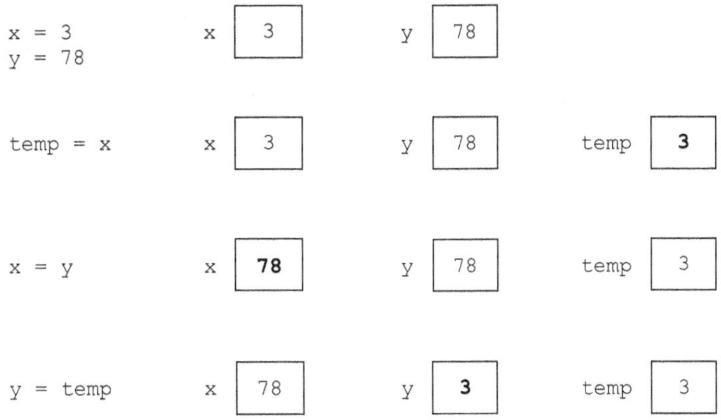

		x	3		y	78		
x = 3								
y = 78								

Figure 7.15 Correct code to swap two integers

You start by copying the old value of x into temp. Next, you copy the old value of x from temp to y. At this point you have successfully swapped the values of x and y, so you don't need temp anymore. Figure 7.15 depicts this process.

Given this swapping code, you can fairly easily write a reversing function. You just have to think about what combinations of values to swap. Start by swapping the first and last values. The sample list has a length of 6, which means that you will be swapping the values at indexes 0 and 5. But you want to write the code so that it works for a list of any length.

In general, the first swap you'll want to perform is to swap element 0 with element len(list) - 1. Then you'll want to swap the second value with the second-to-last value. And so on. The following three swaps are needed for a list of length 6:

- swap list[0] with list[len(list) - 1]
- swap list[1] with list[len(list) - 2]
- swap list[2] with list[len(list) - 3]

There is a pattern to these swaps that you can capture with a loop. If you use a variable i for the first parameter of the call on swap and introduce a local variable j to store an expression for the second parameter to swap, each of these calls will take the following form:

```
# swap list[i] with list[j]
j = len(list) - i - 1
temp = list[i]
list[i] = list[j]
list[j] = temp
```

To implement the reversal, you could put the function inside an indexed `for` loop:

```
# doesn't quite work
for i in range(len(list)):
    # swap list[i] with list[j]
    j = len(list) - i - 1
    temp = list[i]
    list[i] = list[j]
    list[j] = temp
```

If you were to test this code, though, you'd find that it seems to have no effect whatso-ever. The list stores the same values after executing this code as it stores initially. The problem is that this loop does too much swapping. Figure 7.16 shows a trace of the six swaps that are performed on the list [3, 8, 7, 22, 14, 78], with an indication of the values of i and j for each step.

The values of i and j cross halfway through this process. As a result, the first three swaps successfully reverse the list, and then the three swaps that follow undo the work of the first three. To fix this problem, you need to stop it halfway through the process. This task is easily accomplished by changing the loop range:

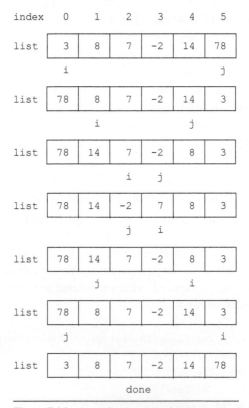

Figure 7.16   Swapping too many elements

```
# this swap code works
for i in range(len(list) // 2):
    # swap list[i] with list[j]
    j = len(list) - i - 1
    temp = list[i]
    list[i] = list[j]
    list[j] = temp
```

In the sample list, `len(list)` is 6. Half of that is 3, which means that this loop will execute exactly three times. That is just what you want in this case (the first three swaps), but you should be careful to consider other possibilities. For example, what if `len(list)` were 7? Half of that is also 3, because of truncating division. Is three the correct number of swaps for an odd-length list? The answer is yes. If there are an odd number of elements, the value in the middle of the list does not need to be swapped. So, in this case, a simple division by 2 turns out to be the right approach.

Including this code in a function, you end up with the following overall solution:

```
# Reverses the order of the elements in the given list.
def reverse(list):
    for i in range(len(list) // 2):
        # swap list[i] with list[j]
        j = len(list) - i - 1
        temp = list[i]
        list[i] = list[j]
        list[j] = temp
```

Let's look at a few variations of this reversal code. Some students find a `while` loop more intuitive than the `for` loop in our previous example. You can initialize your indexes `i` and `j` to the two ends of the list and loop until they cross each other. The code is the following; notice that it in some ways corresponds more closely to our description of the algorithm and the diagrams we showed of it.

```
# Reverses the order of the elements in the given list.
# This version uses a while loop.
def reverse(list):
    i = 0
    j = len(list) - 1
    while i < j:
        # swap list[i] with list[j]
        temp = list[i]
        list[i] = list[j]
        list[j] = temp
        i += 1
        j -= 1
```

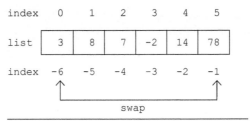

Figure 7.17   Swapping elements with negative indexes

Recall that lists allow negative indexes, such as -1 for the last element, -2 for the second-to-last, etc. You could utilize negative indexing to write the `reverse` function. Figure 7.17 shows a list with the negative indexes labeled.

The following code implements this new algorithm. Instead of defining our variable `j` as a positive index close to the length of the list, we could define it to be `-1` and decrease it each time through the loop. Notice that we also need to change our loop test to continue as long as the variable `i` has not passed the midpoint of the list.

```
# Reverses the order of the elements in the given list.
# This version uses a while loop and negative indexing.
def reverse(list):
    i = 0
    j = -1
    while i < len(list) // 2:
        # swap list[i] with list[j]
        temp = list[i]
        list[i] = list[j]
        list[j] = temp

        i += 1
        j -= 1
```

Shifting Values in a List

You'll often want to move a series of values in a list. For example, suppose you have a list of integers that stores the sequence of values `[3, 8, 9, 7, 5]` and you want to move the value at the front of the list to the back and keep the order of the other values the same. In other words, you want to move the `3` to the back, yielding the list `[8, 9, 7, 5, 3]`. Let's explore how to write code to perform that action. For our example we'll suppose you have a variable called `data` of length 5 that stores the values `[3, 8, 9, 7, 5]`, as shown in Figure 7.18.

The shifting operation is similar to the swap operation discussed in the previous section, and you'll find that it is useful to use a temporary variable here as well. The `3` at the front of the list is supposed to go to the back of the list, and the other values are

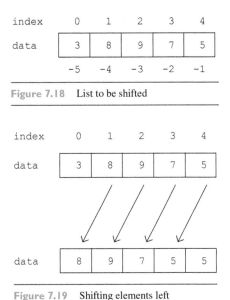

Figure 7.18 List to be shifted

Figure 7.19 Shifting elements left

supposed to rotate forward. You can make the task easier by storing the value at the front of the list (3, in this example) in a local variable:

```
first = data[0]
```

With that value safely tucked away, you now have to shift the other four values to the left by one position. Figure 7.19 depicts the shifts that need to occur.

For this five-element list, the overall task breaks down into four different shifting operations, each of which is a simple assignment statement:

```
data[0] = data[1]
data[1] = data[2]
data[2] = data[3]
data[3] = data[4]
```

Obviously you'd want to write this as a loop rather than writing a series of individual assignment statements. Each of the preceding statements is of the form:

```
data[i] = data[i + 1]
```

You'll replace list element [i] with the value currently stored in list element [i + 1], which shifts that value to the left. You can put this line of code inside an indexed for loop:

```
# shift the rest of the list (does not work)
for i in range(len(list)):
    data[i] = data[i + 1]
```

This loop is almost the right answer, but it has an off-by-one bug. This loop will execute five times for the sample list, but you only want to shift four values (you want to do the assignment for i equal to 0, 1, 2, and 3, but not for i equal to 4). So, this loop goes one too many times. On the last iteration of the loop, when i is equal to 4, the loop executes the following line of code:

```
data[i] = data[i + 1]
```

This line becomes:

```
data[4] = data[5]
```

There is no value data[5] because the list has only five elements, with indexes 0 through 4. So, this code generates an exception. To fix the problem, alter the loop so that it stops one iteration early:

```
# shift the rest of the list
for i in range(len(data) - 1):
    data[i] = data[i + 1]
```

In place of the usual len(data), use len(data) - 1 as the loop bound. You can think of the -1 in this expression as offsetting the +1 in the assignment statement.

Of course, there is one more detail you must address. After shifting the values to the left, you've made room at the end of the list for the value that used to be at the front of the list (which is currently stored in a local variable called first). When the loop has finished executing, you have to place this value in the final slot, which can most easily be indicated with the index -1:

```
# place former first element into last index
data[-1] = first
```

Here is the final function:

```
# Moves each element left by 1 index in the given list,
# wrapping the front element to the back of the list.
def rotate_left(data):
    first = data[0]
    for i in range(len(data) - 1)):
        data[i] = data[i + 1]
    data[-1] = first
```

An interesting variation on this function is to rotate the values to the right instead of rotating them to the left. To perform this inverse operation, you want to take the value that is currently at the end of the list and bring it to the front, shifting the remaining values to the right. So, if a variable called list initially stores the values [3, 8, 9, 7, 5], it should bring the 5 to the front and store the values [5, 3, 8, 9, 7].

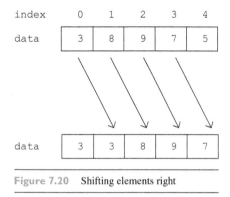

Figure 7.20 Shifting elements right

Begin by tucking away the value that is being rotated into a temporary variable:

```
last = data[-1]
```

Then shift the other values to the right. Figure 7.20 depicts the shifts that need to occur. In this case, the four individual assignment statements would be the following:

```
data[1] = data[0]
data[2] = data[1]
data[3] = data[2]
data[4] = data[3]
```

A more general way to write this is the following line of code:

```
data[i] = data[i - 1]
```

If you put this code inside the standard `for` loop, you get the following:

```
# doesn't work
for i in range(len(data)):
    data[i] = data[i - 1]
```

There is a problem with this code. The first time through the loop, it assigns `data[1]` to what is in `data[0]`, as shown in Figure 7.21.

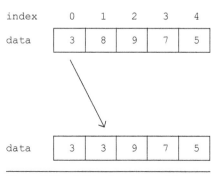

Figure 7.21 Shifting first element right

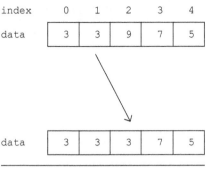

Figure 7.22   Shifting first element right

What happened to the value 8? It's overwritten with the value 3. The next time through the loop, `data[2]` is set to be `data[1]`: The first time through the loop, it assigns `data[1]` to what is in `data[0]`, as shown in Figure 7.22.

You might say, "Wait a minute. `data[1]` isn't a 3, it's an 8." It was an 8 when you started, but the first iteration of the loop replaced the 8 with a 3, and now the 3 has been copied into the spot where 9 used to be. The loop continues in this way, putting 3 into every cell of the list. Obviously, that's not what you want.

To make this code work, you have to run the loop in reverse order, from right to left instead of left to right. We tucked away the final value of the list into a local variable. That frees up the final list position. Now, assign `data[4]` to be what is in `data[3]`, as shown in Figure 7.23.

This wipes out the 5 that was at the end of the list, but that value is safely stored away in a local variable. And once you've performed this assignment statement, you free up `list[3]`, which means you can now set `data[3]` to be what is currently in `data[2]`, as shown in Figure 7.24.

The process continues in this manner, copying the 8 from index 1 to index 2 and copying the 3 from index 0 to index 1, leaving you with the list shown in Figure 7.25, which is the list's state after the loop.

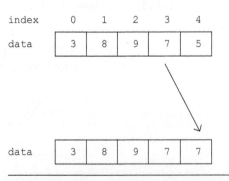

Figure 7.23   Shifting second-to-last element right

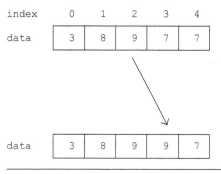

Figure 7.24   Shifting third-from-last element right

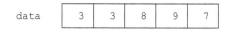

Figure 7.25   List state after right-shift loop

At this point, the only thing left to do is to put the 5 stored in the local variable at the front of the list. You can reverse the for loop by changing the increment to -1 and adjusting the start and stop. The final function is as follows:

```
# Moves each element right by 1 index in the given list,
# wrapping the last element to the front of the list.
def rotate_right(data):
    last = data[-1]
    for i in range(len(data) - 1, 0, -1):
        data[i] = data[i - 1]
    data[0] = last
```

Both of our list rotation functions modified the list in place. If you instead want to create a new list that is rotated, you can perform both of these rotation operations with no loops at all. Python lists have a slicing operation where a subrange of indexes is specified and extracted as a new list. By slicing out all indexes but the first and then concatenating this with another list that contains only the first element, you can shift the elements of a list to the left with a single line of code. You can use similar logic to implement rotate_right, slicing out all but the last index and wrapping the final element to the front. The following shell interaction demonstrates these techniques:

```
>>> nums = [3, 8, 9, 7, 5]
>>> rotl = nums[1:] + nums[:1]      # rotate left
>>> rotl
[8, 9, 7, 5, 3]
```

Continued on next page

Continued from previous page

```
>>> rotr = nums[-1:] + nums[:-1]    # rotate right
>>> rotr
[5, 3, 8, 9, 7]
```

Nested Loop Algorithms

All of the algorithms we have seen have been written with a single loop. But many computations require nested loops. For example, suppose that you were asked to print all inversions in a list of integers. An inversion is defined as a pair of numbers in which the first number in the list is greater than the second number.

In a sorted list such as [1, 2, 3, 4], there are no inversions at all and there is nothing to print. But if the numbers appear instead in reverse order, [4, 3, 2, 1], then there are many inversions to print. We would expect output like the following:

```
(4, 3) (4, 2) (4, 1) (3, 2) (3, 1) (2, 1)
```

Notice that any given number (e.g., 4 in the list above) can produce several different inversions, because it might be followed by several smaller numbers (1, 2, and 3 in the example). For a list that is partially sorted, as in [3, 1, 4, 2], there are only a few inversions, so you would produce output like this:

```
(3, 1) (3, 2) (4, 2)
```

This problem can't be solved with a single traversal because we are looking for pairs of numbers. There are many possible first values in the pair and many possible second values in the pair. Let's develop a solution using pseudocode.

We can't produce all pairs with a single loop, but we can use a single loop to consider all possible first values:

```
for every possible first value:
    Print all inversions that involve this first value.
```

Now we just need to write the code to find all the inversions for a given first value. That requires us to write a second, nested loop:

```
for every possible first value:
    for every possible second value:
        if first value > second value:
            print(first, second)
```

This problem is fairly easy to turn into Python code, although the loop bounds turn out to be a bit tricky. For now, let's use indexed for loops for each of the two dimensions. The following code is an incorrect initial attempt:

```
# look for inversions (initial incorrect attempt)
for i in range(len(data)):
    for j in range(len(data)):
        if data[i] > data[j]:
            print("(", data[i]), ", ", data[j], ")", sep="")
```

The preceding code isn't quite right. Remember that for an inversion, the second value has to appear after the first value in the list. In this case, we are computing all possible combinations of a first and second value. To consider only values that come after the given first value, we have to start the second loop at i + 1 instead of starting at 0. We can also make a slight improvement by recognizing that because an inversion requires a pair of values, there is no reason to include the last number of the list as a possible first value. So the outer loop involving i can end one iteration earlier:

```
for i in range(len(data) - 1):
    for j in range(i + 1, len(data)):
        if data[i] > data[j]:
            print("(", data[i], ", ", data[j], ")", sep="")
```

When you write nested loops like these, it is a common convention to use i for the outer loop, j for the loop inside the outer loop, and k if there is a loop inside the j loop.

Nested loops are also quite common when processing multidimensional lists, which we will discuss in the next section.

List Comprehensions

Python provides a construct called a *list comprehension* that allows you to produce a new list based on the elements of an existing list or sequence. A list comprehension specifies an expression indicating a pattern to apply to each element of a sequence to produce a new list.

> **List Comprehension**
>
> An expression that produces a list by applying an expression to each element of an existing collection.

The general syntax for list comprehensions is the following:

```
[expression for name in sequence]
```
Syntax template: list comprehension

For example, suppose that you have an existing list of integers and you want to produce a list of the squares of those integers. You could build this list of squares using a cumulative list algorithm, starting with an empty list and appending the square of each element in the original list:

```
>>> # create list of squares of 1-5 using cumulative algorithm
>>> nums1 = [1, 2, 3, 4, 5]
>>> nums2 = []
>>> for n in nums1:
...     nums2.append(n * n)
...
>>> nums2
[1, 4, 9, 16, 25]
```

This approach is not bad, but the computation can be more elegantly expressed using a list comprehension:

```
>>> # create list of the squares of 1-5 using list comprehension
>>> nums1 = [1, 2, 3, 4, 5]
>>> nums2 = [n * n for n in nums1]
>>> nums2
[1, 4, 9, 16, 25]
```

The syntax can be a bit terse and hard to understand for new programmers. For a list comprehension such as [n * n for n in nums1], the meaning is, "Create a new list where, for each element with the value n in nums1, my new list will contain the value n * n instead."

Once you get the hang of list comprehensions, you'll find that they can be used to replace many loops and cumulative list algorithms. List comprehensions provide other options, such as an optional if clause at the end to filter the results of the list being produced. We will not explore all aspects of list comprehension syntax just yet, but we will revisit them in Chapter 12 when we explore functional programming.

7.3 Reference Semantics

We have been using parameters since Chapter 3, but we haven't yet discussed in detail how values are passed. List parameters seem straightforward in their usage, but their behavior and semantics are different than when passing simple parameters like integers. To fully understand how lists are passed between functions, we need to explore two types of parameter passing behavior: value semantics and reference semantics.

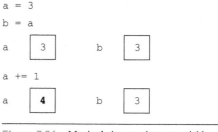

Figure 7.26   Manipulating two integer variables

Values and References

When you have used integer variables, you have seen that the value of one variable is independent of the values of any other variables. This is true even if you assign one variable to another; a statement such as a = b copies the value from b to a at that moment, but otherwise the values of a and b are unrelated to each other. The following code illustrates this idea. Figure 7.26 shows what happens to the two integer variables as their values are assigned. Notice that when the value of a is increased, the value of b does not change.

```
>>> # manipulating integer variables
>>> a = 3
>>> b = a
>>> a += 1
>>> a
4
>>> b
3
```

The preceding code should not surprise you; likely you have written several programs with code like this. This kind of behavior is so commonplace and expected that you probably take it for granted right now. The behavior where a variable's value is copied when assigned to another variable, and that these copies are independent, is called *value semantics*.

> **Value semantics**
> Behavior where values are copied when assigned or passed as parameters.

It may surprise you to see that things do not work quite the same way when you interact with lists. Consider the following code, which interacts with two list variables. This code is meant to mirror the preceding code except using lists instead of integer variables. As in the preceding integer variable code, we assign the second list variable b to store the value a. Then we modify the state of a by changing the value of one of the elements of the list. When we ask for the values of a and b, we see that both lists have changed! What is going on here?

```
>>> # manipulating list variables
>>> a = [1, 2, 3]
>>> b = a
>>> a[0] = 99
>>> a.append(4)
>>> a
[99, 2, 3, 4]
>>> b
[99, 2, 3, 4]
```

The answer has to do with the way Python stores lists and other objects. In Python and many other languages, a variable that stores a list or other object does not directly store the data for that object. Instead, the data are stored in a memory location, and the variable stores that location. So, we have two different elements: the variable and the object.

When we create a list as in the following statement, we end up with a picture like that shown in Figure 7.27. There are two different components to the picture: the list itself, which appears on the right side of the diagram, and a variable called a. We draw the variable a with an arrow pointing to the list to indicate that this variable refers to the location in memory storing that list. We say that a *refers* to the list or that the variable is a *reference* to the list.

This separation between variables and objects is a bit like the difference between a house and its street address. If you see a house at the address 1234 Fifth St, you can write down this address on a piece of paper and take it with you. You are not literally carrying the house in your pocket, but instead you are carrying information about the location of the house. Similarly, when you have a variable that stores a list, that variable does not directly store the data in the list, but rather it stores information that tells Python where in the memory to find that list.

As another analogy, think about how we use mobile phones to communicate with people. The phones can be very tiny and easy to transport because phone numbers don't take up much space. Imagine that, instead of carrying around a set of mobile phone

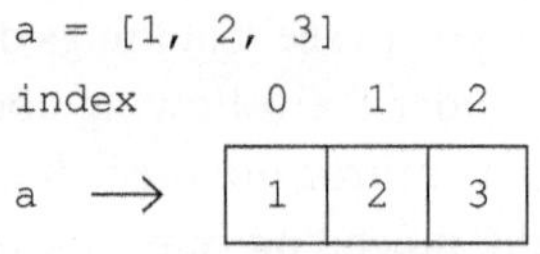

a = [1, 2, 3]
index   0   1   2

a ⟶ | 1 | 2 | 3 |

Figure 7.27　Reference to a list

numbers, you tried to carry around the actual people! Carrying a phone number with you is a way of finding or reaching a person.

This approach is so common that computer scientists have a technical term to describe it. It is known as *reference semantics*. It will take us a while to explore all of the implications of this system.

Reference Semantics

Behavior where variables store memory addresses or locations of objects. When a reference is assigned or passed as a parameter, the second copy refers to the same object as the first.

This concept of referring to a list becomes more interesting when multiple variables are involved. Consider the following lines of code that create three list variables:

```
>>> # three variables for two lists
>>> list1 = [1, 3, 5, 7, 9]
>>> list2 = [1, 3, 5, 7, 9]
>>> list3 = list2
```

The first two lines of code each create a new list and store it into a variable. But what about the third line? We define a variable list3 and set its value equal to list2. This is a very different statement than the two before it. It creates a new reference but not a new list. Figure 7.28 depicts the state of memory after the computer executes the preceding code.

We have three variables but only two different values. The variables list2 and list3 both refer to the same list. Using the mobile phone analogy, you can think of this as two people who both know the mobile phone number for the same person. That means that either one of them can call the person. Or, as another analogy, suppose that both you and a friend of yours know how to access your bank information online. That means that you both have access to the same account and that either one of you can make changes to the account.

The implication of this function is that list2 and list3 are in some sense both equally able to modify the list to which they refer. A line of code that modifies list2

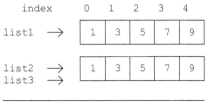

Figure 7.28 Three references to two lists

will produce a change that is also seen in `list3`, as shown in the following shell interaction:

```
>>> # modify a list element
>>> list2[2] = 42
>>> list2
[1, 3, 42, 7, 9]
>>> list3
[1, 3, 42, 7, 9]
>>> list1
[1, 3, 5, 7, 9]
```

Notice that after setting the element of `list2`, we also see that `list3` has been changed. Both variables refer to the same list, and you can access the list through either one. A change made in one also changes the other.

It will take us a while to explore all of the implications of this system. The key thing to remember is that you are always working with references to data rather than the data itself. This system may seem needlessly confusing. Why not just pass actual data? There are two primary reasons:

- **Efficiency.** Values can be complex, which means that they can take up a lot of space in memory. If we made copies of such values, we would quickly run out of memory. A list that stores a large number of elements might take up a lot of space in memory. But even if the list is very large, a reference to it can be fairly small, in the same way that even a mansion has a simple street address.

- **Sharing.** Often, having a copy of something is not good enough. Suppose that your instructor tells all of the students in the class to put their tests into a certain box. Imagine how pointless and confusing it would be if each student made a copy of the box. The obvious intent is that all of the students use the same box. Reference semantics allows you to have many references to a single value, which allows different parts of your program to share a certain value.

Modifying a List Parameter

Suppose we have a function that accepts a parameter of a simple type such as an integer. If the function modifies the value passed for its parameter, the modification does not propagate back to the caller. For example, the following silly function accepts an integer parameter and increases its value by 1:

```
# Increases the value of an integer by 1.
# This does not work.
def increment_number(n):
    n += 1
```

You'll see that when you call this function, it does not change the value of the variable you pass to it. This is due to value semantics; the parameter stores a copy of the value passed to it.

```
>>> # test the increment_number function (it has no effect)
>>> num = 42
>>> increment_number(num)
>>> num
42
```

We could get around this problem by returning the new value of n from the increment_number function and reassigning its new value back into the num variable in the main calling code. This example is just meant to refresh our memory about the behavior we see when passing integer variables as parameters.

Lists exhibit different behavior when passed as parameters. Because of reference semantics, a function is able to change the contents of a list that is passed to it as a parameter. For example, you can write a function that accepts a list as a parameter and increases the value of each element in the list by 1. In the following implementation, we loop over the indexes of the list so that we can reassign new values into those indexes of the list:

```
# Increases the value of each element of the given list by 1.
def increment_all(data):
    for i in range(len(data)):
        data[i] += 1
```

The following shell interaction shows a call to this function along with its result. Notice that the caller sees that its list has been changed:

```
>>> # test the increment_all function
>>> nums = [1, 3, 5, 7, 9]
>>> increment_all(nums)
>>> nums
[2, 4, 6, 8, 10]
```

When the function is called, we make a copy of the variable nums. But the variable nums is not itself the list; rather, it stores a reference to the list. So, when we make a copy of that reference, we end up with two references to the same value, as shown in Figure 7.29.

Because nums and data both refer to the same list, when we change data by saying data[i] += 1, we end up changing the value to which nums refers. That's why, after the loop increments each element of data, we end up with the state shown in Figure 7.30.

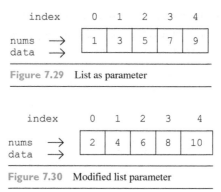

Figure 7.29   List as parameter

Figure 7.30   Modified list parameter

The key lesson to draw from this discussion is that when we pass a list as a parameter to a function, that function has the ability to change the contents of the list. This turns out to be useful, because we can write functions specifically for the purpose of performing various useful manipulations of a list. We wrote several list-traversal algorithms earlier in this chapter, such as reversing a list and replacing values in a list. Those functions took advantage of reference semantics to modify the lists passed to them in place.

The Value None

Before we leave the subject of reference semantics, we should describe in more detail the concept of the special value None. It is a special global constant in Python that is used to represent "no value".

> **None**
>
> A Python constant signifying no value.

You can set any variable to None. This is a way of telling the computer that you want to have the variable, but you haven't yet come up with a value to which it should refer:

```
>>> # set variables to None (absence of a value)
>>> top_student = None
>>> account_list = None
>>> favorite = None
```

Some types have a notion of an "empty" or "default" value, such as 0 for integers, "" for strings, and [] for lists. But there is a difference between setting a variable to an empty/default value and setting it to None. An empty integer value of 0 is still an integer; you can still use it, add or multiply it, ask if it is greater or less than other integers, and so on. An empty string value of "" is still a string; you can still print it, ask for its length (which is 0), concatenate it to other strings, and so on. An empty list value of [] is still a list; you can add and remove values from it. You get the idea.

By contrast, None is still a value, but not a value of any of these preceding types. None is actually a special singleton value of a type called NoneType, and None is the only value of that type. Since None isn't an integer, you cannot add 3 to it. Since None isn't a string or a list, you cannot ask for its length or add elements to it. If you try to do these kinds of operations on a variable that has been set to None, Python will raise an error such as a TypeError or AttributeError:

```
>>> # try to perform operations on None (will not work)
>>> account_list = None
>>> account_list[0]
Traceback (most recent call last):
  File "<stdin>", line 1, in <module>
TypeError: 'NoneType' object is not subscriptable

>>> len(account_list)
Traceback (most recent call last):
  File "<stdin>", line 1, in <module>
TypeError: object of type 'NoneType' has no len()

>>> account_list.append(42)
Traceback (most recent call last):
  File "<stdin>", line 1, in <module>
AttributeError: 'NoneType' object has no attribute 'append'
```

The value None is also implicitly returned by any function that does not explicitly return a value. For example, the built-in print function does not return any value, so if you try to capture its returned result in a variable, that variable will store None:

```
>>> # functions that return None (nothing)
>>> result = print("Hello!")
Hello!
>>> print(result)
None
```

The value None is often used to indicate a lack of a result or an error case. For example, suppose we want to write a function called first_even that returns the first even number in a list. But what if the list contains no even numbers? You could return a default value such as 0 or -1, but this is arguably misleading because those are not numbers that are found in the list. Another option is to return None to indicate that there was no suitable result found. The code of the function would look something like this:

```
# Returns the first even number in the given list,
# or None if no such string is found.
```

Continued on next page

Continued from previous page

```
def first_even(nums):
    for n in nums:
        if n % 2 == 0:
            return n
    return None        # no even numbers found
```

The following shell interaction contains two calls to this function. The first call passes a list that has some even numbers in it, and the first of these values is returned. The second call passes a list that does not contain any even numbers, so the value None is returned. By definition there's not much you can do with None, since it has no real behavior. You can check whether a given value is equal to None using the is keyword.

```
>>> # call the first_even function
>>> numbers = [3, 19, 42, -1, 28, 0, 56]
>>> even = first_even(numbers)
>>> even
42
>>> numbers = [3, 19, 45, -1, 27, 51]
>>> even = first_even(numbers)
>>> even
>>> print(even)
None
>>> even is None
True
```

As a side note, the implementation of first_even did not need to include the return None statement. If that statement were missing, the function would implicitly return None when reaching its end without reaching any other return statement.

Mutability

In the previous sections we have discussed that lists exhibit different behavior because of reference semantics. Actually, every type of value in Python is stored by reference, including basic types like integers. Suppose you define the following two variables. In reality you have created two references to the same integer object storing the value 42, as shown in Figure 7.31.

```
>>> num1 = 42
>>> num2 = num1
```

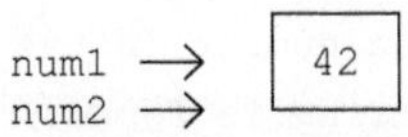

num1 $\rightarrow$
num2 $\rightarrow$ | 42 |

Figure 7.31 Two references to one integer object

But when you have worked with integers and strings and other types, you observed value semantics, not reference semantics. When you assigned one integer or string to another, or passed an integer or string as a parameter and then modified that parameter, you did not see a change back in `main` or whatever function made the call. If integers are really stored and passed by reference, why do they exhibit value semantics?

The answer is that integers, real numbers, strings, and many other types of values are *immutable*. An immutable type is one whose values cannot be changed. An immutable type does not provide any methods or operations that modify the state of its objects. The state of an immutable object is set as the object is being created and is never modified afterward.

> **Immutable**
>
> Unable to be changed.

Most of the types that we have discussed up until now have been immutable. Integers, floats, strings, and Boolean values are all immutable. But this would seem to contradict what we've learned so far; you've done many operations that modify an integer or string, such as `n *= 2` or `s += "hi"`. Don't these operations mutate, or modify, the state of the value?

There is a subtle difference in the behavior of immutable types. They might provide operations that seem to modify the value, but instead of modifying the existing value, they instead create and return an entirely new value. This means that if you try to change them, a new one will be created instead.

Python has a useful global function called `id` that helps us investigate this phenomenon. The call of `id(obj)` returns an integer ID number representing the given object. Every object in a Python program has an ID number that is unique to that object and not used by any other object in the entire program. Let's revisit our code that declares two integer variables. Notice that when we assign `num2` equal to `num1`, the same ID number is used. This is because the two variables refer to the same object. (If you run similar code on your own computer, you may see different ID numbers. The numbers themselves do not matter, only whether two given variables have the same IDs or different IDs.)

```
>>> # investigating object ID numbers
>>> num1 = 42
>>> id(num1)
10936800
>>> num2 = num1
>>> id(num2)
10936800
```

If we now modify or reassign one of the values, Python creates a new integer object with the new value and assigns the appropriate variable to refer to it. Notice in the following code that every time we modify one of the variables, its ID number changes. Figure 7.32 shows the various objects and variables as the code executes.

```
>>> # investigating object ID numbers
>>> num1 = 42
>>> num2 = num1
>>> id(num1)
10936800
>>> num1 = 99
>>> num1
99
>>> num2
42
>>> id(num1)
10938624
>>> id(num2)
10936800
>>> num2 += 5
>>> num2
47
>>> id(num2)
10936962
```

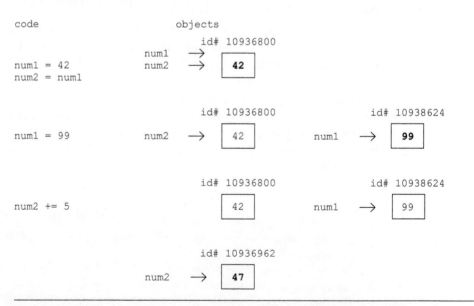

Figure 7.32 References to integer objects

You have seen similar behavior when you have worked with strings. Recall that string methods such as `upper` do not modify an existing string but instead return a new string. You saw that you needed to reassign the returned string into your variable to see the change, as shown in the following code.

```
>>> # converting a string to uppercase
>>> name = "Evelyn Rose"
>>> name.upper()              # does not modify name
'EVELYN ROSE'
>>> name
'Evelyn Rose'
>>> name = name.upper()       # does modify name
>>> name
'EVELYN ROSE'
```

In the preceding code, the value of `name` was not changed until we reassigned it into the variable. That is because the variable `name` refers to an immutable string object storing the characters `"Evelyn Rose"` that cannot be modified. The only way to produce an uppercase version of that string is to create and return an entirely new string object, which is what the `upper` method does. You can observe this by asking for the ID of the string object before and after uppercasing it, as shown in the following shell interaction. Notice that the `id` function returns a different answer after calling `upper`:

```
>>> # converting a string to uppercase
>>> name = "Evelyn Rose"
>>> id(name)
140485929442288
>>> name.upper()              # does not modify name
'EVELYN ROSE'
>>> name
'Evelyn Rose'
>>> id(name)
140485929442288
>>> name = name.upper()       # does modify name
>>> id(name)
140485929442352
```

All of the preceding behavior is typical of immutable types of values. You cannot modify their state after they are created, only create new objects with different state.

Lists are mutable, meaning that they can be modified after creation. This means that you can modify the state of an existing list after creating it. It also means that list methods can modify the list without returning the list's new state. The following code demonstrates that a list variable still refers to the same object (with the same ID number) even as its state is being modified.

```
>>> # modifying a list
>>> nums = [2, 4, 6, 8]
>>> id(nums)
140485929417736
>>> nums[0] = 99          # modify existing list (same ID)
>>> nums.append(10)
>>> nums
[99, 4, 6, 8, 10]
>>> id(nums)
140485929417736
>>> nums.clear()          # clear existing list (still same ID)
>>> nums
[]
>>> id(nums)
140485929417736
>>> nums = [6, 7, 8]      # assign an entirely new list (new ID)
>>> id(nums)
140485943223240
```

The one exception to the mutability rules is when you assign an entirely new list to the variable. This creates a new list object and sets the variable to refer to that list. That's why the ID number changes at the end of the preceding code.

You generally don't need to worry much about mutability and immutability when you are writing code. But when you pass values as parameters, mutability matters. If you pass a parameter of a mutable type, such as a list, the function could modify your list. If the type of value you pass is immutable, such as an integer or string, you don't have to worry that the function will make any modification to your object. Whenever you are learning about a new type of object, it is useful to find out if the type is mutable or immutable so that you know what kind of assumptions you can make about how it will be used.

Tuples

Lists are an example of what Python calls a *sequence type*. A sequence is an object that contains an indexed collection of values and supports certain common operations, such as indexing and slicing. Python has other sequence types, such as ranges (the type of object returned from the range function). Another common sequence type that we will explore in this section is called a tuple.

A *tuple* is a simple, immutable fixed-length sequence that gathers multiple values together into a single structure. (The name "tuple" comes from the general suffix of "tuple" that is often given to groups of things, such as "quadruple," "quintuple," "sextuple," and so on.) Tuples are useful when you want a lightweight way to group a few values together but without all of the complexity and bulk of a list. The immutable nature of tuples is also useful when you don't want to worry about your data being modified when passed as a parameter. Tuples are also used in various library functions, so it is useful to learn the basics about them in order to interact with those libraries.

> **Tuple**
>
> An immutable sequence of values declared in parentheses.

The syntax for creating a tuple is to write its elements separated by commas. Most commonly the elements are also surrounded by parentheses, but in some cases the parentheses are optional. (We will always use the parentheses when we declare tuples in our examples.) This syntax is the same as declaring a list, except that we use ( ) parentheses rather than [ ] brackets.

```
name = (value, value, ..., value)
```
Syntax template: Defining a tuple

For example, the following code defines a few tuples, one for a coordinate stored in (*x*, *y*) form, and another for a calendar date in (*year*, *month*, *day*) order.

```
>>> # define some tuples
>>> pt = (34, 7)
>>> date = (2019, 12, 25)
```

Many of the operations we showed previously for lists also work with tuples. You can ask a tuple for its length with the `len` function; you can convert it to a string with `str`; you can concatenate tuples with the + operator and replicate them with the * operator; and you can access the individual elements of a tuple using the `[i]` bracket notation. You can even use slicing notation to access a subset of the elements of a tuple.

```
>>> # interact with tuples: indexing, concatenation
>>> pt = (34, 7)
>>> pt
(34, 7)
>>> pt[0]
34
>>> pt[1]
7
```

Continued on next page

Continued from previous page

```
>>> pt2 = (-3, 15)
>>> pt + pt2
(34, 7, -3, 15)
>>> pt * 3
(34, 7, 34, 7, 34, 7)
>>> date = (2019, 12, 25)
>>> len(date)
3
>>> date[1:3]
(12, 25)
```

You can even create tuples with zero or one element. A zero-element tuple is just an empty set of parentheses. A one-element tuple has a trailing comma after the single element value in parentheses. These are less useful and not often necessary; we show them for the sake of completeness.

```
>>> # zero and one element tuples
>>> empty_tuple = ()
>>> one_element = (42,)
```

As stated previously, tuples are immutable. This means that a tuple has a fixed length and doesn't have the various modification methods and operations from lists, such as append or insert or del. You also cannot use the [ ] brackets to modify an element of a tuple.

```
>>> # try to modify a tuple
>>> pt = (34, 7)
>>> pt[0] = 15
Traceback (most recent call last):
  File "<stdin>", line 1, in <module>
TypeError: 'tuple' object does not support item assignment
>>> pt.append(45)
Traceback (most recent call last):
  File "<stdin>", line 1, in <module>
AttributeError: 'tuple' object has no attribute 'append'
```

You can convert any sequence of values to a tuple by passing it to the tuple function, which returns the newly created tuple. This is similar to the list function, which converts a sequence to a list. The following code converts a month/day tuple to a list, adds a year to it, and then converts it back to a tuple:

```
>>> # convert between tuple and list
>>> xmas = (12, 25)
>>> xmas_list = list(xmas)
>>> xmas_list
[12, 25]
>>> xmas_list.append(2019)
>>> xmas_list
[12, 25, 2019]
>>> xmas = tuple(xmas_list)
>>> xmas
(12, 25, 2019)
```

While you can access a tuple's elements by [ ] indexing as shown previously, most of the time we do not use indexes with tuples. A more common pattern is to *unpack* the tuple by storing its data into multiple simple variables. Python has an unpacking assignment statement where you write multiple variable names on the left side of an = sign and a sequence on the right side. The elements of the sequence are assigned into the variables in the corresponding order. The syntax of an unpacking assignment statement is the following:

name, name, ..., name = sequence
Syntax template: Unpacking assignment statement

For example, the following assignment extracts the individual elements of the date tuple defined previously. This makes them easier to examine without brackets or indexes:

```
>>> # unpack a tuple
>>> date = (2019, 12, 25)
>>> year, month, day = date
>>> year
2019
>>> month
12
>>> day
25
```

Earlier in this chapter we discussed the idea of writing code to swap two integer values. The unpacking assignment statement can be used as a swapping mechanism. The following code swaps the value of two integers (or values of any type):

```
>>> # swap integers using unpacking assignment statement
>>> a = 35
>>> b = 17
>>> (a, b) = (b, a)
>>> a
17
>>> b
35
```

The unpacking assignment statement can be used with any kind of sequence, including with lists. In fact, in Chapter 6 when we were splitting the lines and tokens of a file and storing them into multiple variables, we were using this same unpacking syntax. We had not yet discussed lists, but we were taking advantage of Python's syntax to unpack a list into its individual values.

Many students don't initially understand the motivation for tuples. Their functionality is a subset of that of lists, so why not just use lists? The primary reasons you'll want to use tuples are as follows:

- **Immutability.** It is useful to know that you can pass a tuple as a parameter to any function without worrying that the function will modify it. Many programmers prefer immutable structures to mutable ones when the choice is available.

- **Simplicity.** Tuples have a clean and simple syntax. They are well integrated into the language and simpler to interact with overall than lists.

- **Used in Python libraries.** Several Python libraries use tuples, so you'll need to know about them in order to interact with those libraries. For example, our own DrawingPanel has some methods that return pixel R/G/B data as three-integer tuples, so if you want to manipulate the pixels of an image, you need a basic understanding of this language feature. (We will explore drawing with pixels later in this chapter.)

Sometimes tuples and lists are used together. For example, our DrawingPanel (first shown in Chapter 3) has several methods that can interact with tuples. Its draw_polygon and fill_polygon methods can accept a list of two-integer (x, y) tuples representing points and draw a polygon between those points. The following code creates a triangle as a list of three tuples and tells the drawing panel to fill it.

```
1  # This program draws a triangle as a list of (x, y) tuples.
2  from DrawingPanel import *
3
4  def main():
5      panel = DrawingPanel(200, 100)
```

Continued on next page

Continued from previous page

```
6        triangle = [(10, 10), (80, 10), (80, 80)]
7        panel.fill_polygon(triangle)
8
9   main()
```

There are some interesting built-in functions that involve tuples. One such function is enumerate, which accepts a list parameter and returns a sequence of (index, value) tuples. The most common use of enumerate is to combine it with the unpacking assignment operator to make a loop that provides both the indexes and values of a list:

```
>>> # demonstrate the enumerate function
>>> pets = ["Abby", "Barney", "Clyde", "Mandy", "Rajah"]
>>> list(enumerate(pets))
[(0, 'Abby'), (1, 'Barney'), (2, 'Clyde'), (3, 'Mandy'), (4, 'Rajah')]
>>> for i, name in enumerate(pets):
...     print("element", i, "is", name)
...
element 0 is Abby
element 1 is Barney
element 2 is Clyde
element 3 is Mandy
element 4 is Rajah
```

Another useful tuple-related function is zip. The zip function accepts two sequences of values as parameters and combines them into a single sequence of two-element tuples. For example, the lists [1, 2, 3] and [4, 5, 6] are combined into [(1, 4), (2, 5), (3, 6)]. This is most useful when the lists correspond to each other in some way, such as a list of first names and a list of last names. As with enumerate, the most common use of zip is in a for-each loop that unpacks the two-element tuples of the combined sequence. The following code demonstrates the zip function. You can even combine zip and enumerate, as we show in the code.

```
>>> # demonstrate the zip function
>>> firsts = ["Allison", "Marty", "Stuart"]
>>> lasts  = ["Obourn",  "Stepp", "Reges"]
>>> list(zip(lasts, firsts))
[('Obourn', 'Allison'), ('Stepp', 'Marty'), ('Reges', 'Stuart')]
```

Continued on next page

Continued from previous page

```
>>> for last, first in zip(lasts, firsts):
...      print("last name is", last, "and first name is", first)
...
last name is Obourn and first name is Allison
last name is Stepp and first name is Marty
last name is Reges and first name is Stuart
>>> for i, (last, first) in enumerate(zip(lasts, firsts)):
...      print(i, first, last)
...
0 Allison Obourn
1 Marty Stepp
2 Stuart Reges
```

Another common trick is to return a tuple as a way of returning multiple values. In Chapter 3 we discussed returning multiple values from a function. In reality, a Python function can return at most one value, but if that value is a tuple, you can essentially bypass the return-one-value restriction. For example, the following function accepts two integer parameters and returns both the quotient and remainder of dividing them:

```
# Returns the quotient and remainder of dividing
# the given integer a by b as a (q, r) tuple.
def divmod(a, b):
    quotient = a // b
    remainder = a % b
    return (quotient, remainder)
```

The following code calls the function and unpacks its tuple return value into two integer variables:

```
>>> # demonstrate the zip function
>>> q, r = divmod(47, 5)
>>> q
9
>>> r
2
>>> 5 * q + r
47
```

7.4 Multidimensional Lists

The list examples in the previous sections all involved what are known as one-dimensional lists (a single row or a single column of data). Often, you'll want to store data in a multidimensional way. For example, you might want to store a two-dimensional grid of data that has both rows and columns. Fortunately, you can form lists of arbitrarily many dimensions. A list of more than one dimension is called a *multidimensional list*.

> **Multidimensional List**
>
> A list of lists, the elements of which are accessed with multiple integer indexes.

Rectangular Lists

The most common use of a multidimensional list is a two-dimensional list of a certain width and height. The syntax for creating a multi-dimensional list involves using two nested sets of [ ] brackets. As with one-dimensional lists, you can create a two-dimensional list by writing down its elements or by repeating a single element value multiple times with the * operator.

```
name = [[value, value, ..., value],
        [value, value, ..., value],
        ...,
        [value, value, ..., value]]
```
Syntax template: Defining a two-dimensional list with given element values
```
name = [[value] * length,
        [value] * length,
        ...,
        [value] * length]
```
Syntax template: Defining a two-dimensional list of a given width/height

For example, suppose that on three separate days you took a series of five temperature readings. You can define a two-dimensional list that has three rows and five columns as shown in the following shell interaction. The resulting list would have the appearance shown in Figure 7.33.

```
>>> # create a multi-dimensional list (first syntax)
>>> temps = [[0, 0, 0, 0, 0],
             [0, 0, 0, 0, 0],
             [0, 0, 0, 0, 0]]
>>>
>>> # create a multi-dimensional list (second syntax)
>>> temps = [[0] * 5, [0] * 5, [0] * 5]
```

		0	1	2	3	4
	0	0	0	0	0	0
temps	1	0	0	0	0	0
	2	0	0	0	0	0

Figure 7.33 Multidimensional list of integers

		0	1	2	3	4
	0	0	0	0	87	0
temps	1	0	0	0	0	0
	2	99	0	0	0	0

Figure 7.34   Multidimensional list after setting some values

As with one-dimensional lists, the indexes start with 0 for both rows and columns. Once you've created such a list, you can refer to individual elements by providing specific row and column numbers, in that order. For example, to set the fourth value of the first row to 87 and to set the first value of the third row to 99, you would write the following code. After the program executes these lines of code, the list would look like Figure 7.34.

```
>>> # get/set element values in a 2D list
>>> temps[0][0]
0
>>> temps[0][3] = 87      # set fourth value of first row
>>> temps[2][0] = 99      # set first value of third row
>>> temps[0][3]
87
```

It is helpful to think of referring to individual elements in a stepwise fashion, starting with the name of the list. For example, if you want to refer to the first value of the third row of Figure 7.34, you obtain it through the following steps:

- `temps` is the entire grid
- `temps[2]` is the entire third row
- `temps[2][0]` is the first element of the third row

This reasoning about the steps of a two-dimensional list are useful to help understand the behavior of the `len` function. When you use the `len` function on a two-dimensional list, it returns the number of rows in the list. To learn how many columns the list has, ask it for the length of one of its rows, such as `len(temps[0])`, as shown in the following shell interaction:

```
>>> # use the len function on a multidimensional list
>>> temps = [[0] * 5, [0] * 5, [0] * 5]
>>> len(temps)        # number of rows
3
>>> len(temps[0])     # length of first row
5
```

You can pass multidimensional lists as parameters just as you pass one-dimensional lists. For example, here is a function that prints a grid on multiple lines:

```
# Prints all elements of a 2D list, one row per line,
# with spaces between each pair of elements.
def print_grid(grid):
    for i in range(len(grid)):
        for j in range(len(grid[i])):
            print(grid[i][j], end=" ")
        print()
```

Notice that to ask for the number of rows you ask for `len(grid)` and to ask for the number of columns you ask for `len(grid[i])`.

Lists can have as many dimensions as you want. For example, if you want a three-dimensional 4 × 4 × 4 cube of integers initialized to 0, you would write the following lines of code:

```
# create a 3D list
outer = []
for i in range(4):
    # add a 2D list element to the outer 3D list
    inner = []
    for j in range(4):
        inner.append([0] * 4)
    outer.append(inner)
```

The normal convention for the order of values is the plane number, followed by the row number, followed by the column number, although you can use any convention you want as long as your code is written consistently.

Jagged Lists

The previous examples have involved rectangular grids that have a fixed number of rows and columns. It is also possible to create a jagged list in which the number of columns varies from row to row.

One way to create a jagged list is to define it with all of its rows and columns specified. A second way is to divide the creation into two steps: create the list for holding rows first, and then create each individual row. For example, to create a list that has two elements in the first row, four elements in the second row, and three elements in the third row, you can write the following lines of code. The result would look like Figure 7.35.

```
>>> # create a jagged multi-dimensional list (first syntax)
>>> jagged = [[0] * 2, [0] * 4, [0] * 3]
>>>
```

Continued on next page

Continued from previous page

```
>>> # create a jagged multi-dimensional list (second syntax)
>>> jagged = []
>>> jagged.append([0] * 2)
>>> jagged.append([0] * 4)
>>> jagged.append([0] * 3)
```

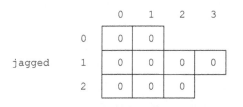

Figure 7.35   Jagged multidimensional list

We can explore this technique by writing a program that produces the rows of what is known as Pascal's triangle. The numbers in the triangle have many useful mathematical properties. For example, row *n* of Pascal's triangle contains the coefficients obtained when you expand the equation:

$$(x + y)^n$$

Here are the results for n between 0 and 4:

$$(x + y)^0 = 1$$
$$(x + y)^1 = x + y$$
$$(x + y)^2 = x^2 + 2xy + y^2$$
$$(x + y)^3 = x^3 + 3x^2y + 3xy^2 + y^3$$
$$(x + y)^4 = x^4 + 4x^3y + 6x^2y^2 + 4xy^3 + y^4$$

If you pull out just the coefficients, you get the following values:

```
        1
      1   1
    1   2   1
  1   3   3   1
1   4   6   4   1
```

These rows of numbers form a five-row Pascal's triangle. One of the properties of the triangle is that if you are given any row, you can use it to compute the next row. For example, let's start with the last row from the preceding triangle:

```
1   4   6   4   1
```

We can compute the next row by adding adjacent pairs of values together. So, we add together the first pair of numbers (1 + 4), then the second pair of numbers (4 + 6), and so on:

```
(1 + 4)  (4 + 6)  (6 + 4)  (4 + 1)
 ⌣⌣      ⌣⌣      ⌣⌣      ⌣⌣
   5        10       10       5
```

Then we put a 1 at the front and back of this list of numbers, and we end up with the next row of the triangle:

```
            1
          1   1
        1   2   1
      1   3   3   1
    1   4   6   4   1
  1   5  10   10  5   1
```

This property of the triangle provides a technique for computing it. We can create it row by row, computing each new row from the values in the previous row. In other words, we write the following loop (assuming that we have a two-dimensional list called triangle in which to store the answer):

```
for i in range(len(triangle)):
    define triangle[i] using triangle[i - 1].
```

We just need to flesh out the details of how a new row is created. This is a jagged list because each row has a different number of elements. Looking at the triangle, you'll see that the first row (row 0) has one value in it, the second row (row 1) has two values in it, and so on. In general, row i has (i + 1) values, so we can refine our pseudocode as follows:

```
for i in range(len(triangle)):
    triangle[i] = [0] * (i + 1)
    fill in triangle[i] using triangle[i - 1].
```

We know that the first and last values in each row should be 1:

```
for i in range(len(triangle)):
    triangle[i] = [0] * (i + 1)
    triangle[i][0] = 1
    triangle[i][i] = 1
    fill in the middle of triangle[i] using triangle[i - 1].
```

And we know that the middle values come from the previous row. To figure out how to compute them, take a look at Figure 7.36, which shows the list we are attempting to build.

	0	1	2	3	4	5
0	1					
1	1	1				
2	1	2	1			
3	1	3	3	1		
4	1	4	6	4	1	
5	1	5	10	10	5	1

triangle

Figure 7.36 Pascal's triangle as multidimensional list

We have already written code to fill in the 1 that appears at the beginning and end of each row. We now need to write code to fill in the middle values. Look at row 5 for an example. The value 5 in column 1 comes from the sum of the values 1 in column 0 and 4 in column 1 in the previous row. The value 10 in column 2 comes from the sum of the values in columns 1 and 2 in the previous row. More generally, each of these middle values is the sum of the two values from the previous row that appear just above and to the left of it. In other words, for column j the values are computed as follows:

triangle[i][j] = (value above and left) + (value above).

We can turn this into actual code by using the appropriate list indexes:

```
triangle[i][j] = triangle[i - 1][j - 1] + triangle[i - 1][j]
```

We need to include this statement in a for loop so that it assigns all of the middle values. The for loop is the final step in converting our pseudocode into actual code:

```
for i in range(len(triangle)):
    triangle[i] = [0] * (i + 1)
    triangle[i][0] = 1
    triangle[i][i] = 1
    for j in range(1, i):
        triangle[i][j] = triangle[i - 1][j - 1] + triangle[i - 1][j]
```

If we include this code in a function along with a printing function similar to the grid-printing function described earlier, we end up with the following complete program:

```
1  # This program creates a jagged two-dimensional list
2  # that stores Pascal's Triangle. It takes advantage of the
```

Continued on next page

Continued from previous page

```
 3   # fact that each value other than the 1s that appear at the
 4   # beginning and end of each row is the sum of two values
 5   # from the previous row.
 6
 7   # Fills Pascal's triangle into the given 2D list up to
 8   # the size of that list.
 9   def fill_in(triangle):
10       for i in range(len(triangle)):
11           triangle[i] = [0] * (i + 1)
12           triangle[i][0] = 1
13           triangle[i][i] = 1
14           for j in range(1, i):
15               triangle[i][j] = triangle[i - 1][j - 1] \
16                               + triangle[i - 1][j]
17
18   # Prints a 2D list with one row on each line
19   # with elements separated by spaces.
20   def print_nice(triangle):
21       for i in range(len(triangle)):
22           for j in range(len(triangle[i])):
23               print(triangle[i][j], end=" ")
24           print()
25
26   def main():
27       triangle = [0] * 11
28       fill_in(triangle)
29       print_nice(triangle)
30
31   main()
```

```
1
1 1
1 2 1
1 3 3 1
1 4 6 4 1
1 5 10 10 5 1
1 6 15 20 15 6 1
1 7 21 35 35 21 7 1
1 8 28 56 70 56 28 8 1
1 9 36 84 126 126 84 36 9 1
1 10 45 120 210 252 210 120 45 10 1
```

Common Programming Error

Multiple References to Inner List

You must be careful not to store multiple references to the same row in a two-dimensional (2D) list. This will happen if you store a list in a variable and store that variable multiple times in a two-dimensional list. For example, the following code mistakenly creates a 2D list where all three rows refer to the same inner list. Modifying any one row will modify all rows.

```
>>> # create 2D list with multiple copies of row (incorrect)
>>> row = [0] * 3
>>> data = [row, row, row]
>>> data[2][2] = 42    # set third value of third row?
>>> data
[[0, 0, 42], [0, 0, 42], [0, 0, 42]]
```

Why does the preceding code fail? The answer has to do with reference semantics. If you create a list, the variable is actually a reference to data in memory. If you create a 2D list with multiple copies of the same inner list variable, all of the rows in the 2D list refer to the same underlying row list of data in memory. Figure 7.37 shows the state of the improperly made list.

You might not be likely to write code like the preceding code. But a more common variation of this mistake is to attempt to create a multidimensional list using multiplication on the inner lists, which has the same issue. For example, the following incorrect code attempts to create a list of lists using the * operator:

```
>>> # create 2D list with * on inner lists (incorrect)
>>> data = [[0] * 3] * 3
>>> data
[[0, 0, 0], [0, 0, 0], [0, 0, 0]]
>>> data[2][2] = 42
>>> data
[[0, 0, 42], [0, 0, 42], [0, 0, 42]]
```

Notice that not only does data[2][2] appear to have been incremented, but so do data[0][2] and data[1][2]. The reason for this comes down to reference semantics as discussed earlier in this chapter. When the multiplication method of creating

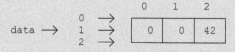

Figure 7.37 Multidimensional list with multiple references to same row

Continued on next page

Continued from previous page

a list is used, it copies a reference to the same value into every spot in the list. If the value is immutable, this is fine because when it is changed the reference is simply switched to point at a new value. However, when the value is mutable, as is the case when the value is another list, this causes a problem. If all three inner lists are references to the same list, then if one changes all the others will change as well. This is why we incremented one location and saw three changes.

We can fix this problem by creating the inner lists in a loop instead of through multiplication. You will notice that we still multiply to get the length of 3 for the inner lists. This is fine because the value inside is immutable.

```
>>> # create 2D list with loop (correct)
>>> data = []
>>> for i in range(3):
...     data.append([0] * 3)
...
>>> data
[[0, 0, 0], [0, 0, 0], [0, 0, 0]]
>>> data[2][2] = 42
>>> data
[[0, 0, 0], [0, 0, 0], [0, 0, 42]]
```

Lists of Pixels

Recall from Chapter 3 that images are stored on computers as a two-dimensional grid of colored dots known as pixels. One of the most common applications of two-dimensional lists is for manipulating the pixels of an image. Popular apps like Instagram provide filters and options for modifying images by applying algorithms to their pixels; for example, you can make an image black-and-white, sharpen it, enhance the colors and contrast, or make it look like an old faded photograph. The two-dimensional rectangular nature of an image makes a 2D list a natural way to represent its pixel data.

Chapter 3 introduced the DrawingPanel class that we use to represent a window for drawing 2D shapes and colors. Recall that an image is composed of pixels whose locations are specified with integer coordinates starting from the top-left corner of the image at (0, 0). The various drawing commands of the panel, such as draw_rect and fill_oval, change the color of regions of pixels. Colors can be specified by (r, g, b) tuples of three integers representing the red, green, and blue components of each pixel from 0 to 255 inclusive.

The DrawingPanel includes several methods for getting and setting the color of pixels; see Table 7.3. You can interact with a single pixel, or you can grab all of the pixels of the image as a 2D list and manipulate the entire list. The list is in *x*-major order; that is, the first index of the list is the *x*-coordinate and the second is the *y*-coordinate. For example, pixels[x][y] represents the pixel at position (*x*, *y*). For efficiency it is

Table 7.3   `DrawingPanel` pixel operations

Method/Property	Description
`panel.get_pixel(x, y)`	returns a single pixel's color as an (r, g, b) tuple
`panel.get_pixel_color(x, y)`	returns a single pixel's color as a hex string such as `"#ff00ff"`
`panel.pixels`	returns all pixels of image as an $[x][y]$ 2D list of (r, g, b) tuples
`panel.pixel_colors`	returns all pixels of image as an $[x][y]$ 2D list of hex strings
`panel.set_pixel(x, y, color)`	sets a single pixel's color to a color specified as an (r, g, b) tuple or hex string

generally recommended to use the list-based versions of the methods; the individual-pixel methods run slowly when applied repeatedly over all pixels of a large image.

The following program uses the `pixels` property to fill a triangular region of the panel with a purple color. Notice that you must set the `pixels` property at the end to see the updated image; changing the 2D list will not produce any effect on the screen until you tell the panel to update itself using the new contents of the list.

```
1   # Draws a triangle using pixels.
2   from DrawingPanel import *
3
4   def main():
5       panel = DrawingPanel(300, 200)
6       px = panel.pixels
7       for x in range(50, 150):
8           for y in range(x, 150):
9               px[x][y] = (255, 0, 255)
10      panel.pixels = px
11
12  main()
```

You can use the pixel list to draw a shape like our purple triangle, but a more typical usage of these methods would be to grab the panel's existing state and alter it in some interesting way. The following program has a `mirror` function that accepts a `DrawingPanel` parameter and flips the pixel contents horizontally, swapping each pixel's color with the one at the opposite horizontal location. You can ask the panel itself for its dimensions as `panel.width` and `panel.height`, or you can use the dimensions of the list. The expression `len(pixels)` returns the panel's width, and `len(pixels[0])` returns its height (the length of the first row of the 2D list). The following is the complete program along with its graphical output before and after `mirror` is called.

```
1   # This program contains a mirror method that flips the appearance
2   # of a DrawingPanel horizontally pixel-by-pixel.
3   from DrawingPanel import *
4
5   # Horizontally flips the pixels of the given drawing panel.
6   def mirror(panel):
7       px = panel.pixels
8       for x in range(panel.width // 2):
9           for y in range(panel.height):
10              # swap with pixel at "mirrored" location
11              opposite = panel.width - 1 - x
12              temp = px[x][y]
13              px[x][y] = px[opposite][y]
14              px[opposite][y] = temp
15      panel.pixels = px
16
17  def main():
18      panel = DrawingPanel(300, 200)
19      panel.fill_oval(20, 100, 30, 70)
20      panel.draw_rectangle(20, 50, 80, 30)
21      mirror(panel)
22
23  main()
```

Often you'll want to extract the individual red, green, and blue components of a color to manipulate them. Each pixel's color is represented as a tuple of three integers representing the red, green, and blue components of the pixel's color from 0 to 255. You can use these individual components to create pixels of different colors or manipulate the colors of an existing image.

The following code shows a method that computes the negative of an image, which is found by taking the opposite of each color's RGB values. For example, the opposite of (red $=$ 255, green $=$ 100, blue $=$ 35) is (red $=$ 0, green $=$ 155, blue $=$ 220). The simplest way to compute the negative is to subtract the pixel's RGB values from the maximum color value of 255.

```
# Produces the negative of the given image by inverting
# the color values of all pixels in the panel.
def negative(panel):
    px = panel.pixels
    for x in range(panel.width):
        for y in range(panel.height):
            # extract red/green/blue components from 0-255
            r, g, b = px[x][y]
            px[x][y] = (255 - r, 255 - g, 255 - b)
    panel.pixels = px
```

All of the previous examples have involved making changes to a 2D pixel list in place. But sometimes you want to create an image with different dimensions, or you want to set each pixel based on the values of pixels around it, and therefore you need to create a new pixel list. The following example shows a `stretch` function that widens the contents of a `DrawingPanel` to twice their current width. To do so, it creates a list called `px2` that is twice as wide as the existing one. (Remember that the first index of the 2D list is *x* and the second is *y*, so to widen the list, the code must double the list's first dimension.) When you set the `pixels` property, it will resize the panel if necessary to accommodate the new larger list of pixels.

The loop to fill the new list sets the value at each index to the value at half as large an *x*-index in the original list. So, for example, the new list's pixel value at (52, 34) comes from the original list's pixel at (26, 34). Because of integer division, the new list's pixel values at (53, 34), (52, 35), and (53, 35) also come from the original list's pixel at (26, 34). Notice that we need to create the inner lists inside the overall 2D list; we initially fill them with the value `None`, but this is quickly overwritten by the pixel values. The following is the stretching function along with an image before and after stretching.

```
# Stretches the given panel to be twice as wide.
# Any shapes and colors drawn on the panel are stretched to fit.
def stretch(panel):
    px  = panel.pixels
    px2 = [None] * (2 * panel.width)
    for x in range(len(px2)):
        px2[x] = [None] * panel.height
        for y in range(len(px2[0])):
            px2[x][y] = px[x // 2][y]
    panel.pixels = px2
```

7.5 Case Study: Benford's Law

Let's look at a more complex program example that involves using lists. When you study real-world data you will often come across a curious result that is known as *Benford's law*, named after a physicist named Frank Benford, who discovered and stated the law in 1938.

Table 7.4   Expected Distribution under Benford's Law

First Digit	Frequency
1	30.1%
2	17.6%
3	12.5%
4	9.7%
5	7.9%
6	6.7%
7	5.8%
8	5.1%
9	4.6%

Benford's law involves looking at the first digit of a series of numbers. For example, suppose that you were to use a random number generator to generate integers in the range of 100 to 999 and you looked at how often the number begins with 1, how often it begins with 2, and so on. Any decent random number generator would spread out the answers evenly among the nine different regions, so we'd expect to see each digit about one-ninth of the time (11.1 percent). But with a lot of real-world data, we see a very different distribution.

When we examine data that matches the Benford distribution, we see a first digit of 1 over 30 percent of the time (almost one-third) and, at the other extreme, a first digit of 9 only about 4.6 percent of the time (less than one in twenty cases). Table 7.4 shows the expected distribution for data that follows Benford's law.

Why would the distribution turn out this way? Why so many 1s? Why so few 9s? The answer is that exponential sequences have properties different from the properties of simple linear sequences. In particular, exponential sequences have a lot more numbers that begin with 1.

To explore this phenomenon, let's look at two different sequences of numbers: one that grows linearly and one that grows exponentially. If you start with the number 1 and add 0.2 to it over and over, you get the following linear sequence:

1, 1.2, 1.4, 1.6, 1.8, 2, 2.2, 2.4, 2.6, 2.8, 3, 3.2, 3.4, 3.6, 3.8, 4, 4.2, 4.4, 4.6, 4.8, 5, 5.2, 5.4, 5.6, 5.8, 6, 6.2, 6.4, 6.6, 6.8, 7, 7.2, 7.4, 7.6, 7.8, 8, 8.2, 8.4, 8.6, 8.8, 9, 9.2, 9.4, 9.6, 9.8, 10

In this sequence there are five numbers that begin with 1, five numbers that begin with 2, five numbers that begin with 3, and so on. For each digit, there are five numbers that begin with that digit. That's what we expect to see with data that goes up by a constant amount each time.

But consider what happens when we make it an exponential sequence instead. Let's again start with 1 and continue until we get to 10, but this time let's multiply each successive number by 1.05 (we'll limit ourselves to displaying just two digits after the decimal, but the actual sequence takes into account all of the digits):

1.00, 1.05, 1.10, 1.16, 1.22, 1.28, 1.34, 1.41, 1.48, 1.55, 1.63, 1.71, 1.80, 1.89,
1.98, 2.08, 2.18, 2.29, 2.41, 2.53, 2.65, 2.79, 2.93, 3.07, 3.23, 3.39, 3.56, 3.73,
3.92, 4.12, 4.32, 4.54, 4.76, 5.00, 5.25, 5.52, 5.79, 6.08, 6.39, 6.70, 7.04, 7.39,
7.76, 8.15, 8.56, 8.99, 9.43, 9.91, 10.40

In this sequence there are 15 numbers that begin with 1 (31.25%), 8 numbers that begin with 2 (16.7%), and so on. There are only 2 numbers that begin with 9 (4.2%). In fact, the distribution of digits is almost exactly what you see in the table for Benford's law.

There are many real-world phenomena that exhibit an exponential character. For example, population tends to grow exponentially in most regions. There are many other data sets that also seem to exhibit the Benford pattern, including sunspots, salaries, investments, heights of buildings, and so on. Benford's law has been used to try to detect accounting fraud under the theory that when someone is making up data, they are likely to use a more random process that won't yield a Benford-style distribution.

For our purposes, let's write a program that reads a file of integers and that shows the distribution of the leading digit. We'll read the data from a file and will run it on several sample inputs. First, though, let's consider the general problem of tallying.

Tallying Values

In programming we often find ourselves wanting to count the number of occurrences of some set of values. For example, we might want to know how many people got a 100 on an exam, how many got a 99, how many got a 98, and so on. Or we might want to know how many days the temperature in a city was above 100 degrees, how many days it was in the 90s, how many days it was in the 80s, and so on. The approach is very nearly the same for each of these tallying tasks. Let's look at a small tallying task in which there are only five values to tally.

Suppose that a teacher scores quizzes on a scale of 0 to 9 and wants to know the distribution of quiz scores. In other words, the teacher wants to know how many scores of 0 there are, how many scores of 1, how many scores of 2, how many scores of 3, and so on. Suppose that the teacher has included all of the scores in a data file called `tally.dat` in the following format:

```
1 7 1 0 7 2 1 9 2 0
8 0 2 3 0 4 6 6 4 1
2 4 7 3 1 6 3 3 7 8
2 3 3 8 1 4 4 1 9 1
```

The teacher could hand-count the scores, but it would be much easier to use a computer to do the counting. How can you solve the problem? First you have to recognize that you are doing ten separate counting tasks: You are counting the occurrences of the number 0, the number 1, the number 2, the number 3, and so on up to 9. You could declare ten separate counters to solve this problem, but a list of length ten is a great way to store the data. In general, whenever you find yourself thinking that you need n of some kind of data, you should think about using a list of length n.

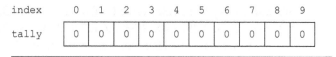

Figure 7.38   List of ten counters

Since you want to count ten things, you will want a list of length ten. Use a cumulative algorithm where our list begins with ten zeros in it, and read each integer from the file and increment those counters. The line below creates the list called `tally` shown in Figure 7.38. The idea is that `tally[0]` will store the count of zeros, `tally[1]` will store the count of ones, and so on, up to `tally[9]`, which stores the count of nines.

```
# define a list of 10 counters
tally = [0] * 10
```

To count up the tallies, read the numbers from the file. As you read each number, you should increment the tally list element at the index that corresponds to that number. For example, if you read a 4, you should increment `tally[4]`.

You're reading from a file, and the white space and line breaks don't matter. It will be easiest to use `read` and `split` to break the input into tokens and loop over the results. You should also convert each string token to an integer before processing it further:

```
# initial loop code to read each number
with open("tally.dat") as file:
    for next in file.read().split():
        next = int(next)
        # process next
```

To complete this code, you need to figure out how to process each value. You know that next will be one of ten different values: 0, 1, 2, and so on, up to 9. If it is 0, increment the counter for 0, which is `count[0]`; if it is 1, increment the counter for 1, which is `count[1]`, and so on. You could solve a problem like this one with nested `if/else` statements:

```
# increment the appropriate element of tally list
if next == 0:
    tally[0] += 1
elif next == 1:
    tally[1] += 1
elif next == 2:
    tally[2] += 1
...
```

But with a list, you can solve this problem much more directly:

```
# increment the appropriate element of tally list
tally[next] += 1
```

This line of code is so short compared to the nested `if/else` construct that you might not realize at first that it does the same thing. Let's simulate exactly what happens as various values are read from the file. When the list is created, all of the counters are initialized to 0. The first few numbers in the file are 1 7 0 1 7. The first value you read is 1, so the program stores that into the variable `next`. Then it executes this line of code:

```
# increment the appropriate element of tally list
tally[next] += 1
```

Because `next` is 1, this line of code becomes:

```
tally[1] += 1
```

So the counter at index `[1]` is incremented. Then you read a 7 from the input file, which means `tally[7]` is incremented. Next, you read another 1 from the input file, which increments `tally[1]` a second time. Then you read a 0 from the input file, which increments `tally[0]`. Then you read a 7 from the input file, which increments `tally[7]` a second time. Figure 7.39 shows the list changing as these first few values are read from the file.

Notice that in just this short set of data you've jumped from index 1 to index 7, then back down to index 1, then to index 0, then back to 7. The program continues executing in this manner, jumping from counter to counter as it reads values from the file. This ability to jump around in the data structure is what's meant by random access.

After processing all of the data, the list ends up with the counter values shown in Figure 7.40.

Figure 7.39   List of ten counters after first five increments

index	0	1	2	3	4	5	6	7	8	9
tally	4	8	5	6	5	0	3	4	3	2

Figure 7.40   List of ten counters after all increments

After this loop finishes executing, you can report the total for each score by using an indexed `for` loop with a `print`. With the addition of a header for the output, the following is the complete program along with the output for the input data shown previously.

```
1   # Reads a series of values and reports the frequency of
2   # occurrence of each value.
3
4   def main():
5       with open("tally.dat") as file:
6           tally = [0] * 10
7           for next in file.read().split():
8               next = int(next)
9               tally[next] += 1
10
11          print("Value\tOccurrences")
12          for i in range(len(tally)):
13              print(i, tally[i], sep="\t")
14
15  main()
```

```
Value    Occurrences
0        4
1        8
2        5
3        6
4        5
5        0
6        3
7        4
8        3
9        2
```

It is important to realize that a program written with a list is much more flexible than programs written with simple variables and `if/else` statements. For example, suppose you wanted to adapt this program to process an input file with exam scores that range from 0 to 100. The only change you would have to make would be to allocate a larger list:

```
tally = [0] * 101
```

If you had written the program with an `if/else` approach, you would have to add 96 new branches to account for the new range of values. When you use a list solution, you just have to modify the overall length of the list. Notice that the list length is one more than the highest score (101 rather than 100) because the list is zero-based and because you can actually get 101 different scores on the test, including 0 as a possibility.

Completing the Program

Now that we've explored the basic approach to tallying, we can fairly easily adapt it to the problem of analyzing a data file to find the distribution of leading digits. As we stated earlier, we're assuming that we have a file of integers. To count the leading digits, we will need to be able to get the leading digit of each. This task is specialized enough that it deserves to be in its own function.

So let's first write a function called `first_digit` that returns the first digit of an integer. If the number is a one-digit number, then the number itself will be the answer. If the number is not a one-digit number, then we can chop off its last digit because we don't need it. If we do the chopping in a loop, then eventually we'll get down to a one-digit number (the first digit). This leads us to write the following loop:

```
# get the first digit of an integer
while result >= 10:
    result = result // 10
```

We don't expect to get any negative numbers, but it's not a bad idea to make sure we don't have any negatives. So putting this into a function that also handles negatives, we get the following code:

```
# Returns the first digit of the given integer.
def first_digit(n):
    result = abs(n)
    while result >= 10:
        result = result // 10
    return result
```

In the previous section we explored the general approach to tallying. In this case we want to tally the digits 0 through 9, so we want a list of length 10. Otherwise the solution is nearly identical to what we did in the last section. We can put the tallying code into a function that creates a list and returns the tally:

```
# Reads integers from input file, computing a list of tallies
# for the occurrences of each leading digit (0 - 9).
def count_digits(file):
    tally = [0] * 10
    for next in file.read().split():
        next = int(next)
        tally[first_digit(next)] += 1
    return tally
```

Notice that instead of tallying n in the body of the loop, we are instead tallying `first_digit(n)` (just the first digit, not the entire number).

The value 0 presents a potential problem for us. Benford's law is meant to apply to data that comes from an exponential sequence. But even if you are increasing exponentially, if you start with 0, you never get beyond 0. As a result, it is best to eliminate the 0 values from the calculation. Often they won't occur at all.

When reporting results, then, let's begin by reporting the excluded zeros if they exist:

```
# report excluded zeros, if present
if tally[0] > 0:
    print("excluding", tally[0], "zeros")
```

For the other digits, we want to report the number of occurrences of each and also the percentage of each. To figure the percentage, we'll need to know the sum of the values. Python includes a global function called sum that accepts a list parameter and returns the sum of its elements. We can use it to compute the total number of digits by calling the function and subtracting the number of zeros:

```
# sum of all tallies, excluding 0
total = sum(tally) - tally[0]
```

Once we have the total number of digits, we can write a loop to report each of the percentages. To compute the percentages, we multiply each count by 100 and divide by the total number of digits:

```
# report percentage of each tally, excluding 0
for i in range(1, len(count)):
    pct = count[i] * 100 / total
    print(i, count[i], pct)
```

Notice that the loop starts at 1 instead of 0 because we have excluded the zeros from our reporting.

Here is a complete program that puts these pieces together. It also includes a header for the table and a total afterward.

```
 1  # This program finds the distribution of leading digits in a set
 2  # of positive integers.  The program is useful for exploring the
 3  # phenomenon known as Benford's Law.
 4
 5  # Reads integers from input file, computing a list of tallies
 6  # for the occurrences of each leading digit (0 - 9).
 7  def count_digits(file):
```

Continued on next page

Continued from previous page

```
 8        tally = [0] * 10
 9        for next in file.read().split():
10            next = int(next)
11            tally[first_digit(next)] += 1
12        return tally
13
14   # Reports percentages for each leading digit, excluding zeros.
15   def report_results(tally):
16        if tally[0] > 0:
17            print("excluding", tally[0], "zeros")
18
19        # sum of all tallies, excluding 0
20        total = sum(tally) - tally[0]
21
22        # report percentage of each tally, excluding 0
23        print("Digit\tCount\tPercent")
24        for i in range(1, len(tally)):
25            pct = tally[i] * 100 / total
26            print(i, tally[i], round(pct, 2), sep="\t")
27        print("Total", total, 100.0, sep="\t")
28
29   # Returns the first digit of the given integer.
30   def first_digit(n):
31        result = abs(n)
32        while result >= 10:
33            result = result // 10
34        return result
35
36   def main():
37        print("Let's count those leading digits...")
38        filename = input("input file name? ")
39        print()
40        with open(filename) as file:
41            tally = count_digits(file)
42            report_results(tally)
43
44   main()
```

Now that we have a complete program, let's see what we get when we analyze various data sets. The Benford distribution shows up with population data because population tends to grow exponentially. Let's use data from the web page https://www.census.gov/, which contains population estimates for various U.S. counties. The data set has information on 3139 different counties with populations varying from 67 individuals to over 9 million for the census year 2000. Here is a sample output of our program using these data:

```
Let's count those leading digits...
input file name? county.txt
Digit   Count   Percent
1       970     30.90
2       564     17.97
3       399     12.71
4       306     9.75
5       206     6.56
6       208     6.63
7       170     5.24
8       172     5.48
9       144     4.59
Total   3139    100.00
```

These percentages are almost exactly the numbers predicted by Benford's law. Data that obey Benford's law have an interesting property. It doesn't matter what scale you use for the data. So if you are measuring heights, for example, it doesn't matter whether you measure in feet, inches, meters, or furlongs. In our case, we counted the number of people in each U.S. county. If we instead count the number of human hands in each county, then we have to double each number. Look at the preceding table and see if you can predict the result when you double each number. Here is the actual result:

```
Let's count those leading digits...
input file name? county2.txt
Digit   Count   Percent
1       900     28.67
2       555     17.68
3       415     13.22
4       322     10.26
5       242     7.71
6       209     6.66
7       190     6.05
8       173     5.51
9       133     4.24
Total   3139    100.00
```

Notice that there is very little change. Doubling the numbers has little effect because if the original data is exponential in nature, then the same will be true of the doubled numbers. Here is another sample run that triples the county population numbers:

```
Let's count those leading digits...
input file name? county3.txt
Digit   Count   Percent
1       926     29.50
2       549     17.49
3       385     12.27
4       327     10.42
5       258     8.22
6       228     7.26
7       193     6.15
8       143     4.56
9       130     4.14
Total   3139    100.00
```

Another data set that shows Benford characteristics is the count of sunspots that occur on any given day. Robin McQuinn maintains a web page at http://sidc.oma.be/html/sunspot.html that has daily counts of sunspots going back to 1818. Here is a sample execution using these data:

```
Let's count those leading digits...
input file name? sunspot.txt
excluding 4144 zeros
Digit   Count   Percent
1       5405    31.24
2       1809    10.46
3       2127    12.29
4       1690    9.77
5       1702    9.84
6       1357    7.84
7       1364    7.88
8       966     5.58
9       882     5.10
Total   17302   100.00
```

Notice that on this execution the program reports the exclusion of some 0 values.

Chapter Summary

- A list groups multiple values under one name. Each individual value, called an element, is accessed with an integer index that ranges from 0 to one less than the list's length.
- Attempting to access a list element with an index of less than negative the list's length or one that is greater than or equal to the list's length will cause the program to crash with an `IndexError`.
- Lists are often traversed using loops. List elements can be accessed in order using a standard `for` loop over the list's elements, also called a for-each loop. You can also traverse a list by looping over its indexes from 0 through the list's length minus 1.
- Several common list algorithms are implemented by traversing the elements and examining or modifying each one.
- Python lists use reference semantics, which means that variables store references to values rather than to the actual values themselves. This means that two list variables can refer to the same list, and if one variable's list elements are modified, the change will also be seen in the other.
- Some Python types, like integers, real numbers, Booleans, and strings, are immutable. This means they cannot be changed.
- Other Python types, like lists, are mutable and can be changed. This means if a list is modified through one of its references, the modification will also be seen in the other.
- A tuple is an immutable sequence of values. Tuples are similar to lists but without all operations that would cause a change to the collection.
- A multidimensional list is a list of lists. Multidimensional lists are often used to store two-dimensional data, such as data in rows and columns or *x/y* data in a two-dimensional space. Multidimensional lists can also be used to represent the pixels of an image.

Self-Check Problems

Section 7.1: List Basics

1. What expression should be used to access the first element of a list called `numbers`? What expression should be used to access the last element of `numbers`, assuming `numbers` contains 10 elements? What expression can be used to access its last element, regardless of its length?

2. Write code that creates a list called `data` with the contents shown in Figure 7.41.

index	0	1	2	3	4
data	27	51	33	-1	101

Figure 7.41   List of data elements

3. Write code that stores all odd numbers between −6 and 38 into a list using a loop. Make the list's size exactly large enough to store the numbers. Then, try generalizing your code so that it will work for any minimum and maximum values, not just −6 and 38.

4. What elements does the list `numbers` contain after the following code is executed?

```
numbers = [0] * 8
numbers[1] = 4
numbers[4] = 99
```

Continued on next page

Continued from previous page

```
numbers[7] = 2
x = numbers[1]
numbers[x] = 44
numbers[numbers[7]] = 11     # uses numbers[7] as index
```

5. What elements does the list `data` contain after the following code is executed?

```
data = [0] * 8
data[0] = 3
data[7] = -18
data[4] = 5
data[1] = data[0]

x = data[4]
data[4] = 6
data[x] = data[0] * data[1]
```

6. Write a piece of code that creates a list called `data` with the elements 7, -1, 13, 24, and 6. Use only one statement to initialize the list.

7. Given the following list, write slicing expressions that would produce the following results:

```
# index     0   1   2   3   4   5   6
letters = ["a", "b", "c", "d", "e", "f", "g"]
```

a. `["a", "b"]`
b. `["d"]`
c. `["d", "e", "f", "g"]`
d. `["g", "f", "e"]`
e. `["b", "d", "f"]`

8. Write a piece of code that examines a list of integers and reports the maximum value in the list. Consider putting your code into a function called `maximum` that accepts the list as a parameter and returns the maximum value. Assume that the list contains at least one element. (Do not use the Python built-in `max` function in this problem.)

9. Write code that computes the average (arithmetic mean) of all elements in a list of integers and returns the answer. For example, if the list passed contains the values `[1, -2, 4, -4, 9, -6, 16, -8, 25, -10]`, the calculated average should be 2.5. You may want to put this code into a function called `average` that accepts a list of integers as its parameter and returns the average.

The next three questions refer to the following list:

```
data = ["It", "was", "a", "stormy", "night"]
```

10. Write code to insert two additional elements, `"dark"` and `"and"`, at the proper places in the list to produce the following list as the result:

```
["It", "was", "a", "dark", "and", "stormy", "night"]
```

11. Write code to change the second element's value to `"IS"`, producing the following list as the result:

```
["It", "IS", "a", "dark", "and", "stormy", "night"]
```

12. Write code to remove from the list any strings that contain the letter `"a"`. The following should be the list's contents after your code has executed:

```
["It", "IS", "stormy", "night"]
```

Section 7.2: List-Traversal Algorithms

13. What is a list traversal? Give an example of a problem that can be solved by traversing a list.

14. Write code that uses a `for` loop to print each element of a list called `data` that contains five integers:

```
element [ 0 ] is 14
element [ 1 ] is 5
element [ 2 ] is 27
element [ 3 ] is -3
element [ 4 ] is 2598
```

Consider generalizing your code so that it will work on a list of any size.

15. What elements does the list contain after the following code is executed?

```
data = [2, 18, 6, -4, 5, 1]
for i in range(len(data)):
    data[i] = data[i] + (data[i] // data[0])
```

16. Write the output produced when the following function is passed each of the following lists:

```
def mystery(lis):
    for i in range(len(lis) - 1, 0, -1):
        if lis[i] < lis[i - 1]:
            element = lis[i]
            lis.pop(i)
            lis.insert(0, element)
    print(lis)
```

a. `[2, 6, 1, 8]`
b. `[30, 20, 10, 60, 50, 40]`
c. `[-4, 16, 9, 1, 64, 25, 36, 4, 49]`

17. Write the output produced when the following function is passed each of the following lists:

```
def mystery(lis):
    for i in range(len(lis) - 1, -1, -1):
        if i % 2 == 0:
            lis.insert(lis[i])
        else:
            lis.insert(0, lis[i])
    print(lis)
```

a. `[10, 20, 30]`
b. `[8, 2, 9, 7, 4]`
c. `[-1, 3, 28, 17, 9, 33]`

18. Write a function called `all_less` that accepts two lists of integers and returns `True` if each element in the first list is less than the element at the same index in the second list. Your function should return `False` if the lists are not the same length.

19. What are the values of the elements in the list `numbers` after the following code is executed?

```
numbers = [10, 20, 30, 40, 50, 60, 70, 80, 90, 100]
for i in range(9):
    numbers[i] = numbers[i + 1]
```

20. What are the values of the elements in the list `numbers` after the following code is executed?

```
numbers = [10, 20, 30, 40, 50, 60, 70, 80, 90, 100]
for i in range(1, 10):
    numbers[i] = numbers[i - 1]
```

21. Consider the following function, `mystery`:

```
def mystery(a, b):
    for i in range(len(a)):
        a[i] += b[len(b) - 1 - i]
```

What are the values of the elements in list `a1` after the following code executes?

```
a1 = [1, 3, 5, 7, 9]
a2 = [1, 4, 9, 16, 25]
mystery(a1, a2)
```

22. Consider the following function, `mystery2`:

```
def mystery2(data, x, y):
    data[data[x]] = data[y]
    data[y] = x
```

What are the values of the elements in the list `numbers` after the following code executes?

```
numbers = [3, 7, 1, 0, 25, 4, 18, -1, 5]
mystery2(numbers, 3, 1)
mystery2(numbers, 5, 6)
mystery2(numbers, 8, 4)
```

23. Consider the following function:

```
def mystery3(lis):
    x = 0
    for i in range(1, len(lis)):
        y = lis[i] - lis[0]
        if y > x:
            x = y
    return x
```

What value does the function return when passed each of the following lists?

a. `[5]`
b. `[3, 12]`
c. `[4, 2, 10, 8]`
d. `[1, 9, 3, 5, 7]`
e. `[8, 2, 10, 4, 10, 9]`

24. Write a piece of code that computes the average string length of the elements of a list of strings. For example, if the list contains `["belt", "hat", "jelly", "bubble gum"]`, the average length is 5.5.

25. Write code that accepts a list of strings as its parameter and indicates whether that list is a palindrome. A palindrome list is one that reads the same forward as backward. For example, the list `["alpha", "beta", "gamma", "delta", "gamma", "beta", "alpha"]` is a palindrome.

26. Given the following list, write list comprehensions that would produce the following new lists:

```
# index       0       1     2      3
letters = ["apple", "ball", "car", "dog"]
```

a. `["A", "B", "C", "D"]`
b. `["appleapple", "ballball", "carcar", "dogdog"]`
c. `[("apple", "a"), ("ball", "b"), ("car", "c"), ("dog", "d")]`

Section 7.3: Reference Semantics

27. What is the output of the following program?

```
def mystery(x, a):
    x = x + 1
    a[x] = a[x] + 1
    print(x, a)


def main():
    x = 0
    a = [0, 0, 0, 0]
    x = x + 1
    mystery(x, a)
    print(x, a)

    x = x + 1
    mystery(x, a)
    print(x, a)
main()
```

28. What is the output of the following program?

```
def mystery(x, lis):
    lis[x] += 1
    x += 1
    print(x, lis)


def main():
    x = 1
    a = [0, 0]
    mystery(x, a)
    print(x, a)
```

Continued on next page

Continued from previous page

```
        x -= 1
        a[1] = len(a)
        mystery(x, a)
        print(x, a)
    main()
```

29. Write a function called `swap_pairs` that accepts a list and swaps the elements at adjacent indexes. That is, elements 0 and 1 are swapped, elements 2 and 3 are swapped, and so on. If the list has an odd length, the final element should be left unmodified. For example, the list `[10, 20, 30, 40, 50]` should become `[20, 10, 40, 30, 50]` after a call to your function.

30. The following code uses tuples and contains four errors. What are they?

```
# incorrect code that interacts with a tuple
t = (10, 20, 30)
t[0] += 1
if len(t) < 5:
    t.append(40)
    print("t is", t)
    t.reverse()
    print("t is", t)
else:
    t.clear()
```

31. Write a function called `nearest_points` that accepts a list of (x, y) tuples representing points on the 2D Cartesian plane and prints out which two points were the closest. To compute the distance between two points, use the Pythagorean theorem, which states that the distance between two points is the square root of the sum of the squares of the differences in the two dimensions. You may assume that the list contains at least two points and that one pair is uniquely the closest pair.

Section 7.4: Multidimensional Lists

32. What elements does the list `numbers` contain after the following code is executed?

```
numbers = [[0, 0, 0, 0],
           [0, 0, 0, 0],
           [0, 0, 0, 0]]
for r in range(len(numbers)):
    for c in range(len(numbers[0])):
        numbers[r][c] = r + c
```

33. Assume that a two-dimensional rectangular list of integers called `data` has been declared with four rows and seven columns. Write a loop to initialize the third row of `data` to store the numbers 1 through 7.

34. Write a piece of code that constructs a two-dimensional list of integers with 5 rows and 10 columns. Fill the list with a multiplication table, so that each list element `[i][j]` contains the value `i * j`. Use nested `for` loops to build the list.

35. Assume that a two-dimensional rectangular list of integers called `matrix` has been declared with six rows and eight columns. Write a loop to copy the contents of the second column into the fifth column.

36. Consider the following function:

```
def mystery2d(a):
    for r in range(len(a)):
        for c in range(len(a[0]) - 1):
            if a[r][c + 1] > a[r][c]:
                a[r][c] = a[r][c + 1]
```

If a two-dimensional list numbers is initialized to store the following integers, what are its contents after the call shown?

```
numbers = [[3, 4, 5, 6],
           [4, 5, 6, 7],
           [5, 6, 7, 8]]
mystery2d(numbers)
```

37. Write a piece of code that constructs a jagged two-dimensional list of integers with five rows and an increasing number of columns in each row, such that the first row has one column, the second row has two, the third has three, and so on. The list elements should have increasing values in top-to-bottom, left-to-right order (also called row-major order). In other words, the list's contents should be the following:

```
1
2, 3
4, 5, 6
7, 8, 9, 10
11, 12, 13, 14, 15
```

Use nested for loops to build the list.

38. When examining a 2D list of pixels, how could you figure out the width and height of the image even if you don't have access to the DrawingPanel object?

39. Finish the following code for a function that converts an image into its red channel; that is, removing any green or blue from each pixel and keeping only the red component.

```
def to_red_channel(panel):
    px = panel.pixels
    for x in range(panel.width):
        for y in range(panel.height):
            # your code goes here

    panel.pixels = px
```

Exercises

1. Write a function called `list_range` that returns the range of values in a list of integers. The range is defined as 1 more than the difference between the maximum and minimum values in the list. For example, if a list called `lis` contains the values [36, 12, 25, 19, 46, 31, 22, the call of `list_range(lis)` should return 35. You may assume that the list has at least one element.

2. Write a function called `is_sorted` that accepts a list of numbers as a parameter and returns `True` if the list is in sorted (nondecreasing) order and `False` otherwise. For example, if lists named `list1` and `list2` store [16.1, 12.3, 22.2, 14.4] and [1.5, 4.3, 7.0, 19.5, 25.1, 46.2], respectively, the calls `is_sorted(list1)` and `is_sorted(list2)` should return `False` and `True`, respectively. Assume the list has at least one element. A one-element list is considered to be sorted.

3. Write a function called `mode` that returns the most frequently occurring element of a list of integers. Assume that the list has at least one element and that every element in the list has a value between 0 and 100 inclusive. Break ties by choosing the lower value. For example, if the list passed contains the values [27, 15, 15, 11, 27], your function should return 15. (*Hint:* You may wish to look at the tallying program from this chapter to get an idea how to solve this problem.) Can you write a version of this function that does not rely on the values being between 0 and 100?

4. Write a function called `median` that accepts a list of integers as its parameter and returns the median of the numbers in the list. The median is the number that appears in the middle of the list if you arrange the elements in order. Assume that the list is of odd size (so that one sole element constitutes the median) and that the numbers in the list are between 0 and 99 inclusive. For example, the median of [5, 2, 4, 17, 55, 4, 3, 26, 18, 2, 17] is 5 and the median of [42, 37, 1, 97, 1, 2, 7, 42, 3, 25, 89, 15, 10, 29, 27] is 25. (*Hint:* You may wish to look at the tallying program from earlier in this chapter for ideas.)

5. Write a function called `price_is_right` that mimics the guessing rules from the game show *The Price Is Right*. The function accepts as parameters a list of integers representing the contestants' bids and an integer representing a correct price. The function returns the element in the bids list that is closest in value to the correct price without being larger than that price. For example, if a list called `bids` stores the values [200, 300, 250, 1, 950, 40], the call of `price_is_right(bids, 280)` should return 250, since 250 is the bid closest to 280 without going over 280. If all bids are larger than the correct price, your function should return -1.

6. Write a function called `contains` that accepts two lists of integers `a1` and `a2` as parameters and that returns a Boolean value indicating whether or not the sequence of elements in `a2` appears in `a1` (`True` for yes, `False` for no). The sequence must appear consecutively and in the same order. For example, consider the following lists:

```
list1 = [1, 6, 2, 1, 4, 1, 2, 1, 8]
list2 = [1, 2, 1]
```

The call of `contains(list1, list2)` should return `True` because the sequence of values in `list2` [1, 2, 1] is contained in `list1` starting at index 5. If `list2` had stored the values [2, 1, 2], the call of `contains(list1, list2)` would return `False`. Any two lists with identical elements are considered to contain each other. Every list contains the empty list, and the empty list does not contain any lists other than the empty list itself.

7. Write a function called `collapse` that accepts a list of integers as a parameter and returns a new list containing the result of replacing each pair of integers with the sum of that pair. For example, if a list called `lis` stores the values `[7, 2, 8, 9, 4, 13, 7, 1, 9, 10]`, then the call of `collapse(lis)` should return a new list containing `[9, 17, 17, 8, 19]`. The first pair from the original list is collapsed into 9 (7 + 2), the second pair is collapsed into 17 (8 + 9), and so on. If the list stores an odd number of elements, the final element is not collapsed. For example, if the list had been `[1, 2, 3, 4, 5`, then the call would return `[3, 7, 5]`. Your function should not change the list that is passed as a parameter.

8. Write a function called `vowel_count` that accepts a string as a parameter and produces and returns a list of integers representing the counts of each vowel in the string. The list returned by your function should hold five elements: the first is the count of A's, the second is the count of E's, the third I's, the fourth O's, and the fifth U's. Assume that the string contains no uppercase letters. For example, the call `vowel_count("i think, therefore i am")` should return the list `[1, 3, 3, 1, 0]`.

9. Write a function called `min_to_front` that accepts a list of integers as a parameter and moves the minimum value in the list to the front, otherwise preserving the order of the elements. For example, if a variable called `lis` stores `[3, 8, 92, 4, 2, 17, 9]`, the value 2 is the minimum, so your function should modify the list to store the values `[2, 3, 8, 92, 4, 17, 9]`.

10. Write a function called `remove_even_length` that accepts a list of strings as a parameter and removes all of the strings of even length from the list.

11. Write a function called `double_list` that accepts a list of strings as a parameter and replaces every string with two of that same string. For example, if the list stores the values `["how", "are", "you?"]` before the function is called, it should store the values `["how", "how", "are", "are", "you?", "you?"]` after the function finishes executing.

12. Write a function called `scale_by_k` that accepts a list of integers as a parameter and replaces every integer of value k with k copies of itself. For example, if the list stores the values `[4, 1, 2, 0, 3]` before the function is called, it should store the values `[4, 4, 4, 4, 1, 2, 2, 3, 3, 3]` after the function finishes executing. Zeros and negative numbers should be removed from the list by this function.

13. Write a function called `remove_duplicates` that accepts as a parameter a sorted list of strings and eliminates any duplicates from the list. For example, if the list stores the values `["be", "be", "is", "not", "or", "question", "that", "the", "to", "to"]` before the function is called, it should store the values `["be", "is", "not", "or", "question", "that", "the", "to"]` after the function finishes executing. Because the values will be sorted, all of the duplicates will be grouped together. Assume that the list contains only string values, but keep in mind that it might be empty.

14. Write a function called `matrix_add` that accepts a pair of two-dimensional lists of integers as parameters, treats the lists as two-dimensional matrixes, and returns their sum. The sum of two matrixes A and B is a matrix C, where for every row i and column j, $C_{ij} = A_{ij} + B_{ij}$. You may assume that the lists passed as parameters have the same dimensions.

15. Write a function called `is_magic_square` that accepts a two-dimensional list of integers as a parameter and returns `True` if it is a magic square. A square matrix is a magic square if all of its row, column and diagonal sums are equal. For example, `[[2, 7, 6], [9, 5, 1], [4, 3, 8]]` is a square matrix because all eight of the sums are exactly 15.

16. Write a function called `grayscale` that accepts a `DrawingPanel` as a parameter and converts its pixels into black-and-white. This is done by averaging the red, green, and blue components of each pixel. For example, if a pixel has RGB values of (red = 100, green = 30, blue = 80), the average of the three components is (100 + 30 + 80)/3 = 70, so that pixel becomes (red = 70, green = 70, blue = 70).

17. Write a function called `transpose` that accepts a `DrawingPanel` as a parameter and inverts the image about both the *x* and *y* axes. You may assume that the image is square; that is, that its width and height are equal.

18. Write a method `zoom_in` that accepts a `DrawingPanel` as a parameter and converts it into an image twice as large in both dimensions. Each pixel from the original image becomes a cluster of 4 pixels (2 rows and 2 columns) in the new zoomed image.

Programming Projects

1. Write a program to reverse the lines of a file and also to reverse the order of the words in each line of the file. Use lists to help you.

2. Write a game of Hangman using lists. Allow the user to guess letters and represent which letters have been guessed in a list.

3. Write a program that plays a variation of the game of Mastermind with a user. For example, the program can use pseudorandom numbers to generate a four-digit number. The user should be allowed to make guesses until she gets the number correct. Clues should be given to the user indicating how many digits of the guess are correct and in the correct place and how many digits are correct but in the wrong place.

4. Write a family database program. Use lists and tuples to represent each person and to store the person's mother, father, and any children the person has. Read a file of names to initialize the name and parent-child relationships of each person. (You might want to create a file representing your own family tree.) Store the overall list of people in a list. Write an overall main user interface that asks for a name and prints the maternal and paternal family line for that person. Here's a hypothetical execution of the program, using as an input file the line of English Tudor monarchs:

```
Person's name? Henry VIII
Maternal line:
Henry VIII
Elizabeth of York

Paternal line:
Henry VIII
Henry VII

Children:
Mary I
Elizabeth I
Edward VI
```

5. Write a program that models a list of possibly overlapping rectangular two-dimensional window regions, like the windows for the programs open on your computer. The order of the rectangles in the list implies the order in which they would display on the screen (sometimes called the "z-order"), from 0 on the bottom to length −1 on the top.

   Each rectangle stores its (x, y) position, width, and height. Your rectangle list class should have a function that takes (x, y) coordinates as parameters, behaves as though the user clicked that point on the screen, and moves the topmost rectangle touching that point to the front of the list.

6. Write a program that reads a file of DNA data and searches for protein sequences. DNA data consists of long strings of the letters A, C, G, and T, corresponding to chemical nucleotides called adenine, cytosine, guanine, and thymine. Proteins can be identified by looking for special triplet sequences of nucleotides that indicate the start and stop of a protein range. Store relevant data in lists as you make your computation. See our text's web site for sample DNA input files and more details about heuristics for identifying proteins.

7. Write a program that plays the game of Tic-Tac-Toe using a 2D list to represent the board.

8. Write a basic Photoshop- or Instagram-inspired program with a menu of available image manipulation algorithms similar to those described in the exercises in this chapter. The user can load an image from a file and then select which manipulation to perform, such as grayscale, zoom, rotate, or blur.

Dictionaries and Sets

Introduction

The previous chapter explored the use of lists. A list is one of many ways to store data in Python. In this chapter we'll explore some of Python's other collections, including dictionaries and sets. We'll see how to use these structures together to manipulate and examine data in many ways to solve programming problems.

The dictionary, in particular, is a structure used frequently in Python programs. A dictionary allows us to store pairs of data values and look them up later, which is useful for tasks like a phone book, thesaurus, or employee database. We'll also discuss a collection called the set, which doesn't allow duplicate elements and is fast and easy to search.

Unlike most other chapters in this textbook, this one does not end with a single Case Study example. Instead, since we want to explore several kinds of collections, we will examine several medium-sized example programs throughout the chapter.

8.1 Dictionary Basics

In Chapter 7 we discussed ways to use lists to store data. The notion of organizing and structuring data is an important one that helps us solve complex problems. Entities that store and manage data are also called *data structures*. Data structures can be used to implement sophisticated data storage objects called *collections*.

> **Collection**
>
> An object that stores a group of other objects, called its elements.

A list is an example of a collection. A collection uses a data structure internally to store its elements, such as a list or a set of linked objects that refer to one another. Collections are categorized by the types of elements they store, the operations they allow you to perform on those elements, and the speed or efficiency of those operations. Here are some examples of collections:

- **List:** An ordered collection of elements, often accessed by integer indexes or by iteration.
- **Set:** A collection of elements that is guaranteed to contain no duplicates.
- **Dictionary:** A collection of key/value pairs in which each key is associated with a corresponding value.

Python provides several useful collections that allow you to store, access, search, sort, and manipulate data in a variety of ways.

Let's look at an example where using lists to store data would be a poor choice. Consider the task of writing a phone book program that allows users to type a person's name and search for that person's phone number. Suppose the data comes from a file such as the following *phonenumbers.txt*:

```
Allison (520)555-6789
Comcast (800)266-2278
DirecTV (800)347-3288
Flowers (800)356-9377
Marty (650)555-1234
Stuart (206)555-6543
Yana (206)555-5683
```

What would be a good way to store this data? You could read this data and store it in a list, where each name is followed by that person's phone number. Another strategy would be to store the data in two lists, one for names and one for phone numbers, which is called *parallel lists*. Neither of these representations is the best choice, for reasons we'll explain in a moment. The following code shows both of these list-based strategies:

```
# phone book as one list (not recommended)
phonelist = ["Allison", "(520)555-6789",
             "Comcast", "(800)266-2278",
             "DirecTV", "(800)347-3288",
             ...]
```

...

```
# look up phone number in list
for i in range(len(phonelist)):
    if phonelist[i] == "Comcast":
        print("Phone number is", phonelist[i + 1])
```

```
# phone book as two lists (not recommended)
namelist  = ["Allison", "Comcast", "DirecTV", ...]
phonelist = ["(520)555-6789",
             "(800)266-2278",
             "(800)347-3288",
             ...]
```

...

```
# look up phone number in pair of lists
for i in range(len(namelist)):
    if namelist[i] == "Comcast":
        print("Phone number is", phonelist[i])
```

With a single list, when you want to search for a phone number, you traverse the list, looking for the name entered by the user, and then return the associated phone number in the next index of the list. With a pair of lists, the searching strategy would be to find the name in the first list, and then go to that same index in the second list to find that person's phone number. For example, if you search the first list for "DirecTV" and find that it is found at index 2 in that list, then you can find DirecTV's phone number at the same index 2 in the second list. There are other list-related solutions, such as making a list of (name, phone number) tuples.

But while these list-based solutions would work, to look up a phone number in either case you need to loop over the entire list, which is clunky and inefficient. If the list of records is large, it would take the program a long time to search for the right name and phone number. Both of these approaches are generally considered to be poor choices for solving this kind of problem.

A key insight here is that we want to perform *lookups* of information in our data structure. The notion of lookups is common when we think about data. For example, if you want to find information about a university student in a computer system, you might type in that student's ID number or name to look up his or her records. Or perhaps you want to write a vocabulary-building program where the user types a word and the program looks up its definition. The idea is that we know something about the item of interest (an ID number, a name, a word, etc.) and want to use what we know to look up some other related piece of information about it (an address, a course list, a definition, etc.). The piece of information that we know is called a *key*. The related information we want to look up that is associated with a given key is called a *value*.

> ### Key
> A unique identifier for a record of data that a user wants to look up.

> ### Value
> Information in a data collection that is related to a given key.

Python has a collection type called a *dictionary* that is built for lookups based on keys. A dictionary stores a collection of pairs, where each pair has two elements: a *key* and a *value*.

A dictionary stores a one-way association from each key to each value such that if you provide the same key later, the associated value will be looked up and returned. A dictionary is also sometimes called an *associative array*, a *hash*, or a *map*.

> ### Dictionary (Associative Array)
> A collection that stores key/value pairs such that a value can be efficiently looked up using its key.

A dictionary is implemented in such a way that it is able to add, remove, and search for pairs within itself much more efficiently than a list. Dictionaries can be used to solve a surprisingly large number of problems, such as:

- Associating chat users with their set of friends and buddies.
- Representing a family tree associating each person with his or her mother and father.
- Grouping all the words in a book by length and report how many words there are of each length.
- Building a thesaurus of words and their synonyms.
- Creating an employee management system where salaries and other data can be looked up given an employee's ID number.

In our phone book example, the data consists of names and phone numbers. You want to store each name together with its phone number in such a way that you can easily look up the phone number for a given name. This indicates that names should be keys in our dictionary and phone numbers should be the values associated with those keys.

Creating a Dictionary

There are several ways to create a dictionary. One way is to define an empty dictionary and then add key/value pairs to it. An empty dictionary is typically written as a pair of curly { } braces, though you can also write `dict()` to create an empty dictionary:

```
name = {}            # syntax 1 (preferred)
name = dict()        # syntax 2
```
Syntax template: Defining an empty dictionary

Once you have created a dictionary, you can add a key/value pair to it using [ ] square brackets with the following syntax:

```
name[key] = value
```
Syntax template: Adding a key/value pair to a dictionary

Once your dictionary stores some key/value pairs, you can look up a value in the dictionary by supplying that key in [ ] square brackets. The general syntax is the following:

```
name[key]
```
Syntax template: Looking up a value in a dictionary using its key

For example, the following statements in the Python Shell show the creation of a dictionary, storing two key/value pairs in it, and looking up each pair's value by supplying its key:

```
>>> phonebook = {}                              # create empty dict
>>> phonebook["Allison"] = "(520)555-6789"      # store a pair
>>> phonebook["Marty"]   = "(650)555-1234"      # store another pair
>>> phonebook["Allison"]                        # look up number by name
'(520)555-6789'
>>> phonebook["Marty"]                          # look up number by name
'(650)555-1234'
```

A dictionary can be thought of as a generalization of the concept of an indexed list. The lists you saw in the previous chapter associate 0-based integer indexes with values, as shown in Figure 8.1. A dictionary is a similar structure except that the "indexes" associated with the values don't need to be 0-based integers. The indexes can be strings, or

index	value
0	"(520)555-6789"
1	"(650)555-1234"
2	"(800)347-3288"

Figure 8.1 A list of phone numbers

key	value
"Allison"	"(520)555-6789"
"Marty"	"(650)555-1234"
"DirecTV"	"(800)347-3288"

Figure 8.2 A dictionary of phone numbers

integers that don't start from 0, or almost any value you want, as shown in Figure 8.2. To highlight this distinction we call them keys instead of indexes.

```
>>> # creating/accessing a list
>>> mylist = [""] * 3
>>> mylist[0] = "(520)555-6789"
>>> mylist[1] = "(650)555-1234"
>>> mylist[2] = "(800)347-3288"
```

```
>>> # creating/accessing a dictionary
>>> mydict = {}
>>> mydict["Allison"] = "(520)555-6789"
>>> mydict["Marty"]   = "(650)555-1234"
>>> mydict["DirecTV"] = "(800)347-3288"
```

If you know the dictionary's initial data ahead of time, you can supply the key/value pairs as you are defining it. The syntax is to put its sequence of pairs in curly braces, where a key/value pair is written with a colon between them. Key/value pairs are separated by commas:

name = {key: value, key: value, ..., key: value}
Syntax template: Defining a dictionary with initial data

For example, the following single statement has the same effect as the first three statements in our original Python Shell interaction, creating a dictionary with two key/value pairs in it:

```
>>> # dictionary with initial data
>>> phonebook = {"Allison": "(520)555-6789", "Marty": "(650)555-1234"}
```

There is also a lesser used syntax for creating a dictionary from a list of (*key*, *value*) tuples. Generally you would favor the preceding syntax unless you had an existing list of tuples that you wanted to treat as a dictionary.

```
name = dict([(key, value), (key, value), ..., (key, value)])
```
Syntax template: Defining a dictionary with data as list of tuples

You can see the contents of a dictionary by printing it or by typing its name into the Python Shell:

```
>>> # printing the contents of a dictionary
>>> print("Contacts:", phonebook)
Contacts: {'Allison': '(520)555-6789', 'Marty': '(650)555-1234'}
>>> phonebook
{'Allison': '(520)555-6789', 'Marty': '(650)555-1234'}
```

The keys in a dictionary must be unique; dictionaries store only one value for each key. If you assign a value to a key and later execute a second assignment for that key, then the new value replaces the old one for that key. The following statements could be typed into the Python Shell after the ones in the previous interaction:

```
>>> # replacing a value in a dictionary
>>> phonebook["Allison"]
'(520)555-6789'
>>> phonebook["Allison"] = "(444)555-8800"
>>> phonebook["Allison"]
'(444)555-8800'
```

Although keys are not duplicated among the key/value pairs in a dictionary, the same value can be associated with two or more keys. For example, the code in the following interaction stores two people who share the same phone number:

```
>>> # dictionary where two keys pair with the same value
>>> phonebook
{'Allison': '(520)555-6789', 'Marty': '(650)555-1234'}
>>> phonebook["Yana"] = "(650)555-1234"   # duplicate value
>>> phonebook["Marty"]
'(650)555-1234'
>>> phonebook["Yana"]
'(650)555-1234'
>>> phonebook
{'Allison': '(520)555-6789', 'Marty': '(650)555-1234',
 'Yana': '(650)555-1234'}
```

Now let's revisit our phone book example and implement a complete program using a dictionary. In this case, the data comes from a file. So the right approach is to create an empty dictionary to represent the phone book, then loop over the lines of the file, storing each line's contents as a key/value pair in the dictionary. To look up a person's phone number afterward, we can use the square bracket notation. The following is the complete program along with a sample log of execution:

```
 1  # This program builds a phone book where the user can
 2  # type a name and look up that person's phone number.
 3  # The program stores the phone book as a dictionary.
 4
 5  def main():
 6      # build phone book as list
 7      phonebook = {}
 8      with open("phonenumbers.txt") as file:
 9          for line in file:
10              name, phone = line.split()
11              phonebook[name] = phone
12
13      # look up phone numbers
14      name = input("Name to look up? ")
15      while name != "":
16          print(name, "phone number is", phonebook[name])
17          name = input("Name to look up? ")
18      print("Have a nice day.")
19
20  main()
```

```
Name to look up? DirecTV
DirecTV phone number is (800)347-3288
Name to look up? Stuart
Stuart phone number is (206)555-6543
Name to look up?
Have a nice day.
```

Dictionary Operations

In this section we'll explore the operations supported by dictionaries in more detail. Dictionaries provide several useful methods and operations. Table 8.1 lists many of the most common ones.

Table 8.1 **Dictionary Operations**

Operation	Description
`dict[key]`	returns the value associated with the given key; raises `KeyError` if not found
`dict[key] = value`	sets the value associated with the given key; replaces if already found
`del dict[key]`	removes the given key and its paired value; raises `KeyError` if not found
`key in dict`	returns `True` if the given key is found
`key not in dict`	returns `True` if the given key is not found
`len(dict)`	number of key/value pairs
`str(dict)`	returns string representation such as `"{'a':1, 'b':2}"`
`dict.clear()`	removes all key/value pairs
`dict.get(key, default)`	returns the value associated with the given key; returns `default` if not found
`dict.items()`	returns the contents of the dictionary as a sequence of (key, value) tuples
`dict.keys()`	returns the keys in the dictionary as a sequence
`dict.pop(key)`	returns the value associated with the given key, and removes that key/value pair
`dict.update(dict2)`	adds all key/value pairs from another dictionary, replacing if keys are already present
`dict.values()`	returns the values in the dictionary as a sequence

One problem with our previous phone book program is that it crashes when you type a name that is not present in the dictionary:

```
Name to look up? Hermione
Traceback (most recent call last):
  File "phonebook.py", line 17, in <module>
    main()
  File "phonebook.py", line 15, in main
    print(name, "phone number is", phonebook[name])
KeyError: 'Hermione'
```

The program crashes because the dictionary's [ ] lookup operation raises a `KeyError` if the specified key is not found. You can avoid this error by checking whether the key is present before trying to access it. This is done using the `in` keyword:

```
if key in dict:
    statement
    statement
    ...
    statement
```

Syntax template: Checking for existence of a key in a dictionary

The following code would fix the crash in our phone book program:

```
name = input("Name to look up? ")
if name in phonebook:
    print(name, "phone number is", phonebook[name])
else:
    print(name, "not found.")
```

The same `len` function that provides the length of strings and lists also works with dictionaries. When used with a dictionary, `len` returns the number of pairs in the dictionary. An empty dictionary has a length of 0.

```
>>> # adding a pair to a dictionary
>>> phonebook = {"Allison": "(520)555-6789",
                 "Marty": "(650)555-1234",
                 "Stuart": "(206)555-6543"}
>>> len(phonebook)
3
>>> phonebook["Yana"] = "(206)555-5683"
>>> len(phonebook)
4
```

The `del` keyword removes a key/value pair from a dictionary. You write only the key's name, but both the key and its associated value are removed. A `KeyError` will be raised if the given key is not found, so be careful not to try to delete a key unless you know it is present in the dictionary. The general syntax for deleting a pair is the following:

```
del dict[key]
```

Syntax template: Deleting a key/value pair from a dictionary

The following code demonstrates removing a pair from a dictionary:

```
>>> # deleting a pair from a dictionary
>>> phonebook
{'Stuart': '(206)555-6543', 'Yana': '(206)555-5683',
 'Marty': '(650)555-1234', 'Allison': '(520)555-6789'}
>>> del phonebook["Marty"]
>>> phonebook
{'Stuart': '(206)555-6543', 'Yana': '(206)555-5683',
 'Allison': '(520)555-6789'}
```

Looping Over a Dictionary

The nature of dictionaries is such that you often don't need to loop over their contents. In particular, you should not use a loop to search through the contents of a dictionary to find a particular key, because the in keyword and [ ] brackets will retrieve the key and its value if present. But there are cases where you might want to loop over a dictionary, such as to print all of its elements.

You can loop over the contents of a dictionary in several ways. The simplest way is to use a standard for loop, which in the case of a dictionary will loop over its keys:

```
>>> # for loop over dictionary keys
>>> phonebook = {"Allison": "(520)555-6789",
                 "Marty": "(650)555-1234",
                 "Stuart": "(206)555-6543"}
>>> for name in phonebook:
...     print(name)
...
Stuart
Allison
Marty
```

If you also want to print the values in the dictionary, you can use the key variable along with the [ ] brackets to look up the value during the loop.

```
>>> # for loop over dictionary keys (and look up values)
>>> for name in phonebook:
...     print(name, "has phone number", phonebook[name])
...
Stuart has phone number (206)555-6543
Allison has phone number (520)555-6789
Marty has phone number (650)555-1234
```

A dictionary has methods called `keys`, `values`, and `items` that return sequences of its keys, values, or both, respectively. A *sequence* in this context means a list-like object that you can generally treat in the same ways as a list. These are sometimes called collection *views* of a dictionary because each is a collection that exists conceptually within the dictionary. Perhaps the most useful collection view is the dictionary's `items` method, which returns the dictionary's data as a sequence of (*key*, *value*) tuples. You can use this method to loop over the dictionary data without having to use the `[ ]` brackets to look up each item. For our phone book example, this lets us easily print each name (key) and phone number (value):

```
>>> for (name, phone) in phonebook.items():
...     print(name, "has phone number", phone)
...
Stuart has phone number (206)555-6543
Allison has phone number (520)555-6789
Marty has phone number (650)555-1234
```

Common Programming Error

Trying to Use Indexed for Loop with Dictionary

You cannot use the index-based `for` loop that we have sometimes used on strings and lists. This is because, unlike lists, dictionaries do not store their elements with 0-based integer indexes; they store them with keys instead. The following type of loop does not work and will raise a `KeyError`:

```
# trying to loop over a dictionary (this style does not work)
phonebook = {"Allison": "(520)555-6789",
             "Marty": "(650)555-1234",
             "Stuart": "(206)555-6543"}
for i in range(len(phonebook)):
    print(phonebook[i])
```

Some new programmers dislike the lack of integer indexes in a dictionary. But different collections work well in different programming situations; the dictionary doesn't do everything that a list does because it is meant to be used in different circumstances. If you are writing a program that needs to store information with numbered indexes, use a list. If you are associating pairs of values and want to look them up, use a dictionary.

Dictionary Ordering

If you were reading the Python Shell output carefully in the examples in the prior sections, you may have noticed that the keys and values do not always print in the same order that they were defined. For example, the following interaction creates a dictionary of names and phone numbers in a given order, but the `for` loop to print the pairs produces them in a completely different order:

```
>>> # loop over a dictionary (keys out of order)
>>> phonebook = {"Comcast": "(800)266-2278",
                 "Marty": "(650)555-1234",
                 "Allison": "(520)555-6789",
                 "Stuart": "(206)555-6543"}
>>> for name in phonebook:
...     print(name)
...
Stuart
Comcast
Allison
Marty
```

This is not a bug or typographical error; it's part of the way a dictionary is built internally. A dictionary is implemented in a way that makes it very fast for adding, removing, and searching for keys. Dictionaries are implemented using a data structure called a *hash table* that causes its elements to be stored in an order that is based on various internal algorithms rather than on the order in which you added the items. We won't go into all of the details of hash tables in this text, but if you're curious, you can search the web to learn more about them. For our purposes we want to focus on how to use a dictionary properly. The idea is that when using a dictionary, you surrender the predictability of element ordering in exchange for very fast searching functionality.

If you do want to iterate over a dictionary's elements in a given order, you can do so in your loop. For example, if you want to loop over the names in the phone book in alphabetical order, you can pass the list of keys of the book (as returned by its `keys` method) to the `sorted` function we saw in the last chapter:

```
>>> # loop over a dictionary (keys in sorted order)
>>> for name in sorted(phonebook.keys()):
...     print(name)
...
Allison
Comcast
Marty
Stuart
```

The other sequence-ordering functions also work here, such as `reversed`.

It is not possible to have complete control over the order of the elements in a dictionary. Python does provide some dictionary-like objects that give you greater control over element ordering. There is a collection called `OrderedDict` that behaves essentially the same as a dictionary, except that it stores its key/value pairs in the order that you insert them. To use `OrderedDict` you must place an `import` statement at the top of your program:

```
from collections import OrderedDict
```

Once you've imported the `OrderedDict` library, you can create an ordered dictionary as follows. After creation, an `OrderedDict` supports all of the same operations as a standard dictionary as listed in Table 8.1. The following interaction shows the creation of an ordered dictionary. Notice that we don't define it with its pairs in { } braces because that is the syntax for creating a regular dictionary. Instead, we initialize it as an empty `OrderedDict` and then add the key/value pairs one by one. Then when looping over the ordered dictionary, the names come out in exactly the same order that we added them.

```
>>> # use OrderedDict to store keys in sorted order
>>> from collections import OrderedDict
>>> phonebook = OrderedDict()
>>> phonebook["Comcast"] = "(800)266-2278"
>>> phonebook["Marty"] = "(650)555-1234"
>>> phonebook["Allison"] = "(520)555-6789"
>>> phonebook["Stuart"] = "(206)555-6543"
>>> for name in phonebook:
...     print(name)
...
Comcast
Marty
Allison
Stuart
```

The `OrderedDict` might seem strictly superior to the standard dictionary at first, since it provides the same operations along with a predictable ordering. But there are many reasons why the standard dictionary is often preferred. In most applications where you'll use a dictionary, the order of the pairs doesn't matter. Looking up individual keys using `in` and `[ ]` is much more common than looping over an entire dictionary. An `OrderedDict` also doesn't support the same { } syntax for creating and initializing a dictionary with a given set of key/value pairs inside the braces. The `OrderedDict` uses slightly more memory and has slightly slower performance than the standard dictionary for standard tasks like looking up the value for a given key. For all of these reasons, we advise you to use a standard dictionary unless the element ordering is critical to the problem you're solving.

If you want to learn more about `OrderedDict` and other dictionary variants, consult the official Python online documentation:

• https://docs.python.org/3/library/collections.html#collections.OrderedDict

8.2 Advanced Dictionary Usage

In this section we will explore other uses of dictionaries that allow you to solve new kinds of programming problems. As you will see, dictionaries are versatile and powerful for solving a variety of programming tasks. Once you become comfortable with dictionaries, you will find yourself using them in many of your programs.

Dictionary for Tallying

There are a variety of computing tasks where you want to count occurrences of various values. The case study in the previous chapter involved counting occurrences of digit values. Dictionaries are very useful for solving these kinds of counting problems For example, suppose you want to find the words that occur most frequently in a large book. To do this, you should count how many times each word in the book occurs, and then examine all of those counts and print the ones with the largest values. The book data would come from a file. Suppose the first several words of the file were the following:

```
to be or not to be that is the question
```

The desired strategy is a cumulative algorithm similar to many other counting problems you have seen. But in this case you want to count many different things; specifically, you need to count the number of occurrences of each individual word. If you read through each word of the file, you can accumulate a count of that word.

The algorithm would progress as follows: We open the file and loop over each word. As the code looks at each word, we keep track of separate counters of every word we have seen. When we look at the next word, if we haven't encountered that word before, we start a new counter for that word with a value of 1. If we have seen the word before, it must already have a counter, so we increase that counter by 1. The algorithm can be described by the following pseudocode:

```
word_counts = Empty dictionary.
For each word in the file:
    If I have never seen this word before:
        Store a count of 1 for this word in the dictionary.
    Otherwise, if I have seen this word before:
        Increase this word's count by 1 in the dictionary.
```

The idea is that the dictionary can store (*word*, *count*) pairs where each key is a word from the file, and each value is the count of occurrences seen so far of that word.

```
to be or not to be that is the question
     ^

counts: {'to': 1}
```

As the loop examines each word, that word is placed into a dictionary pair with a count of 1:

```
to be or not to be that is the question
                ^

counts: {'to': 1, 'be': 1, 'or': 1, 'not': 1}
```

When the code reaches a word that has been seen previously, it increments that word's counter by 1.

```
to be or not to be that is the question
                   ^

counts: {'to': 2, 'be': 2, 'or': 1, 'not': 1}
```

Recall that when you store a key/value pair in a dictionary that already contains that key, the old pair is replaced. For example, if the pair (`"ocean"`, `25`) was present and we put in a new pair (`"ocean"`, `26`), the old pair would be replaced. After the program is done reading the file, we can print each word that occurs more than 2000 times.

   The following is the complete program. We have introduced a function that improves the structure of the program and a constant to store the minimum number of occurrences required to be considered among the most frequent words. We also convert the entire file text to lowercase as we read it in to make the program case insensitive. The program produces the following output for *Moby-Dick*:

```
 1   # Uses a dictionary to implement a word count,
 2   # so that the user can see which words
 3   # occur the most in the book Moby-Dick.
 4
 5   # minimum number of occurrences needed to be printed
 6   OCCURRENCES = 2000
 7
 8   def intro():
 9       print("This program displays the most")
10       print("frequently occurring words from")
11       print("the book Moby Dick.")
```

Continued on next page

Continued from previous page

```
12      print()
13
14  # Reads book and returns a dictionary of (word, count) pairs.
15  def count_all_words(file):
16      # read the book into a dictionary
17      word_counts = {}
18      for word in file.read().lower().split():
19          if word in word_counts:
20              word_counts[word] += 1    # seen before
21          else:
22              word_counts[word] = 1     # never seen before
23      return word_counts
24
25  # Displays top words that occur in the dictionary
26  # at least OCCURRENCES number of times.
27  def print_results(word_counts):
28      for word, count in word_counts.items():
29          if count > OCCURRENCES:
30              print(word, "occurs", count, "times.")
31
32  def main():
33      intro()
34      with open("mobydick.txt") as file:
35          word_counts = count_all_words(file)
36          print_results(word_counts)
37
38  main()
```

```
This program displays the most
frequently occurring words from
the book Moby Dick.

to occurs 4448 times.
a occurs 4571 times.
that occurs 2729 times.
of occurs 6408 times.
the occurs 14092 times.
in occurs 3992 times.
and occurs 6182 times.
his occurs 2459 times.
```

Chapter 8 Dictionaries and Sets

If you want to shorten the code slightly for this algorithm, you can take advantage of the dictionary's `get` method. The `get` method returns the value associated with a given key, and you can pass a default value to return if the given key is not found in the dictionary. This allows us to get rid of the `if` statement that tests whether a given key is in the dictionary; if it isn't there, you can just supply a default value of 0:

```
# read the book into a dictionary (using get method)
word_counts = {}
for word in file.read().lower().split():
    word_counts[word] = word_counts.get(word, 0) + 1
```

Notice that the output shows the top words, but they are not displayed in any particular order. How would you print the words in a better ordering? One simple change would be to use the `sorted` function on the dictionary to display the top words in alphabetical order, but the user would probably prefer to see the words listed in decreasing order based on which ones occur the most frequently.

Printing the top most frequently occurring words is tricky due to the unpredictable ordering of dictionaries. As we have seen, dictionaries order their key/value pairs in a particular way that doesn't make it easy to sort the results. We can solve this problem by putting the key/value pairs into a list and then sorting that list. We'll write a function called `most_common_words` that accepts our dictionary as a parameter and returns a list of (count, word) tuples for all words that occur at least 2000 times.

```
# Returns a list of (count, word) tuples of all words in the
# given (word, count) dictionary that occur at least 2000 times.
def most_common_words(word_counts):
    most_common = []
    for (word, count) in word_counts.items():
        if count > OCCURRENCES:
            most_common.append((count, word))
    return most_common
```

If we produce the list of two-element tuples and sort it, it will sort based on ascending order of the first half of each tuple, breaking ties by the second half of each tuple. We want to sort by word count, so we should store the words in our list in (*count, word*) order. We sort the list by count in reverse order, which gives us the top elements in descending order. The following replacement for the `print_results` function from our previous program should do the trick:

```
# Displays top words that occur most in the dictionary.
def print_results(word_counts):
    wordlist = most_common_words(word_counts)
    wordlist.sort(reverse = True)
    for count, word in wordlist:
        print(word, "occurs", count, "times.")
```

```
the occurs 14092 times.
of occurs 6408 times.
and occurs 6182 times.
a occurs 4571 times.
to occurs 4448 times.
in occurs 3992 times.
that occurs 2729 times.
his occurs 2459 times.
```

Python includes a special variant of a dictionary called a `Counter`, found in the built-in `collections` module, that is tailor made for tallying problems. A `Counter` can be created from a list or sequence and will essentially provide the same functionality as our word count algorithm, making a dictionary of key/value pairs where each key is an element from the sequence and each value is the count of occurrences of that element in the sequence. The general syntax is the following:

```
from collections import Counter
...
name = Counter(sequence)
```
Syntax template: Creating a Counter

A `Counter` works beautifully for tallying words in a book like we did in the previous program. To use a `Counter` here, first create a list of exactly what it is you want to count. In our case, we want to count occurrences of the words from the file, case-insensitively. We can get a list of every word in the file in lowercase by writing `file.read().lower().split()`:

```
# list of all words in the file, in lowercase
words = file.read().lower().split()

# create a Counter to tally counts of all words
word_counts = Counter(words)
```

Once we have our `Counter` collection named `word_counts`, the rest of our program can use it in exactly the same way as a normal dictionary. The following program produces the same output as the previous word count program:

```
1  # Uses a Counter to implement a word count,
2  # so that the user can see which words
3  # occur the most in the book Moby-Dick.
4
5  from collections import Counter
6
```

Continued on next page

Continued from previous page

```
 7  # minimum number of occurrences needed to be printed
 8  OCCURRENCES = 2000
 9
10  def intro():
11      print("This program displays the most")
12      print("frequently occurring words from")
13      print("the book Moby Dick.")
14      print()
15
16  # Displays all words in the dictionary that occur
17  # at least OCCURRENCES number of times.
18  def print_results(word_counts):
19      for word, count in word_counts.items():
20          if count > OCCURRENCES:
21              print(word, "occurs", count, "times.")
22
23  def main():
24      intro()
25      with open("mobydick.txt") as file:
26          words = file.read().lower().split()
27          word_counts = Counter(words)
28          print_results(word_counts)
29
30  main()
```

The use of `Counter` in this case makes the code cleaner and simpler than a standard dictionary, but it is still important to understand the mechanics of using a dictionary for counting and tallying. Many programming languages do not include an equivalent of `Counter`, and `Counter` is not as versatile for all counting tasks as a normal dictionary.

Nested Collections

The basic collections like lists and dictionaries are powerful on their own, but you can solve even more interesting problems when you combine them. A collection can contain other collections; for example, you can make a list of lists, a set of dictionaries, a dictionary of (string, set) pairs, and so on. The nesting can be arbitrarily deep, such as a list of sets of dictionaries of lists of sets. (Phew!) A collection that contains other collections is called a *nested collection* or a *compound collection*.

> **Nested Collection (Compound Collection)**
>
> A collection that contains other collections inside it, such as a list of sets or a dictionary of lists.

There is no special Python syntax for nested collections. You just treat them the same as a collection of any other type of data. For example, the following Python Shell interaction creates a dictionary to represent "friend lists" like you might see on a social network. Each key is a person's name and each value is a list of that person's friends.

```
>>> # creating a nested collection
>>> buddies = {}
>>> buddies["Arya"] = ["Bran", "Catelyn"]
>>> buddies["Dany"] = ["Jorah", "Greyworm", "Missandei"]
>>> buddies["Stannis"] = ["Davos"]
>>> buddies["Theon"] = []
>>> buddies
{'Arya': ['Bran', 'Catelyn'], 'Stannis': ['Davos'],
 'Theon': [], 'Dany': ['Jorah', 'Greyworm', 'Missandei']}
>>> buddies["Dany"]
['Jorah', 'Greyworm', 'Missandei']
>>> buddies["Dany"][0]
'Jorah'
>>> len(buddies["Arya"])
2
>>> buddies["Dany"].append("Barristan")
>>> buddies["Dany"]
['Jorah', 'Greyworm', 'Missandei', 'Barristan']
```

Notice in the preceding interaction that each key is a string and each value is a list of strings. If you look up a value in the dictionary using its key, such as `buddies["Dany"]`, you'll get the entire list. If you want an individual element of that list, you can either store the list into a variable and index into it, or you can write a second set of `[ ]` square brackets, such as `buddies["Dany"][0]` to access the 0th element of Dany's friend list.

Our previous Python Shell code created each key/value pair separately, but you can initialize an entire nested collection all at once if you know its contents ahead of time:

```
>>> # creating a nested collection (quick initialization)
>>> buddies = {
...     "Arya"    : ["Bran", "Catelyn"],
...     "Dany"    : ["Jorah", "Greyworm", "Missandei"],
...     "Stannis" : ["Davos"],
...     "Theon"   : []
... }
...
>>> buddies
{'Arya': ['Bran', 'Catelyn'], 'Stannis': ['Davos'],
 'Theon': [], 'Dany': ['Jorah', 'Greyworm', 'Missandei']}
```

Let's look at another example involving a larger set of data. Consider the following file `thesaurus.txt` containing data from a thesaurus. The file contains lists of synonyms for many English words. The format of the file is that each record contains four lines: the first is the word itself, the second is its part of speech such as noun or adjective, the third line is a sequence of synonyms separated by | characters, and the fourth line is blank. The following is a subset of the data in this file:

```
abate
verb
slake|slack|decrease|lessen|minify|let up|slack off|diminish

abeyance
noun
suspension|inaction|inactivity|inactiveness

...
```

Suppose we want to write a program that prompts the user to type a word and then looks up a randomly chosen synonym for that word from the thesaurus data. The desired output is the following:

```
Word to look up (Enter to quit)? abate
A synonym for abate is decrease
```

The program should allow the user to look up as many words as desired. The file is very large, and it would be inefficient to search the whole file each time the user types a word. So we'll read the file into a collection for fast lookup. We don't want to have to loop over our collection to find the word typed by the user, so a list is a poor choice. A dictionary that uses words as keys is much better.

Since a dictionary stores key/value pairs, the value associated with each word key should be the synonyms of that word. There may be many synonyms for a given word, so a nested collection works well here. Our dictionary will store key/value pairs of the form (*word, list of synonyms of that word*).

The first major task in our code is to read the input file and store its data into our dictionary. We'll read all of the file's lines into a list and then loop over the indexes of that list in steps of 4. Within each group of 4 lines, the first (index `i`) is the word itself; the second (index `i+1`) is the part of speech, which we'll ignore in this program; and the third (index `i+2`) is the sequence of synonyms of that word. We'll split the third line to get a list of word strings and then store the (*word, synonyms*) pair into our dictionary.

```
# read thesaurus into a dictionary
thesaurus = {}
with open("thesaurus.txt") as file:
    lines = file.readlines()
    for i in range(0, len(lines) - 3, 4):
```

Continued on next page

Continued from previous page

```
        word = lines[i].strip()
        synonyms = lines[i + 2].strip().split("|")
        thesaurus[word] = synonyms
```

Once we've built the nested dictionary representing the thesaurus, we can prompt the user for words to look up. After the user types a word, we'll use that word as a key and pull out the word's associated value, which is a list of its synonyms. We want to print a random synonym to the user, and the random module's choice function is perfect for this task. The choice function accepts a list or sequence of values as a parameter and chooses and returns a single random value from that list.

```
word = input("Word to look up (Enter to quit)? ")
synonyms = thesaurus[word]         # a list of synonyms
syn = random.choice(synonyms)    # random element from that list
print("A synonym for", word, "is", syn)
```

The following is the complete program along with a sample log of execution. This final version is decomposed into functions and contains some code to make sure we don't try to look up words that don't exist in the dictionary.

```
 1   # This program reads an input file of thesaurus data
 2   # and allows the user to look up synonyms for words.
 3   # It stores words in a nested dictionary of lists,
 4   # where each key is a word and its value is a list
 5   # of synonyms of that word from the thesaurus file.
 6
 7   import random
 8
 9   # Reads the given input file and converts its data
10   # into a dictionary where each key is a word and each
11   # value is a list of synonyms for that word.
12   def read_thesaurus(filename):
13       thesaurus = {}
14       with open(filename) as file:
15           lines = file.readlines()
16           for i in range(0, len(lines) - 3, 4):
17               word = lines[i].strip()
18               synonyms = lines[i + 2].strip().split("|")
19               thesaurus[word] = synonyms
20       return thesaurus
21
22   # Looks up and prints a randomly chosen synonym
23   # for the given word in the given thesaurus.
24   # If the word is not found, prints an error message.
```

Continued on next page

Continued from previous page

```
25  def find_random_synonym(thesaurus, word):
26      if word in thesaurus:
27          synonyms = thesaurus[word]
28          syn = random.choice(synonyms)
29          print("A synonym for", word, "is", syn)
30      else:
31          print(word, "not found.")
32
33  def main():
34      # introduction
35      print("This program looks up random synonyms")
36      print("for you from a thesaurus.")
37      print()
38
39      # read thesaurus into a dictionary
40      thesaurus = read_thesaurus("thesaurus.txt")
41
42      # look up random synonyms
43      word = input("Word to look up (Enter to quit)? ")
44      while word != "":
45          find_random_synonym(thesaurus, word)
46          word = input("Word to look up (Enter to quit)? ")
47
48      print("Goodbye.")
49
50  main()
```

```
This program looks up random synonyms
for you from a thesaurus.

Word to look up (Enter to quit)? abate
A synonym for abate is decrease
Word to look up (Enter to quit)? alloy
A synonym for alloy is fuse
Word to look up (Enter to quit)? vivacious
A synonym for vivacious is spirited
Word to look up (Enter to quit)? prevaricate
A synonym for prevaricate is misinform
Word to look up (Enter to quit)?
Goodbye.
```

Dictionary Comprehensions

In the previous chapter we introduced list comprehensions for producing variations of an existing list. Python has a similar construct called a *dictionary comprehension* that is the equivalent for dictionaries. A dictionary comprehension specifies a key/value pattern and applies that pattern to every pair in an existing dictionary to produce a new dictionary.

> **Dictionary Comprehension**
>
> An expression that specifies a new dictionary and its elements based on an existing dictionary or other sequence of values.

The general syntax for a dictionary comprehension is the following:

```
{key: value for pattern in sequence}
```
Syntax template: Dictionary comprehension

Dictionary comprehensions have a flexible syntax that allows their data to come from a variety of sources. For example, the following interaction creates a dictionary where the keys are integers and the values are the squares of those integers. You could use this dictionary to look up the square of some integer *k* by asking for `squares[k]`:

```
>>> # dictionary comprehension based on a range of integers
>>> squares = {x: x*x for x in range(1, 7)}
>>> squares
{1: 1, 2: 4, 3: 9, 4: 16, 5: 25, 6: 36, 7: 49}
>>> squares[5]
25
```

The following interaction creates a dictionary where the keys are words in a string, and the values are the lengths of those words:

```
>>> # dictionary comprehension of words in a string
>>> text = "four score and 7 years"
>>> lengths = {s: len(s) for s in text.split()}
>>> lengths
{'four': 4, 'and': 3, '7': 1, 'years': 5, 'score': 5}
>>> lengths["and"]
3
```

You can make a dictionary comprehension that is based on an existing dictionary. As an example, let's revisit our phone book dictionary from the last section. If you have looked up numbers in a phone book or contact list, you have probably wished the book also went in the other direction: What is the name of the person calling me from phone number (555)123-4567? Unfortunately, most phone books don't work that way; they look up a phone number if you know a person's name, but not the other way around. A dictionary has the same limitation; it helps you find the value for a given key, but it doesn't easily reveal the key for a given value.

But you can create a reversed version of the phone book using a dictionary comprehension. The expression we'll use for the new dictionary is to make each value a key and vice versa. This is sometimes called *inverting* the dictionary. The following Python Shell interaction demonstrates this idea using our previous phone book dictionary:

```
>>> # inverting a dictionary using a dictionary comprehension
>>> phonebook = {"Allison": "(520)555-6789",
                 "Marty": "(650)555-1234",
                 "Stuart": "(206)555-6543"}
>>> reversebook = {v: k for k, v in phonebook.items()}
>>> reversebook
{'(206)555-6543': 'Stuart', '(520)555-6789': 'Allison',
 '(650)555-1234': 'Marty'}
```

Inverting a dictionary is not always simple. Recall that a dictionary cannot store two pairs with the same key, but it is allowed to have two keys that both pair with the same value. If you try to invert a dictionary with any duplicate values, those values will collide when trying to become keys, and only one of them will survive into the resulting dictionary. The following phone book with duplicates will lose one of its entries. Notice that the original entry for "Marty" is lost because it overlaps with the value for "Yana":

```
>>> # inverting a dictionary with duplicates
>>> phonebook = {"Allison": "(520)555-6789",
                 "Marty": "(650)555-1234",
                 "Stuart": "(206)555-6543",
                 "Yana": "(650)555-1234"}
>>> reversebook = {v: k for k, v in phonebook.items()}
>>> reversebook
{'(206)555-6543': 'Stuart', '(520)555-6789': 'Allison',
 '(650)555-1234': 'Yana'}
```

One workaround for this problem would be to create a nested collection where each phone number pairs with a list or set of names of people who have that number.

8.3 Sets

A major limitation of lists is that searching them takes a long time. Generally, if you want to search a list, you have to look at each element sequentially to see whether you've found the target. This can take a long time for a large list. (In Chapter 10 we will talk more about searching lists.)

Another limitation of lists is that it's not easy to prevent a list from storing duplicate values. In many cases this isn't a problem, but if, for example, you are storing a collection to count the number of unique words in a book, you don't want any duplicates to exist. To prevent duplicates in a list, you have to search the list sequentially every time you add to it.

When you want to maintain a collection of elements that can be searched quickly and that prevents duplicates, you're better off using another collection type called a *set*.

> **Set**
>
> A searchable collection that cannot contain duplicates.

The set collection is very much like the mathematical notion of a set. Sets do not support all the operations you can perform on lists (namely, any operation that requires an index), but they do offer the benefits of fast searching and effortless elimination of duplicates. The core operations of a set are adding, removing, and testing for membership. A proper set is generally expected to provide efficient implementations of those three operations.

Set Basics

Python contains a built-in collection called `set` to represent sets. You can create an empty set using the `set()` function. The general syntax is the following:

```
name = set()
```
Syntax template: Defining an empty set

You can also create a set with an initial sequence of elements inside it. The syntax for doing this is to write the elements inside { } braces. This is very similar to the syntax for creating a dictionary, except that you do not write colons or key/value pairs, only single elements.

```
name = {expression, expression, ..., expression}
```
Syntax template: Defining a set with initial elements

Note that you cannot use the { } syntax to create an empty set, because Python thinks {} is an empty dictionary instead.

If you wanted to store a set of names, you could write code like the following. After the code executes, the set will contain only four elements, because "Moe" will be placed into the set only once:

```
>>> # interacting with a set
>>> stooges = {"Larry", "Moe", "Curly"}
>>> stooges
{'Curly', 'Moe', 'Larry'}
>>> stooges.add("Shemp")          # add an element
>>> stooges
{'Shemp', 'Curly', 'Moe', 'Larry'}
>>> stooges.add("Moe")            # duplicate; won't be added
>>> stooges
{'Shemp', 'Larry', 'Moe', 'Curly'}
>>> stooges.remove("Curly")       # remove an element
>>> stooges
{'Shemp', 'Moe', 'Larry'}
```

You can also create a new set by calling the set function and passing a list, set, or other sequence of values. The set created will have the same elements as the sequence you pass it but without any duplicates. If you pass a string, the set stores the unique characters in that string.

```
>>> # creating sets from lists and strings
>>> word_list = ["to", "be", "or", "not", "to", "be"]
>>> word_set = set(word_list)
>>> word_set
{'or', 'not', 'to', 'be'}
>>> letters = set("mississippi")
>>> letters
{'i', 'm', 'p', 's'}
```

You can test whether a given value is present in a set using the in keyword.

```
>>> # testing for membership in a set
>>> stooges = {"Larry", "Moe", "Curly"}
>>> "Moe" in stooges
True
>>> "Donald" in stooges
False
>>> if "Curly" in stooges:
...     print("Woop woop woop!")
...
Woop woop woop!
```

The usual `len` function returns the number of elements in a set:

```
>>> # interacting with a set
>>> stooges = {"Larry", "Moe", "Curly"}
>>> len(stooges)
3
```

At first glance a set may not seem much different from a list. You can perform all operations of a set using a list; to avoid duplicates in a list, you'd need to add an `if` statement checking whether a value is in the list before adding it. One of the main benefits of the set is that it handles this for you to make sure that there is no possible way for a duplicate value to slip in. The other main reason to use a set is that it performs its core operations of adding, removing, and searching for elements more efficiently than a list, so you can create a very large set and search it many times without experiencing poor performance.

Sets allow you to examine lots of data while ignoring duplicates. For example, if you wanted to see how many unique words appear in the book *Moby-Dick*, you could write code such as the following. This code produces the following output when run on the text of *Moby-Dick* (available from gutenberg.org):

```
 1  # Uses a set to count words in Moby-Dick.
 2
 3  def main():
 4      words = set()
 5      with open("mobydick.txt") as file:
 6          for word in file.read().lower().split():
 7              words.add(word)
 8      print("Unique words =", len(words))
 9
10  main()
```

```
Unique words = 30368
```

The preceding code can be made even shorter if you use the set's `update` method, which accepts a sequence as a parameter and adds all elements from that sequence to the set, avoiding duplicates. The `for` loop in the preceding code can be replaced by the single line:

```
words.update(file.read().lower().split())
```

One drawback of a set is that it doesn't store elements by indexes. The following loop raises an error on a set, because it doesn't support [ ] integer indexing. It is also missing any methods you might expect from lists that involve indexes. The following code won't work with a set:

```
# does not work; sets do not use integer indexes
stooges = {"Larry", "Moe", "Curly"}
for i in range(len(stooges)):
    print(stooges[i])    # error!
```

Instead, you can examine the elements directly using a `for` loop over the set itself:

```
# this code does work
stooges = {"Larry", "Moe", "Curly", "Shemp"}
for name in stooges:
    print(name)
```

```
Curly
Shemp
Larry
Moe
```

Notice that the elements of the set in our previous example did not print in the order they were written when the set was defined. Like dictionaries, sets store their elements with an unpredictable ordering. This is because sets are implemented using a similar internal structure to dictionaries.

When working with dictionaries, we introduced the `OrderedDict` to represent a dictionary that remembers the order of insertion of its elements. Python does not provide a corresponding `OrderedSet` in its built-in libraries. There are some third-party libraries for ordered sets, but we will not discuss them in this textbook. If you need a collection of individual elements stored in a specific order, you may want a list rather than a set. If you must loop over a set's elements in order, you can call the `sorted` function on the set:

```
# loop over set in sorted order
stooges = {"Larry", "Moe", "Curly", "Shemp"}
for name in sorted(stooges):
    print(name)
```

```
Curly
Larry
Moe
Shemp
```

Set Operations

In this section we'll explore the operations supported by sets in more detail. Sets provide several useful methods and operations. Table 8.2 lists many of the most common ones.

We have already discussed some of the operations such as add and in. Some of the others are similar to the operations you can perform on lists, such as clear and remove. The most interesting functionality we will discuss are the classic *set operations* such as union and intersection. You can use set operations in a variety of programming situations. For example, a school registration system can use set operations to see which students are in common between two courses. A writing analysis program can use set operations to count unique letters used between several strings or unique words

Table 8.2 Set Operations

Operation	Description
value in set	returns True if the given value is found in the set
value not in set	returns True if the given value is not found
len(set)	number of elements in the set
str(set)	returns string representation such as "{'a', 'b', 'c'}"
set.add(value)	adds the given value to the set, if not already present
set.clear()	removes all elements
set.isdisjoint(set2)	returns True if there are no elements in common between set and set2
set.pop()	removes and returns one element from the set
set.remove(value)	removes the given value from the set, if present
set.update(sequence)	adds all values from the sequence to the set, if not already present
set | set2 or set.union(set2)	returns a new set containing all elements present in set or set2 or both
set & set2 or set.intersection(set2)	returns a new set containing all elements that are present in both set or set2
set - set2 or set.difference(set2)	returns a new set containing all elements that are present in set but not in set2
set ^ set2 or set.symmetric_difference(set2)	returns a new set containing all elements that are present in set or set2 but not both
set < set2	returns True if all elements from set are also present in set2 and set is smaller in size than set2
set <= set2 or set.issubset(set2)	returns True if all elements from set are also present in set2
set > set2	returns True if all elements from set2 are also present in set and set is larger in size than set2
set >= set2 or set.issuperset(set2)	returns True if all elements from set2 are also present in set

appearing in a document. A card or dice game program can use set operations to track the categories of cards in play for scoring. And so on.

As a basic example, consider the task of figuring out how many unique elements appear in two given sets. You cannot just add the sets' sizes, since they might have some elements in common that should not be counted twice in your total. Instead, you could count all elements from the first set and then count only the unique elements of the second, by checking to see whether each element from the second is also in the first:

```python
# Returns the number of unique elements contained
# in either set1 or set2. Not a good model to follow.
def total_elements(set1, set2):
    count = len(set1)
    for element in set2:
        if element not in set:
            count += 1
    return count
```

However, a more elegant way to perform this calculation is to compute a *union* between the sets. The union of two sets A and B is the set of all elements contained in either A, B, or both. Union is an example of a set operation. Other examples of set operations are intersection (the set of all elements that are in both A and B) and difference (the set of all elements that are in A but not in B). In Python, set operations do not modify the sets but instead produce and return a new set as their result. The `total_elements` function can be rewritten more elegantly using the `union` method on the two sets:

```python
# Returns the number of unique elements contained
# in either set1 or set2.
def total_elements(set1, set2):
    return len(set1.union(set2))
```

Set operations are often depicted by drawings called Venn diagrams, which depict sets as circles and set operations as shaded overlapping between the circles. Figure 8.3 shows some examples.

The set operations are used so frequently that Python also lets you call them using operators such as | for `union` and & for `intersection`. The following interaction in the Python Shell demonstrates the results of calling the various set operators:

```python
>>> # set operators
>>> s1 = {1, 2, 5, 7, 9}
>>> s2 = {1, 4, 9, 16}
>>> s3 = {1, 5, 9}
```

Continued on next page

Continued from previous page

```
>>> s4 = {1, 3, 4, 9, 16, 22}
>>> s1 | s2                      # union
{1, 2, 4, 5, 7, 9, 16}
>>> s1 & s2                      # intersection
{1, 9}
>>> s1 - s2                      # difference
{2, 5, 7}
>>> s1 ^ s2                      # symmetric difference
{2, 4, 5, 7, 16}
>>> s3 <= s1                     # subset
True
>>> s4 >= s2                     # superset
True
```

Set Efficiency

One of the most important benefits of using a set is that it can be searched incredibly quickly. While we won't go into a detailed discussion of algorithms and efficiency here; Chapter 10 discusses program efficiency and runtime in more detail. But we do want to highlight the noticeable improvements that can be made in the runtime of even a simple program by using a set instead of a list.

Whenever you check whether an element is present in a list using the `in` keyword, it must examine every element of the list in order until it finds the target value. This can take a long time if your list is very large. But a set is implemented in a clever way internally that is optimized for fast searching. The internals of a set use a special data structure called a hash table that places elements into specific positions so that they are easy for the set to look up later. This means that the `in` keyword with a set does

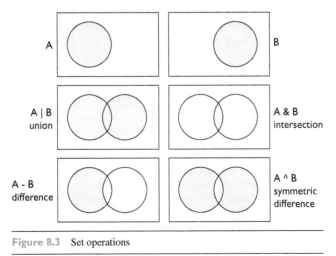

Figure 8.3   Set operations

not need to examine every element. You don't need to understand the details of a set's implementation to use it; the bottom line is that you can add, remove, and search for elements in a set much more quickly than you can with a list.

In a previous section we showed a short piece of code that read the contents of a text file representing a book such as *Moby-Dick* into a set to count the number of unique words in the file. You could write the same code with a list almost as easily, but it would be much slower. Each time the program reads a word from the file, it must examine the entire list of existing words to see whether the new word is present or not. The cost of these traversals and examinations adds up when processing such a large file.

We can measure the runtime of a given piece of Python code using the built-in `time` module. To measure code's runtime in seconds, import the `time` module and then call its `clock` function, which returns a `float` representing a time stamp in seconds. A single time stamp is not very useful by itself, but you can ask for a time stamp both before and after running a given piece of code and then compare their values to see how much time elapsed while the code was running. The general syntax for timing code is the following:

```
import time
...


start = time.clock()


statement
statement
...
statement


end = time.clock()
```
Syntax template: Measuring code runtime in seconds

The following demonstration measures the runtime of counting unique words in *Moby-Dick* using a list and a set. The results are staggering: the list-based program requires over 20 seconds to run on the author's laptop, while the set-based program processes the entire file in under a tenth of one second! The larger the file, the wider the gap in runtimes between these two programs. This example serves as an illustration of the importance of choosing the right collection to solve a given problem.

```
1   # Uses a list to count words in Moby-Dick,
2   # and measures/prints the code's runtime.
3   import time
4
5   def main():
6       # count the unique words in the file
7       start = time.clock()
```

Continued on next page

Continued from previous page

```
8          words = []
9          with open("mobydick.txt") as file:
10             for word in file.read().lower().split():
11                 if word not in words:
12                     words.append(word)
13         end = time.clock()
14
15         # report results
16         print("Unique words =", len(words))
17         print("Runtime:", round(end - start, 2), "sec")
18
19  main()
```

```
Unique words = 30368
Runtime: 20.94 sec
```

```
1   # Uses a set to count words in Moby-Dick,
2   # and measures/prints the code's runtime.
3   import time
4
5   def main():
6       # count the unique words in the file
7       start = time.clock()
8       words = set()
9       with open("mobydick.txt") as file:
10          for word in file.read().lower().split():
11              words.add(word)
12
13      end = time.clock()
14
15      # report results
16      print("Unique words =", len(words))
17      print("Runtime:", round(end - start, 2), "sec")
18
19  main()
```

```
Unique words = 30368
Runtime: 0.08 sec
```

A deeper understanding of program efficiency, along with an ability to analyze a given program or algorithm and reason about its runtime, are crucial skills for a software developer. We will explore algorithm efficiency in more detail in Chapter 10.

Set Example: Lottery

Consider the task of writing a program to play a fake lottery game. The program should randomly generate a winning lottery ticket with six numbers, then prompt the player to enter lotto numbers. Depending on how many numbers match, the player wins various amounts of money.

Sets make excellent collections for storing the winning lotto numbers and the player's numbers. They prevent duplicates, and they allow us to efficiently test whether a number in one set exists in the other. These features will help us to count the number of winning numbers the player has entered.

The following code initializes a set of six randomly chosen winning lottery numbers between 1 and 40. You might think that the code could use a `for` loop that repeats six times to create the winning lottery numbers, but there is a strong possibility that at least one of the six random numbers generated will be a duplicate. So instead the code uses a `while` loop that generates random integers and adds them to the set until its size becomes 6:

```
# generate a set of 6 winning lottery numbers
winning = set()
while len(winning) < 6:
    num = random.randint(1, 40)
    winning.add(num)
```

Next we'll read the player's lottery numbers into a second set. Similarly, to the code to generate the winning lottery ticket, we will continue to re-prompt the user for numbers until they have typed six unique integers:

```
# read the player's lottery ticket from the console
ticket = set()
while len(ticket) < 6:
    num = int(input("next number? "))
    ticket.add(num)
```

To figure out how many lottery numbers the player has chosen correctly, we could search the winning number set to see whether it contains each number from the ticket. However, a more elegant way to perform this test is to determine the intersection between the winning numbers set and the player's ticket set. The following code creates the intersection of the player's ticket and the winning numbers by copying the ticket and then removing any elements from it that aren't winning numbers:

```
# find the winning numbers from the user's ticket
matches = ticket.intersect(winning)
```

The length of the intersection indicates how many of the player's numbers were winning numbers; we can then calculate the appropriate cash prize amount for the player on the basis of that number. (Our version starts with a $100 prize and doubles that figure for each winning number.)

Here is a complete implementation of the lottery program along with one example output from running the program. We've created a few functions for structure and added a few constants to represent the number of numbers, maximum number, and lotto prize amounts.

```
1   # Plays a lottery game with the user, reading
2   # the user's numbers and printing how many matched.
3
4   import random
5
6   NUMBERS = 6
7   MAX_NUMBER = 40
8   PRIZE = 100
9
10  # Generates a set of the winning lotto numbers,
11  # which is returned as a set.
12  def create_winning_numbers():
13      winning = set()
14      while len(winning) < NUMBERS:
15          num = random.randint(1, MAX_NUMBER)
16          winning.add(num)
17      return winning
18
19  # Reads the player's lottery ticket from the console,
20  # which is returned as a set.
21  def read_ticket():
22      ticket = set()
23      print("Type your", NUMBERS, "lotto numbers: ")
24      while len(ticket) < NUMBERS:
25          num = int(input("next number? "))
26          ticket.add(num)
27      print()
28      return ticket
29
30  def main():
31      # get winning number and ticket sets
32      winning = create_winning_numbers()
33      ticket = read_ticket()
34
35      # print results
36      print("Your ticket was:", ticket)
37      print("Winning numbers:", winning)
```

Continued on next page

Continued from previous page

```
38
39      # keep only winning numbers from ticket (intersect)
40      matches = ticket.intersect(winning)
41      if len(matches) > 0:
42          prize = 100 * 2 ** len(matches)
43          print("Matched numbers:", matches)
44          print("Your prize is $", prize)
45
46  main()
```

```
Type your 6 lotto numbers:
next number? 2
next number? 8
next number? 15
next number? 18
next number? 21
next number? 32

Your ticket was: {32, 2, 8, 15, 18, 21}
Winning numbers: {1, 3, 39, 15, 16, 18}
Matched numbers: {18, 15}
Your prize is $ 400
```

If you want to display the lottery tickets and winning numbers in ascending order, you can pass each set to the `sorted` function before you print it:

```
print("Your ticket was:", sorted(ticket))
print("Winning numbers:", sorted(winning))
print("Matched numbers:", sorted(matches))
```

```
Your ticket was: {2, 8, 15, 18, 21, 32}
Winning numbers: {1, 3, 15, 16, 18, 39}
Matched numbers: {15, 18}
```

Chapter Summary

- A collection is an object that stores a group of other objects. Examples of collections are the list, dictionary, and set. Collections are used to structure, organize, and search data.

- A dictionary (dict) is a collection that stores pairs, with each pair containing a key and a value. Dictionaries are used to create associations between pieces of data, such as a person's name and phone number.

- A dictionary stores its pairs in an unpredictable order. The OrderedDict stores its pairs in the order that you add them, but its performance is slightly slower.

- Collections can be nested, storing one collection inside another. For example, you can create a dictionary where each key is a name and each value is a list of that person's friends.

- A set (set) is a collection that does not allow duplicates. Sets can be searched efficiently to see whether they contain a particular element value.

- Sets support many common operations such as union, intersection, and difference.

Self-Check Problems

Section 8.1: Dictionary Basics

1. A dictionary doesn't have the same methods that a list has. How do you examine every key and every value of a dictionary? How do you check whether a given key is found in a dictionary?

2. What happens if you try to add a key/value pair to a dictionary and it already has a pair with that same key? What happens if it already has a pair with the same value, but not with the same key?

3. The key/value pairs in a dictionary are stored in an unpredictable order. How can you loop over the pairs in sorted order by the ordering of the keys?

4. Write the code to declare a dictionary that associates people's names with their ages. Add mappings for your own name and age, as well as those of a few friends or relatives.

5. What keys and values are contained in the following dictionary after this code executes?

```
people = {}
people[7] = "Marty"
people[34] = "Louann"
people[27] = "Donald"
people[15] = "Moshe"
people[84] = "Larry"
people[7] = "Ed"
people[2350] = "Orlando"
del people[7]
people[5] = "Moshe"
del people[84]
people[17] = "Steve"
```

6. What keys and values are contained in the following map after this code executes?

```
number_words = {}
number_words[8] = "Eight"
number_words[41] = "FortyOne"
number_words[8] = "Ocho"
number_words[18] = "Eighteen"
number_words[50] = "Fifty"
number_words[132] = "OneThreeTwo"
number_words[28] = "TwentyEight"
number_words[79] = "SeventyNine"
del number_words[41]
del number_words[28]
if "Eight" in number_words:
    del number_words["Eight"]
number_words[50] = "FortyOne"
number_words[28] = "18"
del number_words[18]
```

7. Write the output produced when the following function is passed each of the following dictionaries:

```
def mystery(dictionary):
    result = {}
    for key in dictionary:
        if key < dictionary[key]:
            result[key] = dictionary[key]
        else:
            result[dictionary[key]] = key
    print(result)
```

a. {"two": "deux", "five": "cinq", "one": "un",
   "three": "trois", "four": "quatre"}

b. {"skate": "board", "drive": "car",
   "program": "computer", "play": "computer"}

c. {"siskel": "ebert", "girl": "boy", "H": "T",
   "ready": "begin", "first": "last", "begin": "end"}

d. {"cotton": "shirt", "tree": "violin", "seed": "tree",
   "light": "tree", "rain": "cotton"}

8. Write the dictionary returned when the following function is passed the following dictionaries:

```
def mystery(dict1, dict2):
    result = {}
    for s in dict1:
        if dict1[s] in dict2:
            result[s] = dict2[dict1[s]]
    return result
```

a. dict1 = {"bar": 1, "baz": 2, "foo": 3, "mumble": 4}
   dict2 = {1: "earth", 2: "wind", 3: "air", 4: "fire"}
b. dict1 = {"five": 105, "four": 104, "one": 101, "six": 106,
            "three": 103, "two": 102}
   dict2 = {99: "uno", 101: "dos", 103: "tres", 105: "cuatro"}
c. dict1 = {"a": 42, "b": 9, "c": 7, "d": 15,
            "e": 11, "f": 24, "g": 7}
   dict2 = {1: "four", 3: "score", 5: "and",
            7: "seven", 9: "years", 11: "ago"}

Section 8.2: Advanced Dictionary Usage

9. Write the dictionary returned when the following function is passed the following lists of numbers:

```python
def mystery(numbers):
    data = {}
    for el in numbers:
        if el in data:
            data[el].append(1)
        else:
            data[el] = []
    return data
```

a. [1, 2, 34, 3, 4, 1, 2, 4, 2, 14]
b. [1, 1, 1, 2, 2, 2, 1, 4, 4, 4]
c. [45, 43, 44, 54, 45, 45, 54, 43]

10. Write the dictionary returned when the following function is passed the following dictionaries:

```python
def mystery(dictionary):
    data = {}
    for (key, value) in dictionary.items():
        if value not in data:
            data[value] = set()
        data[value].add(key)
    return data
```

a. {"hello": 4, "world", 4, "and": 3}
b. {"banana": 1, "peach": 2, "nectarine": 3, "kiwi": 1, "apple": 3}
c. {"the": "and", "and": "the", "is": "the",
     "has": "the", "and": "and"}

11. Assume that there is a preexisting Python file object named `file`. Write code that reads this text file and produces a dictionary of counters based on what letter each word in the file starts with from A to Z, case-insensitively. For example, if the file contains the text `"to be or not to be"`, your dictionary would store `{"b": 2, "n": 1, "o": 1, "t": 2}`. You may assume that every word token in the file begins with a letter from A to Z in upper- or lowercase.

12. Given the following list and dictionary, write list or dictionary comprehensions that would produce the following new collections:

```
# index      0      1      2      3
words = ["apple", "ball", "car", "dog"]
synonyms = {"hirsute" : "hairy",
            "erudite" : "learned",
            "abattoir": "slaughterhouse",
            "kwyjibo" : "ape"}
```

a. {"a": "apple", "b": "ball", "c": "car", "d": "dog"}

b. {"hairy": "hirsute", "learned": "erudite",
   "slaughterhouse": "abattoir", "ape": "kwyjibo"}

c. ["hirsute means hairy", "erudite means learned",
   "abattoir means slaughterhouse", "kwyjiby means ape"]

Section 8.3: Sets

13. A list has every function that a set has, and more. So why would you use a set rather than a list?

14. A set doesn't have the indexes that a list has. How do you examine every element of a set?

15. How do you check whether a set contains a given value? What happens if you try to add a value to a set but that value is already present in the set?

16. What elements are contained in the following set after this code executes?

```
data = set()
data.add(74)
data.add(12)
data.add(18274)
data.add(9074)
data.add(43)
data.remove(74)
data.remove(43)
data.add(32)
data.add(18212)
data.add(9)
data.add(29999)
```

17. What elements are contained in the following set after this code executes?

```
set = set()
set.add(4)
set.add(15)
set.add(73)
set.add(84)
set.add(247)
set.remove(15)
set.add(42)
```

Continued on next page

Continued from previous page

```
set.add(12)
set.remove(73)
set.add(94)
set.add(11)
```

18. How do you merge the contents of two sets? How do you find out what elements are commonly stored between two sets? Give an answer that doesn't require any loops.

19. Suppose you have sets stored as variables named `people`, `male`, `female`, `young`, `old`, `silly`, and `hungry`. Each set contains strings representing people with that quality: the `people` set includes everyone; the `male` set includes all men; etc. Now suppose you want to find all of the men who are not hungry and are old or poor or both. How would you use set operators to find that exact set of people?

20. Write the output produced when the following function is passed each of the following lists of names:

```
def mystery(names):
    result = set()
    for element in names:
        if element < names[0]:
            result.add(element)
        else:
            result.clear()
    print(result)
```

a. `["marty", "stuart", "helene", "jessica", "amanda"]`
   `["sara", "allison", "janette", "zack", "riley"]`

b. `["zorah", "alex", "tyler", "roy", "roy",`
   `"charlie", "phil", "charlie", "tyler"]`

Exercises

1. Write a function `is_unique` that accepts a dictionary whose keys and values are strings as a parameter and returns `True` if no two keys map to the same value (and `False` if any two or more keys do map to the same value). For example, if the dictionary contains the following key/value pairs, your function would return `True`:

```
{"Marty": "Stepp", "Stuart": "Reges", "Jessica": "Wolk",
 "Allison": "Obourn", "Hal": "Perkins"}
```

But calling your function on the following dictionary would return `False`, because of two mappings for Perkins and Reges:

```
{"Kendrick": "Perkins", "Stuart": "Reges", "Jessica": "Wolk",
 "Bruce": "Reges", "Hal": "Perkins"}
```

2. Write a function `intersect` that accepts two dictionaries whose keys are strings and whose values are integers as parameters and returns a new dictionary containing only the key/value pairs that exist in both of the parameter dictionaries. In order for a key/value pair to be included in your result, not only do both dictionaries need to contain a mapping for that key, but they need to map it to the same value. For example, if the two dictionaries passed are:

```
{"Janet": 87, "Logan": 62, "Whitaker": 46, "Alyssa": 100,
 "Stef": 80, "Jeff": 88, "Kim": 52, "Sylvia": 95}
{"Logan": 62, "Kim": 52, "Whitaker": 52, "Jeff": 88,
 "Stef": 80, "Brian": 60, "Lisa": 83, "Sylvia": 87}
```

your function would return the following new dictionary (the order of the key/value pairs does not matter):

```
{"Logan": 62, "Stef": 80, "Jeff": 88, "Kim": 52}
```

3. Write a function `max_occurrences` that accepts a list of integers as a parameter and returns the number of times the most frequently occurring integer (the "mode") occurs in the list. Solve this problem using a dictionary as auxiliary storage. If the list is empty, return 0.

4. Write a function called `is_1_to_1` that accepts a dictionary whose keys and values are strings as its parameter and returns `True` if no two keys map to the same value. For example, for the following dictionary your function should return `False` because both `"Hawking"` and `"Newton"` map to the same value:

```
{"Marty": "206-9024", "Hawking": "123-4567",
 "Smith": "949-0504", "Newton": "123-4567"}
```

but for the following dictionary your function should return `True` because each key maps to a unique value:

```
{"Marty": "206-9024", "Hawking": "555-1234",
 "Smith": "949-0504", "Newton": "123-4567"}
```

The empty dictionary is considered 1-to-1 and returns `True`.

5. Write a function called `reverse` that accepts a dictionary from strings to strings as a parameter and returns a new dictionary that is the reverse of the original. The reverse of a dictionary is a new dictionary that uses the values from the original as its keys and the keys from the original as its values. Since a dictionary's values need not be unique but its keys must be, you should have each value map to a set of keys. For example, if passed the following dictionary:

```
{42: "Marty", 81: "Sue", 17: "Ed", 31: "Dave",
 56: "Ed", 3: "Marty", 29: "Ed"}
```

You should reverse it to become (the order of the keys and values does not matter):

```
{"Marty": [42, 3], "Sue": [81], "Ed": [17, 56, 29], "Dave": [31]}
```

6. Write a function called `rarest` that accepts a dictionary whose keys are strings and whose values are integers as a parameter and returns the integer value that occurs the fewest times in the dictionary. If there is a tie, return the smaller integer value.

7. Write a function called `max_length` that accepts a set of strings as a parameter and that returns the length of the longest string in the set. If your function is passed an empty set, it should return 0.

8. Write a function called `has_odd` that accepts a set of integers as a parameter and returns `True` if the set contains at least one odd integer and `False` otherwise. If passed the empty set, your function should return `False`.

9. Write a function called `symmetric_set_difference` that accepts two sets as parameters and returns a new set containing their symmetric set difference (that is, the set of elements contained in either of the two sets but not in both). For example, the symmetric difference between the sets {1, 4, 7, 9} and {2, 4, 5, 6, 7} is {1, 2, 5, 6, 9}. Do not call the set's `symmetric_difference` method in your solution.

Programming Projects

1. Write a program that solves the classic "random writer" problem. This problem deals with reading input files of text and examining the frequencies of characters. On the basis of those frequencies, you can generate randomized output that appears to match the writing style of the original document. The longer the chains you link together, the more accurate the random text will sound. For example, level 4 random text (text with chains of 4 letters long) generated from Tom Sawyer might look like this:

"en themself, Mr. Welshman, but him awoke, the balmy shore. I'll give him that he couple overy because in the slated snufflindeed structure's kind was rath. She said that the wound the door a fever eyes that WITH him."

Level 10 random text from the same source might look like this:

"you understanding that they don't come around in the cave should get the word beauteous was over-fondled, and that together and decided that he might as we used to do--it's nobby fun. I'll learn you."

Search the Internet for "Random Writer" to learn more about this problem, such as the specification posed by computer scientist Joseph Zachary.

2. Write a program that computes the edit distance (also called the Levenshtein distance, for its creator Vladimir Levenshtein) between two words. The edit distance between two strings is the minimum number of operations that are needed to transform one string into the other. For this program, an operation is a substitution of a single character, such as from "brisk" to "brick". The edit distance between the words "dog" and "cat" is 3, following the chain of "dot", "cot", and "cat" to transform "dog" into "cat". When you compute the edit distance between two words, each intermediate word must be an actual valid word. Edit distances are useful in applications that need to determine how similar two strings are, such as spelling checkers.

Read your input from a text file full of words. From this file, build a dictionary that connects every word to its immediate neighbors; that is, the words that have an edit distance of 1 from it. Once this dictionary is built, you can walk it to find paths from one word to another. A good way to process paths to walk the neighbors is to use a list or set of words to visit, starting with the beginning word, such as "dog". Your algorithm should repeatedly remove the front word of the list and add all of its neighbors to the end of the list, until the ending word (such as "cat") is found or until the list becomes empty, which indicates that no path exists between the two words.

3. Write a program that solves the classic "stable marriage" problem. This problem deals with a group of men and a group of women. The program tries to pair them up so as to generate as many stable marriages as possible. A set of marriages is unstable if you can find a man and a woman who would rather be married to each other than to their current spouses (in which case the two would be inclined to divorce their spouses and marry each other).

The input file for the program will list all of the men, one per line, followed by a blank line, followed by all of the women, one per line. The men and women are numbered according to their positions in the input file (the first man is #1, the second man is #2, and so on; the first woman is #1, the second woman is #2, and so on). Each input line (except for the blank line separating men from women) lists the person's name, followed by a colon, followed by a list of integers. These integers are the marriage partner preferences of this particular person. For example, see the following input line in the men's section:

```
Joe: 10 8 35 9 20 22 33 6 29 7 32 16 18 25
```

This line indicates that the person is named "Joe" and that his first choice for marriage is woman #10, his second choice is woman #8, and so on. Any women not listed are considered unacceptable to Joe.

In 1962 economists David Gale and Lloyd Shapley came up with an algorithm for finding stable marriage pairings. The Gale-Shapley algorithm is as follows:

```
Assign each person to be free.
While some man M with a nonempty preference list is free:
    W = the first woman on M's list.

    If some man P is engaged to W:
        assign P to be free.

    Assign M and W to be engaged to each other.

    For each successor Q of M who is on W's list:
        Remove W from Q's preference list.
        Remove Q from W's preference list.
```

Consider the following input file:

```
Man 1: 4 1 2 3
Man 2: 2 3 1 4
Man 3: 2 4 3 1
Man 4: 3 1 4 2
Woman 1: 4 1 3 2
Woman 2: 1 3 2 4
Woman 3: 1 2 3 4
Woman 4: 4 1 3 2
```

The following is a stable marriage solution for this input:

```
Man 1 and Woman 4
Man 3 and Woman 2
Man 2 and Woman 3
Man 4 and Woman 1
```

(*Note:* The classic version of this problem is heteronormative in that it expects men to want to marry women and vice versa. But this problem really just depends on two sets of people who are interested in each other. If you prefer a version of this problem with male/male, female/female, or other types of pairings, you can certainly work with input files that facilitate such pairings.)

## Chapter 9

Recursion

Introduction

In this chapter we focus on a programming technique known as recursion that allows us to solve certain complex problems in a highly elegant manner. We begin by comparing recursion with the problem-solving techniques you already know. Then we discuss the low-level mechanics that make recursion work in Python. Finally, we examine a number of problems that are easily expressed using this technique.

Recursion turns out to have a surprising range of useful applications, including recursive graphics that are known as fractals. But programming recursively also requires some special techniques that we'll have to explore. Recursive programming also requires a different mind-set in general, so the chapter explores a large set of sample problems to reinforce this new way of thinking.

9.1 Thinking Recursively

The problem-solving techniques we have employed so far fall under the heading of classical *iteration*, also known as the *iterative approach*.

> **Iteration (Iterative)**
>
> A programming technique in which you describe actions to be repeated using a loop.

In this chapter we will explore a new technique known as *recursion*. Recursion is a programming technique where we will write functions that call themselves.

> **Recursion (Recursive)**
>
> A programming technique in which you describe actions to be repeated using a function that calls itself.

The developers who built Google have placed an Easter egg into the Google search page. If you search for "recursion," the page suggests that you search for "recursion," as shown in Figure 9.1.

You have spent so much time writing solutions iteratively that it will take a while to get used to thinking about problems recursively. This chapter will help you get acclimated.

A Nonprogramming Example

If you're standing in line, you might wonder what position you're in. Are you number 10 in the line? Number 20? How would you find out?

Most people would solve this problem iteratively, by counting the people in the line: one, two, three, and so on. This approach is like a `while` loop that continues while there are more people left to count. The iterative approach is a natural one, but it has some limitations. For example, what if the person in front of you is taller than you? Will you be able to see past that person to count all the people in front of him or her? And what if the line goes around the block and you can't see around the corner to count the people there?

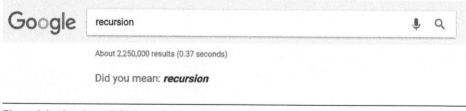

Figure 9.1   Google result for "recursion"

Can you think of another way to determine your position in the line? To think about the problem recursively, you have to imagine that all the people standing in line work together to solve the problem: Instead of having one person do all of the counting, each person is responsible for a little piece.

One cooperative approach would be to ask the person in front of you what your place in line is. That person might ask another person, who might ask another person. But that doesn't help much, because it just leads to a bunch of people saying, "This guy wants to know what place he is in line. Does anyone know?" Someone would probably eventually start counting and solve the problem iteratively.

You have to make the problem simpler. Instead of asking the person in front of you what place you are in line, ask that person what place he or she is in line, as depicted in Figure 9.2.

The key difference is that the person in front of you is closer to the front of the line. Suppose, for example, that you're 4th in line. The person in front of you is 3rd in line, which is closer to the front. But notice that you're asking the person in front of you to think about the exact same kind of question you're considering: you're both trying to figure out your places in line. That's where recursion comes in: the problem recurs because each of you wants to answer the same question.

The idea is to set up a chain reaction of people, all asking the person in front the same question. This process has to end eventually, when someone asks the person who is first in line. At this point you've reached what is sometimes referred to as the *bottom* of the recursion. This is shown in Figure 9.3.

You've gotten a bunch of people involved in collectively solving the problem, and you've finally reached a point where you can start assembling the answer. The person at the front is in position 1. That means the person just before is at position 2, and the person just before that person is at position 3, and so on. Once you reach the bottom of the recursion, you *unwind* it to figure out the answer to your initial problem. Figure 9.4 depicts this process.

Figure 9.2   Asking for place in line, part 1

Figure 9.3   Asking for place in line, part 2

Figure 9.4   Reporting place in line

These diagrams included just four individuals for the sake of brevity, but this process would still work even if there were 30 or even 300 people in the line.

One of the key aspects to notice here is that recursion involves many cooperating entities, each of which solves a little bit of the problem. Instead of one person doing all of the counting, each individual asks one question as we go toward the front of the line and answers one question as we come back down the line.

In programming, the iterative solution of having one person do all the counting is like having a loop that repeats some action. The recursive solution of having many people each do a little bit of work translates into many different function calls, each of which performs a little bit of work. Let's look at an example of how a simple iterative solution can be turned into a recursive solution.

Iteration to Recursion

As a first example, we will explore a problem that has a simple iterative solution. It won't be a very impressive use of recursion because the problem is easily solved with iteration. But exploring a problem that has a straightforward iterative solution allows us to compare the two solutions.

Suppose you want to create a function called `print_stars` that will accept an integer parameter *n* and will print a line of output with exactly *n* stars on it. You could solve this problem with string multiplication or with a `for` loop:

```
# version that uses string multiplication
def print_stars(n):
    print("*" * n)


# version that uses a for loop
def print_stars(n):
    for i in range(n):
        print("*", end="")
    print()
```

The action being repeated here is the call on `print` that prints a star. To write the stars recursively, let's imagine that the Python language did not contain any string multiplication `*` operator and did not contain loops. How would you print multiple stars without these features?

When writing recursive code, you need to think about different cases. You might ask the function to produce a line with 10 stars, 20 stars, or 50 stars. Of all of the possible star-writing tasks you might ask it to perform, which is the simplest?

Students often answer that printing a line of one star is very easy, and they're right that it's easy. We could start by writing code to handle the case where *n* is 1:

```
# version that handles a simple case (print 1 star)
def print_stars(n):
    if n == 1:
        print("*")
    else:
        ...
```

The code in the `else` part will deal with lines that have more than one star on them. Your instinct will probably be to fill in the `else` part with the `for` loop shown earlier, but you'll have to fight the instinct to solve the entire problem that way. To solve this second part of the problem, it is important to think about how you can do just a small amount of work that will get you closer to the solution. What is a small amount of work that each function call could perform? A good choice is for each call to print a single star. If the number of stars is greater than one, you know you have to print at least one star, so you can add that action to the code:

```
# version with partial else case
def print_stars(n):
    if n == 1:
        print("*")
    else:
        # n > 1
        print("*", end="")
        # what is left to do?
        ...
```

At this point in the process you have to make a leap of faith: You have to believe that recursion actually works. Once you've printed a single star, what's left to do? The answer is that you want to write $(n - 1)$ more stars. In other words, after writing one star, the task that remains is to write a line of $(n - 1)$ stars. You may think, "If only I had a function that would produce a line of $(n - 1)$ stars, I could call that function." But you do have such a function: the function you're writing. So, after your function writes a single star, you can call the print_stars function itself to complete the line of output:

```
# version with completed else case
def print_stars(n):
    if n == 1:
        print("*")
    else:
        # n > 1
        print("*", end="")
        print_stars(n - 1)
```

Many novices complain that this seems like cheating. You're supposed to be writing the function called print_stars, so how can you call print_stars from inside print_stars? Welcome to the world of recursion.

In the earlier example, we talked about people standing in a line and solving a problem together. To understand a recursive function like print_stars, it is useful to imagine that each function invocation is like a person in the line. The key insight is that there isn't just one person who can do the print_stars task; there's an entire army of people, each of whom can do the task.

Let's think about what happens when you call the function and request a line of three stars:

```
print_stars(3)
```

Imagine that you're calling up the first person from the `print_stars` army and saying, "I want a line of three stars." That person looks at the code in the function and sees that the way to write a line of three stars is to execute the following lines:

```
# expansion of print_stars(3) call
print("*", end="")
print_stars(2)
```

In other words, the first member of the army writes a star and calls up the next member of the army to write a line of two stars, and so on down the line. Just as in the earlier example you had a series of people figuring out their places in line, now you have a series of people each printing one star and then calling on someone else to write the rest of the line. In the line example, you eventually reached the person at the front of the line. In this case, you eventually reach a request to write a line of one star, which leads you into the `if` branch rather than the `else` branch. At this point, you complete the task with a simple `print` of a single star. Figure 9.5 shows a trace of the calls that would be made to print the line.

A total of three different calls are made on the function. Continuing the analogy, you could say that three members of the army are called up to solve the task together. Each one solves a star-writing task, but the tasks are slightly different (three stars, two stars, one star). This is similar to the example in which the various people standing in line were all answering the same question but were solving slightly different problems because their positions in line were different.

The previous version of `print_stars` gets the job done, but it is not the best possible recursive solution. We identified that the easiest number of stars to print was 1, but there is a task that is even easier. Printing a line of zero stars requires almost no work at all. Our code ought to be able to work properly if passed an

```
print_stars(3)            # n > 1, execute else
 ├── print("*", end="")
 └── print_stars(2)        # n > 1, execute else
      ├── print("*", end="")
      └── print_stars(1)   # n == 1, execute if
               print("*")
```

Figure 9.5 Trace of `print_stars` calls

n value of 0. You can handle that case just by calling `print` with no parameter to print a blank line:

```
# initial version that handles the n = 0 case
def print_stars(n):
    if n == 0:
        print()
    elif n == 1:
        print("*")
    else:
        # n > 1
        print("*", end="")
        print_stars(n - 1)
```

We can make an interesting observation about our code once we add the test for *n* of 0. If you truly understand recursion you will notice that the n == 1 case is no longer necessary. If we simply remove that case, the n == 1 case will fall into the `else` part of the code, will print a single star, and then will make a recursive call to `print_stars(0)`, which will end the line of output. This is the correct behavior, so the n == 1 case is not needed and should be removed. The code in the `else` part will now deal with lines that have more than zero stars on them. The following is the improved version of the code:

```
# version that handles simplest case (print 0 stars)
def print_stars(n):
    if n == 0:
        print()
    else:
        # n > 0
        print("*", end="")
        print_stars(n - 1)
```

Figure 9.6 is an updated version of our trace of the calls that would be made by `print_stars(3)`. Notice that the code now makes one more call, to `print_stars(0)`, to complete its work. This extra call is not a bad thing; it is better to have the most elegant and correct version of this function.

Structure of Recursive Solutions

Writing recursive solutions requires you to make a certain leap of faith, but there is nothing magical about recursion. Let's look a bit more closely at the structure of a

```
print_stars(3)                          # n > 0, execute else
   ├── print("*", end="")
   └── print_stars(2)                   # n > 0, execute else
          ├── print("*", end="")
          └── print_stars(1)            # n > 0, execute else
                 ├── print("*", end="")
                 └── print_stars(0)     # n == 0, execute if
                        └── print()
```

Figure 9.6   Trace of print_stars calls, version 2

recursive solution. The following function is not a solution to the task of writing a line of *n* stars:

```
# does not work; infinite recursion
def print_stars(n):
    print_stars(n)
```

This version never finishes executing, a phenomenon called *infinite recursion*. For example, if you ask the function to write a line of 10 stars, it tries to accomplish that by asking the function to write a line of 10 stars, which asks the function to write a line of 10 stars, which asks the function to write a line of 10 stars, and so on. This solution is the recursive equivalent of an infinite loop.

Every recursive solution that you write will have two key ingredients: a *base case* and a *recursive case*. A base case is a path in the code that performs a simple solution that does not involve any recursive calls, such as printing a single star. A recursive case is a path in the code that does include a recursive call on the same function.

> **Base Case**
>
> A case within a recursive solution that is so simple that it can be solved directly without a recursive call.

> **Recursive Case**
>
> A case within a recursive solution that involves reducing the overall problem to a simpler problem of the same kind that can be solved by a recursive call.

Here is the `print_stars` function again, with comments indicating the base case and recursive case:

```
def print_stars(n):
    if n == 0:
        # base case
        print()
    else:
        # recursive case
        print("*", end="")
        print_stars(n - 1)
```

The base case is the task of writing a line of zero stars. This task is so simple that it can be done immediately. The recursive case is the task of writing lines with one or more stars. To solve the recursive case, you begin by writing a single star, which reduces the remaining task to that of writing a line of $(n - 1)$ stars. This is the task that the `print_stars` function is designed to solve and it is simpler than the original task, so you can solve it by making a recursive call.

As an analogy, suppose you're at the top of a ladder with n rungs on it. If you have a way to get from one rung to the one below and if you can recognize when you've reached the ground, you can handle a ladder of any height. Stepping from one rung to the one below is like the recursive case in which you perform some small amount of work that reduces the problem to a simpler one of the same form (get down from rung $(n - 1)$ versus get down from rung n). Recognizing when you reach the ground is like the base case that can be solved directly (stepping off the ladder).

Some problems involve multiple base cases and some problems involve multiple recursive cases, but there will always be at least one of each case in a correct recursive solution. If you are missing either, you run into trouble. Without the ability to step down from one rung to the one below, you'd be stuck at the top of the ladder. Without the ability to recognize when you reach the ground, you'd keep trying to step down onto another rung even when there were no rungs left in the ladder.

Keep in mind that your code can have infinite recursion even if it has a proper recursive case. Consider, for example, this version of `print_stars`:

```
# does not work; infinite recursion
def print_stars(n):
    print("*", end="")
    print_stars(n - 1)
```

This version correctly reduces from the case of n to the case of $n - 1$, but it has no base case. As a result, it goes on infinitely. Instead of stopping when it reaches the task of writing zero stars, it instead recursively tries to write -1 stars, then -2 stars, then -3 stars, and so on.

Because recursive solutions include some combination of base cases and recursive cases, you will find that they are often written with `if/else` statements, nested `if` statements, or some minor variation thereof. You will also find that recursive programming generally involves a case analysis, in which you categorize the possible forms the problem might take into different cases and write a solution for each case.

Reversing a File

Solving the `print_stars` task with recursion may have been an interesting exercise, but it isn't a very compelling example. Let's look in detail at a problem in which recursion simplifies the work to be done.

Suppose you are reading an input file and you want to print the lines of the file in reverse order. For example, the file might contain the following four lines of text:

```
this
is
fun
no?
```

Printing these lines in reverse order would produce this output:

```
no?
fun
is
this
```

To perform this task iteratively, you could use a collection for storing the lines of text, such as a list. However, recursion allows you to solve the problem without using any collections.

As with many recursive problems, the challenge is for each call to solve only a little bit of the problem. How do you take just one step that will get you closer to completing the task? You can read one line of text from the file:

```
# initial version that reads one line
def reverse_file(file):
    line = file.readline()
    ...
```

Remember that recursive programming involves thinking about cases. What would be the simplest file to reverse? A one-line file would be fairly easy to reverse, but it would be even easier to reverse an empty file. So, you can begin writing your function as follows:

```
# version with if/else to separate cases
def reverse_file(file):
    line = file.readline()
    if line == "":
        # base case (empty file)
        ...
    else:
        # recursive case (nonempty file)
        ...
```

In this problem, the base case is so simple that there isn't anything to do. An empty file has no lines to reverse. Thus, in this case it makes more sense to turn around the if/else statement so that you test for the recursive case. That way you can write a simple if statement that has an implied "else there is nothing to do":

```
# simpler version with a single case
def reverse_file(file):
    line = file.readline()
    if line != "":
        # recursive case (nonempty file)
        ...
```

For the sample file, this code would read the line "this" into the variable line and leave you with the following three lines of text remaining to be read:

```
is
fun
no?
```

Recall that your aim is to produce the following overall output:

```
no?
fun
is
this
```

You might be asking yourself questions like, "Should I read a second line of input to process?" But that's not recursive thinking. If you're thinking recursively, you'll be thinking about what a call on the function will get you. Since the file object is positioned in front of the three lines "is", "fun", and "no?", a call on reverse should read in those lines and produce the first three lines of output that you're looking for. If that works, you'll only have to write out the line "this" afterward to complete the output.

This is where the leap of faith comes in: you have to believe that the reverse_file function actually works. If it does, this code can be completed as follows:

```
def reverse_file(file):
    line = file.readline()
    if line != "":
        # recursive case (nonempty file)
        reverse_file(file)        # print rest of file, reversed
        print(line.rstrip())      # print my line (at end)
```

This code does work. To reverse a sequence of lines, simply read in the first one, reverse the others, and then write out the first one.

The Recursive Call Stack

Novices seem to understand recursion better when they know more about the underlying mechanics that make it work. In this section we'll draw diagrams to represent functions calling each other. We'll look at a nonrecursive program first and then turn to recursive functions.

When one function calls another, the first function waits for the second to finish and then resumes executing. At any given point in a program, the code may be inside of several functions waiting for each other. The set of functions currently active in a program, along with the state of each of those functions, is referred to as the *call stack*. The Python interpreter maintains a structure storing information about the current call stack at a given point in the program. If you envision the call stack as a stack of papers with the most recently called function on top, you'll have a pretty good idea of how it works.

> **Call Stack**
>
> The internal structure that keeps track of the sequence of functions that are currently active.

To illustrate the mechanics of the call stack, let's first consider a simple nonrecursive program for printing triangular figures made of stars. The main function calls a function draw_two_triangles, which in turn calls another function draw_triangle twice:

```
 1   # A simple program that draws three triangles.
 2   def draw_triangle():
 3       print("  *")
 4       print(" ***")
 5       print("*****")
 6       print()
 7
 8   def draw_two_triangles():
 9       draw_triangle()
10       draw_triangle()
11
12   def main():
13       draw_triangle()
14       draw_two_triangles()
15
16   main()
```

Imagine that each function call has been written on a different piece of paper. We begin program execution with the main function, so its piece of paper would be laid down first. We then execute each of the statements in main in turn, from first to last. First we will execute the call on draw_triangle, as shown in Figure 9.7.

We know that at this point, the computer stops executing main and turns its attention to the draw_triangle function. This step is analogous to picking up the piece of paper

```
def main():
→    draw_triangle()
     draw_two_triangles()
```

Figure 9.7 Call stack from `main` function

with `draw_triangle` written on it and placing it over the piece of paper with `main` on it, as shown in Figure 9.8.

```
def main():

     def draw_triangle():
         print("  *")
         print(" ***")
         print("*****")
         print()
```

Figure 9.8 Call stack from `draw_triangle` function

Now we execute each of the statements in `draw_triangle` from first to last, then go back to `main`, removing the `draw_triangle` sheet. When we go back to `main` we will have finished the call on `draw_triangle`, so the next step is the call on `draw_two_triangles`, as shown in Figure 9.9.

```
def main():
     draw_triangle()
→    draw_two_triangles()
```

Figure 9.9 Call stack back in `main` function

So we grab the piece of paper with `draw_two_triangles` on it and place it over the paper with `main` on it. Inside the `draw_two_triangles` function, the first thing to do is the first call on `draw_triangle`, as shown in Figure 9.10.

```
def main():

     def draw_two_triangles():
→        draw_triangle()
         draw_triangle()
```

Figure 9.10 Call stack from `draw_two_triangles` function

To execute this function, we take out the sheet of paper with `draw_triangle` on it and place it on top of the `draw_two_triangles` sheet, as shown in Figure 9.11.

This diagram makes it clear that we started with the function `main`, which called the function `draw_two_triangles`, which called the function `draw_triangle`. So, at this moment, three different functions are active. The one on top is the one that we are actively executing. Once we complete it, we'll go back to the one underneath, and once

```
def main():
    def draw_two_triangles():
        def draw_triangle():
            print("  *")
            print(" ***")
            print("*****")
            print()
```

Figure 9.11   Call stack three levels deep

we finish that one, we'll go back to main. We could continue with this example, but you probably get the idea by now.

Let's use the idea of the call stack to understand how the recursive file-reversing function works. To visualize the call stack, we need to put the function definition on a piece of paper, as shown in Figure 9.12.

```
def reverse_file(file):
    line = file.readline()     # _____
    if line != "":
        reverse_file(file)
        print(line.rstrip())
```

Figure 9.12   Call stack from reverse_file 1

Notice that the paper includes a blank space to store the value of the local variable line. This is an important detail. Suppose that we call this function with the earlier sample input file, which contains the following four lines of text:

```
this
is
fun
no?
```

When we call the function, it reads the first line of text into its line variable, and then it reaches the recursive call on reverse_file, as shown in Figure 9.13.

```
def reverse_file(file):
    line = file.readline()     # _"this"_
    if line != "":
 →       reverse_file(file)
        print(line.rstrip())
```

Figure 9.13   Call stack from reverse_file inside if

Then what happens? In the draw_triangles program, we took the sheet of paper for the function being called and placed it on top of the current sheet of paper. But here we have the function `reverse_file` calling itself. To understand what happens, you have to realize that each function invocation is independent of the others. We don't have only a single sheet of paper with the `reverse_file` function written on it; we have as many copies as we want. So, we can grab a second copy of the same function definition and place it on top of the current one, as shown in Figure 9.14.

```
def reverse_file(file):                          1
    line = file.readline()    # _"this"_
    if line != "":
→       def reverse_file(file):                  2
            line = file.readline()    # _____
            if line != "":
                reverse_file(file)
                print(line.rstrip())
```

Figure 9.14   Call stack from `reverse_file` 2

This new version of the function has a variable of its own, called `line`, in which it can store a line of text. Even though the previous version (the one underneath this one) is in the middle of its execution, this new one is at the beginning of its execution. Think back to the analogy of being able to employ an entire army of people to write out a line of stars. Just as you could call on as many people as you needed to solve that problem, you can bring up as many copies of the `reverse_file` function as you need to solve this problem.

The second call on `reverse_file` reads another line of text (the second line, "is"). After the program reads the second line, it makes another recursive call on `reverse_file`, as shown in Figure 9.15.

```
def reverse_file(file):                          1
    line = file.readline()    # _"this"_
    if line != "":
→       def reverse_file(file):                  2
            line = file.readline()    # _"is"___
            if line != "":
→               reverse_file(file)
                print(line.rstrip())
```

Figure 9.15   Call stack from `reverse_file` 2 inside `if`

So Python sets aside this version of the function as well and brings up a third version. This version of the function also reads in a line (the third line, "fun") and reaches a recursive call on `reverse_file`. The next call will bring up a fourth version of the function, which finds a fourth line of input ("no?"), so it reads that in and reaches the recursive call. These calls are shown in Figure 9.16.

This call brings up a fifth version of the function, as shown in Figure 9.17.

This version turns out to have the easy task, like the final person who was asked to print a line of zero stars. This time around the file has no data left to read

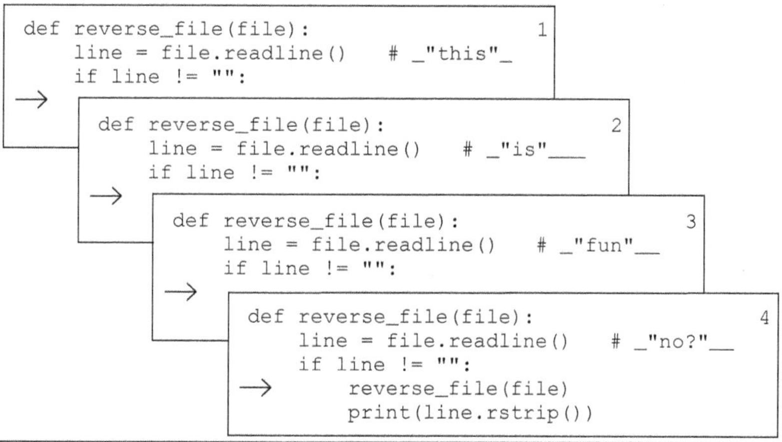

```
def reverse_file(file):                    1
    line = file.readline()     # _"this"_
    if line != "":
→       def reverse_file(file):                2
            line = file.readline()     # _"is"___
            if line != "":
    →           def reverse_file(file):                3
                    line = file.readline()     # _"fun"___
                    if line != "":
        →               def reverse_file(file):                4
                            line = file.readline()     # _"no?"___
                            if line != "":
            →                   reverse_file(file)
                                print(line.rstrip())
```

Figure 9.16   Call stack from reverse_file 3 and 4

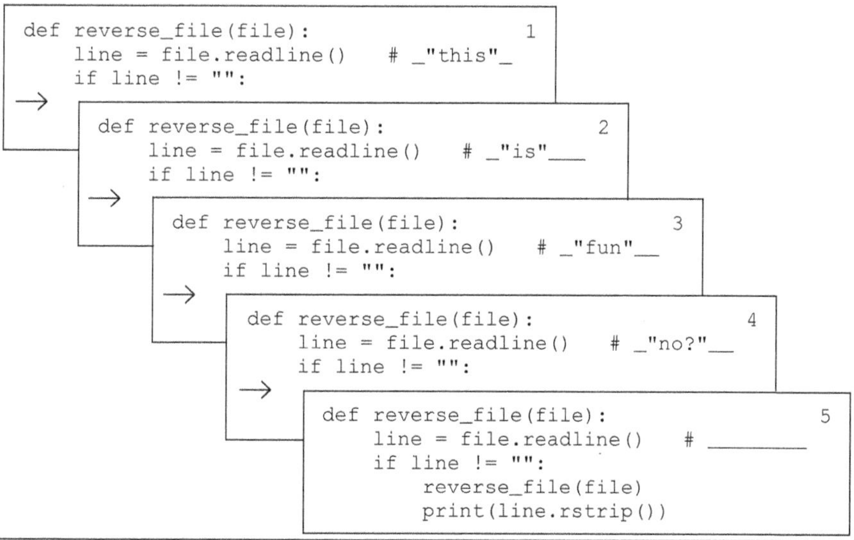

```
def reverse_file(file):                1
    line = file.readline()     # _"this"_
    if line != "":
→   def reverse_file(file):                2
        line = file.readline()     # _"is"___
        if line != "":
    →   def reverse_file(file):                3
            line = file.readline()     # _"fun"___
            if line != "":
        →   def reverse_file(file):                4
                line = file.readline()     # _"no?"___
                if line != "":
            →   def reverse_file(file):                5
                    line = file.readline()     # _____
                    if line != "":
                        reverse_file(file)
                        print(line.rstrip())
```

Figure 9.17   Call stack from reverse_file 5

(file.readline() returns a blank line, ""). The program has reached the very important base case that stops this process from going on indefinitely. This version of the function recognizes that there are no lines to reverse, so it simply terminates.

Then what? Having completed this fifth call, we throw it away and return to where we were just before executing the call, which is in the body of the fourth function call, as shown in Figure 9.18.

We've finished the fifth call on reverse_file and are positioned at the print right after it, so we print the text in the line variable ("no?") and terminate. Where does that

```
def reverse_file(file):                    1
    line = file.readline()    # _"this"_
    if line != "":
→
        def reverse_file(file):                2
            line = file.readline()    # _"is"___
            if line != "":
    →
            def reverse_file(file):                3
                line = file.readline()    # _"fun"___
                if line != "":
        →
                def reverse_file(file):                4
                    line = file.readline()    # _"no?"___
                    if line != "":
                        reverse_file(file)
            →           print(line.rstrip())
```

Figure 9.18   Call stack from reverse_file returning to 4

```
def reverse_file(file):                    1
    line = file.readline()    # _"this"_
    if line != "":
→
        def reverse_file(file):                2
            line = file.readline()    # _"is"___
            if line != "":
    →
            def reverse_file(file):                3
                line = file.readline()    # _"fun"___
                if line != "":
                    reverse_file(file)
        →           print(line.rstrip())
```

Figure 9.19   Call stack from reverse_file returning to 3

leave us? This function has been executed and we return to where we were just before, which is in the body of the third function call, as shown in Figure 9.19.

We then print the current line of text, which is "fun", and this version also goes away, returning us to the body of the second function call, which had read the line "is". That line is printed, and then the code returns to the body of the first function call, as shown in Figure 9.20.

Notice that we've written out three lines of text so far:

```
no?
fun
is
```

Our leap of faith was justified. The recursive call on reverse_file read in the three lines of text that followed the first line of input and printed them in reverse order.

```
def reverse_file(file):
    line = file.readline()    # _"this"_
    if line != "":
        reverse_file(file)
→       print(line.rstrip())
```

Figure 9.20   Call stack from `reverse_file` returning to 1

We complete the task by printing the first line of text, which leads to this overall output:

```
no?
fun
is
this
```

Then this version of the function terminates, and the program has finished executing.

9.2 Recursive Functions and Data

Both of the examples of recursion we have studied so far have been action-oriented functions that do not return values. In this section we will examine some of the issues that arise when you want to write functions that compute and return a result. Such functions are similar to mathematical functions in that they accept a set of input values and produce a set of possible results. We'll also explore an example that involves manipulating recursive data.

Integer Exponentiation

Python provides a built-in function called `pow` that allows you to compute an exponent. If you want to compute the value of x^y you can call `pow(x, y)`. There is also the `**` exponentiation operator, `x ** y`. Let's consider how we could implement a `pow` function ourselves. We'll name our version `power` to keep it separate from the built-in `pow` function.

To keep things simple, we'll limit ourselves to the domain of integers. But because we are limiting ourselves to integers, we have to recognize an important precondition of our function: We won't be able to compute negative exponents because the results would not be integers. The function we want to write will look like the following:

```
# pre : y >= 0
# post: returns x ** y
def power(x, y):
    . . .
```

We could obviously solve this problem by calling pow or using **, or we could write a loop to accumulate the result. But we want to explore how to write the function recursively. Again, we should start by thinking about different cases. What would be the easiest exponent to compute? It's pretty easy to compute x^1, so that's a good candidate. But as with the print_stars function from earlier, there is an even more basic case: zero. By definition, any integer to the power of 0 is considered to be 1. So we can begin our solution with the following code:

```
# version with base case
def power(x, y):
    if y == 0:
        # base case: x to the 0th power
        return 1
    else:
        ...
```

In the recursive case we know that y is greater than 0. In other words, there will be at least one factor of x in the result. We know the following from the mathematical definition of exponentiation:

$$x^y = x \cdot x^{y-1}$$

This equation expresses x to the y power in terms of x to a smaller power, $(y - 1)$. Therefore, it can serve as our recursive case. All we have to do is to translate it into its Python equivalent:

```
# complete recursive version
def power(x, y):
    if y == 0:
        # base case: x to the 0th power
        return 1
    else:
        # recursive case: y > 0
        return x * power(x, y - 1)
```

This is a complete recursive solution. Tracing the execution of a recursive function is a little more difficult than using a function that doesn't return a value, because we have to keep track of the values that are returned by each recursive call. Figure 9.21 shows a trace of execution showing how we would compute 3^5. The code makes a series of six recursive calls in a row until we reach the base case of computing 3 to the 0 power. That call returns the value 1 and then the recursion unwinds, computing the various answers as it returns from each function call.

```
power(3, 5) = 3 * power(3, 4)
    power(3, 4) = 3 * power(3, 3)
        power(3, 3) = 3 * power(3, 2)
            power(3, 2) = 3 * power(3, 1)
                power(3, 1) = 3 * power(3, 0)
                    power(3, 0) = 1
                power(3, 1) = 3 * 1 = 3
            power(3, 2) = 3 * 3 = 9
        power(3, 3) = 3 * 9 = 27
    power(3, 4) = 3 * 27 = 81
power(3, 5) = 3 * 81 = 243
```

Figure 9.21   Trace of power (3, 5) call

It is useful to think about what will happen if someone violates the precondition by asking for a negative exponent. For example, what if someone asked for `power(3, -1)`? The function would recursively ask for `power(3, -2)`, which would ask for `power(3, -3)`, which would ask for `power(3, -4)`, and so on. In other words, it would lead to an infinite recursion. The most common way to handle an illegal parameter value like this is to raise an exception. Our solution is structured as a series of cases, so we can simply add a new case for illegal exponents. Since this error involves an inappropriate parameter (argument) value being passed, the appropriate kind of error to raise is a `ValueError`:

```
# version that raises error on negative exponent
def power(x, y):
    if y < 0:
        raise ValueError("negative exponent: " + str(y))
    elif y == 0:
        # base case: x to the 0th power
        return 1
    else:
        # recursive case: y > 0
        return x * power(x, y - 1)
```

One of the advantages of writing functions recursively is that if we can identify other cases, we can potentially make the function more efficient. For example, suppose that you want to compute 2^{16}. In its current form, the function will multiply 2 by 2 by 2 a total of 16 times. But we can do better than that. If y is an even exponent, then the following mathematical equality holds true:

$$x^y = (x^2)^{y/2}$$

This observation can greatly reduce the number of recursive calls needed by our function. Currently our code would compute 2^{16} by asking for 2^{15}, then 2^{14}, then 2^{13}, and so on. If we modify our function to take advantage of the preceding idea, we can

```
power(2, 16) = power(4, 8)
│   power(4, 8) = power(16, 4)
│   │   power(16, 4) = power(256, 2)
│   │   │   power(256, 2) = power(65536, 1)
│   │   │   │   power(65536, 1) = 65536 * power(65536, 0)
│   │   │   │   │   power(65536, 0) = 1
│   │   │   │   power(65536, 1) = 65536 * 1 = 65536
│   │   │   power(256, 2) = 65536
│   │   power(16, 4) = 65536
│   power(4, 8) = 65536
power(2, 16) = 65536
```

Figure 9.22 Trace of power(2, 16) call

compute 2^{16} by asking for 4^8, which is 16^4, which is 256^2, and so on. This algorithm is much more efficient. The following code adds this case to our function:

```
# version that optimizes on even exponents
def power(x, y):
    if y < 0:
        raise ValueError("negative exponent: " + str(y))
    elif y == 0:
        # base case: x to the 0th power
        return 1
    elif y % 2 == 0:
        # recursive case 1: even exponent
        return x * x * power(x, y // 2)
    else:
        # recursive case 2: odd exponent
        return x * power(x, y - 1)
```

This version of the function is more efficient than the original. Figure 9.22 shows a trace of execution for computing 2^{16}.

Without the special case for even exponents, this computation would have required 17 different calls: 16 recursive cases and one base case.

Greatest Common Divisor

In mathematics, we often want to know the largest integer that goes evenly into two different integers a and b, which is known as the *greatest common divisor* (or GCD) of the two integers. Let's explore how to write a GCD function recursively. For now, let's not worry about negative values of a and b. We want to write the following function:

```
# pre : a >= 0 and b >= 0
# post: returns the greatest common divisor of a and b
def gcd(a, b):
    ...
```

To introduce some variety, let's try to figure out the recursive case first and then figure out the base case. Suppose, for example, that we are asked to compute the GCD of 20 and 132. The GCD is 4, because 4 is the largest integer that goes evenly into both numbers.

There are many ways to compute the GCD of two numbers. One of the most efficient algorithms dates back at least to the time of Euclid and perhaps even farther. This algorithm eliminates any multiples of the smaller integer from the larger integer. In the case of 20 and 132, we know that the following is true:

$$132 = 20 \times 6 + 12$$

There are six multiples of 20 in 132, with a remainder of 12. Euclid's algorithm says that we can ignore the six multiples of 20 and just focus on the value 12. In other words, we can replace 132 with 12:

```
gcd(132, 20) = gcd(12, 20)
```

We haven't figured out the base case yet, but no matter what the base case ends up being, we're making progress if we can reduce the numbers using Euclid's algorithm. When you're dealing with nonnegative integers, you can't reduce them forever.

The proof of this principle is beyond the scope of this text, but that is the basic idea. This algorithm is easy to express in Python terms because the mod operator gives us the remainder when one number is divided by another. Expressing this principle in general terms, we know that the following is true when $b > 0$:

$$GCD(a, b) = GCD(a \% b, b)$$

Again, the proof is beyond the scope of this text, but given this basic principle we can produce a recursive solution to the problem. We might try to write the function as follows:

```python
# version with recursive case
def gcd(a, b):
    if ...:
        # base case
    else:
        # recursive case
        return gcd(a % b, b)
```

This isn't a bad first attempt, but it has a problem: It's not enough for the solution to be mathematically correct; we also need our recursive solution to keep reducing the overall problem to a simpler problem. If we start with the numbers 132 and 20, the function makes progress on the first call, but then it starts repeating itself:

```
gcd(132, 20) = gcd(12, 20)
    gcd(12, 20) = gcd(12, 20)
        gcd(12, 20) = gcd(12, 20)
            gcd(12, 20) = gcd(12, 20)
                ...
```

This pattern will lead to infinite recursion. The Euclidean trick helped the first time around, because for the first call *a* was greater than *b* (132 is greater than 20). But the algorithm makes progress only if the first number is larger than the second number. Here is the line of code that is causing the problem:

```
return gcd(a % b, b)
```

When we compute a % b, we are guaranteed to get a result that is smaller than b. That means that on the recursive call, the first value will always be smaller than the second value. To make the algorithm work, we need the opposite to be true. We can achieve this goal simply by reversing the order of the arguments:

```
return gcd(b, a % b)
```

On this call we are guaranteed to have a first value that is larger than the second value. If we trace this version of the function for computing the GCD of 132 and 20, we get the following sequence of calls:

```
gcd(132, 20) = gcd(20, 12)
    gcd(20, 12) = gcd(12, 8)
        gcd(12, 8) = gcd(8, 4)
            gcd(8, 4) = gcd(4, 0)
                ...
```

At this point we have to decide what the GCD of 4 and 0 is. It may seem strange, but the answer is 4. In general, the GCD of *n* and 0 is *n*. Obviously, the GCD can't be any larger than *n*, and *n* goes evenly into *n*. But *n* also goes evenly into 0, because 0 can be written as an even multiple of *n*: $(0 * n) = 0$.

This observation leads us to the base case. If *b* is 0, the GCD is *a*:

```
# version with base case and recursive case
def gcd(a, b):
    if b == 0:
        # base case
        return a
    else:
        # recursive case
        return gcd(b, a % b)
```

This base case also solves the potential problem that the Euclidean formula depends on *b* not being 0. However, we still have to think about the case in which either or both of *a* and *b* are negative. We could keep the precondition and raise an error when this occurs, but it is more common in mathematics to return the GCD of the absolute value of the two values. We can accomplish this by including one extra case for negatives:

```
# version that handles negative values
def gcd(a, b):
    if a < 0 or b < 0:
        return gcd(abs(a), abs(b))
    elif b == 0:
        # base case
        return a
    else:
        # recursive case
        return gcd(b, a % b)
```

For what it's worth, there is an actual `gcd` function in the Python standard library. You need to import it from the `fractions` module in which it's located:

```
>>> from fractions import gcd
>>> gcd(132, 20)
12
```

You can read more about the built-in `gcd` function and the rest of the `fractions` library in the Python Standard Library documentation:

- https://docs.python.org/3/library/fractions.html

Common Programming Error

Infinite Recursion

Everyone who uses recursion to write programs eventually accidentally writes a solution that leads to infinite recursion. For example, the following is a slight variation of the `gcd` function that doesn't work:

```
# version that handles negative values
def gcd(a, b):
    if a <= 0 or b <= 0:
        return gcd(abs(a), abs(b))
    elif b == 0:
        # base case
        return a
    else:
        # recursive case
        return gcd(b, a % b)
```

Continued on next page

Continued from previous page

This solution is just slightly different than the one we wrote previously. In the test for negative values, this code tests whether *a* and *b* are less than or equal to 0.

The original code tests whether *a* and *b* are strictly less than 0. It doesn't seem like this variation should make much difference, but it does. If we execute this version of the code to solve our original problem of finding the GCD of 132 and 20, the program produces many lines of output that look like the following:

```
File "gcd.py", line 12, in gcd
   return gcd(a % b, b)
File "gcd.py", line 12, in gcd
   return gcd(a % b, b)
File "gcd.py", line 5, in gcd
   if a <= 0 or b <= 0:
RecursionError: maximum recursion depth exceeded in comparison
```

The first time you see this, you are likely to think that something has broken on your computer because you will get so many lines of output. Notice that the output says that the code has raised a `RecursionError`. This is sometimes called a *stack overflow*. Python is letting you know that you have made too many nested recursive calls and the call stack has gotten too big. Why did this happen? Remember the trace of execution for this case:

```
gcd(132, 20) = gcd(20, 12)
    gcd(20, 12) = gcd(12, 8)
        gcd(12, 8) = gcd(8, 4)
            gcd(8, 4) = gcd(4, 0)
                ...
```

Consider what happens at this point, when we call `gcd(4, 0)`. The value of *b* is 0, which is our base case, so normally we would expect the function to return the value 4 and terminate. But the function begins by checking whether either *a* or *b* is less than or equal to 0. Since *b* is 0, this test evaluates to `True`, so the function makes a recursive call with the absolute values of *a* and *b*. But the absolute values of 4 and 0 are 4 and 0. So the function decides that `gcd(4, 0)` must be equal to `gcd(4, 0)`, which must be equal to `gcd(4, 0)`, and so on:

```
gcd(132, 20) = gcd(20, 12)
    gcd(20, 12) = gcd(12, 8)
        gcd(12, 8) = gcd(8, 4)
            gcd(8, 4) = gcd(4, 0)
                gcd(4, 0) = gcd(4, 0)
```

Continued on next page

Continued from previous page

```
gcd(4, 0) = gcd(4, 0)
    gcd(4, 0) = gcd(4, 0)
        gcd(4, 0) = gcd(4, 0)
                ...
```

In other words, this version generates infinitely many recursive calls. Python allows you to make a lot of recursive calls, but eventually it runs out of memory. When it does, it gives you a call stack trace to let you know how you got to the error. In this case, the stack trace is not as helpful as usual because almost all of the calls will involve the infinite recursion.

Again, think in terms of stacking pieces of paper on top of each other as functions are called. You'd wind up with a stack containing hundreds or even thousands of sheets, and you would have to look back through all of these to find the problem.

To handle these situations, you have to look closely at the line number to see which line of your program generated the infinite recursion. In this simple case, we know that it is the recursive call for negative *a* and *b* values. That alone might be enough to allow us to pinpoint the error. If the problem isn't obvious, though, you might need to include print statements to figure out what is going on. For example, in this code, we could add a `print` just before the recursive call:

```python
# version that handles negative values
def gcd(a, b):
    if a <= 0 or b <= 0:
        print("a is", a, "and b is", b)
        return gcd(abs(a), abs(b))
    elif b == 0:
        # base case
        return a
    else:
        # recursive case
        return gcd(a % b, b)
```

When we run the program with that `print` statement in place, the code produces many lines of output of the form:

```
x = 4 and y = 0
```

If we examine that case closely, we'll see that we don't have negative values and will realize that we have to fix the test we are using.

Directory Crawler

Recursion is particularly useful when you're working with data that is itself recursive. For example, consider how files are stored on a computer. Each file is kept in a folder or directory. But directories can contain more than just files: Directories can contain other directories, those inner directories can contain directories, and even those directories can contain directories. Directories can be nested to an arbitrary depth. This storage system is an example of *recursive data*.

Let's write a program that will prompt the user for the name of a file or directory and recursively explore all the files that can be reached from that starting point. If the user provides the name of a file, the program should simply print the name. But if the user gives the name of a directory, the program should print the directory name and list all the directories and files inside that directory.

In Chapter 6, you learned to use file objects to read data from files stored on your computer. In this situation we don't want to read the data inside the files; we just want a list of the names of all files in a given directory. Python contains two modules called os and os.path that have useful functions for asking about properties of files and directories.

```
import os
import os.path
```

Table 9.1 shows a partial list of the functions of these two modules.

You can find a full list of the functions of the os and os.path modules in the Python library documentation:

- https://docs.python.org/3/library/os.html
- https://docs.python.org/3/library/os.path.html

Back to the task at hand. We are trying to write a recursive directory crawler function. The function will be passed the name of a file or directory as a parameter. The function should begin by printing the name of the file or directory, without any preceding directory in front of it. The os.path.basename function can help us do this:

```
# Initial version that prints file name.
def crawl(path):
    print(os.path.basename(path))
    ...
```

If the given path represents a simple file, we have completed the task. But we want to treat directories differently than regular files. You can tell whether a path represents a file or directory using the os.path.isfile and os.path.isdir functions, respectively.

Table 9.1   Functions of `os` and `os.path` Modules

Function	Description
`os.chdir("path")`	changes program's working directory
`os.chmod("path", mode)`	changes permissions on a file/dir
`os.chown("path", user, group)`	changes the owner of a file/dir
`os.getcwd()`	returns program's working directory
`os.listdir("path")`	returns list of all files/dir within a directory
`os.mkdir("path")`	creates a new directory
`os.makedirs("path")`	creates a new directory and any of its parent dirs recursively
`os.remove("path")`	deletes a file
`os.removedirs("path")`	deletes a directory recursively
`os.rename("src", "dst")`	renames a file or directory
`os.rmdir("path")`	deletes a directory
`os.path.abspath("path")`	returns an absolute version of a relative path
`os.path.basename("path")`	returns the filename portion of a path
`os.path.dirname("path")`	returns the directory portion of a path
`os.path.exists("path")`	returns True if a given file/dir exists
`os.path.getmtime("path")`	returns the last-modified time of a file/dir
`os.path.getsize("path")`	returns a file's size in bytes
`os.path.isdir("path")`	returns True if the given path is a directory
`os.path.isfile("path")`	returns True if the given path is a file

If the path represents a directory, we want to print the names of all the files contained in the directory. We can accomplish this task with the `os.listdir` function, which returns a list of strings that represent the contents of the directory. We can use a `for` loop to process each of those files. An obvious approach is to simply print the names of the files in the directory:

```
# Version that prints files inside a directory.
def crawl(path):
    print(os.path.basename(path))
    if os.path.isdir(path):
        # print each file in this directory
        for file in os.listdir(path):
            print(file)
```

This function works in that it prints the names of the files inside the directory. But remember that there can be directories inside this directory, so some of those files might actually be directories whose contents also need to be printed. We could try to fix our code by adding a test for this and another loop:

```
# Version that prints files and directories inside a directory.
# (This code is getting worse, not better!)
def crawl(path):
    print(os.path.basename(path))
    if os.path.isdir(path):
        # print each file in this directory
        for file in os.listdir(path):
            if os.path.isdir(file):
                # print each file in this subdirectory
                for file2 in os.listdir(path + "/" + file):
                    print(file2)
```

But even this won't work, because there might be directories within those inner directories, and those directories might have subdirectories, and so on. There is no simple way to solve this problem with standard iterative techniques.

The solution is to think recursively. You might be tempted to envision many different cases: a file, a directory with files, a directory with subdirectories, a directory with subdirectories that have subdirectories, and so on. However, there are really only two cases to consider: Each object is either a file or a directory. If it's a file, we simply print its name. If it's a directory, we print its name and then print information about every file and directory inside of it. How do we get the code to recursively explore all of the possibilities? We call our own `crawl` function to process whatever appears inside a directory:

```
# Working recursive version
def crawl(path):
    print(os.path.basename(path))
    if os.path.isdir(path):
        for file in os.listdir(path):
            crawl(path + "/" + file)    # recursive call
```

This version of the code recursively explores the structure. Each time the function finds something inside a directory, it makes a recursive call that can handle either a file or a directory. That recursive call might make yet another recursive call to handle either a file or directory, and so on. If we run this version of the function, we'll get output like the following:

```
homework
assignments.doc
hw1
song.py
```

Continued on next page

Continued from previous page

```
hw1notes.txt
hw2
rocket.py
needle.py
```

The problem with this output is that it doesn't indicate the structure to us. We know that the first line of output is the name of the starting directory (homework) and that everything that follows is inside that directory, but we can't easily see the substructure. It would be more convenient if the output used indentation to indicate the inner structure, as in the following example:

```
homework
    assignments.doc
    hw1
        song.py
        hw1notes.txt
    hw2
        rocket.py
        needle.py
```

In this output we can more clearly see that the directory called homework contains three elements, two of which are directories that have their own files (hw1 and hw2). We can get this output by including an extra parameter in the crawl function that indicates the desired level of indentation. On the initial call in main, we can pass the function an indentation of 0. On each recursive call, we can pass it a value one higher than the current level. We can then use that parameter to print some extra spacing at the beginning of the line to generate the indentation.

Here is our complete program, including the new version of the crawl function with indentation:

```
1   # This program contains a recursive directory crawler.
2   import os
3   import os.path
4
5   def crawl(path, indent = 0):
6       print("    " * indent, os.path.basename(path))
7       if os.path.isdir(path):
8           for subfile in sorted(os.listdir(path)):
9               crawl(path + "/" + subfile, indent + 1)
10
11  def main():
12      path = input("Directory to crawl? ")
13      crawl(path)
14
15  main()
```

```
Directory to crawl? /home/jsmith12/homework
homework
    assignments.doc
    hw1
        song.py
        hw1notes.txt
    hw2
        rocket.py
        needle.py
```

9.3 Recursive Graphics

There has been a great deal of interest in the past 30 years about an emerging field of mathematics called *fractal geometry*. A *fractal* is a geometric object that is recursively constructed or self-similar. A fractal shape contains smaller versions of itself, so that it looks similar at all magnifications.

> **Fractal**
>
> A self-similar geometric figure that can be drawn recursively.

Benoit Mandelbrot founded the field of fractals in 1975 with his first publication about these intriguing objects, particularly a specific fractal that has come to be known as the *Mandelbrot set*. The most impressive aspect of fractal geometry is that extremely intricate and complex phenomena can be described with a simple set of rules. When Mandelbrot and others began drawing pictures of their fractals, they were an instant hit.

Many fractals can be described easily with recursion. In this section we will write programs to implement two simple fractals: the Cantor set and the Sierpinski triangle. Both of these fractals use repeated patterns of simple shapes to produce more complex figures.

Cantor Set

The first fractal we will explore is called the *Cantor set*. The fractal was introduced by German mathematician Georg Cantor in 1883. Cantor described the set as a mathematical range of numbers, but it can be drawn as a set of lines on a screen.

The Cantor set is a pattern of horizontal lines. The pattern can be drawn at various *levels*. A level-1 Cantor set is just a single horizontal line of a given length. A level-2 Cantor set also has a second pair of lines below the first line, each being one third as long as the first line. Figure 9.23 shows the first two levels of a Cantor set.

The process continues in this fashion as new levels are added. Figure 9.24 shows the Cantor set figure at levels 3 and 4.

Figure 9.23   Cantor set, levels 1 and 2

Figure 9.24   Cantor set, levels 3 and 4

Because of their self-similar repeating nature, fractals are generally implemented as recursive functions. Let's write a recursive function called `cantor_set` that uses the `DrawingPanel` class from Chapter 3 to draw this figure. We'll pass the panel as a parameter to the function, as well as the (x, y) coordinates of the left edge of the line, along with its horizontal length. We must also pass the number of levels of the figure to draw. We will separate each level of lines by 20 pixels of vertical space. The function's heading will look like this:

```
# Draws a Cantor Set figure of the given level with its left
# endpoint at the given x/y coordinates and the given line length.
def cantor_set(panel, x, y, length, levels):
    . . .
```

One place to start our work would be to think of simple cases of the figure to draw. An easy figure to draw is the level-1 figure, which is just a straight line of the given length. We can use the `DrawingPanel`'s `draw_line` method that accepts the *x/y* coordinates of the start and end points as parameters:

```
# initial version with base case
def cantor_set(panel, x, y, length, levels):
    if levels == 1:
        # base case: draw a single line
        panel.draw_line(x, y, x + length, y)
    else:
        . . .
```

The recursive case consists of many smaller lines, but that doesn't mean the code in the `else` branch should contain many `draw_line` calls. In a recursive function we want each call to do a small portion of the overall work. Writing a recursive function requires you to spot how a problem is self-similar; that is, how smaller instances of that same problem recur. For students who are new to recursion, it can be difficult to see the self-similarity in fractals like these. If you look at the level-4 Cantor set carefully, you'll see that it could be described as a single horizontal line followed by two level-3 Cantor sets of smaller size below it. Figure 9.25 shows this self-similarity.

Figure 9.25   Level-4 Cantor set self-similarity

Recognizing the self-similarity can help us to make two recursive calls from our function. The first recursive call draws the smaller Cantor set on the left. It starts at the same *x*-coordinate, with a *y*-coordinate shifted down by 20 pixels. The length of the smaller Cantor set is one-third as large as the current one, and it has one fewer levels to it. The smaller Cantor set at right uses similar parameters, except that its *x*-coordinate is shifted right by two-thirds of the current figure's length. The recursive code is the following:

```
# version with first attempt at recursive case
def cantor_set(panel, x, y, length, levels):
    if levels == 1:
        # base case: draw a single line
        panel.draw_line(x, y, x + length, y)
    else:
        # recursive case: draw line plus two smaller Cantor sets
        panel.draw_line(x, y, x + length, y)
        cantor_set(panel, x, y + 20, length // 3, levels - 1)   # L
        cantor_set(panel, x + 2 * length // 3, y + 20, \
                   length // 3, levels - 1)                       # R
```

If you look at the code carefully, you'll notice that the base case and recursive case both start with the same line to draw a single line. We can factor this code out of the `if/else` statement since it is drawn in both cases. A more elegant version of this function would be to change the base case to be a level-0 fractal, which draws nothing. The recursive case will draw a line and then make two recursive calls to draw smaller subfigures. This will still work for the level-1 case because the two recursive calls would be to level-0, which would do nothing. The following is the complete program:

```
1   # This program draws the Cantor Set fractal.
2   from DrawingPanel import *
3
4   # Draws a Cantor Set figure of the given level with its left
5   # endpoint at the given x/y coordinates and the given line length.
6   def cantor_set(panel, x, y, length, level):
7       if level >= 1:
8           panel.draw_line(x, y, x + length, y)
9           cantor_set(panel, x, y + 20, length // 3, level - 1)
10          cantor_set(panel, x + 2 * length // 3, y + 20, \
```

Continued on next page

Continued from previous page

```
11                        length // 3, level - 1)
12
13  def main():
14      panel = DrawingPanel(400, 200)
15      panel.color = "black"
16      panel.stroke = 3
17      cantor_set(panel, 50, 20, 300, 4)
18
19  main()
```

Sierpinski Triangle

As a second example, we will explore a recursive function for drawing what is known as the *Sierpinski triangle*. The fractal is an infinitely recurring pattern composed of triangles with subtriangles inside them. We will write a function that produces various levels of the fractal.

At level 1, we draw an equilateral triangle as shown in Figure 9.26. Proceeding to level 2, we draw three smaller triangles that are contained within the original triangle.

We apply this principle in a recursive manner. Just as we replaced the original triangle with three inner triangles, we replace each of these three triangles with three inner triangles to obtain Figure 9.27 with nine triangles in level 3. This process continues indefinitely, making a more intricate pattern at each new level. The figure shows the result at level 6.

As with the Cantor set, we can solve this problem using the DrawingPanel class from Chapter 3. We'll pass the panel as a parameter to the function that is to draw the triangles. The function will need to know the three vertices of the triangle. We could pass them as six integers, but for this problem it is a bit cleaner to pass the coordinates as three (x, y) tuples that we'll call *p1*, *p2*, and *p3*. Recall from Chapter 7 that a tuple is just an object storing multiple values inside it, such as two integers per tuple in this case.

Figure 9.26   Sierpinski triangle, levels 1 and 2

Figure 9.27   Sierpinski triangle, levels 3 and 6

The function will also need the level to use, which we can pass as an integer. Our function will look like this:

```
def sierpinski(panel, p1, p2, p3, level):
    ...
```

Our base case will be to draw the basic triangle for level 1. The DrawingPanel class has functions for filling rectangles and ovals, but not for filling triangles. Fortunately, the DrawingPanel class has a fill_polygon method that accepts an arbitrary number of (*x, y*) points represented as two-integer tuples as parameters and draws a filled polygon between those endpoints. Passing it three tuples representing the three points will draw a triangle. Therefore our base case will look like this:

```
# version with base case
def sierpinski(panel, p1, p2, p3, level):
    if level == 1:
        # base case: draw a single filled triangle
        panel.fill_polygon(p1, p2, p3)
    else:
        # recursive case
        ...
```

Most of the work happens in the recursive case. We have to split the triangle into three smaller triangles. We'll label the vertices of the overall triangle. We then need to compute three new points that are the midpoints of the three sides of this triangle. Figure 9.28 shows these labeled points. From the figure we see the following:

- *p4* is the midpoint of *p1* and *p2*.
- *p5* is the midpoint of *p2* and *p3*.
- *p6* is the midpoint of *p1* and *p3*.

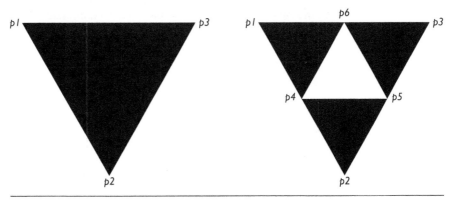

Figure 9.28   Sierpinski triangle endpoints and midpoints

Once we have computed those points, we can describe the smaller triangles as follows:

- In the upper-left corner is the triangle formed by *p1*, *p4*, and *p6*.
- In the bottom middle is the triangle formed by *p4*, *p2*, and *p5*.
- In the upper-right corner is the triangle formed by *p6*, *p5*, and *p3*.

There are three different midpoint computations involved here, so clearly it will be helpful to first write a function that will compute the midpoint of a segment given two endpoints. Computing the midpoints involves finding the arithmetic average (halfway point) of the *x* values and the *y* values. We'll accept the two points as two (*x*, *y*) tuples and return the result as another tuple:

```
# Returns a point that is halfway between the given two points.
def midpoint(p1, p2):
    x1, y1 = p1
    x2, y2 = p2
    x = (x1 + x2) // 2
    y = (y1 + y2) // 2
    return (x, y)
```

Given this function, we can easily compute the three midpoints *p4*, *p5*, and *p6*. The final detail we have to think about is the level. If you look again at the level-2 version of the figure, you will notice that it is composed of three simple triangles. In other words, the level-2 figure is composed of three level-1 figures. Similarly, the level-3 figure is composed of three level-2 figures, each of which in turn is composed of three level-1 figures. In general, if we are asked to draw a level N figure, we do so by drawing three level $(N - 1)$ figures.

We can turn these observations into code to complete the recursive function. The following is the complete program:

```
1   # This program draws the Sierpinski Triangle fractal.
2   from DrawingPanel import *
3
4   # Returns a point that is halfway between the given two points.
5   def midpoint(p1, p2):
6       x1, y1 = p1
7       x2, y2 = p2
8       x = (x1 + x2) // 2
9       y = (y1 + y2) // 2
10      return (x, y)
11
12  # Draws a Sierpinski Triangle figure of the given level with
13  # its endpoints at the three given x/y points.
14  def sierpinski(panel, p1, p2, p3, level):
15      if level == 1:
16          # base case: draw a single filled triangle
17          panel.fill_polygon(p1, p2, p3)
18      else:
19          # recursive case: split into 3 smaller triangles
20          p4 = midpoint(p1, p2)
21          p5 = midpoint(p2, p3)
22          p6 = midpoint(p1, p3)
23          sierpinski(panel, p1, p4, p6, level - 1)
24          sierpinski(panel, p4, p2, p5, level - 1)
25          sierpinski(panel, p6, p5, p3, level - 1)
26
27  def main():
28      panel = DrawingPanel(600, 400)
29      panel.fill_color = "black"
30      p1 = (100, 30)
31      p2 = (500, 30)
32      p3 = (300, 376)
33      level = 6
34      sierpinski(panel, p1, p2, p3, level)
35
36  main()
```

There is a limit to the number of levels down that we can go. The DrawingPanel has a finite resolution, so at some point we won't be able to subdivide our triangles any further. Also bear in mind that at each new level the number of triangles that we draw triples, which means that the number of triangles increases exponentially with the level. This can cause the program to run slowly if passed a large value for levels.

On the authors' test machine the program runs at an acceptable speed for up to roughly 12 levels, which is plenty for our purposes.

9.4 Recursive Backtracking

Many programming problems can be solved by systematically searching a set of possibilities. For example, if you want to find a path through a maze from a starting point to an exit point, you can explore all possible paths through the maze until you find one that works. For many games like tic-tac-toe you can explore all possible moves and countermoves to see if there is some move that guarantees that you win.

Many of these exhaustive search problems can be solved with an approach called *backtracking*. It is a particular approach to problem solving that is nicely expressed using recursion. As a result, it is sometimes referred to as *recursive backtracking*.

> **(Recursive) Backtracking**
>
> A general algorithm for finding solutions to a problem by exploring possible candidate solutions and abandoning ("backtracking") once a given candidate is deemed unsuitable.

Backtracking involves searching all possibilities, so it can be an expensive technique to use. But many problems are small enough in scope that they are nicely solved with a backtracking approach.

Traveling North/East

To introduce the basic concepts and terminology of backtracking, let's explore a simple example. Consider a standard Cartesian plane with (x, y) coordinates. Suppose that you start at the origin, $(0, 0)$, and you are allowed to repeatedly make one of three moves:

- You can move North (abbreviated "N"), which will increase your y-coordinate by 1.
- You can move East (abbreviated "E"), which will increase your x-coordinate by 1.
- You can move Northeast (abbreviated "NE"), which will increase both your x-coordinate and y-coordinate by 1.

Starting from the origin, these three different moves would leave you in the locations shown in Figure 9.29. We can think of this as a traveling problem where we can make a series of moves that take us from the origin to some other (x, y) point. For example, the sequence of moves N, NE, N would leave us at $(1, 3)$.

Every backtracking problem involves a *solution space* of possible answers that you want to explore. We try to view the problem as a sequence of *choices*, which allows us to think of the solution space as a *decision tree*. For our traveling problem the choices are the sequence of moves that we make. Figure 9.30 shows a decision tree showing all of the possible ways to make two moves and where each sequence leaves us. These decision trees can be quite large even for a small problem like this.

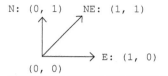

Figure 9.29   Traveling north, east, or northeast from origin

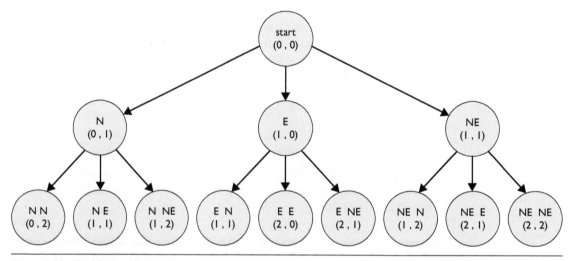

Figure 9.30   Decision tree for two moves

Consider the problem of traveling from the origin to the point (1, 2). What are the possible sequences of moves that would get you there? People are fairly good at solving problems like these, so you can probably pretty easily come up with all five of the possibilities:

- N, N, E
- N, E, N
- N, NE
- E, N, N
- NE, N

How would we write a computer program to find these solutions? For this simple problem, we could devise a specialized algorithm that takes into account the properties of these paths, but backtracking provides a convenient way to exhaustively search all possibilities. When writing functions to solve problems like this, we almost always need extra parameters for the backtracking. We can give them default values so that the initial call does not need to pass them.

The basic form that our backtracking solution will take is a function to explore all possible choices recursively:

```
def explore(a scenario):
    ...
```

Because we are using recursion, we need to identify base cases and recursive cases. Backtracking solutions generally involve two different base cases. You tend to stop the backtracking when you find a solution, so that becomes one of your base cases. Often what you want to do when you find a solution is to report it:

```
def explore(a scenario):
    if this is a solution:
        report it.
    else:
        ...
```

We don't want to search forever, so we also have to be on the lookout for what is called a *dead-end*. We might make a set of choices that lead us to a scenario where it is clear that no solution is possible with this set of choices. We make this a base case in our recursion so that we stop exploring when we reach a dead-end. Stopping at dead-ends is so important that we'll check for it first, before any other tests.

```
def explore(a scenario):
    if this is a dead-end:
        backtrack.
    else if this is a solution:
        report it.
    else:
        ...
```

If our backtracking search has led us to a scenario where we haven't yet solved the problem and haven't yet reached a dead-end, then we want to explore each possible choice available to us. For each possible choice, we recursively explore the scenario of making that choice:

```
def explore(a scenario):
    if this is a dead-end:
        backtrack.
    else if this is a solution:
        report it.
    else, use recursive calls to explore each available choice.
```

This pseudocode captures the essence of the backtracking approach. Not all backtracking solutions will take exactly this form, but they will all have some variation of each of these elements. For example, another variation of the backtracking code is to move the dead-end test down to just before the code to make recursive calls for exploration. This is more suited to some problems.

```
def explore(a scenario):
    if this is a solution:
        report it.
    else if this is not a dead-end:
        use recursive calls to explore each available choice.
```

We can flesh out the pseudocode a bit by filling in some details for this particular problem. We are considering the problem of moving from a current position to a target position, both specified with (x, y) coordinates. And we have three available moves from any given position: N, E, and NE:

```
def explore(current (x, y) and target (x, y)):
    if this is a solution:
        report it
    elif this is not a dead-end:
        explore(moving N).
        explore(moving E).
        explore(moving NE).
```

Often it can be challenging to figure out what parameters to pass to the exploration function. In this case, we need a current x and y and a target x and y (which we'll call tx and ty). We also need some way of keeping track of the choices that we have made so that we can report the path that we have taken. There are many ways to do this, but for simplicity, let's build up a string that stores the sequence of moves. This means that the heading for our recursive function should be:

```
# initial version of function header
def travel(tx, ty, x, y, path):
    ...
```

But the preceding function heading is cumbersome for the caller because they would need to pass five total arguments. Let's supply default values for all but the first two parameters. If no current x or y coordinate is passed, we'll default to $(0, 0)$. If no path has been passed, we'll pass an empty string.

```
# function header with default parameter values
def travel(tx, ty, x = 0, y = 0, path = ""):
    ...
```

We can test whether we have a solution by testing whether the current and target coordinates match. This can form the base case of our recursive solution:

```
# version with base case
def travel(tx, ty, x = 0, y = 0, path = ""):
    if x == tx and y == ty:
        print(path)
    ...
```

But how do we test for a dead-end? In this problem, our *x*-coordinates and *y*-coordinates never go down. So if we reach a point where the current *x* is greater than the target *x* or the current *y* is greater than the target *y*, then we know that we have traveled too far in that direction and we will never reach the target.

```
# version with start of recursive case
def travel(tx, ty, x = 0, y = 0, path = ""):
    if x == tx and y == ty:
        print(path)
    elif x <= tx and y <= ty:
        # haven't reached a dead-end yet
        ...
```

If our code has not reached a dead-end, we should explore in the three possible directions, trying to go N, E, and NE from the current *x/y* position. You might think that the code needs to carefully check before making each of these recursive calls to make sure that none of them goes too far in the *x* or *y* direction. An initial poorly styled attempt to handle this would be the following:

```
# Version with initial recursive code.
# Not a model to follow.
def travel(tx, ty, x = 0, y = 0, path = ""):
    if x == tx and y == ty:
        print(path)
    elif x <= tx and y <= ty:
        # haven't reached a dead-end yet
        if x <= tx and y + 1 <= ty:
            travel(tx, ty, x, y + 1, path + "N ")
        if x + 1 <= tx and y <= ty:
            travel(tx, ty, x + 1, y, path + "E ")
        if x + 1 <= tx and y + 1 <= ty:
            travel(tx, ty, x + 1, y + 1, path + "NE ")
```

There's an old saying, "Look before you leap," meaning that one should not act without looking ahead for possible negative consequences. That's good life advice in general, but it can be bad advice for a programmer trying to write recursive code. The preceding version of the `travel` function "looks before it leaps" by using `if` statements to check the *x* and *y* values to make sure they do not go past the target `tx` and `ty` location. This may seem like a good thing to do, because we don't want our code to go too far in the wrong direction.

If you have a deep understanding of recursion, though, you'll see that the aforementioned `if` tests are not necessary. If we just make the three recursive calls with no test, any calls that move *x* or *y* too far will hit a base case by failing the next call's `elif` test.

This will cause the bad calls to immediately return. The cleanliness and elegance of the code without the `if` tests is preferred over the version with so many extra `if` statements.

The bad practice of writing unnecessary `if` statements in recursive code is sometimes called *arm's length recursion*. Arm's length recursion is most often done by programmers who are still new to recursion and are worried about making a "bad" or "invalid" recursive call. So long as the code has proper base cases that exit when invalid parameter values are passed, a call with invalid values is not a bad thing, and adding lots of `if` statements to avoid such calls is unnecessary and inelegant.

> **Arm's Length Recursion**
>
> A discouraged programming practice where recursive code performs unnecessary `if` tests before making recursive calls.

Modifying our function to avoid arm's length recursive tests, we end up with the following program, including the complete `travel` function and a log of execution:

```
1   # This program recursively prints all paths
2   # to a given target (x, y) position.
3
4   # Prints all paths from (x, y) to target (tx, ty)
5   # that can be made by going N, E, or NE by one step.
6   def travel(tx, ty, x = 0, y = 0, path = ""):
7       if x == tx and y == ty:
8           print(path)
9       elif x <= tx and y <= ty:
10          travel(tx, ty, x, y + 1, path + "N ")
11          travel(tx, ty, x + 1, y, path + "E ")
12          travel(tx, ty, x + 1, y + 1, path + "NE ")
13
14  def main():
15      x = int(input("Target x? "))
16      y = int(input("Target y? "))
17      travel(x, y)
18
19  main()
```

```
Target x? 1
Target y? 2
N N E
N E N
N NE
E N N
NE N
```

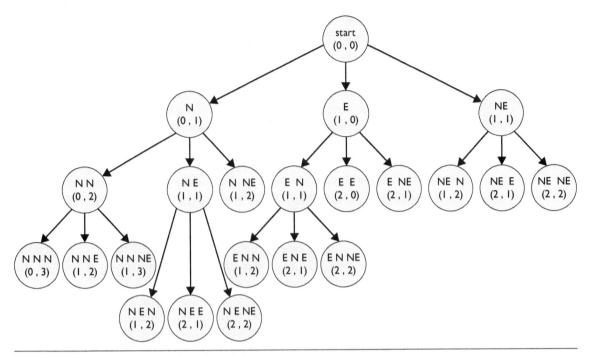

Figure 9.31   Complete decision tree for paths to (1, 2)

Figure 9.31 shows the complete decision tree that is explored by this particular call with the five solutions shaded. Notice that the tree does not contain all of the possible combinations of three moves. That is because we don't explore past a solution and we don't explore past a dead-end, such as (2, 1).

It is useful to consider the order in which the recursive function searches these possibilities. In general, as with most recursive solutions, the recursive calls lead to a depth-first traversal. From the starting point at the top of the tree, it first considers moving North to (0, 1). That entire branch of the tree is explored before any other branches are explored. The next call considers moving North again to (0, 2). Then it considers another move North to (0, 3). So the initial sequence of calls leads it down to the leftmost node of the three. This is a dead-end, so it stops exploring. At that point, it returns to where it last had another choice to consider. So it backs up to where it had chosen two North moves in a row (N N) and it considers moving East instead of moving North. That turns out to be a solution (N N E), so it reports a success. Then it backs up again to where it last had another choice to make and it considers the remaining possibilities.

This property of going back to where it still has other choices to explore is the source of the term "backtracking." As it finds solutions and dead-ends, it goes back (backtracks) to where it last had some other move to consider. It continues to search until it has exhausted all possible sequences of choices.

Eight Queens Puzzle

A classic puzzle that backtracking solves well is to find a way to place eight queens on a chess board so that no two queens threaten each other. Queens can move horizontally, vertically, or diagonally, so it is a challenge to find a way to put eight different queens on the board so that no two of them are in the same row, column, or diagonal. Figure 9.32 shows one example placement.

To solve this problem with backtracking, we have to think of it in terms of a sequence of choices. The simplest way to do this is to think in terms of choosing where the first queen goes, then choosing where the second queen goes, and so on. There are 64 places to put the first queen because the chess board is an 8-by-8 board. So at the top of the tree, there are 64 different choices you could make for placing the first queen. Then once you've placed one queen, there are 63 squares left to choose from for the second queen, then 62 squares for the third queen, and so on.

Because backtracking searches all possibilities, it can take a long time to execute. If we explore all of the possibilities, we'll need to look at 64 × 63 × 62 × . . . states, which is too many even for a fast computer. So we need to be as smart as we can about the choices we explore. In the case of Eight Queens, we can do better than to consider 64 choices followed by 63 choices followed by 62 choices and so on. We know that most of these aren't worth exploring.

One approach is to observe that if there is any solution at all to this problem, then the solution will have exactly one queen in each row and exactly one queen in each column. That's because you can't have two in the same row or two in the same column and because there are eight of them on an 8-by-8 board. So we can search more efficiently if we go row-by-row or column-by-column. It doesn't matter which choice we make, so let's explore column-by-column. Eliminating undesirable candidates from being explored is also called *pruning* the decision tree.

> **Pruning (a Decision Tree)**
>
> Eliminating branches of calls that cannot lead to a solution in a backtracking algorithm.

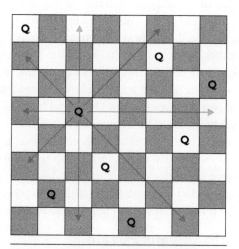

Figure 9.32   The Eight Queens puzzle

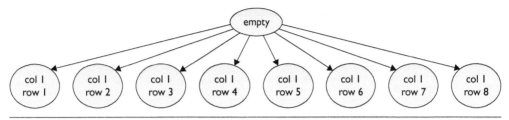

Figure 9.33 Eight Queens decision tree for first column

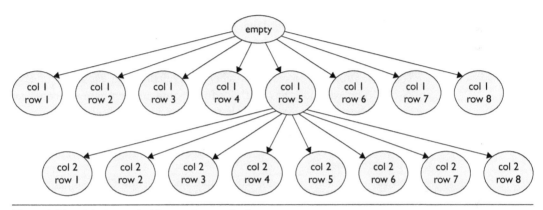

Figure 9.34 Eight Queens decision tree for second column

In this new way of looking at the search space, the first choice is for column 1. We have eight different rows where we could put a queen in column 1. At the next level we consider all of the places to put a queen in column 2. And so on. Figure 9.33 shows the top of our decision tree.

There are eight different branches for each column. Under each of these branches, we have 8 eight branches for each of the possible rows where we might place a queen in column 2. For example, if we think just about the possibility of placing the first queen in column 1 and row 5 and then think about all of the ways to place a second queen, we end up with an extra level of the tree, as shown in Figure 9.34.

The figures don't capture the whole story because the tree is so large. There are eight branches at the top. From each of these eight branches there are eight branches. And from each of those branches there are eight branches. This continues eight levels deep (one level for each column of the board).

It's clear that the eight choices could be coded fairly nicely in a `for` loop. If the rows and columns are numbered with 0-based indexes, something along the lines of the following code would be a start:

```
for row in range(8):
    . . .
```

But what we need for backtracking is something more like a deeply nested `for` loop:

```
for row0 in range(8):           # explore column 0
    for row1 in range(8):       # explore column 1
        for row2 in range(8):   # explore column 2
            for row3 in range(8):   # explore column 3
            ...
```

That's not a bad way to think of what backtracking does, although we will use recursion to write this in a more elegant way.

Before we explore the backtracking code, we need to consider the low-level details of how to keep track of a board that allows us to place queens in specific locations. It is helpful to split off the low level details into a separate class. So let's suppose we already have a `ChessBoard` object that keeps track of the state of the chess board.

The `ChessBoard` object stores whether a queen is on each square of the 8-by-8 (or N-by-N) board, and it has methods for placing and removing queens from a given square. The board also has a methods for asking whether it is safe to place a queen on a square with respect to the other queens already on the board, and for asking whether all existing queens are placed in valid locations. Table 9.2 lists the methods of our `ChessBoard` class.

You can download the complete source code for the `ChessBoard` class from the following URL:

- http://www.buildingpythonprograms.com/chapters/ch09-files/ChessBoard.py

The more interesting code is the backtracking code, which, given this `ChessBoard`, we can now write in a straightforward manner. Our recursive `place_queens` function can be passed a `ChessBoard` as a parameter, and it will recursively perform the backtracking:

```
def place_queens(board):
    ...
```

Table 9.2   ChessBoard Class Methods

Method	Description
`ChessBoard(size)`	creates a board of `size` x `size` squares
`board.has_queen(row, col)`	returns `True` if a queen is on the given board square
`board.place(row, col)`	places a queen on the given board square
`board.remove(row, col)`	removes a queen from the given board square
`board.safe(row, col)`	returns `True` if it is okay to place a queen on the given board square
`board.valid()`	returns `True` if no queens on the board are able to attack each other
`board.size()`	returns the size of the board

Recall that we had this general pseudocode for backtracking solutions:

```
def explore(a scenario):
    if this is a dead-end:
        backtrack.
    else if this is a solution:
        report it.
    else:
        use recursive calls to explore each available choice.
```

The Eight Queens backtracking problem differs in several important ways from the simple backtracking we saw before. Let's consider each of the differences and see how to adapt our pseudocode for each.

In the traveling problem we had just three possibilities to consider, so it made sense to write three recursive calls to explore each possibility. Here we have eight possibilities for the Eight Queens problem and *N* possibilities if the board size is *N* rather than 8. So in this case we want to use a loop to consider the different possibilities. Many backtracking problems will require using a loop instead of individual calls, so it is useful to adapt our pseudocode to fit that approach.

```
def explore(a scenario):
    if this is a solution:
        report it.
    else if this is not a dead-end:
        for each available choice:
            use a recursive call to explore that choice.
```

We can also be more specific about what it means to explore a choice. In our simple example, we were building up a string that stored the path. That meant that we didn't have to undo a choice to move on to the next choice. More complex backtracking problems require a cleanup step where you undo a choice. That will be true of Eight Queens. We will place a queen on the board to explore that branch and when we come back from the recursive exploration, we will need to remove the queen to get ready to explore the next possible choice. So the pseudocode can be expanded to include the pattern of making a choice, recursively exploring, and then undoing the choice:

```
def explore(a scenario):
    if this is a dead-end:
        backtrack.
    else if this is a solution:
        report it.
    else, for each available choice:
        make the choice.
        recursively explore subsequent choices.
        undo the choice.
```

This pseudocode is general enough that it can be used for many backtracking problems. Some programmers refer to this as the "*choose, explore, un-choose*" pattern for backtracking.

In the case of Eight Queens, there are many solutions (over 90 different solutions). The pseudocode we have developed so far will display all of these solutions. This pseudocode is also general enough that it can be used for many backtracking problems when you want to exhaustively find and display all solutions to the problem.

We can adapt our pseudocode to the Eight Queens problem by filling in the details. What parameters will it need to specify a scenario? It certainly needs the `ChessBoard` as a parameter. Recall that each level of the decision tree involves a different column of the board. So the first invocation will handle column 0, the second will handle column 1, and so on. So in addition to the board, the function also needs to know the column to work on. We'll accept the column as a parameter to our `place_queens` function.

How do we know if we've found a solution? This backtracking code doesn't explore dead-ends. So for any given call, we know that all columns prior to the current one must be columns that have queens placed on them in safe locations. That leaves us with this header:

```python
# pre: queens have been safely placed in previous columns
def place_queens(board, col):
    ...
```

If our column parameter reaches 8, that means all eight queens have been placed properly. To make our code work for all sizes and not just 8, we will check whether the column value has reached the board's size. This turns out to be our test for whether we have found a solution:

```python
# pre: queens have been safely placed in previous columns
def place_queens(board, col):
    if col >= board.size():
        # base case: all queens are placed
        print(board)
    else:
        # recursive case: try to place one queen in this column
        ...
```

Now we have to fill in the details of the `for` loop that explores the various possibilities. We have eight possibilities to explore (the eight rows of this column where we might place a queen). A `for` loop works nicely to explore the different row numbers. The pseudocode indicates that we should test to make sure it is not a dead-end. We can do that by making sure that it is safe to place a queen in that row and column:

```python
# recursive case, partial (loop over columns)
for row in range(board.size()):
    if board.safe(row, col):
        ...
```

We now need to fill in the three steps that are involved in exploring a choice: making the choice, recursively exploring subsequent choices, and undoing the choice. We make the choice by telling the board to place a queen in that row and column:

```
# recursive case, partial (place a queen)
for row in range(board.size()):
    if board.safe(row, col):
        board.place(row, col)          # choose
        ...
```

Then we recursively explore subsequent choices (later columns), which will print any solutions found by those subsequent choices:

```
# recursive case with recursive call
for row in range(board.size()):
    if board.safe(row, col):
        board.place(row, col)          # choose
        place_queens(board, col + 1)   # explore
        ...
```

Finally, we have to undo our choice in case that turns out to be a dead-end:

```
# recursive case with un-choosing
for row in range(board.size()):
    if board.safe(row, col):
        board.place(row, col)          # choose
        place_queens(board, col + 1)   # explore
        board.remove(row, col)         # un-choose
```

This code works and solves the problem. The code we developed uses a "look before you leap" approach and does not make a recursive call unless it would be safe to do so. Arguably this is a form of arm's length recursion. We could rewrite this code to try placing the queen, even if it is invalid to do so, but then backtracking immediately from the next call if the placement is invalid. Rather than calling safe on the board before placing a queen, we'll place it, then have the next call use the valid method on the board to see whether all of its queens are in valid spots. If they aren't, we'll backtrack immediately with a return statement.

Putting it all together, we get the following complete program. We need some code in main that prompts the user for the board size and then calls the recursive function to print all of the solutions. The program is shown along a log of execution at size 8. There are many solutions, so we truncate the output and show only the first few.

```
1  # This program solves the Eight Queens problem.
2  # This version prints all solutions.
3
4  from ChessBoard import *
```

Continued on next page

Continued from previous page

```
 5
 6  # Places queens on the given board,
 7  # starting with the given column.
 8  def place_queens(board, col = 0):
 9      if not board.valid():
10          return
11      elif col >= board.size():
12          print(board)
13      else:
14          for row in range(board.size()):
15              board.place(row, col)          # choose
16              place_queens(board, col + 1)   # explore
17              board.remove(row, col)         # un-choose
18          return False
19
20  def main():
21      size = int(input("Board size? "))
22      board = ChessBoard(size)
23      print("Here are all solutions:")
24      place_queens(board)
25
26  main()
```

```
Board size? 8
Here are all solutions:
Q _ _ _ _ _ _ _
_ _ _ _ _ _ Q _
_ _ _ _ Q _ _ _
_ _ _ _ _ _ _ Q
_ Q _ _ _ _ _ _
_ _ _ Q _ _ _ _
_ _ _ _ _ Q _ _
_ _ Q _ _ _ _ _

Q _ _ _ _ _ _ _
_ _ _ _ _ _ Q _
_ _ _ Q _ _ _ _
_ _ _ _ _ Q _ _
_ _ _ _ _ _ _ Q
_ Q _ _ _ _ _ _
_ _ _ _ Q _ _ _
_ _ Q _ _ _ _ _
...
```

Stopping after One Solution

The Eight Queens code from the previous section printed every solution to the board. But what if we wanted to print only a single solution? The code can be modified to do so, but the modifications are not as simple as they might initially seem. In this section we'll talk about differences between code that finds all solutions to a backtracking problem and code that stops after finding just one solution.

Recall the pseudocode we wrote for exploring all solutions:

```
# General backtracking pseudocode to find all solutions
def explore(a scenario):
    if this is a dead-end:
        backtrack.
    else if this is a solution:
        report it.
    else, for each available choice:
        make the choice.
        recursively explore subsequent choices.
        undo the choice.
```

This is appropriate code to use if you want to search all possibilities. In the case of Eight Queens, there are so many solutions (over 90 different solutions for a board of size 8) that we may not want to see them all. If we're happy to have just one solution, we must write a variation that stops when it finds a solution. That means that our recursive function will need to have a way to let us know whether a certain path worked out or whether it turned out to be a dead-end. A good way to do this is to return a Boolean value from the function: `True` if it succeeds, `False` if it is a dead-end. The following pseudocode is an incomplete initial attempt to make such a modification:

```
# General backtracking pseudocode to find a single solution.
# This version does not quite work.
def explore(a scenario):
    if this is a dead-end:
        return False.
    else if this is a solution:
        report it.
        return True.
    else, for each available choice:
        make the choice.
        recursively explore subsequent choices.
        undo the choice.
```

We can incorporate these ideas into our Eight Queens code from the last section. We have two base cases: one where we have reached an invalid state (a dead-end), and

one where we have found a solution to the board. We can modify these two cases to
return `False` and `True`, respectively:

```
# Initial version with Boolean return values.
# This version does not quite work.
def place_queens(board, col):
    if not board.valid():
        return False
    elif col >= board.size():
        return True
    else:
        # recursive case: try to place one queen
        ...
```

You'll find that if you run this modified `place_queens` function to contain the preceding modifications, it will still print all solutions. How can this be, if we're returning
`True` and `False`? The code may not be returning where you think. A `return` statement
doesn't exit us all the way out to `main`; it just sends us back one level in the call stack.
In the case of a recursive function like this, returning will send us back to the previous
call of the function. That previous call is not reacting to these returned values, so it is
not going to stop exploring other solutions.

Let's think about the case where we find a solution and the code returns `True`. This
would be returned by a ninth call to the recursive function. The returned value of `True`
will be sent back to the eighth call that made the ninth call in the first place. That eighth
call needs to notice that the function returned `True` and react to this. If the next call
returns `True`, so should the current call.

For the code to actually stop after finding a single solution, whenever we make a
recursive call, we must examine the Boolean result returned from it. If that result is `True`,
it means that we found a solution, so we should immediately stop the current call and
return `True` from it as well. The following pseudocode contains this important change:

```
# General backtracking pseudocode to find a single solution.
# This version does work properly.
def explore(a scenario):
    if this is a dead-end:
        return False.
    else if this is a solution:
        report it.
        return True.
    else, for each available choice:
        make the choice.
        result = recursively explore subsequent choices.
        if result is True:
            return True.
        undo the choice.
```

You may wonder, does the pseudocode need an `else` case to react to a result of `False` from the recursive call? The answer is no, because if the recursive call returned `False`, it means that the call was unable to find a solution. So our call should keep looking and checking further columns to try to find a solution. You could put the "un-choose" code into an `else` statement, but the existing version already works, so the `else` is not needed.

Let's incorporate these latest changes into our Eight Queens code. We add an `if` statement that checks whether the recursive calls return `True`, and, if so, stops the process since it has found a solution:

```
# recursive case that checks Boolean value
for row in range(board.size()):
    board.place(row, col)
    if place_queens(board, col + 1):
        return True
    ...
```

The following is the complete program that prints a single solution to the Eight Queens puzzle. The program is shown along with two logs of execution, one at size 8 (where a solution does exist) and another at size 2 (where no solution exists):

```
 1  # This program solves the Eight Queens problem.
 2  # This version prints a single solution.
 3
 4  from ChessBoard import *
 5
 6  # Places queens on the given board,
 7  # starting with the given column.
 8  # Returns True if successful and False if no solution found.
 9  def place_queens(board, col = 0):
10      if not board.valid():
11          return False
12      elif col >= board.size():
13          return True
14      else:
15          for row in range(board.size()):
16              board.place(row, col)              # choose
17              if place_queens(board, col + 1):   # explore
18                  return True
19              board.remove(row, col)             # un-choose
20          return False
21
22  def main():
23      size = int(input("Board size? "))
```

Continued on next page

Continued from previous page

```
24      board = ChessBoard(size)
25      if place_queens(board):
26          print("One solution is as follows:")
27          print(board)
28      else:
29          print("No solution found.")
30
31  main()
```

```
Board size? 8
One solution is as follows:
Q _ _ _ _ _ _ _
_ _ _ _ _ Q _
_ _ _ _ Q _ _ _
_ _ _ _ _ _ _ Q
_ Q _ _ _ _ _ _
_ _ _ Q _ _ _ _
_ _ _ _ _ Q _ _
_ _ Q _ _ _ _ _

Board size? 2
No solution found.
```

9.5 Case Study: Prefix Evaluator

In this section, we will explore the use of recursion to evaluate complex numeric expressions. First we will examine the different conventions for specifying numeric expressions and then we will see how recursion makes it relatively easy to implement one of the standard conventions.

Infix, Prefix, and Postfix Notation

When we write numeric expressions in a Python program, we typically put numeric operators like + and * between the two operands, as shown in the examples in Figure 9.35. Putting the operator between the operands is a convention known as *infix notation*.

```
3.5 + 8.2
9.1 * 12.7
7.8 * (2.3 + 2.5)
```

Figure 9.35 Expressions in infix notation

```
+ 3.5 8.2
* 9.1 12.7
* 7.8 + 2.3 2.5
```

Figure 9.36   Expressions in prefix notation

```
3.5 8.2 +
9.1 12.7 *
7.8 2.3 2.5 + *
```

Figure 9.37   Expressions in postfix notation

A second convention is to put the operator in front of the two operands, as shown in the examples in Figure 9.36. Putting the operator in front of the operands is a convention known as *prefix notation*.

Prefix notation looks odd for symbols like + and *, but it resembles mathematical function notation, in which the name of the function goes first. For example, if we were calling functions instead of using operators, we would write:

```
plus(3.5, 8.2)
times(9.1, 12.7)
times(7.8, plus(2.3, 2.5))
```

(There actually are functions for performing basic arithmetic like this, located in Python's `operator` library. These are not currently very useful to us, but in Chapter 12 we will discuss functional programming, which will make the functions more useful.)

There is a third convention in which the operator appears after the two operands, as in the examples in Figure 9.37. This convention is known as *postfix notation*. It is also sometimes referred to as reverse Polish notation, or RPN. For many years Hewlett-Packard has sold scientific calculators that use RPN rather than normal infix notation.

We are so used to infix notation that it takes a while to get used to the other two conventions. One of the interesting facts you will discover if you take the time to learn the prefix and postfix conventions is that infix is the only notation that requires parentheses. The other two notations are unambiguous. Table 9.3 summarizes the three notations.

Evaluating Prefix Expressions

Of the three standard notations, prefix notation is most easily implemented with recursion. In this section we will write a program that reads a prefix expression from a string and computes its value. The core of our program will be a recursive function called `evaluate` that accepts the prefix expression to evaluate and returns its resulting value.

Before we can begin writing the function, we have to consider the kind of input that we are going to get. As the precondition indicates, we will assume that the input contains a legal prefix expression. The simplest possible expression would be a number like `38.9`. There isn't much to evaluate in such a case; we can simply read and return the number.

Table 9.3 Arithmetic Notations

Notation	Description	Examples
infix	operator between operands	`2.3 + 4.7`
		`2.6 * 3.7`
		`(3.4 + 7.9) * 18.6 + 2.3 / 4.7`
prefix	operator before operands	`+ 2.3 4.7`
	(functional notation)	`* 2.6 3.7`
		`+ * + 3.4 7.9 18.6 / 2.3 4.7`
postfix	operator after operands	`2.3 4.7 +`
	(reverse Polish notation)	`2.6 3.7 *`
		`3.4 7.9 + 18.6 * 2.3 4.7 / +`

A more complex prefix expression will involve one or more operators. Remember that the operator goes in front of the operands in a prefix expression.

```
+ 2.6 3.7
* 4.1 + 1.5 2.2
```

The expression represented by a given operator could itself be an operand in a larger expression. For example, we might ask for the result of the following expression:

```
* + 2.6 3.7 + 5.2 18.7
```

At the outermost level, we have a multiplication operator with two operands:

In other words, this expression is computing the product of two sums. Here is the same expression written in the more familiar infix notation:

```
(2.6 + 3.7) * (5.2 + 18.7)
```

These expressions can become arbitrarily complex. The key observation to make about them is that they all begin with an operator. In other words, every prefix expression is of one of two forms:

- A simple number
- An operator followed by two operands

This observation will become a roadmap for our recursive solution.

Since we will want to process each token of input separately, we'll have `main` split the expression into a list of strings and pass that to `evaluate` as its parameter. For example, if the expression is `"* 4.1 + 2.6 3.7"`, we will pass it to our function as the five-element list `["*", "4.1", "+", "2.6", "3.7"]`. Our function's heading will look like this:

```
# pre : tokens represent a legal prefix expression
# post: expression is evaluated and the result is returned
def evaluate(tokens):
    ...
```

Before we can begin writing the function, we have to consider the kind of input that we are going to get. As the precondition indicates, we will assume that the list of tokens represents a legal prefix expression. We'll write our function so that it starts at the front of the list, grabbing a token from it and processing that token. As the code reads and examines a given token of the expression, it will "consume" it by deleting it from the front of the list. If we write the function properly, eventually we will consume every token of the expression as our code examines and evaluates it. The best way to grab and remove a specific value from a list is to call its `pop` method, which accepts an index parameter and removes and returns the value at that index from the list:

```
def evaluate(tokens):
    # extract first token
    first = tokens.pop(0)
    ...
```

What kind of value might the first token be? The simplest prefix expression will be a number, and we can distinguish it from the other case because any other expression will begin with an operator. So we can begin our recursive solution by checking whether the next token in the expression list is a number. If it is, we have a simple case and we can simply read and return the number. In Chapter 5 we wrote a predicate function `is_float` that accepts a string parameter and returns a Boolean value indicating whether that string could be safely converted into a `float`. We'll use that function again here to help us implement this base case of our algorithm:

```
def evaluate(tokens):
    # extract first token
    first = tokens.pop(0)
    if is_float(first):
        # base case: a numeric token
        return float(first)
    else:
        ...
```

Turning our attention to the recursive case, we know that the first token of input must be an operator, and that it is followed by two operands. At this point we reach a critical decision. Our code has already extracted the operator and stored it in the variable `first`. Now we need to extract the first operand and then the second operand. If we knew that the operands were simple numbers, we could write code like the following:

```
# not the right approach!
def evaluate(tokens):
    # extract first token
    first = tokens.pop(0)
    if is_float(first):
        # base case: a numeric token
        return float(first)
    else:
        # recursive case: operator and 2 operands
        left = float(tokens.pop(0))
        right = float(tokens.pop(0))
        ...
```

But we have no guarantee that the operands are simple numbers. They might be complex expressions that begin with operators. Your instinct might be to test whether or not the original operator is followed by another operator (in other words, whether the first operand begins with an operator), but that reasoning won't lead you to a satisfactory outcome. Remember that the expressions can be arbitrarily complex, so either of the operands might contain dozens of operators to be processed.

The solution to this puzzle involves recursion. We need to read two operands from the list, and they might be very complex. But we know that they are in prefix form and we know that they aren't as complex as the original expression we were asked to evaluate. The key is to recursively evaluate each of the two operands:

```
def evaluate(tokens):
    # extract first token
    first = tokens.pop(0)
    if is_float(first):
        # base case: a numeric token
        return float(first)
    else:
        # recursive case: operator and 2 operands
        left  = evaluate(tokens)
        right = evaluate(tokens)
        ...
```

This is the right approach. Of course, we still have the task of evaluating the operator. After the two recursive calls have executed, we will have an operator and two numbers (say, +, 3.4, and 2.6). It would be nice if we could just write a statement like the following:

```
return operand1 operator operand2   # does not work
```

Unfortunately, Python doesn't work that way. We have to use a nested if/else statement to test what kind of operator we have and to return an appropriate value:

```
if operator == "+":
    return operand1 + operand2
elif operator == "-":
    return operand1 - operand2
...
```

We can include this code in its own function called apply so that our recursive function stays fairly short:

```
# pre : input contains a legal prefix expression
# post: expression is evaluated and the result is returned
def evaluate(tokens):
    # extract first token
    first = tokens.pop(0)
    if is_float(first):
        # base case: a numeric token
        return float(first)
    else:
        # recursive case: an operator
        operand1 = evaluate(tokens)
        operand2 = evaluate(tokens)
        return apply(first, operand1, operand2)
```

Complete Program

The following is a complete version of the prefix expression evaluator. The code includes the is_float function discussed previously. The code in main introduces the program, prompts the user to type expressions, and splits each expression into a list of tokens separated by spaces. The main function calls our recursive evaluate function and then prints the returned result value, rounded to two decimal places. The program exits when the user types an empty string for the expression.

```
1   # This program prompts for and evaluates a prefix expression.
2
3   # Returns True if the given string can be converted
4   # into a float successfully, or False if not.
5   def is_float(s):
6       try:
7           n = float(s)
8           return True
9       except ValueError:
```

Continued on next page

Continued from previous page

```
10             return False
11
12   # pre : operator is one of +, -, *, /, or %
13   # post: returns the result of applying the given operator
14   #   to the given operands
15   def apply(operator, operand1, operand2):
16       if operator == "+":
17           return operand1 + operand2
18       elif operator == "-":
19           return operand1 - operand2
20       elif operator == "*":
21           return operand1 * operand2
22       elif operator == "/":
23           return operand1 / operand2
24       elif operator == "%":
25           return operand1 % operand2
26       else:
27           raise ValueError("bad operator: " + operator)
28
29   # pre : tokens represent a legal prefix expression
30   # post: expression is evaluated and the result is returned
31   def evaluate(tokens):
32       # extract first token
33       first = tokens.pop(0)
34       if is_float(first):
35           # base case: a numeric token
36           return float(first)
37       else:
38           # recursive case: an operator
39           operand1 = evaluate(tokens)
40           operand2 = evaluate(tokens)
41           return apply(first, operand1, operand2)
42
43   def main():
44       print("This program evaluates prefix expressions that")
45       print("include the operators +, -, *, /, and %.")
46       print()
47
48       expr = input("Expression? ")
49       while expr != "":
50           tokens = expr.split(" ")
```

Continued on next page

Continued from previous page

```
51              value = evaluate(tokens)
52              print("value =", round(value, 2))
53              expr = input("Expression? ")
54
55       print("Exiting.")
56
57   main()
```

```
This program evaluates prefix expressions that
include the operators +, -, *, /, and %.
Expression? 38.9
value = 38.9
Expression? + 2.6 3.7
value = 6.3
Expression? * + 2.6 3.7 + 5.2 18.7
value = 150.57
Expression? / + * - 17.4 8.9 - 3.9 4.7 18.4 - 3.8 * 7.9 2.3
value = -0.81
Expression?
Exiting.
```

The program can handle simple numbers, like 38.9. It can handle expressions with a single operator, as in + 2.6 3.7. And it can handle the case we considered that involved a product of two sums. In fact, it can handle arbitrarily complex expressions, as in the last expression in the sample log. The expression being computed in that example is the prefix equivalent of the following infix expression:

```
((17.4 - 8.9) * (3.9 - 4.7) + 18.4) / (3.8 - 7.9 * 2.3)
```

When you program with recursion, you'll notice two things. First, the recursive code that you write will tend to be fairly short, even though it might be solving a very complex task. Second, some of your program will generally end up being supporting code for the recursion that does low-level tasks. For our current task of evaluating a prefix expression, we have a short and powerful prefix evaluator, but we need to include some supporting code that explains the program to the user, prompts for a prefix expression, and reports the result. We also found that we needed a function that would apply an operator to two operands. The nonrecursive parts of the program are fairly straightforward, so they are shown without detailed discussion.

Chapter Summary

- Recursion is an algorithmic technique in which a function calls itself. A function that uses recursion is called a recursive function.
- Recursive functions include two cases: a base case that the function can solve directly without recursion, and a recursive case in which the function reduces a problem into a simpler problem of the same kind using a recursive call.
- Recursive function calls work internally by storing information about each call into a structure called a call stack. When the function calls itself, information about the call is placed on top of the stack. When a function

call finishes executing, its information is removed from the stack and the program returns to the call underneath.
- A recursive function without a base case, or one in which the recursive case doesn't properly transition into the base case, can lead to infinite recursion.
- Recursive functions often need parameters in addition to the ones specified. A good way to achieve this is to add extra parameters with default values.
- Recursion can be used to draw graphical figures in complex patterns, including fractal images. Fractals are images that are recursively self-similar, and they are often referred to as "infinitely complex."

Self-Check Problems

Section 9.1: Thinking Recursively

1. What is recursion? How does a recursive function differ from a standard iterative function?

2. What are base cases and recursive cases? Why does a recursive function need to have both?

3. Consider the following function:

```
def mystery1(n):
    if n <= 1:
        print(n, end="")
    else:
        mystery1(n // 2)
        print(",", n, end="")
```

For each of the following calls, indicate the output that is produced by the function:

a. mystery1(1)
b. mystery1(2)
c. mystery1(3)
d. mystery1(4)
e. mystery1(16)
f. mystery1(30)
g. mystery1(100)

4. Consider the following function:

```
def mystery2(n):
    if n > 100:
        print(n, end="")
    else:
        mystery2(2 * n)
        print(",", n, end="")
```

For each of the following calls, indicate the output that is produced by the function:

a. `mystery2(113)`

b. `mystery2(70)`

c. `mystery2(42)`

d. `mystery2(30)`

e. `mystery2(10)`

5. Consider the following function:

```python
def mystery_x_y(x, y):
    if y == 1:
        print(x, end="")
    else:
        print(x * y, ", ", sep="", end="")
        mystery_x_y(x, y - 1)
        print(",", x * y, end="")
```

For each of the following calls, indicate the output that is produced by the function:

a. `mystery_x_y(4, 1)`

b. `mystery_x_y(4, 2)`

c. `mystery_x_y(8, 2)`

d. `mystery_x_y(4, 3)`

e. `mystery_x_y(3, 4)`

6. Convert the following iterative function into a recursive function:

```python
# Prints each character of the string reversed twice.
# double_reverse("hello") prints oolllleehh
def double_reverse(s):
    for i in range(len(s) - 1, -1, -1):
        print(s[i], end="")
        print(s[i], end="")
```

Section 9.2: Recursive Functions and Data

7. The following function is an attempt to write a recursive `power` function to compute exponents. What is wrong with the code? How can it be fixed?

```python
def power(x, y):
    return x * power(x, y - 1)
```

8. What are the differences between the two versions of the `power` function shown in this section of the chapter? What advantage does the second version have over the first version? Are both versions recursive?

9. Consider the following function:

```python
def mystery4(x, y):
    if x < y:
        return x
    else:
        return mystery4(x - y, y)
```

For each of the following calls, indicate the value that is returned:

a. `mystery4(6, 13)`

b. `mystery4(14, 10)`

c. `mystery4(37, 10)`

d. `mystery4(8, 2)`

e. `mystery4(50, 7)`

10. Consider the following function:

```
def mystery5(x, y):
    if x < 0:
        return - mystery5(-x, y)
    elif y < 0:
        return - mystery5(x, -y)
    elif x == 0 and y == 0:
        return 0
    else:
        return 100 * mystery5(x // 10, y // 10) + 10 * (x % 10) + y % 10
```

For each of the following calls, indicate the value that is returned:

a. `mystery5(5, 7)`

b. `mystery5(12, 9)`

c. `mystery5(-7, 4)`

d. `mystery5(-23, -48)`

e. `mystery5(128, 343)`

11. Convert the following iterative function into a recursive function:

```
# Returns n!, such as 5! = 1*2*3*4*5
def factorial(n):
    product = 1
    for i in range(1, n + 1):
        product *= i
    return product
```

12. The following function has a bug that leads to infinite recursion. What correction fixes the code?

```
# Adds the digits of the given number.
# Example: digit_sum(3456) returns 3+4+5+6 = 18
def digit_sum(n):
    if n > 10:
        # base case (small number)
        return n
    else:
        # recursive case (large number)
        return n % 10 + digit_sum(n // 10)
```

13. Sometimes the parameters that a client would like to pass to a function don't match the parameters that are best for writing a recursive solution to the problem. What should a programmer do to resolve this issue?

14. The *Fibonacci sequence* is a sequence of numbers in which the first two numbers are 1 and each subsequent number is the sum of the previous two Fibonacci numbers. The sequence is 1, 1, 2, 3, 5, 8, 13, 21, 34, and so on. The following is a correct, but inefficient, function to compute the nth Fibonacci number:

```
def fibonacci(n):
    if n <= 2:
        return 1
    else:
        return fib(n - 1) + fib(n - 2)
```

The code shown runs very slowly for even relatively small values of *n*; it can take minutes or hours to compute even the 40th or 50th Fibonacci number. The code is inefficient because it makes too many recursive calls. It ends up recomputing each Fibonacci number many times. Write a new version of this function that is still recursive and has the same header but is more efficient. Do this by creating a helper function that accepts additional parameters, such as previous Fibonacci numbers, that you can carry through and modify during each recursive call.

Section 9.3: Recursive Graphics

15. What is a fractal image? How does recursive programming help to draw fractals?

16. Write Python code to create and draw a regular hexagon (a type of polygon).

Section 9.4: Recursive Backtracking

17. Why is recursion an effective way to implement a backtracking algorithm?

18. What is a decision tree? How are decision trees important for backtracking?

19. Draw the decision tree that would have resulted for Figure 9.31 if the backtracking solution had explored NE first instead of last in the recursive explore function. (*Hint:* The tree changes at every level.)

20. The original north/east backtracking solution printed the following ways of traveling to (1, 2) in this order. In what order would they be printed if the solution had explored NE first instead of last?

```
moves: N N E
moves: N E N
moves: N NE
moves: E N N
moves: NE N
```

21. Figure 9.30 shows only part of the decision tree for the first two levels. How many entries are there at the second level of the full tree? How many are at level 3 of the full tree?

22. If our Eight Queens algorithm tried every possible square on the board for placing each queen, how many entries are there at the 8th and final level of the full tree? What does our algorithm do to avoid having to explore so many possibilities?

23. The Eight Queens `explore` function stops once it finds one solution to the problem. What part of the code causes the algorithm to stop once it finds a solution? How could the code be modified so that it would find and output every solution to the problem?

Exercises

1. Write a recursive function called `star_string` that accepts an integer as a parameter and prints to the console a string of stars (asterisks) that is 2^n (i.e., 2 to the nth power) long. The function should throw a `ValueError` if passed a value less than 0. For example:

   `star_string(0)` should print * (because $2^0 == 1$)
   `star_string(1)` should print ** (because $2^1 == 2$)
   `star_string(2)` should print **** (because $2^2 == 4$)
   `star_string(3)` should print ******** (because $2^3 == 8$)
   `star_string(4)` should print **************** (because $2^4 == 16$)

2. Write a recursive function called `write_nums` that accepts an integer n as a parameter and prints to the console the first n integers starting with 1 in sequential order, separated by commas. Your function should throw a `ValueError` if passed a value less than 1. For example, consider the following calls:

   ```
   write_nums(5)
   print() # to complete the line of output
   write_nums(12)
   print() # to complete the line of output
   ```

   These calls should produce the following output:

   ```
   1, 2, 3, 4, 5
   1, 2, 3, 4, 5, 6, 7, 8, 9, 10, 11, 12
   ```

3. Write a recursive function called `write_sequence` that accepts an integer n as a parameter and prints to the console a symmetric sequence of n numbers composed of descending integers that ends in 1, followed by a sequence of ascending integers that begins with 1. The following table indicates the output that should be produced for various values of n:

Function Call	Output Produced
`write_sequence(1)`	1
`write_sequence(2)`	1 1
`write_sequence(3)`	2 1 2
`write_sequence(4)`	2 1 1 2
`write_sequence(5)`	3 2 1 2 3
`write_sequence(6)`	3 2 1 1 2 3
`write_sequence(7)`	4 3 2 1 2 3 4
`write_sequence(8)`	4 3 2 1 1 2 3 4
`write_sequence(9)`	5 4 3 2 1 2 3 4 5
`write_sequence(10)`	5 4 3 2 1 1 2 3 4 5

Notice that when n is odd the sequence has a single 1 in the middle, while for even values it has two 1s in the middle. Your function should throw a `ValueError` if it is passed a value less than 1.

4. Write a recursive function called `double_digits` that accepts an integer *n* as a parameter and returns the integer obtained by replacing every digit of *n* with two of that digit. For example, `double_digits(348)` should return `334488`. The call `double_digits(0)` should return `0`. Calling `double_digits` on a negative number should return the negation of calling `double_digits` on the corresponding positive number; for example, `double_digits(-789)` should return `-778899`.

5. Write a recursive function called `write_binary` that accepts an integer as a parameter and writes its binary representation to the console. For example, `write_binary(44)` should print `101100`.

6. Write a recursive function called `write_chars` that accepts an integer parameter *n* and that prints out a total of *n* characters. The middle character of the output should always be an asterisk (`*`). If you are asked to write out an even number of characters, then there will be two asterisks in the middle (`**`). Before the asterisk(s) you should write out less-than characters (`<`). After the asterisk(s) you should write out greater-than characters (`>`). Your function should raise a `ValueError` if it is passed a value less than 1. For example, the following calls produce the following output:

Function Call	Output Produced
`write_chars(1)`	`*`
`write_chars(2)`	`**`
`write_chars(3)`	`<*>`
`write_chars(4)`	`<**>`
`write_chars(5)`	`<<*>>`
`write_chars(6)`	`<<**>>`
`write_chars(7)`	`<<<*>>>`
`write_chars(8)`	`<<<**>>>`

7. Write a recursive function called `digit_match` that accepts two non-negative integers as parameters and that returns the number of digits that match between them. Two digits match if they are equal and have the same position relative to the end of the number (i.e., starting with the ones digit). In other words, the function should compare the last digits of each number, the second-to-last digits of each number, the third-to-last digits of each number, and so forth, counting how many pairs match. For example, for the call of `digit_match(1072503891, 62530841)`, the function would compare as follows and return 4 because four of the pairs match (2–2, 5–5, 8–8, and 1–1).

```
1 0 7 2 5 0 3 8 9 1
    | | | | | | | |
    6 2 5 3 0 8 4 1
```

8. Write a recursive function called `is_reverse` that accepts two strings as parameters and returns `True` if the two strings contain the same sequence of characters as each other but in the opposite order (ignoring capitalization), and `False` otherwise. For example, the call of `is_reverse("hello", "eLLoH")` would return `True`. The empty string, as well as any one-letter string, is considered to be its own reverse.

9. Write a recursive function called `even_digits` that accepts an integer parameter and that returns the integer formed by removing the odd digits from it. For example, `even_digits(8342116)` returns `8426` and `even_digits(-34512)` returns `242`. If the number is 0 or has no even digits, such as 35159 or 7, return 0. Leading zeros in the result should be ignored.

10. The Sierpinski carpet is a fractal that is defined as follows: The construction of the Sierpinski carpet begins with a square. The square is cut into nine congruent subsquares in a 3-by-3 grid, with the central subsquare removed. The same process is then applied recursively to the eight other subsquares. Figure 9.38 shows the first few iterations of the carpet. Write a program to draw the carpet on a `DrawingPanel` recursively.

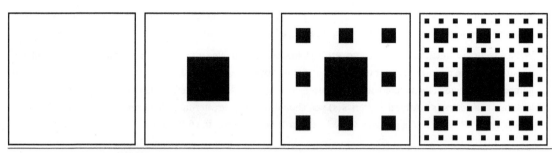

Figure 9.38:   Sierpinski Carpet Levels 0–3

11. Write a recursive function called `ways_to_climb` that accepts a positive integer value representing a number of stairs and prints each unique way to climb a staircase of that height, taking strides of one or two stairs at a time. Do not use any loops. Output each way to climb the stairs on its own line, using a 1 to indicate a small stride of 1 stair, and a 2 to indicate a large stride of 2 stairs. The order in which you output the possible ways to climb the stairs is not important, so long as you list the right overall set of ways. For example, the call `ways_to_climb(3)` should produce the following output:

```
[1, 1, 1]
[1, 2]
[2, 1]
```

The call `ways_to_climb(4)` should produce the following output:

```
[1, 1, 1, 1]
[1, 1, 2]
[1, 2, 1]
[2, 1, 1]
[2, 2]
```

12. Write a recursive function called `count_binary` that accepts an integer n as a parameter and that prints all binary numbers that have exactly n digits in ascending order, each on its own line. All n digits should be shown for all numbers, including leading zeros if necessary. Assume that n is non-negative. If n is 0, a blank line should be produced.

Call	Output
`count_binary(1)`	0
	1
`count_binary(2)`	00
	01
	10
	11
`count_binary(3)`	000
	001
	010
	011
	100
	101
	110
	111

13. Write a recursive function called `subsets` to find every possible sublist of a given list. A sublist of a list L contains 0 or more of L's elements. Your function should accept a list of strings as its parameter and print every sublist that could be created from elements of that list, one per line. For example, if the list stores `['Janet', 'Robert', 'Morgan', 'Char']`, the output from your function would be:

```
['Janet', 'Robert', 'Morgan', 'Char']
['Janet', 'Robert', 'Morgan']
['Janet', 'Robert', 'Char']
['Janet', 'Robert']
['Janet', 'Morgan', 'Char']
['Janet', 'Morgan']
['Janet', 'Char']
['Janet']
['Robert', 'Morgan', 'Char']
['Robert', 'Morgan']
['Robert', 'Char']
['Robert']
['Morgan', 'Char']
['Morgan']
['Char']
[]
```

The order in which you show the sublists does not matter, and the order of the elements of each sublist also does not matter. The key thing is that your function should produce the correct overall set of sublists as its output. Notice that the empty list is considered one of these sublists. You may assume that the list contains no duplicates. Do not use any loops.

14. Write a recursive function called `max_sum` that accepts a list of integers L and an integer limit n as parameters and uses backtracking to find the maximum sum that can be generated by adding elements of L that does not exceed n. For example, if you are given the list `[7, 30, 8, 22, 6, 1, 14]` and the limit of 19, the maximum sum that can be generated that does not exceed is 16, achieved by adding 7, 8, and 1. If the list L is empty, or if the limit is not a positive integer, or all of L's values exceed the limit, return 0. Each index's element in the list can be added to the sum only once, but the same number value might occur more than once in a list, in which case each occurrence might be added to the sum. For example, if the list is `[6, 2, 1]` you may use up to one 6 in the sum, but if the list is `[6, 2, 6, 1]` you may use up to two sixes.

List L	Limit n	Return Value
`[7, 30, 8, 22, 6, 1, 14]`	19	16
`[5, 30, 15, 13, 8]`	42	41
`[30, 15, 20]`	40	35
`[10, 20, 30]`	7	0
`[10, 20, 30]`	20	20
`[]`	10	0

You may assume that all values in the list are non-negative. Your function may alter the contents of the list L as it executes, but L should be restored to its original state before your function returns. Do not use any loops.

Programming Projects

1. Write a recursive program to solve the Towers of Hanoi puzzle. The puzzle involves manipulating disks that you can move among three different towers. You are given a certain number of disks (four in this example) stacked on one of the three towers. The disks have decreasing diameters, with the smallest disk on the top, as shown in Figure 9.39.

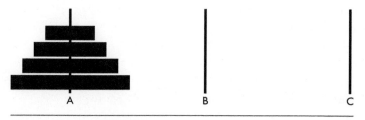

Figure 9.39   Towers of Hanoi

The object of the puzzle is to move all of the disks from one tower to another (say, from A to B). The third tower is provided as a temporary storage space as you move disks around. You are allowed to move only one disk at a time, and you are not allowed to place a disk on top of a smaller one (i.e., one with a smaller diameter).

Examine the rather simple solutions for one, two, and three disks, and see if you can discern a pattern. Then write a program that will solve the Towers of Hanoi puzzle for any number of disks. (*Hint:* Moving four disks is a lot like moving three disks, except that one additional disk is on the bottom.)

2. Write a recursive program to generate random sentences from a given Backus-Naur Form ("BNF") grammar. A BNF grammar is a recursively defined file that defines rules for creating sentences from tokens of text. Rules can be recursively self-similar. The following grammar can generate sentences such as "Fred honored the green wonderful child":

```
<s>::=<np> <vp>
<np>::=<dp> <adjp> <n>|<pn>
<dp>::=the|a
<adjp>::=<adj>|<adj> <adjp>
<adj>::=big|fat|green|wonderful|faulty|subliminal|pretentious
<n>::=dog|cat|man|university|father|mother|child|television
<pn>::=John|Jane|Sally|Spot|Fred|Elmo
<vp>::=<tv> <np>|<iv>
<tv>::=hit|honored|kissed|helped
<iv>::=died|collapsed|laughed|wept
```

3. Write a program that uses recursive backtracking to generate all anagrams from a phrase typed by the user. An anagram is a word or phrase made by rearranging the letters of another word or phrase. For example, the words "midterm" and "trimmed" are anagrams. If you ignore spaces and capitalization and allow multiple words, a multiword phrase can be an anagram of some other word or phrase. For example, the phrases "Clint Eastwood" and "old west action" are anagrams. Your program will read a dictionary file of words and search for all words that can be formed using the letters in the user's phrase. Use backtracking to choose each word, explore what can be made out of the remaining letters, then un-choose the word afterward. Here is a possible example dialogue:

```
Phrase to search? barbara bush
Max words to use? 3
['abash', 'bar', 'rub']
['abash', 'rub', 'bar']
['bar', 'abash', 'rub']
['bar', 'rub', 'abash']
['rub', 'abash', 'bar']
['rub', 'bar', 'abash']
```

4. Write a program that uses recursive backtracking to play the game of Boggle. Boggle is a word game played on a 4-by-4 grid where the player tries to find all valid dictionary words that can be made by tracing a path between adjacent letters from the board. Each link in the path can be horizontal, vertical, or diagonal. Figure 9.40 shows an example path to form the word "ensure." Use recursive backtracking to explore each possible word that can be made using the letters on the board. Your algorithm should choose a starting square, explore what can be made from there, and un-choose the square afterward. (*Hint:* You will need a way to "mark" squares as being chosen or not chosen.)

Figure 9.40   An example Boggle board

Searching and Sorting

Introduction

When you are dealing with large amounts of data, you'll often want to search the data for particular values. For example, you might want to search the Internet for a web page that contains a certain keyword, or you might want to search a phone book for a person's phone number.

It's also useful to be able to rearrange a collection of data into sorted order. For example, you might want to sort a list of students' course grade data by name, student ID, or grade.

In this chapter we'll look at ways to use Python's libraries to search and sort data. We'll practice implementing some searching and sorting algorithms and talk more generally about how to observe and analyze the runtimes of algorithms.

10.1 Searching and Sorting Libraries

Python lists contain several features used for searching for element values. As first mentioned in Chapter 7, the simplest way of checking whether a particular value is found in a list is to use the `in` keyword:

```
if value in collection:
    statements
```

Syntax template: in expression

For example, you could use an `in` expression to see whether a given word is found in a list:

```
>>> # using the 'in' keyword to check for membership
>>> words = ["oh", "beautiful", "for", "spacious", "skies"]
>>> "skies" in words
True
>>> "banana" in words
False
```

(Note that as we saw in Chapter 8, if you are creating a large collection and plan to test many values for membership in that collection, a set is generally preferred over a list. Sets have much faster searching behavior than lists, and the difference will be especially noticeable for large lists or for programs that perform many searches.)

Sometimes knowing that a word is in a list is not enough; you'd also like to know its position in the list. You can use the `index` method of the list to examine each element of the list, looking for a target value. It returns the first index at which the target value occurs in the list. If the value doesn't occur in the list, `index` raises a `ValueError`:

```
>>> # using the index function to search for words
>>> words = ["oh", "beautiful", "for", "spacious", "skies"]
>>> words.index("spacious")
3
>>> words.index("banana")
Traceback (most recent call last):
  File "<stdin>", line 1, in <module>
ValueError: 'banana' is not in list
```

The `index` function performs what is called a *sequential search*, examining each element of the list in sequence until it finds the one that the user is looking for. When it searches a million-element list for an element at index 675,000, a sequential search would have to examine all 675,000 elements that came before the desired element. If it reaches the end of the list without finding the requested word, it raises a `ValueError`.

> **Sequential Search**
>
> One that examines each element of a collection one at a time, starting from the beginning of the collection, until the desired value is found or all elements have been examined.

The following code reads a large text file into such a list, then prompts the user to search for words and displays the index at which they are found in the file:

```
1   # Searches a large file for words and displays
2   # the index at which each word is found.
3
4   def main():
5       words = open("mobydick.txt").read().split()
6       word = input("Word to search for? ")
7       while word != "":
8           try:
9               index = words.index(word)
10              print(word, "is found at index", index, "of", len(words))
11          except ValueError:
12              print(word, "is not found.")
13          word = input("Word to search for? ")
14
15  main()
```

```
Word to search for? the
the is found at index 46 of 208433
Word to search for? of
of is found at index 49 of 208433
Word to search for? end
end is found at index 4659 of 208433
Word to search for? direwolf
direwolf is not found.
Word to search for?
```

Binary Search

Sometimes you'll want to search through elements of a list that you know is in sorted order. For example, if you wanted to know whether "queasy" was a real English word, you could search the contents of an alphabetized dictionary text file. Likewise, you might find yourself looking for a book written by Robert Louis Stevenson in a list of books sorted by the author's last name. If the dictionary is large or the list of books is long, you probably won't want to sequentially examine all the items it contains.

There's a better algorithm called *binary search* that searches sorted data much faster than a sequential search. A normal sequential search of a million-element list may have to examine all the elements, but a binary search will need to look at only around 20 of them. Python's class libraries have functions that implement the binary search algorithm for lists.

> **Binary Search**
>
> An algorithm that searches for a value in a sorted list by repeatedly dividing the search space in half.

The binary search algorithm begins by examining the center element of the list. If the center element is smaller than the target you're searching for, there's no reason to examine any elements to the left of the center (at lower indexes). If the center element is larger than the target you're searching for, there's no reason to examine any elements to the right of the center (at greater indexes). Each pass of the algorithm eliminates half the search space from consideration, so in most cases the algorithm finds the target value much faster than a sequential search would have found it. The algorithm scales extremely well to large input data and is much faster than a sequential search overall.

The logic of the binary search algorithm is similar to the strategy that people use in a high/low guessing game in which the computer generates a random number between 1 and 100 and the user tries to guess it. After each incorrect guess, the program gives a hint about whether the user's guess was too high or too low. A poor algorithm for this game is to guess 1, 2, 3, and so on. A smarter algorithm is to guess the middle number and cut the range in half each time on the basis of whether the guess was too high or too low. Figure 10.1 shows how this works.

The built-in Python libraries contain a module called `bisect` that contains a function called `bisect_left` that implements the binary search algorithm. It accepts a list of any suitable type and a target value as its parameters and returns the index where you can find the target element:

```
>>> # binary search on a list
>>> import bisect
>>>
>>> #            0   1   2    3    4    5    6    7    8    9   10
>>> numbers = [-3,   4,   9,  12,  17,  29,  39,  44,  44,  58,  79]
>>> bisect.bisect_left(numbers, 29)
5
>>> bisect.bisect_left(numbers, 9)
2
>>> bisect.bisect_left(numbers, 44)     # a duplicate value
7
>>> bisect.bisect_left(numbers, 31)     # a value that is not found
6
```

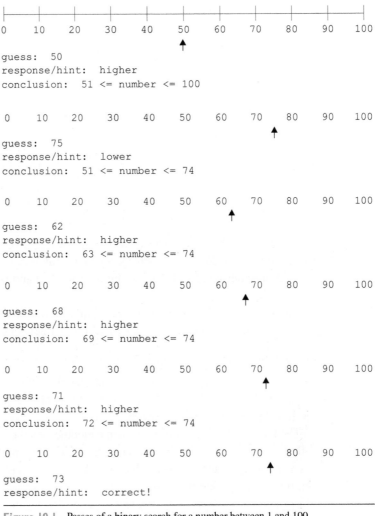

Figure 10.1   Passes of a binary search for a number between 1 and 100

The binary search algorithm needs to examine only indexes 4, 6, and then 5 in order to find the target value of 29 at index 5. A sequential search would need to examine all of indexes 0 to 5 to find the same target value.

If the target value occurs multiple times in the list, `bisect_left` returns the index of the first occurrence, as with 44 in the preceding list, which returns index 7.

Unlike the list `index` function, `bisect_left` does not raise an error if the element isn't found. Instead the function returns an unusual result: the index at which that value *would* have been found if it had been in the list. In the preceding example, the search for 31 returns 6. Index 6 of the list does not contain 31; it contains 39. But if we were to insert the value 31 into the list at index 6, the list would remain sorted. So if you are using `bisect_left` to search a list for a given value, you must make sure to look at the list at that index and ensure that the given value is found there.

There is a similar function called `bisect_right` that also uses the binary search algorithm, but instead of returning the index of the first occurrence of the given value, it returns 1 past the index of the last occurrence of the value. So, for example, `bisect_right` would return 9 when searching for 44 in the previous example. The two functions behave the same when searching for a value that is not found in the list; `bisect_right` would return 6 if searching the preceding list for the value 31. The `bisect` module has another function called `insert` that inserts a new value into a sorted list at the right location to maintain sorted order. For example, the call of `bisect.insort(numbers, 31)` would insert 31 into the preceding list at index 6. We won't explore `insort` further since we are focused on searching in this section. Table 10.1 lists the functions of the `bisect` module.

The list you supply to any `bisect` function must be in sorted order, because the binary search algorithm used by the function relies on the ordering to quickly find the target value. If you call `bisect_left` on unsorted data, the results are undefined and the algorithm doesn't guarantee that it will return the right answer.

If you want to learn more about the `bisect` library, consult the official Python online documentation:

- https://docs.python.org/3/library/bisect.html

Let's look at a short program that benefits from the speed of binary search. In the game of Scrabble, players form words on a board using letter tiles to earn points. Sometimes a player tries to spell a word that is not a legal word in the dictionary, so another player "challenges" the word. The challenger looks up the word in the dictionary, and depending on whether it is found, the move may be revoked from the board. The following program helps resolve Scrabble word challenges by performing binary searches for words in a Scrabble players' dictionary file that contains 172,823 words. The input file's words occur in sorted order, so the list can be properly searched using `bisect_left`.

Table 10.1 Functions of `bisect` Module

Function	Description
`bisect.bisect_left(seq, value)`	returns index of the first occurrence of the given value in a sorted sequence; if not present, returns index of the insertion point where the value could be added to maintain sorted order
`bisect.bisect_right(seq, value)` or `bisect.bisect(seq, value)`	returns index just after the last occurrence of the given value in a sorted sequence; if not present, returns index of the insertion point where the value could be added to maintain sorted order
`bisect.insort(seq, value)`	adds a value to a sorted sequence at the proper location to maintain sorted order

```
1   # Searches a large file for words using a binary search,
2   # and displays the index at which each word is found.
3
4   import bisect
5
6   def main():
7       print("Welcome to Scrabble word challenge!")
8       words = open("scrabble-words.txt").read().split()
9       word = input("Word to challenge (Enter to quit)? ")
10      while word != "":
11          index = bisect.bisect_left(words, word)
12          if 0 <= index < len(words) and words[index] == word:
13              print(word, "is word", index, "of", len(words))
14          else:
15              print(word, "is not found.")
16          word = input("Word to challenge (Enter to quit)? ")
17
18  main()
```

```
Welcome to Scrabble word challenge!
Word to challenge (Enter to quit)? queazy
queazy is word 121788 of 172823
Word to challenge (Enter to quit)? kwyjibo
kwyjibo is not found
Word to challenge (Enter to quit)? building
building is word 18823 of 172823
Word to challenge (Enter to quit)? python
python is word 79156 of 172823
Word to challenge (Enter to quit)? programs
programs is word 118860 of 172823
Word to challenge (Enter to quit)?
```

In this section we've claimed that bisect_left and binary searching in general are much faster than sequential searching. Let's demonstrate this by running both algorithms and measuring the runtime. You can measure how long a given piece of code takes to run by calling the time function from the time module, which returns a real number representing a count of seconds that have elapsed since January 1, 1970. If you call time before and after running a given algorithm, the difference between the two times tells you how long the given code took to run. The following program runs a sequential search (using a list's index function) over a large list to measure its runtime. We run the search hundreds of times so that the program will take longer total time to run, which will give us a better sense of the overall search runtime.

```
 1  # Searches a large file for various words and displays
 2  # the index at which each word is found.
 3
 4  import time
 5
 6  def main():
 7      words = open("words.txt").read().split()
 8      targets = ["the", "of", "banana", "direwolf", "monkey"]
 9      start_time = time.time()
10
11      # Search for a word's index many times
12      REPS = 500
13      for i in range(REPS):
14          for word in targets:
15              try:
16                  index = words.index(word)
17              except ValueError:
18                  pass
19
20      elapsed_time = time.time() - start_time
21      print("Performed", REPS * len(targets), "searches")
22      print("Took", elapsed_time, "sec")
23
24  main()
```

```
Performed 2500 searches
Took 4.316449403762817 sec
```

If we run the same code using `bisect_left`, the program is much, much faster than with the sequential search. Notice that we can perform several orders of magnitude more searches than with the sequential search in less time.

```
 1  # Searches a large file for various words and displays
 2  # the index at which each word is found.
 3
 4  import bisect
 5  import time
 6
 7  def main():
 8      words = open("words.txt").read().split()
```

Continued on next page

Continued from previous page

```
9       targets = ["the", "of", "banana", "direwolf", "monkey"]
10      start_time = time.time()
11
12      # Search for a word's index many times
13      REPS = 500000
14      for i in range(REPS):
15          for word in targets:
16              index = bisect.bisect(words, word)
17
18      elapsed_time = time.time() - start_time
19      print("Performed", REPS * len(targets), "searches")
20      print("Took", elapsed_time, "sec")
21
22  main()
```

```
Performed 2500000 searches
Took 2.2320826053619385 sec
```

Sorting

When you use a computer, you often need to sort data. When you browse your hard drive, for example, you might sort your files by file name, extension, and date. When you play music, you might sort your song collection by artist, year, or genre. You might also want to sort a list so that it can be searched efficiently with the binary search algorithm.

The Python list has a built-in `sort` function that rearranges that list's elements into sorted order. The list's elements must be of a type that can be compared, such as integers (sorted by numeric value) or strings (sorted into case-sensitive alphabetical order). The following code demonstrates:

```
>>> # demonstrate the sort function
>>> letters = ["c", "b", "g", "h", "d", "f", "e", "a"]
>>> letters.sort()
>>> letters
['a', 'b', 'c', 'd', 'e', 'f', 'g', 'h']
```

There is also a global function called `sorted` that accepts a list or collection as a parameter and returns a new list that contains its elements in sorted order. The difference between `sort` and `sorted` is that `sorted` creates a new list and does not modify the existing list. This is useful in several situations, such as when you want to iterate over the keys of a dictionary.

```
>>> # demonstrate the sorted function
>>> letters = ["c", "b", "g", "h", "d", "f", "e", "a"]
>>> sorted(letters)
['a', 'b', 'c', 'd', 'e', 'f', 'g', 'h']
>>> letters    # should be unchanged
['c', 'b', 'g', 'h', 'd', 'f', 'e', 'a']
>>>
>>> # sort the keys of a dictionary
>>> phonebook = {"Stuart": "555-1234", "Marty": "123-4567",
                 "Yana": "999-9999", "Allison": "520-9876"}
>>> list(phonebook.keys())
['Stuart', 'Marty', 'Yana', 'Allison']
>>> sorted(phonebook.keys())
['Allison', 'Marty', 'Stuart', 'Yana']
```

These sorting functions internally use an algorithm called *Timsort*, which in turn is based on a classic sorting algorithm called merge sort. We'll discuss the implementation of merge sort in detail later in this chapter.

Shuffling

The task of shuffling data, or rearranging the elements into a random order, is perhaps the opposite of sorting. One application for shuffling is a card game program. You might have a card deck stored as a list of cards. If the cards are in a predictable order, the game will be boring. You'd like to shuffle the deck of cards, rearranging them into a random ordering each time. This is a case in which chaos is preferable to order.

Another application is a situation in which you want a random permutation of a list of numbers. You can acquire a random permutation of the numbers from 1 through 5, for example, by storing those numbers into a list and shuffling the list.

The `random` library has a function called `shuffle` that accepts a collection as its parameter and rearranges its elements randomly. The following example creates a deck of card strings, shuffles it, and deals the player a random five-card hand consisting of the first five cards in the deck. The program would generate different random output each time it is run.

```
1  # Deals and displays a hand of 5 random playing cards.
2  import random
3
4  def main():
5      ranks = ["2", "3", "4", "5", "6", "7", "8", \
6              "9", "10", "Jack", "Queen", "King", "Ace"]
7      suits = ["Clubs", "Diamonds", "Hearts", "Spades"]
8
```

Continued on next page

Continued from previous page

```
 9       # build sorted deck
10       deck = []
11       for rank in ranks:
12            for suit in suits:
13                 deck.append(rank + " of " + suit)
14
15       # generate random 5-card hard
16       random.shuffle(deck)
17       hand = sorted(deck[:5])
18
19       print("Your hand:")
20       for card in hand:
21            print(card)
22
23  main()
```

```
Your hand:
4 of Clubs
5 of Clubs
5 of Diamonds
Ace of Diamonds
King of Diamonds
```

10.2 Program Complexity

Since searching and sorting are important programming ideas, it's worthwhile to understand how they are implemented. But before we dive into this, let's discuss some background ideas about how to analyze the efficiency of code.

As you progress in this text, you're writing increasingly complex programs. You're also seeing that there are often many ways to solve the same problem. How do you compare different solutions to the same problem to see which is better?

We desire algorithms that solve problems quickly or with high efficiency. The technical term that refers to algorithms' runtime is *complexity*. An algorithm with higher complexity uses more time or resources to solve a problem.

> **Complexity**
>
> A measure of the computing resources that are used by a piece of code, such as time, memory, or disk space.

Usually when we talk about the efficiency of a program we are talking about how long the program takes to run, or its *time complexity*. The time complexity for a program to be "fast enough" depends on the task. A program running on a modern computer that requires five minutes to look up a dictionary word is probably too slow. An algorithm that renders a complex three-dimensional movie scene in five minutes is probably very fast.

One way to determine an algorithm's approximate time complexity is to program it, run the program, and measure how long it takes to run. This is sometimes called an *empirical analysis* of the algorithm. For example, consider two algorithms to search a list: one that sequentially searches for the desired target element, and one that first sorts the list and then performs a binary search on the sorted list. You could empirically analyze the algorithms by writing both as programs, running them on the same input, and timing them.

But empirically analyzing an algorithm isn't a very reliable measure, because on a different computer with a different processor speed and more or less memory the program might not take the same amount of time. Also, in order to empirically test an algorithm, you must write it and time it, which can be a chore.

A more neutral way to measure a program's performance is to examine its code or pseudocode and roughly count the number of statements that are executed. This is a form of *algorithm analysis*, the practice of applying techniques to mathematically approximate the complexity and performance of various computing algorithms. Algorithm analysis is an important tool in computer science. One of the fundamental principles of science in general is that we can make predictions and hypotheses using formal models, which we can then test by experimentation.

> **Algorithm Analysis**
> The process of determining the computational complexity of algorithms.

Not all statements require the same amount of time to execute. For example, a CPU can handle addition faster than multiplication, and a function call generally takes more time than a statement that evaluates the Boolean test of an if/else statement. But for the purposes of simplification, let's assume that the following actions require an equal and fixed amount of time to execute:

- Making variable definitions and assignments
- Evaluating mathematical and logical expressions
- Accessing or modifying an individual element of a list
- Printing a value to the console
- Performing simple function calls (where the function does not perform a loop)

One kind of variable that might not require a fixed amount of time to initialize is a list. When a list is constructed, Python must initialize each list element, which takes more time for longer lists. Some types of objects also have lengthy internal code that makes them take longer to create.

From the preceding simple rules, we can extrapolate the runtimes of larger and more complex pieces of code. For example, the runtime of a group of statements in sequential order is the sum of the individual runtimes of the statements:

```
statement1.  ⎫
statement2.  ⎬  3
statement3.  ⎭
```

The runtime of a loop is roughly equal to the runtime of its body times the number of iterations of the loop. For example, a loop with a body that contains K simple statements and that repeats N times will have a runtime of roughly ($K * N$):

```
for i in range(N):   ⎫
    statement1.       |
    statement2.       ⎬  3N
    statement3.       ⎭
```

The runtime of multiple loops placed sequentially (not nested) with other statements is the sum of the loops' runtimes and the other statements' runtimes:

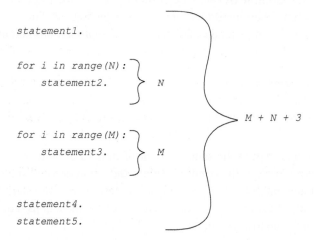

```
statement1.

for i in range(N):   ⎫
    statement2.       ⎬  N

                                          M + N + 3

for i in range(M):   ⎫
    statement3.       ⎬  M

statement4.
statement5.
```

The runtime of a loop containing a nested loop is roughly equal to the runtime of the inner loop multiplied by the number of repetitions of the outer loop:

```
for i in range(M):
    for j in range(N):
        statement1.   ⎫
        statement2.   ⎬  3   ⎬ 3N   ⎬ 3MN
        statement3.   ⎭
```

Normally, the loops in long-running algorithms are processing some kind of data. Many algorithms run very quickly if the input dataset is small, so we generally worry about the performance only for large datasets. For example, consider the following set of loops that process a list of *N* elements:

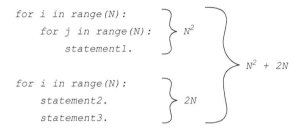

```
for i in range(N):
    for j in range(N):
        statement1.

for i in range(N):
    statement2.
    statement3.
```

When we analyze code like this, we often think about which line is most frequently executed in the code. In programs with several sequential blocks of code that all relate to some common value *N* (such as the size of an input dataset), the block raised to the highest power of *N* usually dominates the overall runtime. In the preceding code, the first N^2 loop executes its statement far more times than the second *N* loop executes its two statements. For example, if *N* is 1000, *statement1* executes (1000 × 1000) or 1,000,000 times, while *statement2* and *statement3* each execute only 1000 times.

When we perform algorithm analysis, we often ignore all but the most frequently executed part of the code, because the runtime of this statement will outweigh the combined runtimes of the other parts of the code. For example, we might refer to the preceding code as being "on the order of" N^2, ignoring the extra 2*N* statements altogether. We'll revisit this idea later in the chapter.

One key concept to take away from this brief discussion of algorithm analysis is how expensive it is to perform nested loops over large sets of input data. Algorithms that make many nested passes over a very large dataset tend to perform poorly, so it's important to come up with efficient algorithms that don't loop over data needlessly.

Now let's take a look at algorithm complexity in action, observing the runtimes of some actual algorithms that can be used to solve a programming problem on a large dataset.

Empirical Analysis

Consider the task of computing the range of numbers in a list. The range is the difference between the lowest and highest numbers in the list. This can be computed by calling the built-in functions `max` and `min` on the list, but for the moment let's assume that we have to find the range by ourselves from scratch. An initial solution might use nested loops to examine every pair of elements in the list, computing their difference and remembering the largest difference found:

```
How to find the range of values in a list:
    max = 0.
    For each pair of indexes (i, j):
        If list elements [i] and [j] differ by more than max:
            Update max.
```

The following code implements the range function as described:

```
# returns the range of numbers in the given list
def range_of_values(numbers):
    max_diff = 0
    for i in range(len(numbers)):
        for j in range(len(numbers)):
            diff = abs(numbers[j] - numbers[i])
            if diff > max_diff:
                max_diff = diff
    return max_diff
```

Since the code has two nested `for` loops, each of which processes the entire list, we can hypothesize that the algorithm executes roughly N^2 statements, or some multiple thereof. We can measure the speed of this range algorithm in milliseconds by calling `range` on various lists and measuring the time elapsed. We measure the time by acquiring the current time before and after calling `range` on a large list and subtracting the start time from the end time.

As you can see in the output from the code below, as the input size N doubles, the runtime of the `range_of_values` function approximately quadruples. This is consistent with our hypothesis. If the algorithm takes N^2 statements to run and we increase the input size to $2N$, the new runtime is roughly $(2N)^2$ or $4N^2$, which is four times as long as the original runtime.

```
 1  # Measures the runtime of an algorithm to find
 2  # the range of values in a large list.
 3  # First version.
 4
 5  import random
 6  import time
 7
 8  # Returns the range of numbers in the given list.
 9  def range_of_values(numbers):
10      max_diff = 0
11      for i in range(len(numbers)):
12          for j in range(len(numbers)):
13              diff = abs(numbers[j] - numbers[i])
14              if diff > max_diff:
15                  max_diff = diff
16      return max_diff
17
18  # Creates and returns a random list of integers of length N.
19  def create_random_list(N):
20      numbers = [0] * N
21      for i in range(N):
```

Continued on next page

Continued from previous page

```
22              numbers[i] = random.randint(0, 999999999)
23        return numbers
24
25  def main():
26        # Search for a word's index many times
27        N = 500
28        MAX_N = 32000
29        print("N", "runtime (ms)", sep="\t")
30        while N <= MAX_N:
31            numbers = create_random_list(N)
32            start_time = time.time()
33            r = range_of_values(numbers)
34            elapsed_time = time.time() - start_time
35            print(N, round(elapsed_time * 1000), sep="\t")
36            N *= 2
37
38  main()
```

N	runtime
500	49
1000	188
2000	755
4000	3030
8000	11987
16000	48001
32000	192110

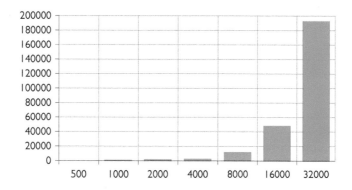

Our code isn't very efficient for a large list. It requires over 12 seconds to examine 32,000 integers on a modern computer. In real-world data-processing situations, we would expect to see far larger input datasets than this, so this runtime isn't acceptable for general use.

Studying a piece of code and trying to find ways to speed it up can be deceptively difficult. It's tempting to approach the problem by looking at each line of code and trying to reduce the amount of computation it performs. For example, you may have noticed that our `range_of_numbers` function actually examines every pair of elements in the list twice: For unique integers i and j, we examine the pair of elements at indexes (i, j) as well as the pair at (j, i).

We can perform a minor modification to our range functions code by starting each inner j loop ahead of i, so that we won't examine any pair (i, j) where $i \geq j$. Performing minor modifications like this is sometimes called tweaking an algorithm. The following code implements our tweaked version of the `range_of_numbers` algorithm. Since about half of the possible pairs of i/j values are eliminated by this tweak, we'd hope that the code would run about twice as fast. The output shows its actual measured runtime:

```
# Returns the range of numbers in the given list.
# Second version that examines j values where j > i only.
def range_of_values2(numbers):
    max_diff = 0
    for i in range(len(numbers)):
        for j in range(i + 1, len(numbers)):
            diff = abs(numbers[j] - numbers[i])
            if diff > max_diff:
                max_diff = diff
    return max_diff
```

N	runtime
500	24
1000	105
2000	382
4000	1505
8000	6022
16000	25455
32000	99626

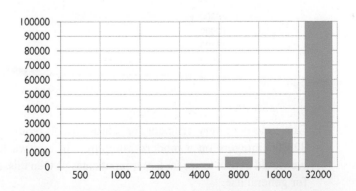

As we estimated, the second version is about twice as fast as the first. When the input size doubles, the runtime of either version of the algorithm roughly quadruples. Consequently, regardless of which version we use, if the input list is very large the function will be too slow.

Rather than trying to further tweak our nested loop solution, let's try to think of a more efficient algorithm. As we noted earlier, the range of values in a list is the difference between the list's largest and smallest elements. We don't really need to examine all pairs of values to find this range; we just need to discover the pair representing the largest and smallest values. We can discover both of these values in a single loop over the list by using a min/max loop, discussed in Chapter 4.

Since this algorithm passes over the list only once, we'd hope that its runtime would be proportional to the list's length. If the list length doubles, the runtime should double, not quadruple. The following new algorithm demonstrates this idea along with its runtime:

```python
# Returns the range of numbers in the given list.
# Third version that sweeps the list once to find its
# max/min element values and then subtracts them.
def range_of_values3(numbers):
    max_value = numbers[0]
    min_value = numbers[0]
    for i in range(1, len(numbers)):
        if numbers[i] > max_value:
            max_value = numbers[i]
        elif numbers[i] < min_value:
            min_value = numbers[i]
    return max_value - min_value
```

N	runtime
500	0
1000	0
2000	0
4000	0
8000	1
16000	2
32000	3
64000	6
128000	13
256000	25
512000	51
1024000	106
2048000	285
4096000	580
8192000	844
16384000	1774

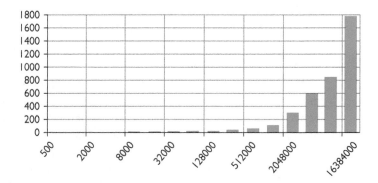

Our runtime predictions were roughly correct. As the size of the list doubles, the runtime of this new range algorithm approximately doubles as well. This means that the algorithm has a linear runtime complexity, or O(N), as opposed to the two other O(N^2) range algorithms shown previously. The overall runtime of this algorithm is much better; we can examine over a hundred million integers in less than a second.

The following output shows the runtime of all three versions of the range algorithm side-by-side. Figure 10.2 shows a graph of these runtimes. (We write "?" for columns where we didn't even bother to run a given algorithm because it was too slow to practically measure.) The difference in runtime is so great that it makes the chart hard to read. The bars from the third and fastest algorithm don't even show up until we reach tens of millions of elements. This staggering difference in runtime underscores the importance of choosing an efficient algorithm.

N	range1	range2	range3
1000	188	105	0
2000	755	382	0
4000	3030	1505	0
8000	11987	6022	1
16000	48001	25455	2
32000	192110	99626	3
64000	?	?	6
128000	?	?	13
256000	?	?	25
512000	?	?	51
1024000	?	?	106
2048000	?	?	285
4096000	?	?	580
8192000	?	?	844
16384000	?	?	1774
32768000	?	?	3458
65536000	?	?	6659
131072000	?	?	13370

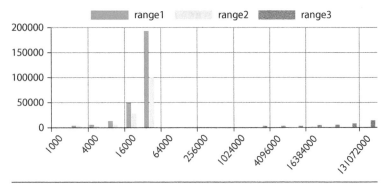

Figure 10.2   Runtime of three range algorithms

There are some important observations to take away from this exercise:

- Tweaking an algorithm's code often isn't as powerful an optimization as finding a better algorithm.
- An algorithm's rate of growth, or the amount by which its runtime increases as the input dataset grows, is the standard measure of the algorithm's complexity.

Did You Know?

Timing Code and the Epoch

Python's `time` function returns the number of seconds that have passed since 12:00 AM on January 1, 1970. This function can be used to measure the runtime of an algorithm. Over one billion seconds have passed since the indicated time. The following lines of code show how a piece of code can be timed:

```
start_time = time.time()
code to be timed
end_time = time.time()
print("Elapsed time (ms):", (end_time - start_time))
```

The choice of January 1, 1970 as the point of reference for system times is an example of an epoch, or an instant chosen as the origin of a particular time scale. This particular epoch was chosen because it matches the epochs of many popular operating systems, including Unix.

For historical reasons, many older Unix operating systems store the time that has passed since the epoch as a 32-bit integer value. However, unspecified problems may occur when this number exceeds its capacity, which is not necessarily a rare event. The clocks of some Unix systems will overflow on January 19, 2038, creating a Year 2038 problem similar to the famous Year 2000 (Y2K) problem.

Complexity Classes

We categorize rates of growth on the basis of their proportion to the input data size N. We call these categories *complexity classes* or *growth rates*.

Complexity Class

A set of algorithms that have a similar relationship between input data size and resource consumption.

The complexity class of a piece of code is determined by looking at the most frequently executed line of code, determining the number of times it is executed, and extracting the highest power of N. For example, if the most frequent line executes $(2N^3 - 4N)$ times, the algorithm is in the "order N^3" complexity class, or $O(N^3)$ for short. The shorthand notation with the capital O is called *big-Oh notation* and is used commonly in algorithm analysis.

Big-Oh Notation

A standard way of describing the growth rate of algorithms relative to their input size N.

Here are some of the most common complexity classes, listed in order from slowest to fastest growth (i.e., from lowest to highest complexity):

- Constant-time, or $O(1)$, algorithms have runtimes that don't depend on input size. Some examples of constant-time algorithms would be code to convert Fahrenheit temperatures to Celsius or numerical functions such as `abs`.
- Logarithmic, or $O(\log N)$, algorithms typically divide a problem space in half repeatedly until the problem is solved. Binary search is an example of a logarithmic-time algorithm.
- Linear, or $O(N)$, algorithms have runtime growth that is directly proportional to N (i.e., roughly they double when N doubles). Many algorithms that process each element of a data set are linear, such as algorithms that compute the count, sum, average, maximum, or range of a list of numbers.
- Log-linear, or $O(N \log N)$, algorithms typically perform a combination of logarithmic and linear operations, such as executing a logarithmic algorithm over every element of a dataset of size N. Many efficient sorting algorithms, such as merge sort (discussed later in this chapter), are log-linear.
- Quadratic, or $O(N^2)$, algorithms have runtimes that are proportional to the square of the input size. This means that quadratic algorithms' runtimes roughly quadruple when N doubles. The initial versions of the `range_of_numbers` algorithm developed in the previous section were quadratic algorithms.

Table 10.2   **Algorithm Runtime Comparison Chart**

Input Size N	$O(1)$	$O(\log N)$	$O(N)$	$O(N \log N)$	$O(N^2)$	$O(N^3)$	$O(2^N)$
100	100 ms	100 ms	100 ms	100 ms	100 ms	100 ms	100 ms
200	100 ms	115 ms	200 ms	240 ms	400 ms	800 ms	32.7 sec
400	100 ms	130 ms	400 ms	550 ms	1.6 sec	6.4 sec	12.4 days
800	100 ms	145 ms	800 ms	1.2 sec	6.4 sec	51.2 sec	36.5 million years
1600	100 ms	160 ms	1.6 sec	2.7 sec	25.6 sec	6.8 min	$4.21 * 10^{24}$ years
3200	100 ms	175 ms	3.2 sec	6 sec	1.75 min	54.6 min	$5.6 * 10^{61}$ years

- Cubic, or $O(N^3)$, algorithms have runtimes that are proportional to the cube of the input size. Such algorithms often make triply nested passes over the input data. Code to multiply two $N \times N$ matrices or to count the number of colinear trios of points in a large list would be examples of cubic algorithms.

- Exponential, or $O(2^N)$, algorithms have runtimes that are proportional to 2 raised to the power of the input size. This means that if the input size increases by just one, the algorithm will take roughly twice as long to execute. One example would be code to print the "power set" of a dataset, which is the set of all possible subsets of the data. Exponential algorithms are so slow that they should be executed only on very small input datasets.

Table 10.2 presents several hypothetical algorithm runtimes as the input size N grows, assuming that each algorithm requires 100 ms to process 100 elements. Notice that even though they all start at the same runtime for a small input size, as N grows the algorithms in higher complexity classes become so slow that they would be impractical.

When you look at the numbers in Table 10.2, you might wonder why anyone bothers to use $O(N^3)$ or $O(2^N)$ algorithms when $O(1)$ and $O(N)$ algorithms are so much faster. The answer is that not all problems can be solved in $O(1)$ or even $O(N)$ time. Computer scientists have been studying classic problems such as searching and sorting for many years, trying to find the most efficient algorithms possible. However, there will likely never be a constant-time algorithm that can sort 1,000,000 elements as quickly as it can sort 10 elements.

For large datasets it's very important to choose the most efficient algorithms possible (i.e., those with the lowest complexity classes). Algorithms with complexity classes of $O(N^2)$ or worse will take a long time to run on extremely large datasets. Keeping this in mind, we'll now examine algorithms to search and sort data.

10.3 Implementing Searching and Sorting Algorithms

In this section we'll implement functions that search and sort data. We'll start by writing code to search for an integer in a list of integers and return the index where it is found. If the integer doesn't appear in the list, we'll return a negative number. We'll examine two major searching algorithms, sequential and binary search, and discuss the tradeoffs between them.

There are literally hundreds of algorithms to sort data; we'll cover two in detail in this chapter. The first, seen later in this section, is one of the more intuitive algorithms, although it performs poorly on large datasets. The second, examined as a case study in the next section, is one of the fastest general-purpose sorting algorithms that is used in practice today.

Sequential Search

Perhaps the simplest way to search a list is to loop over the elements of the list and check each one to see if it is the target number. As we mentioned earlier, this is called a sequential search because it examines every element in sequence. We discussed algorithms that traverse and search lists in Chapter 7. In this case, the code uses an indexed `for` loop and is relatively straightforward. The algorithm returns -1 if the loop completes without finding the target number:

```
# Sequential search algorithm.
# Returns the index at which the given target number first
# appears in the given input list, or -1 if it is not found.
def sequential_search(elements, target):
    for i in range(len(elements)):
        if elements[i] == target:
            return i
    return -1    # not found
```

Using the rules stated in the previous section, we predict that the sequential search algorithm is a linear $O(N)$ algorithm because it contains one loop that traverses at most N elements in a list. (We say "at most" because if the algorithm finds the target element, it stops and immediately returns the index.) Next, we'll time it to verify our prediction.

Figure 10.3 shows actual results of running the sequential search algorithm on randomly generated lists of integers. Searches were conducted for a value known to be in the list and for a value not in the list.

N	found	not-found
100000	3	7
200000	6	13
400000	14	26
800000	24	48
1600000	57	99
3200000	101	196
6400000	203	409
12800000	389	789
25600000	775	1576

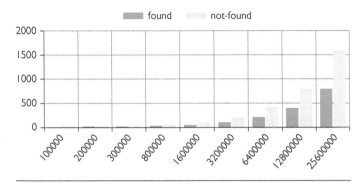

Figure 10.3 Sequential search runtime

When the algorithm searches for an integer that isn't in the list, it runs somewhat slower, because it can't exit its loop early by finding the target. This scenario
raises the question of whether we should judge the algorithm by its fastest or slowest
runtime. Often what's most important is the expected behavior for a typical input,
or the average of its runtime over all possible inputs. This is called an average case
analysis. But under certain conditions, we also care about the fastest possible outcome, the best case analysis, and/or the slowest possible outcome, the worst case
analysis. In this algorithm, the average search looks at approximately half of the list,
which is linear or $O(N)$.

Binary Search

Consider a modified version of the searching problem, in which we can assume that the
elements of the input list are in sorted order. Does this ordering affect our algorithm?
Our existing algorithm will still work correctly, but now we know that we can stop
the search if we ever get to a number larger than our target without finding the target.
For example, if we're searching a list containing the elements $[1, 4, 5, 7, 7, 9, 10, 12, 56]$
for the target value 8, we can stop searching once we see the 9.

We might think that such a modification to our sequential search algorithm would
significantly speed up the algorithm, but in actuality it doesn't make much difference.
The only case in which it speeds up the algorithm noticeably is when it is searching for
a relatively small value that isn't found in the list. In fact, when the modified algorithm
is searching for a large value that requires the code to examine most or all of the list
elements, the algorithm actually performs slower than the original because it has to
perform a few more Boolean tests. Most importantly, the algorithm is still $O(N)$, which
isn't the optimal solution.

Once again, tweaking the algorithm won't make as much difference as finding
another, more efficient algorithm. If the input list is in sorted order, a sequential search
isn't the best choice. If you had to instruct a robot how to look up a person's phone
number in a phone book, would you tell the robot to read through all the entries on
the first page, then the second, and so on until it found the person's name? Not unless

you wanted to torture the poor robot. You know that the entries are sorted by name, so you'd tell the robot to flip open the book to somewhere near the middle, then narrow its search toward the first letter of the person's name.

The binary search algorithm discussed previously in this chapter takes advantage of the ordering of the list. A binary search keeps track of the range of the list that is currently of interest. (Initially, this range is the whole list.) The algorithm repeatedly examines the center element of the list and uses its value to eliminate half of the range of interest. If the center element is smaller than the target, the lower half of the range is eliminated; if the center element is larger than the target, the upper half is eliminated.

As the algorithm runs, we must keep track of three indexes:

- The minimum index of interest (min)
- The maximum index of interest (max)
- The middle index, halfway between the minimum and maximum, which will be examined during each pass of the algorithm (mid)

The algorithm repeatedly examines the element at the middle index and uses it to trim the range of indexes of interest in half. If we examine the middle element and find it's too small, we will eliminate all elements between min and mid from consideration. If the middle element is too large, we will eliminate all elements between mid and max from consideration.

Consider the following list depicted in Figure 10.4.

```
# index      0    1    2    3    4    5    6    7    8    9   10   11   12   13   14
numbers = [11,  18,  29,  37,  42,  49,  51,  63,  69,  72,  77,  82,  88,  91,  98]
```

Let's run a binary search on the list for a target value of 77. We'll start at the middle element, which is at index (14 // 2), or 7. Figure 10.5 shows the min, mid, and max at each step of the algorithm.

What about when we're searching for an element that isn't found in the list? Let's say we're searching for the value 78 instead of 77. The steps of the algorithm will be the same, except that on the fourth pass the algorithm will reach 77 instead of the desired value, 78. The algorithm will have eliminated the entire range without finding the target and will know that it should stop. Another way to describe the process is that the algorithm loops until the min and max have crossed each other.

0	1	2	3	4	5	6	7	8	9	10	11	12	13	14
11	18	29	37	42	49	51	63	69	72	77	82	88	91	98

Figure 10.4 List to be searched

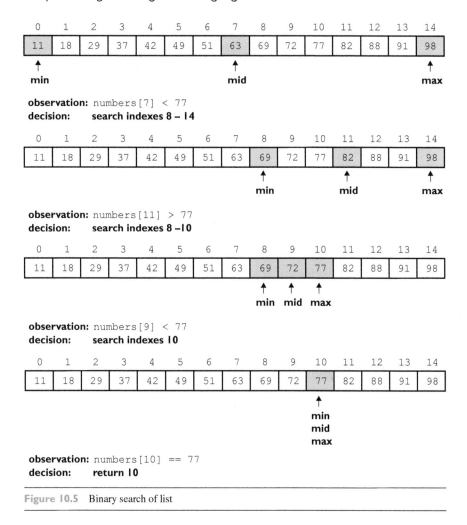

Figure 10.5 Binary search of list

The following code implements the binary search algorithm. Its loop repeats until the target is found or until the min and max have crossed. It is similar to the implementation of the bisect functions, except that it returns -1 if the element is not found.

```
# Binary search algorithm.
# Returns an index at which the target appears
# in the given input list, or -1 if not found.
# Precondition: list is sorted.
def binary_search(numbers, target):
    start = 0
    end = len(numbers) - 1
    while start <= end:
        mid = (start + end) // 2
```

Continued on next page

Continued from previous page

```
        if target == numbers[mid]:
            return mid          # found it!
        elif target < numbers[mid]:
            end = mid - 1       # go left
        else:
            start = mid + 1     # go right
    return -1                   # not found
```

We won't bother to show a runtime chart for the binary search algorithm, because there would be nothing to draw on the chart. This algorithm is so fast that the computer's clock has trouble measuring its runtime. On a modern computer, even a list of over 100,000,000 elements registers as taking 0 milliseconds to search.

While this is an impressive result, it makes it harder for us to empirically examine the runtime. What is the complexity class of the binary search algorithm? The fact that it finishes so quickly tempts us to conclude that it's a constant-time, or $O(1)$, algorithm. But it doesn't seem right that a function with a loop in it would take a constant amount of time to execute. There is a relation between the runtime and the input size, because the larger the input is, the more times we must divide our min-max range in half to arrive at a single element. We could say that 2 raised to the number of repetitions is approximately equal to the input size N:

$$2^{\text{repetitions}} \approx N$$

Using some algebra and taking a logarithm base-2 of both sides of the equation, we find that:

$$\text{repetitions} \approx \log_2 N$$

We conclude that the binary search algorithm is in the logarithmic complexity class, or $O(\log_2 N)$. We often just write $O(\log N)$ and omit the base of 2.

The runtime of the binary search algorithm doesn't differ much between the best and worst cases. In the best case, the algorithm finds its target value in the middle on the first check. In the worst case, the code must perform the full ($\log N$) comparisons. But since logarithms are small numbers ($\log_2 1,000,000$ is roughly 20), the performance is still excellent in the worst case.

Recursive Binary Search

In the previous section, binary search was implemented using an iterative algorithm with a `for` loop. But the algorithm can also be implemented elegantly using the concept of recursion introduced in Chapter 9. The recursive version of the function should accept the same parameters as the standard binary search:

```
# Recursive version of binary search.
def binary_search_r(numbers, target):
    ...
```

But this header will not make it easy to write a recursive solution to the problem.

Recall that the essence of a recursive solution is to break down the problem into smaller pieces and then solve the subproblem(s). In this algorithm, the way to shrink the problem is to examine a smaller and smaller portion of the list until we find the right index. To do this, we can change our function to accept additional parameters for the range of indexes (start and end) that currently are being examined. We can add default values for these parameters so that the function can be called without passing any start or end index values. The required function can start the recursive process by using 0 and the list's length − 1 as its start and end indexes to examine, respectively:

```
# Recursive binary search algorithm.
# Returns an index at which the target appears
# in the given input list, or -1 if not found.
# Precondition: list is sorted.
def binary_search_r(numbers, target, start = 0, \
                    end = len(numbers) - 1):
    ...
```

On each pass of the recursive algorithm, the code examines the middle element. If this element is too small, the code recursively examines only the right half of the list. If the middle element is too large, the code recursively examines only the left half. This process repeats, recursively calling itself with different values of min and max, until it finds the target or until the entire list has been eliminated from consideration. The following code implements the algorithm:

```
# Recursive binary search algorithm.
# Returns an index at which the target appears
# in the given input list, or -1 if not found.
# Precondition: list is sorted.
def binary_search_r(numbers, target, start = 0, \
                    end = len(numbers) - 1):
    if start > end:
        return -1   # not found
    else:
        mid = (start + end) // 2
        if target == numbers[mid]:
            return mid       # found it!
        elif target < numbers[mid]:
            # too small; go left
            return binary_search_r(numbers, target, start, mid - 1)
        else:
            # too large; go right
            return binary_search_r(numbers, target, mid + 1, end)
```

Some instructors don't like recursive versions of functions like binary search because there is a nonrecursive solution that's fairly easy to write and because recursion tends to have poor runtime performance because of the extra function calls it generates. However, that doesn't pose a problem here. The runtime of the recursive version of our binary search function is still O(log *N*), because it's essentially performing the same computation; it's still cutting the input in half at each step. In fact, the recursive version is fast enough that the computer still can't time it accurately. It produces a runtime of under 10 ms even on lists of millions of integers.

In general, analyzing the runtimes of recursive algorithms is tricky. Recursive runtime analysis often requires a technique called recurrence relations, which are mathematical relations that describe an algorithm's runtime in terms of itself. That's a complex topic for a later course that won't be covered in this textbook.

Selection Sort

Selection sort is a well-known sorting algorithm that makes many passes over an input list to put its elements into sorted order. Each time it runs through a loop, it selects the smallest value and puts it in the proper place near the front of the list. Consider the following list:

```
# index   0    1   2    3    4    5
nums = [12, 123, 1, 28, 183, 16]
```

How would you put its elements into order from smallest to largest? The selection sort algorithm conceptually divides the list into two pieces: sorted elements at the front and unsorted elements at the end. The first step of the selection sort makes a pass over the list and finds the smallest number. In the sample list, the smallest is nums[2], which equals 1. The algorithm then swaps the smallest value with the value in the first position in the list, so that the smallest value will be at the front of the list. In this case, nums[0] and nums[2] are swapped, as shown in Figure 10.6.

The element at index 0 now has the right value, and only the elements at indexes 1 through 5 remain to be ordered. The algorithm repeats the process of scanning the unsorted portion of the list and looking for the smallest element. On the second pass, it scans the remaining five elements and finds that nums[2], which equals 12, is the

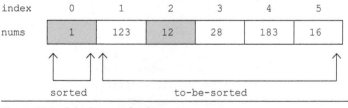

Figure 10.6   Selection sort after first swap

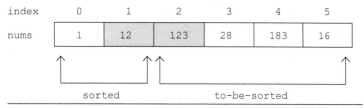

Figure 10.7   Selection sort after second swap

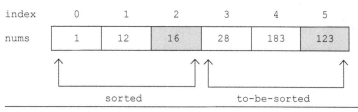

Figure 10.8   Selection sort after third swap

smallest element. The program swaps this value with `nums[1]`. After this swap, the sorted area of the list consists of its first two indexes, as shown in Figure 10.7.

Now `nums[0]` and `nums[1]` have the correct values. The third pass of the algorithm scans the remaining four unsorted elements and finds that the smallest one is `nums[5]`, which equals `16`. It swaps this element with `nums[2]`, as shown in Figure 10.8.

The algorithm continues this process until all the elements have the proper values. Each pass involves a scan followed by a swap. The scan/swap occurs five times to process six elements. You don't need to perform a sixth scan/swap because, if the first five elements have the correct values, the sixth element will be correct as well.

Here is a pseudocode description of the execution of the selection sort algorithm over a list nums that has six elements:

```
for each i from 0 to 4:
    scan nums[i] through nums[5] for the smallest value.
    swap nums[i] with the smallest element found in the scan.
```

You can write pseudocode like the following for the scan:

```
smallest = lowest list index of interest.
for each other index i of interest:
    if nums[i] < nums[smallest]:
        smallest = i.
```

You can then incorporate this pseudocode into your larger pseudocode as follows:

```
for each i from 0 to 4:
    smallest = i.
    for each index j between (i + 1) and 5:
        if nums[j] < nums[smallest]:
            smallest = j.
    swap nums[i] with nums[smallest].
```

You can translate this pseudocode almost directly into Python, except for the swap process. To help us implement the sorting algorithms in this chapter, we will use a swap function that accepts a list and two indexes as parameters and swaps the values at those indexes:

```
# Swaps list[i] with list[j].
def swap(list, i, j):
    temp = list[i]
    list[i] = list[j]
    list[j] = temp
```

We can also modify the code to work with lists of any size. The following code implements the overall selection sort algorithm. Our examples have used lists of integers, but the current selection sort code will sort lists of any type of value that can be compared using a < operator.

```
# Places the elements of the given list into sorted order
# using the selection sort algorithm.
# post: list is in sorted (nondecreasing) order
def selection_sort(lst):
    for i in range(len(lst)):
        smallest = i
        for j in range(i + 1, len(lst)):
            if lst[j] < lst[smallest]:
                smallest = j
        swap(lst, i, smallest)
```

N	runtime (ms)
500	10
1000	42
2000	160
4000	659
8000	2617
16000	10783
32000	45588

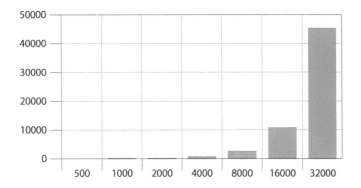

Since selection sort makes roughly N passes over a list of N elements, its performance is O(N^2). Technically, it examines $N + (N - 1) + (N - 2) + \ldots + 3 + 2 + 1$ elements, because each pass starts one index ahead of where the last one started. There is a mathematical identity which states that the sum of all integers from 1 to any maximum value N equals $(N)(N + 1)/2$, which is just over $\frac{1}{2} N^2$. Our output supports this analysis, because the runtime quadruples every time the input size N is doubled, which is characteristic of an N^2 algorithm. The algorithm becomes impractically slow once the number of elements reaches tens of thousands.

10.4 Case Study: Implementing Merge Sort

There are other algorithms similar to selection sort that make many passes over the list and swap various elements on each pass. An algorithm that searches for inverted pairs of elements and swaps them into order in this way cannot run faster than O(N^2), on average. However, there is a better algorithm that breaks this barrier.

The *merge sort* algorithm is named for the observation that if you have two sorted sublists, you can easily merge them into a single sorted list. For example, consider the following list:

```
nums = [14, 32, 67, 76, 23, 41, 58, 85]
```

You can think of it as two sublist halves, each of which (because of the element values we chose) happens to be sorted, as shown in Figure 10.9.

The following pseudocode provides the basic idea of the merge sort algorithm:

```
merge_sort(list):
    split the list into two halves.
    sort the left half.
    sort the right half.
    merge the two halves.
```

Let's look at splitting the list and merging halves first; then we'll talk about how to sort each half.

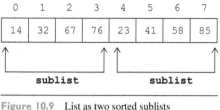

Figure 10.9   List as two sorted sublists

Splitting and Merging lists

Splitting one list into its two halves is relatively straightforward. We'll set a midpoint at one half of the length of the list and consider everything before this midpoint to be part of the "left" half and everything that follows it to be in the "right" half. We can use the standard [] operator to extract the halves of a list as new lists. The "left" half is from range 0 to half the length, and the "right" half is from half the length to the full length:

```
def merge_sort(lst):
    # split list into two halves
    mid = len(lst) // 2
    left  = lst[ : mid]
    right = lst[mid : ]
    ...
```

We will need to sort these left/right halves, then merge them into a sorted whole. For now, let's think about how we would merge two *sorted* sublists. (We'll come back to how to sort them later.) Suppose that you have two stacks of exam papers, each sorted alphabetically by name, and you need to combine them into a single stack sorted by name. The simplest algorithm is to place both stacks in front of you, look at the top paper of each stack, pick up the paper that comes first in alphabetical order, and put it face down into a third pile. You then repeat this process, comparing the papers on the top of each stack and placing the one that comes first face down on the merged stack, until one of your two original stacks is empty. Once one is empty, you just grab the entire remaining stack and place it on your merged pile.

The idea behind merging two sorted lists is similar, except that instead of physically removing papers (integers) from the piles (sublists), we'll keep an index for each sublist and increment that index as we process a given element. Here is a pseudocode description of the merging algorithm:

```
merging sorted sublists 'left' and 'right' into 'list':
    i1 = 0.    # left index
    i2 = 0.    # right index
    for each element in entire list:
        if left value at i1 <= right value at i2:
            include value from left list in new list.
```

Continued on next page

Continued from previous page

```
        increase i1 by 1.
    else:
        include value from right list in new list.
        increase i2 by 1.
```

Figure 10.10 shows a trace of the eight steps to merge the two sublists into a sorted list.

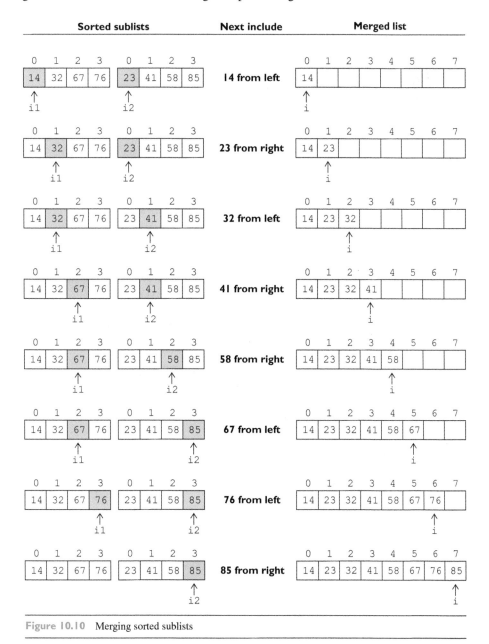

Figure 10.10 Merging sorted sublists

The following code is an initial incorrect attempt to implement the merge algorithm that was just described:

```
# initial incorrect attempt
def merge(result, left, right):
    i1 = 0   # index into left list
    i2 = 0   # index into right list
    for i in range(len(result)):
        if left[i1] <= right[i2]:
            result[i] = left[i1]     # take from left
            i1 += 1
        else:
            result[i] = right[i2]    # take from right
            i2 += 1
```

The preceding code is incorrect and will cause an out-of-bounds exception. After the program completes the seventh step of the preceding diagram, all of the elements in the left sublist will have been consumed and the left index i1 will run off the end of the sublist. Then, when the code tries to access element left[i1], it will crash. A similar problem would occur if the right index i2 exceeded the bounds of the right list.

We need to modify our code to remain within the bounds of the lists. The if/else logic needs to ensure that the index i1 or i2 is within the list bounds before the program attempts to access the appropriate element. The simple test in the pseudocode needs to be expanded:

```
if i2 has passed the end of the right list,
or left value at i1 <= right value at i2:
    take from left.
else:
    take from right.
```

The following second version of the code correctly implements the merging behavior. The preconditions and postconditions of the function are documented in comments:

```
# Merges sorted left/right lists into given result list.
# pre:  left and right must be sorted
# post: result contains merged sorted results of left and right
def merge(result, left, right):
    i1 = 0   # index into left list
    i2 = 0   # index into right list
```

Continued on next page

Continued from previous page

```
    for i in range(len(result)):
        if i2 >= len(right) or \
            i1 < len(left) and left[i1] <= right[i2]:
            result[i] = left[i1]     # take from left
            i1 += 1
        else:
            result[i] = right[i2]    # take from right
            i2 += 1
```

Recursive Merge Sort

We've written the code to split a list into halves and to merge the sorted halves into a sorted whole. The overall merge sort function now looks like this:

```
# Merge sort code so far (incomplete).
def merge_sort(lst):
    # split list into two halves
    mid = len(lst) // 2
    left  = lst[ : mid]
    right = lst[mid : ]

    # sort the two halves
    ...


    # merge the two sorted halves back into the original list
    merge(lst, left, right)
```

The last piece of our program is the code to sort each half of the list. How can we sort the halves? We could call the `selection_sort` function created earlier in this chapter on each of the two halves. But in Chapter 9 we discussed the recursive "leap of faith," the belief that our own function will work properly to solve a smaller version of the same problem. In this case, a better approach is to merge sort the two smaller halves. We can recursively call our own `merge_sort` function on the list halves. If our function is written correctly, it'll put each half into sorted order. Our original pseudocode can now be rewritten as the following pseudocode:

```
merge_sort(list):
    split the list into two halves.
    merge sort the left half.
    merge sort the right half.
    merge the two halves.
```

If we're making our merge sort algorithm recursive, it needs to have a base case and a recursive case. The preceding pseudocode specifies the recursive case, but for the base case, what are the simplest lists to sort? A list with either no elements or just one element doesn't need to be sorted at all. At least two elements must be present in order for them to appear in the wrong order, so the simple case would be a list with a length less than 2. This means that our final pseudocode for the merge sort function is the following:

```
merge_sort(list):
    if list length is 2 or more:
        split the list into two halves.
        merge sort the left half.
        merge sort the right half.
        merge the two halves.
```

We don't need any explicit code for the base case. We can just check that the list length is at least 2 with no `else` statement, because if the list size is 0 or 1, we don't need to do anything to the list. This recursive algorithm has an empty base case. The following function implements the complete merge sort algorithm:

```
# Places the elements of the given list into sorted order
# using the merge sort algorithm.
# post: list is in sorted (nondecreasing) order
def merge_sort(lst):
    if len(lst) >= 2:
        # recursive case: split list into two halves
        mid = len(lst) // 2
        left  = lst[ : mid]
        right = lst[mid : ]

        # (recursively) sort the two halves
        merge_sort(left)
        merge_sort(right)

        # merge the two sorted halves back into the original list
        merge(lst, left, right)
```

To get a better idea of the algorithm in action, we'll temporarily insert a few `print` statements into its code and run the function on the eight-element sample list shown previously in this section. We'll insert the following `print` statement at the start of the merge_sort function:

```
# at start of merge_sort function
print("sorting", lst)
```

We'll also put the following `print` statement at the start of the `merge` function:

```
# at start of merge function
print("merging", left, "and", right)
```

Here is the output from running `merge_sort` on the example list. Though the actual console output is not indented, we have indented the lines of output to help indicate the nesting of calls. Notice that each call leads to three overall steps: sorting a left half, sorting a right half, and merging the two halves.

```
sorting [14, 32, 67, 76, 23, 41, 58, 85]
    sorting [14, 32, 67, 76]
        sorting [14, 32]
            sorting [14]
            sorting [32]
            merging [14] and [32]
        sorting [67, 76]
            sorting [67]
            sorting [76]
            merging [67] and [76]
        merging [14, 32] and [67, 76]
    sorting [23, 41, 58, 85]
        sorting [23, 41]
            sorting [23]
            sorting [41]
            merging [23] and [41]
        sorting [58, 85]
            sorting [58]
            sorting [85]
            merging [58] and [85]
        merging [23, 41] and [58, 85]
    merging [14, 32, 67, 76] and [23, 41, 58, 85]
```

It's also important to test the code on a list that doesn't divide into sublists of exactly equal size (i.e., one whose overall length is not a power of 2). Because it employs integer division, our code makes the left sublist one element smaller than the right sublist when the size is odd. Given an initial five-element list of [14, 32, 67, 76, 23], the algorithm prints the following output, which is once again indented to show the nesting of calls:

```
sorting [14, 32, 67, 76, 23]
    sorting [14, 32]
        sorting [14]
        sorting [32]
        merging [14] and [32]
    sorting [67, 76, 23]
        sorting [67]
        sorting [76, 23]
            sorting [76]
            sorting [23]
            merging [76] and [23]
        merging [67] and [23, 76]
    merging [14, 32] and [23, 67, 76]
```

Runtime Performance

The following is the complete program containing the merge sort code along with its console output. The program's `main` function constructs a sample list and sorts it using the algorithm.

```
 1  # This program implements merge sort for lists of integers.
 2
 3  # Places the elements of the given list into sorted order
 4  # using the merge sort algorithm.
 5  # post: list is in sorted (nondecreasing) order
 6  def merge_sort(lst):
 7      if len(lst) >= 2:
 8          # recursive case: split list into two halves
 9          mid = len(lst) // 2
10          left  = lst[ : mid]
11          right = lst[mid : ]
12
13          # (recursively) sort the two halves
14          merge_sort(left)
15          merge_sort(right)
16
17          # merge the two sorted halves back into the original list
18          merge(lst, left, right)
19
20  # Merges sorted left/right lists into given result list.
21  # pre:  left and right must be sorted
22  # post: result contains merged sorted results of left and right
```

Continued on next page

Continued from previous page

```
23  def merge(result, left, right):
24      i1 = 0   # index into left list
25      i2 = 0   # index into right list
26      for i in range(len(result)):
27          if i2 >= len(right) or \
28              i1 < len(left) and left[i1] <= right[i2]:
29              result[i] = left[i1]    # take from left
30              i1 += 1
31          else:
32              result[i] = right[i2]   # take from right
33              i2 += 1
34
35  def main():
36      nums = [14, 32, 67, 76, 23, 41, 58, 85]
37      print("before:", nums)
38      merge_sort(nums)
39      print("after :", nums)
40
41  main()
```

```
before: [14, 32, 67, 76, 23, 41, 58, 85]
after : [14, 23, 32, 41, 58, 67, 76, 85]
```

Figure 10.11 demonstrates the performance of our merge sort algorithm on a modern computer. The merge sort algorithm's performance is much better than that of the selection sort algorithm. For example, whereas our selection sort test run needed over 45 seconds to sort 32,000 elements, the merge sort algorithm handled the same job in only 221 milliseconds. In those same 45 seconds, merge sort can process around four million elements.

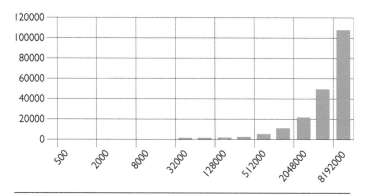

Figure 10.11   Merge sort runtime

```
N          runtime
500        2
1000       5
2000       12
4000       32
8000       49
16000      123
32000      221
64000      473
128000     1023
256000     2222
512000     4996
1024000    10745
2048000    21519
4096000    49435
8192000    108131
```

But what is merge sort's complexity class? It looks almost like an O(N) algorithm, because the runtime only slightly more than doubles when we double the list size. However, merge sort is actually an O($N \log N$) algorithm.

A formal proof of merge sort's complexity is beyond the scope of this text, but a common-sense chain of reasoning is as follows: We have to split the list in half repeatedly until we hit the algorithm's base case, in which the sublists each contain 1 element. For a list of size N, we must split the list $\log_2 N$ times. At each of those $\log_2 N$ steps, we have to do a linear operation of order N: merging the halves after they're sorted. Multiplying these operations' runtimes together produces a O($N \log N$) overall runtime. Figure 10.12 shows this visually. Think of the algorithm's runtime as the area of the rectangle whose width is the list size N and whose height is the number of layers of recursive calls we need to make, which is $\log_2 N$.

The preceding algorithm runtime analysis is informal and not rigorous. As with other recursive algorithms, a precise analysis of merge sort's performance is complicated and requires mathematical techniques such as recurrence relations, which are not discussed in this text.

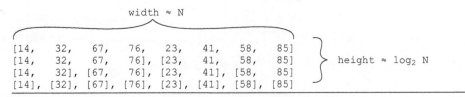

Figure 10.12 Merge sort runtime diagram

Hybrid Approach

The actual sorting algorithm used by Python's `sort` and `sorted` functions is called Timsort. Invented by programmer Tim Peters in 2002, Timsort is a hybrid sorting algorithm that takes advantages of multiple algorithms to sort a list more efficiently. In this section we will implement an algorithm that uses some ideas from Timsort to improve performance.

Timsort relies on two key observations about sorting. The first observation is that regions of data that are already sorted do not need to be re-sorted. The second observation is that when the list size N is small, function call overhead can cause a sorting algorithm with a technically better big-Oh complexity class such as merge sort to run more slowly than a sorting algorithm with worse complexity class such as selection sort. Timsort takes advantage of the first observation by examining the input data for sorted and unsorted regions, flagging the unsorted regions separately, sorting them, and then merging the pieces. It takes advantage of the second observation by switching the sort algorithm used to sort a given unsorted region based on that region's size: if the region is large, it uses merge sort, but if the region is small, it uses an algorithm with less function call overhead, such as selection sort. (Timsort actually uses an algorithm called insertion sort for small unsorted regions, but we have not discussed insertion sort in this chapter.)

We won't implement the full Timsort in this section. But we can use the sorts written in this chapter to test its second hypothesis, that small lists can be sorted more efficiently with selection sort than merge sort. We'll use a selection sort if the list in question has 20 elements or fewer, and perform a merge sort if the list size is larger than 20. We choose the threshold of 20 based on a few runtime tests that seem to show 20 being better than, say, 10 or 40.

```
# constant for minimum length before our hybrid sort switches algorithms
TIM_SORT_MIN_LENGTH = 20
```

The following is the code for the `hybrid_sort` function. The hybrid sort is a merge sort except that it calls our existing `selection_sort` function if the list length is less than our constant of 20:

```
# Places the elements of the given list into sorted order
# using a hybrid sort based on the "TimSort" algorithm.
# This algorithm uses merge sort unless the list in question is
# very small, in which case it falls back to another algorithm
# such as insertion sort or selection sort.
# post: list is in sorted (nondecreasing) order
def hybrid_sort(lst):
    length = len(lst)
    if length < 2:
```

Continued on next page

Continued from previous page

```
        # base case: already trivially sorted
        return
    elif length < TIM_SORT_MIN_LENGTH:
        # base case: small list, sort with selection sort
        selection_sort(lst)
    else:
        # recursive case: split list into two halves
        mid = length // 2
        left  = lst[ : mid]
        right = lst[mid : ]
```

Figure 10.13 shows the runtime of `hybrid_sort` when passed lists of various sizes. For comparison purposes we have included the runtime of the original `merge_sort` in the output. At input sizes over 1,000,000 elements, the benefits of the hybrid approach become apparent. The hybrid sort seems to result in a 15 to 20 percent runtime savings over the original merge sort in our tests.

```
N         merge    hybrid
500       2        2
1000      5        4
2000      12       8
4000      32       19
8000      49       40
16000     123      89
32000     221      185
64000     473      418
128000    1023     956
256000    2222     2069
512000    4996     4284
1024000   10745    9002
2048000   21519    18952
4096000   49435    40196
8192000   108131   86854
```

The example shown in Figure 10.13 helps to illustrate that there is much more to sorting than we can cover in this chapter alone. There are many other sorting algorithms that use clever tricks and strategies to sort various data more efficiently, and advances are still being made in sorting despite it being a problem as old as computing itself. A particular area of advancement in sorting is the development of sorting algorithms that utilize multiple processors and/or machines to sort giant data sets in parallel. We will discuss the basics of parallel programming near the end of Chapter 11.

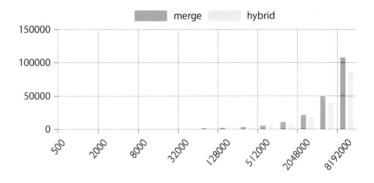

Figure 10.13   Hybrid sort runtime

Chapter Summary

- Searching is the task of attempting to find a particular target value in a collection or list.
- Sorting is the task of arranging the elements of a list or list into a natural ordering.
- Python's class libraries contain several functions for searching and sorting lists and lists, such as `index`, `bisect_left`, `sort`, and `sorted`.
- Empirical analysis is the technique of running a program or algorithm to determine its runtime. Algorithm analysis is the technique of examining an algorithm's code or pseudocode to make inferences about its complexity.
- Algorithms are grouped into complexity classes, which are often described using big-Oh notation such as $O(N)$ for a linear algorithm.
- Sequential search is an $O(N)$ searching algorithm that looks at every element of a list until it finds the target value.

- Binary search is an $O(\log_2 N)$ searching algorithm that operates on a sorted dataset and successively eliminates half of the data until it finds the target element.
- Selection sort is an $O(N^2)$ sorting algorithm that repeatedly finds the smallest unprocessed element of the list and moves it to the frontmost remaining slot of the list.
- Merge sort is an $O(N \log N)$ sorting algorithm, often implemented recursively, that successively divides the input dataset into two halves, recursively sorts the halves, and then merges the sorted halves into a sorted whole.
- Python's built-in sorting functions use a hybrid sorting algorithm named Timsort, which performs merge sort on larger lists and insertion sort on smaller lists.

Self-Check Problems

Section 10.1: Searching and Sorting in the Python Class Libraries

1. Describe two ways to search an unsorted list of strings using the Python class libraries.

2. If you perform a binary search on a list of one million integers, which of the following is closest to the number of elements that the search algorithm will need to examine?
   a. all 1,000,000 of the integers
   b. roughly 3/4 (750,000) of the integers
   c. roughly half (500,000) of the integers
   d. roughly 1/10 (100,000)
   e. less than 1 percent (10,000 or fewer)

3. Should you use a sequential or binary search on a list of strings, and why?

Section 10.2: Program Complexity

4. Approximate the runtime of the following code fragment, in terms of n:

```
sum = 0
j = 1
while j <= n:
    sum += 1
    j *= 2
```

5. Approximate the runtime of the following code fragment, in terms of n:

```
sum = 0
for j in range(1, n):
    sum += 1
    if j % 2 == 0:
        sum += 1
```

6. Approximate the runtime of the following code fragment, in terms of n:

```
sum = 0
for i in range(1, n * 2 + 1):
    for j in range(1, n + 1):
        sum += 1

for j in range(1, 100):
    sum += 1
    sum += 1
```

7. Approximate the runtime of the following code fragment, in terms of n:

```
sum = 0
for i in range(1, n + 1):
    for j in range(1, i + 1, 2):
        sum += 4
for k in range(-50, -2):
    sum += 1
```

8. Determine the complexity classes of the algorithms that could be used to perform the following tasks:

a. Finding the average of the numbers in a list of integers

b. Finding the closest distance between any pair of numbers in a list

c. Finding the maximum value in a list of real numbers

d. Counting the median length of the strings in a list

e. Counting the number of lines in a file

f. Determining whether a given integer representing a year stores a leap year (a year divisible by 4, but not divisible by 100 unless also divisible by 400)

9. Suppose an algorithm takes exactly the given number of statements for each value below, in terms of an input size N. Give a tight big-Oh bound for each algorithm, representing the closest complexity class for that algorithm based on that runtime.

a. $\frac{1}{2} N \log_2 N + \log_2 N$

b. $N^2 - (N + N \log_2 N + 1000)$

c. $N^2 \log_2 N + 2N$

d. $\frac{1}{2} (3N + 5 + N)$

e. $2N + 5 + N^4$

f. $\log_2 (2^N)$

g. $N! + 2N$

Section 10.3: Implementing Searching and Sorting Algorithms

10. What is the runtime complexity class of a sequential search on an unsorted list? What is the runtime complexity class of the modified sequential search on a sorted list?

11. Why does the binary search algorithm require the input to be sorted?

12. How many elements (at most) does a binary search examine if the list contains 60 elements?

13. What indexes will be examined as the middle element by a binary search for the target value 8 when the search is run on the following input lists? What value will the binary search algorithm return?

a. `numbers = [1, 3, 6, 7, 8, 10, 15, 20, 30]`

b. `numbers = [1, 2, 3, 4, 5, 7, 8, 9, 10]`

c. `numbers = [1, 2, 3, 4, 5, 6, 7, 8, 9]`

d. `numbers = [8, 9, 12, 14, 15, 17, 19, 25, 31]`

14. What indexes will be examined as the middle element by a binary search for the target value 8 when the search is run on the following input list? Notice that the input list isn't in sorted order. What can you say about the binary search algorithm's result?

`numbers = [6, 5, 8, 19, 7, 35, 22, 11, 9]`

15. Consider the following sorted list of integers. When a binary search is performed on this list for each of the following integer values, what indexes are examined in order? What result value is returned?

```
# index      0   1    2    3    4    5    6    7   8   9   10   11   12   13
numbers = [-30, -9, -6, -4, -2, -1,  0,  2,  4, 10, 12, 17, 22, 30]
```

a. -5

b. 0

c. 11

d. -100

16. Consider the following list:

`numbers = [29, 17, 3, 94, 46, 8, -4, 12]`

After a single pass of the selection sort algorithm (a single swap), what would be the state of the list?

a. `[-4, 29, 17, 3, 94, 46, 8, 12]`

b. `[29, 17, 3, 94, 46, 8, 12]`

c. `[-4, 29, 17, 3, 94, 46, 8, -4, 12]`

d. `[-4, 17, 3, 94, 46, 8, 29, 12]`

e. `[3, 17, 29, 94, -4, 8, 46, 12]`

17. Trace the execution of the selection sort algorithm as shown in this section when run on the following input lists. Show each element that will be selected by the algorithm and where it will be moved, until the list is fully sorted.

    a. `[29, 17, 3, 94, 46, 8, -4, 12]`
    b. `[33, 14, 3, 95, 47, 9, -42, 13]`
    c. `[7, 1, 6, 12, -3, 8, 4, 21, 2, 30, -1, 9]`
    d. `[6, 7, 4, 8, 11, 1, 10, 3, 5, 9]`

Section 10.4: Implementing Merge Sort

18. How many calls on the `merge_sort` function are generated by a call to sort a list of length 32?

19. Consider the following list of elements:

    `numbers = [7, 2, 8, 4, 1, 11, 9, 5, 3, 10]`

    a. Show the state of the elements after five passes of the outermost loop of selection sort have occurred.
    b. Show a trace that is two levels deep of the merge sort algorithm.
    c. Show the splitting of the overall list, plus one level of the recursive calls.

20. Consider the following list of elements:

    `numbers = [7, 1, 6, 12, -3, 8, 4, 21, 2, 30, -1, 9]`

    a. Show the state of the elements after five passes of the outermost loop of selection sort have occurred.
    b. Show a trace that is two levels deep of the merge sort algorithm. Show the splitting of the overall list, plus one level of the recursive calls.

21. Which one of the following statements about sorting and big-Oh is true?

    a. Selection sort can sort a list of integers in $O(N)$ time.
    b. Merge sort achieves an $O(N \log N)$ runtime by dividing the list in half at each step and then recursively sorting and merging the halves back together.
    c. Merge sort runs faster than selection sort because it is recursive, and recursion is faster than loops.
    d. Selection sort runs in $O(N)$ time if the list is already sorted to begin with, or $O(N^2)$ if it is not.
    e. Sorting algorithms that rely on comparing elements can only be used with numbers, because values from other types of data cannot be compared to each other.

22. Trace the complete execution of the merge sort algorithm when called on each list below. Show the sublists that are created by the algorithm and show the merging of sublists into larger sorted lists.

    a. `[29, 17, 3, 94, 46, 8, -4, 12]`
    b. `[6, 5, 3, 7, 1, 8, 4, 2]`
    c. `[33, 14, 3, 95, 47, 9, -42, 13]`

Exercises

1. Suppose the following list has been declared:

   ```
   # index   0   1    2    3    4    5    6    7    8    9
   lst   = [-2,  8,  13,  22,  25,  25,  38,  42,  51,  103]
   ```

What indexes will be examined as the middle element by a binary search for each of the following target values? What value will be returned?

a. 103

b. 30

c. 8

d. −1

2. Suppose the following list has been declared:

```
# index      0   1   2   3   4   5   6   7   8   9  10  11
numbers = [-1,  3,  5,  8, 15, 18, 22, 39, 40, 42, 50, 57]
```

What indexes will be examined as the middle element by a binary search for each of the following target values? What value will be returned?

a. 13

b. 39

c. 50

d. 2

3. To which complexity class does the following algorithm belong? Consider N to be the length or size of the list or collection passed to the function. Explain your reasoning.

```
def mystery1(lis):
    result = [0] * (2 * len(lis))
    for i in range(len(lis)):
        result[2 * i] = lis[i] // 2 + list[i] % 2
        result[2 * i + 1] = lis[i] // 2
    return result
```

4. To which complexity class does the following algorithm belong?

```
def mystery2(lis):
    for i in range(len(lis) // 2):
        j = len(lis) - 1 - i
        temp = list[i]
        list[i] = list[j]
        list[j] = temp
```

5. To which complexity class does the following algorithm belong?

```
def mystery3(lis):
    for i in range(len(lis) - 1, 2):
        first = list.pop(i)
        list.insert(i + 1, first)
```

6. To which complexity class does the following algorithm belong?

```
def mystery4(lis):
    for i in range(0, len(lis) - 1, 2):
        first = lis[i]
        lis[i] = lis[i + 1]
        list[i + 1] = first
```

7. Write the state of the elements of each of the following lists after each pass of the outermost loop of the selection sort algorithm has occurred (after each element is selected and moved into place). Suppose the following lists have been declared:

```
numbers1 = [63, 9, 45, 72, 27, 18, 54, 36]
numbers2 = [37, 29, 19, 48, 23, 55, 74, 12]
```

8. Using the same lists from the previous problem, trace the complete execution of the merge sort algorithm when called on each list. Show the sublists that are created by the algorithm and show the merging of sublists into larger sorted lists.

9. Write the state of the elements of each of the following lists after each pass of the outermost loop of the selection sort algorithm has occurred (after each element is selected and moved into place).

```
numbers3 = [8, 5, -9, 14, 0, -1, -7, 3]
numbers4 = [15, 56, 24, 5, 39, -4, 27, 10]
```

10. Using the same lists from the previous problem, trace the complete execution of the merge sort algorithm when called on each list. Show the sublists that are created by the algorithm and show the merging of sublists into larger sorted lists.

11. Write the state of the elements of each of the following lists after each pass of the outermost loop of the selection sort algorithm has occurred (after each element is selected and moved into place).

```
numbers5 = [22, 44, 11, 88, 66, 33, 55, 77]
numbers6 = [-3, -6, -1, -5, 0, -2, -4, -7]
```

12. Using the same lists from the previous problem, trace the complete execution of the merge sort algorithm when called on each list. Show the sublists that are created by the algorithm and show the merging of sublists into larger sorted lists.

    a. Write the state of the elements of each list after each pass of the outermost loop of the selection sort algorithm has occurred (after each element is selected and moved into place).

    b. Trace the complete execution of the merge sort algorithm when called on each list. Show the sublists that are created by the algorithm and show the merging of sublists into larger sorted lists.

13. Write code to read a dictionary from a file; then prompt the user for two words and tell the user how many words in the dictionary fall between those two words. Here is a sample run of the program:

```
Type two words: goodbye hello
There are 4418 words between goodbye and hello
```

Use the binary search algorithm in your solution.

14. Write a modified version of the selection sort algorithm that selects the largest element each time and moves it to the end of the list, rather than selecting the smallest element and moving it to the beginning. Will this algorithm be faster than the standard selection sort? What will its complexity class (big-Oh) be?

15. Write a modified "dual" version of the selection sort algorithm that selects both the largest and smallest elements on each pass and moves each of them to the appropriate end of the list. Will this algorithm be faster than the standard selection sort? What predictions would you make about its performance relative to the merge sort algorithm? What will its complexity class (big-Oh) be?

16. Implement an algorithm to shuffle a list of numbers or objects. The algorithm for shuffling should be the following:

```
for each index i:
    choose a random index j where j >= i.
    swap the elements at indexes i and j.
```

(The constraint about *j* being greater than or equal to *i* is actually quite important, if you want your shuffling algorithm to shuffle fairly. Why?)

17. Implement a "bogus" sorting algorithm called bogo sort that uses your shuffling algorithm from the previous exercise to sort a list of numbers. The bogo sort algorithm is the following:

```
while list is not sorted:
    shuffle list.
```

Obviously, this is not a very efficient sorting algorithm, but it eventually does shuffle the list into order if you let it run long enough. Try running it on a very small list, such as 8 or 10 elements, to examine its runtime. What is your best guess about the complexity class (big-Oh) of this silly algorithm?

Programming Projects

1. Write a program that reads a series of input lines and sorts them into alphabetical order, ignoring the case of words. The program should use the merge sort algorithm so that it efficiently sorts even a large file.

2. Perform a "Sort Detective" challenge to run several sorting algorithms without knowing which is which. Try to figure out which sorting algorithm is which on the basis of the runtime and characteristics of each algorithm. Search the Web for "sort detective" for more ideas on such a project.

3. Write a program that discovers all anagrams of all words listed in an input file that stores the entries in a large dictionary. An anagram of a word is a rearrangement of its letters into a new legal word. For example, the anagrams of "share" include "shear," "hears," and "hares." Assume that you have a file available to you that lists many words, one per line. Your program should first read in the dictionary file and sort it, but instead of sorting in alphabetical order it should sort according to each word's canonical form. The canonical form of a word contains the same letters as the original, but in sorted order. Thus, the canonical form of "computer" is "cemoprtu," and the canonical form of "program" is "agmoprr." When your dictionary file is sorted, the word "program" would be placed before the word "computer" because its canonical form comes first in alphabetical order. Write code to retrieve a word's canonical form.

Classes and Objects

Introduction

Now that you've mastered the basics of procedural-style programming in Python, you're ready to explore another major paradigm: object-oriented programming. This chapter introduces the basic terminology that you should use to talk about objects and shows you how to define your own classes to create your own objects.

Objects are entities that contain state and behavior and that can be used as parts of larger programs. We'll discuss the concepts of abstraction and encapsulation, which allow you to use objects at a high level without understanding their inner details. We'll also discuss ideas for designing new classes of objects and implementing the programs that utilize them.

11.1 Object-Oriented Programming

Most of our focus so far has been on procedural decomposition, the technique of breaking complex tasks into smaller subtasks. This is the oldest style of programming, and even in a language like Python we still use procedural techniques. But Python also provides a different approach to programming that we call *object-oriented programming*.

> **Object-Oriented Programming (OOP)**
>
> Reasoning about a program as a set of objects rather than as a set of actions.

Object-oriented programming involves a particular view of programming that has its own terminology. Let's explore that terminology with nonprogramming examples first. You first saw objects in Chapter 3 when you interacted with a `DrawingPanel`. More broadly, an *object* is an entity in a program that combines data and code. An object encapsulates a state and then provides behavior to manipulate and interact with that state.

> **Object**
>
> A programming entity that contains state (data) and behavior (methods).

To truly understand this definition, you have to understand the terms "state" and "behavior." These are some of the most fundamental concepts in object-oriented programming.

Let's consider the class of objects we call radios. A radio can be in different states. It can be turned on or turned off. It can be tuned to one of many different stations, and it can be set to one of many different volumes. Any given radio has to "know" what state it is in, which means that it has to keep track of this information internally. We call the collection of such internal values the *state* of an object.

> **State**
>
> A set of values (internal data) stored in an object.

What are the behaviors of a radio? The most obvious one is that it produces sound when it is turned on and the volume is turned up. But there are actions that we can perform on a radio that manipulate its internal state. We can turn a radio on or off, and we can change the station or volume. We can also check what station the radio is set to right now. We call the collection of these operations the *behavior* of an object.

> **Behavior**
>
> A set of actions an object can perform, often reporting or modifying its internal state.

Objects themselves are not complete programs; they are components that are given distinct roles and responsibilities. Objects can be used as part of larger programs to solve problems. The pieces of code that create and use objects are known as *clients*.

> **Client (or Client Code)**
>
> Code that interacts with a class or objects of that class.

Client programs interact with objects by sending messages to them and asking them to perform behaviors. A major benefit of objects is that they provide reusable pieces of code that can be used in many client programs. You've already used several interesting objects, such as file objects, `DrawingPanel` objects, and lists. In other words, you and your programs have been clients of these objects. Python's provided libraries contain thousands of existing classes of objects.

As you write larger programs, however, you'll find that Python doesn't always have a preexisting object for the problem you're solving. For example, if you are creating a calendar application, you might want to use objects to represent dates, contacts, and appointments. If you are creating a three-dimensional graphical simulation, you might want objects to represent three-dimensional points, vectors, and matrices. If you are writing a financial program, you might want classes to represent your various assets, transactions, and expenses. In this chapter you'll learn how to create your own classes of objects that can be used by client programs like these.

Our definition of object-oriented programming is somewhat simplified. A full exploration of this programming paradigm includes other advanced concepts called polymorphism and inheritance that will be discussed in the next chapter.

Classes and Objects

A class describes a type of objects. When you create a class, you describe the state that will be stored in each object of that class, the behavior each object of that class can perform, and how to create objects of that class.

> **Class**
>
> A blueprint for a type of objects that describes the state and behavior of each object of that type.

Once we have written the appropriate code, we can use the class to create objects of its type. We can then use those objects in our client programs. We say that the created objects are *instances* of the class because one class can be used to construct many objects. This is similar to the way that a blueprint works: One blueprint can be used to create many similar houses, each of which is an instance of the original blueprint.

Did You Know?

Operating Systems History and Objects

In 1983 the IBM PC and its "clones" dominated the PC market, and most people ran an operating system called DOS. DOS uses what we call a "command-line interface," in which the user types commands at a prompt. The console window is a similar interface. To delete a file in DOS, for example, you would give the command "del" (short for "delete") followed by the file name:

```
del data.txt
```

This interface can be described in simple terms as "verb noun." In fact, if you look at a DOS manual, you will find that it is full of verbs. This structure closely parallels the procedural approach to programming. When we want to accomplish some task, we issue a command (the verb) and then mention the object of the action (the noun, the thing we want to affect).

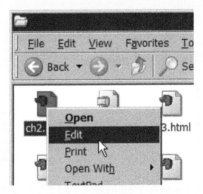

In 1984, Apple Computer released a new computer called a Macintosh that used what we call a graphical user interface, or GUI. The GUI interface uses a graphical "desktop" metaphor that has become so well known that people now tend to forget it is a metaphor. Later, Microsoft brought this functionality to IBM PCs with its Windows operating system.

To delete a file on a Macintosh or on a Windows machine, you locate the icon for the file and click on it. Then you have several options. You can drag it to the trash/recycling bin, or you can select a "delete" command from the menu. Either way, you start with the object you want to delete and then give the command you want to perform. This is a reversal of the fundamental paradigm: With a GUI it's "noun verb." This different form of interaction is the core of object-oriented programming.

Most modern programs use GUIs because we have learned that people find it more natural to work this way. We are used to pointing at things, picking up things, grabbing things. Starting with the object is very natural for us. This approach has also proved to be a helpful way to structure our programs, enabling us to divide our programs into different objects that each can do a certain task, rather than dividing up the central task into subtasks.

Date Objects

To learn about objects we will implement a class called Date. Each Date object will represent a specific date of the year, such as March 11 or November 29. The object will store a month and day as integers. Date objects are useful for applications that need to store and manipulate dates, such as a calendar app, appointment scheduler, or event reminder.

While we haven't written the Date class yet, it can be helpful to think about how a client would want the class to function. Here is a hypothetical example of client code that someone might want to write using our class:

```
# desired usage of Date class
from Date import *

valentines = Date(2, 14)
print("v.day is on:", valentines)

today = Date(11, 29)
print("today's date is:", today)
print("the month is:", today.month)
print("the day is:", today.day)
...
```

```
v.day is on: 2/14
today's date is: 11/29
the month is: 11
the day is: 29
```

11.2 Object State and Behavior

In the next few sections, we'll explore the structure of classes by writing a new class incrementally. We'll write our version of the Date class that was just described.

Here are the main components of a class that we'll see in the sections that follow:

- Attributes (the data stored in each object)
- Constructors (code that initializes an object as it is being created)
- Methods (the behavior each object can execute)
- Encapsulation (protects an object's data from outside access)

We'll focus on these concepts by creating several major versions of the Date class. The first version will give us Date objects that contain only data. The second version will allow us to construct Dates representing any calendar date. The third version will add behavior to the objects. The finished code will encapsulate each `Date` object's internal data to protect it from unwanted outside access.

The early versions of the class will be incomplete and will be used to illustrate each feature of a class in isolation. Only the finished version of the `Date` class will be written in proper object-oriented style. We choose to show the syntax and concepts of classes incrementally so that we can understand each concept one at a time, rather than jumping into a complete class right away.

Data Attributes

The first version of our `Date` class will be a completely empty class. We will create objects of our class in the client code.

In general we will define each class in its own `.py` file with the same name as the class. The following code, written in the file `Date.py`, defines the first version of our `Date` class. The class has an empty body, indicated by the `pass` keyword. Each object of type `Date` will start out with nothing inside it, but the client can add elements to it after creating it.

```
1  # A Date object represents a month and day such as 12/25.
2  # First version: a completely empty class.
3
4  class Date:
5      pass
```

The `Date` class isn't itself an executable Python program; it simply defines a new class of objects for client programs to use. The client code that uses `Date` will be a separate class that we will store in a separate file. The client program needs to import the `Date` class in order to use it. After that, client programs can create `Date` objects by writing the class name `Date` followed by empty parentheses:

```
# client program that creates two Date objects
from Date import *

birthday = Date()
xmas = Date()
```

Empty objects aren't very interesting, but the client can add variables to our objects after we create them. We define special variables called *data attributes*, or just *attributes* for short. Attributes are like normal variables except that they live inside an object; in this way an object is like a data structure such as a list or dictionary in that it serves as a holding place for multiple pieces of data. There are many synonyms for "attribute" that come from other programming languages and environments, such as "field," "instance variable," or "member variable." An object with attributes is a bit like a dictionary where the attributes' names are the keys and the attributes' values are the values.

> **Data Attribute (Attribute)**
>
> A variable inside an object that makes up part of its internal state.

The syntax for adding an attribute to an object (or modifying the value of an existing attribute) is the following:

```
object.attribute = value
```
Syntax template: Adding or modifying an attribute of an object

For example, the following client code creates a `Date` object and adds two integer attributes to it named `month` and `day`. Typically we would put the client code into another file, not into `Date.py`.

```
# create a Date object and add attributes to it
xmas = Date()
xmas.month = 12
xmas.day   = 25
```

The syntax to access the value of an existing data attribute is the following. If no attribute with the given name exists in that object, Python will raise an `AttributeError`.

```
object.attribute
```
Syntax template: Accessing an attribute of an object

It is important to understand that each `Date` object stores its own data that is separate from other `Date` objects. The following shell interaction demonstrates the creation of two `Date` objects. Notice that each one has its own `month` and `day` attribute:

```
>>> # create multiple Date objects
>>> from Date import *
>>> xmas = Date()
>>> xmas.month = 12
>>> xmas.day   = 25

>>> bday = Date()
>>> bday.month = 9
>>> bday.day   = 19

>>> bday.month
9
>>> xmas.month
12
```

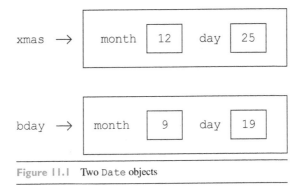

Figure 11.1 Two Date objects

After the shell executes the previous lines of code, you have the situation depicted in Figure 11.1. Each variable refers to an object of the Date class, and each of xmas and bday contains a month and day attribute inside it.

The following is a complete client program that uses our Date class. The code is saved in a file called *date_main.py*, which should be in the same folder or project as *Date.py* in order for the program to work successfully. The client program is inelegant and has some redundancy that we'll eliminate as we improve our Date class in the sections that follow.

```
1   # A client program that deals with dates.
2   # First version, to accompany Date class with state only.
3
4   from Date import *
5
6   def main():
7       # create two Date objects
8       d1 = Date()
9       d1.month =  2
10      d1.day   = 14
11
12      d2 = Date()
13      d2.month =  9
14      d2.day   = 19
15
16      # print each date's state
17      print("d1 is", d1.month, "/", d1.day)
18      print("d2 is", d2.month, "/", d2.day)
19      print()
20
21      # change the state of each date
22      d1.month +=  2
```

Continued on next page

Continued from previous page

```
23      d1.day   -= 13
24      d2.month += 1
25      d2.day   += 12
26
27      # print the dates again
28      print("d1 is", d1.month, "/", d1.day)
29      print("d2 is", d2.month, "/", d2.day)
30
31  main()
```

```
d1 is 2 / 14
d2 is 9 / 19

d1 is 4 / 1
d2 is 10 / 31
```

Our initial `Date` class essentially serves as a way to group two integer values into one object. This technique is somewhat useful for the client program, but the client could have been written using integer variables instead, or with a collection like a list, tuple, or dictionary. Using `Date` objects is not yet substantially better than using `int` values, because our `Date` objects do not yet have any behavior. An object that contains state, but no behavior, is sometimes called a record or structure. In the sections that follow, we'll grow our `Date` class from a minimal implementation into a proper Python class.

Initializers

A clumsy aspect of our existing client code is that it takes three lines to create and initialize the state of one `Date` object:

```
# client needs 3 statements to initialize one Date object (bad)
d1 = Date()
d1.month =  9
d1.day   = 19
```

In general, when we have created objects, we have been able to initialize their state in a single statement. For example, when creating a `DrawingPanel` object, we wrote two integer values in parentheses representing the panel's width and height in pixels. We might expect that we could initialize a `Date` by writing its initial month and day values in parentheses as we created it:

```
# desired behavior; does not work yet
d1 = Date(9, 19)
```

However, such a statement wouldn't be successful for our Date class, because we haven't written any code specifying how to create a Date with an initial month/day state. Our second version of the Date class will add this ability. Classes can contain methods that provide behavior to the objects of that class. The initial state of an object is specified by writing a special method called a *constructor*. A constructor is sometimes also called an *object initializer* or an *initializer method*.

> **Constructor (Initializer)**
>
> A special method that initializes the state of an object as it is created.

The constructor is special code that executes when the client creates a new object. A constructor's header looks like a function or method header, though it must have the special name of __init__ with two underscores on either side of the word init. When you write a constructor, you specify what parameters must be passed when clients create an object of your type and how those parameters should be used to initialize the newly created object. The constructor also accepts an initial parameter named self that represents the object that is being created.

The general syntax for a constructor is the following:

```
class ClassName:
    def __init__(self, name, parameters):
        statement
        statement
        ...
        statement
```
Syntax template: Constructor

Our constructor for the Date class will accept month and day values as parameters and store them as attributes in the Date object:

```
class Date:
    # Constructor initializes the state of new
    # Date objects as they are created by client code.
    def __init__(self, month, day):
        self.month = month
        self.day = day
```

Constructors can be confusing for students who are just learning how classes work. Once you have an __init__ method, if you write the following line of client code:

```
d1 = Date(9, 19)
```

Python will perform all of the following actions when that line of code is executed:

1. Create a new `Date` object in memory.

2. Execute the `Date` class's `__init__` method, referring to the newly created object as `self`, and passing `9` and `19` as the `month` and `day` parameter values.

3. (Implicitly) return the newly created `Date` object as the return value from the constructor call.

4. Store a reference to the `Date` object in the variable named `d1` in the client code.

Figure 11.2 shows the steps that occur when a constructor is executed. In this diagram we attempt to separate the client's code and perspective from the code that runs in the `Date` class itself. The `Date` class does the work of creating the object and initializing its state, and then it sends the new object back to the client to use.

Part of what makes constructors confusing is that several important things happen implicitly. The client code does not explicitly write `__init__` to invoke the constructor; it is called implicitly when you write `Date(...)` in client code. And in the code for the `__init__` method inside the `Date` class, the step of creating the new `Date` object and referring to that object as `self`, is not indicated explicitly anywhere in the code; it is done implicitly when the client calls the constructor by calling `Date(...)`. Lastly, the `__init__` method does not explicitly return the `Date` object that was created, but Python implicitly returns that object so that the client can store that object in its `d1` variable. It can be hard to understand what is going on with so many details and so much happening under the hood, but this is part of the process of learning how to write new classes of objects.

Calling a constructor with parameters is similar to ordering a car from a factory: "I'd like the yellow one with power windows and a dashboard navigation system." You might not need to specify every detail about the car, such as the fact that it should have four wheels and headlights, but you do specify some initial attributes that are important to you.

Here is the complete code for the new version of our `Date` class, which now contains a constructor:

```
1   # A Date object represents a month and day such as 12/25.
2   # This version adds a constructor to initialize object state.
3
4   class Date:
5       # Constructor initializes the state of new
6       # Date objects as they are created by client code.
7       def __init__(self, month, day):
8           self.month = month
9           self.day = day
```

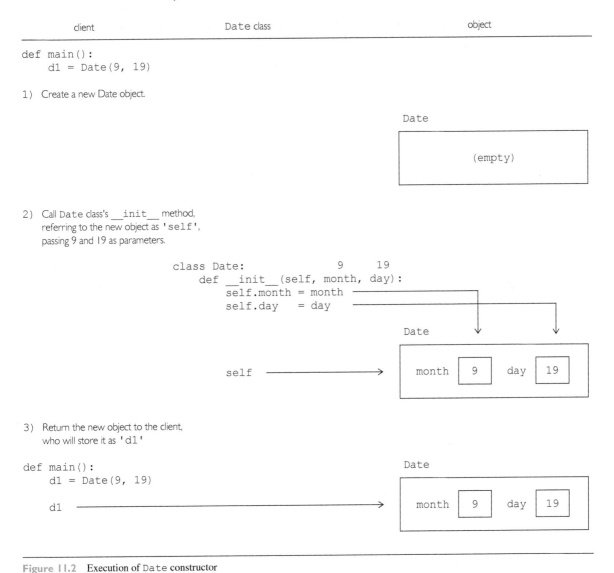

Figure 11.2 Execution of Date constructor

The parameters to the constructor are often given the same names as the object's attributes, but this is not required. Some programmers prefer to give them different names to avoid ambiguity. For example, if we had chosen to call our constructor's parameters m and d, the constructor code would be the following:

```
class Date:
    # constructor with shorter/different parameter names
    def __init__(self, m, d):
        self.month = m
        self.day = d
```

As with functions and methods, constructors can utilize default parameter values. Default parameters allow creating objects with an explicitly provided initial state or a default state. In the case of our `Date` class, we can make the month and day parameters optional as follows:

```
class Date:
    # Constructs a date object representing the given month and day.
    # If no month and day are passed, initializes to January 1.
    def __init__(self, month = 1, day = 1):
        self.month = month
        self.day = day
```

The client code to create `Date` objects can now use either form:

```
# client code
def main():
    d1 = Date(9, 19)    # initial state of 9/19
    d2 = Date()         # default state of 1/1
    ...
```

Methods

The next version of our `Date` class will contain both state and behavior. Behavior of objects is specified by writing *methods*. A method is like a function, but while a function stands on its own, a method lives inside of an object. A method interacts with the data of its object to perform useful behavior related to that object. Some programmers describe methods of an object as "messages" that can be sent to the object.

> **Method**
>
> A function inside an object that operates on that object.

The objects introduced in previous chapters all contained methods that represented their behavior. For example, a file object has a `read` method, and a `DrawingPanel` object has a `draw_line` method. We think of these methods as being stored inside the object. As you recall, they use different call syntax than functions: You write the object's name, then a dot, and then the method's name and parameters. Each object's methods are able to interact with the data stored inside that object.

For example, suppose we want to write code to compute the number of days in a given month. Since `Date` objects store a month, it would be nice to be able to ask a `Date` how many days there are in its month. Recall the mnemonic device for remembering the number of days in each month of the year:

- Thirty days have September, April, June, and November.
- February has 28 days (in a non–leap year).
- All other months have thirty-one days.

To represent this logic in the program, one option would be to write a regular function in the client code that accepts a `Date` as a parameter and returns the desired information. (This is not the best way to represent such logic, as we'll see in this section.) The function assumes that the `Date` passed has a `month` attribute. Its code would look like the following.

```
# A function to return days in a given month;
# not a good choice in this case.
def days_in_month(d):
    if d.month in {4, 6, 9, 11}:
        return 30
    elif d.month == 2:
        return 28
    else:
        return 31
```

A call to the function would look like the following line of code in the client program:

```
# client code to use the bad days_in_month function
d1 = Date(9, 19)
days = days_in_month(d1)
print("There are", days, "days in month #", d1.month)
```

```
There are 30 days in month # 9
```

However, a standard function isn't the best way to implement the behavior; we should use a method instead. The `Date` class is supposed to be reusable so that many client programs can use it. If the `days_in_month` method is placed into our client program *date_main.py* client, other clients won't be able to use it without copying and pasting its code redundantly. Also, one of the biggest benefits of programming with objects is that we can put related data and behavior together. The ability of a `Date` to translate data is closely related to that `Date` object's data, so it is better to specify that each `Date` object will know how many days are in its month. We'll do this by writing a method in the `Date` class.

We know from experience with objects that you can call a method using "dot notation":

object.method(parameters)
Syntax template: Calling a method of an object

If we were to turn `days_in_month` into a method, a call to the method in the client code would look like this:

```
days = d1.days_in_month()
```

Notice that the client doesn't pass the `Date` as a parameter, nor the month. Instead, the call begins by indicating which `Date` object it wants to interact with (`d1`). In our example, the client is sending a `days_in_month` message to the object to which `d1` refers.

Let's look at how a `days_in_month` method would be implemented. A method has the same syntax as a standard function with two differences: it appears inside of a class, and it accepts an initial parameter named `self` that represents the object on which the method was called:

```
class ClassName:
    def method_name(self, parameters):
        statement
        statement
        . . .
        statement
```
Syntax template: Defining a method

You saw the `self` parameter when we implemented a constructor, and its meaning is similar here. The parameter `self` refers to the object on which the method was called. For example, if the client code calls `d1.days_in_month()`, during that call the `self` variable refers to `d1`. Though in the client code the object of interest comes before the `.` dot character, inside the class itself the object of interest is declared explicitly as the first parameter to the method. The code for the method has a knowledge of the object on which it operates. This is sometimes called the *object parameter* or the *self reference*.

> **Object Parameter (Self Reference)**
>
> A parameter that refers to the object on which a method is called. Commonly named `self` in Python code.

Naming this parameter `self` is a convention but not a requirement. The name `self` is not a special keyword in Python, but the official Python documentation recommends

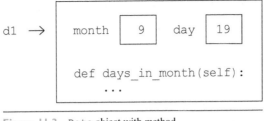

Figure 11.3   Date object with method

it and most programmers consistently use this name, so it is considered good style to follow this practice for consistency.

When we define a method in the Date class, think of it as if each Date object has its own copy of that method. Each Date object also has its own month and day attribute values. A Date object would look like Figure 11.3.

It's helpful to know at this point that an object's methods can refer to that object's attributes. The methods of an object can refer to the data attributes of that object by interacting with the self parameter. For example, the expression self.month or self.day would refer to either of the attributes of the Date object on which the method was called.

To convert days_in_month from a standard function into a method, we would therefore rename the parameter d to self and paste the method's code into the Date class in Date.py. The following are the two versions of the code:

```
# A function to return days in a given month. (bad)
def days_in_month(d):
    if d.month in {4, 6, 9, 11}:
        return 30
    elif d.month == 2:
        return 28
    else:
        return 31
```

```
class Date:
    # A method to return days in a given month. (good)
    def days_in_month(self):
        if self.month in {4, 6, 9, 11}:
            return 30
        elif self.month == 2:
            return 28
        else:
            return 31
```

Figure 11.4   Two Date objects with method

Methods like days_in_month are useful because they give our objects useful behavior that lets us write more expressive and concise client programs. If multiple clients use our Date class, all of the client programs will be able to call the days_in_month method without needing to rewrite it.

The following client code contains two calls to the days_in_month method. The first call is d1.days_in_month(), which means that for that execution of the code, self refers to d1. This means that the method returns the number of days in d1's month of September, which is 30. The second call is d2.days_in_month(), so self refers to d2, which has a month value of 11, causing a return value of 31. The objects created by this client code are diagrammed in Figure 11.4.

```
def main():
    d1 = Date(9, 19)
    d2 = Date(12, 24)
    print("days in Sep:", d1.days_in_month())
    print("days in Dec:", d2.days_in_month())
```

Accessors and Mutators

The days_in_month method is an example of a category of methods called accessors. An *accessor* is a method that helps the client examine or utilize information based on the state of an object, often by returning a value. Using our radio analogy, an accessor might return the current station or volume. Examples of accessor methods you have seen in previous chapters include the tell method of file objects and the get_pixel_color method of DrawingPanel objects.

> **Accessor**
>
> A method that provides information about the state of an object without modifying it.

Mutators form a second important category of methods. A *mutator* is a method that modifies the state of an object in some way, usually by assigning a new value to one or more of its data attributes. If you think of an object as a radio, the mutators would be the switches and knobs that turn the radio on and off or change the station or volume.

> **Mutator**
>
> A method that modifies the object's internal state.

Some mutator methods' names begin with "set," as in `set_id` or `set_title`. Usually a mutator method does not return a value. Mutators often accept parameters that specify the new state of the object or the amount by which to modify the object's current state. You can think of accessors as read-only operations while mutators are read/write operations.

Let's write a mutator method in our `Date` class. A common useful operation would be to move a `Date` forward by one day; for example, September 19 would advance to September 20; or October 31 would advance to November 1. We could represent this logic with a method called `advance` in the `Date` class. Its header would look like the following:

```
class Date:
    ...


    # Advances the Date's state to the next day.
    def advance(self):
        ...
```

As with the `days_in_month` method, `advance` can refer to the state of the object on which it was called through the `self` parameter. In this case we will write statements that modify that state by assigning new values to `self`'s data attributes. The simplest case would be to increase the object's `day` value by 1:

```
# incomplete/partial version
def advance(self):
    self.day += 1
    ...
```

This initial code will work correctly for dates in the early parts of a month, such as advancing September 19 into September 20. But it will fail if this is the last day of the month; the current code would advance November 31 to be November 32, which is an invalid date. The easiest way to handle the month-wrapping case is to utilize the `days_in_month` method we wrote previously. Methods of an object are allowed to call other methods on `self` using the usual syntax. In this case, we can advance the day of the object, and then use `days_in_month` to see whether we have exceeded the boundaries of the month, adjusting the date's state to the next month if so. If we advance to the next month, we increase the `month` attribute by 1 and also set the `day` attribute back to 1 to indicate the first day of the next month:

```
# second version that wraps months
def advance(self):
    self.day += 1
    if self.day > self.days_in_month():
        # wrap to next month
        self.month += 1
        self.day = 1
```

This version is nearly correct, but there is one more case to consider. What if the date object represents December 31, the very last day of the year? Advancing from 12/31 should cause the date to wrap around to January 1. Our existing code can be modified to handle this case as well.

Here's the complete version of our `Date` class that now contains the finished `advance` method:

```
 1   # A Date object represents a month and day such as 12/25.
 2   # This version adds behavior (methods).
 3
 4   class Date:
 5       # Constructor initializes the state of new
 6       # Date objects as they are created by client code.
 7       def __init__(self, month, day):
 8           # set the attributes (the state in each Date object)
 9           self.month = month
10           self.day = day
11
12       # Advances the Date's state to the next day,
13       # wrapping into the next month/year as necessary.
14       def advance(self):
15           self.day += 1
16           if self.day >= self.days_in_month():
17               # wrap to next month
18               self.month += 1
19               self.day = 1
20               if self.month > 12:
21                   # wrap to next year
22                   self.month = 1
23
24       # Returns the number of days in this Date's month.
25       def days_in_month(self):
```

Continued on next page

Continued from previous page

```
26          if self.month in {4, 6, 9, 11}:
27              return 30
28          elif self.month == 2:
29              return 28
30          else:
31              return 31
```

The client program can now use the new behavior and methods of the Date class. Notice that we test all three cases of the advance method: a date in the middle of a month, a date at the very end of its month, and a date at the end of the year.

```
1   # A client program that deals with dates.
2   # This version accompanies Date class with methods.
3
4   from Date import *
5
6   def main():
7       # create three Date objects
8       d1 = Date( 9, 19)
9       d2 = Date( 7, 31)
10      d3 = Date(12, 31)
11
12      # advance each date and print its state
13      d1.advance()
14      print("d1 is", d1.month, "/", d1.day)
15      d2.advance()
16      print("d2 is", d2.month, "/", d2.day)
17      d3.advance()
18      print("d3 is", d3.month, "/", d3.day)
19
20   main()
```

```
d1 is 9 / 20
d2 is 8 / 1
d3 is 1 / 1
```

Making Objects Printable

The designers of Python felt that it was important for it to be easy to print many types of values to the console, and for many types of values to interact well with strings. But if you write a class, by default Python does not know how to print the state of your class's objects. If you try to print a Date object as in the following code, for example, the output is unhelpful:

```
def main():
    d1 = Date(9, 19)
    print("d1 is", d1)
```

```
d1 is <Date.Date object at 0x7f1085d5e7b8>
```

When Python doesn't know how to print a value of a given type, it displays a default message indicating that value's type and the address where it is stored in the computer's memory. The memory address is shown as a base-16 hexadecimal integer. But this is not very useful; we'd rather have it print the object's state of 9/19.

When a Python program is printing an object or converting it to a string, the program calls a special method called __str__ on the object. (The name is the word str with two underscores on either side, a naming convention similar to the __init__ method.) The __str__ method accepts no parameters other than self and returns a string representing the state of the object. Its general syntax is the following:

```
class ClassName:

    ...

    def __str__(self):
        code to produce and return the desired string
```
Syntax template: __str__ method for converting objects to strings

The following code implements a __str__ method for our Date objects and returns a string such as "9/19":

```
# returns a string representation of this date
def __str__(self):
    return str(self.month) + "/" + str(self.day)
```

Now that our class has this method, the preceding client code produces the following output:

```
d1 is 9/19
```

Note that the client code didn't explicitly call the __str__ method; the Python interpreter did it automatically because the Date object was being printed. The __str__ method is also called when you use the str conversion function on an object, as in the following code:

```
def main():
    d1 = Date(9, 19)
    s = str(d1)
    print("s is", s, "with length", len(s))
```

```
s is 9/19 with length 4
```

In order for this implicit calling behavior to work properly, your __str__ method's signature must exactly match the one shown in this section. Changing the name or signature even slightly (for example, naming the method _str_ with a single underscore, or __Str__ with a capital S) will cause the class to produce the old output (e.g., "<Date.Date object at 0x7f1085d5e7b8>").

Common Programming Error

Print Statement in __str__ Method

Since the __str__ method is closely related to printing, some students mistakenly think that they should place print statements in their __str__ method, as in the following example:

```
# this method is flawed;
# it should return the string rather than printing it
def __str__(self):
    print(str(self.month) + "/" + str(self.day))
```

A key idea to understand about __str__ is that it doesn't directly print anything: It simply returns a string that the Python interpreter or client can use in a print statement.

In fact, many well-formed classes of objects do not contain any print statements at all. The inclusion of print statements in a class binds that class to a particular style of output. For example, the preceding code prints a Date object on its own line, making the class unsuitable for a client that doesn't want the output to appear exactly this way (say, a client that wants to print many Date objects on the same line).

You may wonder why the designers of Python chose to use a __str__ method rather than, say, a print_date method that would output the object to the console. The reason is that __str__ is more versatile. You can use __str__ to output the object to a file, display it on a graphical user interface, or even send the text over a network.

Object Equality and Ordering

For several chapters now, you have used relational operators like == and < to compare values for equality and ordering. By default these operators do not behave as expected when used on objects. For example, Python doesn't know how to compare two Date objects for equality:

```
>>> # try to compare Dates for equality
>>> d1 = Date(2, 14)
>>> d2 = Date(2, 14)
>>> d3 = Date(12, 31)
>>> d1 == d2
False
>>> d1 == d3
False
>>> d1 == d1
True
```

When trying to compare two `Date` objects with the same state, such as `d1` and `d2` in the interaction above, the result is surprisingly `False`. This is because Python doesn't understand how to compare objects of classes you write, and so by default it compares only the objects' *identity*. An object has an identity and is distinct from other objects, even if another object happens to have the same state. This means that the only time you will receive a `True` result on an `==` test is when you literally compare an object to itself.

A nonprogramming analogy would be if you and your friend both purchased identical pairs of shoes. They are in some ways equivalent, but you still consider them distinct and separate items. You might not want to share them. And the items' states are not linked in any way. Over time, their state might become visibly unequal, such as if one of you wore your new shoes more often than the other.

The `==` operator does not behave as expected with objects because it tests whether two objects have the same identity. The `==` comparison actually tests whether two variables refer to the same object, not whether two distinct objects have the same state. This relates to the concept of reference semantics as discussed in Chapter 7. Consider the following three variable definitions:

```
d1 = Date(2, 14)
d2 = Date(2, 14)
d3 = d2
```

The diagram in Figure 11.5 represents the state of these objects and the variables that refer to them. Notice that `d3` is not a reference to a third object but a second reference to the object that was referred to by `d2`. This means that a change to `d2`, such as a call of its `advance` method, would also be reflected in `d3`, as shown in Figure 11.5.

In the case of the preceding objects, the expression `d1 == d2` would evaluate to `False` because `d1` and `d2` do not refer to the same object. The object referred to by `d1` has the same state as `d2`'s object, but these objects have different identities. The expression `d2 == d3` would evaluate to `True`, though, because `d2` does refer to the same object as `d3`. This is the default behavior Python uses when comparing objects.

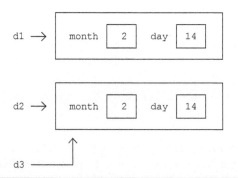

Figure 11.5   Defining three variables to refer to two unique objects

For many kinds of objects, we don't want to compare objects for identity but instead for *equivalence*. In other words, we want to know whether the objects have the same state. You can imagine a piece of client code that examines two `Date` objects to see whether they have the same `month` and `day` values:

```
# client code to compare Date object state (bad style)
if d1.month == d2.month and d1.day == d2.day:
    # the objects have equal state
    ...
```

The preceding code works properly, but the comparison logic should actually be implemented in the `Date` class itself, not in the client code. To change the `==` and `!=` operators so that they compare based on state, we can write a special predicate method named `__eq__` (short for "equal") that accepts the object to compare as a parameter and returns a Boolean value indicating whether the two objects are the same. Rather than having two `Date`s d1 and d2, the `__eq__` method accepts `self` as the first object and accepts the second object as a parameter. It returns `True` if the two objects are equal.

A proper `__eq__` method performs a comparison of two objects' states and returns `True` if the states are the same. With the preceding `Date` objects, we'd like the expressions d1 `==` d2, d1 `==` d3, and d2 `==` d3 to all evaluate to `True` because the `Date`s all have the same month/day values.

The following code is a correct implementation of the `__eq__` method, followed by the client code to use it. We utilize Boolean Zen by returning a Boolean value directly rather than writing an `if/else` statement.

```
# Date class with equality method
class Date:
    ...

    # Compares Dates for equality.
    def __eq__(self, other):
        return self.month == other.month and self.day == other.day

# Date client that uses equality method
d1 = Date(2, 14)
d2 = Date(2, 14)
d3 = d2


if d1 == d2:
    print("The dates are the same!")
```

The `__eq__` method fixes the `==` and `!=` for our class. If you want to be able to use operators like `<` and `>` for ordering, you can write similar methods named `__lt__`, `__gt__`, and `__cmp__`. Python has even more special methods, such as `__hash__` for storing objects as keys in a dictionary or set. These are outside the scope of this chapter, but you may want to consult the official Python documentation on classes and special methods for more information.

11.3 Encapsulation

Our next version of the `Date` class will protect its data from unwanted access using a concept known as encapsulation. *Encapsulation* is the programming practice of hiding internal details about a piece of code (in this case, details about a class of objects) from clients of that code.

> **Encapsulation**
>
> Hiding the implementation details of an object from the clients of the object.

To understand the notion of encapsulation, recall the analogy of radios as objects. Almost everyone knows how to use a radio, but few people know how to build a radio or understand how the circuitry inside a radio works. It is a benefit of the radio's design that we don't need to know those details in order to use it.

The radio analogy demonstrates an important dichotomy of external versus internal views of an object. From the outside, we just see behavior. From the inside, we see the internal state that is used to accomplish that behavior.

Focusing on the radio's external behavior enables us to use it easily while ignoring the details of its inner workings that are unimportant to us. This is an example of an important computer science concept known as *abstraction*.

> **Abstraction**
>
> Focusing on essential properties rather than inner details.

Figure 11.6 shows this idea when applied to a radio. In fact, a radio (like most other electronic devices) has a case or chassis that houses all of the electronics so that we don't see them from the outside. Dials, buttons, and displays on the case allow us to manipulate the radio without having to deal with all of the circuitry that makes it work. In fact, you wouldn't want someone to give you a fully functional radio that had wires and capacitors hanging out of it, because they would make the radio less pleasant to use.

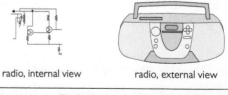

radio, internal view   radio, external view

Figure 11.6   The internal and external views of a radio

In programming, the concept of hiding internal state from outside view is called encapsulation. When an object is properly encapsulated, its clients cannot directly access or modify its internal workings, nor do they need to do so. Only the implementer of the class needs to know about those details. Encapsulation leads to abstraction; an encapsulated object presents a more pure abstraction than one that has data which can be accessed directly.

In previous chapters you have taken advantage of the abstraction provided by well-encapsulated objects. For example, you have used `DrawingPanel` objects to draw graphics without knowing exactly how the graphics appear on the screen, and you have used file objects to read from files without knowing the computer's file system in great detail.

But so far, our `Date` class is not encapsulated. We've built a working radio, but its wires (its `month` and `day` attributes) are still hanging out. Using encapsulation, we'll put a bit of casing around our `Date` objects so that clients will only need to use the objects' methods and will not access the attributes directly.

Motivation for Encapsulation

Encapsulation can help us protect an object's state from unwanted or invalid modifications. We'll explore this by discussing issues involving invalid states with our `Date` class.

In the case of dates, there is a finite set of legal values that represent valid dates of the year. For example, a valid month is between 1 and 12 inclusive, and a valid day is between 1 and the number of days in the given month. What if the client tries to supply a value outside these ranges? The following code demonstrates that it is currently possible to do so:

```
>>> # create a Date with illegal values
>>> bogus1 = Date(13, 55)

>>> # create legal Date, but then change to invalid state
>>> bogus2 = Date(2, 17)
>>> bogus2.month = 13
>>> bogus2.day   = 55
```

If a `Date` object has an invalid state, we cannot guarantee that our various methods and operations will work properly. For example, the `advance` and `days_in_month` methods implicitly assume that the `month` and `day` values in the `Date` have valid values. It would be best for the `Date` class to protect itself by forbidding clients from setting invalid month and day values like this.

Once we properly encapsulate our class, it will be much harder for a malicious or buggy client to put one of its objects into an invalid state.

Private Attributes and Properties

Some programming languages support a concept called private access, where attributes of an object can be defined in a way that outside code is not able to directly access them.

Python does not directly support any such feature. Instead, Python programmers have a convention that attributes with certain names are to be thought of as *private attributes*, which are ones that are not to be directly accessed or modified by client code.

Private Attribute

An attribute of a class that is not to be modified by client code.

Some languages support the concept of strictly private access and will not allow programs to run if any client code tries to access an object's private attribute. The Python language does not enforce privacy of attributes, but all Python programmers are expected to understand that they should not directly refer to such attributes in inappropriate ways.

The general syntax for defining such an attribute is to precede its name by an underscore. You can define a private attribute by assigning it a value in a constructor:

```
class ClassName:
    def __init__(self, parameters):
        self._name = value
```
Syntax template: Private attribute (with leading underscore)

The attributes of our Date class would be defined as follows:

```
# Date class with private attributes
class Date:
    def __init__(self, month, day):
        self._month = month
        self._day   = day
    ...
```

Declaring private attributes indicates to clients that the author of the class wants to encapsulate the state of the object, in the same way that a radio's casing keeps the user from seeing the wires and circuitry inside it. Private attributes are meant to be accessed or modified by all of the code inside the Date class (i.e., inside the Date.py file), but not anywhere else. This means that a client is expected to no longer directly refer to a Date object's _month or _day attributes. The following client code still runs just fine, but it is considered bad style; the underscores are supposed to be a visual cue to help alert the client code author to this.

```
# client code that directly accesses private attributes
# (this is discouraged and considered poor style)
d1 = Date(9, 19)
print("d1 month is", d1._month)
print("d1 day is", d1._day)
```

If you name your attributes with two leading underscores instead of one, Python provides even further protection on their values. The interpreter will dynamically rename the attributes internally to have mangled names like `_Date__month` so that it is almost impossible for clients to accidentally access or modify their values. But in general the Python community prefers the single-underscore style; this latter double-underscore style is not as common in real Python code bases. The prevailing opinion seems to be that the inconvenience and ugliness of using two underscores is not worth the additional protection. We will use the single-underscore naming convention for attributes in the rest of this text.

Now we have a `Date` whose attributes should not be accessed. But the preceding constraints are a bit too strict. We do have a sense that clients should be allowed to look at the state of a `Date`. We also don't mind if clients modify a `Date`'s state, so long as they only set them to legal values. Forbidding all access to a `Date`'s month and day seems excessive.

To allow client code to access a `Date` object's attribute values, we can add some new methods to the `Date` class. If we write a method whose sole purpose is to return the date's `_month` or `_day` value, this amounts to a read-only access to that attribute, since a client can see a copy of its value but cannot directly change it. In other programming languages, we would write methods with names like `get_month` and `get_day` to achieve this functionality, though this is not the preferred style in Python.

Python has a better way to provide read-only access to an object's attributes. Python supports a special kind of method called a *property* that is meant to be used as an accessor to return an attribute's value. A special aspect of properties is that though they are methods, the syntax for calling them is the same as the syntax for directly accessing data attributes.

> **Property**
>
> A method for accessing or modifying a data attribute of an object. Allows special client code syntax to make it look like a direct access to that attribute rather than a method call.

You may have used properties when you interacted with a `DrawingPanel` in Chapter 3. For example, you can set the title text and background color of a `DrawingPanel` by setting its `title` and `background` properties:

```
# properties of a DrawingPanel object
panel = DrawingPanel(500, 300)
panel.title = "My window"
panel.background = "yellow"
...
```

Now that we have learned more about classes and objects, the preceding code looks as though we are directly setting data attributes inside the drawing panel. But we are actually calling special property methods that modify the state of the panel. A property combines the simple client syntax of directly accessing data attributes with the encapsulation semantics of calling methods. (When a language provides a clean and simple syntax for an operation like this, it is sometimes called "syntactic sugar.")

You can provide this same kind of functionality in your own classes by defining properties. The syntax for defining a property is the same as writing a method, except preceded by a decorator of `@property`:

```
class ClassName:
    @property
    def property_name(self):
        code to return the property's value
```
Syntax template: Defining a property

Typically we name the property with the same name that the previously public attribute used to have, such as `month` or `day`. The following code shows property methods that provide access to a `Date` object's `month` and `day` attributes: Properties are distinct from other accessor methods in that a client can execute them without writing parentheses after the property's name. The benefit of this is that the client can use a cleaner syntax that looks more like directly accessing the attribute while making sure that the access is read-only. The client code to print a `Date` object's state must be changed to the following:

```
# Date class with private attributes and properties (good style)
class Date:
    def __init__(self, month, day):
        self._month = month
        self._day   = day

    @property
    def month(self):
        return self._month

    @property
    def day(self):
        return self._day

    . . .


# Date client using properties (good style)
d1 = Date(9, 19)
print("d1 month is ", d1.month)
print("d1 day is ", d1.day)
```

It probably seems odd to grant access to a `Date` object's `month` and `day` attributes when we said our goal was to encapsulate those attributes, but having properties doesn't actually violate the encapsulation of the object. The properties just return a copy of the attributes' values to the client, so that the client can see the month or day values but not change them. In other words, these properties give the client read-only access to the state of the object. If a client tries to set the month or day of a `Date` directly, the interpreter will raise an `AttributeError` and halt the program:

```
# client of Date class trying to set a read-only property
d1 = Date(9, 19)
d1.month = 13
print("d1 month is ", d1.month)
```

```
Traceback (most recent call last):
  File "date_main.py", line 25, in <module>
    main()
  File "date_main.py", line 16, in main
    d1.month = 13
AttributeError: can't set attribute
```

One drawback of encapsulating the `Date`'s state with properties is that it is no longer easy for the client code to set a `Date` to a new month or day. This is somewhat by design, as we wanted to prevent clients from setting a `Date`'s state to values outside the valid ranges. In most other programming languages, the workaround for this problem would be to write a mutator method for each attribute, with names like `set_month` and `set_day`. Python provides a better mechanism called a *property setter* that allows property syntax to be used when setting values as well as accessing them.

```
class ClassName:
    @property_name.setter
    def property_name(self, parameter):
        code to set the property's value
```
Syntax template: Property setter

The simplest property setter accepts the new property value as a parameter and simply stores that value into the object's data attribute. For example, a simple setter for the `month` property of a `Date` object is shown below along with client code to call it. The syntax for a client to call a property setter looks the same as the syntax for setting a public attribute, with the parentheses omitted. When the client writes `d1.month = 11`, it invokes the `month` setter with `self` set to `d1` and `value` set to 11.

```
# Date class with basic property setter
class Date:

    ...


    # The month property allows get/set access
    # to the Date's month value.
    @property
    def month(self):
        return self._month

    @month.setter
    def month(self, value):
        self._month = value
# Date client using property setter
d1 = Date(9, 19)
d1.month = 11    # use property setter
print("d1 month is ", d1.month)
```

But the preceding setter is inadequate; it allows clients to set the month or day to any value. While the code for each property accessor was fairly simple, just returning the corresponding attribute's value, the code for a property setter is often more complex. The property setter is the place where the class can enforce constraints on the values of its attributes.

In the case of our Date class, the valid values of a month are between 1 and 12. If the client passes a value outside this range, our code should not store it in the object's attribute. We could resolve the problem by printing an error message or by setting the attribute's value to some other arbitrary value. But in cases like this, the invalid value often comes from a bug or a mistake in the client's understanding of our class. The best way to handle a violation like this is to raise an error so that the client will know the parameter values passed were illegal. So we will raise an error (specifically, a ValueError) when an invalid value is passed. The following is a better version of the month property setter:

```
# Date class with better month property setter
class Date:

    ...


    # The month property allows get/set access to the Date's month value.
    # The month must be between 1-12 inclusive, else a ValueError is
    raised.
    @property
    def month(self):
        return self._month
```

Continued on next page

Continued from previous page

```
    @month.setter
    def month(self, value):
        if value >= 1 and value <= 12:
            self._month = value
        else:
            raise ValueError("Invalid month: " + str(value))
```

We can write a `day` property with similar constraints. The range of valid values for the `day` property is less obvious than with the month, however. The minimum legal `day` value is `1`, and the maximum legal day value depends on what month the `Date` represents. This is a case where we can reuse existing logic from other parts of the class. The `day` property setter can call the `days_in_month` method on the `Date` object itself to find out the maximum legal `day` value:

```
# Date class with day property setter
class Date:

    ...

    # The day property allows get/set access to the Date's day value.
    # Must be between 1 and # of days in the month, inclusive.
    @property
    def day(self):
        return self._day

    @day.setter
    def day(self, value):
        if value >= 1 and value <= self.days_in_month():
            self._day = value
        else:
            raise ValueError("Invalid day: " + str(value))
```

Class Invariants

In the previous section we wrote properties and property setters to help stop clients from setting a `Date` object to have an invalid state. We decided that we wanted every `Date` object to store only valid months between 1 and 12, and only valid days between 1 and the number of days in the given month. We wrote code in our property setter to ensure that this would be true if the client tries to directly modify the month or day. But the checks in the property setter are insufficient, because it is still possible for a client to create an invalid Date by passing invalid values to its constructor:

```
# client code constructing invalid date
d1 = Date(13, 55)    # oops!
```

This buggy code slips through because we currently don't check the validity of the parameters passed to our `Date` constructor:

```
class Date:
    ...


    # This constructor doesn't check for valid parameters.
    def __init__(self, month, day):
        self._month = month
        self._day = day
```

We want to ensure that every `Date` object's state is valid throughout its entire lifespan, not just when its properties are modified. Such a claim that is always true of every object of a class is called a *class invariant*.

Class Invariant

An assertion about an object's state that is true for the lifetime of that object.

Typically a class that has invariants announces them in its top comment header so that clients of the class know about them. In the case of our `Date` class, we might write the following comment header to announce our intent to enforce invariants on each `Date` object's state:

```
# A Date object represents a month and day such as 12/25.
# Invariant: Every Date's month value is from 1-12 inclusive,
# and its day value is from 1 to # of days in its month inclusive.
class Date:
    ...
```

Now that we've announced our intent, we must follow through on that intent by enforcing it throughout our class's code. Class invariants are related to preconditions, postconditions, and assertions, as presented in Chapters 4 and 5. We cannot allow any object to be created in an invalid initial state. We also cannot allow any mutator or setter to break the invariants we have chosen. A class invariant should be treated as an implicit postcondition of every method and setter in the class. Enforcing an invariant may cause you to add preconditions and tests to the constructors, mutator methods, and property setters of your class.

We could insert new code in every place where we modify a `Date` object's state that would check for invalid values. But the best way to avoid invalid states for our objects is to funnel all object mutation through a single place in the code. To do this, we'll add a mutator method called `set_date` that accepts a month and day as parameters and sets the date's internal state to those values. If either value is invalid, the method will raise a `ValueError`:

```
class Date:
    ...
    # Modifies the date's month and day state.
    # Raises a ValueError if values are out of range.
    def set_date(self, month, day):
        if month >= 1 and month <= 12:
            self._month = month
        else:
            raise ValueError("Invalid month: " + str(month))
        if day >= 1 and day <= self.days_in_month():
            self._day = day
        else:
            raise ValueError("Invalid day: " + str(day))
```

The `set_date` method could be used by client code such as the following:

```
# Date client using set_date method
d1 = Date(9, 19)
print("d1 is", d1)
d1.set_date(11, 30)      # change to Nov 30
print("d1 is", d1)
```

Now that we have the `set_date` method, we will update the rest of the class to call `set_date` every time it modifies the state of the object. This includes the constructor and the `month` and `day` property setters. The only other mutator in our class right now is `advance`, which moves the `Date` forward by one day. The code for `advance` already abides by our invariant because it properly wraps month and day values within the valid ranges. If we were to introduce any other mutators or setters in our class, we would need to ensure that they did not violate our invariants.

Here is the fourth complete version of our `Date` class, including encapsulated attributes and properties, that declares and maintains our class invariants throughout its code:

```
1   # A Date object represents a month and day such as 12/25.
2   # This version adds private attributes and properties.
3   #
4   # Invariant: Every Date's month value is from 1-12 inclusive,
5   # and its day value is from 1 to # of days in its month inclusive.
6
7   class Date:
```

Continued on next page

Continued from previous page

```
 8      # Constructor initializes the state of new
 9      # Date objects as they are created by client code.
10      # Raises a ValueError if values are out of range.
11      def __init__(self, month, day):
12          self.set_date(month, day)
13
14      # Returns a string representation of a Date, such as "9/19".
15      def __str__(self):
16          return str(self._month) + "/" + str(self._day)
17
18      # month property allows get/set access to Date's month value
19      # must be between 1-12 inclusive, else a ValueError is raised
20      @property
21      def month(self):
22          return self._month
23
24      @month.setter
25      def month(self, value):
26          self.set_date(value, self._day)
27
28      # day property allows get/set access to Date's day value
29      # must be between 1 - # of days in month, inclusive
30      @property
31      def day(self):
32          return self._day
33
34      @day.setter
35      def day(self, value):
36          self.set_date(self._month, value)
37
38      # Advances the Date's state to the next day,
39      # wrapping into the next month/year as necessary.
40      def advance(self):
41          self._day += 1
42          if self._day >= self.days_in_month():
43              # wrap to next month
44              self._month += 1
45              self._day = 1
46              if self._month > 12:
47                  # wrap to next year
48                  self._month = 1
49
```

Continued on next page

Continued from previous page

```
50      # Returns the number of days in this Date's month.
51      def days_in_month(self):
52          if self._month in {4, 6, 9, 11}:
53              return 30
54          elif self._month == 2:
55              return 28
56          else:
57              return 31
58
59      # Modifies the date's month and day state.
60      # Raises a ValueError if values are out of range.
61      def set_date(self, month, day):
62          if month >= 1 and month <= 12:
63              self._month = month
64          else:
65              raise ValueError("Invalid month: " + str(month))
66          if day >= 1 and day <= self.days_in_month():
67              self._day = day
68          else:
69              raise ValueError("Invalid day: " + str(day))
```

Invariants bring to light the importance of proper encapsulation. If the Date class weren't encapsulated, we would not be able to properly enforce our invariants. Even if our constructor and methods carefully checked for valid values, a buggy or malicious client would be able to make a Date object's state invalid by setting its attributes' values directly. When the class is encapsulated, it has much better control over how clients can use its objects, making it impossible for a misguided client program to violate the class invariant.

11.4 Case Study: Designing a Stock Class

So far we have written several classes, but we have not talked about how to design a class or how to break apart a programming problem into classes. In this section we'll examine a larger programming problem and design a class and client to solve it. We will create a class called Stock and a client program that compares the performance of stocks that the user has purchased.

Consider the task of writing a financial program to record purchases of shares of two stocks and report which has the greater profit. The investor may have made several purchases of the same stock at different times and prices. The interaction with the program might look like this:

```
First stock's symbol? AMZN
How many purchases? 2
1: How many shares? 50
   Price per share? 35.06
2: How many shares? 25
   Price per share? 38.52
Today's price per share? 37.29
Net profit/loss: $ 80.75

Second stock's symbol? INTC
How many purchases? 3
1: How many shares? 15
   Price per share? 16.55
2: How many shares? 10
   Price per share? 18.09
3: How many shares? 20
   Price per share? 17.15
Today's price per share? 17.82
Net profit/loss: $ 29.75


AMZN was more profitable than INTC
```

The program must perform several actions: prompting the user for input, calculating the amount spent on each purchase of stock, reporting profits, and so on. The client program could perform all of these actions and could keep track of the financial data using existing types such as real numbers and strings. However, recall that we began this chapter by talking about object-oriented reasoning. When you are studying complex programs, it is often useful to think about the problem in terms of the relevant objects that could solve it, rather than placing all behavior in the client program. In this particular program, we must perform several computations that involve keeping track of purchases of shares of a particular stock, so it would be useful to store the purchase information in an object.

One possible design would be to create a `Purchase` class that records information about a single purchase of shares of a particular stock. For example, if the user specified three purchases, the program should construct three `Purchase` objects. However, a more useful abstraction here would be to hold the overall information about all purchases of one stock in one place. The investor may make many purchases of the same stock, so you want to have an easy way to accumulate these shares and their total cost into a single object.

Therefore, instead of a `Purchase` class, we'll write a `Stock` class. Each `Stock` object will keep track of the investor's accumulated shares of one stock and can provide profit/

loss information. Our `Stock` class will reside in a file called `Stock.py`, and the client program itself will reside in a separate file called `stock_main.py`.

Object-Oriented Design Heuristics

We now face the important task of deciding on the contents of our `Stock` class. It can be tricky to choose a good set of classes and objects to solve a complex programming problem. Chapter 4's case study introduced a set of procedural design *heuristics*, or guidelines for good design, for effectively dividing a problem into methods. There are similar guidelines for effectively breaking a large program into a set of classes and objects. The heuristics we'll discuss here are based on those listed in computer scientist Arthur Riel's influential book *Object-Oriented Design Heuristics*.

First let's look at the overall set of responsibilities, the things that a class must know or do to solve the overall problem:

- Prompt the user for each stock's symbol and store the information somewhere.
- Prompt the user for the number of purchases of each stock.
- Read each purchase (number of shares and price per share) from the console and store the information somewhere.
- Compute the total profit/loss of each stock.
- Print the total profit/loss of each stock to the console.
- Compare the two total profits/losses and print a message to the console about which stock performed better.

It might be tempting to make most or all of these tasks responsibilities of our `Stock` class. We could make a `Stock` object store all the purchases of both stocks, prompt for information from the console, print the results, and so on. But a key guideline when writing classes is that they should have *cohesion*.

> Cohesion
>
> The extent to which the code for a class represents a single abstraction.

Placing all the responsibilities in the `Stock` class would not allow that class to represent a single clear abstraction. The abstraction we want to represent in the `Stock` class is the accumulated purchases of a single stock.

One set of responsibilities that `Stock` objects should not handle is producing the console input and output. We need to prompt the user for information and print messages, but these methods are specific to the current client program. Objects are meant to be reusable pieces of software, and other programs might wish to track stock purchases without using these exact messages or prompts. If the `Stock` class handles the prompts and printing, it will be heavily intertwined with this client program and will not be easily reusable by other clients.

In general, we want to reduce unnecessary dependencies among classes. Dependencies among classes in an object-oriented program contribute to *coupling*, the degree to which one part of a program depends on another.

Striving to avoid unnecessary coupling is a second design heuristic commonly used in object-oriented programming. A design that avoids this problem is sometimes said to have loose coupling.

Let's divide some of the responsibilities now, based on our heuristics. Since the client program will perform the console I/O, it should handle the following responsibilities:

- Prompt for each stock's symbol.
- Prompt for the number of purchases of each stock.
- Read each purchase (number of shares and price per share) from the console.
- Print the total profit/loss of each stock.
- Compare the two total profits/losses and print a message about which stock generated higher profits.

Since the client program will be performing the console I/O, it might seem natural for it also to store the information about each stock purchase (that is, the number of shares and the price paid). But our `Stock` object should contain the functionality to compute a stock's total profit or loss, and it will need to have the data about all purchases to do so. This leads us to a third design heuristic: Related data and behavior should be in the same place. With that in mind, we can write out the responsibilities for the `Stock` class as follows:

- Store a stock's symbol.
- Store accumulated information about the investor's purchases of the stock.
- Record a purchase of the stock.
- Compute the total profit/loss for the stock.

When they are designing large object-oriented programs, many software engineers write information about classes as we've done here. A common technique to brainstorm ideas for classes is to write information on index cards. Each card is called a *CRC card* and lists the Class, its Responsibilities, and its Collaborators (other classes to which it is coupled). The following list summarizes the design heuristics discussed in this section:

1. A class should be cohesive, representing only one abstraction.

2. A class should avoid unnecessary coupling.

3. Related data and behavior should be in the same class.

Note that we began our design by looking at responsibilities rather than by specifying attributes as we did when we developed our Date class. We began writing the Date class by discussing attributes because the data associated with a date is simple and more obvious than the data associated with stock purchases. But in many larger problems like this one, working backward from behavior and responsibilities is a better technique.

Stock Attributes and Method Headers

In this section we'll decide on a design for the method names and signatures the Stock should use to implement its behavior. We'll use this design to determine which attributes are required to implement the behavior.

We've decided that a Stock object should allow clients to record purchases and request the total profit or loss. Each of these tasks can be represented as a method. The recording of a purchase can be represented as a method called purchase. The retrieval of the total profit or loss can be represented as a method called profit.

The purchase method should record information about a single purchase. A purchase consists of a number of shares that the user bought (which we can assume is a whole number) and a price per share (which can include real numbers with both dollars and cents). Our purchase method should accept two parameters: an integer for the number of shares bought and a real number for the price per share. The method does not need to return any value. Its heading might look like this:

```
class Stock:
    # Records a purchase of the given number of shares
    # at the given price per share.
    def purchase(self, shares, price_per_share):
        ...
```

The profit method will return the amount of money that the user made or lost on all accumulated purchases of this stock. Consider an investor who has made the following three purchases of a stock:

1. 20 shares × $10 per share = $200 cost
2. 20 shares × $30 per share = $600 cost
3. 10 shares × $20 per share = $200 cost

These purchases total 50 total shares at $1000 total cost. If today's price per share is $22, the current market value of the investor's 50 shares is (50 × 22) or $1100. Since the investor paid $1000 total for the shares and they are now worth $1100, the investor has made ($1100 − $1000) = $100 of profit. The general formula for the profit is the following:

$$profit = ((total\ shares) \times (current\ share\ price)) - (total\ cost)$$

The total number of shares and total cost figure needed for this calculation are the accumulated information from all the purchases that have been made of this stock. This means that information will need to be stored during each call of the purchase method to be used later in the `profit` method. A key observation is that we do not need to store the number of shares, price per share, and cost for every purchase. We only need to store cumulative sums of the total shares purchased so far and the total dollars spent so far to acquire those values.

The third value we need in order to calculate the profit is the current share price. We could choose to make this an attribute in the `Stock` class as well, but the share price is a dynamic value that changes regularly. We use it during a single call to the `profit` method, but the next call may come at a later date when the price per share has changed.

This problem leads us to another design heuristic: attributes should represent values of core importance to the object and values that are used in multiple methods. Adding too many attributes clutters a class and can make its code harder to read. If a value is used in only one method of the class, it's best to make it a parameter to that method rather than an attribute. Therefore, we'll make the current share price a parameter to the `profit` method.

```
# Computes and returns the profit on all purchases
# of stock, given the current price per share.
def profit(self, current_price):
    ...
```

One piece of state that we haven't discussed yet is that each stock has a symbol, such as `"AMZN"`. We'll store the symbol as a string attribute in each `Stock` object. Taking all of this together, we need our `Stock` object to keep track of the following three pieces of information, each of which should be represented as a private data attribute:

1. The stock's symbol (as a string)
2. The total number of shares (as an integer)
3. The total cost to purchase all of those shares (as a real number)

We'll need to write a constructor (an `__init__` method) to set up the state of these three data attributes. The symbol is something that the client should pass to the `Stock` object's constructor. It may be tempting to write a constructor that accepts three parameters: the symbol, the total number of shares purchased, and the total cost. But our `Stock` objects are accumulators of purchases, and we may want to be able to create new `Stock` objects before the program records initial purchases. When you know the initial value of an attribute like this, you do not need to ask the client to pass it to your constructor. Our constructor can take `self` and the symbol as its two parameters and initialize the other attributes to `0`.

Here's a skeleton of our `Stock` class so far:

```
# incomplete Stock class
class Stock:
    # Initializes a new Stock object for the given symbol,
    # with 0 shares purchased.
    def __init__(self, symbol):
        self._symbol = symbol
        self._total_shares = 0
        self._total_cost = 0.0

    # Computes and returns the profit on all purchases
    # of stock, given the current price per share.
    def profit(self, current_price):
        ...

    # Records a purchase of the given number of shares
    # at the given price per share.
    def purchase(self, shares, price_per_share):
        ...
```

Stock Method and Property Implementation

Now that we've decided on some of the Stock's state and behavior, let's think about how to write the bodies of the various methods. First we will handle the purchase method. The task of recording the purchase consists of adding the new number of shares to the total number of shares and adding the new price paid for these shares to the total cost. The price paid is equal to the number of shares times the price per share. Here's the code for the purchase method to implement this behavior:

```
# Records purchase of the given shares at the given price.
def purchase(self, shares, price_per_share):
    self._total_shares += shares
    self._total_cost += shares * price_per_share
```

Earlier in this chapter we discussed class invariants. It makes sense that a reasonable invariant here would be that you cannot purchase negative shares nor purchase at a negative price per share. To perform this test, we can insert the following lines at the start of our purchase method:

```
# Records purchase of the given shares at the given price.
# pre: shares >= 0 && price_per_share >= 0.0
def purchase(self, shares, price_per_share):
    if shares < 0 or price_per_share < 0.0:
        raise ValueError("Shares/price cannot be negative")
    self._total_shares += shares
    self._total_cost += shares * price_per_share
```

Next, we'll write the body of the `profit` method. As we noted previously, the profit is equal to its current market value minus the amount that was paid for it:

$$profit = ((total\ shares) \times (current\ share\ price)) - (total\ cost)$$

We can implement this formula in a straightforward manner using the `_total_shares` and `_total_cost` attributes along with the `current_price` parameter:

```
# Returns the total profit or loss earned on this stock,
# based on the given price per share.
def profit(self, current_price):
    return self._total_shares * current_price - self._total_cost
```

Note that parentheses are not needed in the code because multiplication has a higher precedence than subtraction. As we did for the other methods, we should check for illegal parameter values. In this case, we shouldn't allow a negative current price per share. To ensure that this doesn't happen, we can place the following code at the start of the method:

```
# Returns the total profit or loss earned on this stock,
# based on the given price per share.
# pre: current_price >= 0.0
def profit(self, current_price):
    if current_price < 0.0:
        raise ValueError("Current price cannot be negative")
    return self._total_shares * current_price - self._total_cost
```

The last touch we'll add to our `Stock` class is to define read-only properties so that clients can see the stock's symbol, total shares, and total cost. The client program we'll write may not need all of these properties, but it is considered good practice to make useful object state visible to clients.

After we've written all the attributes, the constructor, methods, and properties of our `Stock`, the class will look like this:

```
1   # A Stock object represents purchases of shares of a stock.
2   class Stock:
3       # Initializes a new Stock with no shares purchased.
4       def __init__(self, symbol):
5           self._symbol = symbol        # stock symbol, e.g. "YHOO"
6           self._total_shares = 0       # total shares purchased
7           self._total_cost = 0.0       # total cost for all shares
8
9       # Read-only properties to access Stock's state.
10      @property
```

Continued on next page

Continued from previous page

```
11        def symbol(self):
12            return self._symbol
13
14        @property
15        def total_cost(self):
16            return self._total_cost
17
18        @property
19        def total_shares(self):
20            return self._total_shares
21
22        # Returns the total profit or loss earned on this stock,
23        # based on the given price per share.
24        # pre: current_price >= 0.0
25        def profit(self, current_price):
26            if current_price < 0.0:
27                raise ValueError("Current price cannot be negative")
28            return self._total_shares * current_price - self._total_cost
29
30        # Records purchase of the given shares at the given price.
31        # pre: shares >= 0 && price_per_share >= 0.0
32        def purchase(self, shares, price_per_share):
33            if shares < 0 or price_per_share < 0.0:
34                raise ValueError("Shares/price cannot be negative")
35            self._total_shares += shares
36            self._total_cost += shares * price_per_share
```

Here's the client code to use the Stock class. It would generate the sample log of execution listed at the start of this Case Study:

```
1   # This client program tracks a user's purchases of two stocks,
2   # computing and reporting which stock was more profitable.
3   # It makes use of the Stock class, representing the user's
4   # purchases of each unique stock as a Stock object.
5
6   from Stock import *
7
8   def main():
9       # create first stock
10      symbol1 = input("First stock's symbol? ")
11      stock1 = Stock(symbol1)
12      profit1 = make_purchases(stock1)
```

Continued on next page

Continued from previous page

```
13
14      # create second stock
15      symbol2 = input("Second stock's symbol? ")
16      stock2 = Stock(symbol2)
17      profit2 = make_purchases(stock2)
18
19      # report which stock made more money
20      if profit1 > profit2:
21          print(symbol1, "was more profitable than", symbol2)
22      elif profit2 > profit1:
23          print(symbol2, "was more profitable than", symbol1)
24      else:
25          print(symbol1, "and", symbol2, "are equally profitable")
26
27  # make purchases of stock and return the profit
28  def make_purchases(stock):
29      num_purchases = int(input("How many purchases? "))
30
31      # ask about each purchase
32      for i in range(num_purchases):
33          shares = int(input(str(i + 1) + ": How many shares? "))
34          price = float(input("   Price per share? "))
35
36          # ask the Stock object to record this purchase
37          stock.purchase(shares, price)
38
39      # use the Stock object to compute profit
40      current_price = float(input("Today's price per share? "))
41      profit = stock.profit(current_price)
42
43      print("Net profit/loss: $", profit)
44      print()
45      return profit
46
47  main()
```

It would be useful to have a few other methods in our `Stock` class. For example, it would be good to implement a `__str__` method to easily print `Stock` objects. We could even add optional parameters to our constructor for an initial number of shares and cost. These features are left for you to implement as exercises.

Chapter Summary

- Object-oriented programming is a different philosophy of writing programs that focuses on nouns or entities in a program, rather than on verbs or actions of a program. In object-oriented programming, state and behavior are grouped into objects that communicate with each other.
- A class serves as the blueprint for a new type of object, specifying the object's data and behavior. The class can be asked to construct many objects (also called "instances") of its type.
- The data for each object are specified using special variables called data attributes.
- A class can define special code called a constructor (represented as a method named __init__) that initializes the state of new objects as they are created. The constructor will be called when client code creates a new object of your type.

- The behavior of each object is specified by writing methods in the class. Methods exist inside an object and can access that object's internal state.
- To make objects easily printable, write a __str__ method that returns the object's text representation.
- Objects can protect their internal data from unwanted external modification, an action known as encapsulation. Encapsulation provides abstraction so that clients can use objects without knowing about their internal implementation. Encapsulation also helps the author of a class maintain promises that the objects' states will always be valid. Encapsulation in Python is not strictly enforced and is instead indicated by the informal convention of naming object attributes with a leading underscore.
- A class should represent only one key abstraction with related data and behavior, and its code should be independent from its clients.

Self-Check Problems

Section 11.1: Object-Oriented Programming

1. Describe the difference between object-oriented programming and procedural programming.

2. What is an object? How is an object different from a class?

3. What is the output of the following program?

```
def main():
    a = 7
    b = 9
    p1 = Date(2, 2)
    p2 = Date(2, 2)
    add_to_month_twice(a, p1)
    print(a, b, p1.month, p2.month)
    add_to_month_twice(b, p2)
    print(a, b, p1.month, p2.month)

def add_to_month_twice(a, p1):
    a = a + a
    p1.month = a
    print(a, p1.month)

main()
```

4. Imagine that you are creating a class called `Calculator`. A `Calculator` object could be used to program a simple mathematical calculator device like the ones you have used in math classes in school. What state might a `Calculator` object have? What might its behavior be?

Section 11.2: Object State and Behavior

5. Explain the differences between an attribute and a parameter. What is the difference in their syntax? What is the difference in their scope and the ways in which they may be used?

6. Create a class called `Name` that represents a person's name. The class should have attributes representing the person's first name, last name, and middle initial. (Your class should contain only attributes for now.)

7. What is the difference between an accessor and a mutator? What naming conventions are used with accessors and mutators?

8. Suppose we have written a class named `BankAccount` with a method inside it, defined as:

```
def compute_interest(rate)
```

If the client code has defined a `BankAccount` variable named `acct`, which of the following would be a valid call to the above method?

a. `result = compute_interest(acct, 42)`
b. `acct.compute_interest(42.0, 15)`
c. `result = BankAccount.compute_interest(42)`
d. `result = acct.compute_interest(42)`
e. `BankAccount(42).compute_interest()`

9. (You must complete Self-Check Problem 11.6 before answering this question.) Add two new methods to the `Name` class:

```
def normal_order(self)
```

This method returns the person's name in normal order, with the first name followed by the middle initial and last name. For example, if the first name is `"John"`, the middle initial is `"Q"` and the last name is `"Public"`, the method returns `"John Q. Public"`.

```
def reverse_order(self)
```

This method returns the person's name in reverse order, with the last name preceding the first name and middle initial. For example, if the first name is `"John"`, the middle initial is `"Q"`, and the last name is `"Public"`, the method returns `"Public, John Q."`.

10. How do you write a class whose objects can easily be printed on the console?

11. The following `print` statement (the entire line) is equivalent to which of the following?

```
d1 = Date()
...
print(d1)
```

a. `print(__str__(d1))`
b. `d1.__str__()`
c. `print(d1.__str__())`
d. `print(Date.__str__())`

12. (You must complete Self-Check Problem 11.6 before answering this question.) Write a ___str___ method for the Name class that returns a string such as "John Q. Public".

Section 11.3: Encapsulation

13. What is abstraction? How do objects provide abstraction?

14. When attributes are made private, client programs are not supposed to access them directly. How do you allow classes access to read these attributes' values without letting the client break the object's encapsulation?

15. (You must complete Self-Check Problem 11.6 before answering this question.) Encapsulate the Name class. Indicate that its attributes are private by giving them appropriate names, and add properties that clients can use to access them outside the class.

16. (You must complete the previous problem before answering this question.) Add property setters to your Name class so that clients can set the values of the first name, middle initial, and last name.

17. How does encapsulation make it easier to change the internal implementation of a class?

Section 11.4: Case Study: Designing a Stock Class

18. What is cohesion? How can you tell whether a class is cohesive?

19. Why didn't we choose to put the console I/O code into the Stock class?

20. Add property setters to the Stock class that allow the client to modify the stock's symbol, total shares, and total cost. (What are reasonable values you should accept? What values should be rejected?)

Exercises

1. Add the following accessor method to the Date class described in this chapter:

```
def absolute_day(self)
```

Your method should return the absolute day of the year that is represented by the given date from 1 to 365.
For example, January 1 is absolute day #1; January 2 is absolute day #2; January 31 is absolute day #31; February 1 is absolute day #32; February 2 is absolute day #33; and so on, up to December 31, which is absolute day #365.

2. Add the following accessor method to the Date class described in this chapter:

```
def from_absolute_day(self, absday)
```

Your method should accept an integer parameter representing an absolute day of the year from 1 to 365 as described in the previous problem. You should modify the Date object's state to represent the month and day of the year that corresponds to that absolute day. For example, if the client calls your method with the parameter value 33, you should set the date to store February 2.

3. Add the following mutator method to the Date class described in this chapter:

```
def shift(self, days)
```

Your method should move the date forward or backward in time by the given number of days, wrapping months as necessary. For example, September 19 shifted by 7 days is September 26, and September 30 shifted by 1 day is October 1. You should also handle negative numbers; September 19 shifted by −7 days is September 12, and September 12 shifted by −15 days is August 28.

4. Add a `year` property to the `Date` class so that it represents not only a month and date but also a specific year. Also add a method `is_leap_year` that returns `True` if the given year is a leap year. Leap years are ones that are divisible by 4, except for those that are divisible by 100 but not by 400. For example, 1996 is a leap year, as is 2000; but 1997, 1979, 1700, 1800, and 1900 are not. Modify any other methods as appropriate to respond to your new year state. For example, modify the `advance` method to properly advance the year if you go from December 31 to January 1, and modify the `__str__` method to include the year at the end of the returned string, such as `"9/19/1979"`.

5. Add the following mutator method to the `Stock` class described in this chapter's case study:

```
def clear(self)
```

Your method should reset the `Stock`'s number of shares purchased and total cost to 0.

6. (The next several exercises refer to the following `BankAccount` class.) Suppose the following `BankAccount` class has been created:

```
# Each BankAccount object represents one user's account
# information including name and balance of money.
class BankAccount:
    def __init__(self, name):
        self.name = name
        self.balance = 0.0

    def deposit(self, amount):
        self.balance += amount

    def withdraw(self, amount):
        self.balance -= amount
```

Notice that the class is not encapsulated. Modify it to be encapsulated with private data attributes and read-only properties representing the name and balance.

7. Modify the `BankAccount` class to enforce the invariant that the account's balance cannot ever become negative. This means that you should forbid negative deposits and forbid withdrawals that are more than the balance on the account.

8. Add a property to the `BankAccount` class named `transaction_fee` for a real number representing an amount of money to deduct every time the user withdraws money. The default value is $0.00, but the client can change the value. Deduct the transaction fee money during every withdraw call (but not from deposits). Make sure that the balance cannot go negative during a withdrawal. If the withdrawal (amount plus transaction fee) would cause it to become negative, don't modify the balance at all.

9. Add a `__str__` method to the `BankAccount` class from the previous exercises. Your method should return a string that contains the account's name and balance separated by a comma and space. For example, if an account object named `yana` has the name "Yana" and a balance of 3.03, the call `str(yana)` should return the string `"Yana, $3.03"`.

10. Add a `transfer` method to the `BankAccount` class from the previous exercises. Your method should move money from the current bank account to another account. The method accepts two parameters aside from `self`: a second `BankAccount` to accept the money, and a real number for the amount of money to transfer. There is a

$5 fee for transferring money, so this much must be deducted from the current account's balance before any transfer. The method should modify the two `BankAccount` objects such that the current object has its balance decreased by the given amount plus the $5 fee, and the other account's balance is increased by the given amount. If this account object does not have enough money to make the full transfer, transfer whatever money is left after the $5 fee is deducted. If this account has under $5 or the amount is 0 or less, no transfer should occur and neither account's state should be modified. The following are some example calls to the method:

```
# client code using the BankAccount class
ben = BankAccount("Ben")
ben.deposit(80.00)
hal = BankAccount("Hal")
hal.deposit(20.00)
ben.transfer(hal, 20.00)    # ben $55, hal $40   (ben -$25, hal +$20)
ben.transfer(hal, 10.00)    # ben $40, hal $50   (ben -$15, hal +$10)
hal.transfer(ben, 60.00)    # ben $85, hal $ 0   (ben +$45, hal -$50)
```

11. (The next several exercises refer to the following `Rectangle` class.) Write a class `Rectangle` that represents a rectangular two-dimensional region. Your `Rectangle` objects should have the following methods:

Method	Description
def __init__(self, x, y, w, h)	Initializes a new `Rectangle` whose top-left corner is specified by the given (x, y) coordinates and with the given width and height, w by h. Raise a `ValueError` on a negative width or height.
def height(self)	A property representing the rectangle's height.
def width(self)	A property representing the rectangle's width.
def x(self)	A property representing the rectangle's x-coordinate.
def y(self)	A property representing the rectangle's y-coordinate.
def __str__(self)	Returns a string representation of this `Rectangle`, such as `"Rectangle[x=1,y=2,width=3,height=4]"`.

12. Add the following accessor method to your `Rectangle` class:

```
def contains(self, x, y)
```

Your method should return `True` if the given coordinates lie inside the bounds of this `Rectangle`.

13. Add the following method to your `Rectangle` class:

```
def union(self, rect)
```

Your method should accept another `Rectangle` as a parameter, and return a new `Rectangle` that represents the area occupied by the tightest bounding box that contains both the current `Rectangle` (`self`) and the given other `Rectangle`.

14. Add the following method to your `Rectangle` class:

```
def intersection(self, rect)
```

Your method should accept another `Rectangle` as a parameter, and return a new `Rectangle` that represents the largest rectangular region completely contained within both the current `Rectangle` (`self`) and the given other `Rectangle`. If the rectangles do not intersect at all, returns a `Rectangle` with its width and height both equal to `0`.

15. Add the following method to your `Rectangle` class:

    ```
    def __eq__(self, rect)
    ```

    Your method should accept another `Rectangle` as a parameter and return `True` if the two rectangles have exactly the same state, including their `x`, `y`, `width`, and `height` values.

Programming Projects

1. Write a class `RationalNumber` that represents a fraction with an integer numerator and denominator. A `RationalNumber` object represents the ratio (numerator / denominator). The denominator cannot be 0, so raise a `ValueError` if 0 is passed.

Method	Description
`def __init__(self)`	Initializes a new rational number to represent the ratio 0/1.
`def denominator(self)`	A property representing the rational number's denominator value; for example, if the ratio is 3/5, returns 5.
`def numerator(self)`	A property representing the rational number's numerator value; for example, if the ratio is 3/5, returns 3.
`def __str__(self)`	Returns a string representation of this rational number, such as `"3/5"`. You may wish to omit denominators of 1, returning `"4"` instead of `"4/1"`.
`def __eq__(self, other)`	Returns `True` if this rational number represents a value equal to the given other rational number.

An extra challenge would be to maintain your `RationalNumber` objects in reduced form, avoiding rational numbers such as 3/6 in favor of 1/2, or avoiding 2/−3 in favor of −2/3. Another possible extra feature would be methods to add, subtract, multiply, and divide two rational numbers.

2. Write a class `GroceryList` that represents a list of items to buy from the market, and another class named `GroceryItemOrder` that represents a request to purchase a particular item in a given quantity (example: four boxes of cookies). The `GroceryList` class should use a list attribute to store the grocery items and to keep track of its size (number of items in the list so far). A `GroceryList` object should have the following methods:

Method	Description
`def __init__(self)`	Initializes a new empty grocery list.
`def add(self, item)`	Adds the given item order to this list.
`def total_cost(self)`	A property that returns the total sum cost of all grocery item orders in this list.

The `GroceryItemOrder` class should store an item quantity and a price per unit. A `GroceryItemOrder` object should have the following methods:

Method	Description
def __init__(self, name, quantity, price_per_unit)	Initializes an item order to purchase the item with the given name, in the given quantity, which costs the given price per unit.
def cost(self)	A property that returns the total cost of the item in its given quantity. For example, four boxes of cookies that cost 2.30 per unit have a total cost of 9.20.
def quantity(self) def quantity(self, quantity)	A property that returns the grocery item's quantity, with a setter that changes the quantity to be the given value.

Functional Programming

Introduction

This chapter introduces a new style of programming called functional programming. Functional programming involves the use of functions to decompose complex tasks. In this style a program consists of a series of nested function calls. We have already decomposed programs into functions throughout this text, but a true functional programming approach takes this further. Functional programming is an approach that views the function as the fundamental unit of program composition.

Functions are referred to as "first-class citizens" in functional programming. A function can be stored in a variable, used as a parameter to another function, or applied to a set of data such as a list to manipulate its data. Functional programming is connected to other programming language concepts such as mutable state and scope. A functional style works best in a program with minimal mutable state.

Functional programming also turns out to be an approach that lends itself well to concurrency. With new computers containing multiple processors and processor cores, it is important to write programs that leverage all of the computing power available in modern machines. Near the end of this chapter we will explore techniques for writing concurrent functional code that can utilize many processors at once.

12.1 Functional Programming Concepts

Every ten to fifteen years the computer science education community updates the suggested curriculum for computer science majors. In the most recent curriculum revision in 2013, a joint task force from the Association for Computing Machinery and the Institute of Electrical and Electronics Engineers (ACM/IEEE) updated the suggestions for coverage of programming languages. As the task force writers explained in the introduction to that section:

> Software developers must understand the programming models underlying different languages and make informed design choices in languages supporting multiple complementary approaches. Computer scientists will often need to learn new languages and programming constructs, and must understand the principles underlying how programming language features are defined, composed, and implemented.

The writers went on to describe specific concepts from various programming paradigms that should be studied by every undergraduate computer science major. Two of the paradigms that they emphasize are the procedural and object-oriented paradigms that have been discussed thoroughly in this book. Python is a hybrid language that supports both approaches. We began the book by studying procedural programming with static functions that we used to decompose a large program into action-oriented components. Then, starting in Chapter 11, we moved on to the object-oriented approach, in which a large program is decomposed into a set of interacting objects each with their own class defining their state and behavior. In this chapter we will explore a third approach to programming that is known as *functional programming*.

> **Functional Programming**
>
> A style of programming that emphasizes the use of functions to decompose a complex task into subtasks.

The new curriculum guidelines list five specific topics that undergraduates should study related to functional programming:

1. Side effects and effect-free programming
2. Processing structured data via functions
3. First-class functions
4. Function closures
5. Higher-order operations on collections

The first three are categorized as Core Tier-1, and items 4 and 5 are categorized as Core Tier-2. As the guidelines explain, "computer-science curricula should cover all the Core Tier-1 topics" and "all or almost all of the Core Tier-2 topics." Each of these concepts has its own section in this chapter. The chapter ends with a short case study that picks up an additional Core Tier-1 concept of using concurrency to speed the execution of a complex computation. As we will see, the functional programming approach is particularly well suited to safe and reliable concurrency, which is becoming increasingly important in modern computing, where the average PC now comes with multiple processors (sometimes described as "multi-core processing"). The terminology can sometimes be intimidating, but as we will see, these concepts are fairly straightforward when explored using Python constructs.

Side Effects

Consider the following two lines of code. The first code computes a result by calling a function two different times and adding together the results. The second code calls the same function once but multiplies the result by 2.

```
>>> # call function twice
>>> result = f(x) + f(x)
>>> # call function once and double result
>>> result = 2 * f(x)
```

Offhand it seems that we would get the exact same behavior from both of these two statements. In reality, sometimes the two are equivalent and sometimes not. The question to consider is whether the function produces a *side effect*.

Side Effect

A change to the state of an object or program variable produced by a call on a function (i.e., a function).

As an example, consider the following program:

```
1   # This program demonstrates a function with a side effect.
2   # Each time f is called, the variable x's value changes.
3
4   x = 5
5
6   def f(n):
7       global x
8       x = x * 2
9       return x + n
10
```

Continued on next page

Continued from previous page

```
11  def main():
12      global x
13      x = 5
14      result = f(x) + f(x)
15      print("result is", result)
16      print("x is", x)
17
18  main()
```

```
result is 45
x is 20
```

This confusing program begins with the declaration of a variable x that has the entire program as its scope. Such variables are called *global variables*. We have discouraged the use of global variables because they can lead to the kind of confusing code we have here.

The program begins by initializing the global variable x to the value 5. Then on line 14 the program calls the function f twice, passing it the value of x each time. But f doubles the value of x before returning the sum of the value passed as a parameter and x. If you find this all highly confusing, you're not alone. This style of programming is very bad.

On the first call to f, the variable x has the value 5. This is passed from main as the parameter called n. Inside function f, we first double x, which gives it the value 10. The function then returns the sum of x, which is now 10, and n, which is 5. So it returns 15 for the first call. On the second call, it passes the current value of x, which is 10, to the function and uses this to initialize n to be 10. Then it doubles x from 10 to 20 and returns the sums of x and n, which are 20 and 10, respectively. So it returns the value 30 on the second call. The variable result is set to the sum of these two return values, which is 15 plus 30, or 45.

What happens if we substitute our other line of code for setting result on line 14?

```
result = 2 * f(x)
```

The first call on the function behaves as it did before, returning the value 15. We double that to 30 and set result to 30. So we end up with a program that has different behavior because the function f has a side effect.

Because functional programming focuses so much on individual functions, the community of programmers who use functional programming regularly have concluded that side effects should be avoided when possible, leading to what are called *effect-free functions*.

> **Effect-Free Function**
>
> One that produces no side effects; one that does not change the state of an object or program when it is called.

The object-oriented community has been less wary of functions with side effects. A central idea of object-oriented programming is that objects have states that change as functions are called. Recall that accessor methods of objects can be thought of as read-only operations accessing the object's state, while mutators can be thought of as read/write operations that change the state of the object. Using the terminology from functional programming, we would say that accessors are usually effect-free functions while mutators are functions with a side effect. Even accessors can have side effects because they might change the state of other objects.

One of the simplest and most pervasive sources of side effects we have seen is the printing of values. Continuing our example of a function f that might be called once or twice, if the function includes a call on `print`, then it will produce more output when called twice than when it is called once. So even though the variable result in our example might be set to the same value, there is still a possible side effect caused by the function if it produces output.

As we will see in the case study at the end of the chapter, there are great advantages to writing code that is free of side effects. It is easier to take advantage of concurrency using such code and it is easier to prove formal properties of programs that are written using the effect-free approach.

First-Class Functions

When you study any particular programming language, you soon learn the basic elements of the language. For example, almost every programming language allows you to manipulate numbers as basic elements. You can store a number in a variable, you can pass a number as a parameter, you have various operations for manipulating numbers, and you can return a number from a function call. Strings are also basic elements of Python because they are easy to declare, store, and pass as parameters.

Not every data type is a first-class citizen of every language. For example, not every programming language allows you to manipulate Boolean values as basic elements the way Python does. For decades the C programming language did not have a proper type for storing Boolean values, and programmers instead used the integer values 1 and 0 to represent True and False. Some languages like Python consider collections such as lists and maps to be first-class citizens and provide special syntax for declaring and manipulating them; others do not.

> **First-Class Citizen**
>
> An element of a programming language that is tightly integrated with the language and supports the full range of operations generally available to other entities in the language.

What does it mean for a function to be a first-class citizen? The answer is that a function can be stored in a variable, passed as a parameter, put into a list or other collection, or do anything else you would do with most any data type in the language. Functions are first-class citizens in Python. For example, suppose you have three functions called `larger`, `add`, and `multiply` defined as follows:

```
# Returns the larger of two numbers passed.
def larger(a, b):
    if a > b:
        return a
    else:
        return b


# Returns the sum of the given two numbers.
def add(a, b):
    return a + b


# Returns the product of the given two numbers.
def multiply(a, b):
    return a * b
```

Since functions are first-class citizens in Python, you can create a variable that refers to a function. By writing that variable's name with parentheses and parameter values, you can call the function to which it refers:

```
>>> # store a function in a variable
>>> f = larger
>>> f
<function larger at 0x7fede3e0dae8>
>>> f(3, 4)
4
```

Note, crucially, that the line `f = larger` does not include any parentheses. When you write parentheses after a function's name, you are telling Python to call that function immediately. When you write the function's name without parentheses, you are giving that function an alias called `f` so that you can call it later.

You could even store a list of functions and then apply all of those functions to a given pair of values. Notice how the following code prints 4, 7, and 12, which are the results of calling `larger`, `add`, and `multiply`, respectively, on the values 3 and 4.

```
>>> # store several functions in a list
>>> funcs = [larger, add, multiply]
>>> for f in funcs:
...     print("the result is", f(3, 4))
...
the result is 4
the result is 7
the result is 12
```

The ability to use, store, and manipulate functions in this way is powerful. We can use it to elegantly write programs where various behavior is supplied by providing functions to execute under various conditions.

Higher-Order Functions

In a language where functions are first-class citizens, it is possible to write a function that accepts another function as a parameter. Such a function is known as a *higher-order function*.

Higher-Order Function
A function that accepts another function as a parameter.

In this section we'll explore an example that points out the motivation for and useful-ness of higher-order functions. Consider the task of writing a "math quiz" program that performs drill and practice with a user; the program makes up random addition problems involving two numbers between 1 and 12, and you keep track of how many answers the user got right. The following is a typical interaction:

```
10 + 6 = 16
you got it right
9 + 6 = 15
you got it right
3 + 7 = 9
incorrect...the answer was 10
12 + 10 = 22
you got it right
9 + 12 = 20
incorrect...the answer was 21
3 of 5 correct
```

Suppose that the preceding quiz is represented as a function called `quiz_problems` that is passed a number of problems as a parameter, as in:

```
# ask user to solve 5 math problems
quiz_problems(5)
```

This is a straightforward task to solve building on material from Chapters 1 through 5:

```
# Asks the user to solve the given number of addition problems.
def quiz_problems(num_problems):
    correct = 0
```

Continued on next page

Continued from previous page

```
    for i in range(num_problems):
        x = random.randint(1, 13)
        y = random.randint(1, 13)
        answer = x + y
        response = int(input(str(x) + " + " + str(y) + " = "))
        if response == answer:
            print("you got it right")
            correct += 1
        else:
            print("incorrect...the answer was", answer)
    print(correct, "of", num_problems, "correct")
```

We now have a function that allows us to have a user practice addition problems. What if we wanted to also practice multiplication problems? Most of the code stays the same, but we would have to change the addition in the two lines of code below from addition to multiplication:

```
# version that performs addition
answer = x + y
response = int(input(str(x) + " + " + str(y) + " = "))


# version that performs multiplication
answer = x * y
response = int(input(str(x) + " * " + str(y) + " = "))
```

In a sense, we want to replace the plus with an asterisk in both of these lines of code. If we want the code to work for both addition and multiplication, the first line of code is easier to generalize. The only part that needs to change is the text to be printed, and we have the ability to manipulate text as a basic element of Python using a string. We can change the function header to accept a parameter specifying the text to print:

```
def quiz_problems(num_problems, operator):
    ...
    response = int(input(str(x) + operator + str(y) + " = "))
    ...
```

We can then make two calls on the function to have it use a plus the first time and an asterisk the second time:

```
quiz_problems(5, "+")
quiz_problems(5, "*")
```

So far so good. But now we run into the problem that the function is computing the right answer as the sum of the two numbers, even if an asterisk is passed as the text.

That will make for a very frustrating experience on the second call, where the console indicates to the user that the problem is a multiplication problem.

The question is how to change the computation of the right answer. It would be great if we could say:

```
answer = x operator y
```

If Python somehow filled in "+" or "*" appropriately and then used the corresponding operator for the computation, then it would work. But Python doesn't work this way. The way that we usually get around this in Python is by introducing an `if/else` structure that tests whether the string is a plus or an asterisk. But then the code works for only those two operators, and additional branches must be added to the code later to make it support subtraction and other operations.

What we really want is the ability to pass an additional parameter that specifies the calculation to perform. We want to say, "Use the addition operation the first time and the multiplication operation the second time." A functional programmer would say that what we want to be able to do is to pass in a function as a parameter, making `quiz_problems` into a higher-order function. This is an example of what we mean by elevating functions to first class status in the language. We want to be able to introduce a third parameter that specifies the function to use for computing the right answer. That requires thinking of the function as a thing in the language that can be passed as a parameter.

We could now write the complete math quiz program with a higher-order function. But before we do so, let's explore some Python syntax called a lambda expression that makes it easier to call a higher-order function.

Lambda Expressions

In the last section we discussed a desire for passing a function as a parameter. We could certainly do this by writing standard functions and passing their names as parameters. But Python provides a nicer mechanism for easily creating and passing a small function to use as a parameter for a higher-order function. We can write a short unnamed function called a *lambda expression*.

Lambda Expression (Lambda)

An expression that describes a function by specifying its parameters and the value that it returns.

The term "lambda" was coined by a logician named Alonzo Church in the 1930s. The term is used consistently across many programming languages, so it is worth becoming familiar with it. Python actually uses `lambda` as a keyword for forming this type of anonymous function, as we'll see.

Lambda expressions are formed in Python by writing the keyword `lambda`, then specifying the parameters of the function followed by a colon, followed by an expression that represents the value to return:

```
lambda parameter_name, parameter_name, ..., parameter_name: expression
```
Syntax template: lambda expression

For example, we can use the following lambda expression to represent a function that adds together two arguments:

```
lambda x, y: x + y
```

In reading this expression, we typically describe it as, "Given the parameters x and y, we return x + y." We could also write this as a function with a name, as in:

```
def sum(x, y):
    return x + y
```

Notice how the lambda expression takes the parameter list from the function header and the expression used in the `return` statement to form a simple expression. Once you get used to reading lambda expressions, you will find that lambda statements are a concise way to read and reason about the underlying computation being performed.

For our sample code, we will be able to use this lambda expression to describe multiplication:

```
lambda x, y: x * y
```

Given this new option, we can rewrite our client code as follows to perform three each of addition and multiplication problems.

```
quiz_problems(3, "+", lambda x, y: x + y)
quiz_problems(3, "*", lambda x, y: x * y)
```

Below is the complete math quiz program using lambdas, along with a sample log of execution:

```
1  # This program presents random addition or multiplication
2  # problems to the user using numbers from 1-12.
3  # The correct answers are calculated using lambda expressions.
4
5  import random
6
7  # Asks the user to solve the given number of problems.
```

Continued on next page

Continued from previous page

```
 8  # 'operator' is a lambda function to calculate the right answer.
 9  # 'text' is a string to represent the operator, like "*".
10  def quiz_problems(num_problems, text, operator):
11      correct = 0
12      for i in range(num_problems):
13          x = random.randint(1, 13)
14          y = random.randint(1, 13)
15          answer = operator(x, y)
16          response = int(input(str(x) + text + str(y) + " = "))
17          if response == answer:
18              print("you got it right")
19              correct += 1
20          else:
21              print("incorrect...the answer was", answer)
22      print(correct, "of", num_problems, "correct")
23      print()
24
25  def main():
26      quiz_problems(3, " + ", lambda x, y: x + y)
27      quiz_problems(3, " * ", lambda x, y: x * y)
28
29  main()
```

```
9 + 1 = 10
you got it right
4 + 4 = 8
you got it right
6 + 2 = 9
incorrect...the answer was 8
2 of 3 correct


10 * 11 = 110
you got it right
9 * 6 = 64
incorrect...the answer was 54
5 * 7 = 45
incorrect...the answer was 35
1 of 3 correct
```

Lambdas are most commonly used inline without giving them a name. But it is also fine to name a lambda function and use it as though it were a standard function:

```
>>> f = lambda x, y: x + y
>>> f(1, 1)
2
>>> f(3, 5)
8
```

This ability to pass a lambda expression as a parameter points out the benefit of treating functions as first-class elements of the language. Just as we can provide a different number of problems to perform or a different text to use for displaying the problems, we can also provide a different function for computing the right answer. This is a much more flexible approach than having to write tedious if/else constructs that say exactly what to do for each different possibility. Instead we provide a simple definition of the function we want to use and the function is stored in a parameter of the function.

Lambdas are not always the right tool for the job; they cannot replace every situation where a function would be used. For example, a lambda cannot contain multiple statements, only a single expression based on its parameters. If you want to pass a function as a parameter that uses multiple statements to compute its result, you can do so using the regular def function declaration syntax. In the case of our math quiz program, we could craft a complex computation such as the following:

```
def doublepow(x, y):
    z = x ** y
    return z + z

...
def main():
    quiz_problems(3, " doublepow ", doublepow)
```

It's worth noting that Python has a module named operator that contains several useful functions that are essentially equivalent to various operators. For example, the module's add function accepts two parameters and returns their sum; similarly, sub and mul perform subtraction and multiplication, respectively. If we were to import operator into our program, we could write our main as follows:

```
def main():
    quiz_problems(3, " + ", operator.add)
    quiz_problems(3, " * ", operator.mul)
```

12.2 Functional Operations on Collections

In this section we will discuss several common functional operations that are applied to collections such as lists. These operations are provided with Python and are among the most commonly useful ones in functional programming.

Specifically, we will explore higher-order functions called map, filter, and reduce. Each one accepts a parameter that is an iterable collection, such as a list, along with a function to apply. The higher-order function applies that function to the elements of the collection to produce a result.

Before we dive into processing collections in a functional way, it may be helpful to look at a more procedural example. Suppose we want to compute the sum of the squares of the integers from 1 to 5 inclusive. We could write a standard cumulative sum loop to accomplish this:

```
>>> # sum the squares of integers 1-5
>>> total = 0
>>> for i in range(1, 6):
...     total += i * i
...
>>> total
55
```

This code specifies exactly how to perform this computation, using a loop variable called i that varies from 1 to 5 and accumulating the calculated values into a total called sum. We could also have done this calculation using lists, along with the built-in function sum that accepts a collection of numbers and returns their sum:

```
>>> # sum the squares of integers 1-5 using lists
>>> nums1 = [1, 2, 3, 4, 5]
>>> nums2 = []
>>> for i in nums1:
...     nums2.append(i * i)
...
>>> nums2
[1, 4, 9, 16, 25]
>>> total = sum(nums2)
55
```

It is also possible to perform computations like these on lists in a functional style. You will see that when we use functional programming, we describe *what* we want computed more than *how* to compute it. This can make the coding itself simpler, but, more importantly, it gives the computer more flexibility to decide how to implement the computation.

Table 12.1 lists the three higher-order functional operations we will discuss in detail in the coming sections: map, filter, and reduce.

Table 12.1 **Functional Operations on Collections**

Function Name	Description
map(f, seq)	applies the given function f to each value in seq, producing a new sequence of results
filter(f, seq)	applies the given predicate function f to each value in seq, retaining any values for which f returns True, producing a new (possibly shorter) sequence of results
reduce(f, seq)	applies the given function f to each neighboring pair of values in seq, producing a single unified value as a result

Using Map

Python has a higher-order function called map that applies a function to each element of a list or collection to produce a new collection. It takes two parameters: the function to apply to each element, and the collection of elements. The function to apply to each element should accept a single parameter and return a value. It returns a new iterable collection representing the modified elements.

> map
>
> Functional operation that applies a function to each element of a collection, producing a new collection from it.

We can use map to greatly simplify our previous example of computing the sum of the squares of the integers 1 to 5. Rather than a manual cumulative sum loop, or a loop to create a list of squares before calling sum on it, we can simply call map on our list of integers, passing a lambda that squares a value. Our previous code becomes:

```
>>> # sum the squares of integers 1-5 using map
>>> nums1 = [1, 2, 3, 4, 5]
>>> total = sum(map(lambda n: n * n, nums1))
>>> total
55
```

The value returned by map is an iterable collection of values, but it is not a list. If we wanted to capture the result of the mapping as a new list called nums2 we could do so as follows. We could also loop over the values produced by map in a for-each loop if desired:

```
>>> # create list of the squares of integers 1-5
>>> nums1 = [1, 2, 3, 4, 5]
>>> nums2 = list(map(lambda n: n * n, nums1))
```

Continued on next page

Continued from previous page

```
>>> nums2
[1, 4, 9, 16, 25]
>>> sum(nums2)
55
>>> for i in map(lambda n: n * n, nums1):
...     print(i)
...
1
4
9
16
25
```

Figure 12.1 diagrams the behavior of the map operation. The lambda is applied to each element of the list, and its result becomes part of the resulting collection. Note that map doesn't modify the list you pass it; it returns a new collection of values.

```
nums1 = [1, 2, 3, 4, 5]
         ↓   ↓   ↓
       lambda n: n * n
         ↓   ↓   ↓
        [1, 4, 9, 16, 25]
```

Figure 12.1   Application of map function

The map function can work with data of any type. Here is an example that processes a list of strings:

```
>>> # using map with strings
>>> words = ["so", "long", "and", "thanks", "for", "all", "the", "fish"]
>>> list(map(lambda s: s.upper() + "!", words))
['SO!', 'LONG!', 'AND!', 'THANKS!', 'FOR!', 'ALL!', 'THE!', 'FISH!']
```

Since map applies the same function to each element of the collection you pass it, the collection it returns will have the same number of elements as the one you pass it. In the next section we'll look at producing a resulting collection with a different number of elements.

Using Filter

Suppose that instead of using sequential integers, we decide to work with the first ten digits of pi. We can make a list of those digits, so let's use the same code as before but using those ten digits:

```
>>> # sum squares of the digits of pi
>>> pi_digits = [3, 1, 4, 1, 5, 9, 2, 6, 5, 3]
>>> total = sum(map(lambda n: n * n, pi_digits))
>>> total
207
```

But suppose that we are interested in only the odd digits of pi rather than all digits. We could rewrite the lambda function we used in map to return 0 for even numbers and the square of the number for odd numbers, but there is a better way.

Python has a function called filter that can be used to restrict a collection to those values that pass some test. While map gives you a collection of new values of the same length as the original, filter gives you a stream of unchanged values, but not necessarily of the same length because not all values might pass the given test. The filter function takes two parameters: a function (often a lambda) that accepts a value and returns a Boolean indicating whether it should be kept in the result, and a collection of items to examine.

> filter
>
> Functional operation that applies a Boolean function to each element of a collection, keeping elements that cause the function to return True and discarding elements that return False.

In our case, since we want to sum the odd digits of pi, we will test that the remainder when divided by 2 is not 0.

```
>>> # sum squares of the odd digits of pi
>>> pi_digits = [3, 1, 4, 1, 5, 9, 2, 6, 5, 3]
>>> total = sum(filter(lambda n: n % 2 != 0, pi_digits))
>>> total
27
```

To help illustrate exactly what filter returns, we'll capture its returned collection of results as a list and display it in the command shell:

```
>>> # sum squares of the odd digits of pi
>>> pi_digits = [3, 1, 4, 1, 5, 9, 2, 6, 5, 3]
>>> odd_digits = list(filter(lambda n: n % 2 != 0, pi_digits))
>>> odd_digits
[3, 1, 1, 5, 9, 5, 3]
>>> sum(odd_digits)
27
```

```
pi_digits = [3, 1, 4, 1, 5, 9, 2, 6, 5, 3]
             ↓   ↓   ↓
          lambda n: n % 2 != 0
             ↓   ↓   ↓
       T   T   F   T   T   T   F   F   T   T
             ↓   ↓   ↓
          [3, 1, 1, 5, 9, 5, 3]
```

Figure 12.2   Application of `filter` function

Figure 12.2 diagrams the behavior of the `filter` operation. The lambda is applied to each element of the list, and if it returns `True`, the element is kept. The new filtered collection is returned as the result of `filter`.

As another example, suppose we want to write a function to test whether a number n is prime. By definition a prime is a number that is divisible by 1 and itself but nothing else. Another way of saying this is that primes have exactly two factors. We can express this by producing a list of the values 1 through n, then filtering them to get only the factors, then seeing whether there are exactly two of them:

```
# Returns True if the given integer n is prime,
# meaning that its only factors are 1 and itself.
def is_prime(n):
    nums = range(1, n + 1)
    factors = filter(lambda x: n % x == 0, nums)
    return len(list(factors)) == 2
```

Remember that the second parameter to `range` is exclusive, which is why we use `n + 1` to go all the way up to and including n. It is worth considering the special case of 1. This function says that it is not prime, because there is only one value between 1 and 1 that is divisible by 1. That is the right answer because the value 1 is not considered a prime. This computation is inefficient because it only needs to test values up to the square root of `n`, but we will delay that discussion for the case study at the end of this chapter.

Using Reduce

Now let's consider the task of computing the factorial of an integer n, which is defined as the product of the integers 1 through n. This is fairly straightforward to implement using a loop:

```
# Iterative function to compute n!, which is
# defined as the product of the integers 1-n.
def factorial(n):
    result = 1
    for i in range(1, n + 1):
        result *= i
    return result
```

Let's think about how to compute a factorial with a functional approach. This is a slightly different task and requires a slightly different strategy. In this case, we want to take all of the integers in a range and combine them into one integer using multiplication. This one can't be solved using `map` or `filter` alone. Recall that the `map` function performs an operation on each element of a collection to produce a collection of the same length, and `filter` examines the elements of a collection, keeping some and discarding others. We don't want either of these behaviors here; rather, we want to process the elements of a range and combine all of them into a single result. In functional programming we would say that we want to *reduce* the collection values into a result.

Python has a function in its `functools` module called `reduce` that combines elements from a collection into a single result. The `reduce` function accepts two parameters: a function (often a lambda) to apply to a pair of elements, and a collection to process. Each pair of elements is passed to the lambda function, which is expected to return a single value. The eventual outcome of this process is that the collection is merged (reduced) into a single overall result. The operations `map`, `filter`, and `reduce` are often thought of as a core trio of operations necessary to program in a functional style.

> reduce
>
> Functional operation that applies a function to each neighboring pair of elements of a collection, combining them into a single result.

Below is a function that computes a factorial using `reduce`:

```
from functools import reduce


# Functional function to compute n!, which is
# defined as the product of the integers 1-n.
def factorial(n):
    return reduce(lambda a, b: a * b, range(1, n + 1))
```

Figure 12.3 diagrams the behavior of the `reduce` operation when applied to the range from 1 through 4. The lambda is applied to each pair of elements of the list, and its single result is passed to the next lambda call. For example, if the list contains [a, b, c], first

```
                                    [1,   2,   3,   4]
          lambda a, b: a * b         1 * 2
                                      ⌣⌣⌣
                                        2  *   3
                                        ⌣⌣⌣
                                           6   *   4
                                           ⌣⌣⌣
                                              24
```

Figure 12.3   Application of reduce function

the lambda is applied to (a, b), producing result d; then the lambda is applied to (d, c). The single result value is returned as the result of `reduce`.

An interesting special case occurs when you try to call `factorial` with a value of `0`. There are no elements in the range, so the `reduce` function doesn't have any values to merge and therefore does not know what to return:

```
>>> factorial(0)
Traceback (most recent call last):
  File "<stdin>", line 1, in <module>
  File "<stdin>", line 2, in factorial
TypeError: reduce() of empty sequence with no initial value
```

To guard against cases like this, you can pass a third parameter to `reduce` indicating a starting value. This starting value is implicitly prepended to the list of items passed to `reduce`. In the case of computing a factorial, the best starting value to use is 1, since multiplying by 1 does not change the overall result:

```
# Version of factorial with an initial value to reduce.
# This makes the function work correctly when 0 is passed.
def factorial(n):
    return reduce(lambda a, b: a * b, range(1, n + 1), 1)
```

The above change essentially means that for an n value of 5, the code would be reducing the list `[1, 1, 2, 3, 4, 5]`. For an n value of 0, the code would be reducing the list `[1]`, with the value 1 coming from our third parameter to `reduce`. When the list contains only a single element, `reduce` returns that element without applying the lambda.

Our change allows the expression to guarantee that it returns a value even if the range is empty. That means that 0! is now correctly reported as 1.

```
>>> factorial(0)
1
```

Our new version also returns `1` when passed a negative integer, which is technically incorrect because the factorial is undefined for negative numbers. We could fix this with a test that raises an error in that case.

As another example, suppose you want to find the length of the longest word in a list. The `reduce` function can help solve this problem. You can start by converting each string into its length by writing a lambda function. Once we have mapped each string to its length, we can find the largest one using a `reduce` operation that uses another lambda that picks the max of each pair of values:

```
>>> # find length of longest word (first attempt)
>>> words = ["so", "long", "and", "thanks", "for", "all", "the", "fish"]
>>> list(map(lambda s: len(s), words))
[2, 4, 3, 6, 3, 3, 3, 4]
>>> reduce(lambda a, b: max(a, b), map(lambda s: len(s), words))
6
```

This code is correct but unnecessarily verbose; in this case the lambdas are unnecessary.
The lambda function passed to map does exactly what len itself does: accepts a string
parameter and returns its length. In such a case, we can directly pass the len function
rather than wrapping it in an unnecessary lambda. The same is true for the lambda that
wraps the built-in function max in our reduce call; we can just pass max directly, since
the lambda does nothing except forward its arguments on to max. The following is the
improved code:

```
>>> # find length of longest word (improved)
>>> words = ["so", "long", "and", "thanks", "for", "all", "the", "fish"]
>>> reduce(max, map(len, words))
6
```

What if we wanted the longest word itself as a string, rather than its length? We could
achieve this by reducing the list in a different way. Rather than mapping words to their
length, we could write a function that examines each pair of strings and returns the
longer of the two. Reducing the entire list in this manner would leave the very longest
word as the only one left at the end. But returning the longer string from our lambda
would require if/else statements, and a lambda function cannot contain entire statements. We could write a normal non-lambda function, but there is a better way. Python
has a syntax called a *conditional expression* (sometimes called a ternary expression)
that selects between two values based on a test. Its general syntax is the following:

expression1 if *test* else *expression2*
Syntax template: Conditional expression (ternary expression)

This looks a lot like a normal if/else statement with a few differences. The main
behavioral difference is that here we are choosing between two values rather than
choosing between two blocks of statements to execute. A conditional expression can
be used as the body of a lambda function to find the longest word in a list:

```
>>> # find the longest word as a string
>>> words = ["so", "long", "and", "thanks", "for", "all", "the", "fish"]
>>> reduce(lambda s1, s2: s1 if len(s1) > len(s2) else s2, words)
'thanks'
```

List Comprehensions

Python includes a syntax called a *list comprehension* that is roughly equivalent to the map function. We briefly introduced list comprehensions in Chapter 7, but it is worth examining them again in the context of functional programming. Recall that a list comprehension specifies an expression indicating a pattern to apply to each element of a collection to produce a new list.

> **List Comprehension**
>
> An expression that produces a list by applying an expression to each element of an existing collection.

For example, recall the previous code that used map to produce a list of the squares of the integers from 1 to 5:

```
>>> # create list of the squares of integers 1-5, using map
>>> nums1 = [1, 2, 3, 4, 5]
>>> nums2 = list(map(lambda n: n * n, nums1))
>>> nums2
[1, 4, 9, 16, 25]
```

The same computation can be elegantly expressed using a list comprehension.

```
>>> # create list of squares of integers 1-5, using list comprehension
>>> nums1 = [1, 2, 3, 4, 5]
>>> nums2 = [n * n for n in nums1]
>>> nums2
[1, 4, 9, 16, 25]
```

The meaning of the preceding comprehension is, "Create a new list where, for each element with the value n in num1, my new list will contain the value n * n instead." As described in Chapter 7, the general syntax for list comprehensions is the following:

```
[expression for name in collection]
```
Syntax template: list comprehension

The list comprehension syntax can essentially replace map in most places where we would want to call map. Another nice side benefit of list comprehensions is that they inherently produce lists as their results, while the result of `map` instead produces a map structure that must be explicitly converted into a list by wrapping it with `list(...)`.

A list comprehension can contain an optional `if` clause at the end, which is roughly equivalent to the `filter` function. The general syntax for list comprehensions with an `if` filter is the following:

```
[expression for name in collection if test]
```
Syntax template: list comprehension with if filter

For example, in a previous section we used `filter` and `sum` to compute the sum of the odd digits of pi:

```
>>> # sum squares of the odd digits of pi, using filter
>>> pi_digits = [3, 1, 4, 1, 5, 9, 2, 6, 5, 3]
>>> list(filter(lambda n: n % 2 != 0, pi_digits))
[3, 1, 1, 5, 9, 5, 3]
>>> total = sum(filter(lambda n: n % 2 != 0, pi_digits))
>>> total
27
```

The same computation can be done using a list comprehension with an `if` clause to test for odd digits:

```
>>> # sum squares of the odd digits of pi, using filter
>>> pi_digits = [3, 1, 4, 1, 5, 9, 2, 6, 5, 3]
>>> [n for n in pi_digits if n % 2 != 0]
[3, 1, 1, 5, 9, 5, 3]
>>> total = sum([n for n in pi_digits if n % 2 != 0])
>>> total
27
```

There is no list comprehension syntax equivalent to the `reduce` function, but it largely replaces `map` and `filter` in most modern Python code.

Python also contains dictionary and set comprehensions using similar syntax except surrounded by `{}` braces. Chapter 8 briefly introduced dictionary comprehensions. Otherwise these are outside the scope of this chapter, but you can read about them in the Python online language documentation:

- https://docs.python.org/3/tutorial/datastructures.html

12.3 Function Closures

We have seen that Python has extensive rules about the scope of variables that guarantees that every reference to a variable will work out. Consider, for example, the following program, which attempts to count how many factors of 10 there are:

```
 1   # Attempts to count the factors of 10.
 2   # Raises an error; not an example to follow.
 3
 4   # Returns true if n is a multiple of (is divisible by) x.
 5   def is_multiple(x):
 6       return n % x == 0
 7
 8   def main():
 9       n = 10
10       count = 0
11       for i in range(1, n + 1):
12           if is_multiple(i):
13               count += 1
14       print("count =", count)
15
16   main()
```

```
Traceback (most recent call last):
  File "bad_scope.py", line 15, in <module>
    main()
  File "bad_scope.py", line 11, in main
    if is_multiple(i):
  File "bad_scope.py", line 5, in is_multiple
    return n % x == 0
NameError: name 'n' is not defined
```

This program does not run properly. The Python interpreter raises an error that the variable n referred to in the function is_multiple is not defined. You might argue that it is defined in the main function and is set up before the function is called. But as we have seen, Python has strict rules about this and requires that the variable n be visible in the scope of the function or in the outer program scope. Being available in the scope of a different function isn't good enough.

The usual fix is to pass n as a parameter:

```
 1   # Counts the factors of 10.
 2
 3   # Returns true if n is a multiple of (is divisible by) x.
```

Continued on next page

Continued from previous page

```
 4  def is_multiple(x, n):
 5          return n % x == 0
 6
 7  def main():
 8          n = 10
 9          count = 0
10          for i in range(1, n + 1):
11                  if is_multiple(i, n):
12                          count += 1
13          print("count =", count)
14
15  main()
```

```
count = 4
```

This program now correctly reports that there are four factors of 10 (1, 2, 5, and 10). But consider the following functional code, which uses `filter` and `len` to count the factors:

```
>>> n = 10
>>> count = len(list(filter(lambda x: n % x == 0, range(1, n + 1))))
>>> count
4
```

It also correctly reports that there are four factors of 10. Similar code is used in the `is_prime` function included in the previous section. But how does this work? Think about the lambda expression being passed as a parameter to filter:

```
lambda x: n % x == 0
```

This is supposed to represent an independent function. In fact, it looks a lot like the `is_multiple` function from the *bad_scope.py* program. It has a single parameter called x and it returns a Boolean value based on whether the variable n is divisible by x. It has access to the variable x because it is the parameter, but how does it have access to the variable n?

You might say that you can see the variable n defined in the scope in which this lambda expression occurs, and that is the key to understanding this. But it is important to recognize that something special is going on here. Remember that you are passing a lambda function to the `filter` function that it will execute. That `filter` function is in a different scope that doesn't have access to the variable n that is defined here. So somehow the value of n is being passed along with the code.

When you form a lambda expression, some of the variables you refer to will be included as parameters to the function. We call such references *bound variables* because they are each connected to a parameter. Any reference that is not to a parameter in a lambda expression is considered a *free variable*. Variables cannot be completely free of definition because then they would be undefined. But because a lambda expression occurs in the middle of code that potentially has variables defined, the lambda expression can refer to free variables that are defined in its outer scope.

> **Bound/Free Variable**
>
> In a lambda expression, parameters are bound variables while variables in the outer containing scope are free variables.

In our sample lambda expression, the outer code defines a local variable called n, which means that the reference to n in the lambda expression makes sense. But Python has to perform some work behind the scenes to include this variable definition along with the code. We refer to such a combination as a *closure*.

> **Function Closure**
>
> A block of code defining a function along with the definitions of any free variables that are defined in the containing scope.

Let's use another example that goes to an extreme to make the point. Suppose we have a function called compute that takes a function of two arguments as a parameter. (Note the distinction: compute doesn't accept two parameters; it accepts a single parameter, which is a function. The function that compute accepts must accept two parameters.) We might call it like this:

```
compute(lambda x, y: x + y)
```

This lambda expression refers to x and y, which are both parameters, which means they are bound. There are no free variables in this expression. But suppose the code instead had been:

```
a = 10
b = 50
mult = 3
compute(lambda x, y: max(x, a) * max(y, b) * mult)
```

This lambda expression has references to x and y just like the other one, but those aren't a problem because parameters are bound variables. But it also has references to variables called a, b, and mult, which are not parameters of the lambda expression, which means they are free variables. Python has to include those definitions along with the code in order for the compute function to be able to do its job.

For a visual representation, imagine that Python puts together the code of the lambda expression along with the definitions of the parameters and these three free variables into one big object, as shown in Figure 12.4.

```
parameters    : (x, y)
free variables: a = 10, b = 50, mult = 3
code          : max(x, a) * max(y, b) * mult
```

Figure 12.4   Diagram of a function closure

This object is the closure. It contains both the code and the relevant context in which the code occurs. The free variables `min`, `max`, and `multiplier` have been included so that the code can be executed. We say that they have been *captured* in forming this closure.

The word "closure" comes from mathematics (e.g., the concept of a transitive closure), but here is a way to think about it that might be helpful to remember the concept. We all seek closure in our lives, which means that we don't want any loose ends from our past left around to upset us. Free variables are loose ends in a lambda expression that would make it impossible to evaluate the code. By including their definition in the closure, we are tying up those loose ends so that there isn't anything left that is undecided. Once we've done that, we've reached a kind of closure with this computation.

We run into potential problems if any of the free variables included in a closure change in value. If the value of a free variable changes, then the computation isn't well defined. For example, it means that the order in which we perform the individual computations for a function like `map` or `filter` could change the overall result. This relates to the concept of effect-free programming described earlier in this chapter. We want to write code that does not have these potential sources of inconsistency.

Generator Functions

Most of the functional programming examples we've seen so far operate on lists. But this has a drawback: a functional algorithm over a list must create that entire list and store it in memory while the program runs. This can lead to problems if the list is very large.

Consider the example of the hailstone sequence that was introduced in Chapter 4. This was the mathematical function that begins with a given integer value n and then successively changes n into $3n + 1$ if n is odd, or $n / 2$ if n is even, until n reaches 1. We could write a function to produce all the values in a hailstone sequence, starting from a given n value passed as a parameter, returning all of the intermediate values as a list. The following program contains this code:

```
1   # This program implements the hailstone sequence
2   # as a procedural algorithm.
3
4   # Returns a list of all integers in a hailstone
5   # sequence starting with n until n reaches 1.
6   def hailstone_sequence(n):
7       result = [n]
```

Continued on next page

Continued from previous page

```
 8        while n != 1:
 9            if n % 2 == 0:
10                n = n // 2
11            else:
12                n = 3 * n + 1
13            result.append(n)
14        return result
15
16  def main():
17      n = int(input("Value of N? "))
18      values = hailstone_sequence(n)
19      print("Hailstone sequence starting with", n, ":")
20      for k in values:
21          print(k, end=" ")
22      print()
23
24  main()
```

```
Value of N? 17
Hailstone sequence starting with 17 :
17 52 26 13 40 20 10 5 16 8 4 2 1
```

However, the hailstone list for some integers can be quite long. In fact, it is unproven (though strongly suspected) that every hailstone list will eventually reach 1 for every possible integer value *n*. It's a shame to create a list of such large size when all we really want to do is iterate over the list's elements one at a time to process or print them.

To deal with these kinds of situations, Python has a language feature called generators. A *generator* is a function that returns a sequence of values one at a time, emitting one value from the sequence each time it is called.

> **Generator**
>
> A function that emits ("yields") a sequence of values one at a time so that they can be iterated over, such as by a for-each loop or higher-order function.

The code for a generator effectively builds and returns a list of values without the author of the function having to create or fill that list. The values are provided to the caller of the function as an iterable sequence object that can be processed by a for-each loop or by a higher-order function such as `map`, but without having to build and store the entire sequence of values in memory all at once. For this reason, generators are very important for improving memory usage and performance of functional code.

The syntax for writing a generator function is the same as writing a standard function, with one important difference. Instead of emitting result values using a `return` or `print` statement, the function instead uses a `yield` statement. A `yield` statement has the following general syntax:

```
yield expression
```
Syntax template: yield statement

The meaning of a `yield` statement is similar to a `return` statement. However, where a `return` completely exits a function and discards any local state, a `yield` statement exits the function and emits the given value but remembers all local state from the function's closure at that point in the function. If the function is ever called again to ask for another value, the function resumes from the point of the `yield`.

For comparison, the following is a function that returns a hailstone sequence as a list:

```
# Returns a list of all integers in a hailstone
# sequence starting with n until n reaches 1.
def hailstone_sequence(n):
    result = [n]
    while n != 1:
        if n % 2 == 0:
            n = n // 2
        else:
            n = 3 * n + 1
        result.append(n)
    return result
```

A generator that returns an entire hailstone sequence has the following code:

```
# Generates all integers in a hailstone sequence
# starting with n until n reaches 1.
def hailstone_sequence(n):
    yield n
    while n != 1:
        if n % 2 == 0:
            n = n // 2
        else:
            n = 3 * n + 1
        yield n
```

Notice that the places where we used to write `result.append(n)` become the places where we now write `yield n`. This means that the generator's overall result of returned values is the same as the content of the list returned by the procedural version.

When client code calls a generator, the value returned is called a *generator object*. A generator object contains the remembered state of the function. The most common usage of a generator object is to iterate over its elements using a for-each loop:

```
>>> # using a generator object
>>> values = hailstone_sequence(17)
>>> values
<generator object hailstone_sequence at 0x7eff52436f10>
>>> for k in values:
...     print(k, end=" ")
...
17 52 26 13 40 20 10 5 16 8 4 2 1
```

Notice that the loop over the generator object produces the same list of values as the list in the procedural version of the code. A generator object's sequence of values can be converted into a list by passing the generator to the `list` function, but we don't want to do that in this case.

Generators are closely related to the idea of function closures. When a generator function yields a value, it must keep track internally of the function's closure, including the values of any free and bound variables used by the function at that point. The `yield` statement is quite a powerful tool for remembering this state without any real work by the function's author.

Generator objects are very useful in functional programming because you can pass one as a sequence of values to a higher-order function. For example, the result of `hailstone_sequence` can be passed to `map`, `filter`, or `reduce`:

```
>>> # compute sum of squares of hailstone sequence
>>> sum(map(lambda x: x*x, hailstone_sequence(17)))
6304
```

An interesting aspect of generators is that once you loop over their contents, the generator object becomes "used up" and no longer provides any way to access the values again. If you want to loop over the sequence again, you would have to call `hailstone_sequence` a second time to acquire a fresh generator object:

```
>>> # trying to iterate over a generator twice
>>> values = hailstone_sequence(17)
>>> values
<generator object hailstone_sequence at 0x7eff52436f10>
```

Continued on next page

Continued from previous page

```
>>> for k in values: print(k, end=" ")
...
17 52 26 13 40 20 10 5 16 8 4 2 1
>>> # second time (no output is printed)
>>> for k in values: print(k, end=" ")
...

>>> # re-initialize generator and try again
>>> values = hailstone_sequence(17)
>>> for k in values: print(k, end=" ")
...
17 52 26 13 40 20 10 5 16 8 4 2 1
```

Lazy Evaluation

An interesting detail about generator objects is that they do not compute and yield all of their results unless those results are actually asked for by client code. For example, our `hailstone_sequence` generator function will not finish its overall `while` loop if the client stops asking for values from the sequence. Suppose our client wants to loop until a certain value is found. This can be done by breaking out of the loop early:

```
>>> # use partial results from a generator (lazy evaluation)
>>> values = hailstone_sequence(17)
>>> for k in values:
...     print(k, end=" ")
...     if k >= 40: break
...
17 52 26 13 40
```

The remaining elements of the hailstone sequence, 20 10 5 16 8 4 2 1, are never computed, printed, or stored by the preceding code. When functional code describes the process of computing but does not actually compute results that are not needed, we say that it uses *lazy evaluation*.

> **Lazy Evaluation**
>
> Process in which results are described but not calculated unless needed by client code.

The implications of lazy evaluation can be seen in unexpected places. For example, suppose you want to use the `map` function to print each element of a list. Since `print` is a function, rather than writing a `for` loop over the list, why don't we just call `map` on the list and pass `print` to it? Doing so does not actually print any of the elements:

```
>>> # map the print function over a list? (attempt #1)
>>> nums = [10, 20, 30, 40]
>>> map(print, nums)
<map object at 0x7f62c3bc3b00>
```

This is because the result of `map` is lazily evaluated. It does not actually apply the function (`print` in this case) to the elements of the sequence unless you actually process those elements in some way, such as by iterating over the object returned by `map`. If we convert the results of `map` into a list, oddly enough, the printed output suddenly appears. This is because the `list` conversion needs to iterate over the `map` result, forcing it to evaluate itself, which calls `print` on each element. The `list` call returns a strange result of four occurrences of the value `None`. This is because `print` does not return a value; therefore the result of mapping `print` to a sequence is to replace each value with `None`, with the side effect of printing the value to the console:

```
>>> # map the print function over a list? (attempt #2)
>>> nums = [10, 20, 30, 40]
>>> list(map(print, nums))
10
20
30
40
[None, None, None, None]
```

Lazy evaluation makes it possible to write a generator function that produces an infinite sequence of values. The following generator produces an infinite sequence of random numbers in a given range. A client usually wouldn't directly perform a for-each loop over the result of a `inf_rand_seq` call, nor pass such a result to `map` or `filter`, because the loop would never terminate. But you can extract individual values from the sequence by passing it to the global function `next`:

```
# A generator that produces an infinite sequence.
def inf_rand_seq(min, max):
    while True:
        yield random.randint(min, max)
```

```
>>> r = inf_rand_seq(1, 10)
>>> next(r)
5
```

Continued on next page

Continued from previous page

```
>>> next(r)
1
>>> next(r)
2
>>> next(r)
8
>>> next(r)
5
```

The lazy evaluation approach is powerful because you can create a generator object that potentially contains or computes a large or infinite number of values, but the client code does not need to pay the cost of such computation except for the values they actually use.

Iterable Objects

The generator objects returned by calls to generator functions are examples of a general class of objects in Python called *iterable objects*. An iterable object is any object that can be used as the target of a for-each loop to yield a sequence of values. Several functions you have already seen in Python, such as `range`, `map`, and `filter`, return iterable objects. You may have noticed that if you call such functions and try to directly examine or print their results, you may have expected the result to be a list, but instead you find that they return their own types of objects.

```
>>> # examining return values from various functions
>>> r = range(1, 10)
>>> r
range(1, 10)
>>> m = map(lambda x: x*x, r)
>>> m
<map object at 0x7eff5243cb70>
>>> f = filter(lambda x: x % 2 == 0, r)
>>> f
<filter object at 0x7eff5243cc18>
```

These iterable objects returned by `range`, `map`, and `filter` are similar to generator objects in that they are lazily evaluated and do not gather all of their contained values into a collection. Instead, they each compute and emit (yield) the next value as you loop over them. This helps keep their memory usage low and improve performance when used in functional programming. You can essentially think of `range`, `map`, `filter`, and others as generator functions that yield the sequence of values that are the result of these functions.

As an intellectual exercise, we could use the syntax of generator functions to write our own versions of higher-order functions like map, filter, and reduce. Let's re-implement map and filter, each of which accepts two parameters: a function to apply to each element, and a sequence of elements. The code for map and filter is essentially equivalent to the following:

```
# Our own version of map and filter,
# written as generator functions.

def my_map(f, seq):
    for value in seq:
        yield f(value)

def my_filter(f, seq):
    for value in seq:
        if f(value):
            yield value
```

```
>>> # using my_map and my_filter
>>> # (they behave the same as the built-in ones)
>>> result = my_map(lambda x: x * x, range(10))
>>> for k in result: print(k, end=" ")
...
0 1 4 9 16 25 36 49 64 81
>>> result = my_filter(lambda x: x % 2 == 0, range(10))
>>> for k in result: print(k, end=" ")
0 2 4 6 8
```

We could re-implement other functions like range and reduce in a similar fashion. Doing so is not useful since the existing versions work just fine, but it illustrates the utility of generator functions in functional programming.

Generator Expressions

Let's look at one last application of generators. We saw earlier in this chapter that a list comprehension is an elegant replacement syntax for the map and/or filter functions. But list comprehensions defy the lessons in this section, because they create actual lists that store all of their result values in one combined collection. This has all of the drawbacks discussed previously about memory usage and performance. For example, the following code computes a sum of squares of integers, but it creates two unnecessary lists: the initial list nums1 of 1 to 5, and the second list nums2 produced by the list comprehension.

```
>>> # sum squares of integers 1-5, using list comprehension
>>> nums1 = [1, 2, 3, 4, 5]
>>> nums2 = [n * n for n in nums1]
>>> nums2
[1, 4, 9, 16, 25]
>>> total = sum(nums2)
>>> total
55
```

The only reason we're creating lists and list comprehensions in the example is so that we can iterate over the elements or process them with a function like sum. For such cases, Python has a feature called *generator expressions* for creating lazily evaluated iterable generator objects. A generator expression uses essentially the same syntax as a list comprehension, except that it is surrounded by ( ) parentheses rather than [ ] square brackets. The result of such an expression is equivalent to that of a list comprehension, except that it is a lazily evaluated iterable object rather than a list.

Generator Expression

A Python expression similar to a list comprehension that produces a lazily evaluated iterable object based on applying an operation to every value from some other sequence of values.

The general syntax for a generator expression is the following:

```
(expression for name in sequence)
(expression for name in sequence if test)
```
Syntax template: generator expression (with and without filter)

Notice that, just like a list comprehension, a generator expression can contain an optional if filter at its end. The following client code uses generator expressions to avoid creating any lists. We call range to get the initial sequence of integers 1 to 5 because range produces a lazily evaluated iterable object, thus avoiding the need to create an entire list.

```
>>> # sum squares of integers 1-5, using generator expressions
>>> nums1 = range(1, 6)
>>> nums2 = (n * n for n in nums1)
>>> total = sum(nums2)
>>> total
55
```

Rather than separating out each step, an experienced functional programmer would more likely combine them into a single computation as follows. The extra parentheses around the call to sum are technically not needed, but we include them for clarity:

```
>>> # sum squares of integers 1-5 (shorter)
>>> total = sum((n * n for n in range(1, 6)))
>>> total
55
```

It is recommended to use generator expressions rather than list comprehensions if the only reason you are creating the list is to iterate over its elements once. If you actually need to store the data as a list or iterate over it many times, a list comprehension is likely the better choice.

12.4 Case Study: Perfect Numbers

To complete our exploration of functional programming, we will look at a classic problem from mathematics whose solution takes a lot of computational power. We are going to write a program that looks for perfect numbers. A perfect number is defined as one that is equal to the sum of its divisors other than itself. For example, the divisors of 6 are [1, 2, 3, 6]. If you exclude 6, the other divisors add up to 6 (1 + 2 + 3). In fact, 6 is the smallest perfect number. The next perfect number is 28 whose divisors are [1, 2, 4, 7, 14, 28].

If you search for "perfect number" in your web browser, you will find several web sites that chronicle the fascination that many people have had over the years with this concept. Some ancient Greeks believed that the world was created in 6 days because 6 is the first perfect number. St. Augustine repeats this claim in his writings. The ancient Greeks also believed that the moon completes an orbit every 28 days because 28 is the second perfect number.

The first four perfect numbers have been known since ancient times, but the earliest known references to the fifth perfect number date from the fifteenth century (between 1456 and 1461, according to Wikipedia). In this section we will write a program to find the fifth perfect number. In doing so, we will be able to explore one of the biggest benefits of functional programming: that it can speed up the execution of programs that require a lot of computational power.

Computing Sums

This problem, as with many problems from mathematics, lends itself naturally to a functional approach. In this first version, let's write code that finds the sum of the divisors of a number not including the number itself; and let's include debugging code that will allow us to have confidence that our code is working correctly.

We can use `range` to produce a collection of integers and filter it with a test for divisibility and then compute the sum. We produce a generator expression over the factors of `n`, and then call `sum` on this generator to add the divisors. Let's put it into a function so that we can call it easily:

```
# returns the sum of the proper divisors of n
def sum_divisors(n):
    return sum((k for k in range(1, n) if n % k == 0))
```

Normally we would have the range go up to `n + 1` so that it will include `n`, but in this case we want to exclude `n` from the sum because we are looking for the sum of the divisors other than the number itself.

In the `main` function we can test computing the sums for the first 10 integers and print them out again using a call on `range` and a call on `map` to apply our function. The following is the code and its output:

```
def main():
    for i in range(1, 11):
        print("sum of divisors of", i, "=", sum_divisors(i))
```

```
sum of divisors of 1 = 0
sum of divisors of 2 = 1
sum of divisors of 3 = 1
sum of divisors of 4 = 3
sum of divisors of 5 = 1
sum of divisors of 6 = 6
sum of divisors of 7 = 1
sum of divisors of 8 = 7
sum of divisors of 9 = 4
sum of divisors of 10 = 8
```

This output indicates that the sum of divisors for 1 is 0, the sum of divisors for 2 is 1, the sum of divisors for 3 is 1, and so on. This sounds wrong, but remember that we are excluding the number `n` itself from these divisors. For example, the proper divisors of 8 are 1, 2, and 4, leading to a total of 7.

We can modify `main` so that it looks at a lot of integers (say, up to one million) and filters on those that are equal to their sum of divisors. To gauge the performance of our program, we can also use the `time` function from the time module introduced in Chapter 10 to keep track of how much time we spend computing the result. Since the general task of running and timing a function comes up often, this is a nice opportunity to write a higher-order function called `measure_runtime` that accepts another function as a parameter, runs that function, and returns the runtime needed. The following is the relevant code along with its output:

```
# Runs the given function f, measuring how long it took to run.
# Returns the elapsed runtime at the end of the call.
def measure_runtime(f):
    start_time = time.time()
    f()
    elapsed_time = time.time() - start_time
    return elapsed_time

# Finds and prints all perfect numbers from 1-1000000.
def find_perfect_numbers():
    print("Searching for perfect numbers:")
    perfects = filter(lambda n: n == sum_divisors(n), \
                    range(1, 1000001))
    for p in perfects:
        print(p)

def main():
    runtime = measure_runtime(find_perfect_numbers)
    print("time =", runtime, "sec")
```

```
6
28
496
8128
time = 2261.290875628907 sec
```

When one of the authors ran this on a local server machine, the program reported taking over 2260 seconds to complete, which is over 37 minutes. It correctly reported the first four perfect numbers, but it didn't manage to find the fifth. We could increase the maximum value, but this algorithm isn't going to find the fifth in a reasonable amount of time.

We need to improve the efficiency of our computation. The easiest way to do this is to notice that each divisor that is less than the square root of a number is paired with a divisor that is greater than the square root. If, for example, we are looking for the divisors of 100, we find that the divisor 1 is paired with 100, the divisor 2 is paired with 50, the divisor 4 is paired with 25, and so on. So instead of finding each divisor by checking all the way up to the number, we can instead find pairs of divisors by checking up to the square root. If you search for the divisors in this way, for each divisor k you find, you know that you have also found its pair, whose value is n // k. So we can modify our sum_divisors function to add in each divisor's pair to our sum.

Remember that we want to exclude the number n itself from the sum. It is always paired with 1, so an easy way to do this is to start our search for divisors at 2 rather than 1. If we do that, however, then we have to remember to add 1 to the final result because 1 is supposed to be included in the sum. The code below attempts to implement this strategy:

```
# returns the sum of the proper divisors of n
# (optimized version that computes up to square root only)
def sum_divisors(n):
    root = int(math.sqrt(n))
    return sum((k + n // k for k in range(2, root + 1) if n % k == 0)) + 1
```

We can go back to our old client code that prints output for the numbers 1 through 10, which now produces the following output:

```
sum of divisors of 1 = 0
sum of divisors of 2 = 1
sum of divisors of 3 = 1
sum of divisors of 4 = 5
sum of divisors of 5 = 1
sum of divisors of 6 = 6
sum of divisors of 7 = 1
sum of divisors of 8 = 7
sum of divisors of 9 = 7
sum of divisors of 10 = 8
```

Our new function computes the wrong answers for some of these values. In particular, it has the wrong answer for 4 and 9. The problem comes for numbers that are perfect squares, integers that are the square of another integer. It is true that every divisor that is strictly less than the square root of a number has a different divisor that it is paired with that is strictly larger than the square root. But for numbers that are perfect squares, their square root isn't paired with another divisor. Let's take 4. Its divisors other than itself are 1 and 2, so that should add up to 3. Instead we get a sum of 5. This is because 4 has a pair of divisors 2 and 2; these combine with the divisor of 1 to make a total of 5. We can handle this special case after the computation of the sum by checking for perfect squares with the following code:

```
if n == root * root:
    result -= root
```

Below is the complete program that checks numbers up to one million. This version takes only around 42 seconds to run on our server, which is quite a bit better than 37 minutes.

```
 1  # Searches for perfect numbers among the integers 1 - 1,000,000.
 2  # This version has an optimization to compute the sum of
 3  # n's factors more quickly by examining only up to sqrt(n).
 4
 5  import math    # for sqrt
 6  import time
 7
 8  # returns the sum of the proper divisors of n
 9  def sum_divisors(n):
10      root = int(math.sqrt(n))
11      result = sum((k + n // k for k in \
12                  range(2, root + 1) if n % k == 0)) + 1
13      if n == root * root:
14          result -= root
15      return result
16
17  # Runs the given function f, measuring how long it took to run.
18  # Returns the elapsed runtime at the end of the call.
19  def measure_runtime(f):
20      start_time = time.time()
21      f()
22      elapsed_time = time.time() - start_time
23      return elapsed_time
24
25  # Finds and prints all perfect numbers from 1-1000000.
26  def find_perfect_numbers():
27      print("Searching for perfect numbers:")
28      perfects = filter(lambda n: n == sum_divisors(n), \
29                      range(1, 1000001))
30      for p in perfects:
31          print(p)
32
33  def main():
34      runtime = measure_runtime(find_perfect_numbers)
35      print("time =", runtime, "sec")
36
37  main()
```

```
6
28
496
8128
time = 41.983463287353516 sec
```

The Fifth Perfect Number

We are ready to see if we can find the fifth perfect number. We have checked up to one million and didn't find it. We could try going up to ten million or one-hundred million or some other large number. But it isn't ideal to use `range` here because we don't know the upper bound of the maximum integer at which to stop. Luckily Python provides a nice alternative.

Python has a library called `itertools` that contains a function called `count`. This function produces an infinite iterable sequence of integers starting from a given value. The `count` function takes a starting integer value as a parameter and produces an iterable sequence of integers starting from that value. (The implementation of `count` is essentially a generator function that maintains a counter integer that is `yielded` and incremented over and over.) So our code will contain the following call.

```
itertools.count(1)
```

This is potentially an infinite range of numbers because we say to start at 1 but we never say when to stop. You can imagine client code using the `count` function as follows:

```
# find all the perfect numbers?
perfects = filter(lambda n: n == sum_divisors(n), itertools.count(1))
...
```

But the preceding code will never stop, not even once it finds the elusive fifth perfect number. When you work with an iterable sequence like this, you have to limit how many values you want it to produce. In Python, you can achieve this with the `itertools` function `islice`, which accepts two parameters: the iterable sequence of interest, and an integer k representing how many items you want from the sequence. `itertools.islice` returns a new iterable sequence of just those first k values. While we are improving this code, we'll change our call on `filter` into a generator expression.

The following code prints the first five integers that are equal to the sum of their divisors (in other words, the first five perfect numbers):

```
perfects = (n for n in itertools.count(1) if n == sum_divisors(n))
for k in itertools.islice(perfects, 5):
    print(k)
```

This is another place where it is important to understand in general the order of operations and lazy evaluation. If you think of the generator expression as producing all of its results immediately, then the code would never finish running. Remember that the generator expression computes values only as they are needed. The call on `itertools.slice` with the second parameter of 5 asks the generator for its first 5 values, which causes the generator to look through integers as far as needed to find 5 perfect numbers and no further.

The authors ran this version of the program on our server, but it took over five hours to run without finding the fifth perfect number. So we need an even better approach.

Leveraging Concurrency

Our program is functionally complete, but it is too slow to be practical. Computer scientists have realized for a while now that speeding up a single processor cannot be achieved indefinitely and that eventually we will have to leverage the power of concurrency. It is typical now for desktops, laptops, and even mobile devices to include dual-core or quad-core or some other form of multi-core where there is more than one processor. But it isn't easy to take advantage of multiple processors.

The pitfalls are beyond the scope of this discussion, but think about something as simple as preparing a meal to be served at a restaurant. It is easy to see how one chef would complete the task by doing everything. Adding additional chefs might be helpful if you can divide up the task somehow. For example, one might prepare an appetizer while another prepares the main dish and a third prepares a dessert. Even in this case the timing matters because if the dessert is completed quickly and the main dish comes out last, then it is possible that the dessert will spoil because the customer won't want to eat it until the end of the meal. And if you try to have a dozen cooks work on the meal, you generally end up with the well-known disaster of "too many cooks in one kitchen."

In programming for multiple processors, we leverage two distinct but related concepts. *Concurrent* computations are ones that can occur in any order. For example, if your program needs to download a large collection of files, you may not care which file is downloaded first, second, and so on, so long as they all arrive eventually. *Parallel* computations are ones that happen at the same time. If computations are considered to be concurrent, they can safely be performed in parallel without changing the program's functionality.

> Concurrency
>
> The ability of parts of an algorithm to be executed out of order without affecting the outcome.

> Parallelism
>
> Computation in which many calculations are carried out simultaneously.

When Google was faced with the problem of performing massive calculations over vast databases, it quickly turned to concurrency with multiple machines to speed things up. Google programmers realized that many computations can be decomposed into a mapping operation and a reducing operation similar to the approach we have described in this chapter. For example, if you want to count how many web pages have a particular search phrase, you can map a function over the pages that returns 0 or 1 depending on whether the search term appears in that particular page and then you can reduce all of those 0s and 1s using simple addition. Google computer scientists built a system called MapReduce that uses exactly this approach. Typical computations are executed with hundreds of processors working on each problem. Hadoop is an open source version of Google's system and has also been popular for applying concurrency effectively to large-scale computations.

The increasing importance of concurrency has led many to realize that functional programming is a powerful way to take advantage of parallel computation. An emphasis on effect-free programming allows us to avoid many of the common pitfalls of running code on multiple processors. The model of expressing a computation in terms of mapping, filtering, and reducing lends itself naturally to a concurrent solution because usually these operations can be performed in parallel without affecting the overall result.

Many people enjoy functional programming because they like to express problems in a functional manner. Others appreciate the fact that you can write short code that has a certain elegance to it because complex computations can be expressed very concisely. But in the world of modern computing, the truly compelling reason to study functional programming is that it provides a practical solution to the problem of taking advantage of concurrency. In other words, concurrency is the "killer app" for functional programming that convinced the ACM/IEEE joint task force among others that every undergraduate majoring in computer science must understand the basics of functional programming.

If you are curious about the number of processors or cores available on your computer, you can import the os library and call its `cpu_count` function:

```
>>> # how many CPU cores does my machine have?
>>> import os
>>> os.cpu_count()
8
```

To execute a parallel algorithm in Python, we will import a class named `Pool` from a library called `multiprocessing`:

```
from multiprocessing import Pool
```

We can construct a `Pool` object and call its `imap` method, passing two parameters: the function to call, and the sequence of values to process. The `imap` method, short for "iterable map," returns a lazily evaluated iterable object containing the results. (The pool also has a `map` method, but that method isn't lazily evaluated, so it won't serve our purposes.) In the case of our code, the expensive computation we want to perform concurrently is computing the sum of divisors of each integer:

```
pool = Pool()
divisors = pool.imap(sum_divisors, nums)
...
```

This is essentially the same as a call to `map`, except that the computation is performed in parallel across all processors on the current machine. It's okay for Python to use as many cooks as it has available to work on the individual problems. Imagine, for example, that a thousand different processors are working on this. There is no reason you can't say, "Processor #1, you figure out whether 1 is a perfect number while processor #2 figures out whether 2 is and processor #3 figures out whether 3 is, etc."

One unfortunate aspect of using a `Pool` and `imap` is that we can't use the generator expression syntax here when performing the mapping. This means that we can't include an `if` clause at the end to perform filtering. We could write a small lambda function to filter the numbers, but the `Pool` library also doesn't work with lambdas. (This is due to an implementation detail called "pickling" where multiprocess functions are stored and loaded by their names, which doesn't work with lambdas since they are anonymous functions.) Such things are outside the scope of this chapter, but suffice it to say that we will have to introduce a new function to perform filtering:

```
# returns n if n is a perfect number, else None
def is_perfect_number(n):
    if n == sum_divisors(n):
        return n
```

We'll now use our new `is_perfect_number` function as the parameter to `imap`. This will lead to an iterable result from `imap` with perfect numbers and `None`s in it. We can filter these using a generator expression as in the following code:

```
results = pool.imap(is_perfect_number, itertools.count(1))
perfects = (n for n in results if n is not None)
first_five = itertools.islice(perfects, 5)
```

When this final version was run on the same server, it produced the following output. The runtime was around 4497 seconds, or roughly 75 minutes. The server in question has eight different processors. If we were to let the previous non-parallelized version of the program finish running, it likely would have had a runtime less than eight times this long. This is common because not all of the program runs in parallel, and because there is overhead involved in spawning processes and combining their results. The following are the final program and its output from our server, including the discovery that the fifth perfect number is 33,550,336:

```
1   # Searches for the first five perfect numbers.
2   # This version uses a multi-process pool for concurrency.
3
4   import itertools
5   import math    # for sqrt
6   import os
7   import time
8   from multiprocessing import Pool
9
10  # returns the sum of the proper divisors of n
11  def sum_divisors(n):
12      root = int(math.sqrt(n))
13      result = sum((k + n // k for k in \
```

Continued on next page

Continued from previous page

```
14                 range(2, root + 1) if n % k == 0)) + 1
15      if n == root * root:
16          result -= root
17      return result
18
19   # returns n if n is a perfect number, else None
20   def is_perfect_number(n):
21       if n == sum_divisors(n):
22           return n
23
24   # Runs the given function f, measuring how long it took to run.
25   # Returns the elapsed runtime at the end of the call.
26   def measure_runtime(f):
27       start_time = time.time()
28       f()
29       elapsed_time = time.time() - start_time
30       return elapsed_time
31
32   # Finds and prints the first 5 perfect numbers.
33   def find_perfect_numbers():
34       print("Searching for perfect numbers on", \
35             os.cpu_count(), "CPUs:")
36       pool = Pool()
37       results = pool.imap(is_perfect_number, itertools.count(1))
38       perfects = (n for n in results if n is not None)
39       first_five = itertools.islice(perfects, 5)
40       for k in first_five:
41           print(k)
42
43   def main():
44       runtime = measure_runtime(find_perfect_numbers)
45       print("time =", runtime, "sec")
46
47   main()
```

```
Searching for perfect numbers on 8 CPUs:
6
28
496
8128
33550336
time = 4496.814912080765 sec
```

Chapter Summary

- Functional programming is a style that emphasizes the use of functions to decompose problems. Python added new constructs to the language to support functional programming.
- A side effect is a change made to the state of a program that occurs when a function is called, such as modifying a global variable or printing output. Functional programmers try to avoid side effects as much as possible.
- A first-class function is one that can be treated like other types of data, such as being passed as a parameter or composed with other functions.
- A higher-order function is one that accepts another function as a parameter.
- Python provides a shorthand syntax for defining anonymous functions called lambda expressions or lambdas for short.
- Typical functional operations performed on a collection include map (apply an operation to each element),

filter (keep or remove some elements based on various criteria), and reduce (combine multiple elements into a single element).
- A list comprehension is similar to a map or filter operation, producing a list based on applying a transformation or test on each element of a sequence of values.
- A closure is a function definition along with the definitions of any variables declared outside the function ("free variables") that the function utilizes.
- A generator function is one that produces (yields) a sequence of values one at a time, so that its result can be passed as the sequence of values for a functional operation such as map or reduce.
- A parallel algorithm is one where computations occur on multiple CPUs or cores at the same time. Functional programming makes it easier to write efficient parallel code, which can greatly speed up computationally intensive programs.

Self-Check Problems

Section 12.1: Functional Programming Concepts

1. Why do functional programmers want to avoid side effects?

2. Why is calling print considered a side effect? Does this imply that calling print is a bad thing?

3. What side effect does the following function have? How could it be rewritten to avoid side effects?

```
# Doubles the values of all elements in a list.
def double_all(a):
    for i in range(len(a)):
        a[i] = 2 * a[i]
```

4. Write a lambda expression that converts an integer into the square of that integer; for example, 4 would become 16.

5. Write a lambda expression that accepts two integers and chooses the larger of the two; for example, if given 4 and 11, it would return the 11.

6. Write a lambda expression that accepts two strings representing a first and last name and concatenates them together into a string in "Last, First" format. For example, if passed "Cynthia" and "Lee", it would return "Lee, Cynthia".

Section 12.2: Functional Operations on Collections

7. What is the output of the following code?

```
lis = [10, -28, 33, 28, -49, 56, 49]
lis = list(map(lambda num: abs(num), lis))
print(lis)
```

8. Suppose you have a list of integers called `numbers`. Write a piece of code that uses functional operations to make a new list called `positives` that stores only the positive integers from numbers.

9. Suppose you have a list of strings declared as follows. Write functional code to produce all of the three- or four-letter words in the list.

```
words = ["four", "score", "and", "seven", "years", "ago"]
```

10. Write functional code to print all lines from the file `notes.txt` that are at least 40 characters long.

Section 12.3: Function Closures

11. What is the difference between a free variable and a bound variable?

12. What are the free variables and bound variables in the lambda function in the following code?

```
a = 1
b = 2
lambda b, c: c + b - a
```

Exercises

For the exercises in this chapter, write all of your solutions in a functional style. That is, use functional operations like `map` and `reduce`, or list comprehensions, rather than loops whenever appropriate.

1. Write a function called `double` that takes a list as a parameter and returns a list of integers that contains double the elements in the initial list. For example, if the initial list is `[2, -1, 4, 16]`, the new list should contain `[4, -2, 8, 32]`.

2. Write a function called `abs_sum` that takes a list as a parameter and returns the sum of the absolute values of a list of integers. For example, the sum of `[-1, 2, -4, 6, -9]` is 22.

3. Write a function called `largest_even` that takes a list as a parameter and returns the largest even number from a list of integers. An even integer is one that is divisible by 2. For example, if the list is `[5, -1, 12, 10, 2, 8]`, your function should return 12. You may assume that the list contains at least one even integer.

4. Write a function called `total_circle_area` that takes a list as a parameter and returns the sum of the areas of a group of circles, rounded to the nearest whole number. Your function accepts a list of real numbers representing the radii of the circles. For example, if the list is `[3.0, 1.0, 7.2, 5.5]`, return `289.0`. Recall that the area of a circle of radius r is $\frac{1}{2} \pi r^2$.

5. Write a function called `count_negatives` that takes a list as a parameter and returns how many numbers in a given list of integers are negative. For example, if the list is `[5, -1, -3, 20, 47, -10, -8, -4, 0, -6, -6]`, the function should return 7.

6. Write a function `pig_latin` that takes a string parameter to convert a string into its "Pig Latin" form. For this problem we'll use a simple definition of Pig Latin where the first letter should be moved to the end of the word and followed by "ay." For example, if the string passed is `"go seattle mariners"`, return `"o-gay eattle-say ariners-may"`.

7. Write a function `count_vowels` that uses functional programming to count the number of vowels in a given string. A vowel is an A, E, I, O, or U, case-insensitive. For example, if the string is `"SOO beautiful"`, there are 7 vowels.

8. Write a function `glue_reverse` that accepts a list of strings as its parameter and uses functional programming to return a single string consisting of the list's elements concatenated together in reverse order. For example, if the list stores `["the", "quick", "brown", "fox"]`, the function should return `"foxbrownquickthe"`.

9. Write a function `the_lines` that accepts a file name as a parameter and uses functional programming to return a count of the number of lines in the file that start with the word "The", case-insensitive.

10. Write a function `four_letter_words` that accepts a file name as a parameter and returns a count of the number of unique lines in the file that are exactly four letters long.

11. Write a function `odds` to generate a list of all the odd numbers between 0 and 20.

Programming Projects

1. Write a file searching program that uses functional programming to efficiently search a set of files for a given substring. Write two versions of the code, one that sequentially reads each file with `read` and checks each line to see if it contains the substring, and a second that uses functional programming to open all of the files and search the lines using multiple parallel processes. The most efficient version of the stream code will open all of the files in parallel. Test how much more efficient than `read` the functional programming is by using `time` to measure the elapsed time for both versions of the code when run on a collection of large files, and by printing output such as the following:

```
Searching 15 files for "the" using read:
there were 84530 total matching lines.
Took 546 ms.

Searching 15 files for "the" using functional programming:
there were 84530 total matching lines.
Took 160 ms.
```

2. Write a program that prompts the user for an integer value n and that reports the sum of the first n prime numbers, reporting a sum of 0 if the user enters a value less than 1. Structure your program to be similar to the case study, using a generator to produce the sequence 1, 2, 3, . . . , and filtering using the `is_prime` function, which we discussed in Section 12.2. Include timing code and print how long it takes to compute the sum. Once you have a working program, explore the following efficiency improvements and note how the time changes with each using a fairly large value of n such as 10,000:

Modify `is_prime` to check only up to the square root, as in the case study (remember that 1 is not a prime).

Modify the iterating function to examine only odd numbers and manually add 2 to the sum (because 2 is the only even prime).

Appendix A:
Python Summary

Keywords and Operators

Keywords

and	as	assert	break	class
continue	def	del	elif	else
except	False	finally	for	from
global	if	import	in	is
lambda	None	nonlocal	not	or
pass	raise	return	True	try
while	with	yield		

Commonly Used Data Types

Type	Description	Examples
int	integers (whole numbers)	42, 3, 18, 20493, 0
float	real numbers	7.35, 14.9, 19.83423, 6.022e23
str	sequences of text characters (strings)	"hello", 'X', "abc 1 2 3!", ""
bool	logical values	True, False

Arithmetic Operators

Operator	Meaning	Example	Result
+	addition	2 + 2	4
-	subtraction	53 - 18	35
*	multiplication	3 * 8	24
/	division	9 / 2	4.5
//	integer division	9 // 2	4
%	remainder or mod	19 % 5	4
**	exponentiation	3 ** 4	81

Appendix A Python Summary

Relational Operators

Operator	Meaning	Example	Value
==	equal to	2 + 2 == 4	True
!=	not equal to	3.2 != 4.1	True
<	less than	4 < 3	False
>	greater than	4 > 3	True
<=	less than or equal to	2 <= 0	False
>=	greater than or equal to	2.4 >= 1.6	True

Logical Operators

Operator	Meaning	Example	Value
and	conjunction	(2 == 2) and (3 < 4)	True
or	disjunction	(1 < 2) or (2 == 3)	True
not	negation	not (2 == 2)	False

Operator Precedence

Description	Operators
exponentiation	**
unary operators	+, -
multiplicative operators	*, /, //, %
additive operators	+, -
relational operators	<, >, <=, >=
equality operators	==, !=
logical not	not
logical and	and
logical or	or
assignment operators	=, +=, -=, *=, /=, %=

Syntax Templates

Control Statements:

```
for name in range(max):
    statement
    statement
    ...
    statement
```
Syntax template: for loop over range of integers

```
if test1:
    statement1
```

Continued on next page

Continued from previous page

```
elif test2:
    statement2
else:
    statement3
```
Syntax template: nested if statements ending in else
```
raise ExceptionType("error message")
```
Syntax template: raising an exception and displaying an error message
```
while test:
    statement
    statement
    ...
    statement
```
Syntax template: while loop
```
try:
    # statements that might raise an error
    statement
    statement
    ...
    statement
except ExceptionType:
    # statements to handle error if it occurs
    statement
    statement
    ...
    statement
```
Syntax template: try/except statement

Input and Output:

```
print(expression, expression, ..., expression)
```
Syntax template: Printing multiple values
```
variable_name = input("message ")
```
Syntax template: Read user input as a string
```
type(expression)
```
Syntax template: Type conversion
```
with open("filename") as name:
    statement
    statement
    ...
    statement
```
Syntax template: Opening a file for input

Continued on next page

Continued from previous page

```
with open("filename", "w") as name):
    ...
```

Syntax template: Opening a file for output

```
for name in file.read().split():
    statement
    statement
    ...
    statement
```

Syntax template: Reading an entire file by tokens

```
name, name, ..., *name = string.split("delimiter")
```

Syntax template: Splitting a line into arbitrary number of tokens

```
print("text", file=file_object)
```

Syntax template: Printing output to a file

```
import urllib.request

with urllib.request.urlopen("url") as name:
    statement
    statement
    ...
    statement
```

Syntax template: Reading data from a URL

Functions:

```
def name():
    ...


def name(parameter_name, parameter_name, ..., parameter_name):
    ...
```

Syntax template: Function definition without/with parameters

```
return expression
```

Syntax template: Return statement

```
name()
name(expression, expression, ..., expression)
variable = name(expression, expression, ..., expression)
```

Syntax template: Function call without/with parameters, and with return

Libraries:

```
import module
```

Syntax template: import statement

```
from module import *
```

*Syntax template: import * statement*

```
module.function_name(parameters)
```

Syntax template: Calling a function from a library

Collections:

```
name = [value, value, ..., value]
name = [value] * length
```
Syntax template: Defining a list
```
list[index] = value
```
Syntax template: Modifying a list element value by index
```
list[start:stop]
list[start:stop:step]
```
Syntax template: Slicing a list
```
for name in list:
    statement
    statement
    ...
    statement
```
Syntax template: for loop over list elements
```
for name in range(len(list)):
    statement
    statement
    ...
    statement
```
Syntax template: Indexed for loop over a list
```
[expression for name in sequence]
[expression for name in sequence if test]
```
Syntax template: list comprehension
```
name = (value, value, ..., value)
```
Syntax template: Defining a tuple
```
name, name, ..., name = sequence
```
Syntax template: Unpacking assignment statement
```
name = [[value, value, ..., value],
        [value, value, ..., value],
           ...,
        [value, value, ..., value]]
```
Syntax template: Defining a two-dimensional list with given element values
```
name = {key: value, key: value, ..., key: value}
name = {}
```
Syntax template: Defining a dictionary
```
name[key] = value
```
Syntax template: Adding a key/value pair to a dictionary
```
{key: value for pattern in sequence}
```
Syntax template: Dictionary comprehension
```
name = {expression, expression, ..., expression}
name = set()
```
Syntax template: Defining a set

Classes:

```
class ClassName:
    # constructor
    def __init__(self, parameters):
        self.attribute = value
        self.attribute = value
        ...

    @property
    def property_name(self):
        code to return the property's value

    @property_name.setter
    def property_name(self, parameter):
        code to set the property's value

    # method
    def method_name(self, parameters):
        statement
        statement
        ...
        statement

    # str method
    def __str__(self):
        code to produce and return the desired string
```

Syntax template: Class

```
object.property = value
```

Syntax template: Modifying a property of an object

```
object.method(parameters)
```

Syntax template: Calling a method of an object

Useful Functions/Methods

Built-In Global Functions

Function	Description	Example	Result
abs(n)	absolute value	abs(-308)	308
chr(n)	returns a string representing the character with the given numeric value	chr(65)	'A'
max(a, b) max(a, b, c, ..., n) max(sequence)	largest of two or more values	max(11, 8)	11
min(a, b) min(a, b, c, ..., n) min(sequence)	smallest of two or more values	min(7, 2, 4, 3)	2
ord(str)	returns the numeric value equivalent to the given character	ord('A')	65
pow(base, exp)	exponentiation (like **)	pow(3, 4)	81
round(n) round(n, digits)	number rounded to a given decimal place	round(3.647) round(3.647, 1)	4 3.7

Dictionary (dict) operations

Operation	Description
dict[key]	returns the value associated with the given key; raises KeyError if not found
dict[key] = value	sets the value associated with the given key; replaces if already found
del dict[key]	removes the given key and its paired value; raises KeyError if not found
key in dict	returns True if the given key is found
key not in dict	returns True if the given key is not found
len(dict)	number of key/value pairs
str(dict)	returns string representation such as "{'a':1, 'b':2}"
dict.clear()	removes all key/value pairs
dict.get(key, default)	returns the value associated with the given key; returns default if not found
dict.items()	returns the contents of the dictionary as a sequence of (key, value) tuples
dict.keys()	returns the keys in the dictionary as a sequence
dict.pop(key)	returns the value associated with the given key, and removes that key/value pair
dict.update(dict2)	adds all key/value pairs from another dictionary, replacing if keys are already present
dict.values()	returns the values in the dictionary as a sequence

DrawingPanel Methods and Properties

Method/Property	Description
`panel = DrawingPanel(width, height)`	creates and returns a new window of the given size
`panel.background`	background color of panel's drawing canvas
`panel.clear()`	erases all drawn shapes and resets canvas to initial state
`panel.close()`	hides and closes the window
`panel.color`	outline color used for future shapes
`panel.draw_arc(x, y, w, h, angle, extent)`	outlined arc (partial oval) over the given angle range
`panel.draw_image("filename", x, y)`	image from a file with top-left corner at (x, y)
`panel.draw_line(x1, y1, x2, y2)`	line from $(x1, y1)$ to $(x2, y2)$
`panel.draw_oval(x, y, w, h)`	outlined oval with bounding box's top-left corner (x, y) of given size
`panel.draw_polyline(x1, y1, x2, y2, ...)`	outlined multiple line segments between given endpoints
`panel.draw_polygon(x1, y1, x2, y2, ...)`	outlined many-sided polygon with given endpoints
`panel.draw_rect(x, y, w, h)`	outlined rectangle with top-left corner at (x, y), of given width/height
`panel.draw_string("text", x, y)`	text with top-left corner at (x, y)
`panel.fill_arc(x, y, w, h, angle, extent)`	filled arc (partial oval) over the given angle range
`panel.fill_color`	fill color used for future shapes
`panel.fill_oval(x, y, w, h)`	filled oval with bounding box's top-left corner at (x, y) of given width/height
`panel.fill_polygon(x1, y1, x2, y2, ...)`	filled many-sided polygon with given endpoints
`panel.fill_rect(x, y, w, h)`	filled rectangle with top-left corner at (x, y) of given width/height
`panel.font`	font used for future text
`panel.get_pixel_color(x, y)`	color of pixel at position (x, y) as a hexadecimal string
`panel.get_pixel_color_rgb(x, y)`	color of the pixel at position (x, y) as three integer values
`panel.get_pixel(x, y)`	a single pixel's color as an (r, g, b) tuple
`panel.height`	height of panel's canvas in pixels
`panel.location`	drawing panel window (x, y) location on screen
`panel.pixels`	all pixels of image as an $[x][y]$ 2D list of (r, g, b) tuples
`panel.pixel_colors`	all pixels of image as an $[x][y]$ 2D list of hex strings
`panel.set_pixel(x, y, color)`	sets a single pixel's color to a color specified as an (r, g, b) tuple or hex string
`panel.size`	width and height of panel's canvas in pixels
`panel.sleep(ms)`	pauses program for given number of milliseconds

Continued on next page

Continued from previous page

Method/Property	Description
panel.stroke	thickness of shape outlines in pixels
panel.title	window title text as a string
panel.width	height of panel's canvas in pixels
panel.x	drawing panel window x location on screen
panel.y	drawing panel window y location on screen

Exception Types

Exception Type	Description
ArithmeticError	invalid numeric operation such as dividing by zero
AttributeError	invalid attempt to access data within an object
ImportError	failure to load a library or module
IndexError	attempt to access an illegal index of a sequence such as a string
IOError	failure to perform input or output (I/O) on a file
KeyError	attempt to look up invalid data in a dictionary
RecursionError	a function that calls itself too many times
RuntimeError	a general error that does not fall into any other category
SyntaxError	invalid syntax in Python code
SystemError	a problem in the operating system or Python interpreter
TypeError	an operation is applied to a value of the wrong type
ValueError	an operation is applied to an inappropriate value

Methods of File Objects

Method Name	Description
file.close()	indicates that you are done reading/writing the file
file.flush()	writes any buffered data to an open output file
file.read()	reads and returns the entire file as a string
file.readable()	returns True if the file can be read
file.readline()	reads and returns a single line of the file as a string
file.readlines()	reads and returns the entire file as a list of line strings
file.seek(position)	sets the file's current input cursor position
file.tell()	returns the file's current input cursor position
file.writable()	returns True if the file can be written
file.write("text")	sends text to an output file
file.writelines(lines)	sends a list of lines to an output file

Functions of `os.path` Library

Function	Description
os.path.abspath("path")	returns absolute path string for the given file
os.path.basename("path")	returns filename of the given file without directory in front of it
os.path.dirname("path")	returns directory the given file is in
os.path.exists("path")	returns True if the given file or directory exists
os.path.getmtime("path")	returns the time the given file was last modified
os.path.getsize("path")	returns the size of the given file in bytes
os.path.isfile("path")	returns True if the given file exists
os.path.isdir("path")	returns True if the given directory exists

List Operations

Operation	Description
list[index]	returns the element at a given index of a list; IndexError if out of bounds
list[start:stop:step]	returns a slice of elements between the given start/stop indexes of a list
list[index] = value	sets the element at a given index of a list
del list[index] del list[index:index]	removes an item or slice from a given index of list, shifting elements left to cover
list1 + list2	concatenates the elements of two lists to produce a new list
list * n	produces a new list of *n* repetitions of the given list
value in list	returns True if the given element occurs in the list
value not in list	returns True if the given element does not occur in the list
list.append(value)	adds an item to the end of the list
list.clear()	removes all items from the list
list.count(value)	returns the number of times the value occurs in the list
list.extend(seq)	extends the list by adding all the elements from the passed in sequence to the end
list.index(value)	returns the first index where the value occurs; raises an error if the value isn't in the list; can optionally also take starting and ending indexes indicating what part of the list to search in
list.insert(index, value)	inserts an item at a given index
list.pop(index)	removes the value at the passed in index and returns it; if no index is passed, will remove and return the last item in list
list.remove(value)	removes first occurrence of specified value from list; raises an error if the value isn't in the list
list.reverse()	reverses the order of list's elements
list.sort() list.sort(reverse=True)	rearranges list elements into sorted order (or into reverse order, if reverse=True is passed)

Global Functions That Operate on Lists/Sequences

Function	Description
enumerate(seq)	returns a sequence of index/value pairs for each element in sequence
filter(seq, predicate)	returns a subset of the elements of the sequence based on some criteria
len(seq)	number of elements in sequence
map(seq, function)	applies a function to each element of the sequence to make a new sequence
max(seq)	returns the largest value in a sequence
min(seq)	returns the smallest value in a sequence
reversed(seq)	returns a new sequence with the same elements in reverse order
sorted(seq)	returns a new sequence with the same elements in sorted order
str(seq)	returns a string representation of the sequence
sum(seq)	returns the sum of the numbers in a sequence

Math Constants

Constant	Description	Value
e	base used in natural logarithms	2.718281828459045
inf	a special float value representing infinity	∞
nan	"not a number"; represents results of invalid math operations	nan
pi	π ratio of circumference of a circle to its diameter	3.141592653589793
tau	τ twice as large as pi	6.283185307179586

Functions in the math Module

Function	Description	Example	Result
ceil	ceiling (round upward)	math.ceil(2.13)	3.0
cos	cosine (radians)	math.cos(math.pi)	-1.0
degrees	convert radians to degrees	math.degrees(math.pi)	180.0
exp	exponent base e	math.exp(1)	2.7182818284590455
factorial	product of [1 .. n]	math.factorial(5)	120
floor	floor (rounds downward)	math.floor(2.93)	2.0
gcd	greatest common divisor	math.gcd(24, 36)	12
log	logarithm (default is base e); pass base as optional second parameter	math.log(math.e) math.log(8, 2)	1.0 3.0
log10	logarithm base 10	math.log10(1000)	3.0
pow	power (exponentiation)	math.pow(3, 4)	81.0
radians	convert degrees to radians	math.radians(270.0)	4.71238898038469
sin	sine (radians)	math.sin(3 * math.pi / 2)	-1.0
sqrt	square root	math.sqrt(2)	1.4142135623730951

Functions of `random` Module

Function Name	Description	Example
choice, choices, shuffle	choosing random elements from lists and sequences	`random.choice([10, 20, 30])`
randrange	integer in `range(start, stop, step)`	`random.randrange(1, 100, 3)`
randint	integer in [min, max]	`random.randint(1, 10)`
random	real number in [0.0, 1.0)	`random.random()`
seed	sets value that influences sequence of numbers generated	`random.seed(42)`
uniform	real number in [min, max]	`random.uniform(2.5, 10.75)`

Set (`set`) Operations

Operation	Description
`value in set`	returns True if the given value is found in the set
`value not in set`	returns True if the given value is not found
`len(set)`	number of elements in the set
`str(set)`	returns string representation such as `"{'a', 'b', 'c'}"`
`set.add(value)`	adds the given value to the set, if not already present
`set.clear()`	removes all elements
`set.isdisjoint(set2)`	returns True if there are no elements in common between set and set2
`set.pop()`	removes and returns one element from the set
`set.remove(value)`	removes the given value from the set, if present
`set.update(sequence)`	adds all values from the sequence to the set, if not already present
`set	set2` or `set.union(set2)`	returns a new set containing all elements present in set or set2 or both
`set & set2` or `set.intersection(set2)`	returns a new set containing all elements that are present in both set or set2
`set - set2` or `set.difference(set2)`	returns a new set containing all elements that are present in set but not in set2
`set ^ set2` or `set.symmetric_difference(set2)`	returns a new set containing all elements that are present in set or set2 but not both
`set < set2`	returns True if all elements from set are also present in set2 and set is smaller in size than set2
`set <= set2` or `set.issubset(set2)`	returns True if all elements from set are also present in set2
`set > set2`	returns True if all elements from set2 are also present in set and set is larger in size than set2
`set >= set2` or `set.issuperset(set2)`	returns True if all elements from set2 are also present in set

String Methods

Method	Description	Example	Returns
`str.capitalize()`	first character capitalized and rest lowercased	`"hi".capitalize()`	`"Hi"`
`str.count(text)`	number of non-overlapping occurrences of text	`"banana".count("an")`	`2`
`str.endswith (text)`	whether the string ends with text	`"world".endswith("hi")`	`False`
`str.find(text)`	index of first occurrence of text (-1 if not found)	`"banana".find("n")`	`2`
`str.format(args)`	perform advanced string formatting operations	`"{0} is {1}".format ("Bob", 42)`	`"Bob is 42"`
`str.join(list)`	the concatenation of the strings with *str* separating them	`"-".join([1, 2, 3])`	`"1-2-3"`
`len(str)`	length of string	`len("Hi there!")`	`9`
`str.lower()`	a string with all lowercase letters	`"HeLLO".lower()`	`"hello"`
`str.lstrip()`	removes leading whitespace	`" hello".lstrip()`	`"hello"`
`str.replace (old, new)`	replaces each *old* with *new*	`"seen".replace("e", "o")`	`"soon"`
`str.rfind(text)`	index of last occurrence of text (-1 if not found)	`"banana".rfind("n")`	`4`
`str.rstrip()`	removes ending whitespace	`" hello ".rstrip()`	`" hello"`
`str.split(sep)`	list split by sep	`"1:2:3:4".split(":")`	`["1", "2", "3", "4"]`
`str.splitlines()`	list split by line breaks	`"1\na\nbcd".splitlines()`	`["1", "a", "bcd"]`
`str.startswith (text)`	whether string begins with text	`"hello".startswith("he")`	`True`
`str.strip()`	removes beginning and ending whitespace	`" hello ".strip()`	`"hello"`
`str.swapcase()`	capitalizes lowercase letters and lowercases uppercase letters	`"HellO".swapcase()`	`"hELLo"`
`str.title()`	starts each word with uppercase letter and lowercases remaining letters	`"HellO world".title()`	`"Hello World"`
`str.upper()`	capitalizes all letters	`"hello".upper()`	`"HELLO"`

Index